THE NEW TESTAMENT

Proclamation and Parenesis,
Myth and History

THIRD EDITION

THE NEW TESTAMENT

Proclamation and Parenesis, Myth and History

THIRD EDITION

DENNIS C. DULING
Canisius College

NORMAN PERRIN
Late of the University of Chicago

UNDER THE GENERAL EDITORSHIP OF ROBERT FERM

MIDDLEBURY COLLEGE

HARCOURT BRACE COLLEGE PUBLISHERS

Fort Worth   Philadelphia   San Diego   New York   Orlando   Austin   San Antonio
Toronto   Montreal   London   Sydney   Tokyo

EDITOR IN CHIEF	Ted Buchholz
ACQUISITIONS EDITOR	David Tatom
DEVELOPMENTAL EDITOR	Mary K. Bridges
PROJECT EDITOR	Angela Williams
SENIOR PRODUCTION MANAGER	Kenneth A. Dunaway
ART DIRECTOR	Peggy Young
PHOTO EDITOR	Elizabeth Banks
ELECTRONIC PUBLISHING SUPERVISOR	Michael Beaupré
ELECTRONIC PUBLISHING COORDINATOR	Barbara S. McGinnis

For my loving and caring parents,
Alice and Lester

PREFACE

The New Testament is both a book and a collection of books. When we read the New Testament we are immediately aware that it is trying to convince us that certain things are true and therefore affect our lives. There is, in other words, a strong element of *proclamation* in the New Testament. Its writers sought to exhort and instruct, to guide and comfort, to advise and encourage, and often to reprimand. Scholars call this *parenesis*. These considerations account for the first part of the subtitle of this book, "Proclamation and Parenesis." The second part of the subtitle, "Myth and History," derives from the further observation that the New Testament is a fascinating blend of *history* and *myth*. On one level we are being presented with the historical facts of how the Romans crucified a potentially dangerous leader (they crucified many such persons) and of the story of a wandering missionary for a new religion or philosophy who ran into trouble with his rivals in the city of Corinth. On another level we are being presented with the same facts as they reveal the nature of God's judgment on the wisdom and power of the world as they become stories through which believers identify the basic truths about their origins and destinies.

The New Testament tells of events, ideas, and persons surrounding a Jew who lived in ancient Palestine and spoke Aramaic. However, Palestine was part of the Roman Empire, and the texts of the New Testament reflect the historical, cultural, and religious circumstances of that larger environment; and they were written in Greek, then the international language of the empire. Chapter One uses the Lord's Prayer as a model text to sort out some of the various methods that have developed to interpret the books, sources, and traditions, that make up the New Testament, and the contexts in which they were written. Chapters Two and Three survey the world of the New Testament by taking up the social history, culture, and religions of the Greek and Roman periods, with special concentration on Palestinian Judaism. Moreover, the texts of the New Testament can properly be understood historically only if they are placed firmly in the context of the particular circumstances of each phase of the New Testament Christianity from which they came. In order to make this possible, Chapter Four presents a systematic account of the social history of New Testament Christianity. Chapters Five through Fourteen each discuss part of the New Testament against the background of its place in the spectrum of that history. Chapter Fifteen concludes with a presentation of Jesus and his teaching.

SPECIAL FEATURES

1. Emphasis on traditional literary factors. The discussion of the books that make up the New Testament emphasizes literary factors and includes a literary analysis of the longer books. Several years of intensive research on the gospels and the Acts of the Apostles indicate that the authors of these books signaled their intentions by the literary structure they gave to their work and by various literary devices they utilized within that structure. While some attention has been given to "new" literary criticism, the accent of this textbook falls on history.

2. Social factors in early Judaism and early Christianity. Scholars have attempted to describe and explain the social contexts of various early Christian communities by analyzing various factors, including the significance of social environment (whether it was urban or rural, for example), social status, social stratification, the distribution of power, and social groups. Where appropriate, such social factors have been commented on in these pages.

3. The Synoptic Gospels and the Acts of the Apostles. Without de-emphasizing the rest of the New Testament, considerable space is devoted to the evangelists Matthew and Mark and the author of Luke-Acts. This feature will become clear in the chapters on methods, the history of New Testament Christianity, earliest non-Pauline Christianity, the special chapters on these writers, and the final chapter on Jesus.

4. The history and earliest phases of Christianity. Chapter Four attempts to synthesize a great deal of scholarship on the highly debated question about the course of several early Christian movements. Chapter Five builds on Chapter Four and, with source and tradition analysis, presents some of the early developments in Christianity before and during the time of Paul.

5. Material ascribed to Jesus in the synoptic gospels. The synoptic gospels (Matthew, Mark, and Luke) contain both the teachings of Jesus and stories about him. All this material, however, reflects the teaching, understanding, and concerns of early Christian communities, and much of it was in fact created by prophets and scribes in those communities. This view of the synoptic gospel material is given serious consideration in several chapters.

6. Jesus as the presupposition of the New Testament. It is usual to begin a survey of the New Testament with Jesus—that is, with the historical Jesus—and then go on to examine developments in the later church, understanding those developments as moving forward from the mission and message of the historical Jesus. However, in accordance with the views of Rudolf Bultmann, who viewed Jesus as a Jew whose teaching was a "presupposition for the theology of the New Testament," the chapter on Jesus comes last (see "Comment about the Third Edition").

7. The exegetical surveys. This textbook makes extensive use of exegetical surveys. Every major book in the New Testament is surveyed, and when limitations of space have made it impossible to treat a book in this way, it is outlined and the contents briefly discussed. This procedure was chosen deliberately to encourage readers to read the New Testament itself, rather than only a book about it, and to help them understand what they are reading. We regard these exegetical surveys as the heart of the book. They are designed to be read in conjunction with a good English translation of the Bible.

8. Student aids. The student will find much bibliographical material in this book. At the ends of the chapters only authors and titles are given, but studies are organized mainly by topics. The same bibliography in complete form can be found at the end of the book. There is also a research bibliography for writing term papers, and it includes a section on computer research, which is clearly of growing importance.

9. Inclusive language. This edition has been especially attentive to eliminating certain aspects of male dominance in the English language. In accord with that objective, the quotations have been taken mostly from the New Revised Standard Version of the Bible.

COMMENT ABOUT THE THIRD EDITION

The success of the second edition and advancements in the study of the New Testament during the last decade brought about a decision by Harcourt Brace and Company to move toward a third edition. Suggestions for changes were solicited by the publisher from some of those who were using the second edition, from the general editor Robert Ferm, and by me from a few colleagues at a forum on Introductions at the Eastern Great Lakes Biblical Society (1991), and from my students at Canisius College. An extensive revision was completed and then masterfully critiqued by several unidentified scholar-teachers. It was revised again, and then expertly edited at Harcourt Brace. The net result is that the third edition once again has been virtually rewritten, without, however, totally removing the plan of the first and second editions.

Some of the most obvious changes and their rationale are as follows:

1. There is a new chapter on methods for studying the New Testament (Chapter One). That change is a return to the format of Perrin's first edition, but it was motivated by the need to deal creatively with the recent methodological explosion in New Testament study in a more complete, but simplified, way. To that end I have organized the discussion around the interpretation of a familiar text, the Lord's Prayer. In this chapter I have also included some of the discussion about manuscripts and English translation formerly found in Appendixes Two and Three in the second edition, but I have treated them in a simplified form. This latter change is partly because these appendixes addressed problems of interpretation, but primarily because students argued that if materials in appendixes are important enough to assign for study, they should be placed in the main body of the text. The chapter continues the second edition's treatment of traditional literary and historical methods, but expands on social science contributions and adds several other methods currently in use in New Testament study. It deals more briefly with contemporary literary criticism because there are current literary introductions for those who wish to emphasize this approach, and because my own recent research interests have focused more on developments in social history and the social sciences.

2. The second edition's Chapter One, "The World of the New Testament," has now become "The Social-Historical Context of the New Testament" and "The Cultural and Religious Environment of the New Testament" (Chapters Two and Three). The new Chapter Two concentrates on political history but has been given a social historical cast. The new Chapter Three on cultural and religious environment, also influenced by social scientific study, includes many of the ancient text examples originally found in the second edition's Appendix Five. This division of one chapter into two is admittedly artificial. It has been done for pedagogical reasons: many students claim that if they have not studied ancient history, the

environment of the New Testament is easier to understand by approaching it first through a sequential, or chronological, framework.

3. Most of the second edition's Chapter Two, with its heavy concentration on myth, has been omitted, primarily for three reasons. First, while the shadow of Rudolf Bultmann's demythologization project is a long one, the Bultmannian and post-Bultmannian eras in the USA have been eclipsed by other moods, movements, and interests, especially literary/rhetorical and social-historical/social-science criticism. Second, despite the attempt to make this chapter simpler in the second edition, many students still found it difficult. Third, other changes and additions required that something go, and a difficult chapter, parts of which were somewhat dated, seemed to be the best choice for omission.

4. Chapters Three and Four in the second edition have been extensively rewritten as Chapters Four and Five. The new Chapter Four attempts to take into account the *way* early Christian history can be written on the basis of methods presented earlier in the book, and then offers a social-historical sketch of early Christianity on the basis of oral traditions, written sources (including the *Gospel of Thomas*), dates of documents, social conditions, and the like. Gnostic Christianity and the development of the canon from Appendix One in the second edition have been placed here.

5. The new Chapter Five has been changed from "Apocalyptic Christianity" to "The Earliest Non-Pauline Christians" for two reasons. First, apocalyptic remains an essential part of the chapter but Revelation, the only New Testament apocalypse, has now been placed in a later chapter of its own (Chapter Thirteen). In its place are sections on social stratification, early Christian groups, worship and liturgies, wisdom and prophecy, parables, anecdotes, miracles, death and resurrection traditions, and Christological Hymns (even though some of them are found in Paul's writings). Chapters Six to Twelve, Fourteen, and Fifteen are also much-updated chapters, with many added emphases on social factors.

6. There has been a great deal of discussion with colleagues about whether the final chapter on Jesus as the presupposition of the New Testament, initially a Bultmannian emphasis (see above, special features), should remain at the end of the book. After an open discussion at the Eastern Great Lakes Biblical Society in the spring of 1991 an informal poll on this question revealed that the scholars present were split almost exactly 50–50. Since placing the chapter on Jesus at the end has the added merit that readers will have encountered numerous interpretations of Jesus in the New Testament, and will be aware of the difficulties in literary, historical, and social analysis in examining his teaching and commenting about his life, the chapter remains in its original position. It is written in such a way that those who prefer to take it first may do so.

7. There remains only one appendix, "Major Archeological, Textual Discoveries, and Publications." It, too, has been updated, and slightly expanded, and videos have been added to its bibliography.

8. The Bibliography for Research Papers has been revised (see below), and to it I have added a brief section on electronic aids for bibliographical research, clearly something of growing importance.

9. At the suggestion of students, footnotes in this edition have been removed as an unnecessary distraction. This was done with much hesitation since a general introduction is obviously indebted to many scholars, some more than others. To compensate, I have occasionally indicated special indebtedness to scholars in the Further Reading sections. As in the other editions, the general bibliography at the end of the book has been correlated with the bibliographies at the end of each chapter, and it is now quite extensive. It is also due to student suggestions that the Glossary has been expanded and the time line of Christian and pre-Christian eras has been clarified. Many other changes in this edition have been made to clarify language and concepts for students.

10. There is much awareness today about sexist features of the English language. While some improvements were made in the second edition, there has been a much more thorough attempt to be inclusive in this edition. With this feature in mind, quotations from the Bible have been taken primarily from the inclusive language New Revised Standard Edition, though it has been abandoned occasionally to make a particular exegetical point or literal text correlation sometimes lost in the NRSV's inclusive paraphrase.

I noted in the second edition that Professor Norman Perrin died unexpectedly just before Thanksgiving in 1976. He was a distinguished and internationally known New Testament scholar, an unusually clear-headed thinker and writer, and a spunky personality who had developed and defended his own views on a number of central issues in New Testament interpretation. Perrin had moved through several stages in his scholarly career; he himself would have made revisions of his textbook in accord with his most recent perspective. Since that was not possible, I, his former student and continuing friend, agreed to attempt these revisions in the second edition, not without some initial hesitation. In this third edition revisions are much more extensive.

I would like to acknowledge the following people and institutions for their part in the production of the third edition. Bill McLane of Harcourt Brace and Company originally encouraged me to undertake it, and after Harcourt's merger with Holt, Rinehart, and Winston, I corresponded with David Tatom and the developmental editor, Mary K. Bridges. As with the second edition, extremely helpful suggestions and much encouraging support were offered by the general editor, Professor Robert Ferm of Middlebury College, who read and critiqued the entire manuscript. The task of editing fell to Ms. Bridges and project editor Angela Williams at Harcourt Brace and Company. Peggy Young created the design for this edition, Elizabeth Banks edited the photos, and Barbara McGinnis developed the artwork, maps, and charts.

As noted above, comments were offered and solicited from a number of teachers, scholars, and students. For the seeds of the reorientation of the second edition I was most indebted to Professor Wayne Meeks of Yale University and to his 1979 seminar on the social world of early Christianity, which was made possible by a grant from the National Endowment for the Humanities. Prof. Edward C. Hobbs of Wellesley College offered some criticisms of the second edition. The Canisius College sophomore Honors students of 1986 and 1987 tactfully and without reluctance found weaknesses in the second edition that scholars would not notice, and offered many suggestions for improvement. I would like to recognize my Canisius College colleague and friend, Benjamin Fiore, S.J., for organizing the open forum on Introductions to the New Testament at the 1991 Eastern Great Lakes Biblical Society, a regional section of the Society of Biblical Literature, Catholic Biblical Association, and American Schools of Oriental Research. The following reviewers made many helpful suggestions: John J. Collins, University of Notre Dame; Joah A. Darr, Boston College; Florence Gilman, University of San Diego; Paul Mirecki, University of Kansas; Pamela Thimmes, OSF, The University of Dayton; Tomas H. Tobin, S.J., Loyola University of Chicago; and Joseph B. Tyson, Southern Methodist University. A special thanks should be given to Dr. K. C. Hanson of the School of Theology at Claremont, California, who read and offered many suggestions on several of the early chapters. As in the case of the second edition, Fr. Bonaventure Hayes, professor and librarian at Christ the King Seminary in East Aurora, New York, kindly provided the basis for the research bibliography noted above. A very special word of thanks is due Canisius College in Buffalo, New York, which not only encourages its faculty to do research, but backs them financially. In this connection I would like to thank two students, Andrew Moynahan, who helped with reformatting and critiqued the manuscript, and Michael Watz, who helped prepare the Index.

In an indirect way, I have also been influenced by a number of groups and persons in the decade since the second edition was published. With the support of the National Endowment for the Humanities, Prof. Louis Feldman and the members of his NEH Summer Seminar on Judaism and Hellenism at Yeshiva University, New York City, in 1983, contributed to my understanding of the world in which Christianity was born. An NEH Fellowship also made it possible for me to extend my understanding of social history begun with Prof. Meeks. To that end I went to Heidelberg, Germany, where I engaged in helpful discussions with Prof. Gerd Theissen. I would also like to acknowledge the stimulating discussions about Jesus in Dr. Robert Funk's Jesus Seminar of the Westar Institute, in which I participated actively from 1985–1989. More recently I have profited most directly from the members of Context Group convened by Prof. John Elliott of the University of San Francisco, and the Social Sciences and New Testament Section of the Society of Biblical Literature currently under the leadership of Prof. Bruce J. Malina of Creighton University and Dr. John Pilch. At Canisius College, the personnel of the library, especially Karen Perone, and the Computer Center, especially Mark Castner and Kenneth Wigel, have also been very helpful for information and technical assistance. My colleagues in the Religious Studies Department, Fr. Daniel Jamros, S. J., and especially Fr. Martin Moleski, S.J., also gave me invaluable help with computer problems. The former Vice President for Academic Affairs, Fr. Edmund Ryan, his associate, Dr. Jerome Neuner, and the deans, Prof. Walter Sharrow and Prof. Ellen Conley, have been extremely supportive, and my chairperson, Prof. James McDermott, has offered his continued support and encouragement.

Finally, I am most fortunate of human beings to have a marvelous family. I am grateful to my two children, Teddie Anne and Stephen, now grown, who have endured looking at the back of my head for many of their formative years. I am indebted beyond expression to my devoted and loving spouse of thirty-three years, Gretchen, who has occasionally made her own learned observations about the manuscript. Finally, I have dear parents, Alice and Lester Duling, retired in Lakeland, Florida; to them this edition is dedicated.

Again, I recall with fondness the author of the first edition of this book, and I hope the third edition will continue to be of as much service to students as the first two editions have been.

Dennis C. Duling

A NOTE ABOUT
THE RESOURCE BOOKS

The following are some of the works continually referred to in the Further Reading sections at the end of each chapter and in the appendix.

The Anchor Bible Dictionary. Ed.-in-chief, D. N. Freedman. 6 vols. New York: Doubleday, 1992. (Quoted as *ABD.*) This "mega"-Bible dictionary is virtually an encyclopedia with more than 1000 contributors. The entries include articles about methods of interpretation and summaries of scholarship, as well as the usual word studies. It contains the best up-to-date scholarship.

The New Jerome Biblical Commentary. Englewood Cliffs, NJ: Prentice-Hall, 1990. (Quoted as *NJBC.*) This is a one-volume commentary on the Bible plus excellent general articles, revised from the 1968 *Jerome Biblical Commentary.* It is a product of some of the very best American Roman Catholic scholarship.

The Interpreter's Dictionary of the Bible. 4 vols. New York and Nashville: Abingdon Press, 1962. (Quoted as *IDB.*) Though dated, it is still a valuable, comprehensive reference work, and especially helpful for quick reference about Biblical words. The articles vary in quality, but at their best they are very good and always extremely informative.

IDB Suppl. Volume 5 of the *IDB,* published in 1976.

TABLE OF CONTENTS

ABBREVIATIONS AND EXPLANATIONS

Books of the Bible and the Apocrypha are abbreviated to the first three or four letters of their titles; for example, Gen = Genesis, Matt = Matthew, 1 Cor = 1 Corinthians. We have followed the example of the Oxford Annotated Bible in using *Sir* for ben Sira, or The Wisdom of Jesus the Son of Sira, a book in the Apocrypha sometimes called Ecclesiasticus. The abbreviation *par.* (for parallel) is used to refer to passages in the gospel passages that are parallel to the one cited; for example, "Mark 13 par." means "Mark chapter 13 and its parallels in Matthew and Luke." Qumran materials are abbreviated according to the standard established in the official publication *Discoveries in the Judaean Desert*, edited by J. T. Milik and D. Barthélemy (Oxford: Clarendon Press, 1955–   ). The following is a list of other abbreviations used.

ABD	*The Anchor Bible Dictionary*
ASV	American Standard Version (of the Bible) = SV
AV	Authorized Version (of the Bible) = KJV
ERV	English Revised Version (of the Bible) = RV
IDB	*Interpreter's Dictionary of the Bible* (4 vols.)
IDB Suppl.	*Interpreter's Dictionary of the Bible*, vol. 5
NJBC	*New Jerome Biblical Commentary*
KJV	King James Version (of the Bible) = AV
LXX	Septuagint (the Greek translation of the Jewish Scriptures, transmitted as the Old Testament by Christians)
NAB	New American Bible
NEB	New English Bible
NRSV	New Revised Standard Version (of the Bible)
OAB	Oxford Annotated Bible
RSV	Revised Standard Version (of the Bible)
RV	Revised Version (of the Bible) = ERV
SV	Standard Version (of the Bible) = ASV
TEV	Today's English Version (of the Bible)

Unless otherwise identified, quotations from the Bible are from the NRSV. "Matthew," "Mark," "Luke," and "John" are often used to refer both to the evangelists (gospel writers) and to the gospels themselves. Further definition ("the evangelist Matthew" or "the Gospel of Matthew") is given for the sake of emphasis or where it is necessary to avoid confusion. This usage is purely a matter of convenience and is not intended to imply anything about the actual names of the evangelists. Publication details of all books and articles quoted or referred to are given in the bibliography at the end of the book, except that individual articles in the resource books (*ABD, NJBC, IDB,* and *IDB Suppl.*) are not further listed there.

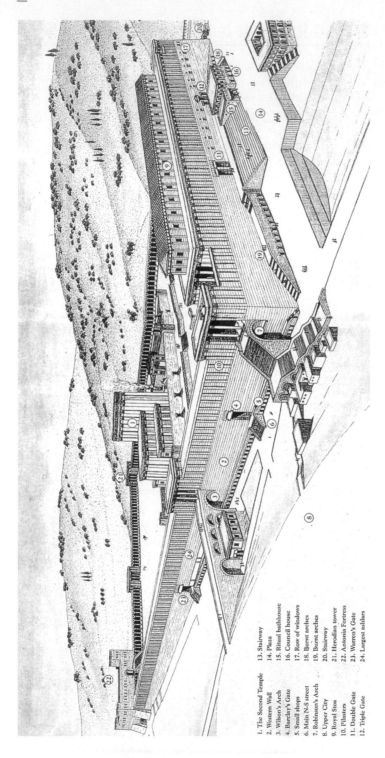

1. The Second Temple	13. Stairway
2. Western Wall	14. Plaza
3. Wilson's Arch	15. Ritual bathhouse
4. Barclay's Gate	16. Council house
5. Small shops	17. Row of windows
6. Main N-S street	18. Burnt arches
7. Robinson's Arch	19. Burnt arches
8. Upper City	20. Stairway
9. Royal Stoa	21. Herodian tower
10. Pilasters	22. Antonia Fortress
11. Double Gate	23. Warren's Gate
12. Triple Gate	24. Largest ashlars

The magnificent Temple of Jerusalem. Its rebuilding, which doubled its size, was launched by Herod the Great (37–4 B.C.E.) about 20 B.C.E. and mostly completed in eighteen months, though some rebuilding continued virtually up to the time of its destruction by the Romans in 70 C.E. Its floor plan is on p.xxi, and a photo of remaining sections of its western wall is at the beginning of Chapter Nine. (Drawing by Leen Ritmeyer, *Biblical Archeology Review* 15/6 [Nov/Dec 1989], pp. 24–25; reprinted in Kathleen and Leen Ritmeyer, *Reconstructing Herod's Temple Mount in Jerusalem*. Used by permission.)

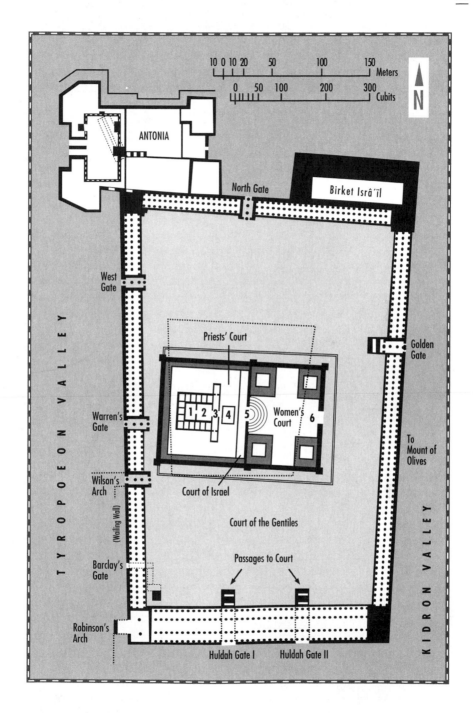

Floor plan of Herod's Temple and courts: (1) Holy of Holies; (2) Holy Place (Nave); (3) Porch; (4) Altar; (5) Nicanor Gate; (6) Beautiful Gate? (Based on Vincent-Steve [W.F. Stinespring, *IDB* R-Z, p. 556] and C. L. Meyers [*Harpers Bible Dictionary*, p. 1028 (Maplewood, NJ: Hammond Incorporated)]). For Ritmeyer's reconstruction, see p. xx; for a photo of the remains of its western wall, see the beginning of Chapter Nine.

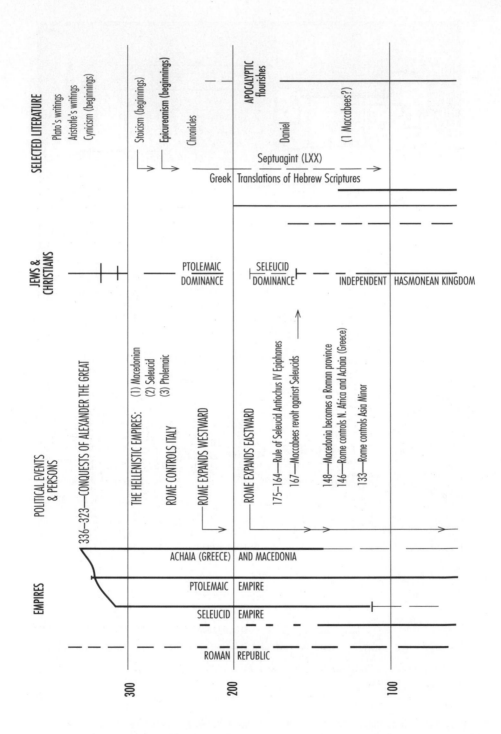

SELECTED LITERATURE

Plato's writings
Aristotle's writings
Cynicism (beginnings)

Stoicism (beginnings)
Epicureanism (beginnings)
Chronicles

APOCALYPTIC
flourishes

Daniel

(1 Maccabees?)

Septuagint (LXX)
Greek Translations of Hebrew Scriptures

JEWS & CHRISTIANS

PTOLEMAIC DOMINANCE   SELEUCID DOMINANCE   INDEPENDENT HASMONEAN KINGDOM

POLITICAL EVENTS & PERSONS

336–323—CONQUESTS OF ALEXANDER THE GREAT

THE HELLENISTIC EMPIRES: (1) Macedonian
                            (2) Seleucid
                            (3) Ptolemaic

ROME CONTROLS ITALY

ROME EXPANDS WESTWARD

ROME EXPANDS EASTWARD

175–164—Rule of Seleucid Antiochus IV Epiphanes
167—Maccabees revolt against Seleucids

148—Macedonia becomes a Roman province
146—Rome controls N. Africa and Achaia (Greece)
133—Rome controls Asia Minor

EMPIRES

ACHAIA (GREECE) AND MACEDONIA

PTOLEMAIC EMPIRE

SELEUCID EMPIRE

ROMAN REPUBLIC

300   200   100

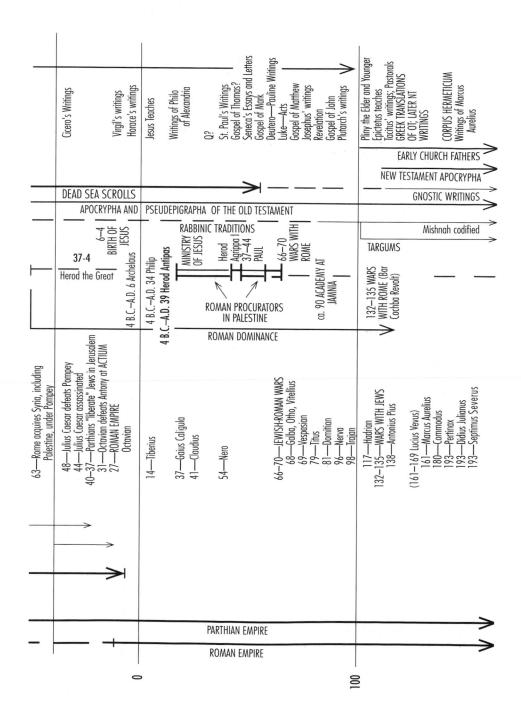

The Scribe Eadwine, from the *Canterbury Psalter*, ca. 1150 C.E., Trinity College, Cambridge, England. Manuscripts were copied by hand (sometimes by groups of monks in monasteries) until the invention of the printing press in the 1450s. Despite great care, they were subject to error (and occasionally intentional changes to defend doctrine). From such hand-written copies that vary from each other modern Textual Critics attempt to reconstruct what the New Testament writers originally wrote. See the modern Jewish scribe at the beginning of Chapter Ten.

INTERPRETING THE NEW TESTAMENT
The Lord's Prayer

Sometimes it is hard to understand what other people are trying to say. Their choice and stress of words, body language, sexual differences, and actions and the motivations for them enter into the communication process. This is true with friends and acquaintances. How much more difficult it is with strangers!

The task as we begin our study of the New Testament is to interpret what some religious people said and did in a different culture with a different language about 2000 years ago. The New Testament is not one book written by one person, but a collection of twenty-seven books written by a variety of persons. Generally, it contains gospels, acts, letters, and a "revelation." Some authors are indicated by name, some are not. The individual books are similar to other such books in antiquity, but they do not normally say anything explicit about when they were written, though they sometimes show evidence of their origin and destination. Years later they were translated from Greek into many other languages. Scribes hand-copied all the language versions for many centuries, giving rise to various errors. Finally, they came from an environment in which people thought and acted in ways different from our own, as we shall show in Chapter Two.

Of course, some people may not consider these human dimensions of interpretation seriously. They may sincerely believe that the very words of the "word of God" are divinely inspired, that the Truth is literal, word-for-word correspondence, perhaps in a particular English translation. Others can admit that errors have indeed crept into the manuscripts of the Bible down through the centuries, and that translation is often a problem, but they claim that the original Greek documents were without error. Still others do not take the New Testament so literally, but see in it living tradition, religious myth, beautiful poetry, and much else.

Most scholars fall into the latter category. They often speak of "Biblical criticism." By this expression they do not mean simply the study of its manuscripts, though that is included; rather, they include various historical and literary methods of interpretation that have developed in the last two centuries to solve certain interpretative problems. Discerning students will perceive that critical interpretations of human factors in the formation of the books of the New Testament do not automatically or necessarily exclude reading it for inspiration or comfort. For some students, however, it may be important to rethink what theologians have sometimes called "divine inspiration and authority" from a more critical perspective.

This book assumes the importance of New Testament criticism for interpreting the books of the New Testament. These sources, combined with a few other ancient Christian books, present us with several critical problems, and these problems have in turn generated methods to solve them. As a prelude to discussion, we shall outline the situation as follows:

Problem	Method for Solving the Problem
A) Foreign-language documents	A) English Translation
B) Many manuscripts with many variants in them	B) Textual Criticism
C) Literary and historical questions	C) Historical Criticism
1) Authors, dates, places, major ideas of writers	1) General Historical Criticism
2) Written sources used by New Testament authors	2) Source Criticism
3) Oral traditions, their histories and settings	3) Form Criticism
4) Authors' special emphases The genre of whole books	4) Redaction Criticism; Composition Criticism; Genre Criticism
5) Christian groups, their symbols and relations	5) Social-Historical and Social-Science Criticism
6) Material remains and newly discovered texts	6) Archeology
D) Understanding the New Testament plot; characters; reader perspectives; and so forth	D) Recent Literary Criticism

To introduce some of the critical methods of interpretation, we shall focus on a familiar New Testament passage, a prayer attributed to Jesus. Christians call it the "Our Father" or "the Lord's Prayer." A familiar version reads:

Our Father who art in heaven,
    Hallowed be Thy name.
Thy Kingdom come.
    Thy will be done,
    On earth as it is in heaven.
Give us this day our daily bread;
And forgive us our debts,
    As we forgive our debtors,
And lead us not into temptation,
    But deliver us from evil.
For Thine is the Kingdom,

And the power,
And the glory forever. Amen.

(Matthew 6:9b–13)

This version is similar to the one found in the influential King James Version of the Bible of 1611 C.E. (or A.D.). It is the prayer used in most English-speaking Protestant churches. Roman Catholics and some Protestants will note a major difference; that is, they pray,

And forgive us our *trespasses*
As we forgive *those who trespass against* us.

Catholics will note a second important difference: They do not immediately pray the concluding "doxology," or words praising God,

For thine (yours) is the Kingdom
(And) the power
And the glory forever (and ever). Amen.

Yet, a modern translation of these words is recited slightly later in the liturgy of the Mass. These two differences in the prayer illustrate our first two problems for interpreting the New Testament, English translation and manuscript variants.

ENGLISH TRANSLATION

It is easy to describe the first difference. "Debts"/"debtors" and "trespasses"/"those who trespass against" are alternative translations of ancient Greek terms *opheilēmata/tois opheiletais*. Translation is our first problem of interpretation.

The books of the New Testament were written in *koinē* ("common") Greek, the commonly spoken, international language of politics, trade, and culture. This culture began with the expansion of the Greeks to the Middle East in the fourth century B.C.E. and continued into the early Roman Empire, the period when Christianity was born. By about 200 C.E., Latin, the language of Rome and the Roman Empire, was replacing Greek as the international language. The Christian Bible was often translated into Latin, but it was the famous Latin **Vulgate of St. Jerome,** completed in 383 C.E., that eventually become *the* Bible of the church in the regions of the western Mediterranean and the official Catholic church down to modern times. The Vulgate translated the two Greek words for "debts"/"debtors" or "trespasses"/"those who trespass against" with the Latin *debita/debitoribus.*

Certain select Biblical passages for liturgical and devotional purposes in monasteries and convents required translations into other vernacular languages. These were translated from Latin into Old English by about 700 C.E. and into Middle English after the eleventh century. In such a collection towards the end of the fourteenth century C.E., the two key words looked similar to those of the Vulgate, from which they were translated:

And foryeue us oure *dettys,*
as we foryeue oure *dettourys.*

Yet, about the same time an English translation associated with **John Wycliffe,** about 1330–1384 C.E., read:

> And forgeve vs oure *treaspases,*
> even as we forgeve *them whych treaspas* vs.

In these very early translations we see the roots of the modern "debts" and "trespasses." The latter was perpetuated by the sixteenth-century Protestant reformers William Tyndale (1526) and Myles Coverdale (1535), and this was picked up in the Church of England's official prayer books (1537, 1549, 1552), primers, and ABC books. Eventually, Roman Catholics in England also came to prefer "trespasses." The "debts" translation continued in the Coverdale Bible (1535, "dettes"/"detters"), the official "Thomas Matthew" Bible (1537), and the Great Bible (1539–68). The first official English translation for the Roman Catholic Church, the **Rheims New Testament** of 1582 C.E., based on the Latin, also contained "debts"/"debtors." Most important, the extremely influential Protestant-sponsored English **King James Version** of 1611 C.E., translated from the original Biblical languages, also followed this translation.

In short, the official prayer books that followed the Wycliffe/Tyndale translations rendered "trespasses," and this translation determined the prayer practice of the established English church (the Church of England), as well as the Catholic Church. However, whole Bible translations that had "debts," especially the King James Version, determined most other Protestant forms of the prayer.

This sketch clarifies the entrance of the translations into the history of English translation of the prayer. Which translation is *better?* This question is not as simple as it looks. In the first place, we actually have two Greek words to consider. The Gospel of Luke has a version of this prayer (Luke 11:2–4) containing a different Greek term (Luke 11:4: *tas hamartias*), usually translated literally as "sins." Are these Greek terms alternate translations of the same term in Aramaic, the mother tongue spoken by Jesus? It is sometimes so argued, and scholars who do so sometimes take this into account in their English translation of Matthew. However, all of this implies a problem about what the historical Jesus of Nazareth said and meant. Did he mean "monetary" debts or trespasses in the sense of sins? To answer this question requires exploring some of the methods that attempt to arrive at what Jesus actually said. We shall attempt to do this later. For the time being, we shall narrow our focus to language in Matthew.

Again, which is the better translation of Matthew, "trespasses"/"those who trespass against us" or "debts"/"debtors"? Even this narrower form of the question is not easy. The Greek terms *opheilēmata/tois opheiletais* come from the verb *opheilō,* "I owe." In the literal sense, the verb and its cognates refer to owing a debt to someone, especially money. The best literal translation would be "debts"/"debtors" in the sense of monetary debts or their equivalent.

However, words often have more-than-literal meanings. Did the author of Matthew mean them literally? Or do they have broader connotations? The "trespasses" translation probably implies a broader sense. While "to trespass" in Elizabethan English referred to property in legal contexts (contemporary "No trespassing"), it could also mean in general "to offend against," "to wrong," "to violate a person," and thus "to sin." This more general sense also passed over to the noun "trespass." So a "trespass" was something like a "sin." This general sense of "trespass" is not so common today, except perhaps when Christians mean something like "sins" when they pray "trespasses"! It may also be that this broader sense of trespasses became a common translation because it coincided with the term "sins" in the Lukan form of the prayer. Yet, again, this is not the literal meaning of the Greek *opheilē mata* in Matthew; it means "debts," primarily of money.

It should be noted that translation differences on the basis of the historically different religious beliefs of Catholics and Protestants is not really the issue, especially today. To illustrate this point, the Revised Standard Version of the 1940s and 1950s was a translation by Protestant scholars, but the New Revised Standard Version of 1989 had on its translation committee five Roman Catholic scholars and one Jewish scholar.

In summary, "debts," not "trespasses," is the better translation of Matthew. It comes closer to the literal rendering of the Greek more than the modern, ordinary-language meaning of "trespasses." An obvious problem is whether the literal sense was really intended in the gospel, and this is separate from the question whether the gospel accurately represents what Jesus intended in Aramaic, his mother tongue. A further complication is whether "debts" itself (in English) now conveys a more-than-literal sense. In fact, those who pray "debts" today may also think something more like "sins." Nonetheless, the better literal translation of the text of Matthew is "debts." We would have to engage in further analysis to determine what Jesus himself might have said and meant.

TEXTUAL CRITICISM

The second well-known difference between Catholic and Protestant versions of the prayer attributed to Jesus is the presence or absence of the final doxology, the final words praising God. It can be seen as a simple problem. Some ancient manuscripts contained the doxology and others did not. Early Protestant gospel translations and most of the liturgies based on them used one set of manuscripts, and the Roman Catholic gospel translations and the liturgies based on them used another set. This explanation is correct, but again we must go a little deeper into the problem.

The study of ancient writing scripts and habits, called "palaeography," shows that none of the surviving manuscripts of the New Testament is early enough to be an original, that is, directly from the hand of its author. Only copies, and copies of copies, survive. These manuscripts were produced by hand for hundreds of years, down to the invention of the printing press in the fifteenth century. They contain many copying errors. While most of them are minor, some are very important and significantly alter the meaning of the texts. In addition, some intentional changes were made for doctrinal reasons, for example, "proving" the Trinity. The phenomena posed by these manuscripts and their variants has given rise to another kind of analysis, **textual criticism.** It has two aims: to classify the surviving manuscripts and to evaluate them in order to reconstruct hypothetically what the authors originally wrote. Only then is there a Greek "New Testament text" to translate.

Classification of Manuscripts

The modern system for classifying New Testament manuscripts developed slowly and is therefore not always logical. Some manuscripts are classified by the *material* on which they are written, such as **papyrus;** others by the *kind of script* that they contain, namely, **uncials,** or block "capital" letters, and **minuscules,** or cursive script; and still others by their *content,* such as **lectionaries,** or Biblical passages read on special days of the church year. There are also early Christian writers who quote the New Testament, giving rise to **patristic citations,** and translations into vernacular languages, or **versions.** Most of these manuscripts are now in the libraries and museums of Europe and the Middle East. We shall briefly describe their character.

Papyri (second to eighth century)

These manuscripts were made from the fibers of the papyrus plant, which grew in the Nile River marshes. Such manuscripts were accidently preserved over many centuries in the hot and dry climate of Egypt. Today, ninety-six papyri are cited in official scholarly lists. Almost all come from "codices," or books (Latin *codex,* "book"), which were replacing rolled scrolls. They have a type of script formed with capital block letters, called uncial script. Scholars designate papyri by the letter "P" followed by a number. Though they have only been published within the last century, they are very valuable because most are among our earliest surviving manuscripts. The earliest of all is P^{52}, a tiny fragment of John 18:31–33 (front side) and 18:37–39 (back side), which dates back to about 125 C.E.

New Testament Uncials (second/third to tenth century)

Uncial manuscripts, named for their uncial characters, are written on parchment, or "vellum," that is, scraped, smoothed, and lined animal hide. In age some are almost as early as the papyri but most are later. There are about 300 uncials. Scholars designate them by letters of the alphabet, and since there are more manuscripts than the alphabet has letters, also by numerals prefixed by a zero (for example, B = 03, C = 04, etc.). Two of the most important uncials are S or 01, Codex Sinaiticus (middle fourth century), and B or 03, Codex Vaticanus (early fourth century).

New Testament Minuscules (ninth to sixteenth century)

In the ninth century, smaller, more easily and quickly written cursive characters were developed. From then on "minuscule" codices predominate. More than 2800 minuscules have survived. They are designated by Arabic numerals (not preceded by 0).

Lectionaries (fourth century [?] to sixteenth century)

Quotations from the New Testament used as lessons for the special days of the church year were also preserved. These lectionaries are both uncial and minuscule scripts. Limited in value, they can sometimes help to explain manuscript changes based on familiar liturgical usage. Scholars designate them by the letter "l" plus an Arabic numeral. There are more than 2280 lectionaries.

Here is a summary of the first four classifications of New Testament manuscripts by quantity known and century produced:

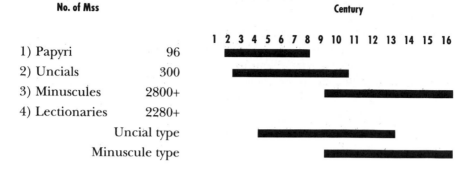

No. of Mss		Century

This chart shows that more than 5000 hand-copied Greek manuscripts of the New Testament or parts thereof were produced between the second century and the first printed editions in the sixteenth century. There are two other types of manuscript material important for reconstructing the text of the New Testament.

Patristic Citations

Important Christian thinkers from the second to the tenth centuries are called "Church Fathers." They copied, combined, quoted, alluded to, and wrote commentaries on passages from the New Testament. If their citations are used with caution, they sometimes offer information about variants that were current in the time when, and location where, the Church Father was active.

Early Versions

As Christianity spread, the Greek Bible was translated into other tongues, and these translations are called "versions." Like the patristic citations, these translated versions had their own internal copying history; thus, they can be used to reconstruct the original Greek only with great caution.

1. Latin.
   a. "Old Latin" (second century C.E. on)
   b. Vulgate (383 C.E.). About 8,000 Vulgate manuscripts have survived.
2. Syriac.
   a. The Diatessaron (originally written about 170 C.E.)
   b. The "Old Syriac" (fourth century C.E.)
   c. The Peshitta (fifth century)
3. Coptic (Egyptian).
4. Other Early Versions
   a. Armenian
   b. Georgian
   c. Ethiopic
   d. Gothic
   e. Slavonic

Evaluating the Manuscripts and "Establishing the Text"

Copying manuscripts by hand through the centuries led to more than 200,000 "mistakes" by copyists in the 5000-plus manuscripts. Most are minor, but some are very important, and a few are intentional. If one includes lectionaries and versions, there are many more variants. Thus, we come to the second major problem of textual criticism: How can all these manuscripts be evaluated to arrive at a close approximation of what an author of a New Testament book *originally* wrote?

The most basic principle of Textual Criticism for establishing the text is: When variant word(s), phrase(s), or sentence(s) occur, those that explain the origin of the other variant readings are most likely to be the best readings. To use a modern example, if there are several versions of a sentence in a film, you could compare them to decide which is earlier. If you are inclined to rate one version "PG-13," one "R," another "X," you would probably decide that the "X" version came first and that offensive words were removed from the "R" and again from the "PG-13" versions to "clean up" the film for family consumption. In Textual Criticism the principle is related to two types of evidence, external evidence and internal evidence. External evidence evaluates the manuscripts according to their age, family relationships, and geographical distribution. Internal evidence evaluates the characteristic vocabulary, style, or ideas of their authors, as well as changes typical of most copyists.

Evaluation of manuscripts has produced a number of family trees that have been further grouped into more comprehensive "text types." Two of these text types are clearly distinguishable and very important historically. The first text type is represented by the most Greek manuscripts, more than 800, mostly minuscules. Between the sixteenth and nineteenth centuries, this text type was thought to be the New Testament and was thus called the **Received Text** or in Latin, the *Textus Receptus*. It became the basis for the printed editions of the Greek New Testament in these centuries and, in turn, the basis for the early English translations discussed above. With the discovery and publication of the earlier uncials and the papyri in the late nineteenth and early twentieth centuries, it was realized that what we call the **Alexandrian text type** (associated with Alexandria, Egypt) is earlier and better. Today, a **Standard Text,** based primarily on this second text type, is now accepted by the Protestant International United Bible Societies and the Roman Catholic Church.

We can now be more specific about the concluding doxology of the prayer in Matthew 6. With regard to external evidence, there are, unfortunately, no surviving papyrus manuscripts of Matthew 6. The next most reliable manuscripts, the early and important uncials of the Alexandrian text type (S 01, or Codex Sinaiticus, and B 03, or Codex Vaticanus), both from the fourth century, *do not contain the doxology*. Indeed, it is found in only four uncials, the earliest being from the fifth century. In contrast, the late minuscule manuscripts of the inferior Received Text include the doxology. External evidence therefore suggests that the prayer did not originally have the doxology. Indeed, we would go no further except that an early manuscript and the *Didachē* (di-dah-káy) contain shorter *variations* of a doxology ("k": "for thine is the power forever and ever"; *Didachē*: for thine is the power and the glory forever"). External evidence favors the probability that a doxology was not original, but added to the prayer very early.

The main question from the perspective of internal evidence is this: If the doxology was part of the prayer in Matthew, why would a later copyist have omitted it? In either private devotion or public worship it would have been natural to have added something to conclude the prayer. Moreover, we know of a similar doxology in the Bible, namely, 1 Chronicles 29:11–13. Verse 11 reads:

> "*Thine,* O LORD, is the greatness, and *the power, and the glory,* and the victory, and the majesty; for all that is in the heavens and in the earth is thine; thine is *the kingdom,* O LORD, and thou art exalted as head above all." (KJV)

Since copyists usually added to and improved on their manuscripts, it is likely that very early in Christian history—the *Didache* and "k" noted above is evidence for this—a doxology similar to (based on?) the doxology found in scripture and in use in various liturgies was added. Thus, internal evidence also supports the omission of the doxology.

Textual critics conclude on the basis of external and internal evidence that the Lord's Prayer in the Gospel of Matthew did not originally contain the doxology; rather, it was added at an early date.

With respect to the Roman Catholic and Protestant liturgies, the Catholic liturgy was derived from the Latin Vulgate, which in this particular instance follows the best Greek manuscripts in omitting the doxology. In contrast, the *Textus Receptus,* based on late minuscule manuscripts and used as the basis for Protestant translations, including the influential King James Version, contained the doxology. It became the basis for the Protestant liturgies. On the basis of the above conclusion, the familiar Catholic liturgical form of the prayer is more likely to be representative of what the author of the Gospel of Matthew originally wrote, and that is the form of the prayer we shall discuss in the rest of this chapter.

HISTORICAL CRITICISM

Suppose that we now have a relatively accurate text of the New Testament and a relatively good translation of it. Further questions persist. Who wrote the Gospel of Matthew? What was the background of the author? Where was the gospel written? To whom? Why? Why is this prayer included? Was it derived from a source? If it was, was the source written or oral? What was the religious situation in which the prayer was prayed or taught? What were the social conditions represented by the prayer? Did Jesus actually pray this prayer or some version of it? These are some of the main questions of **historical criticism.**

Scholars have developed several methods for attempting to solve these literary and historical problems. We can again summarize these methods:

1. General Historical Criticism.
2. Source Criticism.
3. Form Criticism.
4. Redaction Criticism; Composition Criticism; Genre Criticism.
5. Social-Historical and Social-Science Criticism.
6. Archeology.

Each of these methods has arisen to solve certain specific problems of interpretation. We shall now consider each of them.

General Historical Criticism

Who wrote the Gospel of Matthew? To answer this question we need to keep in mind several facts. First, the titles of the gospels ("superscriptions") with their formula ("According to X") were added to distinguish one from the other according to *second-century opinion,* that is, "(This one was written) according to X," "(that one) according to Y," and so on. Second, not one of the four gospels identifies its author within the book. Third, the surviving writings of Church Fathers between 95 and 150 C.E. do not mention them by author. Finally, about 140–150 C.E., a certain **Papias,** a bishop in Hieropolis in Asia Minor (modern Turkey), wrote about "Mark" and "Matthew." Of Matthew, he said: "Matthew collected the sayings *(logia)* in the Hebrew language, and each interpreted them as best he could" (Eusebius, *Ecclesiastical History* 3.39.16). By "Hebrew" Papias may have meant Aramaic. By "Matthew" Papias undoubtedly meant one of Jesus' twelve disciples (Matt 10:3; Mark 3:18; Luke 6:15; compare Acts 1:13) who, in the Gospel of Matthew, and *only in this gospel,* is the "toll collector" at Capernaum along the Sea of Galilee (Matt 9:9; 10:3). By the late second century C.E. this Matthew was secured as the author (Irenaeus, *Against Heresies* 3.11.7; compare 16.2 [185 C.E.]).

Papias says nothing about when or where the first gospel was written. Presumably, he had in mind the years soon after the death of Jesus, and because of its "Hebrew" language, some place in Palestine, as later writers claimed (for example, fourth-century Jerome, "Prologues to the Four Gospels," *Commentary on Matthew; Illustrious Men* 3).

Does this information tally with what we know about the Gospel of Matthew? There are complications. First, our Gospel of Matthew is not simply a collection of "sayings" *(logia),* as Papias says; rather, it is a long narrative (twenty-eight chapters) and contains shorter narratives, for example, miracle stories. Second, experts are convinced that our Greek Matthew is not a translation from Hebrew or Aramaic, the language Papias mentions. Third, it is usually argued that the first gospel used Greek sources. None of this tallies with Papias' information.

There are also complications about the implied date. References within the gospel speak about someone or something "abominable" that defiled the Jerusalem Temple (24:15–16 [Mark 13:14]; compare Dan 9:27; 11:31; 12:11; 1 Macc 1:54; 2 Macc 6:2). Such evidence points to the probability that the author knew about the destruction of Jerusalem by the Roman general Titus in 70 C.E. (**Flavius Josephus** [37–100? C.E.], *Wars of the Jews* 6.1.1–6.4.8 paragraphs 1–248; see Chapter Two), as the author of the Lukan gospel seems to think (Luke 21:20; compare 19:43). The Gospel of Matthew also hints at this destruction in 22:7. There are other facts converging to date the first gospel sometime in the late first century C.E. Those facts include its use of Mark as a source (see below, the Two-Source Theory) and the heightened conflict between Christians and Pharisees in this period, also typical of the Gospel of Matthew. Thus, the generally accepted view is that the Gospel of Matthew was written about 85 to 90 C.E. Such a date is very late for a disciple of Jesus, and it adds to the difficulty of maintaining the Papias and church tradition about "Matthew."

Finally, was the first gospel written in Palestine? Modern critics most often suggest that the probable location is Antioch, Syria, north of Palestine. The primary reason for this logic is that the gospel is known to have been in use there in the early second century (Ignatius *Smyrneans* 1:1 [Matt 3:15]; compare also *Polycarp* 2:2 [Matt 10:16]; *Ephesians* 19:2–3 [Matt 2:2]). Not everyone agrees with this Antioch location, but it is probably still the majority view.

The usual conclusion of general historical criticism is that Papias' information about "Matthew" as author is inaccurate. The usual theory is that an anonymous person composed it about 85–90 C.E., perhaps in Antioch. Since a well-known and authoritative name was later attached to the book, it is called **pseudonymous.** It is important to see at this point that pseudonymity was a common phenomenon among the ancients, who apparently had not developed the modern notion of "intellectual property." Thus, books could be associated with an author's opinion, or be believed to have been written by an author, or be named with the conscious intention to give them authority, or all these reasons simultaneously (see Chapters Three, Eight, Fourteen).

The implication of pseudonymity for the Gospel of Matthew is important for interpreting the prayer of Jesus in this gospel: it was not recorded simply because Jesus' disciple, the toll collector Matthew, heard it, memorized it, and then wrote it in his memoirs. Rather, an unknown author must have taken it from some written source or learned it from some familiar oral/liturgical tradition.

The background to the Gospel of Matthew is only one sample of general historical reconstruction of the first century. We shall consider many others throughout this book.

Source Criticism (written sources)

If the Lord's Prayers in Matthew and Luke are placed side by side, a modern translation (New Revised Standard Version, 1989, altered) looks like this:

Matthew 6:9b–13	Luke 11:2–4
Our **Father** in heaven,	**Father,**
hallowed be your name.	**hallowed be your name.**
Your kingdom come,	**Your kingdom come.**
Your will be done,	
On earth as it is in heaven.	
Give **us** this day **our daily bread;**	*Give* **us** each day **our daily bread;**
And forgive us our debts,	**And forgive us our** sins,
As we **also** *have forgiven*	As we **also** *have forgiven*
our debtors.	everyone who is indebted
	to us;
And do not bring us to the test,	**And do not bring us to the test.**
But rescue us from the	
Evil One.	

These parallels reveal that the two prayer versions contain words and phrases that are exactly alike (boldface), somewhat alike (italics, not visible in English translation), and very different (Note: Some expressions, like "this day" and "each day," are different phrases in Greek; therefore, "day" is not the same word). If we accept the pseudonymous conclusion and late dating about this gospel, but posit some connection between the two versions of the prayer, five possibilities suggest themselves(the references to Mark, Matthew, and Luke are to three *writings,* not persons):

1. Luke used Matthew as a source, shortening the prayer;
2. Matthew used Luke as a source, lengthening the prayer;
3. Matthew and Luke independently modified a written source;
4. Matthew and Luke independently modified an oral/liturgical tradition;
5. some mixture of solutions 1–4.

Which solution is most likely? Certain facts that will become clear require that we first address solutions 1–3. **Source criticism** is the method for analyzing texts to discover their written sources.

The view that became accepted down through the centuries was a version of the first one: The gospels were composed in the order in which they are found in the New Testament. Matthew, Jesus' disciple, came first; Mark used and shortened Matthew's gospel; Luke knew and used both gospels, Matthew and Mark; and John, another disciple, used the first three, but wrote a "spiritual gospel."

There are difficulties with this traditional theory. First, the Gospel of John might be described as "spiritual," but it is so different in outline, vocabulary, style, and subject matter that its *direct* literary dependence on the three others is not very likely. Second, most modern critics find it incredible that the Lukan writer used the Gospel of Matthew as a direct literary source, because there are irreconcilable differences in long, crucial passages such as the birth and resurrection stories. Yet, it cannot be denied that all three have the same general outline and that they have the same or similar content. It is therefore possible to place the first three gospels in parallel columns and compare them. A book placing them together in parallel columns is called a "synopsis" (Greek *syn,* "together"; *optic,* from the verb "to see"), and the first three gospels are usually called the **"synoptic gospels."** *The problem of explaining the similarities and differences of the synoptic gospels in both order and content is called "the Synoptic Problem."* On the one hand, it is a problem of sources—who used what—but it is also more: Its results are crucial for determining the sequence, dating, and authorship of the gospels.

To understand the problem, study a passage found in all three gospels ("the triple tradition"), the Baptism of Jesus. Certain agreements are in italics; they will be be explained below.

Matthew 3:13–17	**Mark 1:9–11**	**Luke 3:21–22**
Then Jesus came from *Galilee* to John at the Jordan, to be baptized by him.	In those days Jesus came from Nazareth of *Galilee*	Now when all the people were baptized

14) John would have prevented him, saying, "I need to be baptized by you, and do you come to me?" 15) But Jesus answered him, "Let it be so now; for it is proper for us in this way to fulfill all righteousness." Then he consented.

16) And when Jesus had been baptized,	and was baptized by John in the Jordan. 10) And	and when Jesus also had been baptized
just as he came up from *the water,* suddenly the heavens were opened to him and *he saw* the Spirit of God descending like a dove and alighting on him; 17) and a voice from heaven said "This is my Son, the Beloved, with whom I am well pleased."	just as *he* was coming out of *the water,* *he saw* the heavens torn apart and the Spirit descending like a dove on him 11) and a voice came from heaven, "*You* are my Son, the Beloved; with *you* I am well pleased."	and was praying, the heaven was opened 22) and the Holy Spirit descended upon him in bodily form like a dove. And a voice came from heaven, "*You* are my Son, the Beloved; with *you* I am well pleased."

These parallels reveal that Matthew and Mark agree against Luke (Jesus from Galilee; Jesus comes up from the water; he sees things), and Mark and Luke agree against Matthew (absence of reason Jesus baptized by John; no "and alights"; "you" [twice]), but *Matthew and Luke do not agree against Mark. Such a pattern suggests that Mark is the common factor, or source, of Matthew and Luke.* The most obvious additions to Mark are found in Matthew 3:14–15.

A similar pattern exists in the order of the major events (not sayings) throughout the three gospels. Study of a synopsis will show that when the Gospel of Luke deviates from the Markan order, the Gospel of Matthew, where parallel, does not, and vice versa. However, *Matthew and Luke do not normally agree against Mark. Thus, the Gospel of Mark seems to be the common thread.*

There is a third and related argument, namely, it is easier to explain how and why Matthew and Luke changed Mark than how and why Mark and Luke changed Matthew. This argument involves the more detailed perspectives of the writers of the gospels themselves (see "Redaction Criticism" below).

A fourth, related argument stresses the length of the gospels, the kind of material they contain, and the length of the various passages within them.

	Matthew	Mark	Luke
Verses	1,068	661	1,149
Words	18,293	11,025	19,376

The Gospel of Mark is the shortest of the three. Yet, in "the triple tradition," Mark's version of any given passage is often longer. If the Markan author had known the important material just listed, would he have omitted it from a source (Matthew) and then expanded the other stories? It is easier to explain why and how the authors of Matthew and Luke shortened their versions of various passages to make room for what seem to be very important passages.

Other, less impressive, arguments are these: Matthew and Luke revised Mark's "inferior" grammar and Mark's explanations of Aramaic terms, colloquialisms, and redundancies.

Cumulatively, these arguments lead to the theory that Mark, not Matthew, is the earliest gospel and a source for Matthew and Luke. This theory is called **the Markan priority.** It will explain passages where Matthew or Luke, or both together, agree with Mark. However, if the Lukan author did not know the Gospel of Matthew (or vice versa), as the theory holds, it will *not* explain the exact or close parallels between Matthew and Luke not found in Mark (the "double tradition"). Neither will it explain single traditions (only in Matthew, or only in Luke). Let us consider the "double tradition" first.

If a *direct* literary connection between the gospels of Matthew and Luke is unlikely, how can they share so many word-for-word verses that are not found in Mark? The usual solution is that these verses come from another written source that has not survived. Since the late nineteenth century, scholars have called this hypothetical source **"Q"** (German *Quelle*, "source," is one common explanation for the symbol). Q can be easily seen in a synopsis by observing parallel passages in Matthew and Luke that are not in Mark. This material consists of sixty-eight passages, or about 235 verses, or about 22 percent of Matthew (4290 words) and 20 percent of Luke (3559 words). It is distributed differently throughout the two gospels. Since the Lukan gospel is thought to have the better sequence of Q, scholars designate the sixty-eight passages in Q by the Lukan chapter and verse preceded by the letter "Q" (that is, Q 4:3–8 = Luke 4:3–8 = Matt 3:3–10).

Q scholars usually think that Q was written 50–70 C.E. References to Galilean towns point to a possible Galilean origin. There is also a general consensus about what it contained: mostly sayings of Jesus. Linguistic analysis will show that Matthew and Luke had access to a written version in Greek, but that the original was written in Aramaic. Indeed, Aramaic Q comes closer to Papias' description of what "Matthew" composed (a collection of sayings in "Hebrew") than our present Gospel of Matthew. A "sayings gospel" analogous to Q in form, but only partially sharing some of the same content, was discovered at Nag Hammadi, Egypt, in 1945; it is called the *Gospel of Thomas* (see Chapters Four, Five, Fifteen).

Finally, what about the passages that are found in only one gospel? Since most of Mark is in Matthew and Luke (about 94 percent), these are mostly sections in Matthew and Luke. Many of these sections represent other sources, written or oral. They are called **"Special M"** and **"Special L."** One must be cautious; in some cases they may be totally new compositions by the author.

We may now represent the relation of the synoptic gospels:

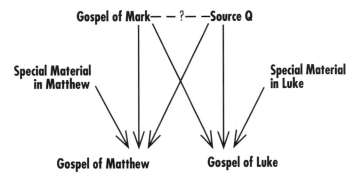

This solution to the Synoptic Problem is called the **"Two-Source Theory,"** "two" referring to the two main *written* sources, Mark and Q. *The Two-Source Theory, built on the acceptance of the priority of the Gospel of Mark and the existence of Q, is the simplest and most widely held solution to the Synoptic Problem.*

However, not everyone accepts the Two-Source Theory. One major reason is that in a few instances of the triple tradition, the wording in Matthew and Luke agrees *against* Mark (for example, Mark 1:7–8; Matt 3:11–12; Luke 3:16–18). How could this happen if their authors did not know each other? These "minor agreements" raise the question whether the gospels of Matthew and Luke were really literarily independent after all. An alternative solution to the Synoptic Problem is that Matthew came first, Luke modified Matthew, and then Mark shortened both (a renewal of the "Griesbach [or Two-Document] hypothesis" [Griesbach was a nineteenth-century scholar]). Defenders of the Two-Source Theory sometimes offer an alternative explanation for the "minor agreements": Mark and Q occasionally contained the same material ("Mark-Q overlaps"— note the dotted line and question mark between Mark and Q in the Two-Source Theory diagram above). Other scholars have put forth theories about more complicated interrelationships among the synoptic gospels. For example, some say that there are multiple editions of gospels that have complex interrelationships difficult to track or use oral alongside written traditions.

In this textbook we follow the Two-Source Theory, but we recognize that the challenges to it have important points to make and that the multiple gospel theories also have merit. Thus, the simple, wooden form represented by the diagram above can serve as a simplified solution to the problem, but it is not adequate to gospel complexity.

We shall look again at the Lord's Prayer. This time, we shall number the "petitions," or direct requests to God, in the Matthean form of the prayer.

The prayer is not found in Mark. The boldface lines show the terms and phrases that Matthew and Luke share in common. The third and seventh petitions are found only in Matthew. Would the Lukan author have omitted them if they had been in Q? This is not likely. A better hypothesis would be that the author of Matthew added them to Q. We can refine the point. First, observe that in Matthew the first three petitions refer to God with second-person singu-

Matthew 6:9b–11	Luke 11:2–4
Our **Father** in heaven,	**Father,**
1) **hallowed be your name.**	**hallowed be your name.**
2) **Your kingdom come,**	**Your kingdom come.**
3) *Your will be done,*	
On earth as it is in heaven.	
4) Give **us** this day **our daily bread;**	Give **us** each day **our daily bread;**
5) **And forgive us our** debts,	**And forgive us our** sins,
As we **also** have forgiven our debtors;	As we **also** *have forgiven* everyone who is indebted to us;
6) **And do not bring us to the test,**	**And do not bring us to the test.**
7) *But rescue us from the Evil One.*	

lar pronouns ("your"), but the last four petitions refer to human beings with first- or third-person plural pronouns. Second, an additional phrase in Matthew occurs after each division, that is, (1) after the initial address to God (Greek word order, "Father, our in heaven," makes the point forcefully); (2) after the petitions to God ("Your will be done on earth as it is in heaven"); and (3) after the human petitions ("But rescue us from the Evil One"). The wording of Matthew, however, is probably closer to what Q originally contained in a few instances. We shall return to the reasons for this judgment below (see "Redaction Criticism"). For now, we offer a hypothetical reconstruction of the Q form of the prayer:

Father,
Hallowed be your name.
Your kingdom come.
Give us this day our daily bread.
And forgive us our debts,
As we also have forgiven our debtors.
And do not bring us to the test.

Summarizing, the Lord's Prayer does not occur in the first gospel simply because a disciple, an eyewitness of Jesus' life, heard what Jesus had said, remembered it, and recorded it. Rather, an unknown author from the late first century derived it from the Q source and expanded on it. A historical result is that the Q form of the prayer is earlier than the Matthean or Lukan forms.

However, is it possible that the author of Matthew knew (also?) an *oral* form that influenced his version of the prayer—for example, a form used in worship—or alternatively, that behind the shorter Q written form was an *oral* history? Let us shift from written sources to oral tradition and the method used to study it, form criticism.

Form Criticism (oral traditions)

You will easily recognize oral forms in our own culture, for example, the joke (three parts followed by a punch line), or the thirty-second TV ad (beer ads about macho males and sexy females). You can also analyze and comment on the social or psychological functions of these oral forms in their typical contexts (joke: racial, ethnic, or sexual stereotypes; ad: age, social status, economic bracket, gender and sex roles, marketing techniques). Finally, you also know something about the history of joke or ad forms (joke: more four-letter words than before; ad: changes in male-female relationships; more technical sophistication in presentation).

There were also well-known oral forms in antiquity. The spoken word and oral transmission were more highly valued. Well into the second century, the Christian Papias could still write: "For I did not suppose that the things from the books would aid me so much as the things from the living and continuing voice" (Eusebius, *Ecclesiastical History* 3.5). The recognition of oral tradition as common in primitive Christianity led German New Testament critics of the early twentieth century to study the phenomenon. The study is called **form criticism**. Form critics have been interested in the three matters we have cited above in relation to contemporary jokes and ads:

1. *Forms.* Smaller isolated, individual units (called "pericopes" [pur-`ik-ko-pees])—stories, sayings, hymns, and the like—that can be analyzed in isolation from their present literary contexts and compared with similar, well-known forms in the ancient cultural environment.

2. *Sitz im Leben* (German: literally, "setting in life," or loosely, "socioreligious context"), referring to socioreligious settings—preaching, teaching, moral exhortation, worship, convincing others—in which these forms functioned before authors placed them in their literary contexts. These functions and settings are also understood in relation to comparative religion in the environment (German: *Religionsgeschichte,* or "history of religions").

3. *The history of oral traditions.* As the settings and functions changed, the forms of sayings and stories changed. For example, Jesus' parables, told to challenge accepted religious and social attitudes in a particular context, were often transformed into symbolic allegories used to give more generalized moral teachings in the early church. In the process, the content shifted. Form critics usually argue that simpler, purer, or shorter oral forms developed into more complex, mixed, or longer forms. Study of this gradual buildup, or "accretions," reveals later stages of the oral tradition. By removing the later accretions, one can move back to earlier stages of the tradition. In other words, there are layers of tradition in each unit or pericope. Form criticism thereby becomes an aid to recovering the history of earliest Christianity (German *Formgeschichte* is literally, "form history").

For some form critics, the following aim should be added:

4. *Rediscovering Jesus' teaching and typical aspects of Jesus' life.*

Let us now return to the Lord's Prayer. Though all its forms (Luke, Matthew, the *Didachē*) are in couplets, or "parallel members," typical of oral prayer and poetry in Judaism, form critics expect that the shorter form of the prayer in Luke would have been earlier than the more developed form in Matthew (and the *Didachē*). Similarly the reconstructed Q form above would be argued as earlier on formal grounds.

Let us now arrange the prayer in metrical structure, translate it back into Aramaic, and write it in accented English characters so it can be pronounced by an English-speaking person.

1. *'Abbā'*	Father,
	Hallowed be your name.
2. *yit-qaddásh shʿmák*	Your kingdom come.
teté malkuták	
3. *lachmán d'limchár*	Give us this day
hab lán yoma dén	Our daily bread.
ushʿboq lán chobénan	And forgive us our debts/sins,
kʿdishʿbáqnan	As we also have forgiven
lʿchayyabénan	our debtors.
4. *wʿla' tá' 'elínnan lénisyón.*	And lead us not to the test.

Say aloud the left column. You will hear that the prayer sounds poetic. The *form* of the prayer can be outlined like this:

1. an invocation (addressing God, asking for God's presence);
2. two short petitions (requests);
3. two long (positive) petitions; and
4. a short, closing (negative) petition.

The invocation and two short petitions center on God, and the two long and last petitions center on humans.

In the "invocation" the Aramaic term *'Abbā'* behind "Father" as a direct address to God in an Aramaic prayer is distinctive. It is the more familiar term for the father within the family. It is used by children and adult sons and daughters; formal Jewish prayers do not use it. The Gospel of Mark attributes it to Jesus himself (Mark 14:36), but it persists as a liturgical utterance in the Greek-speaking Christianity of Paul's circles (Gal 4:6; Rom 8:15).

Next come the two short, second-person petitions. Compare their form and content with what is usually held to be a first-century prayer from the Jewish synagogue liturgy, the Kaddish.

> Exalted and *hallowed be his great name*
>   in the world which he has created according to his will.
> *May he let his kingdom rule* in your lifetime and in your days
>   and in the lifetime of the whole house of Israel, speedily and soon.
>   (Dalman, *Die Worte Jesu*, 305; Jeremias, *Theology*, 198)

In both prayers, the petitions fall together without conjunctions (form), and in both prayers a petition sanctifying God's name comes before another about the Kingdom of God (content). In Judaism, God was holy, and God's name, "YHWH" or Yahweh, was so holy that it was not uttered. "Circumlocutions" such as "the Lord" (= God, not Jesus) or "the Name" were used. Neither was God's name usually written; sometimes an abbreviation, for example "YY," was used. There may be irony here: the statement glorifying the Divine Name follows *'Abbā'*, the familiar term. The "Kingdom of God" is also central to Jesus' teaching, and in both the Kaddish and the Lord's Prayer it refers to something in the near future. The expression Kingdom "come" in the New Testament version is distinctive (see Chapter Fifteen).

The next two lines are the long petitions about "daily bread" and "debts." They are joined by a conjunction and they are longer, each consisting of two half-lines. The Matthean wording in Greek is more immediate ("this day"; "*[begin to]* give") and therefore probably more original (see below, "Redaction Criticism"). The precise sense of the rare term for "daily" (Greek *epiousios*) in "daily bread" is difficult to determine. It could mean "future," "what is necessary to subsist," or "tomorrow's." If the latter is correct, the phrase would be "give us tomorrow's bread today" (*Gospel of the Nazareans,* quoted by fourth-century Jerome, *Commentary on Matthew* 6:11 [Aramaic *māchar*]). Yet, either of the future senses does not exclude the daily bread needed to exist (Prov 30:8; the Ninth of the Eighteen Benedictions; compare Mark 6:8; Luke 12:29 = Matthew 6:31). As we shall see in Chapter Fifteen, eating together was important for the practice of Jesus and his peasant and outcast followers.

The "debts" term has been discussed above. Greek *opheilēmata* and Aramaic *hōbā'* clearly mean "debts" of money, but the Aramaic also can have the meaning "sins." The Greek term for "sins" is found in Luke (Luke 11:4: *tas hamartias*). Was the original emphasis on debts, sins, or both, perhaps in some ambiguous sense? Jewish morning and evening prayer puts several meanings together:

> Bring me not into the power of *sin,*
> bring me not into the power of *debt,*
> bring me not into the power of *temptation,*
> bring me not into the power of *what is shameful.*
> (Babylonian *Berakot* 60b; Jeremias, *Theology,* 202)

Some scholars think that the Matthean "debts" and the Lukan "sins" are simply alternate translations of Aramaic *hōbā'* (compare Mark 11:25). In Q Jesus is the "friend of tax collectors and sinners" (Q Luke 7:34 [Matt 11:19]), a much-discussed phrase that included debtors, and early Christians practiced "baptism of repentance for the forgiveness of sins" (Mark 1:4). Yet, at the written Greek level it is more likely that the Lukan writer changed Greek "debts" (*opheilēmata*) in Q to "sins" (*tas hamartias*) for two reasons: The Gospel of Luke places a stronger emphasis on the theme "forgiveness of sins" (Luke 15), and both Matthean and Lukan writers have the term for "debt(s)" in the following clause (*opheiletais*). Thus, the Matthean Greek word "debts" probably stood in Q. However, if Jesus spoke a word in Aramaic that could mean both "debts" and "sins," what did he mean (see Social-Science and Social-Historical Criticism below)? Another question: Does "as we have forgiven our debtors" imply that God's forgiveness depends on human forgiveness? While the Gospel of Matthew seems to think so (Matthew 6:14–15; compare 18:21–22, 35; 5:23–26), Aramaic specialists say that the Aramaic sense is that God requires humans to be willing to forgive.

Formally, the last, single line of the prayer with its negative prohibition seems to be out of place; it is abrupt after two sets of parallel members. Perhaps some sort of "ad lib" conclusion followed (the "seal"), and we have seen that a doxology was added. In any case, prayers for deliverance from trial and testing were common in Judaism (Ben Sira 51:10), and there are also prayers for removing one's transgressions (Benedictions 6 and 7 of the Eighteen Benedictions) and temptation (Morning and Evening Prayer cited above; 1QM 1:12 in the Dead Sea Scrolls). Christianity also stresses deliverance from trial (Mark 14:36).

We have briefly discussed form and content. What about a socioreligious context for its function *(Sitz im Leben)*. In the Gospels of Matthew and Luke and the

Didachē Jesus instructs his followers in prayer. The order of material in the *Didachē* (*Did* 1–6, the two ways; 7 baptism; 8 fasting and Lord's Prayer; 9–10 eucharist) also suggests that it was used to instruct those who, following baptism, were formally initiated into an early Christian community. Yet, the addition of the doxology in Matthew/*Didachē* circles shows that by about 100 C.E. Christians prayed the prayer. In short, written sources indicate that from the last decades first century on, the Our Father was taught, memorized as a model and example prayer in religious instruction, and prayed in worship. Was this the setting earlier in the century? Possibly. At least part of Q—some recent study argues that this part was earlier and a source for the final form of Q—was Christian wisdom teaching.

Is this the prayer that Jesus himself prayed? Form critics apply several criteria for recovering the teaching of Jesus. One important criterion is distinctiveness in content in comparison with Judaism and the rest of early Christianity. The three most distinctive elements in the prayer are: use of the familiar term *'Abbā'*; the petition that the Kingdom "come"; and the willingness of humans to forgive as a condition for God's forgiveness of them. Another criterion is the consistency or "coherence" of the prayer with the rest of Jesus' characteristic teaching and activity. Some interpreters have argued that the above reconstructed prayer in Aramaic was prayed and taught by Jesus. As a Jew Jesus would also have seen God's name as holy, have petitioned God for "bread," and have stressed God's forgiveness of debts/sins. Its *Sitz im Leben* would probably have been Jesus' everyday meals with his disciples and disreputable people (Matt 8:11; 11:16–19). Other interpreters have argued that Jesus prayed some of the individual phrases that were later incorporated into a more formalized prayer. Whether the interpreter accepts the whole or only some of the parts as going back to Jesus, the result is that we are closer to the Jesus of history (at least the "echo of his voice"). This is one goal of some form critics.

Redaction Criticism; Composition Criticism; Genre Criticism

We have stated that according to carefully controlled criticism one can explain how and why the Matthean and Lukan writers changed the Markan order. We have also affirmed that while the shorter Lukan prayer form is earlier, in a few cases the Gospel of Matthew preserves the more original wording. Such judgments are in part based on conclusions about the special interests of the individual authors of Q, Matthew, and Luke.

The method that studies the way Biblical writers accepted or rejected, changed or expanded, or otherwise reformulated their oral and written sources, as well as how they reordered and regrouped them to make a certain point, composed new materials, and structured their accounts is called **redaction criticism.** It assumes that the writers were more than simple compilers of tradition; they were creative authors who intended to put forth their own perspectives or "theologies." When redaction criticism is combined with source criticism and form criticism, one can observe how authors of Matthew and Luke make use of Q, Mark, oral traditions, and perhaps other written traditions. Where the traditions and sources do not empirically exist, but must be theoretically reconstructed as in the case of the Acts of the Apostles or what "lies behind" the Gospel According to Mark, the method has sometimes been called **composition criticism.** Since its practice is very similar, we shall refer to both as redaction criticism.

If you examine the Lord's Prayer in the Lukan context, you will see:

11:1	Jesus at prayer in a lonely place
11:2–4	**The Lord's Prayer**
11:5–8	Parable of the friend making a demand that is answered at midnight
11:9–10	**Exhortations and promises about "ask," "seek," and "knock"**
11:11–13	**Rhetorical questions about asking and answering in human situations and "how much more" God is willing to answer**

The boldface passages are from Q. We cannot go deeply into the total redactional perspective of Q itself until Chapter Five; at this point we note only that these passages are part of an important interest in Q: "wisdom"-instruction for members of the community. One passage, Q 11:9–10, has a parallel in the *Gospel of Thomas* 92.

Let us focus on the Gospel of Luke. The author has inserted a parable from Special L about God's response to persistence (11:5–8) into a block of Q material (Q 11:2–4, 11:9–13). The whole is then introduced by Jesus himself praying "in a certain place" (Luke 11:1). This last feature corresponds with the Lukan writer's unique emphasis on Jesus as one who prays before or during important events (see Chapter Eleven).

Within this section Jesus is also asked to teach prayer as John the Baptist has taught his disciples. In the Lukan gospel, John is viewed positively as Jesus' blood relative and a forerunner of the Messiah, and the story of his infancy is narrated (Luke 1; 3:1–6, 3:19–20; [compare Mark 1:1–6]; 7:18–35; Luke 9:9 [contrast Mark 6:17–29 = Matt 14:3–12]); yet, he is subordinate to Jesus (Luke 3:15–18), his water-baptism is not enough in comparison to Jesus' Spirit-baptism (Luke 3:16; Acts 19:1–7), and he is said to belong to a time prior to Jesus (Luke 16:16). The Baptist comment may therefore reflect a rivalry between Jesus' and John's followers (compare John 4:1–2).

A third observation about the Lukan gospel is that if the Christian asks God for the Holy Spirit, it will be granted (11:12). The gift of the Holy Spirit is also a central Lukan theme. It often accompanies baptism and it guides Jesus and the early church in its mission to the world (see further, Chapter Ten).

Finally, the Lukan author has placed this set of passages in the larger context of Jesus' journey from Galilee to Jerusalem (Luke 9:51–18:14). During the journey the teachings and actions of Jesus demonstrate that his message of salvation is available to all kinds of people, for example, Samaritans (Luke 9:51–56; 10:25–37), Gentiles (10:17–20; 13:29), women (10:38–42; 11:27–28), sinners (15:1–32; 17:3–4; 18:9–14); and the poor (12:13–21; 16:19–31).

For the Lukan writer, the Lord's Prayer is instruction from the Jesus who prayed at decisive moments in his life. It is a model prayer for any Christian who has been baptized, who has received the Holy Spirit (granted also in prayer), who is part of the ongoing church in time, and who prays, whether Jew or Gentile, man or woman, rich or poor. If the Christian prays persistently, God will answer.

The Gospel of Matthew places the Q material in a different context. Jesus is still in Galilee and portrayed as teaching the Sermon on the Mount (Matt 5–7). The beginning of the Sermon shows that Jesus is on a mountain before larger crowds. He is sitting, the usual position for a Jewish teacher (5:1). The key theme is that Jesus is a more authoritative teacher than contemporary Jewish teachers (7:28–29; compare 23:8). We can outline the more immediate context like this:

6:1	Beware of showing off your piety before others
6:2–4	Do not show off giving alms, like the hypocrites; give in secret.
6:5–6	Do not show off when you pray, like the hypocrites; pray in secret.
6:7–8	Do not pray like the Gentiles who heap up empty phrases.
6:9–13	**Lord's Prayer**
6:14–15	*Forgive others their transgressions.*
6:16–18	Do not show off when you fast, like the hypocrites; fast in secret.

In this context, the Lord's Prayer from Q (Matt 6:9–13) and the forgiveness of sins from Mark (Matt 6:14–15; Mark 11:25) have been inserted into a Matthean-sounding section about three common acts of piety in Judaism and Jewish Christianity: almsgiving, prayer, and fasting (6:1–4; 6:5–8; 6:16–18). The Q section about "asking," "searching," and "knocking" (Q 11:9–13; Luke 11:9–13 above) has been deferred until later (Matt 7:7–11). The major point is that when Jesus' followers practice the three acts of piety they should not show off like the hypocritical Jewish religious leaders (6:1, 2, 5, 16; compare 23:1–36). Rather, they should practice them in secret and their heavenly Father will reward them in secret (6:1, 4, 6, 18). In the prayer section itself, one should not "heap up empty phrases as the Gentiles do." One should, then, "pray like this . . ." Then comes the Lord's Prayer, followed by the correlation between human and divine forgiveness (Matt 6:14–15; Mark 11:25).

In the Matthean context the prayer instructs and serves as a model and an example of a superior way that contrasts with long-winded Gentiles, but much more, with hypocritical Jewish leaders. In the words of the Sermon, "For I tell you, unless your righteousness exceeds that of the scribes and Pharisees, you will never enter the kingdom of heaven" (Matt 5:20).

Redaction critical analysis of vocabulary and themes will also yield reasons for the additions to the Q prayer in the Gospel of Matthew. They indicate that the Matthean writer was not merely following an alternative oral/liturgical prayer tradition.

1. *"Our . . .in heaven"* is typical Matthean editorial practice to surround references to "Father" with "heavenly" or "my/your . . . in the heavens" (5:45, 48; 6:1, 9, 14, 26, 32; 7:11, 21; 12:50, etc.).
2. *"Your will be done"* corresponds to the Matthean emphasis on doing the "will of the ('my') Father" (7:21; 26:42; 21:31; compare 12:50) or "your will" (6:10; 18:14), and may reflect Jesus' prayer language elsewhere (compare Mark 14:36 = Matt 26:39 = Luke 22:42); it also means producing "fruits" superior to that of the "hypocritical" Jewish leaders.

3. *"On earth as it is in heaven"* is especially typical of the heaven/earth contrast in Matthew (Matthew thirteen times; Mark two times; Luke five times).
4. In *"But rescue us from the Evil One,"* the "Evil One" is a Matthean term for the devil (Matt 13:19; 13:38).

Redaction criticism also gives reasons for the judgment that the original Q *wording* is sometimes preserved in the Gospel of Matthew:

1. The Lukan emphasis on the guidance of the Spirit as time marches on makes it likely that the Lukan author changed the more immediate "this day" to the continuing "each day" than the reverse (Luke 9:23 adds "daily" to the Markan text);
2. The Greek forms of "give" and "forgive" in the Lukan version also imply a continuation of time (English: "keep on giving," "keep on forgiving") and thus the more immediate Matthean verb forms were probably in Q;
3. The Lukan emphasis on the forgiveness of sins/sinners makes it more likely that the Lukan author changed "debts" to "sins" rather than the reverse, especially when "debtors"/"everyone indebted" is in the Q context (Matt 6:12 = Luke 11:4).

Form criticism analyzes the form of smaller units such as aphorisms, parables, allegories, anecdotes, miracle stories, creeds, confessions, and prayers, and it does so in relation to comparable cultural forms. Redaction criticism analyzes larger units, or wholes in relation to their parts. Closely related to form criticism and redaction criticism is **genre criticism.** Its major concern is the classification of forms in comparison with comparable forms in Hellenistic antiquity, but in this case, of whole documents, or literary genres. For example, twenty-one of the twenty-seven books of the New Testament might be classified "letters." Yet, there are short, more personal letters, a long essay letter, and some letters that are not even letters! What was the general form of the letter in antiquity? Were there different types? How did letters function? There are four so called gospels in the New Testament. What is a gospel? Is it a literary type? Would understanding its type help to understand the purpose of its various units, for example, the Lord's Prayer?

Summarizing, redaction criticism tries to uncover the special emphases of an individual writer by determining the placement of traditions within an overall structure and observing the way in which these traditions have been chosen, connected, modified, expanded, reworked, and reordered. These changes show the author's special perspective as revealed in the minute details of vocabulary, style, emphases, creation of new material, and the like. Redaction criticism adds valuable historical information about the author's intentions at the time of writing. When there are no available sources to compare to the final composition, some critics prefer the term "composition criticism." Such final products can often be compared to similar genres, thus making it possible to learn more about the way literary products function. Finally, by removing the author's emphases, the interpreter can more easily see earlier sources and traditions, and thus gain insight into the prewritten history of early Christianity.

Social-Science Criticism and Social-Historical Criticism

One of the three major goals of the early form critics was to isolate the socioreligious settings *(Sitze im Leben)* of oral traditions in the early Christian communities. The settings they discovered, however, were primarily "church-related" settings. The Lord's Prayer, for example, was preserved in teaching and worship. However, other social questions need to be asked. How did everyday social relations and arrangements within and among groups affect the meaning of the prayer? How, for example, did ancient Jews like Jesus think about *'Abbā'* as part of the family, for example, in relation to mothers, brothers, and sisters? Why would any group "hallow" someone's name? What were political and social relations in ancient kingdoms like? What would the need for "daily bread" have meant in relation to poverty or repressive taxation? What social circumstances contributed to owing debts? What social problems were associated with "the test"?

Questions similar to these were asked by scholars in the early part of this century. About 1960 a renewed interest in such social questions took place. Answering them has not been easy, because the ancient sources do not intend to give direct information about, or explain, social relations. Moreover, there is no way of generating new data comparable to the modern opinion poll or of joining an ancient group and observing their behavior ("participant observation"). Rather, it is necessary to "read between the lines," to try to compare and contrast the New Testament information with what is otherwise known about social arrangements in that society or in comparable societies.

Two related methods have arisen, social-science criticism and social-historical criticism. **Social-science criticism** is interested in the general theory of social relations in fields such as sociology, sociology of religion, social psychology, social anthropology, and cultural anthropology. It wants to develop typical models of social arrangements, either from the same or distant cultures, or both, to see if the groups of the Bible fit any of them. For example, can we look at male dominance and hereditary family arrangements in distant societies of the Far East or in closer Mediterranean societies as a means to understand, even explain, male dominance in Judaism and the New Testament? What models for understanding Biblical differences between the rich and the poor can be learned from the study of the economies of preindustrial peasant societies? Can the study of religious groups around the world, of social organization and social conflict, of the way cultural symbols work, and of attitudes toward status, values, and norms of behavior help us understand the New Testament? **Social-historical criticism,** recognizing the paucity of data and need for some social science theory, begins with archeological information and historical texts. It is interested in describing specific historical conditions and early Christian responses to them. It would like to explain how they developed and changed over time. Thus, social historians emphasize the usual sources of historical reconstruction ("social description"; "social location"; "social context").

How does such study help to interpret the Lord's Prayer? A *social-historical* approach tries to determine the successive *social* contexts in which the prayer was used and transmitted. For example, in Q the challenge to conventional beliefs by teaching unconventional "wisdom" (Q 6:27, 29), stress on the poor (Q 6:20), and judgment on "this generation" (Q 7:31–35) and its Pharisaic teachers

(Q 11:39b–44, 46–52; 13:34–35; 12:51–59), point to early Palestinian Jewish Christian groups that were from the lower social and economic strata who opposed the rich and powerful. In the villages of Galilee, the Lord's Prayer was revolutionary "wisdom" and "prophetic" teaching in these circles.

There is a shift in the social-historical context in the Gospel of Matthew. By the late first century there had emerged a sharper conflict between a "Jewish–Christian" group and the Jewish group that had become dominant, the Pharisees. In Matthew the prayer is used to illustrate the proper way to pray in opposition to the style used by outsiders they labeled "hypocrites." Another social-historical context is represented by the Gospel of Luke, which reflects a Christian group that believed it had received the gift of the Holy Spirit through baptism. This group probably competed with the followers of the Baptist; yet, it was more fluid and stressed the inclusion of the poor, outcasts, women, and non-Jews. The prayer now represented the teaching of the founder of this group, believed to be the universal "benefactor" or "patron" of all humankind. In short, from a social-historical perspective, we witness a shift in the use of the prayer from an early Jewish Christian reform movement to other Christian groups.

The prayer (Q 11:2–4) can also be illuminated by social-science interpretation. "Worship" in antiquity is related to family, kinship, male-female roles, and village life, as well as the politics of empire and monarchy and the economics of agriculture. 'Abbā' fits family relations dominated by men; the son honors, respects, and obeys his father, who is also his teacher. "Hallowed be your name" is associated with the sanctity of the Divine Name. "Your kingdom come" derives its imagery from ancient middle eastern monarchies as political systems. "Give us this day our daily bread" suggests meal customs: Who is permitted to eat together (men? women? children? non-Jews? slaves? outcasts?); different types of meals (daily meals? community meals? banquets? religious feasts?); where meals are eaten (temples? shrines? houses? fields?); when meals are eaten (ordinary; holy days and seasons); status, who sits where, and the position of eating (head and foot of the table); extended family structures (fathers, mothers, children, household servants); hosts, guests, invitations, and hospitality; who cooks and who serves (men? women? slaves? leaders?); pure/impure foods (kosher foods, foods offered to foreign gods, bread, wine, who cooks); the order of foods served; and so on. Normally the father of a Jewish household began a meal by giving thanks, breaking the bread, and distributing it, features typical of early Christian eucharistic practice. "Forgive us our debts" is bound up with agricultural societies and the ancient economy: the control and redistribution of agricultural products; social roles and status; urban and rural forms of poverty; the burdens of taxes and tolls; hereditary wealth and inheritance by sons; repression of peasants and peasant revolts; "social welfare" in relation to family and village life; alms-giving and begging; and so on. Yet, in Jewish prayer debts are parallel to sin—the Aramaic word "debts" can sometimes mean "sins" (hōbā')—as well as temptation, and the important values of honor and shame. "Lead us not to the test" implies persecution and perhaps final judgment, as well.

In short, social-science criticism leads to theories, models, and cross-cultural parallels that help to analyze and explain social phenomena like the Lord's Prayer above and beyond worship and teaching contexts.

Archeology

In the narrow sense, archeology refers to the science of recovering and evaluating the material remains of everyday life from past civilizations, for example, buildings (temples, government buildings, houses), statues, objects of worship, magical paraphernalia, pottery, gems, and the like. It also includes literary remains of material objects, that is, inscriptions on stones, coins, pottery, burial stones, and amulets. In the broader sense, newly discovered manuscripts are often associated with archeology (see Appendix).

Material remains have political, social, religious, economic, and thus cultural relevance for any period of history. With respect to the Lord's Prayer, we can better understand kingdom language and poverty by the opulence of the kingdom of Herod, religious practices of the Jerusalem Temple, life in Palestinian and Hellenistic villages and cities, and so forth.

Archeology in the broader sense includes **manuscript discoveries.** The two most important discoveries for early Christianity are the Dead Sea Scrolls and the Nag Hammadi Texts. The Dead Sea Scrolls, discovered near the Dead Sea in 1947, give insight into a Jewish sect. Most scholars have identified it with the Essenes, and this identification is probably correct. Like the early Christians, this group experienced social, economic, and political repression. It baptized, celebrated a sacred meal with bread and wine, held beliefs about messiahs, and preserved revelations. The scrolls also contain prayers and songs that sanctify God's name and information about sin and temptation. The absence of '*Abbā*' reinforces the view that this name for God was distinctive in early Christianity. A similar form, '*Abî*, has been found in Aramaic Genesis Apocryphon (2:19, 24; 3:3). We shall have more to say about the "Dead Sea Sect" (probably the Essenes) in Chapter Three and the Appendix.

The texts of the Nag Hammadi Library, discovered in Egypt in 1945, contain Jewish, Christian, and Greco-Roman thought. One of the books, called the *Gospel of Thomas* can be compared to Q, especially in form. It is also very important for understanding unconventional wisdom in early Christianity (see Chapter Five), as well as the teaching of Jesus. Interestingly, this gospel is even more unconventional about the traditional Jewish practices of fasting, praying, and almsgiving than Matthew 6: "If you fast, you will give rise to sin for yourselves; and if you pray, you will be condemned; and if you give alms, you will do harm to your spirits" (Saying 14; compare Sayings 6, 104, 75; Irenaeus *Against Heresies* 121.3). We shall say more about the *Gospel of Thomas* in Chapters Five and Fifteen.

LITERARY CRITICISM

The above methods have been developed to solve specific literary and historical problems related to ancient history and literature. Beginning in the 1960s some New Testament interpreters, convinced that much was being lost in the attempt to probe behind the texts for historical information, predocument sources, and theological beliefs, turned to alternative methods of interpretation. We cannot do justice to the many varieties of this literary perspective, but will note three related variations.

New Literary Criticism

Some interpreters do not deny that the New Testament contains forms of ancient literature—genre remains important—as well as history, but their interests are not basically historical. Drawing upon the new literary criticism used to interpret modern literature, especially fiction, they claim that the critic should not just probe a Biblical text for the author's intention ("the intentional fallacy") and the text's date of composition, place of writing, and historical or social context. Rather, one should concentrate on the text's own *imaginary* "world," a world that understands life in subtle, indirect, metaphorical, and sometimes ironic ways. To use a favorite image, the text is not a "window" through which one looks to gaze upon the past, what was thought or what happened, the histories of individuals and groups, or the perspectives of authors living in those communities; rather, it is a "mirror" that reflects what one "sees" now, a creative work of art with meanings going beyond what was originally intended. Once produced, it takes on a life of its own, and like a painting, a piece of fiction, or a film, interpretation involves the perspective of the interpreter. From this perspective, numerous interpretations are possible.

Narrative Criticism

Narrative criticism seeks to recapture the story features of the Bible. It stresses how the story is told, how scenes are used, how the plot unfolds, and what the characters are like. It analyzes the "point of view" consciously adopted by an author in light of his or her intended readers (imaginary or not) , and especially the "world" of the text (imaginary or not). Like redaction criticism, it is interested in the final form, and like genre criticism it is concerned with the genre as a whole; however, the critic's main interest is on the effect of the total story as a work of art. Some narrative critics go further. They suggest that even nonnarrative genres, such as letters, have a story underlying them. For example, behind Paul's letters (the letter genre is not narrative as such) stands the story of Paul's relationship with his churches. To this extent, narrative criticism remains very interested in historical matters.

Reader Response Criticism

Somewhat similar to narrative criticism is reader response criticism. Reader response critics note that the point of view assumed in the text is not necessarily the point of view of the real author, who can assume an alternative stance as "implied author." Similarly, like narrative critics, reader response critics say that the text has in view an imaginary or intended reader who may not conform to actual readers, past or present. We, for example, may read a New Testament text quite differently than its intended respondents. Moreover, multiple levels of authors/speakers and readers/hearers are possible within a text, for example, the narrator of Mark tells a story; within that story is another narrative about Jesus in which Jesus teaches his disciples and they respond; further, his teaching may involve still another story, a parable in which there are other speakers and respondents. Thus, we see a response embedded within a response embedded within a story written to achieve an intended response. Such analyses often move us one or two steps away from what were "actual" authors/speakers and readers/hearers external to the text in antiquity, but the analysis claims that the latter are mediated to the interpreter through the text understood in this way.

Such interpretative approaches have often been criticized. The objection is that they do not appreciate that Biblical stories often refer to actual persons or events outside the imaginative story world, and that they are often different from modern fiction. Such outside factors are precisely what the other historical and literary criticisms have attempted to discover.

How do these rather different literary approaches affect the interpretation of the Lord's Prayer? One emphasis would be that the prayer must be seen within the context of the whole story about Jesus from beginning to end. We cannot offer an analysis of a whole gospel story at this point but we can offer a few observations from the Gospel of Matthew.

In the Matthean story, the narrator is an unidentified, unnoticed figure behind the scenes. All-seeing and all-knowing, this storyteller transports us from this scene to that scene, like film directors, camera people, and editors. The narrator gains our trust and attempts to convince us of the Truth. Thus, he gives us the "right" point of view, or as he implies, God's point of view (Matt 16:23).

The major characters in the Matthean story are the protagonist Jesus, his immediate followers, and the opposing religious leaders. Jesus is portrayed as the Messianic King descended from King David, as the special Son of God, and as the authoritative preacher, teacher, and healer. The immediate followers, the disciples, are of "little faith" and come into minor conflicts with Jesus, but ultimately they will carry on his mission. The opponents on the supernatural level are the Evil One and his demons; on the natural level they are the Jewish leaders who by the end of the story are joined by the crowds.

The time of the plot is from the conception of Jesus to his resurrection. There is also a greater expanse of time implied, from the creation (Matt 19:4) through the time of the author to the "end of the age" (Matt 28:20). The plot turns on conflict between good and evil. Jesus wins the supernatural conflict by not yielding to the test of the Evil One and by overcoming the evils of disease and demon possession; indeed, he has authority over nature itself. He appears to be defeated by his human adversaries, but his resurrection shows that he is ultimately victorious. In passing, the narrator steps outside the story to indicate to the "implied reader" that Jesus' followers are still spreading his message down to the present. In all of this, of course, we do not get the point of view of the Jewish leaders; had we done so, the story would look quite different! We are told with "proof texts" from Scripture that the story is the plan of God and fulfills his promises.

In the Gospel of Matthew, the plot is interrupted on five important occasions to portray the protagonist as the authoritative teacher or speaker. Thus, within the story is speech and reception. Jesus is portrayed as being unlike the hypocritical Jewish religious leaders. He properly interprets the religious traditions to his followers and lives according to his teaching, thus generating a great following. In Jesus' first sermon (Matt 5–7), the narrator takes us to an unknown mountain in Galilee (Matt 5:1) where Jesus interprets the "Law and the prophets" and their proper mode of observance (5:17–20) to disciples and crowds, an embedded audience. Jesus' interpretation of alms-giving, prayer, and fasting contrasts with the showy piety of the religious leaders. The Lord's Prayer is taught as a model prayer by Jesus to his followers; it is the way to pray in contrast to publicly observant prayer practices of religious leaders. It can be correlated with the whole story especially in the request not to be led to the test, in rescue from the Evil One, and in the religious leaders actions leading to Jesus' death. Ultimately it generates opposition and leads to the plot on Jesus' life (Matt 12:14). Finally, the Lord's Prayer lesson is for the "implied reader" of the story, but it may speak to other readers, as well. Insofar as the text has a life of its own, the teaching does not have one simple interpretation; indeed, it may have a number of different responses.

OTHER METHODS

The major methods we have outlined above do not by any means cover the whole "methods explosion" in New Testament study. Theory of interpretation, sometimes called **hermeneutic(s)** (Greek: *hermēneuō,* "I interpret"), opens up many possibilities for seeing meaning in texts. There are other varieties of literary criticism. "Structuralists," who have influenced literary criticism, usually derive their approach from the fields of linguistics and structural anthropology. They are interested either in the way a story fits a certain set of actions and roles, somewhat like the literary critics, or in a "deep structure" related to the way human beings think in opposites that have to be mediated, for example, "heaven" and "earth" as related to life and death. There are also poststructural interpreters (deconstructionists), who challenge virtually all previous interpretations in the history of Western civilization, leaving our texts open-ended. Other interpreters base their insights on their understanding of the psychoanalytic theories of Freud or Jung. One might , for example, relate the "father figure" in the prayer to Freud's view of the father. In contrast, there are interpreters interested in New Testament theology, which usually attempts to think consistently and coherently about major themes in the Bible. Finally, we should note feminist hermeneutics, that is, specialized insights that deal with gender issues often ignored by mainly male-dominated texts and male interpreters down through the centuries. What, for example, is the significance, historically or otherwise, of God's being addressed in patriarchal terms, that is, as "Father"?

SUMMARY

In summary, we list again, add to, and give the general period of dominance of several forms of interpretation.

1. English translation	Foreign-language documents
2. Textual	Manuscripts for reconstructing the New Testament
3. General Historical	Authors, dates, places, major ideas of writers

4. Source	Written sources used by New Testament authors
5. Form	Oral traditions, their histories, and settings
6. Redaction/Composition/	Special emphases and "final" forms of writings
Genre	Relation of final forms to cultural analogies
7. Social-Historical; Social-Scientific	Relations within, and symbols of, Christian groups
8. Archeology	Material remains and newly discovered texts
9. Literary	Plot, characters, implied authors/readers
OTHER METHODS:	
10. Psychoanalytic	Attempting to discover psychological insights
11. Theological	Common ways of thinking about God, Jesus, church, etc.
12. Structuralist	Relational ways human minds think, expressed in narrative
13. Poststructural	Meaning cannot be captured, is indefinitely deferred
14. Feminist	Strategic reorientation to neglected women's issues

If placed in a chronological chart, the critical methods and other orientations look like this:

There are many ways to approach the New Testament. In this chapter we have highlighted traditional historical and literary methods, along with social-historical and social-scientific methods. One must have some translated texts to interpret, and these texts have to be reconstructed from copies that have errors in them. It is also necessary to determine, where possible, authorship, time, and place, as well as sources and oral traditions used, contributions of authors, social contexts, and genres. Such methods will be used in this textbook. We have also noted some literary interpretations that for some analysts provide an alternative to the dominant historical-literary approaches. Such methods can be better understood through other textbooks. Though we have focused on the New Testament documents, we have noted some other early Christian literature. In accord with our continuing traditional literary, social historical, and sociological approaches, our next step will be to sketch the social-historical context of the New Testament. That will be the focus of Chapter Two.

FURTHER READING

The Lord's Prayer

ABD: "Abba" (J. Ashton); "Amen" (B. Chilton); "Semiticisms in the NT" (M. Wilcox); "Lord's Prayer" (J. L. Houlden).

> J. Barr, *"Abbá* Isn't 'Daddy',*" Journal of Theological Studies* 39 (1988), pp. 28–47.
> R. Guelich, *The Sermon on the Mount.*
> J. Jeremias, *New Testament Theology.*
> ———, *The Lord's Prayer.*
> N. Perrin, *The Kingdom of God in the Teaching of Jesus.*
> M. Smith, *Tannaitic Parallels to the Gospels.*
> G. Strecker, *The Sermon on the Mount. An Exegetical Commentary.*
> H. Taussig, "The Lord's Prayer," *Forum* 4/4 (1988), pp. 25–41.

General Surveys on Methods of Interpretation

ABD: "Biblical Criticism" (J. C. O'Neill); "Exegesis" (D. Stuart); "Historiography" (D. Latainer); "Scriptural Authority in the Post-Critical Period" (W. Brueggemann).

> E. J. Epp and G. W. MacRae, eds., *The New Testament and Its Modern Interpreters.*
> D. J. Harrington, *Interpreting the New Testament.*
> J. H. Hayes and C. R. Holladay, *Biblical Exegesis. A Beginner's Handbook. Theological Studies* 50 (1989).
> O. Kaiser and W.G. Kümmel, *Exegetical Method: A Stu* ' *Handbook.*

English Translation

ABD: "Versions, English" (J. P. Lewis); "Versions, English (Authorized Versions)" (J. P. Lewis); "Versions, English (King James Version)" (J. P. Lewis); "Versions, English (American)" (E. S. Frerichs); "Versions, Modern Era" (H. G. Grether); "Theories of Translation" (E. A. Nida).

> F. F. Bruce, *The English Bible. A History of Translations.*
> H. Thurston, *Familiar Prayers. Their Origin and History.*
> J. P. M. Walsh, "Contemporary English Translations of Scripture," *Journal of Theological Studies* 50 (1989), pp. 336–358.

Textual Criticism

ABD: "Chester Beatty Papyri" (A. Pietersma); "Codex" (H. Y. Gamble); "Codex Alexandrinus" (J. C. Slayton); "Codex Sinaiticus" (J. H. Charlesworth); "Codex Vaticanus" (D. C. Parker); "Lectionary" (K. Junack); "Textual Criticism (NT)" (E. J. Epp); "Vulgate" (D. C. Parker); "Versions, Ancient (Survey)" (S. N. Birdsall).

NJBC, pp. 1083–1112 (Texts and Versions: R. E. Brown; D. W. Johnson; K. G. O'Connell).

    K. and B. Aland, *The Text of the New Testament.*

    B. Metzger, *The Text of the New Testament* (3d ed.).

General Historical Criticism

ABD: "New Testament Criticism" (W. Baird).

    K. Aland, "The Problem of Anonymity and Pseudonymity in Christian Literature of the First Two Centuries," *Journal of Theological Studies 12* (1961), pp. 39–49.

    V. H. Harvey, *The Historian and the Believer.*

    E. Krentz, *The Historical Critical Method.*

Source Criticism

ABD: "Q" (C. M. Tuckett); "Source Criticism (NT)" (D.-A. Koch); "Two Source Theory" (D. L. Dungan); "Synoptic Problem" (C. M. Tuckett); "Two Source Hypothesis" (M.-É. Boismard, trans. T. Prendergast).

NJBC, pp. 587–595 ("Synoptic Problem": F. Neirynck).

    R. H. Klein, *The Synoptic Problem. An Introduction.*

    J. S. Kloppenborg, M. W. Meyer, S. J. Patterson, M. C. Steinhauser, *Q–Thomas Reader.*

    E. P. Sanders and Margaret Davies, *Studying the Synoptic Gospels.*

Form Criticism

ABD: "Form Criticism (NT)" (V. K. Robbins); "Tradition History" (D. A. Knight).

    R. Bultmann, "The Study of the Synoptic Gospels," in R. Bultmann and K. Kundsin, *Form Criticism: Two Essays on New Testament Research.*

    W. Kelber, *The Oral and Written Gospel.*

    E. V. McKnight, *What is Form Criticism?*

Redaction Criticism

ABD: "Redaction Criticism (NT)" (R. H. Stein).

    J. R. Donahue, *The Gospel in Parable.*

    N. Perrin, *What Is Redaction Criticism?*

    R. H. Stein, "What is *Redaktionsgeschichte?" Journal of Biblical Literature* 88 (1969), pp. 45–56.

Sociological, Anthropological, and Social-Historical Criticism

ABD: "Christianity" (L. Michael White); "Community, New Testament *Koinónia"* (R. W. Wall); "Sociology (Early Christianity)" (S. R. Garrett).

    J. Elliott, "Introduction," *A Home for the Homeless.* (2d ed.).

    B. Holmberg, *Sociology and the New Testament An Appraisal.*

    H. Kee, *Knowing the Truth: A Sociological Approach to New Testament Interpretation.*

    B. Malina, *The New Testament World. Insights from Cultural Anthropology.*

    C. Osiek, *What Are They Saying About the Social Setting of the New Testament?* (2d ed.)

    ——,"The New Handmaid: The Bible and Social Sciences," *Theological Studies* 50 (1989), pp. 260–278.

    Listening. Journal of Religion and Culture 21/2 (Spring, 1986).

Archeology (For further works, see Appendix)

ABD: "Archeology, Syro-Palestinian and Biblical" (W. G. Dever); "Coinage" (J. W. Bet-lyon); "Nag Hammadi" (B. A. Pearson); "Palestine Funerary Inscriptions" (E. Puech, trans. S. Rosoff); "Papyri, Early Christian" (S. R. Pickering); "Palestine, Archaeology of (NT)" (J. F. Strange).

IDB: "Archeology" (G. W. Van Beek).

IDB Suppl.: "Archeology" (W. G. Dever); (pp. 992–993, map of archeological sites); "Archeological Sites" (listed); "Manuscripts from the Judean Desert" (G. Vermes).

NJBC, pp. 1196–1218 "Biblical Archeology:" (R. North; P. J. King).

L. J. Hoppe, *What Are They Saying About Biblical Archeology?*

E. M. Meyers and J. F. Strange, *Archaeology, the Rabbis, and Early Christianity. The Social and Historical Setting of Palestinian Judaism and Christianity.*

Literary Criticism

ABD: "Reader Response Theory" (B. C. Lategan); "Rhetoric and Rhetorical Criticism" (R. Majercik).

D. Aune, *The New Testament in Its Literary Environment.*

D. Rhodes and D. Michie, *Mark as Story.*

J. Kingsbury, *Matthew as Story.*

R. A. Culpepper, *Anatomy of the Fourth Gospel.*

R. Fowler, *Let the Reader Understand: Reader-Response Criticism and the Gospel of Mark.*

P. Perkins, "Crisis in Jerusalem? Narrative Criticism in New Testament Studies," *Theological Studies* 50 (1989), pp. 296–313.

Other

ABD: "Computers and Biblical Studies" (H. Van Dyke Parunak); "Feminist Hermeneutics" (E. Schüssler Fiorenza); "Hermeneutics" (B. C. Lategan); "Linguistics and Biblical Studies" (W. R. Bodine); "Poststructural Analysis" (M. Davies); "Statistical Research on the Bible" (A. Dian Forbes); "Theology (NT)" (R. Morgan).

J. R. Donahue, "The Changing Shape of New Testament Theology," *Theological Studies 50* (1989), pp. 314–335.

D. and A. Patte, *Structural Exegesis: From Theory to Practice.*

P. Perkins, *Hearing the Parables.*

E. Schüssler Fiorenza, *In Memory of Her.*

———, *Bread not Stone: The Challenge of Feminist Biblical Interpretation.*

D. O. Via, *Kerygma and Comedy in the New Testament: A Structuralist Approach to Hermeneutic.*

———, "The Prodigal Son: A Jungian Reading." *Society of Biblical Literature 1975 Seminar Paper,* pp. 219–232.

Masada (Hebrew for "stronghold"), a majestic mesa 1900 feet by 600 feet, located about 50 miles southeast of Jerusalem near the shores of the Dead Sea. Originally built by the Maccabeans, it was further fortified and developed by Herod the Great (ruled 37–4 B.C.E.) who added a casemate wall around the top, a three-tiered palace-villa on the north end, enormous cisterns for water, a bath-house, and store-rooms. Two ritual baths were also unearthed there. The dramatic story of the last stand of the Jewish rebels against Rome on Masada (73 C.E.) is recorded by the Jewish historian Josephus (*Wars* 7.8–9, paragraphs 252–406).

CHAPTER TWO

THE SOCIAL-HISTORICAL CONTEXT OF THE NEW TESTAMENT

Christianity did not emerge in a vacuum. It arose out of a rich and varied historical background. It was the child of Judaism, but a Judaism that had been dominated politically by a sequence of foreign powers: Assyria, Babylonia, Persia, Macedonia-Greece, and, most recently, Rome. Thus, Judaism was a pluralistic or multicultural religion whose groups had come in contact with, and in varying degrees become assimilated to, a wide variety of influences from these colonial powers.

In this chapter, we shall isolate the sociohistorical background of Christianity in the Judaism of the Greco-Roman period, touching on religious matters only where they are necessary for understanding the main course of events. This approach is admittedly somewhat artificial, but it will have the advantage of greater clarity. We shall take up more fully other cultural trends, that is, religious ideas, groups, and movements in the next chapter.

EARLY HISTORY AND RELIGION OF THE LAND OF ISRAEL

EARLY CHRONOLOGY

B.C.E. (B.C.E. = Before the Common Era of Jews and Christians = Christian B.C.; C.E. = the Common Era of Christians and Jews = Christian A.D.)

1000	**Independent monarchy** under Kings David and Solomon
921	**Independent divided monarchy:** ISRAEL (NORTH) and JUDAH (SOUTH)
721	**Assyrians** overcome Israel, deport and import populations (origin of SAMARITANS)
587	**Babylonians** defeat Southern Kingdom (Judah), and destroy Jerusalem and the Temple
587–539	**Babylonian exile** of Jewish leaders

539	**Persians** under Cyrus the Great defeat Babylonians
	538 Edict of Toleration for Jews; some return
	515 Second Temple dedicated
	437? Nehemiah rebuilds Jerusalem's walls
	428? Ezra promulgates the Jewish "Law"
332	**Greeks** (Macedonians) march through Palestine
	301 Ptolemies (Greek–Egyptians) control Palestine
	198 Seleucids (Greek–Syrians) control Palestine
	167 Maccabean revolt of Jews against Seleucids
142	**Independent Maccabean (Hasmonean) Kingdom**
63	**Romans** assume control of Palestine; end of Jewish independence

The Israelite Monarchy and Religion Prior to the Babylonian Exile (1000–587 B.C.E.)

The lands surrounding the Mediterranean Sea are mostly rugged and dominated by great rivers and their flood plains, with a few arid regions to the East. Several major cities are found on these rivers and along the coasts. While attempts to correlate ecology and civilization are complex and debated, it is obvious that the sea is what these regions share in common; it creates a communication and trade network, carried into the interior by rivers and overland trade routes. It is also obvious that the rivers and their floodplains are the basis for the ancient agricultural economy. The rugged terrain and desert lands tend to produce independent communities, some of them nomadic tribespeople. Finally, the cities with their culture and civilization dominate the hinterlands. What emerges in this environment is a competitive, hierarchically arranged system of mostly male-dominated relationships. Kin groups and villages provide some relief from these pressures.

Palestine (the name first occurs in fifth-century B.C.E. Herodotus) is a small region about 150 miles "from Dan [in the North] to Beersheba [in the South]" and about 60 miles wide (see map, p. 53). It is bounded on the north by the foothills of Mount Hermon, on the west by the Mediterranean Sea, on the east by a region just east of the Jordan River, and on the south by the wilderness called the Negeb. It has no great river with a flood plain. The Jordan River, which flows south from the springs of Mount Hermon into the Sea of Galilee and then winds on to the Dead Sea, which is below sea level, is relatively small. The central hill country gradually slopes down to the sea in the West and to the Jordan Valley in the East. The northern and central regions have heavy rainfall and are more suited to agriculture; the southern area is barren and rocky. The region has a Mediterranean climate typified by winter rains and summer drought.

In antiquity Palestine was an agrarian, or peasant, society, although there was also some mining, fishing on the Sea of Galilee and small businesses. Its strategic location meant that before the coming of the Greeks and Romans it was a buffer state between the larger, more powerful empires to the north and east (Assyrians, Babylonians, Persians) and the south (Egyptians), and that it was positioned along the major overland trade routes between these civilizations.

Thus, there was much trading, with some exports in figs and dates. As in all such societies, the cities took the lead in cultural development, economic control of the agricultural surplus, and political power. Social arrangements were characterized by a certain suspicion of, and competitiveness with, those outside the family, clan, or village, and, of course, all relationships were dominated by men who lived according to the code of honor and shame.

The Hebrew Monarchy

Late in the second millennium B.C.E., groups that spoke a language called Hebrew could be found in "the land of Israel," the phrase for Palestine in the **Hebrew Bible.** About 1000 B.C.E., David, a young bandit and mercenary from Bethlehem, came to power and made Jerusalem his capital. In a period when the surrounding empires were in decline, he set up an independent monarchy with agriculture as its economic base. After David came his son Solomon, renowned for his wisdom, his many wives, and his execution of his father's plan to build the **Jerusalem Temple.**

The Divided Monarchy and the Continuation of the Southern Kingdom

About 921 B.C.E., the northern tribes, dissatisfied with forced labor practices, revolted and set up their own monarchy with a rival capital in Samaria and a rival temple on Mount Gerizîm. Thus emerged the **Divided Monarchy.** It consisted of the Northern Kingdom (Israel) and the Southern Kingdom (Judah; in later Roman times, Judea).

In **721 B.C.E.** the invading **Assyrians** crushed the Northern Kingdom. The resulting population, created by the Assyrian deportations and importations of peoples, became the **Samaritans.** The Southern Kingdom continued as the Davidic monarchy until the **Babylonians** destroyed Jerusalem and the Temple in **587 B.C.E.**

Basics of Religion during the Monarchies

Religion in antiquity was related to politics, economics, and family life. Among the Israelites, it was characterized by **monotheism,** the belief in one God. According to sacred stories, the god **YHWH,** or **Yahweh,** had made a treaty with one patriarchal ancestor, Abraham. God had promised Abraham that his descendants would be many and that they would inherit the land of Canaan (Genesis 12; 15). This **covenant** was said to have been ratified by the rite of **circumcision,** or cutting off the foreskin of baby boys on the eighth day after birth (Genesis 17). There were also traditions about other patriarchs, the twelve sons of Jacob [= the twelve tribes of Israel], the exodus from slavery in Egypt, the wilderness wanderings, the giving of the Law of Moses in the desert on Mount Sinai, and the conquest of the "promised land" of Canaan. These stories were molded by the deeply felt conviction that Yahweh directed the course of human affairs.

To these were added literature in which three institutions were important: **kingship,** in which the king was believed to be the mediator between the Divine and the human, the "Son of God" (2 Sam 7:14; Ps 2:7); the **priesthood,** which administered the sacrifices for sin and atonement at the Jerusalem Temple; and **prophecy,** which was Spirit-filled, but which often challenged the political, religious, and social conditions of the day. Finally, there were added accounts about Yahweh's creating the world and resting on the seventh day, a foundation for the **Sabbath** rest, as well as several agricultural **festivals** (Leviticus 23). More will be said about these institutions and festivals in Chapter Three.

THE JEWS UNDER THE BABYLONIANS AND PERSIANS (587–332 B.C.E.)

Destruction of Jerusalem and the Temple; The Babylonian Exile (587–539 B.C.E.)

In 597 B.C.E. **Babylonia,** located in Mesopotamia ("Between the Rivers"; in modern Iraq) conquered the southern kingdom, Judah. Jerusalem and its holy Temple were destroyed in 587 B.C.E. The Babylonians deported the Jewish leaders to Babylonia. Known as the **Babylonian Exile,** this period marked the beginning of the dispersion of Hebrew peoples to foreign countries (Greek *Diaspora,* "dispersion"; see "Diaspora Judaism" at the end of Chapter Three). From this point forward we call the Israelite people **Jews** and their culture and religion **"Judaism"** (from "Judah").

Jewish History and Religion in the Persian (Post-Exilic) Period (539–332 B.C.E.)

The Babylonian Exile was a major turning point in the history and religion of the Jews. Having overcome the Babylonians in 539 B.C.E., **Cyrus the Great of Persia** issued an **Edict of Toleration** in 538. Though many deported Jews chose to stay in Babylonia, which remained a center of Judaism for a thousand years, other exiles returned over time to Palestine. They hoped for the reestablishment of an independent monarchy under Zerubbabel (compare Haggai 2:23 and Zechariah 3:8; 6:12). That event did not happen. Yet, about 515 B.C.E. a modest Temple, the **"second Temple,"** was dedicated. Despite Samaritan opposition, the Jews rebuilt the walls of Jerusalem under the direction of the prophet Nehemiah (437 B.C.E.).

Meanwhile, the priests were gradually establishing a temple-state governed by a priestly aristocracy and high priest, the head of state. Probably about 428 B.C.E., Ezra, "a scribe skilled in the Law of Moses" (Ezra 7:6), came from Babylonia bringing with him the sacred Law, or **Torah** (Hebrew *tōrāh,* "instruction"), that is, the sacred laws and legends of the people.

Monotheism, covenant, circumcision, and the commandments were the heart of the Torah and thus the Jewish religion. By now, however, many Jewish people no longer spoke Hebrew. Rather, they spoke a sister language, **Aramaic,** the standardized international language of administration and trade in the Persian

Empire. Nonetheless, Ezra put the Torah into effect, and the people celebrated its newfound identity by celebrating the grape harvest festival, **Succōth** ("Booths," see Chapter Three). To establish group identity, some marriages with non-Jews were dissolved (Ezra 10:18–44). The book of Nehemiah also emphasizes the necessity to follow the Torah, to avoid trade with non-Jews on the Sabbath, to pay Temple taxes promptly, and to observe the rule that the land was to lie fallow and that slaves were to be released every seventh year (the Sabbatical Year).

These emphases should not lead to the view that the Jewish people were totally withdrawn and isolated, dominated by some sterile "legalism" and isolationism. This point of view, especially characteristic of an earlier generation of Christian scholars, is a caricature that must be corrected by archeological evidence that shows commercial and cultural contact with the outside world and creative impulses leading to the composition of parts of what was to become the **Hebrew Bible.**

Summarizing this sketch, there were three major changes in early post-exilic Judaism:

1. In place of an independent monarchy with its "sacred king" was a temple-state governed by the high priest and a priestly aristocracy subject to a foreign power.
2. While prophecy continued (Haggai and Zechariah; compare Zechariah 13:2–6), there was also concern for its decline (1 Maccabees 9:27; Josephus, *Against Apion* 1.37–41; T. Sotah 13.2).
3. The growing centrality of the **Torah,** that is, the **Pentateuch** (the first five books of the Hebrew Bible) and the necessity of its interpretation for the affairs of everyday life.

We shall consider the major aspects of postexilic Jewish religion in more detail in Chapter Three; here, we shall continue with social-historical developments.

THE JEWS IN THE GREEK PERIOD (332–63 B.C.E.)

Alexander the Great and Hellenization

The New Testament is written in the Greek language. It is a product of the **Hellenistic Age** (Greek *Hellas,* "Greece") which came into being as a result of the conquests of the **Alexander the Great (356–323 B.C.E.)** of Macedonia (the northern Balkan peninsula). In 336 B.C.E., after the assassination of his father, Philip II, who had united most of the Balkan peninsula, Alexander launched a campaign eastward to capture the territories of the Persian Empire. After a victory in southeastern Asia Minor (modern Turkey), the young commander moved down the eastern Mediterranean coast and overcame resistance at coastal cities. He induced the submission of the Jews of Palestine in 332 B.C.E., and was welcomed in Egypt as a conquering hero. Unsatisfied, he moved eastward, decisively defeated the Persians, and took possession of the wealth of the eastern cities. When he advanced into India in 326 B.C.E., his battle-fatigued army resisted following him any further. Alexander settled in the ancient city of Babylon and

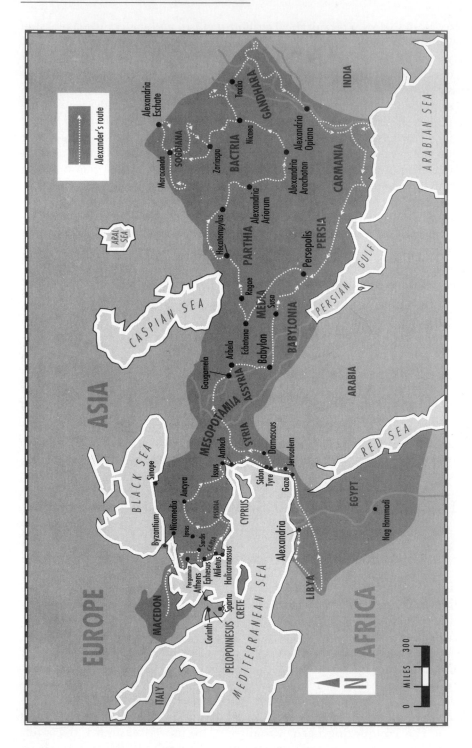

Alexander's empire.

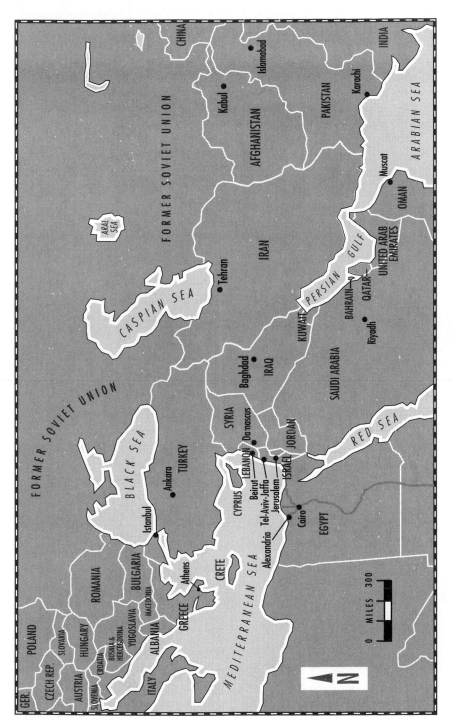

Modern area of Alexander's empire.

began to consolidate his huge empire. However, he did not enjoy it long. He died in the summer of 323 B.C.E., apparently of a fever.

Alexander was a brilliant military strategist, but he was much more. He had been tutored by Aristotle. Attached to his general staff were historians, ethnographers, geographers, botanists, zoologists, mineralogists, and hydrographers. Intentionally or not, Alexander became an emissary of the classical Greek culture. As a result of his conquests Greek language, ideas, culture, religion, and philosophy became much more pervasive throughout the East, mainly in the cities. Historians call this process **Hellenization.** Two of Alexander's activities illustrate this cultural assimilation. First, Alexander and his officers wed Persian women. Second, Alexander built a network of about thirty strategic Greek cities throughout the empire. These cities became centers of commerce, trade, administration, and Greek culture. Here gymnasia, baths, and theaters were built, and the upper classes, attracted to Greek ways, spoke Greek, wore Greek dress, absorbed Greek learning, adopted Greek customs, and took part in Greek athletics. For example, Alexandria, Egypt, founded by, and named for, Alexander became one of the most important cities of Hellenistic civilization.

Despite this cultural revolution, however, the Hellenization of the East was only partial. The urban nature of the phenomenon meant that age-old traditional cultures persisted, especially in the countryside, where most people lived. Eventually a revival of Eastern ways took place. The result was a reverse effect: The West began to be affected by the East.

In short, Alexander's conquests created a network of trade and communication among the eastern cities of the Mediterranean world. There Greek language, ideas, and culture flourished. While rural areas retained much of their traditional culture, and even had some influence on the West, Hellenization persisted through the period of the Roman Empire.

The Jews in the Early Greek Period (301–167 B.C.E.)

The death of Alexander the Great in 323 B.C.E. led to a bitter political power struggle among his Macedonian generals. In the period after 301 B.C.E. four distinct Hellenistic kingdoms emerged:

1. The **Ptolemaic Kingdom** in **Egypt** and the North African coast, along with some islands in the Mediterranean, established by Ptolemy I of Egypt.
2. The **Seleucid Kingdom,** including most of **Asia Minor** (modern Turkey), northern **Syria** through Mesopotamia almost to India, the earliest boundaries established by Seleucus I of Syria;
3. The **Antigonid Kingdom** (Macedonia and parts of **Greece**); and
4. The **Attalid Kingdom** in **western Asia Minor.**

Meanwhile, a fifth power was rising over the western horizon: **Rome.**

How did the Jews fare in the early Greek period? Archeological evidence and the writings of Ben Sira of Jerusalem (200–175 B.C.E.) show that, left alone, the Hellenization of Judaism might have continued uninterrupted, at least among the Jerusalem aristocratic elite. Such a smooth transition, however, did not happen.

The Egyptian Ptolemies allowed the Jews relative independence during the third century B.C.E. In 198 B.C.E., however, the Seleucids gained control of Palestine. At first, the Jews welcomed this Syrian presence. However, in 190 B.C.E. the Romans defeated the Seleucids and forced them and their colonies to pay a huge compensation. Then, in 175 B.C.E. **Antiochus IV Epiphanes,** who claimed to be divine (*Epiphanes* in Greek means "[god] manifest"), took the Seleucid throne. He sought to *enforce* Hellenization throughout his empire and to raise the indemnity demanded by Rome. The Jewish urban aristocracy complied. Some priests began to bid for the High Priesthood. They also tried to carry out a "Hellenistic reform," that is, to abolish the ancestral laws and transform Jerusalem into a Hellenistic city-state.

These events produced an internal Jewish conflict that had momentous results. When rumors of Antiochus' death circulated, civil war broke out between priestly families. In Jerusalem this seems to have developed into a revolt of the urban poor, now linked with the peasants of the countryside, against the wealthy Hellenizing aristocracy. Meanwhile, Antiochus, whose march on Egypt in 168 B.C.E. was thwarted by Roman diplomatic intervention, apparently interpreted the Jerusalem conflict as a revolt against his Hellenizing demands. He attacked the city, exterminated all males who resisted, and sold women and children into slavery. The city walls were torn down, and the old citadel of the Temple was fortified as a Greek garrison (the Akra). Then Antiochus forbade Temple sacrifices, traditional festivals, Sabbath worship, and the rite of circumcision upon pain of death. Torah scrolls were ordered destroyed, and every town in Judea was commanded to sacrifice to the Greek gods. Syrian troops settled Jerusalem, and they brought their gods with them. Moreover, they erected an altar over the altar of burnt offering in the Jerusalem Temple and offered sacrifices to the Greek high god, Zeus. This polluting act became etched on the memory of the Jews as **"the abomination that makes desolate"** (1 Macc 1:54, 59; Dan 11:31; 12:11; compare Mark 13:14 ["the desolating sacrilege"]).

This was no gradual assimilation of Greek ways by the Jewish urban elite; this was a forced Hellenization that threatened to annihilate the Jewish religion altogether.

The Maccabean Revolt (167–164 B.C.E.) and the Independent Maccabean (Hasmonean) Kingdom (142–63 B.C.E.)

The Jewish response to forced Hellenization was a war of social, religious, and national liberation. The initial phase was the **Maccabean Revolt** (167–164 B.C.E.). When Antiochus' emissary came to the Judean town of Modein and demanded that the people offer sacrifices to Greek gods, Mattathias, of priestly stock, refused. Seeing one of the Jews about to comply, he rushed forward and slew him at the altar and then killed the king's emissary, "acting zealously for the law of God, as Phinehas had done" (1 Maccabees 2:26; compare Numbers 25:6–15). Then he and his sons fled to the hills. There they were joined by those nonaristocratic elements from Jerusalem led by a group called the *Hasîdîm* ("Pious Ones," or scribal scholars of Torah; compare 1 Maccabees 2:42). At his death, Mattathias' son **Judas Maccabeus** (died 162 B.C.E.) became the hero of the revolt. He retook Jerusalem and in 164 B.C.E. restored and rededicated the Temple, giving birth to the **Feast of Hanukkah** ("Dedication"), later called the "Festival of Lights."

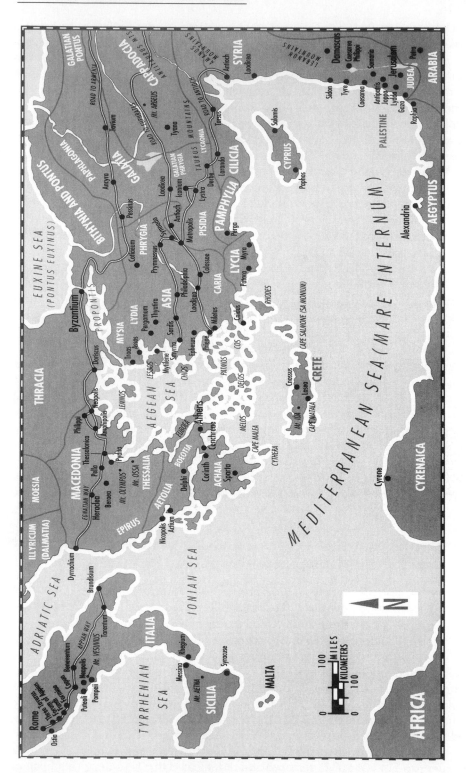

The Roman empire in the first century.

The Maccabean Revolt led to a long guerilla war that, despite tremendous odds, ended in victory. Thus, in 142 B.C.E. the Maccabeans were able to establish an independent Maccabean (or Hasmonean) kingdom. Though its history is a very important chapter in story of the Jews, in this brief survey we shall simply note the following points: The Maccabeans engaged in major territorial expansion; destroyed many Greek cities; forcefully converted and circumcised many of their subjects; and, despite their priestly lineage, began to see themselves also as kings. Eventually, the Jewish people became disenchanted with their rule. It is during their reign that the first Jewish apocalypse was produced (Daniel 7–12). This type of literature became widespread in the next three centuries. In addition, several religious groups first appeared, including the Sadducees, the Pharisees, and the Essenes (see Chapter Three).

The independent Maccabean Kingdom ended in 63 B.C.E. when the Jews invited the Roman general **Pompey** to settle an internal dispute. From that point forward, the Romans were in Palestine to stay.

In summary, two trends dominated the Greek period in Palestine (332 B.C.E. to 63 B.C.E.):

1. The gradual Hellenization of the Jewish aristocracy; and
2. The reaction of the religiously conservative peasant classes to *forced* Hellenization, resulting in the Maccabean Revolt and the independent Maccabean (Hasmonean) kingdom. Their banner was "zeal for the Law."

In addition, three religious groups appear for the first time: the Sadducees, the Pharisees, and the Essenes (see Chapter Three). This stormy period will help us to understand how the Jews and their leaders responded to colonial control during the rise of Christianity when the new colonial power was Rome.

THE RISE OF ROME, THE ROMAN EMPIRE, AND THE EARLY ROMAN EMPERORS

B.C.E.
753   **The Roman Monarchy**
509   **The Roman Republic**
      509–203—Rome controls Italy and western Mediterranean lands
      203–27—Rome gains control of the Hellenistic empires in the eastern Mediterranean
27   **The Roman Empire**
410   The Capture of Rome

Roman history can be divided into three major periods:

1. The Roman Monarchy, established about 753 B.C.E.;
2. The Roman Republic, established in 509 B.C.E.; and
3. The Roman Empire, established in 27 B.C.E.

The Empire lasted until its western lands began to fall to Germanic invaders from northern Europe in the fourth century C.E. Indeed, the city of Rome was captured in 410 C.E.

During the Republic, Rome gradually gained control of the western Mediterranean and then the Hellenistic empires to the East. While Rome could not hold lands to the east—there the Parthian Empire emerged as a rival empire—the Roman conquest in the West gradually included Spain, Gaul (modern France), southern Germany, and southern Britain. These regions were partitioned into Roman provinces. As noted above, Palestine came under Roman control in 63 B.C.E.; it eventually became part of the Roman province of Syria.

In the first century B.C.E., the extension of Roman power put an immense strain on the Republic. The need for a stronger, more centralized rule became urgent. Thus, the Romans looked to their military leaders. They, in turn, struggled with each other for total control. Pompey, successful in the East, was defeated by the western commander, Julius Caesar. After Caesar's assassination in 44 B.C.E., **Octavian** assumed control of the West and Antony took charge of the East. When Antony began to lose the easternmost territories to the Parthians and—though already married to Octavian's sister—married Cleopatra VII of Egypt, Octavian convinced the Senate to declare war on Antony. In **31 B.C.E.** Octavian routed Antony's forces on the sea at the **Battle of Actium.** The suicides of Antony and Cleopatra in Egypt left Octavian in full control. At Rome, he was made *Imperator,* or supreme commander of the army. The Senate then conferred upon him the additional titles *Augustus,* "the August," and *Princeps,* the first of the Senate. Thus, in 27 B.C.E. the Roman Empire was born, and Octavian, called *Caesar Augustus,* was its first emperor.

Roman Emperors

B.C.E.

27	**Octavian** (Caesar Augustus)

C.E.

14	**Tiberius**
37	**Gaius Caligula**
41	**Claudius**
54	**Nero**
68	Galba, Otho, Vitellius
69	**Vespasian**
79	**Titus**
81	**Domitian**
96	Nerva
98	Trajan
117	Hadrian
138	Antonius Pius
161	Marcus Aurelius (d. 180)

While the details of Roman history in the first and early second centuries are not our concern here, a brief look at the first-century Roman emperors will provide some indication of the vacillating political fortunes of the empire in which Christianity was born.

Caesar Augustus was a wise ruler. He secured the borders of the empire, built roads, and established a new era of peace and stability, the famous "peace of Rome" (Latin *pax Romana)*. He reorganized the provinces to achieve a more just administration, instituted tax reform, developed a civil service, and engaged in many public works projects, especially in Rome. During his reign as emperor, Jesus of Nazareth was born.

However, not all of Augustus' successors were capable. **Tiberius (14–27 C.E.)** became unpopular and spent his last eleven years in a life of debauchery on the island of Capri. One of his infamous appointees was the governor of Judea and Samaria in Palestine, **Pontius Pilate (26–36 C.E.),** during whose rule Jesus was crucified. Tiberius was followed by his grandnephew, the great-grandson of Augustus, **Gaius Caligula (37–41).** Caligula became consumed with power, demanded that he be addressed as a god, and proposed that his horse be made a consul (he rewarded the animal with a marble stall and a purple blanket!). He fomented a crisis among the Jews by demanding that statues of himself be set up in the Temple at Jerusalem. The crisis abated only when his bodyguards assassinated him.

Caligula's uncle and successor, **Claudius (41–54 C.E.)** unexpectedly turned out to be a competent ruler. Various pieces of evidence from the reign of Claudius help date the movements of Paul the Apostle (The Edict of Claudius; The Gallio Inscription; see Chapters Four, Six). Claudius was poisoned by his fourth wife, Agrippina.

Nero (54–68 C.E.), Agrippina's son by a previous marriage, became the next emperor. Although the Empire ran smoothly at first, there were many intrigues and murders. For example, Nero poisoned Claudius' son, executed his own wife, and arranged for the assassination of his mother. In 64 C.E., a fire devastated Rome, and Nero found his scapegoat in the Christians. According to church traditions, Peter and Paul were martyred during Nero's reign. Finally, military commanders seized several provinces. Nero fled from Rome and eventually committed suicide in 68 C.E.

Widespread unrest led to a quick succession of emperors in 68–69 C.E.: Galba, Otho, and Vitellius. In 69 C.E., **Vespasian (69–79 C.E.),** who had been dispatched to Palestine to crush **the Jewish Rebellion (66–70 C.E.),** was acclaimed emperor. Vespasian provided a decade of peace and prosperity for the Empire. Vespasian's son and successor, **Titus (79–81 C.E.),** who had concluded the war with the Jews, reigned for two years. Ancient Roman historians and Christian writers remembered his second son, **Domitian (81–96 C.E.),** as a tyrant. Probably his reign provides the backdrop for the most anti-Roman book in the New Testament, Revelation (see Chapter Thirteen). The following emperors were some of Rome's best: Nerva (96–98 C.E.), Trajan (98–117 C.E.), Hadrian (117–138 C.E.), Antonius Pius (138–161 C.E.), and the Stoic philosopher-emperor Marcus Aurelius (161–180 C.E.).

SOCIAL AND ECONOMIC CONDITIONS IN THE GRECO-ROMAN (HELLENISTIC) PERIOD

The Ancient Economy

Modern industrial economies are based on labor, capital, investment, production, business cycles, financial planning, money markets, and real estate investment. As implied by our discussion of ecology at the beginning of this chapter, ancient economies were based primarily on land and agriculture, along with some herding, mining, and fishing. From about 1200–800 B.C.E., the availability of iron implements, especially the iron plow, led to increased productivity and farm surplus. With the growth in cities, there was extensive trade in agricultural produce, especially in spices, handicrafts, and the byproducts of olives.

The landholders, a minuscule upper strata of society, became rich and powerful through their control of production and redistribution. Though there were some traditional family land holdings (compare the Prodigal Son parable, Luke 15:11–32), there was an increasing tendency for emperors, kings, military personnel, and urban aristocrats to hold large estates as absentee landlords. Those who performed the labor were usually poor tenant farmers who paid rents.

The eastern economies were dominated by large temple and palace complexes where there was housed the national treasury; otherwise, banking concerns were small. There was no system of public works. These were usually accomplished by certain **benefactors** or **patrons** of status and wealth who obtained and maintained honor by gift giving. There was also no social security. When times were difficult, people had to depend on family and friends.

The Roman Provincial System and the Impact of Taxation

In the Roman Empire two types of provinces emerged, senatorial provinces and imperial provinces. **Senatorial provinces** were administered by the Roman Senate. **Imperial provinces,** considered more politically volatile, were governed by a Roman military governor from the highest senatorial classes, that is, a "legate," who was directly responsible to the emperor.

There were also mini-imperial provinces called "districts." These were governed by a less powerful Roman governor, usually from the next highest, or equestrian class, called a "prefect" (later called a "procurator"). Like the legate, he was responsible to the emperor. Finally, in some regions, the Romans permitted local "client kings" to rule. When Jesus was born, for example, a client king (Herod the Great) ruled all of Palestine. During Jesus' adult life, Galilee, the major area of his activity, was ruled by a client king of lower rank called a "tetrarch" (Herod's son, Herod Antipas, called "king" in the gospels). In Judea, where Jesus met his death, the prefect/procurator, Pontius Pilate, ruled.

The chief responsibilities of the various Roman governors were civil order, the administration of justice, including the judicial right of capital punishment, and the collection of various taxes and tolls. This system was enforced by a police force. Client kings carried out similar responsibilities, though their right to inflict capital punishment was often restricted. Taxes on individuals and land were normally collected by the agents of Romans and local client kings. Tolls, however, were "farmed out" to the highest bidders. Their income was whatever they collected in excess of the amount due Rome. Greedy toll collectors abused this system. In addition, client kings such as Herod the Great, who had ambitious building projects, added their own taxes. There were also religious taxes, such as the Jewish half-shekel Temple tax for Jewish men, due once a year.

The effect of the social and economic system combined with the various forms of taxation was that the urban poor, rural tenant farmers, and peasant folk in Palestine were subject to an almost unbearable tax burden. Such people were forced to live at a bare subsistence level. Some sold themselves or their children into slavery; others were forced into begging or banditry, or they chose some alternative form of religious life. Such conditions are common among most Jews and early Palestinian Christians.

Social Status and Stratification

In antiquity, **social status** was based on **honor** and came as a result of birth, grant by persons of higher status, or acquisition in social competition with equals. **Shame** meant a decline in social status. The fictional character Trimalchio was a former slave who acquired a vast fortune through land, rents, and interest, but as a former slave, or freedman, he was never able to break into the higher social circles.

There was no large, dominant middle class. Rather, at the top was a tiny aristocratic group and at the bottom a large body of peasants, slaves, men and women set free from slavery, and people considered expendables. Slavery in the ancient world was not like that in the pre-Civil War South. Educated slaves could become teachers, librarians, and administrators, and household servants were sometimes secretaries, tutors, or financial overseers. Some emperor's slaves had powerful positions, owned land, and accumulated assets. There were infrequent movements to abolish slavery. Loyal slaves were sometimes given their freedom, or if their assets were enough, they could occasionally purchase their freedom. Freedmen, however, usually had obligations to their former masters. The image of master and slave occurs frequently in the New Testament. Between the minute upper strata and the great masses of lower strata were a few priests, merchants, small-business people, independent well-to-do farmers who were able to hold on to their ancestral lands, middle and lower ranks of the military personnel, artisans (carpenters, tentmakers, and so forth), fishermen (such as some of the disciples), and seminomadic herders.

A tiny group of rulers and aristocrats, perhaps 1 to 2 percent, controlled most of the wealth. The remaining 98 to 99 percent of the population, especially the peasants and expendables, understood that the good things in life—power, privilege, prestige, status, honor, land, possessions, wealth, friendship, love—were scarce. Workdays were long and only rarely interrupted by holidays, feasts, or games. Most people were barely able to survive. Getting ahead or moving up the social ladder was rare.

The result of the social, economic, and political situation can be illustrated by a model of social stratification in an advanced agrarian society.

To get along in this vertically arranged social system, it was important to have good connections. Thus, there emerged an informal set of contractual arrangements called **patron-client relations.** Patrons, those of higher social status, provided protection, support, and favors for their clients. Clients, beneath the patrons social status, offered something in return, such as loyalty, services, and military or political support. There were also the necessary intermediaries, or brokers. This system operated up and down the social ladder. Indeed, there were patrons of whole cities and, when the Roman emperor and Senate granted local rulers the status of king, such rulers operated as client kings.

The traditional Greco–Roman household was dominated by men (the *paterfamilias*) in three ways: husbands over wives, fathers over children, and masters over slaves (see the "household codes" in Chapter Seven). Among the Greeks and Romans, some upper-class women had varying degrees of education, wealth, and status. Male dominance was even more pronounced in the traditional patriarchal societies of the eastern provinces, which included the Jews.

Travel and Hospitality

After 67 B.C.E., the high seas became mostly free of pirates. Sea travel on the many cargo ships of the Mediterranean became common. There was also a network of well-built Roman roads linking major cities, along which travelers stayed at the many inns and wayside stations. For those who found the inns too unruly and vulgar, correspondence between relatives, distant friends, or acquaintances, often accompanied by letters of reference, made entry to private homes possible. The host's **hospitality** was an extremely important social virtue in antiquity. We shall have more to say about this in connection with the travels of the apostle Paul (Chapter Six; see also Chapter Twelve).

Life in the City and Countryside

Hellenization was primarily an urban phenomenon. Anyone who strolled through an ancient Hellenistic city could observe Greek design and architecture: city walls, socially segregated districts (often by walls within the city), one or more central *agoras* (town squares used for market places or government and administrative buildings), colonnaded streets and porticoes, stadiums, baths, temples, theaters, amphitheaters, hippodromes, gymnasiums, fountains, aqueducts, gates, and arches. Major eastern cities were also dominated by temple and palace complexes. The Greek language was spoken and fashionable Greek dress was common.

In the cities with stronger Roman influence, there was usually a *forum* with temples for the Roman gods, statues of the emperor and his family, statues of patrons, and buildings for the town council and legal and business transactions. Houses of the wealthy usually turned inward toward a central courtyard, where various family units congregated. The less fortunate lived in smaller, often crowded apartments, the upper stories of which contained few amenities.They had to contend with lack of sanitation and its accompanying odors. The problem of feeding the increasing urban populations was never adequately solved and famine was a recurring phenomenon.

The cities, where political power and social status were concentrated, were linked by trade and taxation to the countryside, where agriculture predominated. In the countryside traditional languages and age-old cultural patterns and religious ideas stubbornly persisted. There were to be found poor peasants under control of a wealthy urban absentee landlords. In addition, there were a few nomadic tribes in the steppes.

Social Dislocation

In established local cultures, it was natural for people to perceive themselves as belonging to familiar groups such as family, clan, or village. Such groups dominated conventional morality and the individual's sense of honor and identity (for example, marriage according to kinship lines and taboos against incest). However, the shift to more Hellenistic urban settings with their changing, international environments, as well as political and economic repression of the poor, led to frequent social dislocation. Such was situation of the Jews under Roman domination.

SOCIAL HISTORY OF THE JEWS IN THE EARLY ROMAN PERIOD (63 B.C.E.–135 C.E.)

B.C.E.

63	**Romans,** under the general **Pompey,** take charge of Palestine, ending Jewish independence
37	**Herod the Great** begins to rule
6/4	**Jesus of Nazareth** born
4	**Archelaus** in Judea/Samaria (to 6 C.E.)
4	**Herod Antipas** in Galilee/Perea (to 39 C.E.)
4	**Philip** in region northeast of Sea of Galilee (to 34 C.E.)
0?	**Paul of Tarsus** born

C.E.

6	Procurators replace Archelaus in Judea/Samaria
26	**Pontius Pilate** rules (to 36 C.E.)
37	**Herod Agrippa I** (d. 44 B.C.E.) rules Philip's lands (to 44 C.E.)
39	Herod Agrippa I also rules Galilee/Perea (to 44 C.E.)
41	Herod Agrippa I also rules Samaria/Judea (to 44 C.E.)
44	Procurators again rule whole land
49/50	**Edict of Claudius** expels Jews (and Jewish Christians) from Rome
66–70	**Wars with Rome**
73	**Masada** taken by Romans
90	**Academy at Jamnia (Yavneh)**
115–117	Jewish Diaspora revolts
132–135	Wars with Rome (**The Bar Cochba Revolt**)

Herod "the Great"

Recall that in 63 B.C.E. the Roman General Pompey "settled" the dispute between the Maccabean priest-kings on the side of Hyrcanus II. From that time forward, Palestine was under control of the Romans. One of Hyrcanus' supporters was a crafty Idumean, Antipater II, who gradually gained Roman favor as governor of Idumea. His most important son, Herod, was made ruler of Galilee.

In 40 B.C.E. the Parthians to the east set up the rival Maccabean Antigonus II as a client king in Jerusalem. Herod, having fled the city with his family, eventually went to Rome, where he was appointed king of the Jews. Returning to Palestine, he gathered an army and in 37 B.C.E. retook Jerusalem with Roman help. Palestine now became a frontier "buffer state" of the Romans against the Parthians. Thus, an Idumean whose ancestors had been forcibly converted by the Maccabeans and who was later derided as a "half-Jew" by the Jews, rose to power as a client king under the Romans.

Herod ("the Great") (ruled 37–4 B.C.E.) was both an oriental tyrant and an extremely competent ruler. He had hundreds of opponents executed. The brother of one of his wives, a Maccabean high priest, "accidentally" drowned at a pool party. Her grandfather, the old Maccabean ruler Hyrcanus II, was strangled. When Herod ordered his Hasmonean wife, Mariamme, executed should he not return from Rome, she angrily responded by refusing to have sex with him; he had her tried and executed for adultery. Then he mourned and almost committed suicide. He also killed three of his sons. Since Herod attempted to abide by the Jewish law, which prohibited eating pork, the pun arose, "It is better to be Herod's *hus* (Greek for "pig") than his *huios* (Greek for "son")!"

Herod was a Hellenizer. He surrounded himself with Greek scholars and undertook many ambitious building projects (see Chapter One, "Archeology"; Appendix). In non-Jewish areas he built Hellenistic cities. Ancient Samaria was transformed into a Greek city, Sebaste, dedicated to the emperor (Greek *Sebastos* = Latin *Augustus*). At Jericho he built a marvelous summer palace. The complete transformation of the Mediterranean coastal city, Strato's Tower, into an artificially constructed seaport of **Caesarea,** was an amazing feat of engineering, and it became the capital for the Roman governors.

Jerusalem saw a hippodrome; an amphitheater; a theater; a fortified palace; the rebuilding of the second **Jerusalem Temple** (see reconstruction on p. 54); a colonnaded Greco-Oriental structure with courts, ritual baths, and a central sanctuary; and a palatial Roman fortress, Antonia (named for Antony). Herod also built or rebuilt many outlying military fortresses, including Masada.

Herod had ten wives, and in his final years he was plagued by domestic problems. He passed away unloved and unmourned in 4 B.C.E. At his death, a popular uprising occurred. According to the gospels of Matthew and Luke, Jesus of Nazareth was born near the end of his reign (6–4 B.C.E.).

Herodians, Roman Prefects/Procurators, and the Jews

Herod's final will, altered by Augustus, divided his kingdom among his three sons:

1. **Archelaus** became ethnarch (lower in status than king) of Samaria, Judea, and Idumea in the south. Because of opposition by Antipas and the revolt of his subjects, Archelaus was dismissed and banished to Gaul in 6 C.E.
2. **Philip** (4 B.C.E.–33/34 C.E.) was named tetrarch (slightly lower in status than ethnarch) of the largely non-Jewish regions northeast of the Sea of Galilee.
3. **Herod Antipas** (4 B.C.E.–39 C.E.) became tetrarch of Galilee and Perea beyond the Jordan River (called the king of Galilee in the gospel stories,

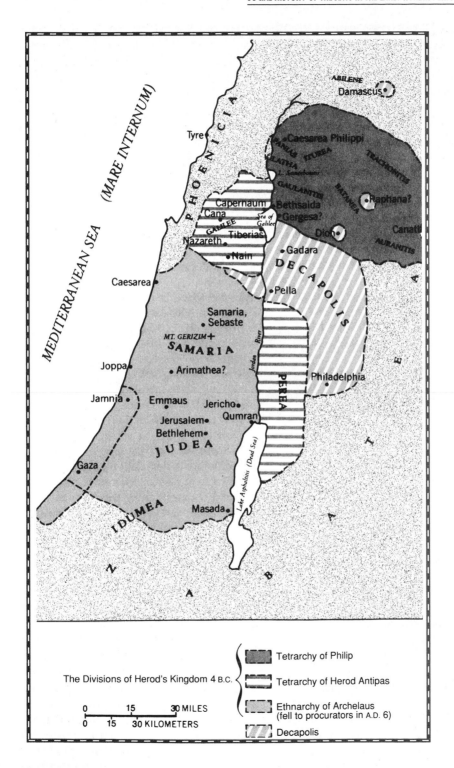

Herod's kingdom, as divided among his three sons.

Modern reconstruction of Caesarea by the Sea, originally constructed along the Mediterranean coast by Herod the Great's builders. Since no natural harbor had existed there, it was an amazing engineering feat. It became the Roman "capital" of Palestine. [From Holum et al., *King Herod's Dream: Caesarea on the Sea* (1988).]

compare Mark 6:17–29; Luke 13:31–33; 23:6–12); he was finally exiled by the Roman emperor Caligula.

With the exception of a short period (41 to 44 C.E.), Samaria, Judea, and Idumea fell under the authority of governors appointed by the emperor, or **prefects** (later called **procurators**). So did most of Palestine after the death of Agrippa I in 44 C.E. According to the ancient Alexandrian Jewish philosopher **Philo,** the fifth prefect, **Pontius Pilate (26–36 C.E.),** was described by King Agrippa I as " . . . by nature unbending and severe with the stubborn," and was accused of " . . . the taking of bribes, wanton insolence, rapacity, outrages, countless and continuous murders, endless and most painful cruelty" (Philo, *Embassy to Gaius* 38). This portrait contrasts with that in the gospels, but is confirmed by the first-century Jewish historian Josephus.

All this accounts for the complex political situation in the gospels. Again, Herod (37–4 B.C.E.) ruled at Jesus' birth. When Jesus was an adult, Herod's son, the tetrarch Philip (4 B.C.E.–33/34 C.E.), still ruled the region northeast of the Sea of Galilee, and his son, the tetrarch Herod Antipas (4 B.C.E.–39 C.E.), still ruled Galilee and Perea. However, the prefect Pilate had replaced his third son, Archelaus, in the district of Judea, Samaria, and Idumea.

How did the Jews fare politically under the Romans and Herodian client kings? The Romans were sensitive enough to permit the stubborn Jews special exemptions: from military service; from appearance in court on the Sabbath; from portraying the emperor's head on their coins (Jewish law prohibited images, that is, idolatry); and from offering sacrifices *to* the emperor as a deity. This latter was replaced by sacrifices "*for* Caesar and the Roman nation" twice daily. In areas of heavy Jewish population, the Romans were not to represent the image of the emperor on their military standards, used in religious practices.

However, these concessions were not always implemented. At the death of Herod, demonstrators demanded that taxes be lowered, duties be removed, certain prisoners be freed, and a new High Priest be instated. When a group protested Herod's execution of two teachers who had encouraged youths to remove the image of a golden eagle that Herod had placed on the Temple gate, Archelaus' Temple troops attacked and, according to Josephus (who likes to inflate figures), killed 3000 of them. Pilate brought military standards containing idolatrous images into Jerusalem at night. They were removed only when the Jews demonstrated their willingness to die for their religion. Pilate also confiscated Temple funds to finance construction of an aqueduct, and, when the Jews protested, he killed many of the unarmed protestors. For these and other abuses, Pilate was eventually removed by the legate of Syria.

One other important event needs to be mentioned. In 40–41 C.E., the emperor Gaius Caligula (37–41), who wished to be worshipped as a deity, took revenge for an incident of Jewish insubordination by commanding the legate of Syria to erect his statue in the Jerusalem Temple. The legate delayed and held conferences with the Jews, who vowed to go to war if he carried out the orders. The incident was averted only when Gaius was assassinated. Herod Agrippa I's rule over the whole of Palestine for a brief period (41–44 C.E.) brought better times for the Jews, though early Christians remembered him for persecuting their leaders (compare Acts 12:20–23).

After Herod Agrippa I's death in 44 C.E., the prefects/procurators assumed control over all of Palestine and the situation worsened. Josephus claimed that on one occasion 20,000 Jews were killed in a riot prompted by a Roman soldier's "mooning" some Passover pilgrim (*Antiquities* 20, 108, 112).

Social Stratification in the Herodian Period

Herodian Palestine reflected in miniature the social stratification of the Greco-Roman world, that is, of an advanced agrarian society. However, certain modifications need to be made to account for its position as a client kingdom. If we adjust the model and make it regional, it would appear as on the following page.

Resistance, Reform, and Terrorist Movements and Leaders

The colonial social context, along with natural calamities such as drought and famine, contributed to much social dislocation and unrest in the first century, especially among the urban poor and the rural peasants. Reform, resistance, and terrorist movements, known from other hot spots in the Mediterranean world, also arose in Palestine. The following are examples (see Horsley and Hanson).

Brigands (Social Bandits)

One type of movement that is known throughout the ancient Mediterranean and that emerged among the Palestinian peasants is often portrayed by Josephus as mere plundering. Modern sociological study, however, suggests they might have been **"social bandits,"** that is, rural bandit-chiefs and their followers who rise from the ranks of the peasants, rob the rich, sometimes give to the poor, and sometimes find support among local villagers who hope for a better future. Yet, such figures are sometimes recruited, supported, and protected by those in power, and thus terrorize the populace in general, including the peasants. In ancient Palestine, the bandits may have been influenced by millennarian or apocalyptic dreams and hopes, although there is scarcely any evidence, mainly because apocalyptic ideas are preserved in the literature of literate scribes. In any case, after 44 C.E.—there was a famine in 46–48 C.E.— such bandit-led rural peasant groups, according to Josephus, increased. They converged in Jerusalem about 67–68 C.E. to become part, probably the dominant part, of the revolutionary **Zealots.** For example, one Zealot leader during the war was John of Gischala, a bandit-chief in upper Galilee. In an earlier day, Jesus of Nazareth was crucified between two such bandits.

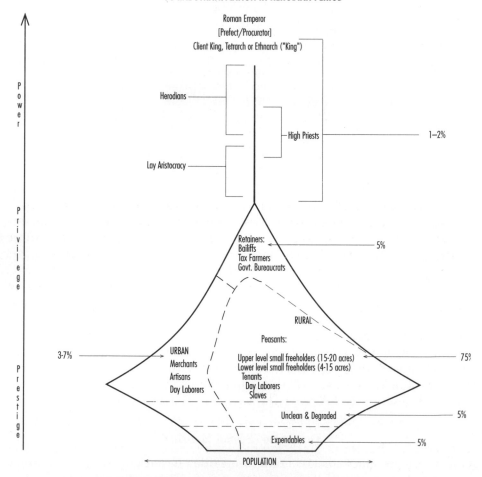

SOCIAL STRATIFICATION IN HERODIAN PERIOD

Adapted from D. Fiensy, *The Social History of Palestine in the Herodian Period,* p. 158, based on G. and J. Lenski, *Human Societies,* p. 203, and G. Alfödy, *Die römische Gesellshaft*

Popular Prophets

There were also self-styled, politically active **popular prophets,** whom Josephus sometimes confuses with bandits. During Pilate's rule a Samaritan prophet led his followers to Mount Gerizim to see sacred vessels supposedly buried by Moses. Josephus claims that they were armed, and that many were killed or routed and others taken into captivity. There was also a certain Theudas (compare Acts 5:36), who in the 40s C.E. led his followers to the Jordan River, telling them that at his command it would divide, presumably like the Red Sea was supposed to have done at the command of Moses. However, the procurator's troops attacked and killed many of them. Theudas was beheaded. A third example was a Jew named "The Egyptian" who in 56 C.E. told his followers that at his command the walls of Jerusalem would fall down, as in the story of Joshua. Again, they were attacked, many were killed, and the Egyptian fled. Several such prophets appeared at the time of revolt against Rome in 66–70 C.E. Anthropologists sometimes associate such figures with magicians. They are often influenced by apocalyptic thought, and are thus called millennial prophets. In this regard, John and Jesus were believed to have been prophets and both were influenced by apocalyptic and prophecy. The author of the Apocalypse, or Revelation, in the New Testament considered himself to be a prophet (see Chapter Thirteen).

Popular Kings or Messiahs

In Chapter Three, we shall discuss messianic hopes. In practice, there arose popular kings or messiahs. These were self-styled strongmen, believed to have superior size or ability, whose followers accepted them as kings. At the unrest that followed the death of Herod in 4 B.C.E. three such popular kings appeared: Judas, son of the bandit-chief Hezekiah, who in "zealous pursuit of royal rank" (Josephus *Antiquities* 17.271–72) led a revolt against the Romans in Galilee; Simon of Perea, who donned the royal diadem, was proclaimed king by the masses, and after plundering Herod's royal palace in Jericho was finally caught and beheaded; and the shepherd Athronges, supported by his four brothers and their troops, who also donned the diadem, claimed to be king, and went about attacking both Roman and Herodian troops. During the wars with Rome from 66–70 C.E., two popular kings surfaced: Menahem, who led a band of radical assassins called **"Sicarii"** (see below) and entered Jerusalem as a king to gain control; and Simon bar Giora, whom the peasants obeyed "like a king" and who also joined the Sicarii in Jerusalem. At the end of the war, Simon appeared in royal robes and was taken to Rome where he was executed.

"Fourth Philosophy"

The "Fourth Philosophy" (according to Josephus, the three other "philosophies" were the Pharisees, Sadducees, and Essenes) may have been a group of nonviolent, activist intellectuals. As Herod lay dying in 4 B.C.E., two "teachers" who incited their disciples to tear down the golden eagle on the Temple gate seem to have been of this type; they and their followers were arrested and executed. In 6 C.E., when direct Roman rule in Judea/Samaria by procurators began and the Roman census was established, a "teacher" named **Judas the Galilean** allied himself with the Pharisee Saddok and opposed the newly instituted taxes, believing that no one should rule the land of Palestine but God, a principle he based on the First Commandment, "Thou shalt have no other gods before me" (Exodus 20:3). As a result, "the nation was filled with unrest" (Josephus *Antiquities* 18:3–9; compare 18:23–25). It may be that the Fourth Philosophy went underground. It is recorded that Judas' sons, James and Simon, were crucified in 47 C.E.

Sicarii

In the 50s C.E. an urban group called the **Sicarii** (Latin *sicarius*, "dagger") appeared in Jerusalem. One of their leaders during the wars with Rome, the popular king Menahem, was Judas the Galilean's (grand?)son, as well as a "teacher" (Josephus *Wars* 2.445). Another leader who made the final defense of Masada, Eleazar son of Ja'ir, was also related. If these two groups were related, a shift in ideology had apparently occurred since the Sicarii were clandestine, *urban-based guerrilla terrorists* identified by their means of assassination, the dagger. They selected specific, symbolic targets for elimination among the aristocracy; they assassinated more generally and plundered the property of the elite; and they kidnapped hostages for ransom. Their religious philosophy was now "No Lord but God."

We have distinguished five revolutionary groups: followers of social bandits, popular messiahs, prophets, the Fourth Philosophy, and Sicarii. There appear to be certain family connections among some of their leaders (Hezekiah and son Judas; Judas the Galilean, sons James and Simon, (grand)son Menahem, and relative Eleazar ben Ja'ir, the latter two of whom led bands of Sicarii). Some scholars have argued that the bandit Judas and the leader of the Fourth Philosophy, Judas the Galilean, were one and the same. Moreover, these groups shared in common what the Maccabees and *Hasîdîm* shared some two hundred years earlier: opposition to the political, economic, and religious repression by a foreign power and the native wealthy aristocracy. Perhaps they were influenced by apocalyptic ideas, as well. Thus, some scholars have argued for a single, unified Jewish resistance movement. While this judgment is probably an oversimplification, some of their common interests in first-century Palestine raise a very important historical question: what was their relation, if any, to Jesus and the Christian movement?

The War with Rome (66–70 C.E.)

Herod Agrippa I died in 44 C.E. His successor, Herod Agrippa II, was relatively powerless. The procurators were again in control, now over all Palestine. Unfortunately, however, conflict persisted. In the spring of 66 C.E., after tensions between Jews and Greeks provoked an incident in Caesarea, Procurator Gessius Florus (64–66 C.E.) confiscated a large sum of money from the Temple treasury "for governmental purposes." The outraged Jewish populace mocked him by taking up a collection in the streets. Florus took revenge by allowing his troops to plunder part of Jerusalem and to execute some prisoners. Attempts at mediation by the priests failed. When Roman troops did not respond to friendly overtures by the Jewish crowds, the people responded by slinging insults at Florus. A slaughter ensued. In a bloody street battle, the people gained the upper hand, took possession of the Temple mount, and cut off the passage between the Temple and the Roman-held fortress of Antonia. Further attempts at mediation by Agrippa II, some leading Pharisees, and the priestly aristocracy failed. The fortress of Masada, taken earlier by the Romans, was retaken by Menahem and his Sicarii. At the direction of Eleazar, the rebellious son of the High Priest, the sacrifices for the emperor were stopped. This was, in effect, a declaration of war.

In Judea, an initial success of the bandit-led rebels in routing the Roman Army encouraged resistance. The land was loosely organized for battle. Nero (54–68 C.E.) dispatched his seasoned commander, **Vespasian,** who organized the legions at Antioch and sent his son, **Titus,** to Alexandria to bring up the fifteenth legion. This newly organized army, containing a formidable force of 60,000 soldiers, marched on Galilee. **Josephus,** the Galilean commander, attempted negotiations and offered only moderate resistance. More radical elements came to believe that Josephus' leadership was not fully dedicated. They were probably correct, for in 67 C.E. Josephus deserted to the Romans and eventually became the official historian of the Jews. Meanwhile, under the leadership of bandit-chief John of Gischala, more dedicated patriots were put in charge. A much disputed Christian tradition states that just before hostilities broke out, Christians fled to a town called Pella across the Jordan River (cf. Eusebius, *Ecclesiastical History* 3.5.3).

Meanwhile, in Jerusalem a chaotic civil war broke out. At first, aristocratic priestly royalists, wealthy families, and Roman soldiers were opposed by the populace and some lower order priests led by Eleazar, son of the High Priest. However, when the popular king Menahem and his Sicarii killed Eleazar's father, the Eleazar group turned on Menahem and assassinated him. The remaining Sicarii, now led by Eleazar ben Ja'ir, escaped to **Masada,** which other Sicarii had retaken from the Romans. Despite the lack of unity, an assault on the city by the Romans was repelled.

Other factions arose in Jerusalem. The Zealots (Greek *zealos* = "zeal" [for the Law]), a coalition of rural bandits, city folk, and lower priests, overthrew the aristocratic government. After plundering the aristocracy, they established their own government and chose their own high priest. However, they, too, broke up into two competing factions. One was led by a priest, Eleazar ben Simon; a second was led by the Galilean bandit-chief, John of Gischala, joined by some Idumeans. The Idumeans then broke from John to form a third group that sought to overthrow John with the help of the popular king, Simon ben Giora.

Confusion reigned in Jerusalem. The experienced Vespasian shrewdly decided to let the Jews in Jerusalem exhaust themselves. Then, in 68 C.E., news came of Nero's suicide. Vespasian continued to delay. In quick succession, Galba, Otho, and the western commander, Vitellius, ruled the empire. In the eastern empire, Vespasian was acclaimed emperor. After the assassination of Vitellius, Vespasian left for Rome to assume his new role, leaving his son Titus to conclude the war.

In the spring of 70 C.E. Titus began the siege of Jerusalem. The Jewish factions of the city now united under Simon ben Giora against a common enemy. While the Jews fought valiantly, Titus' armies surrounded the city. Hunger and thirst began to take their toll. Gradually the walled sections of the city fell, one by one, and the fortress of Antonia was retaken. The Temple was ravaged by fire. The Jews refused to surrender. Women, children, and the elderly, were butchered, and the city and most of its walls were destroyed. The major battle over, Titus set sail for Rome with 700 handsome prisoners for the victory parade through Rome, later commemorated by the arch of Titus, still to be seen in the Roman Forum.

While the victory belonged to the Romans, several fortresses remained. The most difficult was Masada. Now commanded by Eleazar ben Ya'ir and the Sicarii, it was almost impenetrable. The task fell to Roman Commander Flavius Silva, who, because of the steepness of the cliffs, built a wall of earth as a bridge across which a battering ram could be rolled into place. When Eleazar saw that the Jewish cause was hopeless, he addressed the garrison. He asked that they kill their families, and then each other. The deed was done. The Romans finally breached the wall (73 C.E.), but there was no battle left to be fought.

The Post-War Years

The destruction of Jerusalem and the Temple pierced the heart of Palestinian Judaism. What survived was a Judaism gradually reorganized under the Pharisees whom the Romans permitted to meet not far from the Mediterranean coast at the town of Jamnia **(The Academy at Jamnia)** about 90 C.E. Still, hatred simmered. Between 115 and 117 C.E., Jews in North Africa and on the island of Cyprus revolted. Then, from 132 to 135 C.E. Palestinian Judaism again revolted in Judea. Rabbi Akiba acclaimed the leader of the revolt, bar Kosiba, to be "the king, the Messiah." Dubbed Bar Cochba ("Son of the Star," compare the messianic star of Num 24:17), the Bar Cochba Revolt probably arose in response to the emperor Hadrian's empire-wide ban on circumcision (not exclusively a Jewish practice), his attempt to establish Jerusalem as a Greco-Roman city (Aelia Capitolina), and his intention to build a temple to Jupiter Capitolinus on the site of the previous Jerusalem Temple. This revolt also failed. Bar Cochba's detractors renamed him Bar Koziba ("Son of the Lie" = "Liar"). Hadrian's plans were carried out. While there is archeological evidence that Jews and Christians lived side by side in Galilee after the revolt, Jews living in Jerusalem were mostly driven out and officially not permitted to return upon punishment by death. From that time on, Judaism became primarily Diaspora Judaism, a Judaism without a homeland, until the establishment of the state of Israel in 1948 (see Chapter Three).

In summary, we have concentrated our historical sketch on the Jewish people in Palestine before and during the rise of early Christianity. This story shows that it was the fate of the masses of Jewish people to live under the yoke of foreign oppressors and their agents. This colonial situation resulted in social repression, economic deprivation worsened by heavy taxation, and periodic political turmoil. It also brought about linguistic, cultural, and religious contact with powerful, colonial forces. While there is much evidence for assimilation to these influences, from time to time, religiopolitical resistance movements arose to combat them. These historical, economic, political, and religious elements converged in the late first century, precisely the period of the emergence of the earliest surviving Christian literature.

Before we take up that literature, we must look more closely at the cultural environment, especially the religious environment in which Christianity arose. That will be the subject of our next chapter.

FURTHER READING

ABD: "Abomination of Desolation" (D. Wenham); "Agriculture" (O. Borowski); "Agrippa" (D. C. Braund); "Akiba, Rabbi" (J. Klein); "Alexander the Great" (R. D. Milns); "Antiochus" (J. Witherhorne); "Antipas" (F. E. Wheeler); "Archelaus" (D. C. Braund); "Augustus" (D. S. Potter); "Banditry" (B. Isaac); "Bar Cochba, Revolt" (B. Isaac; A. Oppenheimer); "Benefactor" (F. W. Danker); "Caesarea" (R. H. Hohlfelder); "Caligula" (S. T. Carroll); "Client Kings" (D. C. Braund); "Foreigner" (C. T. Begg); "Geography and the Bible" (C. N. Raphael); "Herod the Great" (L. I. Levine); "Hospitality" (J. Koenig); "Israel, History of Post-Monarchic Period" (R. P. Carroll); "Jerusalem" (P. King); "Jewish War" (L. I. Levine); "King and Kingship" (K. W. Whitelam); "Languages (Aramaic)" (S. A. Kaufman); "Languages (Greek)" (G. Mussies); "Languages (Hebrew)" (G. M. Schramm); "Palestine, Administration of" (F. F. Bruce); "Pontius Pilate" (D. R. Schwartz); "Roman Empire" (C. M. Wells); "Sanhedrin" (A. J. Saldarini); "Zealots" (D. Rhoads).

IDB: "History of Israel," the latter part of a longer article (H. H. Rowley).

IDB Suppl.: "Masada" (Y. Yadin).

HDB: "Economics in New Testament Times" (R. F. Hock); "Herod" (F. O. Garcia-Treto); "Maccabees" (F. O. Garcia-Treto); "Roman Empire" (P. P. and P. J. Achtemeier); "Zealots" (P. Perkins).

NJBC, pp. 1219–1252, "A History of Israel," the latter part of a longer article (A. G. Wright; R. E. Murphy; J. A. Fitzmyer).

E. Bickerman, *From Ezra to the Last of the Maccabees.*

D. Cowan, *Bridge Between the Testaments.*

M. I. Finley, *The Ancient Economy.*

W. Foerster, *From the Exile to Christ.*

S. Freyne, *Galilee from Alexander the Great to Hadrian: 323 B.C.E. to 135 C.E.*

E. Lohse, *The New Testament Environment.* Part I.

R. MacMullen, *Roman Social Relations.*

B. Reicke, *The New Testament Era.*

D. Rhoads, *Israel in Revolution 6–74 C.E.: A Political History Based on Josephus.*

C. Roetzel, *The World That Shaped the New Testament.*

S. Safrai, S., and M. Stern, eds. *The Jewish People in the First Century.*

A. Schalit, ed. *The World History of the Jewish People, v. 6: The Hellenistic Age; Political History of Jewish Palestine from 332 B.C.E. to 67 B.C.E.*

E. Schürer, G. Vermes, and F. Millar, *The History of the Jewish People in the Age of Jesus Christ,* vol.1.

E. M. Smallwood, *The Jews Under Roman Rule.*

J. E. Stambaugh and D. L. Balch, *The New Testament in its Social Environment,* esp. chs. 2 ("Mobility and Mission"), 3 ("The Ancient Economy"), and 5 ("City Life").

W. W. Tarn and G. T. Griffith, *Hellenistic Civilization.*

V. Tcherikover, *Hellenistic Civilization and the Jews.*

Y. Yadin, *Masada.*

E. Yamauchi, *Harper's World of the New Testament.*

On Jewish culture and religion, see **Further Reading,** Chapter Three.

Sociological, Social-Historical, and Cultural-Anthropological Theory and Orientation

S. Baron, *A Social and Religious History of the Jews.*

S. J. D. Cohen, *From the Maccabees to the Mishna.*

J. D. Crossan, *The Historical Jesus.*

J. H. Elliott, "Patronage and Clientism in Early Christian Society," Polbridge Press Bookshelf, *Forum* 3/4 (1988), pp. 39–48.

D. Fiensy, *The Social History of Palestine in the Herodian Period: The Land Is Mine.*

S. Freyne, *The World of the New Testament.*

J. G. Gager, *Kingdom and Community*, pp. 20–49.

P. Hanson, *The Dawn of Apocalyptic*, Appendix, pp. 427–444.

R. A. Horsley, *Sociology and the Jesus Movement.*

R. A. Horsley and John S. Hanson, *Bandits, Prophets, and Messiahs. Popular Movements at the Time of Jesus.*

G. and J. Lenski, *Human Societies.* 5th edition.

G. W. E. Nickelsburg, "Social Aspects of Palestinian Jewish Apocalypticism," pp. 641–654 in D. Hellholm, ed., *Apocalypticism in the Mediterranean World and the Near East.*

B. Malina, *Christian Origins and Cultural Anthropology.*

———, *The New Testament World. Insights from Cultural Anthropology.*

J. H. Neyrey, "Unclean, Common, Polluted and Taboo," *Forum* 4/4 (1988), pp. 72–82.

D. Oakman, *Jesus and the Economic Questions of His Day.*

E. Schüssler Fiorenza, *In Memory of Her.*

R. Scroggs, "The Earliest Christian Communities as Sectarian Movement," in J. Neusner, ed., *Christianity, Judaism, and Other Greco-Roman-Cults.*

J. E. Stambaugh and D. L. Balch, *The New Testament in its Social Environment* especially ch. 4 ("Society in Palestine").

G. Theissen, *Sociology of Early Palestinian Christianity.*

B. Wilson, *Religion in Sociological Perspective*, ch. 4 ("The Sociology of Sects").

Josephus

Loeb Classical Library (Greek text and English translation)

P. Bilde, *Josephus Between Jerusalem and Rome: His Life, His Works, and Their Importance.*

L. Feldman, *Josephus and Modern Scholarship (1937–1980).*

S. Mason, *Josephus and the New Testament.*

T. Rajak, *Josephus: The Historian and His Society.*

A third-century C.E. Coptic fresco from Karganis, Egypt, portrays the Egyptian goddess Isis suckling her son Horus. To the Greeks and Romans, Horus was Harpocrates, the god of silence, symbolized by the finger held to his mouth. The motif probably influenced Christian art portraying the Madonna and child. (From A. Toynbee, *The Crucible of Christianity*, pp. 236–237.)

CHAPTER THREE

THE CULTURAL AND RELIGIOUS ENVIRONMENT OF THE NEW TESTAMENT

The cultural and religious environment of the New Testament is very different from that of the modern West. Instead of democracy, individual freedom, and human rights, there are emperors, kings, governors, and aristocrats supported by a military machine and secret police. Instead of capitalism, socialism, and communism, a tiny elite controls the agricultural surplus, profits from heavy taxation, and benefits from slave labor. Instead of a middle class, there are masses of lower classes, the urban poor, rural peasants, and slaves. Instead of the ideal of equality, hierarchies are taken for granted: masters over slaves, men over women, parents over children. Social security is found only in families, tribes, and villages, the main networks of relationships and support, rather than in government. Yet, the elites of this culture offer many contributions to civilization through literature, sculpture, philosophy, law, art, and architecture. Most of the voices we hear from the past are from the educated, mostly male, elites, not the masses. Yet, we know that the masses were there, and with a little bit of interpretative effort, aided by archeology, we can gain some insight about them. Finally, and most important for this chapter, we know something of the religious life of antiquity, though the religious beliefs and practices were often bizarre by modern western standards.

It is neither possible nor desirable to study all of ancient Mediterranean culture and religion; similarly, we cannot do justice to the rich spiritual legacy of the Jewish people. However, we can try to gain enough perspective to help interpret the religious movement that issued from Judaism, early Christianity. Thus, in this chapter we shall concentrate on some culture, some popular philosophies, some religious beliefs and practices, and some religious groups.

HELLENISTIC INTELLECTUAL LIFE AND POPULAR PHILOSOPHY

Science and Literature

A flowering of the natural and mathematical sciences and philology took place in the last two centuries B.C.E., but there were few scientific advances in the Roman period, with the possible exception of medicine. By contrast, there were significant developments in international law, especially in relation to imperial administration of non-Romans, and in literature: comedy, mime, and poetry, the revival of Greek tragedy, and the flourishing of historiography (see Chapter Eleven). With a new-found appreciation of the individual, biographies of rulers and those endowed with great wisdom stressed philosophical ideas, right conduct, and character formation. These often merged with stories of miraculous deeds of powerfuly endowed persons modeled after similar stories of the gods and goddesses (see below, "Heroes and Heroines"). Such themes, as well as many others, for example, travel adventures and erotic descriptions, became typical of the Hellenistic romance.

Popular Platonism

In the Hellenistic world, many popular philosophies functioned like religions. **Plato** (died 347 B.C.E.) argued that the fleeting, material world we perceive through our senses is only a shadowy imitation of the true reality, which is the eternal world of abstract ideas known through reason, especially by the philosopher. In his famous **allegory of the cave,** Plato pictured humans who have been chained immovably in an underground cave since childhood. On the opposite wall, they can see only the shadows of moving figures outside the cave, cast on the cave wall by a blazing fire behind them. They hear voices they think are coming from the shadowy figures. Then one of the people gets loose from his chains, ascends from the cave, sees the true reality, the Light. He is blinded by the Light, but he is unable to convince the others of the truth he has seen.

For Plato the material, mortal body is a prison for the divine, immortal soul. The good and just person disciplines the body and its emotions, allowing the reasonable side of the soul to achieve the virtue of knowledge. This philosophical **"dualism"** (mortal/immortal; material/immaterial; vice/virtue; evil/good) is present when the earthly realm is seen as a shadowy imitation of the heavenly realm, or when human origins and destinies lie in a higher world, or when this world is evil. Views such as these influenced some of the early Christians, for example, the Corinthians, the writer(s) of the Gospel of John, the Apostle Paul (1 Cor 2–4; 2 Cor 5), the author of Hebrews, and the Gnostic Christians (see Chapter Four).

Stoicism and Cynicism

Stoicism took its name from the Greek word *stoa,* a colonnaded outdoor mall. Its founder, **Zeno** (ca. 336–263 B.C.E.), taught under such a mall in Athens. The Stoics saw the world as ordered by a divine Reason, the *Logos* (a Greek term for "word," "reason"). The *Logos* was also God, or Zeus, and associated with fire. A spark or seed of the Logos dwelt within human beings who, if they obeyed it, were at home in the world. In contrast to Platonic dualism, Stoicism represented **"monism"**: all reality is one. Such views can be seen in Cleanthes' *Hymn to Zeus,* where the law of God is right reason. It begins:

> Thou, O Zeus, art praised above all gods:
>> many are thy names and thine is all power for ever.
> The beginning of the world was from thee:
>> and with law thou rulest over all things.
> Unto thee may all flesh speak: for we are
>> thy offspring.
> Therefore will I raise a hymn unto thee:
>> and will ever sing of thy power.
> The whole order of the heavens obeyeth thy
>> word: as it moveth around the earth:
> With little and great lights mixed together:
>> how great art thou, King above all forever!
>> (C. K. Barrett, *Background,* p. 63)

Stoicism sought to teach a person to attain happiness by maintaining harmony with Nature. This led to inner peace and contentment in a world full of troubles. Stoic virtues were self-sufficiency, tranquillity, suppression of emotion, freedom from external constraints and material things, and the natural and innate rights of all people, including slaves and women. Its ethical orientation stressed the importance of the will and a certain detachment from property, wealth, suffering, and sickness. Stoics often formed associations stressing these noble ethical themes.

Zeno, the founder of Stoicism, was a follower of Crates, who was a disciple of Diogenes, the first to call himself "dog," from which the philosophical movement called **Cynicism** derives (Greek *kyōn,* "dog"). The Cynics were not cynical in the modern sense. They were counterculture street preachers who tried to convert people from normative human values such as the quest for fame, fortune, and pleasure to a life of austere virtue. This was the path to true freedom and happiness. Many Cynics wandered from town to town, restricted their diets, begged for food, wore short cloaks, carried only a wallet and staff, and rejected social institutions such as marriage and the state. The Cynic way of life was revived as an ideal among first-century Stoics who wanted to appeal to the masses. The following passage from Epictetus, recorded by his follower Arrian, illustrates ethical thinking.

> He is free whom none can hinder, the man who can deal with things as he wishes. But the man who can be hindered or compelled or fettered or driven into anything against his will, is a slave. And who is he whom none can hinder? The man who fixes his aim on nothing that is not his own.

And what does "not his own" mean? All that it does not lies in our power to have or not to have, or to have of a particular quality or under particular conditions. The body then does not belong to us, its parts do not belong to us, our property does not belong to us. If then you set your heart on one of these as though it were your own, you will pay the penalty deserved by him who desires what does not belong to him. The road that leads to freedom, the only release from slavery is this, to be able to say with your whole soul:

Lead me, O Zeus, and lead me, Destiny,
Whether ordained is by your decree.
                    (Epictetus, *Discourses* 4.1 in W. J. Oates, *The Stoic
                    and Epicurean Philosophers,* 418.)

There are some parallels between Cynic-Stoic lifestyles and those of Jesus and the early apostles, most visible in austerity and apostolic mission (for example, Matt 10:5–23). Also, the Cynic-Stoic literary style of arguing with an imaginary opponent (the *diatribe)* and the habit of listing virtues and vices are characteristic devices of the apostle Paul (for example, Gal 5:19–23; compare James 2:14ff.).

Philosophical Schools

In the larger Hellenistic world, the ideas, beliefs, and even the lifestyles of religious-philosophical leaders were often perpetuated in "schools." Many schools were formed in Athens, the most famous being Plato's Academy, Aristotle's Lyceum, Epicurus' Garden, and Zeno's open-air Stoa. The school tradition was also prevalent among the Jewish teachers, though its origins probably lay in the prophetic guilds of the ancient Near East. There were many differences among the various schools, but there were also similarities. One study has summarized them like this:

(1) they were groups of disciples which usually emphasized *philia* [love] and *koinōnia* [fellowship]; (2) they gathered around, and traced their origins to a founder whom they regarded as an exemplary wise, or good man; (3) they valued the teaching of their founder and the traditions about him; (4) members of the schools were disciples or students of the founder; (5) teaching, learning, studying, and writing were common activities; (6) most schools observed communal meals, often in memory of their founders; (7) they had rules or practices regarding admission, retention of membership, and advancement within the membership; (8) they often maintained some degree of distance or withdrawal from the rest of society; and (9) they developed organizational means of insuring their perpetuity.
                    (A. Culpepper, *The Johannine School,* p. 259)

Early Christianity, as we shall see, also developed "schools," especially those who followed the ideas of Paul, the Fourth Evangelist, and perhaps also the First Evangelist.

HELLENISTIC RELIGIONS AND RELIGIOUS MOVEMENTS

Traditional Gods and Goddesses

The Greeks (and Romans) had their traditional myths, associated with the city-state, that is, the original deities living at some sacred center of the universe, such as the sacred mountain to the north (Olympus), which also became heaven. The main members of this divine family were the supreme, majestic, but humanly promiscuous god of the sky, Zeus (Jupiter); his brothers, Poseidon (Neptune), god of the sea, and Hades (Pluto), god of the underworld, with his wife, Persephone (Proserpine); their sister Hestia (Vesta); Zeus' spouse, the goddess Hera (Juno), protector of marriage; their son, Ares (Mars); and the rest of the children, Zeus' daughter Athena (Minerva), Apollo, Aphrodite (Venus), Hermes (Mercury), and Artemis (Diana); and Hera's son, Hephaestus (Vulcan). They were usually associated with the rhythms of the seasons. Occasionally they were believed to descend from heaven to earth for some redemptive mission on behalf of humankind. Occasionally they were identified with historical figures. Essentially, however, they were eternal gods and goddesses, not human beings.

Heroes and Heroines

In Greco-Roman antiquity, there existed recitations of the virtues of the mighty deeds of gods and goddesses, such as Isis, who in declarations beginning "I Am..." lauded herself as ruler of heaven and earth, and who was said to perform cures in dreams ("incubation"; see below, "Mystery Religions"). "I Am" sayings of a similar sort were also attributed to Jesus in the Gospel of John (for example, John 8:24, 28, 58). Comparable recitations or "biographies" existed about historical or mythical human beings believed to have been so endowed with divinity that they were able to perform superhuman feats. They could be the offspring of divine-human unions, and were most often characterized by wisdom, prophecy, and other special powers, including working miracles, especially healing. They were considered to be the benefactors of humankind. In this type were all manner of rulers, military conquerors, politicians, philosophers, physicians, healers, poets, and athletes.

There was also a special class of such figures who, it was believed, were rewarded with immortality at death. One of the most famous was the itinerant Pythagorean philosopher **Apollonios of Tyana** (Asia Minor), who, it was said, was sired by the Egyptian god Proteus. He gathered followers, taught, helped the poor, healed the sick, raised the dead, cast out demons, and appeared to his followers after death to discourse on immortality. He lived through most of the first Christian century, and shortly after 217 C.E. the *Life of Apollonios of Tyana* was written by Philostratus. Scholars often compare his miracles to those in the

Christian gospels and some think that Paul's opponents in 2 Corinthians 10–13 stressed just such virtues about Jesus.

Sympathy, Divination, Astrology, and Alchemy

In the Hellenistic period, the conviction arose that there were mysterious forces in heaven and on earth that united everything (**"sympathy"**). Some believed that the universe was too mysterious to fully understand. For example, the early Greeks had accepted the view that each person had his or her own Fortune, Chance, or Destiny, whether good or ill, deified as the goddess *Tychē* (Latin *Fortuna*). A somewhat more deterministic and less friendly deity was called Fate (Greek *Heimarmenē*). Nonetheless, there arose those specialists who sought to understand the mysterious order by **divination.** On the one hand, one could employ intuitive skills akin to prophecy. On the other hand, one could "divine" the mysterious order by lots, involuntary acts of speech, animal entrails, oil floating on water, or, as the ancient Babylonians had taught, by investigating the effects on the earth of the impersonal, fixed order of the stars and planets, who were also deified as gods, goddesses, and demons (compare Gal 4:8–10; Col 2:8). With the aid of Greek mathematics and astronomy, a person's "fortune" or "destiny" could be ascertained by the position of the stars at birth; by a knowledge of the stars, or **astrology** (Greek *astēr,* "star"), one could learn about his or her fate. Astrology was extremely widespread in the Hellenistic world, and it affected most religions or religious philosophies, including Judaism and early Christianity. The most obvious reference to astrology in the New Testament is the star of the Magi (Matt 2:1–12, 16). Note also that there also emerged attempts to divine the process of transformation of base metals into precious metals, and to hasten the process (**"alchemy"**).

Healing and Magic

In antiquity the art of healing included much more attention to the whole person rather than mere physical disease. There were many different sorts of healing shrines, persons, and practices. There were the famous health spas of Asclepius, the Greek god of healing (for example, Epidauros, Pergamum, the island of Cos), where the healing arts ranged from dream cure in the holy sanctuary to cures by attending physicians. Additionally, as noted in relation to heroic figures, there were all manner of miracle-working healers traversing the Mediterranean world, and amazing cures were ascribed to them.

A means of healing among the common folk was the practice of **magic.** The Greek term *magos* was borrowed from the Persian language, in which it originally referred to a Persian priest who practiced magic. In antiquity the line between magic and medicine was usually not clearly drawn. Magic was an attempt to combat the mysterious powers that determined one's fate and to provide protection against demonic powers often associated with stars (astrology). To know the correct formula, and to recite it correctly, was a "scientific" way to deal with life's evil tragedies. The following selection from the Egyptian magical papyri shows the attractiveness of Hebrew names, including Jesus of Nazareth.

A tested charm of Pibechis for those possessed by daimons: Take oil of unripe olives with the herb mastigia and the fruit pulp of the lotus, and boil them with colorless marjoram while saying, "IŌĒL OS SARTHIŌMI EMŌRI THEŌCHIPSOITH SŌTHĒ IŌE MIMIPSŌTHIŌŌPH PHERSŌTHI AEĒ IOYŌ IŌĒ EŌCHARI PHTHA, come out from NN [insert name]" (add the usual). **The phylactery [amulet]:** On a tin lamella write "IAĒO ABRAŌTH IŌCH PHTHA MESENPSIN IAŌ PHEŌCH IAĒŌ CHARSOK, and hang it on the patient. It is terrifying to every daimon, a thing he fears. After placing [the patient] opposite [to you], conjure. **This is the conjuration:** "I conjure you by the god of the Hebrews, Jesus, IABA IAĒ ABRAŌTH AIA THOTH ELE EL AEO EOYIIBAECH ABARMAS IABARAOU ABELBEL LONA ABRA MAROIA BRAKIŌN, who appears in fire, who is in the midst of land, snow, and fog....

(Paris Magical Papyrus IV.3008–3025 in H. D. Betz, ed., *The Greek Magical Papyri in Translation*, p. 96).

Magic was castigated, but paradoxically practiced, by many Jews and early Christians (compare Mark 8:22–26; Acts 8:9–24; 19:18–19). Jesus' opponents did not deny that he worked miracles; rather, they said he was in league with the Prince of Demons (for example, Mark 3:20–27) or, as later Jewish writings put it, that he was a magician who led the people astray.

Mystery Religions

For many people during the Hellenistic period, the traditional Greek and Roman humanlike deities had become remote in their far distant heaven, and too formal, too sedate; at the same time, exotic, originally local deities from other religious shrines became internationalized, widespread, and very popular, often filling the void. These **"mystery religions"** (Greek *myein:* "to close" the eyes or lips) were secret religious societies closed to outsiders; only insiders could "see" the true mysteries and become enlightened. Initiates were not born into these religions; they freely joined and went through rites of cleansing and formal initiation. They took vows of silence not to defile the most holy mysteries, and so did not reveal them to outsiders. As a result, outsiders did not know much about their private utterances, practices, and revelations (and neither do modern re-searchers!). However, they also had a public side that displayed colorful pageantry. Usually there was a recital or reenactment of a myth to celebrate the death and resurrection of a hero or heroine, which had its parallel with the death and rebirth of vegetation during the cycle of the agricultural year. Often there was a theme of wandering in quest of some deity or attribute. Devotees also celebrated a sacred meal and were promised immortality, mystical communion with their god, membership in a close-knit community, and thus a true "home." The gods and goddesses of the mysteries, as well as their attributes and practices, tended to mix with those of the old Greco-Roman mythical deities **("syncretism")**; thus, for example, Greek Zeus (Roman Jupiter) was identified with the Syrian Ba`al high god of the sky, both seen as hurling their thunderbolts, and Greek Aphrodite (Roman Venus), the goddess of love and beauty, was identified with Syrian Ashtoreth, or Astarte, goddess of fertility.

Some of the better known mystery religions were the Eleusinian Mysteries of Greece (at Eleusis, a few miles from Athens); the religion of Dionysus or Bacchus, god of wine and the vintage harvest, which also became associated with Greece; Cybele and her consort, Attis, whose priests were castrated in imitation of Attis, driven mad by the jealous Cybele, from Asia Minor; the Adonis fertility cult from Syria-Palestine; Mithras, the transformed Persian god of light and patron of the soldier; and Isis and Osiris from Egypt. While Mithraism was increasingly practiced by men, especially soldiers in the Roman army, other religions stressed the feminine and attracted women devotees, for example, the Eleusinian mysteries (Demeter and Persephone, archetypal mother ["Grain Mother"] and daughter); the Syrian Cybele or Great Mother; the originally Egyptian Isis, queen of the cosmos; and the Dionysiac practices. Moreover, as religions whose myths celebrated the seasons and fertility, some were explicitly sexual, such as the exotic Dionysiac rites; and by Jewish and Christian standards of taste, some were bizarre, for example, initiation by standing in a pit under a slain bull and drinking its blood (the *taurobolium*) in the Cybele initiations.

In a second-century C.E. morality tale called *The Golden Ass,* Apuleius came almost to the point of describing his initiation into the most secret mysteries. According to a dream, the goddess Isis instructed him to find an old high priest, Mithras, who then led him to the temple, performed sacrifices, and instructed him from secret holy books. The priest ritually washed and purified him, presented him to the goddess in the temple, and taught him "certain secret things unlawful to be uttered." Apuleius then fasted for ten days. The account continues:

> Then behold the day approached when as the sacrifice of dedication should be done; and when the sun declined and evening came, there arrived on every coast a great multitude of priests, who according to their ancient order offered me many presents and gifts. Then was all the laity and profane people commanded to depart, and when they had put on my back a new linen robe, the priest took my hand and brought me to the most secret and sacred place of the temple. Thou wouldest peradventure demand, thou studious reader, what was said and done there: verily I would tell thee if it were lawful for me to tell, thou wouldest know if it were convenient for thee to hear; but both thy ears and my tongue should incur the like pain of rash curiosity. Howbeit I will not long torment thy mind, which peradventure is somewhat religious and given to some devotion; listen therefore, and believe it to be true. Thou shalt understand that I approached near unto hell, even to the gates of Proserpine [Persephone, daughter of Demeter in the Eleusinian mysteries], and after that I was ravished throughout all the elements, I returned to my proper place: about midnight I saw the sun brightly shine, I saw likewise the gods celestial and the gods infernal, before whom I presented myself and worshipped them. Behold now have I told thee, which although thou has heard, yet it is necessary that thou conceal it; wherefore this only will I tell, which may be declared without offence for the understanding of the profane.
>
> (Apuleius, *The Golden Ass* 11.22–26, quoted from
> C. K. Barrett, *Background Documents,* 127–128.)

Apuleius continued by reporting that he was then sanctified with twelve stoles and dressed in a religious habit. Torch in hand and garland of flowers on his head, he was permitted to be seen by the people, an act that solemnized the feast. Apuleius then gave an oration to Isis and embraced his spiritual father.

Direct influence of the mysteries on early Christianity is difficult to show, but they nonetheless shared a common environment and some similar practices, such as initiation and common meal. Thus, many non-Christians perceived Christians as members of some Jewish mystery cult, and post-New Testament Christian writers were willing to think of Christianity as the truly sacred mystery.

The Emperor Cult (Emperor Worship)

The emperor cult was an adaptation of middle eastern beliefs about the divinity of the pharaoh or the partial deity of the oriental king. The Greeks and Romans cautiously tolerated such views abroad as one means to political unity and stability, but they discouraged them at home. True, it was usual to pay worthy emperors divine homage after they died, but emperors who claimed for themselves divine prerogatives while still alive met stiff resistance, sometimes contributing to their removal by assassination. Nonetheless, titles of majesty were often bestowed on, or demanded by, the emperor. Examples were "Lord," "God," "Son of God," and "Savior." Moreover, in the provinces some people believed that the emperor's birth, works, and enthronement brought about "good news" for the world. These same themes were also associated with Jesus.

Gnosticism

The term Gnosticism comes from the Greek word *gnōsis,* meaning "knowledge." Knowledge in this case is not just intellectual; it is revealed religious knowledge necessary for salvation. As the late second-century Gnostic Theodotus once summarized it, this is *gnōsis* about our origins, existence, and destiny, or

Who we were, what we have become;
Where we were, whither we were thrown;
Whither we are hastening, from what we are redeemed;
What birth is, and what rebirth.
(Clement of Alexandria, *Excerpts from Theodotus* 78.2)

Theodotus' description points to second-century Gnostic myths in which the evil world and matter are not created by the good God, but by an inferior Deity. The world is an evil place. The true self is a divine spark of light from the world of light above ("who we were"; "where we were"), but is now trapped in an alien body with all of its sensual passions ("what we have become"; "whither we were thrown"; "birth"). This body-spirit dualism is reminiscent of Platonism. Expressed in Gnostic terms, the evil powers attempt to keep the true self in a state of "sleep" or "drunkenness" to hold the creation of the evil world together. The only possible means of liberation from this evil body and this evil world is *gnōsis,* secretly revealed knowledge about God, the world, and the origin, condition, and destiny of humankind. Those who have it ("rebirth") will be enabled to escape this evil world and the body's prison ("from what we are redeemed") to return to the world of light ("whither we are hastening").

In the Hermetic literature, composed sometime in the second century C.E., the Egyptian god Thoth, who is given the Greek name Hermes Trismegistus ("Thrice-Greatest Hermes"), usually reveals the secret knowledge *(gnōsis)* about God, creation, and salvation to a disciple. The dualistic view of the world is parallel to the body-soul dualism. It is described by the myth of the fall of the First or Primal Man, which leads to the slavery of humanity, to the lower powers, and to death.

> And he who had all authority over the world of mortal beings and of beasts without reason bent down through the harmony (of the spheres), broke through the encirclement, and disclosed God's godly form to the lower nature. When she (the lower nature) saw him who had in himself infinite beauty, all power over the governors, and the form of God, she smiled in love, because she beheld man's most beautiful form reflected in the water and in the shadow upon the earth. When he beheld in the water the figure like himself that was to be found in (the lower) nature, he loved it too and willed to dwell there. But the fulfillment followed at once with his intention, and thus he took his abode in the form devoid of reason. And nature (thereby) received the beloved and wholly embraced him, and they were united and loved each other. Therefore man, in contrast to all other living creatures on earth, is a dual being, mortal, to be sure, because of the body, but immortal because of the essential man. Although he is immortal and is given power over all things, he suffers the lot of a mortal and is subject to fate. Although he is placed above the harmony (of the spheres), he became a slave within this harmony. Although he is bisexual, because he is born of a bisexual father, and although he is sleepless, because he comes from one who is sleepless, he is under the dominion (of desire and the longing for sleep).
>
> *(Corpus Hermeticum* tractate Poimandres 14–15,
> quoted from W. Foerster, *Gnosis: A Selection of
> Gnostic Texts,* vol. 2.)

In general, Gnostics believe that *gnōsis* can be taught or transmitted through a secret ritual, but ultimately that it comes from above as a "call." In mythical terms, a Gnostic Redeemer descends from the world of light, disguises himself in human form without becoming bodily, teaches *gnōsis,* and returns or ascends. However Gnostics gain their *gnōsis,* they learn that this world and this body are not their true homes, that they have been thrown into an alien world. Often they totally renounce the body and its passions (asceticism) or, knowing that the world is not their true place and cannot really affect them, allow themselves the utmost freedom (libertinism). Either way, they experience rebirth and become part of the privileged few. It is clear that there are certain affilities between Gnosticism and early Christianity, as we shall see in subsequent chapters.

MAJOR FEATURES OF JEWISH RELIGION IN THE GREEK AND ROMAN PERIODS

In Chapter Two we noted a few beliefs and practices that pious Jews would not compromise when Hellenization was forced upon them. Three points should be kept in mind. First, Judaism was (and is) primarily a religion of practice, or religious observance, not a religion of orthodox dogmas and creeds. Second, by the early Roman period, Judaism consisted of a variety of beliefs, practices, groups and movements, some of them influenced by Hellenistic religions. Indeed, it is somewhat artificial to separate Judaism from Hellenism, since Judaism was a Hellenistic religion. Moreover, one should think of *Judaisms*. Nonetheless, for clarity we have decided to discuss Judaism separately and to consider Diaspora Judaism at the end of this chapter. While several generalizations about beliefs and practices follow, it will be necessary to include observations about varieties.

Clean and Unclean

From an anthropological perspective (see Neyrey), classifications of "clean," "holy," "pure," or "sacred" are made based on what is "in place" according to social norms. Classifications of "unclean," "defiled," "polluted," "impure," or "profane" are based on what is "out of place." The earth is "soil" in the garden; it is "dirt" and considered "unclean" in the house.

Traditional societies set aside people (priests, medicine men), places (temples, shrines), times (special days of the week or year), and things (sacrificial animals, important books) as especially holy, sacred, pure, or clean. They also set aside people (outsiders, lepers), places (other lands, places outside the city gate), and things (contaminated objects, certain foods) as especially unholy, profane, impure, or unclean. Normally, the two realms are separated by boundaries: walls, gates, and curtains. A tightly knit social group may also be symbolically mirrored ("replicated") by its attitudes about the human body, for example, the food that enters it (pork, cf. Leviticus 11), the fluids that come out of it (semen or menses), and the cleanliness of the hands that controls such functions (ritual hand washing; toilet practices). Women in traditional Jewish culture are thus labeled "unclean" more often than men (compare Leviticus 12, 15; compare the woman with a hemorrhage, Mark 5:25–34).

Holy God, Holy People, Holy Land

As already noted, Judaism maintained a special belief, **monotheism:** "Hear, O Israel, the Lord our God, the Lord is one..." (Deuteronomy 6:4, called the *Shema'* [Hebrew, "Hear..."]). According to Genesis 15 and 17, God made a **covenant** with Abraham that his descendants would be many, and that the land of Canaan would be given to them as their special inheritance. This agreement was sealed by a sign, the **circumcision** of every boy on the eighth day after birth. Thus, the Jews believed themselves to be the God's elect, holy, and chosen people. Their mission was to be "a light to the nations." God made other covenants. One was with Moses (the holy Law to guide the people). Another was with David (a king to rule the land). If the king or the people disobeyed the covenants, God would punish them. According to the Bible, then, as God is holy, so the people of God must be holy (Lev 11:44–45; 1 Pet 1:16), and thus God has given them a holy land. By New Testament times, even God's name, "Yahweh," had become too holy to utter. So one substituted *Adonai* ("[my] lord"). All this meant that most observant Jews separated themselves from outsiders by all sorts of physical and social barriers, for example, not eating with non-Jews.

Holy Temple and Holy Priesthood

Within God's holy people and holy land, there were especially holy people, places, times, and things. Within the holy land was the holy city, Jerusalem, surrounded by walls; within the holy city was the holy Temple, surrounded by walls; and within the Temple were holy courts, surrounded by walls. Non-Jews, or Gentiles, were permitted only in the outermost "court of Gentiles." Posted there was a warning that Gentiles proceeded beyond this point "under penalty of death." Moving inward, the Sacred Enclosure for Jews alone consisted of the Court of Women—they were considered more unclean than men—then the Court of Israel (men), then the Court of Priests (especially holy men), and then the forecourt where the holy sacrifices (animals "without blemish") took place to atone for sin. In the very center was the holiest place of all, the Holy of Holies, where the presence of God was said to reside, and into which the holiest of men, the High Priest, entered only on a very holy day, the Day of Atonement (see below).

Priests had to maintain purity. Priestly genealogies were necessary and a priest was required to marry a Jewish woman who had never been a divorcee, prostitute, convert, prisoner of war, or a widow, that is, she had to be a Jewish virgin (Lev 21:13–14). Among priests' duties were purification rites performed on those with diseases, especially disorders of the skin ("leprosy," compare Leviticus 13; Mark 1:40–45) or physical impurities; preservation of holiness in the Temple; and maintenance of their own purity, especially by avoiding contact with a corpse (see the Good Samaritan parable, Luke 10:29–37). They could not officiate in the Temple if they were ritually impure, had a physical defect, were under the influence of alcohol, or had married an impure woman.

About 180 B.C.E., Ben Sira, a Jewish writer from Jerusalem, idealized the Jerusalem High Priest Simon, son of Onias (ca. 219–196 B.C.E.), like this:

5) How glorious he was when the people gathered round
   him as he came out of the inner sanctuary!
6) Like the morning star among the clouds,
   like the moon when it is full;
7) Like the sun shining upon the temple of the Most High,
   and like the rainbow gleaming in glorious clouds;
8) like roses in the days of the first fruits,
   like lilies by a spring of water,
   like a green shoot on Lebanon on a summer day;
9) like fire and incense in the censer,

     like a vessel of hammered gold adorned with all kinds
       of precious stones;
10) like an olive tree putting forth its fruit,
       and like a cypress towering in the clouds.
11) When he put on his glorious robe and clothed himself
       with superb perfection
       and went up to the holy altar, he made the court of the
       sanctuary glorious.
                  (Ben Sira 50:5–11, RSV)

This, again, was an idealized picture of the High Priest. We cannot forget that in New Testament times the high priests' families were also among the elite who tended to support the Romans.

The center of official Jewish religion was the Temple, a political, religious, social, and economic hub of Jewish life and culture. Connected with the Temple were not only the sacrifices, but also the seasonal festivals, the meeting place of **Sanhedrin** (the ruling senate and "supreme court" of Judaism), the laws and system of courts, education, and the Temple treasury, supported by the half-shekel tax. The wealthy priestly aristocracy established the norms for religious life and thought in Judaism ("the great tradition"). In theory, these were emulated by the people ("the little tradition"). Thus, the destruction of the Temple in 70 C.E. was the end of a central cultural institution.

The Holy Scriptures (Tanak)

In the post-exilic period the Jewish people sought to learn God's will through sacred writings and their interpretations. From the record that Moses had written a book (compare Deuteronomy 29:20), they accepted a collection of five books, or **Pentateuch,** as the "book of Moses" (Nehemiah 13:1), or **Torah.** According to sacred tradition, it had been handed down from Moses to Joshua, to the Elders, to the prophets, and finally to the men of the "Great Synagogue." All phases of life and thought were inspired and guided by it. To study the Torah was a "delight" (Ps 1:2; compare Ps 19), and the heroes and heroines of Judaism were frequently those who kept the Torah despite adversity, war, or persecution (Tobit; Judith; Daniel).

We have evidence for varying Torahs and different attitudes toward them. The Samaritans had **the Samaritan Pentateuch,** which recognized a hill in Samaria (Mount Gerizim), not Jerusalem, as the holy mountain. Many Jews and Samaritans were willing to fight and die for their sacred Torah. Some Jews eventually added other books, the **"Prophets"** (including "historical" writings from Joshua to Kings) and the **"Writings"** (primarily wisdom literature such as Psalms and Proverbs). These three divisions—Torah, Prophets, Writings—emerged during the first century C.E. While other books continued to be used in Greek-speaking Judaism and Christianity (see below "Diaspora Judaism"), in Palestine in the period after 70 C.E., books thought to have been inspired or revealed by God were accepted, while those venerated by the more esoteric Jewish groups were omitted. What emerged at the end of the first century C.E., or at least in the second century C.E., became the *Tanak* (T for *Tōrāh;* N for *Nebîîm,* or "Prophets"; K for *Ketubîm,* or "Writings"), the full "Hebrew Scriptures." Excluded books are now collected in the Old Testament Apocrypha and Pseudepigrapha.

The sect of the Pharisees (see below) believed that it was necessary to "build a fence around the Torah," that is, to protect people from transgressing the laws by applying them to specific cases. Such interpretations became authoritative oral tradition ("the tradition of the elders," Mark 7:3). It was believed to have come from Moses, as well. The elaboration of kosher food laws and Sabbath regulations (see below) are excellent examples.

Feasts and Fasts

Feasts and fasts are holy times. Most Jews followed a lunar-solar calendar. The length of the year was determined by the sun (from vernal equinox to vernal equinox), but the length of the months was determined by the phases of the moon (from new moon to new moon). The shorter 30-day months required the intercalation of an extra month every few years.

Judaism's six major feasts and one major fast follow the agricultural year. Following the Jewish months, they are (compare Exodus 23:14–17; 34:22–24; Deuteronomy 16:1–17; Leviticus 23; 1 Macc 4:36–61):

1. Tishri 1 (Sept./Oct.)	New Year *(Rōsh Hashānāh),* Lev 23:24.
2. Tishri 10	**Day of Atonement** *(Yōm Kippūr),* Lev 16 and 23:26–32. (A fast)
3. Tishri 15 (8 days)	**Booths** *(Succōth),* Exod 23:14–17; Lev 23:34–36. (See also *Simhath Tōrāh,* "the Joy of the Law")
4. Kislev 25 (Nov./Dec.) (8 days)	Dedication *(Hanūkkāh),* 1 Macc 4:42–58; 2 Macc 10:1–8. Also known as the "Festival of Lights."
5. Adar 14 (Feb./Mar.) (2 days)	Lots *(Purîm),* Esther.
6. Nisan 15 (Mar./Apr.) (7 days)	**Passover** *(Pesach* and the **Feast of Unleavened Bread** *(Mazzōth),* Exod 12–13.
7. Sivan 6 (May/June),	**Weeks** *(Shāvuōth;* in the New Testament, "Pentecost") 50 days after Passover, Lev 23:15–16.

Three feasts—Booths, Passover, and Weeks—were "Pilgrim Festivals," that is, (male) pilgrims were supposed to make a pilgrimage to Jerusalem. **Booths** was a festival of harvesting grapes when booths were built in the vineyards for grape pickers; it also came to represent the wilderness wanderings. (The ninth day of Booths, called *Simhath Tōrāh* ["the Joy of the Law"] eventually became a separate feast [compare 1 Esdras 9:50]). There may be hints of "Booths" in Mark 9:2-5.

Passover was a spring festival. In popular etymology it referred to when the angel of death "passed over" the houses of the Israelites in Egypt if the house's lintel and doorposts were marked with the blood of the sacrificial lamb. Originally a rite of sacrifice to maintain the fertility of the flock, it commemorated the exodus of the Israelites from Egyptian captivity to freedom. It became associated with the weeklong Feast of Unleavened Bread, originally marking the barley harvest. In the first century, goats and lambs were ritually slaughtered at the Temple in the afternoon before the feast began ("the Day of Preparation," compare Mark 14:12) and the blood was sprinkled on the altar. While the sun was setting, the feast proper began with a common meal at a house or an apartment within the city walls of Jerusalem. Later tradition says the pilgrim should find a room in the city; procure a male yearling sheep or goat for sacrifice; buy wine, unleavened bread dough, and spices; and celebrate with a minimum of ten males. In the gospels, this festival is the occasion for the passion and death of Jesus.

Weeks (New Testament **"Pentecost"**) was originally a celebration of the fertility of the land at the end of the grain harvest. It became associated with the giving of the Law to Moses on Mount Sinai. It is connected with the coming of the Spirit to the early church (Acts 2).

New Year *(Rōsh Hashānāh,* "Head [First] of the Year"), originally celebrating the ascent of the king to the throne, became a day of sanctity marked by blowing the *shōphār,* or ram's horn. *Hanūkkāh* was the "rededication" of the Temple after its defilement by the Seleucid Greeks (see the Maccabean Revolt, Chapter Two). *Purîm* ("Lots") celebrated the victory of Persian Jews over Haman, who cast lots in his attempt to exterminate them; customarily the book of Esther, which tells the story, was read on this day.

The only prescribed *fast* in the Hebrew Scriptures—custom developed others—was *Yōm Kippūr,* the **"Day of Atonement,"** when purification from sins took place (Leviticus 16). On this day of fasting, rest, and penance, the high priest sacrificed a bull for the sins of himself and the Aaronic priests; then, and only on this day, he entered the Holy of Holics and sprinkled the bull's blood on the "mercy seat" of the Ark of the Covenant, that is, God's symbolic throne above the Ark, or box, the place from which God dispensed mercy to his people. Two goats were presented by the people, one for God, one "for Azazel" (the goat? a place? a desert demon?). The High Priest sacrificed the first goat to atone for the sins of the people. Then he placed his hands on the second goat, transferring to it the sins of the people. It was led into the desert to die, after which the High Priest purified himself. Thus, the sins of the community were driven off into the desert (the "scapegoat").

Sabbath

Jewish days are from sunset to sunset. Sabbath (Hebrew *shabbāt)* is the name given to the seventh day of the week, from sunset Friday to sunset Saturday. Popular priestly etymology explained that on the seventh day God ceased (Hebrew *shabbāt,* "he ceases"; compare also *shāvuōth,* "period of seven days," from *sheva*ᵉ, "seven") from his work of creation, blessed the day, declared it holy, and required that no one work on that day (Gen 2:1–3; compare Exodus 23:12). The requirement to observe the Sabbath became part of the Ten Commandments (Exodus 20:8). Similar ideas about refraining from work were associated with the holiness of the "sabbatical," or seventh, year when the land was not to be worked (Leviticus 16:31 and elsewhere), debts were to be released (Deuteronomy 15:2), and taxes were not to be paid (Josephus *Antiquities* 14.202). The following tradition, later than New Testament times, illustrates the attempt to "build a fence around the Law" of the Sabbath command to rest, not work:

> The main classes of work are forty save one: sowing, ploughing, reaping, binding sheaves, threshing, winnowing, cleansing crops, grinding, sifting, kneading, baking, shearing wool, washing or beating or dyeing it, spinning, weaving, making two loops, weaving two threads, separating two threads, tying (a knot), loosening (a knot), sewing two stitches, tearing in order to sew two stitches, hunting a gazelle, slaughtering or flaying or salting it or curing its skin, scraping it or cutting it up, writing two letters, building, pulling down, putting out a fire, lighting a fire, striking with a hammer and taking out aught from one domain into another. These are the main classes of work: forty save one.
> (Babylonian Talmud, *Shabbat* 7.1–2)

The gospels report many controversies about the Sabbath.

Synagogue

The word synagogue comes from the Greek *synagōgē* ("gathering together"), which also translates *qāhal* ("assembly" [of God]) in the Hebrew Bible. Though the Greek term is found frequently in the gospels (compare Mark 1:21; Luke 4:16), Acts (6:9), and in Josephus' writings, indicating literary evidence for the widespread existence of synagogues in Palestine, archeological evidence for synagogue *buildings* there prior to 70 C.E. is extremely scarce and debated. At best, structures at Masada and Herodium in the South, and Gamla in Galilee, might be called synagogue buildings. However, such buildings in the pre-70 period were well known outside of Palestine (Philo of Alexandria; inscriptions). Thus, it is likely that some sort of place for "gathering together," perhaps a large room in a house (a "house-synagogue" or "meeting house"), had developed in Palestine. Such a view would help to lessen the apparent contradiction between the literary and archeological evidence.

In contrast to the Temple, no sacrifice was offered in the synagogue. Rather, services probably consisted of a recitation of the *Shema'* ("Hear, O Israel, the Lord our God, the Lord is one . . ."), Scripture readings, a sermon, blessings, and prayer. Synagogues also became places for meditation and meetings. When buildings did come into existence, they became community centers for education, common meals, and in some cases places where Jewish travelers might be housed.

Prayer and Song

Prayer is communication with a holy God. The psalms of the Hebrew Scriptures were the hymnbook of the Temple and, in New Testament times, psalms and chants had become the special province of a lower order of Temple priests, the Levites. However, prayers were also offered in house-synagogues, synagogues, or at any time and place. Prayers were oriented toward Jerusalem—specifically the Holy of Holies—and it was customary to offer them three times a day: morning, midday, and evening. Standing or kneeling with hands raised to heaven were the usual praying positions.

The following prayer, perhaps as early as the first century C.E., is called "The Kaddish." It is often compared to Jesus' prayer, "Hallowed be thy name, Thy kingdom come" (Matt 6:9–10; Luke 11:12; see Chapter One):

> Exalted and hallowed be his great name
> in the world which he has created according to his will.
> May he let his kingdom rule in your lifetime and in your days
> and in the lifetime of the whole house of Israel, speedily and soon.
> (Dalman, *Die Worte Jesu*, 305; Jeremias, *Theology*, 198)

This prayer became a standard synagogue prayer.

Wisdom

Wisdom had a venerable tradition in the religions of the Ancient Near East. Examples from the Old Testament, some of which were borrowed from non-Israelite Wisdom traditions, are Proverbs, Job, Ecclesiastes, and some of the psalms. There are also many examples from postexilic Judaism, all after 200 B.C.E. (the Wisdom of Jesus ben Sira [Ecclesiasticus], the Wisdom of Solomon, Tobit, Baruch, the Letter of Aristeas, and the Sayings of the Fathers). The Wisdom movement was fostered by "wise men" who were originally part of the royal court. Though the most characteristic form of Wisdom was the proverb, a wide variety of other forms existed, including the parable. Wisdom usually dealt with the practical knowledge about the world and human relations that would help the individual to prosper and lead a long and fruitful life. The first example illustrates everyday wisdom from a male perspective:

> A continual dripping on a rainy day and a contentious woman
> are alike.
> (Proverbs 27:5)

Another example illustrates the centrality of the Torah.

> He [Hillel] used to say: If I am not for myself, who is for me? And when I am for myself, what am I? And if not now, when? Shammai said: Make thy Torah a fixed duty; say little and do much; and receive every man with the look of a cheerful face.
> (*Sayings of the Fathers* 1:14–15)

Such wisdom was believed to be from God. We should also note the **Wisdom myth,** that is, that Wisdom was the personified expression or extension of God. The term "wisdom" is feminine gender in both Hebrew and Greek.

> Wisdom went forth to make her dwelling among the children of men,
> Wisdom found no place where she might dwell;
> Then a dwelling-place was assigned her in the heavens.

Wisdom went forth to make her dwelling among the children of men,
And found no dwelling-place.

Wisdom returned to her place,
And took her seat among the angels.
(Enoch 42:1–2)

As in Greco-Roman religions at large, the descent/ascent motif is present.

Wisdom and the Wisdom myth were very important to many Christians. Jesus was a teacher of wisdom (see Chapter Fifteen), and the Wisdom myth appears to have influenced early Christian view of Jesus as a redeemer from heaven (for example, Phil 2:6–11; John 1:1–18; see Chapters Five, Seven).

Prophecy

It is impossible to give a simple definition of prophecy (see D. Aune). The word "prophet" comes from the Greek *prophētēs*, which in the Septuagint translates *nabî'* in the Hebrew Bible, literally "one who is called" [by God]. A prophet can be a "seer" who sees in the Spirit or a "diviner" and "soothsayer," and such figures are also known among the Greeks and Romans. The prophet is an unusually senstitive person who has a special vocation, who sees or divines what others do not see, or do not care to see, for example, political abuse, religious indifference, social injustice, or simply the outcome of a battle. Prophets articulate revelations in concrete social situations. They *speak* for the gods. In the Hebrew scriptures, prophetic messages often begin, "Thus says the Lord (= YHWH or Yahweh) . . ." As intermediaries between the divine and the human, prophets often have the power to work miracles. There is some prediction of events, but more often interpretations of *current* events were interpreted as predictions later, sometimes centuries later.

While a number of famous premonarchic Israelite figures (prior to 1000 B.C.E.) were remembered as prophets and prophetesses—Abraham (Gen 20:7), Aaron (Exod 7:1), Miriam and Deborah (15:20; Judg 4:4), and Moses (Deut 18:18; 34:10)—during the monarchy several types of prophets could be distinguished. There were official court and cultic prophets at religious shrines, including the Jerusalem Temple, whose oracles were solicited (1 Sam 28:6; 1 Kgs 22:5–6), for example, prior to war (1 Kgs 22:13–28); 20:13–15, 22, 28). Isaiah may have been a cult prophet (Isa 6), and others, like Jeremiah and Ezekiel, were of priestly descent.

More explicitly described were "shaman" prophets, that is, those who experienced altered states of consciousness such as spirit-possession or trances, hallucinations, and visions of the "out-of-the-body" sort. In such states of ecstasy, sometimes induced by musical rhythms (1 Sam 10:5; 1 Kgs 3:15), dancing (1 Kgs 18:21) or self-flagellation (1 Kgs 18:28–29; Zech 13:6), they were said to receive revelations from God. They were believed to be intermediaries between God and human beings and were also known for their wisdom and miracle working. Sometimes they prophesied in bands, or prophetic associations, and were typified by unusual dress such as hairy sheepskins or leather loincloths. Two prophets of the shaman type from the early monarchic period were Elijah and Elisha. Early

Christians often identified John the Baptist with Elijah (for example, Mark 1:2–11; Matthew 11:14), and both Elijah and Elisha figures are echoed in the miracle working of Jesus.

The final type of prophet was the "free prophet." Free prophets came forth especially before, and during periods of national crisis to announce God's word. They were reformers who condemned complacency and injustice, and sought social, political, economic, and religious change. As a result, they often came into conflict with the established authorities, especially the kings, and also with the official cult prophets who supported the kings. Claiming to know the will of the True King, God, they called the people back to God's just rule as represented by the ancient, premonarchial covenant traditions. For example, about 750 B.C.E., when Assyria was threatening, Amos went to the northern capital to denounce the self-indulgence of urban life, to demand justice for the poor peasants, and to condemn the corruption of the official prophets. Other eighth-century B.C.E. free prophets were Hosea, Isaiah, and Micah, and in the seventh century came Jeremiah. Finally Deutero[Second]-Isaiah (Isa 40–55) spoke oracles that reflect the concluding days of the Babylonian Exile (587–539 B.C.E.; compare 48:20), and Ezekiel, taken captive to Babylon in 598 B.C.E., had many visions and prophesied judgment, especially against Jerusalem, false prophets, and the nations.

Prophecy continued in the postexilic period, though in dialogue with, even opposition to, the growing power of the priests, and it showed evidence of emergent apocalyptic. About 520 B.C.E. Haggai urged the rebuilding of the Temple and declared Zerubbabel to be the messianic king (Haggai 2). The group of prophecies that go under the name Zechariah 1–8 were similar, though Zechariah stressed two Messiahs, priestly and royal (compare Zech 3:8; 6:12). In contrast, Zechariah 9–14, which may be later, heightened the attack on the Jerusalem priesthood. Malachi, from about 450 B.C.E., emphasized the correct practice of the Temple liturgy. Isaiah 24–27 showed signs of emergent apocalyptic, and thus is usually considered post-exilic. Finally, the Isaiah traditions continued ("Trito-Isaiah," Isa 56–66)..

Though prophecy had become rare in postexilic Judaism, there also arose a hope for a righteous prophet, either a new or returning Elijah (1 Kings 17–21; 2 Kings 2) or a "prophet like Moses" (Deut 18:15) who would establish the Torah. The Samaritans called the latter type the Taheb. In the Dead Sea Scrolls, the prophet is yoked with the two Messiahs and is a "prophet like Moses" who adheres to the Torah:

> And they shall not depart from any maxim of the Law to walk in all the stubbornness of their heart.
> And they shall be governed by the first ordinances in which the members of the Community began their instruction, until the coming of the Prophet and the Anointed (Ones) of Aaron and Israel.
> (The Manual of Discipline 9:9–11)

In early Christianity many sayings of the ancient prophets were believed to predict the teachings and life of Jesus and early Christian events (for example, Matt 1:18–2:23; 8:17), Jesus himself was considered to be a prophet (for example, Mark 6.1–6; 8.27–9:1), and both male and female prophets continued in the early churches (1 Cor 11:4–5; Matt 10:41; Acts 2:17; 21:8–12). It needs to be added that there were many forms of prophetic speech, usually an oracular utterance in poetic form, and typical forms of utterances about judgment, salvation, combined judgment, assurance, admonition, divine self-disclosure, woes, and God's justice. There are also typical call scenes, prophetic visions, and symbolic actions. Such speech played an enormous role in early Christian speech forms.

Jewish Magic and Other Miracle Traditions

A special form of wisdom was magic. We have seen that in the Greco-Roman world there were many magicians and miracle workers, healers, and physicians. Palestine was no exception, though pious, educated Jews believed that God, not the miracle worker, was the real source of healing. In the Dead Sea Scrolls, Abraham was said to have exorcised a demon from Pharaoh by prayer, the laying on of hands, and rebuking the evil spirit (GenApoc 20:16–19). David was said to have done the same by playing his harp (LibAntBib 60:1–3), and Noah by medicines and herbs (Jub 10:10–14). Solomon was remembered especially for his wisdom, which included his knowledge of magic and medicine. Josephus tells the story of the Jewish exorcist Eleazar, who performed an exorcism:

> He put to the nose of the possessed man a ring which had under its seal one of the roots prescribed by Solomon, and then, as the man smelled it, drew out the demon through his nostrils, and, when the man at once fell down, adjured the demon never to come back into him, speaking Solomon's name and reciting the incantations which he had composed.
> (Josephus *Antiquities* 8:2)

In Josephus and in the Talmud, the *Hāsîd* ("Pious One") "Honi the Circle Drawer" was remembered for bringing rain by prayer. Another *Hāsîd,* Hanina ben Dosa, was remembered for healing by prayer.

> When the son of Yohanan ben Zakkai became ill, Yohanan said, "Hanina, my son, pray for him that he may live." He put his head between his knees and prayed; and he lived.
> (Babylonian Talmud, *Berakot* 34b)

In such stories, the cure is said to have been effected through prayer to God, the real miracle worker. Nonetheless, particular holy men were famous for the ability to heal. Jesus of Nazareth was one such man.

Apocalyptic: Apocalypses, Apocalyptic Eschatology, and Apocalyptic Movements ("Apocalyticism")

The adjective "apocalyptic," from the Greek noun *apocalypsis* ("revelation," compare Rev 1:1), is used as a noun by scholars to encompass three overlapping phenomena: (1) writings called apocalypses; (2) a perspective called apocalyptic eschatology; and (3) apocalyptic movements that accept apocalyptic eschatology as their main religious ideology (see P. D. Hanson; J. Collins).

The name **apocalypse** refers to books or parts of books that record visual and auditory revelations. They are said to come from an otherworldly medium such as God or an angel, sometimes in the form of dreams about the heavenly world. They are given to a human seer who sees in an ecstatic state ("in the Spirit"). A written apocalypse, of course, requires literacy, and apocalypses are normally written down by scribes. Apocalypses usually begin and end with a narrative. They stress *temporal matters* (the origin of the world, history, contemporary or future crises, resurrection of the dead, final judgment of sinners, salvation of the elect, the afterlife) and *spatial matters* (heavenly regions, heavenly beings [angelic or demonic], often revealed to one who takes a heavenly journey to one or several of seven heavens, where he is awestruck and receives assurance). The revelation is full of symbols. The writing usually concludes with the seer's return to a normal state and his reception of instructions about concealing or publishing the revelation. Yet, the author is normally identified with some venerable worthy from the remote past—Abraham, Moses, David—who is represented as prophesying the future. This phenomenon is called **pseudonymity** (attributed authorship [literally, "false name"]). The Jewish apocalypses show the influence of Persian ideas, but they flourished in the Greek and Roman periods, 250 B.C.E. to 250 C.E.

A common perspective of apocalypses is **apocalyptic eschatology,** which may be defined as "revealed teaching about the end of the world" (Greek *eschaton,* "end"). Its most important characteristics are: a sense of alienation and of despair about history that fosters a belief that the world is rushing to a foreordained tragic climax; a hope that God will act in the climactic moment to change things; and a conviction that it will be possible to recognize the signs of the end.

The third term, **apocalypticism,** describes a movement that accepts apocalyptic eschatology as its dominant ideology. Apocalyptic movements embrace apocalyptic eschatology because it helps to resolve the contradictory experience of despair about the terrible course of present human history and hope in the invincible power of God and his purpose for his chosen people. The vision is that the world will become much the same as it was in some earlier, more perfect time; then God's elect people will be vindicated. This reversal of fortunes will be marked by historical and cosmic catastrophes. In the meantime the people of God should prepare themselves for the change and watch for the signs of its coming. Anthropologists often call such groups "millenarian movements" (from Christ's interim 1000-year reign in Revelation 20) or "revitalization movements" because the believers want to revitalize the old ideas and practices. Because ancient apocalypses were written down by scribes, many of whom served the ruling classes, the extent of their influence among the peasant classes is not always clear. Yet, their ideology would certainly have appealed to oppressed classes, and thus it is probable that apocalyptic movements were populated by peasant classes whose leaders appealed to millenarian hopes and dreams.

Daniel 7–12 and Revelation are examples of apocalypses in the Bible. An example outside the Bible is the Assumption of Moses, a work contemporary with the New Testament. It implies a reference to the kingdom of God, a key expression in the teaching of Jesus.

And then **his [God's] kingdom** shall appear throughout all his creation,
And then Satan shall be no more.
And sorrow shall depart with him.
Then the hands of the angel shall be filled
Who has been appointed chief,
And he shall forthwith avenge them of their enemies.
For the Heavenly One will arise from his royal throne,
And he will go forth from his holy habitation
With indignation and wrath on account of his sons.
And the earth shall tremble: to its confines shall it be shaken.
And the high mountains shall be made low
And the hills shall be shaken and fall.
And the horns of the sun shall be broken and he shall be turned
    into darkness;
And the moon shall not give her light, and be turned wholly into blood.
And the circle of the stars shall be disturbed.
And the sea shall retire into the abyss,
And the fountains of waters shall fail,
And the rivers shall dry up.
For the Most High will arise, the Eternal God alone,
And he will appear to punish the Gentiles,
And he will destroy all their idols.
Then thou, O Israel, shalt be happy,
And thou shalt mount upon the necks and wings of the eagle,
And they shall be ended.
And God will exalt thee,
And he will cause thee to approach to the heaven of the stars,
In the place of their habitation.
And thou shalt look from on high and shalt see thy enemies in Gehenna,
And thou shalt recognize them and rejoice,
And thou shalt give thanks and confess thy Creator.
                              (*The Assumption of Moses* 10:1–10)

Messianic Ideology

The Jewish literature points to several types of messiahs (Hebrew *meshîach,* Greek
Christos, "anointed [one]"). Some apocalyptic groups held messianic hopes.
There is a vision of a heavenly ideal ruler in Daniel 7:14–15, "one like a human
being," or literally, a **Son of Man.**

I saw in the night visions,
and behold, with the clouds of heaven
there came one like a son of man,
and he came to the Ancient of Days
and was presented before him.
And to him was given dominion
and glory and kingdom,
that all peoples, nations, and languages

should serve him;
his dominion is an everlasting dominion,
which shall not pass away,
and his kingdom one that shall not be destroyed.
                    (Daniel 7:14–15)

A "son of man" in this text is not a messianic title, but an Aramaic idiom for "man" in the generic sense, that is, "human being" (see Ps 8:4); thus, one like a human being appears before God in the clouds of heaven. In a non-Biblical text, l Enoch 37–71, however, this heavenly Son of Man was said to save "the righteous" and judge "the sinners." He was also called "the Chosen One," "the Righteous One," and the "Messiah" (1 Enoch 48:10; 52:4). A similar development took place in IV Ezra. In other words, we seem to see a general reference to a human being gradually referring to a specific figure described in the same document as the Messiah. The gospels went a step further: The Son of Man became an explicit messianic title for Jesus who had authority on earth, would suffer, and would return on the clouds as judge of sinners.

In the Dead Sea Scrolls it was said that the heavenly Angel of Darkness is opposed by the heavenly Prince of Light (lQS 13:10–12; CD 5:18) and the demonic Belial is opposed by the heavenly High Priest named Melchizedek (11 Q Melchizedek; compare Hebrews in the New Testament; Melchireshah in the Testament of Amram). The scrolls also contained a belief in *two messiahs,* a priestly Messiah of Aaron and a royal Messiah of Israel.

The best example of the royal conception, however, was the hope that a descendant of David would come, overthrow the enemies, and reestablish the Davidic kingdom. This type of expectation is found in The Psalms of Solomon, probably dating from Pompey's coming into Palestine in 63 B.C.E.; most probably it came from a pious Jewish group that, like the Pharisees and Essenes (see below), descended from the *Hasîdîm.* Parts of chapter 17 read:

Behold, O Lord, and raise up unto them their king, the son of David,
At the time in which thou seest, O God, that he may reign over Israel
        thy servant.
And gird him with strength, that he may shatter unrighteous rulers,
And that he may purge Jerusalem from nations that trample her
        down to destruction.
Wisely, righteously he shall thrust out sinners from the inheritance,
He shall destroy the godless nations with the word of his mouth;
At his rebuke nations shall flee before him,
And he shall reprove sinners for the thoughts of their heart.
And he shall gather together a holy people, whom he shall lead in
        righteousness,
And he shall judge the tribes of the people that has been sanctified
        by the Lord his God.
And he shall not suffer unrighteousness to lodge anymore in their midst,
Nor shall there dwell with them any man that knoweth wickedness,
For he shall know them, that they are all sons of their God.
And he shall divide them according to their tribes upon the land,
And neither sojourner nor alien shall sojourn with them any more.

He shall judge peoples and nations in the wisdom of his righteousness.
And he shall have the heathen nations to serve him under his yoke;
And he shall glorify the Lord in a place to be seen of all the earth;
And he shall purge Jerusalem, making it holy as of old:
So that nations shall come from the ends of the earth to see his glory,
Bringing as gifts her sons who had fainted,
And to see the glory of the Lord, wherewith God hath glorified her.
(Psalms of Solomon 17:23–35)

Another example of the royal conception is found in the synagogue prayer called "the Eighteen Benedictions" (The *Shemōneh Esreh*, "eighteen," or *Amîdāh*, "standing," the usual position for prayer) and some form of it may have been recited in the first century.

Be merciful, O Lord our God, towards Jerusalem, Thy City, and towards Zion, the abiding place of Thy glory, and towards the kingdom of the house of David, Thy righteous anointed one. Blessed art Thou, O Lord, God of David, the Builder of Jerusalem!

Though prophecy had become rare in postexilic Judaism, there also arose a hope for a righteous prophet, either a new or returning Elijah (1 Kings 17–21; 2 Kings 2) or a "prophet like Moses" (Deuteronomy 18:15) who would establish the Torah. The Samaritans (see below) called the latter type the Taheb. In the Dead Sea Scrolls, he is yoked with the two Messiahs and is a "prophet like Moses" who adheres to the Torah:

And they shall not depart from any maxim of the Law to walk in all the stubbornness of their heart.
    And they shall be governed by the first ordinances in which the members of the Community began their instruction, until the coming of the Prophet and the Anointed (Ones) of Aaron and Israel.
(The Manual of Discipline 9:9–11)

GROUPS IN FIRST-CENTURY PALESTINE

Regional Groups: Samaritans and Idumeans

Several kinds of groups existed in first-century Palestine. "Regional groups" were marked especially by their geographical location, national-political heritage, language or dialect, regional beliefs and practices, and ethnic self-identity. Except for Gentiles, the **Samaritans** were considered the least pure of all peoples in the eyes of more purist Jews. In the period after 721 B.C.E. the Assyrians had deported many native Israelites from the Northern Kingdom and settled others there. This region (between Galilee and Judea) became Samaria. By the first century C.E., Samaria contained many ethnic groups and had become largely Gentile. The Samaritans themselves accepted only the Pentateuch as scripture, and in their version of it **(The Samaritan Pentateuch)** Mount Gerizim in Samaria, not Mount Zion in Judea, is the holy mountain. They also hoped for a "messianic" figure, the Taheb, who was a "prophet like Moses."

In Greco-Roman times, Idumea ("land of the Edomites") refers to the region just south of Judea. To this region refugees from Edom, southeast of the Dead Sea, migrated. Idumea was forcefully converted to Judaism under the Maccabeans. The Herodian kings came from this region and, says Josephus, were considered by the more purist Jews to be only "half-Jews." In the civil wars in Jerusalem during the wars with Rome, one of the major factions was a group of **Idumeans.**

Religious Groups

There were also religious groups—Josephus calls them "philosophies"(*Wars* 8)—that is, interest groups whose identity was associated primarily with special religious beliefs, norms, and practices mostly related to the scope and interpretation of the Torah.

Sadducees

The Sadducees were a well-established religious group in Jewish society. Since their own literature has not survived, our understanding of them must rely upon sometimes-conflicting sources such as Josephus; the **rabbinic literature,** which has roots in the Pharisaic movement; and the New Testament, which was not friendly to them. Thus, we are not always clear about their social status, beliefs, and practices.

The name Sadducee may have come from the Hebrew *tsaddîqîm* ("righteous ones"), but more likely it was derived from the High Priest Zadok of David's time (tenth century B.C.E.). First mentioned during the rule of the Maccabeans (John Hyrcanus I, 134–104 B.C.E.), the Sadducees had probably become an important part of the wealthy power elite of Jerusalem, and thus leaders of the local aristocratic establishment. Historically, they had from time to time come into conflict, sometimes severe, with their rivals, the Pharisees, whose legal rulings they nevertheless sometimes probably followed. They were probably considered an illigitimate priesthood by a group called the Essenes that seems to have rejected sacrifice in the Jerusalem Temple (see below).

Sadducees also seem to have dominated the **Sanhedrin,** a Jerusalem body of arisocrats that apparently combined executive, legislative, and judicial functions, thus serving as a ruling senate and high court. As political leaders, many of them appear to have accepted a degree of Hellenization and to have maintained cordial relations with their Roman overlords. In the gospels, they are portrayed as opponents of Jesus from the Jerusalem establishment. When the war with Rome became imminent in the 60s, they attempted to mediate, but to no avail.

Despite some political accommodation to the Romans, the Sadducees seem to have remained conservative in religion. Among the Sadducees were priests who carried out sacrifices at the Jerusalem Temple. Like the Samaritans, they accepted only the Pentateuch (in its Jewish form) as "scripture" and they probably interpreted it more literally. They therefore rejected the Pharisees' new traditions (see below), especially Pharisaic interest in personal immortality, and there seem to have been many debates with the Pharisees about purity regulations, for example, Sabbath purity and the condition of women. Undoubtedly the Sadducees would not have welcomed the Essenes to Temple worship. They rejected fate and determinism, and espoused a form of free will; thus, God could not be held responsible for evil. In the New Testament, they are portrayed as not accepting belief in the resurrection of the dead, in contrast to the Pharisees and Jesus (Acts 23:6–10; Mark 12:18–27).

Pharisees

The **Pharisees** were a very different kind of group, but also difficult to describe from our sources: Josephus, the New Testament, and the rabbinic literature that stems from them. Their name was probably derived from the Hebrew *perūshîm* or the Aramaic *perishaya*, which means "the separated (ones)," though from what or whom they were separated is debated. Like the Sadducees, they are first mentioned during the rule of the Maccabeans (John Hyrcanus I, 134–104 B.C.E.), and perhaps come from the *Hasîdîm* (see Chapter Two). In this early period they were a politically oriented reforming faction often in conflict with the Maccabeans and their Sadducee rivals, but eventually they became more established, well organized, and in favor. Their continued political involvement persisted during the reign of Herod (37–4 B.C.E.) and some of the leaders of the revolt against Rome in 66 C.E. came from their ranks. At least by the late first century, when the synagogue was becoming an important institution, they became synagogue leaders. By this time their renowned teachers were called **rabbis.** Unlike the Sadducees, most Pharisees were not priests, but lay scholars and were divided into various schools, the most well-known being those of Rabbi Hillel and Rabbi Shammai.

The early rabbinic literature, which stems from the Pharisees, agrees with the New Testament on certain crucial themes about pre-70 C.E. Pharisaic piety. Especially characteristic was the preservation and development of their oral traditions, an attempt to extend the laws of Temple purity to everyday life. As noted above, the Pharisees "built a fence around the Torah" with respect to laws about Sabbath observance, festivals, oaths, tithes, lawful divorce, kosher food, and those with whom one eats. There nonetheless appears to have been a liberalization of attitudes towards the purity of women who were responsible for preparing food. In contrast to the Sadducees, the Pharisees accepted the larger body of Scriptures and the oral traditions, as well as newer views such as belief in angels and demons and the resurrection of the dead.

After the war with Rome, the Pharisees were well situated to assert their authority and to reestablished Judaism along Pharisaic lines at an academy established at **Yavneh (Jamnia)** near the Mediterranean coast. At the Yavneh Academy certain books that were eventually accepted into the canon of the Jewish Scriptures were debated and oral traditions were collected. Also, the Pharisees added the "prayer" against the *Minîm* ("heretics") to the Eighteen Benedictions (see above, Messianic Ideology). Though the early Jewish Christians may have been included among the *Minîm*, most scholars do not think that the "prayer" was meant for them alone (see Chapter One).

> 12. For the apostates may there be no hope unless they return to your Torah. As for the [*Nōzrîm* and the] *Minîm*, may they perish immediately. Speedily may they be erased from the Book of the Life and may they not be registered among the righteous. Blessed are You, O Lord, who subdue the wicked.
>
> (Translation after L. Schiffman)

In the New Testament, Jesus is pictured as frequently in debate with the Pharisees. Since evidence for Pharisees in Galilee apart from the gospels is sparse, some scholars think that they were primarily representatives, or retainers, of the Jerusalem establishment.

The Dead Sea Sect (Essenes)

Pliny the Elder and the Jew Philo and Josephus (see below) are ancient writers who describe a group called the **Essenes.** The name "Essene" (Greek *Essēnoi, Essaioi,* probably from Aramaic *Hāsayyāh,* "Pious Ones," or perhaps '*asayyah,* "healers") reflects their possible origins among the *Hasidîm,* which also means "Pious Ones," at the time of the Maccabean Revolt (see Chapter Two). It was a group that withdrew from the rest of society. Having surfaced during the period of the Maccabean High Priest Jonathan (161–143/2 B.C.E.), it disappeared during the wars with Rome, about 68 C.E. Though some Essenes lived in the towns and cities, the discovery of the Dead Sea Scrolls in 1947 and the later excavation of nearby Khirbet Qumran (see Chapter One, Appendix) convinced many scholars that at least most of the scrolls came from the Essenes who lived there, apparently in the caves in the cliffs. Though this theory is being challenged by some scroll experts and archeologists as the rest of the scrolls are published and as other suggestions are made about the Qumran ruins (for example, a military outpost?), it has been the prevailing theory, and to us it still seems probable.

The founder of the Dead Sea Sect was a certain **Teacher of Righteousness,** a Zadokite priest who opposed one of the Maccabean priests as "the wicked priest" some time in the second half of the second century B.C.E. In fulfillment of Isaiah 40:3 ("... in the wilderness prepare the way of the Lord..."; compare Mark 1:3), the Teacher took his followers to the Dead Sea and established a community there. Its leaders were priests and its scribes interpreted the prophecies to refer to the community.

At Qumran the group worked, copied religious texts, wrote religious literature, worshipped according to their own calendar and customs, baptized, celebrated a common meal, and sought to live pure and undefiled lives. Their literature, community organization, and eschatological orientation have become extremely important for understanding the rise of early Christianity. The following passage illustrates their liturgical meal in anticipation of the great banquet that will take place when the two Messiahs, the Messiahs of Aaron and Israel, come.

[The Priest] shall enter [at] the head of all the Congregation of Israel, then all (13) [the chiefs of the sons] of Aaron, the priests called to the assembly, men of renown; and they shall sit (14) [before him], each according to his rank.

And afterwards, [the Mess]iah of Israel [shall enter]; and the chiefs (15) of [the tribes of Israel] shall sit before him, each according to his rank, . . . then all (16) the heads of the fa[milies of the Congre]gation, together with the wise me[n of the holy Congregation], shall sit before them, each according to (17) his rank.

And [when] they gather for the Community tab[le], [or to drink w]ine, and arrange the (18) Community table [and mix] the wine to drink, let no man [stretch out] his hand over the first-fruits of bread (19) and [wine] before the Priest; for [it is he who] shall bless the first-fruits of bread (20) and w[ine, and shall] first [stretch out] his hand over the bread. And after[wards], the Messiah of Israel shall [str]etch out his hands (21) over the bread. [And afterwards], all the Congregation of the Community shall [bl]ess, each according to his rank. And they shall proceed according to this rite (22) at every mea[l where] at least ten persons [are as]sembled.

(1QSa 11–22)

The New Testament never mentions "Essenes" or any Jewish group along the Dead Sea, but it is certainly testimony for a variety of Jewish movements. It is possible that John the Baptist had been associated with the Dead Sea Sect. Though their strict interpretation of the Law and withdrawal to the desert are quite distinctive, their eschatology, worship, messianic expectations, and interpretation of Scripture offer many parallels to the New Testament.

DIASPORA JUDAISM

While the focus of our sketch of the history and religion of Judaism has been Palestine, many Jews—indeed, the majority—no longer lived in Palestine. These were Jews of the **Diaspora** (Greek *diaspora*, "dispersion"), noted in connection with the revolts against the Romans in 115–117 C.E. Many Jews had been in Babylonia since the Babylonian Exile; others had been dispersed throughout the Mediterranean, for example, Rome, Antioch, and Damascus, Syria. The largest and most famous Jewish community was at Alexandria, Egypt, where it, like other ethnic groups, formed a legal ghetto within the city (the *politeuma*).

The native tongue of most Diaspora Jews, like many urban Palestinian Jews, was the commonly spoken *koinē* Greek. So the need arose in Diaspora synagogue worship for Greek translations of the Hebrew Scriptures. The legend arose that 70 (or 72) Greek-speaking priests from Jerusalem were invited to Alexandria, where they translated the scriptures independently and miraculously arrived at precisely the same translations (Philo, *Life of Moses* 2.26–42; *Letter of Aristeas* 301–316)! Both the legend and manuscripts of the translations indicate that at least the Torah was translated by the third century B.C.E.

As the Prophets and the Writings began to take on the value of holy texts, they were also translated and the legend came to apply to them. These were supplemented by Greek translations of other Hebrew books and books originally written in Greek. Though they were not eventually included among the 39 books of the Hebrew Bible, they were in use in the Diaspora and became the Bible of the majority of Christians. This longer Greek version is known as the **Septuagint (LXX).** It greatly influenced Hellenistic Jewish and Christian language and thought.

Some other Hellenistic Jewish books were written at Alexandria, the most important of which were the works of a contemporary of Jesus named **Philo of Alexandria** (ca. 20 B.C.E.–45 C.E.). Philo was influenced by Platonic and Stoic ideas, as well as Jewish Wisdom. In his commentaries on the Septuagint, he sought to find and present to educated Greeks its deeper allegorical meaning.

The Jews were exempt from emperor worship and were permitted a number of special privileges based on their observance of the Sabbath and the festivals (see above). They were also permitted to settle inter-Jewish legal disputes according to their own Law and traditions, to administer their own funds, and to send money to Jerusalem, especially the Temple tax. Scholars debate whether Jews also had *civic* rights as citizens of the empire, that is, participation in public life, election of magistrates, and the like. Josephus says they did; other sources during the Roman period indicate they did not, a condition that seems more likely. No doubt many Jews of the Diaspora became less inclined to follow the Torah as strictly as they did in Palestine, especially since much of it dealt with issues about the Temple and purity.

Non-Jewish reactions to the Jews were mixed. On the one hand, Jewish monotheism and practices such as the rite of circumcision and ritual purity kept them separate, and the formation of distinct ghettos, such as the *politeuma*, along with their special privileges under the Romans, brought them ill will. There have survived various "pagan" criticisms of circumcision, pork eating, and Jewish "laziness" (the Sabbath command), as well as Christian charges about Pharisaic hypocrisy. Pro-Roman, anti-Jewish stories about the crucifixion of Jesus testify to "anti-Judaism." (Antisemitism as a *racial* ideology supported by a certain kind of Christian theology is of more recent history.) Yet, some non-Jewish writers admired the Jews' high sense of morality and defended them ("philo-Judaism"). Indeed, as the stories of the Ammonite General Achior (Judith 14:10) and King Izates of Adiabene (an independent kingdom far to the northeast) reveal, the Jews attracted proselytes (that is, converts from another religion), especially women, who did not need to be circumcised, and what the book of Acts calls "God-fearers" (especially men who were attracted to Judaism and its morality, but were not circumcised).

While some early Christian groups had their origins in the Jewish groups of Palestine, other Christian groups quickly migrated to the urban centers of the larger Greco-Roman world where Diaspora Judaism, as well a great variety of Greco-Roman religious and religious philosophies, were planted. Thus, most early Christian literature, including the New Testament, was written in *koinē* Greek and most of its scriptural citations were from the Septuagint.

Our next task will be to narrow down to the early history, ideas, and groups of early Christianity itself. From this vantage point we shall then take up in more detail the various Christian communities and the religious and theological ideas as portrayed in the literature of the New Testament.

FURTHER READING

(See Further Reading, Chapter Two.)

Hellenism; Hellenistic Religions

ABD: "Aretalogy" (D. L. Tiede); "Artemis" (H. N. Martin, Jr.); "Asclepius, Cult of" (T. R. Robinson); "Associations, Clubs, Thiasoi" (F. D. Danker); "Cynics" (R. F. Hock); "Hellenism" (H. D. Betz); "Phrygia" (F. F. Bruce); "Platonism" (J. M. Dillon); "Pythagoreanism" (J. C. Thom); "Stoics, Stoicism" (T. Schmeller).

IDB: "Greek Language" (E. C. Colwell); "Greek Religion and Philosophy" (F. W. Beare); "Roman Empire" (R. M. Grant); "Roman Religion" (F. C. Grant).

IDB Suppl.: "Hellenism" (F. E. Peters); "Nag Hammadi" (G. MacRae).

D. Aune, *Prophecy in Early Christianity and the Ancient Mediterranean World.*

U. Bianchi, *The Greek Mysteries* .

W. Burkert, *Religion in Greece and Rome.*

F. Cumont, *Oriental Religions in Roman Paganism.*

E. R. Dodds, *The Greeks and the Irrational.*

A. J. Festugiére, *Personal Religion Among the Greeks.*

J. Godwin, *The Mystery Religions in the Ancient World.*

M. Grant, *The World of Rome.*

M. Hadas, *Hellenistic Culture.*

————, *Imperial Rome* (Time-Life).

M. Hadas and M. Smith, *Heroes and Gods.*

J. Hull, *Hellenistic Magic and the Synoptic Tradition.*

H. Koester, *Introduction to the New Testament, vol. 1: History, Culture and Religions of the Hellenistic Age* (sections 1–4, 6).

E. Lohse, *The New Testament Environment,* Part II.

L. H. Martin, *Hellenistic Religions. An Introduction.*

J. H. Neyrey, "Unclean, Common, Polluted, and Taboo," *Forum* 4/4 (1988), pp. 72–82.

F. E. Peters, *The Harvest of Hellenism.*

S. Pomeroy, *Goddesses, Whores, Wives, and Slaves: Women in Classical Antiquity* .

C. Roetzel, *The World That Shaped the New Testament.*

W. W. Tarn and G. T. Griffith, *Hellenistic Civilization.*

A. Toynbee, ed. *The Crucible of Christianity.*

Judaism, Jewish Religions and Groups

For a recent survey of interpretations of Judaism, see R. A. Kraft and G. W. E. Nickelsburg, eds., *Early Judaism and Its Modern Interpreters.*

ABD: "Angels (NT)" (D. F. Watson); "Apocalypses and Apocalypticism" (P. D. Hanson); "Early Jewish Apocalypticism" (J. J. Collins); "Art and Architecture, Early Jewish" (R. Hachlili); "Astrology in the Ancient Near East" (F. Rochberg-Halton); "Calendars, Ancient Israelite and Early Jewish" (J. C. Vanderkam); "Dead Sea Scrolls" (J. J. Collins); "Dead, Cult of the" (C. A. Kennedy); "Dress and Ornamentation" (D. Edwards); "Eschatology (Early Jewish)" (G. W. E. Nickelsburg); "Essenes" (M. L. Stone); "Family" (C. J. Wright); "Fast, Fasting" (J. Muddiman); "Galileans" (S. Freyne); "Galilee" (R. Frankel); "Holiness (OT)" (D. P. Wright); "Holiness (NT)" (R. Hodgson, Jr.); "Idumea" (U. Hubner); "Josephus (Person)" (L. H. Feldman); "Judaism, Greco-Roman Period" (S. A. Overman); "Languages (Aramaic)" (S. K. Kaufman); "Languages (Coptic)" (S. Emmel); "Languages (Greek)" (G. Mussies); "Languages (Hebrew)" (G. M. Schramm); "Languages (Latin)" (F. F. Bruce); "Medicine and Healing" (H. C. Kee); "Messiah" (M. De Jonge); "Nag Hammadi" (B. A. Pearson); "Pharisees" (A. J. Saldarini); "Philo of Alexandria" (P. Borgen); "Qumran,

Khirbet" (J. Murphy-O'Connor); "Sadducees" (G. G. Porton); "Samaritan Pentateuch" (B. K. Waltke); "Samaritans" (R. T. Anderson); "Sanhedrin" (A. J. Saldarini); "Satan" (V. Hamilton); "Scribes" (A. J. Saldarini); "Septuagint" (M. Peters); "Sex and Sexuality" (R. Frymer-Kensky); "Unclean and Clean (NT)" (H. Hübner, trans. R. B. Thomas, Jr.).

IDB: "Dead Sea Scrolls" (O. Betz); "Essenes" (W. R. Farmer); "Hebrew Religion" (J. Bright); "Pharisees" (M. Black); "Sadducees" (A. C. Sundberg); "Samaritans" (T. H. Gaster); "Synagogue" (I. Sanne).

IDB Suppl.: "Aaron, Aaronides" (E. Rivkin); "Aramaic" (J. Greenfield); "Apocalypticism" (P. D. Hanson); "Dead Sea Scrolls" (G. Vermes); "Essenes" (O. Betz); "Exorcism in the NT" (J. M. Hull); "Ezra and Nehemiah" (S. Talmon); "Jerusalem" (R. Amiran; Y. Israeli); "Judaism, Hellenistic" (M. Cook); "Pharisees" (E. Rivkin); "Priests" (B. A. Levine); "Samaritans" (J. D. Purvis); "Septuagint" (R. A. Kraft); "Synagogue, the Great" (L. M. Barth); "Synagogue, architecture" (E. M. Meyers); "Targums" (M. McNamara); "Temple of Herod" (M. Ben-Dov); "Torah" (J. A. Sanders).

NJBC, pp. 1055–1082, "Apocrypha; Dead Sea Scrolls; Other Jewish Literature" (R. E. Brown; P. Perkins; A. J. Saldarini).

M. Avi-Yonah, *Oriental Art in Roman Palestine.*

J. J. Collins, *Apocalypse: The Morphology of a Genre.*

———, *Between Athens and Jerusalem: Jewish Identity in the Hellenistic Diaspora.*

———, *The Apocalyptic Imagination: An Introduction to the Matrix of Christianity.*

F. Cross, *The Ancient Library of Qumran and Modern Biblical Studies.*

L. Finkelstein, *The Pharisees: The Sociological Background of Their Faith.*

E. R. Goodenough, *An Introduction to Philo Judaeus.*

J. Gutman, *The Synagogue: Studies in Origins, Archeology, and Architecture.*

P. D. Hanson, *The Dawn of Apocalyptic.*

P. D. Hanson, ed., *Visionaries and Their Apocalypses.*

D. Hellholm. ed., *Apocalypticism in the Mediterranean World and the Near East.*

M. Hengel, *Judaism and Hellenism.*

J. Jeremias, *Jerusalem in the Time of Jesus.*

H. Koester, *Introduction to the New Testament. vol. 1: History, Culture, and Religions of the Hellenistic Age* (section 5).

K. Koch, *The Rediscovery of Apocalyptic.*

S. Libermann, *Hellenism in Jewish Palestine.*

M. McNamara, *Targum and Testament.*

G. F. Moore, *Judaism in the First Centuries of the Christian Era.*

J. Neusner, *From Politics to Piety: The Emergence of Pharisaic Judaism.*

———, *Judaisms and Their Messiahs at the Turn of the Christian Era.*

G. W. E. Nickelsburg, *Jewish Literature Between the Bible and the Mishnah.*

H. Ringgren, *The Faith of Qumran.*

D. S. Russell, *Between the Testaments.*

S. Safrai and M. Stern, eds., *The Jewish People in the First Century.* 2 vols.

T. Saldarini, *Pharisees, Scribes, and Sadducees.*

E. P. Sanders, A. Baumgarten, and A. Mendelson, eds., *Jewish and Christian Self-Definition: Aspects of Judaism in the Greco-Roman World.*

S. Sandmel, *Philo of Alexandria: An Introduction.*

M. Stone, *Scriptures, Sects and Visions.*

G. Vermes, *Jesus the Jew.*

A standard collection of texts that includes the works of Josephus and Philo of Alexandria is the Loeb Classical Library.

Collections of Texts:

C. K. Barrett, *The New Testament Background: Selected Documents,* 2nd ed.

S. Baron and J. Blau, *Judaism, Postbiblical and Talmudic Period.*

H. D. Betz, ed., *The Greek Magical Papyri in Translation.*

D. R. Cartlidge and D. Dungan, *Documents for the Study of the Gospels.*

J. H. Charlesworth, ed., *The Old Testament Pseudepigrapha.* 2 vols.

W. Foerster, *Gnosis: A Selection of Gnostic Texts.* 2 vols.

F. C. Grant, *Hellenistic Religions.*

E. Hennecke and W. Schneemelcher, *The New Testament Apocrypha.* 2 vols.

Josephus, *Jewish Antiquities* (Loeb Classical Library).

———, *Wars* (Loeb Classical Library).

H. Kee, *The Origins of Christianity, Sources and Documents.*

B. Layton, *The Gnostic Scriptures.*

N. Lewis and M. Reinhold, *Roman Civilization: Sourcebook II, The Empire.*

A. Malherbe, *Moral Exhortation: A Greco-Roman Sourcebook.*

———, *The Cynic Epistles: A Study Edition.*

M. W. Meyer, *The Ancient Mysteries. A Sourcebook.*

W. J. Oates, ed., *The Stoic and Epicurean Philosophers.*

M. G. Reddish, ed. *Apocalyptic Literature. A Reader.*

D. G. Rice and J. Stambaugh, *Sources for the Study of Greek Religion.*

H. J. Rose, *A Handbook of Greek Literature.*

M. Stern, *Greek and Latin Authors on Jews and Judaism.*

G. Vermes, *The Dead Sea Scrolls in English,* 2d ed.

NOTE: New editions of the Dead Sea Scrolls will contain texts not yet published.

Josephus (See Further Reading, Chapter Two.)

The Egnatian Way *(Via Egnatia)* was the major Roman road across Macedonia, linking the Adriatic and Aegean seas. Paul probably traveled this road between Philippi and Thessalonica. (See map of important cities and regions of Paul, p. 193).

CHAPTER FOUR

A BRIEF SOCIAL HISTORY OF EARLY CHRISTIANITY

Most sources for the history of early Christianity are in the New Testament itself. Yet, these sources do not easily yield historical information. They must be studied carefully and evaluated in relation to the history of the period.

In this chapter we shall build on the methods illustrated in Chapter One in relation to external information of the type discussed in Chapters Two and Three. Our object will be to develop a foundation for, and offer a brief historical reconstruction of, earliest Christianity. This history will provide a rationale for the rest of our study.

THE NEW TESTAMENT DOCUMENTS

The twenty-seven New Testament books fall into four literary types or "genres."

Gospels (4)	History (1)	Letters (21)	Apocalypse (1)
1. Matthew	5. Acts of	6. Romans	27. Revelation
2. Mark	the Apostles	7. 1 Corinthians	
3. Luke		8. 2 Corinthians	
4. John		9. Galatians	
		10. Ephesians	
		11. Philippians	
		12. Colossians	
		13. 1 Thessalonians	
		14. 2 Thessalonians	
		15. 1 Timothy	
		16. 2 Timothy	
		17. Titus	
		18. Philemon	
		19. Hebrews	
		20. James	
		21. 1 Peter	

22.   2 Peter
23.   1 John
24.   2 John
25.   3 John
26.   Jude

Down through the ages the Christian churches have considered all the New Testament books to be "apostolic." In other words, these books were believed to have been written by eyewitnesses of Jesus' ministry (relatives and disciples) and Paul. James and Jude were named as Jesus' brothers (Mark 6:3 = Matt 13:55; compare Gal 1:19). Peter, John, and Matthew were listed among Jesus' twelve disciples (Mark 3:16–19 = Matt 10:2–4 = Luke 6:14–16; compare Acts 1:13). Revelation claimed to have been written by John of Patmos, whom Christian tradition identified with John son of Zebedee, Jesus' disciple. Philemon was a slave owner whom Paul converted to Christianity (Phlm). Timothy and Titus were Paul's companions (see, for example, 1 Thess 3:1–9; 1 Cor 4:17; 16:10–11; Acts 16:1–4; Gal 2:1–10), and so were Mark and Luke (Phlm 23–24; Col 4:14), to whom was also attributed Acts (Luke 1:1–4; Acts 1:1–2). The remaining names were derived from the place to which Paul, or someone writing in his name, wrote; that is, the cities Rome, Corinth, Philippi, Thessalonica, Ephesus and Colossae, and the region of Galatia. Tradition eventually attributed the book to the Hebrews to Paul, as well.

Can the conviction of "apostolic" be substantiated? To answer this question we shall first offer enough information to establish a relative chronological sequence of early Christian writings.

Internal and External Historical Evidence

Within the New Testament books there are often hints about a book's author, sources, traditions, community, place, time, and recipients. There are also occasional statements about, or allusions to, persons or events in the world at large. Historians call this **internal evidence.** It must be evaluated in relation to whatever else is known from archeology, inscriptions, and literary documents outside these books. Historians call this **external evidence**. Here are four examples that correlate internal and external evidence.

Roman and Jewish References to Rulers

Ancient documents and inscriptions date events by rulers. For example, Luke 2:1–2 states that the birth of Jesus took place in Bethlehem when Caesar Augustus was emperor (27 B.C.E.–14 C.E.), more specifically, when Quirinius was governor of Syria and the first Roman census took place in 6 C.E. (Tacitus, *Annals* 3.21.48; Josephus *Antiquities* 17.8.5; 18.1.1; compare Acts 5:37). We might conclude that Jesus was born in 6 C.E. However, Luke 1:5 and Matthew 2:1 say that Jesus was born during the rule of Herod the Great, who died ten years earlier, in 4 B.C.E. (Josephus *Antiquities* 18.8.1 paragraph 191; *War* 1.33.8 paragraph 665). An explanation for this discrepancy is that the Lukan writer used the Roman census to get Joseph and Mary from Nazareth to Bethlehem, the prophesied location for the Messiah's birth (Micah 5:2). In short, the rules of Augustus and Herod, but not the rule of Quirinius and the census, help date Jesus' birth, about 6–4 B.C.E. (The reason Jesus was born "before the common era" is that in the sixth century C.E. the date of his birth was miscalculated by four to six years!).

Archeology (The Delphi [Gallio] Inscription)

Acts 18:1–3 states that Paul found two Jewish Christians, the tentmaker Aquila and his wife, Priscilla (see also 1 Cor 12:28; 16:19; Rom 16:3–4; compare 2 Tim 4:19), at Corinth (southern Greece). They had arrived there from Italy because the **Edict of Claudius** expelled Jews (and Jewish Christians) from Rome (compare Suetonius *Life of Claudius* 25). Claudius was emperor from 41–54 C.E. According to fifth-century Orosius, Claudius issued the edict in his ninth year, or about 49/50 C.E. Thus, Paul would have been in Corinth about 49/50 C.E. Further, Acts 18:11–12 says that when Paul had been there eighteen months, he was dragged before the judgment seat of Gallio, the Roman Proconsul or chief magistrate. An archeological inscription from Delphi (northwest of Athens), the **Gallio (or Delphi) Inscription,** combined with other inscription evidence from Rome, shows that Gallio was proconsul about July 1, 51 C.E., to July 1, 52 C.E. If Paul had reached Corinth eighteen months earlier, this is further evidence that he would have arrived about 49/50 C.E. In this case a piece of archeological evidence, the Gallio Inscription, confirms Acts (which must always be cautiously evaluated).

Two important results follow: (1) we can calculate a relative chronology of Paul's life; and (2) since Paul's earliest surviving letter, 1 Thessalonians, was probably written from Corinth (compare 1 Thess 3:1, 6; Acts 17:15; 18:1, 5, 18), we can date Paul's letters to the 50s (see Chapter Six).

The Destruction of Jerusalem and the Temple, 70 C.E.

Dating the four gospels is mostly derived from allusions to the catastrophic destruction of Jerusalem and the Temple in 70 C.E., especially the "desolating sacrilege" (Mark 13:14; Matt 24:15; see also 22:7). The Lukan author interprets the reference as "Jerusalem surrounded by armies" (Luke 21:20) and elsewhere describes the destruction of Jerusalem (19:43–44). The Gospel of John also appears to allude to the event (after the fact): " . . . the Romans will come and destroy both our holy place and our nation" (11:48).

The Yavneh (Jamnia) Academy and the Prayer Against the Heretics, About 80–90 C.E.

After the Romans destroyed the Temple, the Pharisees at the Academy of Yavneh (Jamnia) sought to reorganize the Jewish people. According to a Rabbinic tradition in the Talmud *(Berakoth* 28b), the benediction against the *Minîm* ("heretics") was added to the synagogue prayers at this time (see Chapter Three), which impled exclusion from the Jewish synagogues, among whom were Jewish Christians who believed in Jesus as the Messiah (Justin, *Dialogue with Trypho* 16). Some scholars have argued that such an exclusion is implied in the Gospel of John (John 9:22, 34; compare 12:42; 16:2a) and will help explain the intensified anti-Pharisee attitude in the Gospel of Matthew (especially Matt 23), in which case both would be dated in the late first century C.E.

Acts of the Apostles

The only book called "history" in the above list of New Testament books is Acts. We must therefore evaluate this book.

History is a reasonable genre classification for Acts, but it is "history" only in the ancient sense. Ancient Greek and Roman historians told stories to illustrate national values and heroic virtues. Speeches by heroes or heroines were composed on the basis of what the writer thought was said or believed was appropriate for the occasion. Moreover, as history in the Hebrew Bible was told with a *religious* purpose, so in Acts: God was guiding history through his Spirit. Finally, since the same person wrote Luke and Acts (Luke 1:1–4; Acts 1:1–2), and this same writer extensively rewrote the Gospel of Mark (see Chapters One and Eleven), it is likely that sources were used and imaginatively rewritten in Acts.

The value of Acts as history has been much debated. Our position will be that its beginning chapters about the early Jerusalem church, the martyr Stephen, and the first missions are full of legends, miracle stories, and well-constructed speeches by the author about God's plans for his new people as promised in Scripture. They are exciting, but are of limited historical value. The later chapters of Acts look better historically, but they also have miraculous and legendary elements and must be judged with caution. Fortunately, Paul's letters occasionally cover the same ground. In such cases, the interpretive principle is to give priority to the writings of Paul.

Careful comparison of Galatians 1:18–24 with Acts 9:19b–30 and 11:25–26 will illumine the point. In Galatians Paul is at Damascus *three years;* in Acts he is there an *indefinite number of days.* In Galatians Paul portrays himself as directly under *God's* direction (compare Gal 2:2: "by revelation"); in Acts he is directed by *Jewish Christian authorities at Jerusalem* who dispatch him on his mission, that is, they *bring* him to Caesarea and *send* him to Tarsus. In Galatians Paul is virtually *unknown in Jerusalem,* since he makes only a short visit with Cephas (Peter) and meets James; in Acts he is something of *a public hero who disputes with "Hellenists"* (Jews who speak Greek and follow Greek ways).

According to our interpretative principle, Paul's version of the events, even if a little exaggerated by his anger at the Galatians, is preferable. Yet, Acts does give us some general impression of Paul's movements. Moreover, it covers much more ground about Paul's movements than can be gleaned from Paul's letters; read critically, it is invaluable for historical reconstruction, as in the case of Paul before Gallio at Corinth (above), especially where it agrees with the letters.

Given this perspective on the only historical book in the New Testament, we must rely upon other methods to recover the history of early Christianity. We have already given the major methods in Chapter One. Now we need to show their usefulness for reconstructing early Christian history.

Gospels

Source Criticism and Internal/External Evidence

In Chapter One, we illustrated Source Criticism by the Synoptic Problem and its widespread solution, the Two-Source Theory. On the basis of this theory, Mark was the earliest of the first three gospels (the "Markan priority"). Matthew and Luke were written after Mark.

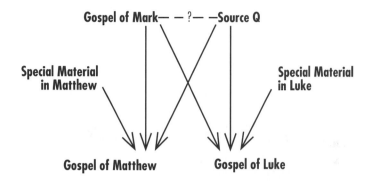

The Matthean gospel was probably quoted by Ignatius of Antioch early in the second century, and the earliest papyrus fragment of the Gospel of John (P [52]) dates from about 125 C.E. Thus, the early second century is the latest possible period for Matthew and John. If the Gospel of Mark was written during or just after the Temple destruction in 70 C.E. (Mark 13:14), then the authors of the three other gospels knew this event (see Matt 24:15; cf. 22:7; Luke 21:20; compare 19:43–44; John 11:48); and if Matthew and Luke were written after Mark, then Matthew and Luke were probably composed about a generation later, about 85–90 C.E., and John slightly later, about 90–100. This dating of Matthew and John receives further support from the events at Yavneh about 80–90 C.E. (see above; Chapters Ten, Twelve).

Redaction Criticism

The results of source and historical criticism can be augmented by noting that an author's redaction betrays her or his interests in relation to certain historical and social contexts. We have illustrated this principle in relation to Matthew's and Luke's use of Q in Chapter One.

The *Gospel of Thomas*

A number of gospels that were not included in the New Testament have been passed on in Christian history or rediscovered in modern times. Though some scholars evaluate several gospels and gospel fragments highly (The Secret Gospel of Mark; the *Gospel of Peter;* Egerton Papyrus 2; isolated sayings ["Agrapha"]), the most important is the *Gospel of Thomas,* one of the more than fifty tractates discovered at Nag Hammadi, Egypt, in 1945. It is a collection of 114 sayings attributed to Jesus, most of which begin with "Jesus said . . . ." According to its introductory statement, its author is Judas Didymos Thomas (See John 21:20), who in Syria was thought to be Jesus' brother. Modern scholarship, however, holds that it is pseudonymous (attributed authorship, or "false name"; see Chapters One [apocalypses], Eight, Fourteen).

The *Gospel of Thomas* was written in an ancient Egyptian language called Coptic, probably in the late fourth century C.E. However, most scholars hold that the Coptic texts are translations from an earlier Greek version. This corresponds with the fact that manuscript hunters had previously discovered a few Thomas sayings in Greek at Oxyrhynchus, Egypt. At least one of them was written before 200 C.E. Thus, the *Gospel of Thomas* was known in the second century. Some experts argue that it was written even earlier, about 70–100 C.E., or even earlier, about 50–70 C.E. (see Chapters One, Five).

As a collection of Jesus' sayings, the *Gospel of Thomas* is similar in form to Q, and it has some of the same sayings as Q. Other sayings offer parallels to those scattered in the four gospels, and still others either occur outside the New Testament gospels or have no known parallels. Comparison often reveals that the Thomas forms are simpler and earlier than the New Testament forms, especially in the parables. In short, while the *Gospel of Thomas* is not in the New Testament, its possible early date, its form as a collection of sayings analogous to Q, and its early forms of specific Jesus sayings make it a valuable addition to the materials for reconstructing early Christian history.

In summary, many scholars date the five gospels like this:

Gospel of Thomas, about 50–70 C.E. (70–100?)
Gospel of Mark, about 70 C.E.
Gospel of Matthew, about 85–90 C.E.
Gospel of Luke, about 85–90 C.E.
Gospel of John, about 90–100 C.E.

This chronology is very helpful for understanding some varieties of early Christianity in the latter part of the first century C.E. However, it is only part of the historical problem.

The New Testament Letters

The twenty-one letters and letterlike books of the New Testament can be divided into three groups: seven letters of Paul, undisputed; seven letters of Paul, disputed; and seven letters attributed to other apostles:

Undisputed Pauline	Disputed Pauline	Other
1 Thessalonians	2 Thessalonians	James
1 Corinthians	Colossians	1 Peter
2 Corinthians	Ephesians	1 John
Philippians	Hebrews	2 John
Philemon	1 Timothy	3 John
Galatians	2 Timothy	Jude
Romans	Titus	2 Peter

If Paul arrived in Corinth about 49/50 C.E. and stayed eighteen months (the Gallio discussion), he wrote 1 Thessalonians there about 51 C.E. It is usually held that this letter, Paul's most apocalyptic, was written first, and that the seven letters in the first column were written in the 50s. *Thus, the undisputed Pauline letters are the earliest written material in the New Testament.* The sequence in the column is our view of their relative chronological order, though this is complicated by the fact that 2 Corinthians and Philippians (boldface) contain several letter fragments.

2 Thessalonians and Colossians, at the top of the second column, are different in vocabulary, style, ideas, and social relationships from those in the first column. Ephesians, the third, is similarly distinctive, probably lacked special recipients (Ephesians 1:1; textual variants), and thus is thought to have circulated as a "cover letter" to a Pauline collection (the seven plus these three). In addition, source criticism shows that Ephesians also copies phrases from Colossians (compare Col 4.7–8 with Eph 6.21–22; see Chapter Eight for the reasons); it therefore follows Colossians. Modern study suggests that these three letters were written by persons who knew the thought of Paul well and wrote in his name, but lived in a somewhat later period, a common practice in antiquity (again, **pseudonymity).** We call these second-generation Pauline letters **deutero('secondary')-Pauline.** They are usually dated to the generation after the undisputed Pauline letters, that is, sometime after 70 C.E. Again, they are probably in relative chronological sequence.

Passing over Hebrews, there is a second set of three letters in the "disputed Pauline" group, 1 and 2 Timothy and Titus. Traditionally, they are called the **pastoral letters** because they purport to be Paul's pastoral advice to two of his companions, Timothy and Titus. On the basis of vocabulary, style, and ideas associated with the more formal organization of Christian communities, they were probably composed early in the second century C.E. by a third-generation "Paulinist." They are also called deutero-Pauline, even though one might consider them trito-Pauline. These second- and third-generation Paulinists lead to the theory of a continuing **Pauline School.** It gains further support from insertions into the Pauline manuscripts (for example, 1 Cor 14:33b–36, which the NRSV places in parentheses; compare "Schools" in Chapter Three).

The "letter" to the Hebrews is radically different from the first thirteen letters attributed to Paul. It is not even a letter in the usual sense. Its vocabulary, style, and ideas are different from those of Paul; indeed, its theme of Jesus as the great high priest is nowhere to be found in the rest of the New Testament. The ancients doubted its Pauline authorship and modern scholars do not include it in the Pauline School. The date of Hebrews in relation to 70 C.E. cannot be established with certainty; most scholars favor about 80–90 C.E.

We can now regroup the traditional Pauline letters (columns one and two).

Pauline (50s)	Pauline School (70–90)	Pauline School (100–125)	Non-Pauline (80–90)
1 Thessalonians	2 Thessalonians	1 Timothy	Hebrews
1 Corinthians	Colossians	2 Timothy	
2 Corinthians	Ephesians	Titus	
Philippians			
Philemon			
Galatians			
Romans			

The seven letters and letterlike books in the final, "other," column (Nos. 20–26 in the first chart) have been traditionally called the **Catholic Epistles** because they are not written to a single Christian group. Specific arguments about vocabulary, style, and content will show that they are pseudonymous. All are judged to have been written between 90 and 125 C.E. This whole group of letters represents the interests and concerns of Christian communities that are on the way to becoming more established groups in the Greco-Roman world.

Revelation

We can date the book of Revelation, or the Apocalypse (Greek *apocalypsis,* "revelation"), to about 95 C.E. This date is chosen primarily because the book's references to persecution and martyrdom fit fears of local persecution related to Christians' refusal to worship Domitian in western Asia Minor about that time, even if there was no actual Domitian persecution. Though its author, John of Patmos, was traditionally identified with Jesus' disciple John son of Zebedee, its language, style, ideas, and context are so different from the Gospel of John and 1, 2, and 3 John that it does not belong in this "Johannine School."

THE EARLIEST "CHURCH FATHERS"; THE NEW TESTAMENT APOCRYPHA

From a historical perspective, it is necessary to include a number of acts, gospels, letters, apocalypses, and other writings that were used during the early phases of Christianity, but that were ultimately rejected for the New Testament. In this group are those "Church Fathers," or writings thought very valuable by emergent orthodoxy, for example, the letters of *1 Clement* (90–95 C.E.) and *2 Clement* (90–110 C.E.), a collection of early Christian exhortations called the *Didachē* ("teaching"; ca. 90–110 C.E.), the letters of bishop Ignatius of Antioch (ca. 110 C.E.), perhaps Polycarp's *Letter to the Philippians* (ca. 110–115), and the *Letter of Barnabas* (100–125 C.E.). There were also gospels that were used by some Christian groups, but often judged heretical. In addition to the *Gospel of Thomas,* some scholars would include the *Gospel of Peter* (an account of Jesus' resurrection), the Secret Gospel of Mark (probably a longer version of Mark, passages of which are purported to have been discovered in 1957), and Egerton Papyrus 2 (a few variant passages of the gospel stories). We shall note them again below in connection with which books were accepted and which were not (see "Canon").

WRITTEN SOURCES USED BY NEW TESTAMENT WRITERS

If we move backward and attempt by analysis to discover written sources used by some of the New Testament authors (source criticism), some of the most important sources include the following:

Mark, Colossians, and Jude

We have maintained that Mark was a written source for Matthew and Luke and that Colossians was a written source for Ephesians. A third example of this type is 2 Peter's use of Jude (Jude 4–16; 1 Peter 2:1–22; see Chapter Fourteen). In all three cases, a chronological sequence results.

The Q Source

There are also written sources that can be isolated by critical analysis. Q, reconstructed from Matthew and Luke, is primarily a collection of Jesus' sayings. Unfortunately, there is no saying in Q that would precisely determine its date. The basic argument is that Q has no reference to the climactic events of 70 C.E. Thus, scholars usually date it to 50–70 C.E.

Parable Collections

Critical analysis shows that sharp breaks or dislocations ("aporiae") occur in ancient texts, and, when they have different vocabulary or ideas, they usually signal insertions by an author or later editor. An example is Mark 4:1–34, which can be outlined as follows:

		[4:1–2a	*Introduction: setting by the sea]*
4:2b–8	The Parable of the *Sower*		
		4:9	Aphorism: "he who has ears . . ."
		[4:10–12	*Private instruction about speaking in parables]*
4:13–20	Explanation of the Parable of the *Sower* (an allegory)		
		4:21	Aphorism: The Lamp
		4:22	Aphorism: Hidden made manifest
		4:23	Aphorism: "he who has ears . . ."
		4:24	Aphorism: The Measure and Measured
		4:25	Aphorism: Having and Receiving
4:26–29	The Parable of the *Seed Growing Secretly*		
4:30–32	The Parable of the *Mustard Seed*		
		[4:33–35	*Conclusion: the Reason for speaking in parables]*

The boldface introduction (4:1–2a) and conclusion (4:33–35), which portray Jesus teaching a large crowd at the Sea of Galilee, are held by redaction critics to be the writer's vocabulary and style. The reason for speaking in parables (that they are meant to confuse outsiders, 4:10–12) is also an important theme of the writer. Curiously, these three verses have a setting in which Jesus and his followers are alone, in sharp contrast with the introduction and conclusion (a dislocation). The six aphorisms (short wisdom-type sayings, see below), which are formally distinct, some of which are found elsewhere, were no doubt once independently circulating sayings (4:9, 21, 22, 23, 24, 25). What remains are three parables that center on a similar theme, seed or its sowing, and an allegorical explanation of the Sower. These parables may have been a collection. Such collections were undoubtedly preserved to illustrate Jesus as a parable teacher, and some (in this case, the allegory) preserved interpretations from a time later than Jesus.

Miracle Collections

Dislocations or aporiae are often evident in relation to miracle stories. If several of these stories can be isolated, it is likely that they were taken from earlier collections and placed in their present context by the author. One miracle source is the well-known "Signs (-Miracles) Source," suggested by the seven miracle stories called "signs" in the Gospel of John (2:1–11; 2:12a + 4:46–54; 21:1–14; 6:1–25; 11:1–45; 9:1–8; 5:2–9; see Chapter Twelve). Another example are the possible miracle collections behind the Gospel of Mark (especially 2:3–5a, 11–12; 3:1–6; 4:35–5:42 + 6:34–51 + 7:25–8:10 + 8:22–25). These collections may well have been made by Christians who believed that Jesus was a miracle working "hero" (see Chapter Three); perhaps they were told not just for entertainment and reinforcement of believers, but for attracting nonbelievers to the faith.

Controversy Dialogues

Less certain but widely accepted are conflict story collections (see below, "Anecdotes," or "Chreiai"). One example is Mark 2:1–3:6, which includes miracle stories in the form of controversies (from the above or another collection?). These short stories progressively heighten the Pharisees' opposition to Jesus because of his association with sinners and tax collectors and his looseness about fasting and the Sabbath. Another is a series of question/answer debates ("challenge and response") with chief priests, scribes, elders, Pharisees, Herodians, Sadducees placed in the Temple (Mark 12:1–37).

Special M and Special L

The Two-Source Theory suggests that the authors of the Gospels of Matthew and Luke had access to other sources. Parts of these "strata," however, were probably oral.

ORAL TRADITIONS

You will recall that one of the tasks of form criticism is to reconstruct the small units and then to theorize about their developing history through early Christian groups (see Chapter One).

The Jesus Tradition

Two types of material about Jesus—his words and actions—are commonly broken down into the following forms:

I. Jesus' Words.
    A. Aphorisms: separate, individualistic, wisdom-like sayings that go against conventional wisdom. These sayings can generate anecdotal contexts similar to the following category.
    B. Anecdotes ("*Chreiai*," "Pronouncement Stories"): sayings spoken by Jesus in a brief context. Whether the context is integral or not, these two types can be subdivided as follows:
        1. Controversy Dialogues.
        2. Teaching Dialogues.
        3. Biographical Accounts.
    C. Prophetic and apocalyptic sayings.
    D. Sayings about Torah laws and behavior among followers.
    E. Similes.
    F. Metaphors.
    G. Parables.
    H. Example Stories.
II. Jesus' Actions.
    A. Miracle stories.
        1. Exorcisms.
        2. Healings.
        3. Feedings.
        4. Resuscitations from the dead.
        5. Nature miracles.
    B. "Biographical" legends and action-oriented anecdotes.
    C. Passion stories.

Sermons, Hymns, Confessions, Creeds, Prayers, and Benedictions

Form criticism is also useful for isolating liturgical traditions. The letter writers quoted all or parts of sermons, hymns, confessions, creeds, prayers, benedictions, and other elements from early Christian worship. We have already discussed the Lord's Prayer in some detail (Chapter One); we shall look at some of the other early liturgical traditions in Chapter Five.

Ethical Lists, Household Codes, and Lists of Sufferings

Early Christians also cited commonly known lists of virtues and vices (for example, Gal 5:19–23), and duties of household members (e.g., Eph 3.18–4:1), both well-known means of moral instruction in Greco-Roman culture. We shall consider these in detail in our discussions of the letters.

Once such forms have been isolated, it has been the task of form critics to determine what is earlier and later in the material, and then to theorize about the developing history of oral traditions through the various early Christian communities (*Sitze im Leben,* "settings in life"). A further extension of this task is based on the view that early Christians may have used lists of scriptural passages ("testimonies") to support their arguments, especially with Jewish opponents, and it is possible to observe shifting interpretations of them. Another approach is to analyze the various dislocations and shifting ideas within the documents in a "School," for example, the Johannine school (the gospel; 1, 2, 3 John), and to track the history of the community. Again, if the writer of Matthew came from a school, perhaps his formulaic use of Scripture quotations were in use there.

The task of analyzing the settings, however, has tended to be neglected. Thus, form criticism is constantly undergoing revision. Contemporary literary critics suggest that more attention should be paid to the *function* of a particular form within a given community. Anthropological and sociological research into oral traditions and their transmission in other cultures have led scholars to evaluate the significance of "orality" and the shift from oral to written communication. Sociologically oriented research tries to learn more about the neglected social settings, and to reconstruct *everyday* settings, not just "church settings" valuable for liturgical traditions and the like (see Chapter One). Though modifications like these are taking place, our view is that form criticism in the broad sense remains a useful tool for attempting to understand the history of early Christian traditions and their functions in the early churches.

CHRONOLOGICAL SUMMARY OF TRADITIONS, SOURCES, AND DOCUMENTS IN RELATION TO EXTERNAL EVIDENCE

We may now summarize Christian traditions, sources, and literature, giving authors and approximate dates in relation to external events.

6/4 B.C.E.–30(?) C.E.   Jesus of Nazareth was born under **Caesar Augustus** (reigned 27 B.C.E.–14 C.E.) and **Herod the Great** (reigned 37–4 B.C.E.) and died under **Caesar Tiberius** (14 C.E.–37 C.E.), **Pontius Pilate** (ruled 26–36 C.E.), and **Herod Antipas** of Galilee (4 B.C.E.–39 C.E.). If Jesus wrote anything down, it did not survive. Jesus wandered from town to town, spoke aphorisms (challenging proverbial-type sayings), parables, and prophetic sayings; associated and ate with peasants, expendables, and outcasts; exorcised and healed; and was crucified for sedition against the state.

30–50 C.E.	Oral traditions. Aphorisms, other wisdom-type sayings, parables, simple stories punctuated by a pronouncement, miracle stories, some passion materials, baptismal and meal traditions, scriptural testimonies, and liturgies, creeds, confessions, hymns. These are found in Q, the Gospel of Thomas, Mark, Special M, Special L, pre-Pauline materials, James, Acts, and the Gospel of John. There are a few isolated sayings in manuscripts and early Church Fathers ("agrapha").
30–70 C.E.	Parables collections; miracle collections; controversy collections; testimonia; passion stories. Continuation of oral traditions.
50–60 C.E.	(compare *Gallio Inscription; Edict of Claudius*). Paul writes 1 Thessalonians; 1 Corinthians and (the collection of letters that is now) 2 Corinthians; (the collection of letters that is now) Philippians; Philemon; Galatians; and Romans probably in that order, though we cannot be sure of the place in the order of the individual elements in 2 Corinthians and Philippians. *Paul's undisputed letters are the earliest New Testament writings to survive intact.* Continuation of oral traditions.
50–70 C.E.	The Q Source; perhaps the Gospel of Thomas. *The remaining early Christian traditions and books come after the* ***fall of Jerusalem*** *to the Romans and the destruction of its Temple, in 70 C.E.* Continuation of oral traditions; Special M and Special L.
70–90 C.E.	Pupils and followers of Paul write the earliest deutero-Pauline letters: 2 Thessalonians, Colossians, and Ephesians. Unknown Christians write what we now know as the gospels of Matthew, Mark, and Luke, the Acts of the Apostles, the letter to the Hebrews, and perhaps the letter of James. Some scholars would add a few extra canonical gospels or their sources here.Continuation of oral traditions.

90–100 C.E.   The Gospel and letters of John are produced
                             most probably not by one individual but by
                             persons who were members of a tightly knit
                             group. We do not know their names but for
                             convenience we will call them the Johannine
                             School. A church leader named John writes the
                             book of Revelation while in exile on the island of
                             Patmos; it is usually dated more precisely in
                             relation to fears of persecution in Asia Minor. 1
                             Peter, which reflects persecution, is probably
                             from this period. Continuation of oral traditions.

90–125 C.E.   Leaders in various churches write the
                             pseudonymous literature of the merging
                             institutional church: the Pastorals, Jude, and 2
                             Peter. To this period we may assign early
                             extracanonical Christian literature, the "Apostolic
                             Fathers." These include the *Didachē*, *1 Clement, 2
                             Clement,* Ignatius of Antioch, the *Epistle of Barnabas,*
                             and perhaps Polycarp's *Letter to the Philippians.*
                             Continuation of oral traditions.

Further reasons for these conclusions will be given in the chapters that follow.

SOCIAL FACTORS IN THE HISTORY OF EARLY CHRISTIANITY

Oral and Written

Jesus wrote nothing that has survived. Oral communication and dramatic actions, both highly valued in both Judaism and early Christianity, were his forté. Oral communication did not suddenly cease when writing became important. Indeed, most people did not write. Yet, Greco-Roman and Jewish societies were not non-literate societies. Texts, especially holy texts and their interpretation, had ancient roots. Moreover, even if popular writing preserved some of the dynamics of oral discourse, there was a cultural shift from an oral environment to written communication. We see here a shift to communities interested in preserving the Jesus tradition and other important documents for posterity.

From Palestine to the Larger Greco-Roman World

The influence of Hellenism in Palestinian towns and cities was extensive. Still, the geographical move from Palestine to the larger Greco-Roman world implied a shift in cultural environment: from the Jewish homeland, with its dominant Jewish population, its holy city, holy temple, holy persons, and holy texts to an environment of greater cultural and religious diversity.

From Mainly Jewish to Mainly Gentile

Jesus and the first disciples were Jews who in diverse ways derived their beliefs from the Torah, though their interpretations of it differed from those of other Palestinian parties and factions, and some scholars argue for certain Greek influences (see Chapter Fifteen). There is some evidence for continuing groups of Jewish Christians in Galilee, Jerusalem, and other eastern localities, but the new movement had its greatest success among Gentiles attracted to moral rather than ritual teachings and practices.

From Aramaic and Some Hebrew to Greek

The Greek language was used for trade and commerce in Palestine, including many Galilean towns. However, the traditional language was Hebrew, the language of the holy texts and, as archeology shows, it was still in use. Yet, the commonly spoken language of Palestinian Jews had long since become Aramaic (see Chapter Two). As Christianity moved into the larger Hellenistic world, Greek predominated. Among Greek-speaking Jews and Greek-speaking Christians, the holy texts were learned and studied from the Greek Septuagint. The shift from the Semitic languages, Hebrew and Aramaic, to Greek was a cultural shift already present in the Hellenistic towns of Palestine and among Greek-speaking Jews of the Diaspora.

From Rural to Urban

The Jesus movement had its initial successes among the villages and towns of Galilee; archeological evidence suggests that some communities continued there. Its greatest success, however, was in the urban centers: Jerusalem, Caesarea, Damascus, Antioch, Ephesus, Philippi, Thessalonica, Corinth, and Rome. Thus, a Jewish movement of the Galilean countryside soon became primarily a Hellenistic urban religion with the attendant problems of, and accommodations to, especially Greco-Roman urban life.

From Reforming Faction to Emergent Institution

The Jesus movement was initially a Jewish faction led by spontaneous, prophetic, Spirit–filled leaders. It spawned a variety of factions that experienced themselves standing against the world. Eventually somewhat more ordered groups emerged. We can see in this process a response to opposition by outsiders, increasing self-definition, and growing organization, institutional authority, fixed offices of leadership, and internal struggles.

Religious Ideologies and Their Social Contexts

The sayings and actions of Jesus that survived were interpreted for new contexts and in the process often transformed; it was also believed that he continued to speak through Spirit-filled prophets. Who, then, was Jesus? A prophet? A messiah? A "Divine Man"? A manifestation of God? Christian reflection about the identity of Jesus is traditionally called **Christology,** or thinking about "the Messiah," "the Christ." Early types of Christology are found throughout the New Testament literature, and it becomes quite explicit in the hymns, creeds, and confessions cited in the texts and isolated by form critics (see above; Chapter Five). It is also implied in titles of honor derived from the culture, for example, Messiah or Christ, Lord, Son of God, Son of Man, and Son of David.

Many early Christians believed Jesus had been vindicated by God through his resurrection from the dead. As opposition to them increased, they increased the intensity of their belief that this world would end and another, different and more perfect, world would be created. Thus, Jewish apocalyptic (see Chapter Three) was transformed into early Christian apocalyptic. It came to dominate most early Christian thinking.

Part of early Christian apocalyptic was the expectation that Jesus would return as Son of Man or Lord to judge the evil and redeem the good. Several New Testament writers used the Greek term *parousia,* a technical term for the official visit of a high official or deity (epiphany), for the expected return of Jesus. However, months and years passed by and the parousia did not take place. The hope for his return surfaced again with the fall of Jerusalem (compare Mark 13) and when the Christians of Asia Minor felt threatened by persecution (compare the book of Revelation). Still Jesus did not return. Much early Christian literature had to come to terms with the **"delay of the parousia."** Broadly speaking, the early Christians took three alternatives. First, the hope was intensified, as if doubts could be overcome by shouting louder (compare 2 Peter). Second, the expectation was maintained but pushed into the more distant future and combined with the attempt to make sense of the extended interim period or present (for example, Luke). Third, the claim was made that the parousia had already taken place, that the Cross and resurrection of Jesus were the final ("eschatological") events, and that the new life was already being experienced by Christians in the present (for example the Gospel of John).

THE PHASES OF NEW TESTAMENT CHRISTIANITY

A simple, step-by-step development of New Testament Christianity eludes modern historians. Nonetheless, using the dating of traditions, sources, and documents, as well as social changes, noted above, we shall now attempt to gain some general impression of the important phases of early Christianity.

Early Palestinian Christianity

The basis for reconstructing the history of Palestinian Christianity lies in the early oral traditions, the earliest history of the Johannine communities, the Q sayings material and the *Gospel of Thomas,* a few reminiscences in the letters of Paul, some scriptural testimonies, a few passion stories, and the critical interpretation of the Acts of the Apostles. We also must rely on historical imagination and sociologically informed models.

Early Galilee

The book of Acts says nothing about continuing Christianity in the villages and towns of Galilee, the locales associated with the activity of Jesus. However, since Q contains woes against Galilean towns (Q 10:13–15), it was probably handed on there. Precisely who preserved it and put it together is uncertain. Some texts indicate there were early Christians who, like Jesus, became itinerant missionaries, leaving home, family, and security to preach the Kingdom of God, teach the wisdom of Jesus, and perform miracles in the Galilean villages, taking with them only the bare necessities of life, begging for their food. Many Galilean towns show Hellenistic influence, and some scholars have suggested that these wandering preachers preserved Cynic-style virtues. Perhaps they collected sayings that supported their message and life-style. Nonetheless, the inclusive concerns for the poor and outcast in Q would have appealed to the peasants. Another theory is that village leaders, that is, scribes who did not represent the Jerusalem establishment, collected such teachings.

A most important point about the Q source is its *form.* The Christians of the Q group(s) may have begun their proclamation by repeating Jesus' proclamation of the Kingdom of God. They were led to the emphasis on the coming of Jesus as Son of Man by what they believed to be the spirit of Jesus inspiring prophets in their gatherings. The early Christians were particularly conscious that the spirit of prophecy had been renewed among them. The Q prophets spoke some sayings, and they were also cast in the form of Jesus' sayings. Thus, Q took the form of sayings. It began with the preaching of John, the temptations of Jesus, and then continued with Jesus' words. It was a "sayings gospel."

Behind this final form, however, there are two kinds of material, wisdom and apocalyptic (see J. Kloppenborg). Traditional Jewish wisdom is represented by the book of Proverbs. For example, though the desire for riches may make one greedy (28:22), overconfident (28:11), or arrogant (18:23), more typically riches are considered the result of industry (10:2, 27) and praised as a basis for security (10:5; 11:18), protection (13:8), and friendship (19:4). By contrast, Q wisdom says, "Blessed are you poor, for yours is the kingdom of God. Blessed are you that hunger now, for you shall be satisfied" (Q 6:20–21). It has the *form* found in ancient wisdom, the beatitude. Its *content,* however, tends to be subversive. It challenges accepted values. Its wisdom is unconventional. It is subtle criticism of acceptable beliefs, norms, and values, somewhat like Cynic wisdom. It is moderate social critique.

Other nonnormative teachings of this type in Q include sayings about breaking family ties, leaving home, turning the other cheek, being a good pupil, lending money without expecting return, love of enemies, begging, mission etiquette, openness to Gentiles, the Lord's Prayer, and some important sayings about the Kingdom of God (see further, Chapters Five, Fifteen). Many of these sayings are aphorisms, that is, short proverbial sayings that, unlike proverbs, are personal, individual challenges to ancient, conventional wisdom. All of this is consistent with the itinerant ethos of a Q group in Galilee. This stratum of Q also contains parables (Q 6:46–49; 14:16–24) and the Lord's Prayer (Q 11:2–4).

There is a second stratum of Q. It is dominated by apocalyptic. It contains strong judgmental sayings against "this generation," usually considered a reference to Israel, or the Jews. This stratum is centered on the imminent parousia of Jesus as Son of Man to judge these outsiders who do not accept his message. It shows a faction preparing for that coming and challenging others to do the same. Thus, it discloses the experience of "we" and "they" related to "their" oppression and persecution of "us." Such conflict is a typical context for the emergence of apocalyptic movements.

The wisdom stratum of Q gently criticizes accepted cultural values; in contrast, the apocalyptic sharply condemns this generation. Moreover, some sayings appear to be new creations spoken by early Christian prophets under the inspiritation of the spirit. Note that there is some correlation here: All the strata in varying degrees offer a critique of norms and values held by most members of the dominant culture.

Is there a historical sequence to these literary strata within Q? An earlier generation of scholars argued that Jesus was an eschatological prophet and that apocalyptically oriented prophecy was earliest. Some recent scholars, however, have given strong literary arguments that Q material became increasingly apocalyptic when the group encountered more and more opposition from "this generation." Some have gone further and seen historical development in the literary sequence, which is possible, but not inevitable since later literary material can often contain earlier sayings. Judgments here are related to one's view of the historical Jesus. We have followed the wisdom-apocalyptic sequence, but have made the reservation that there are certain threads of commonality between countercultural wisdom, countercultural prophecy, and countercultural apocalyptic.

A collection that took virtually the same form as Q, with some of the same sayings, was the *Gospel of Thomas*. Especially remarkable is the paucity, and sometimes the criticism, of eschatology and, most important, the absence of sayings about the apocalyptic Son of Man, the center of Q's version of Jesus. Thus, Thomas preserves the wisdom focus of Jesus' sayings and in that regard is similar to the wisdom stratum of Q.

Jesus was an itinerant, and accounts of Jesus' wanderings were preserved by his disciples, some of whom followed in his footsteps. Thus, the themes of disciples on a mission are present: disciples should take only minimal provisions (Mark 6:8–9), abandon their families (3:31–35; compare 6:1–6), and be prepared for rejection. The parable collection about sowing and seed in Mark 4 shows that there were varying responses to early Christian preaching (Mark 4:13–20).

Jesus was also an exorcist and healer, and stories about his miracles were preserved by some followers. Some of them were remembered as miracle workers, as well. The miracles were elaborated and supplemented with resuscitations, feedings, and nature miracles, eventually ending up in collections used as sources in the Gospels of Mark and John (see above). While such stories might have had entertainment and propaganda value, they also preserved an image of Jesus as a powerful and compassionate Jewish Holy Man, like, but surpassing, other famous Jewish Holy Men, such as Elijah, Elisha, Honi the Circle Drawer, Hanina ben Dosa (see Chapter Three). One also can see in this material a few ingredients of magic—Moses and Solomon were also believed to have been magicians (see Chapter Three)—but there is evidence that magical elements were gradually eliminated. Yet, the elaboration and creation of such stories enhanced Jesus' divine power. These epic elements of power and compassion were very attractive to some groups of early Christians, especially if they were sick or demon-possessed. They were perpetuated beyond the confines of Palestine (2 Cor 10–13) and were accepted by those open to belief in miracle-working heroes.

Another dimension of Jesus' activity was that he ate with his disciples (1 Cor 11:23–25; Mark 14:22–25) and marginal people ("tax collectors and sinners"). His table fellowship thus broke with those who emphasized purity (compare Q 7:24–35; Mark 2:13–17). Early materials refer to meals, meal practices, meal discussions, and the like (Q 14:16b–23; GTh 64:1; Q 6:21a; GTh 69:2; Mark 7; GTh 14:3; Q 11:39–41; Didachē 9–10). These meal practices continued as part of Christian social life and ritual among Christians who met in homes ("house-churches"; compare 1 Cor 11:23–26; 10:14–22; compare Acts 2:43–47). Indeed, meals were probably the context for perpetuating many of the Jesus traditions (see Chapter Five).

As far as we know, Jesus did not baptize. Early Christians probably took over the rite of baptism from John the Baptist (Mark 1:2–11; Q 7:18–20, 22–23, 24–35; John 1:15, 35–51), who in turn may have evolved his practice from the Essenes, though there is no surviving evidence for this connection. John's baptism stressed repentance and the forgiveness of sins—the Gospel of Matthew implies that Jesus' baptism was for different reasons (Matt 3:13–17)—and was connected with spiritual phenomena (Mark 1:8; many Acts passages). Within a generation it had become an initiation rite into Christian groups and stated as an ideal that there should be no distinction between Jew and Greek, male and female, slave and free (Gal 3:28; Rom 6:1–6).

A special dimension of Jesus' activity was perpetuated in groups that emphasized prophetic reform. The ancient prophets had attacked political and economic abuses of the rulers and pious preoccupation with purity, especially when these trends were accompanied by failure to perform acts of mercy, justice, and compassion for the poor, the stranger, the widow, and the orphan. Similarly, Jesus was remembered for his looseness about Sabbath observance, table fellowship with unclean people, and lack of strictness about food rules, as well-as his attack on well-established Temple practices in Jerusalem. Anecdotes were told about his controversial interpretations of the Torah, his conflict with religious authorities, especially members of the Pharisee faction. Aphorisms and other sayings were also made into anecdotes of conflict with religious authorities. Such anecdotes were preserved by those who wished to reform Judaism along the lines of Jesus' precedent.

Early Judea (Jerusalem)

We have no direct literary remains from the early Jerusalem church. Our impressions come from statements by Paul, some pre-Pauline traditions embedded in Paul's letters, an analysis of early, but legendary, sections of Acts, and a few possibilities from later church writers. Often, we must speculate.

Paul's letters show that a generation or so after the death of Jesus there were in Jerusalem conservative Christians who believed that circumcision was the sign of the covenant people of God, that Christians should therefore be circumcised, and that such views were the proper interpretation of the Torah. Paul himself had come to the opposite view. There was in Jerusalem a leading group, "the Twelve" (1 Cor 15:5), and from among them came two Jerusalem leaders, Peter and John (son of Zebedee). There was also a third leader, James (the brother of Jesus, not John's brother, the second son of Zebedee). These pillars, who were somewhat more moderate on the circumcision issue, had to mediate the Torah dispute between the conservatives and Paul at the Jerusalem Conference (Gal 2:1–10). Yet, when "men from James" came from Jerusalem to Antioch later, Peter stopped eating with Gentiles (Gal 2:11–14). The issue in this case was purity in relation to food and table fellowship.

Thus, we learn from Paul's discussions that Jewish Christians ranged from very conservative adherents of Temple and Torah purity to somewhat more moderate positions regarding circumcision. Paul himself was more broad-minded. Yet, he had respect for the Jerusalem group and its leaders. Thus, in connection with the Jerusalem Conference, Paul stated that " . . . they (James, Peter, and John) would have us remember the poor, which thing I was very eager to do" (Gal 2:10). This referred to the "poor among the saints of Jerusalem" (Rom 15:26). Yet, Paul also recalled that there was a split in the Christian mission, "we (Paul and company) to the Gentiles, they (Peter and company) to the Jews" (Gal 2:9).

An even sharper division is implied by the tensions between the Aramaic-speaking Hebrews and the Greek-speaking Hellenists (Stephen and others) in in Jerusalem (Acts 6:1–8:3). The Hellenists were driven out of Jerusalem probably because of their attack on the traditionalists' views of Torah and Temple (Acts 7); since Paul did not go this far, they were more radical than Paul. The conservative to moderate Jewish Christians, or Christianized Jews, were allowed to remain, and these were some of those with whom Paul came in conflict later, especially over meal practices. Although the Letter of James came from a non-Palestinian environment, its stress on the Torah (2:8–13), the ideal of poverty (2:1–7; 5:1–6), some eschatology (5:7–11), and sayings elsewhere attributed to Jesus (for example, James 5:12), may have come from traditions preserved among these Jerusalem Christians.

Again, we see a spectrum of early Christian belief: ultratraditionalists, who stressed Temple and Torah purity, traditionalists willing to forgo circumcision but not meal purity ("men from James"); moderate traditionalists (Peter, who had been eating with Gentiles); reformers like Paul, who preached freedom from the Torah; and radical reformers, like the Hellenists, who attacked both Temple and Torah traditionalists outright. There was no clear concensus at Jerusalem on how the life and teachings of Jesus should be interpreted.

Prophecy and spiritual phenomena may have developed at Jerusalem, as well. To be sure, this conclusion is somewhat speculative. The coming of the Spirit on the Jerusalem Christians in the story of Pentecost as it now exists in Acts 2 is legendary and comes from a later period. However, Acts also knows of a prophet Agabus who was in Jerusalem (Acts 11:28; 21:20), and we may ask whether some of the Jerusalem disciples did not share in the prophetic traditions known in Galilee.

Another strong possibility for Jerusalem is material now found in the passion story. Form critics used to argue that the passion story was the earliest connected narrative about Jesus' life. However, some more recent scholars contend that the passion story was the creation of the Markan author from his traditions. Either way, several episodes probably came from the oral tradition, most likely Jerusalem, if only because the Jerusalem Christians lived in the locale where the final events of Jesus' life took place. There were also old stories about Jesus' appearances in Jerusalem (Luke 24; Acts 1; John 20). No doubt Jerusalem Christians would have interpreted these matters. They did so with Jewish liturgies (Passover) and scriptural prophecies (Ps. 22; 69 [suffering and death]; 16:8–11; 7:2; 110:1 [resurrection]), some perhaps from collections of proof texts ("testimony books"). A related probability is that the Jerusalem community preserved interpretations of Jesus' last meal with his disciples. In any case, Paul cites the "Lord's Supper" as a tradition (1 Cor 11:23–25; compare Mark 14:22–25; compare John 13:1–30; 6:11).

Finally, we should remember that, as in some Galilean towns, the inhabitants of Jerusalem were subject to Hellenistic influences, though the Herodian kings were cautious about offending Jews in the Holy City. Bilingual Aramaic and Greek inscriptions show that Greek had been spoken in Jerusalem since the period of the Ptolemies in the third century B.C.E. Acts claims that there were Greek-speaking synagogues in the city. The Temple itself was influenced by Hellenistic architectural style, and there was protest about Herod's having placed an eagle on the Temple gate (Chapter Two). Recall also that the Hellenists were Greek-speaking Christians in Jerusalem (6:1–8:3).

We are also bound to ask whether the shadowy figure known as the "Beloved Disciple" in the Gospel of John was in any way related to the Jerusalem groups. The matter is speculative. Some interpreters of the history of Johannine groups suggest that the Beloved Disciple had been a disciple of John the Baptist, that he began to follow Jesus in Judea when Jesus was associated with John (compare John 1:35–40), that he was present again during Jesus' last days in Jerusalem (13:23; 19:26; 20:2–5) and that he was known to the high priest (18:15–16). Others doubt the existence of such a figure.

For all the Hellenistic influences, the dominant picture of Jerusalem Christianity is that conservative to moderate Jewish Christians were in charge, and that the Torah and Temple remained holy to them. Despite traditions about Jesus' "hard sayings" concerning his family (Mark 3:31–35; 6:1–6; compare Q 14:26–27), Jesus' relatives came into power among the Jerusalem Christians. Jesus' brother, the conservative, law-minded James, became the primary leader—he was martyred in 62 C.E. (Josephus *Antiquites* 20.9.1)—and there are later church traditions that members of Jesus' family succeeded him (Eusebius, *Ecclesiastical History* 3.11.1; 3.12.1; 3.19.1–20.7). We also may speculate that Jerusalem Christians thought of Jesus as the King-Messiah, Son of David (Rom 1:3–4; 2 Tim 2:8; *Didachē* 10:6), and expected him to return as "Lord" (1 Cor 16:22; Rev 22:20; *Didachē* 10:6; compare Acts 2:36).

Later groups of Jewish Christians in the East were called the Ebionites, or "the poor." We do not know if they were connected to the Jerusalem Christians, though Paul promised to remember "the poor" at Jerusalem (Gal 2:10). Otherwise, there remains a somewhat suspect legend that the Jerusalem Christians fled from Jerusalem across the Jordan River to a town named Pella before the outbreak of the war with Rome in 66 C.E. (Eusebius *Ecclesiastical History* 3.5.2–3).

Samaria

Jesus' parable of the Good Samaritan (Luke 10:30–36) suggests an openness to Samaritans, and there are signs that the early Palestinian Christians broke down the barriers between Jews and Samaritans (compare Luke 17:16; Acts 8.4–25; John 4:1–42). Apparently some Samaritans joined the Jesus movement (John 4:35–38; 8:48). If there were radical Jerusalem Christian Hellenists who opposed the Jerusalem Temple (Acts 7:48–50), they would have gained a hearing from the Samaritans, whose holy place was on Mount Gerizim in Samaria (see Chapter Three). Moreover, the Samaritans hoped for a *prophetic* Messiah (the *Taheb*, "the one who returns," "the one who restores"), sometimes identified with a returning Moses. Moses themes are also prominent in the Gospel of John, but in relation to Jesus (3:13, 31; 5:20; 6:46; 7:16). Thus, the mission to Samaria in Acts (Acts 8:1–25; compare John 4) may reflect a historical reminiscence.

Christianity in the Larger Greco-Roman World

Early Christianity shifted from mainly Jewish to mainly Gentile environments, from Aramaic and some Hebrew to Greek, from rural to urban, and from a Jewish reform movement to more ordered groups. These movements were accompanied by shifts in religious beliefs, ideas, and practices.

Transitions

The book of Acts implies that Christianity existed in Damascus, Syria, before Paul arrived (Acts 9:10–22), and Paul implies the same for Rome (Rom 1:8–15; 15:19, 22–33). We do not know exactly how Christianity came to these places. The earliest movements of Christianity to Egypt and the rest of the African continent are shrouded in legend, as well. A certain Simon of Cyrene (North Africa) was said to have carried Jesus' cross, and his sons are mentioned by name as though they were well known (Mark 15:21). Nothing is otherwise said about a mission to Cyrene. The book of Acts has a story about Philip's enlightening the Ethiopian eunuch (Acts 8:26–40), but no mission to Ethiopia is otherwise mentioned. The Secret Gospel of Mark relates that Mark went to Egypt from Rome, and a few scholars have tried to locate Matthew there, though these are minority views. Scholars debate whether the *Gospel of Thomas* was written in Syria or Egypt. Thus, our explicit information about the spread of Christianity beyond Palestine to the larger Greco-Roman world is very hazy, except for Paul's missions to Asia Minor, Greece, and Rome.

Some of the transitions to the larger Greco-Roman environment are especially reflected in changing beliefs about the nature of Jesus. In Palestinian Christianity, Jesus was characteristically the prophet like Moses (Acts 3:21; John 4), the hoped-for Son of Man as eschatological judge and redeemer (Q; compare Mark 13:26), the royal Son of David resurrected to heaven as Son of God (Ps. 2:7; 2 Sam 7:14; Rom 1:3–4; 2 Tim 2:8; *Didachē* 10:6), and expected to return as "Lord," or *mar,* the Aramaic term for those with authority to judge (1 Cor 16:22; Rev 22:20; *Didachē* 10:6). In more Gentile environments, the "prophet like Moses" was increasingly the "Man from Heaven," the "Savior of the world" (John 4:4–42). The "Son of Man" title in Pauline circles was apparently abandoned because in Greek it had no meaning. "Son of God" and "Lord," in contrast, were maintained because these titles implied divine qualities, as they did with the emperors (see Chapter Three). While "Son of God" could still be used in apocalyptic contexts (1 Thess 1:10), it was often used in the retelling of miracle stories that took place in Gentile regions, for example, Geresa, the Decapolis, and Syrophenicia (see Mark 3:11; 5:7). The major Christological development focused on the title "Lord." This title of respect in Judaism, also applied to the parousia of Jesus (Aramaic *mar)*, became in Hellenistic environments the most common honorific title (Greek *kyrios*). It was used for gods, emperors, and kings, as well as for men of power and authority everywhere (1 Cor 8:5). The author of the Gospel of John has the doubting Thomas exclaim "My Lord and my God" when he believes in Jesus (John 20:28; Suetonius, *Domitian* 13; compare Ps 35:23). The confession "Jesus [Christ] is Lord" (1 Cor 12:3) became the characteristic Christian confession (Rom 10:9; 1 Cor 12:3; compare 8:6).

Transitions can also be seen in the extensive and imaginative use of the Septuagint, or Greek Old Testament, passages of which may have been collected in testimony books. While the speeches in Acts were the creations of its author, they may have relied upon synagogue interpretations transformed by Christian reflection. These lay weight on Jesus' resurrection, which became central to the Pauline theology. Paul recalled one of these confessions when he said, "If you confess with your lips that Jesus is Lord and believe in your heart that God raised him from the dead, you will be saved" (Rom 10:9).

Early Gentile Christianity Besides Paul

The Greco-Roman environment was full of contrasts. Greek culture offered a conception of a good, harmonious life, but daily experience was neither good nor harmonious. The precariousness of life led to a focus on fate and a longing for security and salvation. This was especially clear in mystery cults or mystery religions that centered on a hero or heroine, a divine figure who had conquered life and achieved immortality, a benefit offered to devotees through initiation (see Chapter Three).

The Christians did not borrow directly from the mystery cults; nonetheless, outsiders could have easily interpreted Christianity as a Jewish mystery cult. It had its initiation rite, baptism, its sacred meal, its message of redemption to a better form of existence, and most of all, its myth of the hero, the gospel story of Jesus. Thus, we hear less and less about the apocalyptic eschatology of the Palestinian groups and the early Paul, with its stress on the final resurrection of the dead. Rather, we hear about possession by the Spirit, the transformation of life to a higher level, and especially continuing reflection on the nature of Jesus.

In the Christological hymns, for example (see Chapter Five), we can see the pattern of a redeemer figure who descends to the earth from a higher sphere, achieves his redemptive purpose on earth, and ascends to the higher, heavenly sphere. This pattern of thought appears to have influenced both Hellenistic Judaism—recall the Wisdom myth (Chapter Three)—and Christianity. It is found in the New Testament with quite remarkable consistency wherever there is strong contact with the Hellenistic Gentile world. There is also some evidence in the history of the Johannine community that, in addition to Samaritans, Greeks were now being admitted to the group. Thus, the Johannine Prologue (compare John 1:1–18) seems to have been modeled on Hellenistic versions of the Jewish Wisdom myth, emphasizing the descent of Wisdom to earth. Some scholars speculate that the group migrated from Palestine to Asia Minor, a more Hellenistic environment. In any case, the understanding of Jesus as a descending-ascending redeemer is one of Gentile Christianity's contributions to developing Christianity.

Early Christianity participated in the Hellenistic Gentile tendency to believe in heroes and heroines, that is, figures who particularly represented the power of a god, who had about them the aura of divinity. We noted that Christianity in its transition to the Greco-Roman environment responded to this aspect of its environment by interpreting Jesus in this way, for example, in the miracle stories now found in Mark 5 and 7. This emphasis led to a particular understanding of Jesus as miracle worker. It also led to a particular understanding of the nature of Christian discipleship. The Hellenistic Christian churches often understood their heroes as miracle workers, as we can see from the portrayal of Peter and Philip in the early chapters of Acts and from the note about Paul's garments possessing miraculous powers (Acts 19:12). In Corinth Paul ran into a related problem in that his opponents there, especially those against whom he argued in 2 Corinthians, understood a Christian apostle as one who exhibited such an aura and power, and they claimed it of themselves and wanted Paul to demonstrate it of himself (2 Cor 10–13). The Gospel of Mark also wants to go beyond this heroic view of Jesus.

The Apostle Paul

The apostle Paul is discussed in detail in Chapters Six and Seven, but he is so important in the development of New Testament Christianity that some brief indication of his place in it must be given here. A Jewish Christian missionary, he became its outstanding representative and natural leader.

Paul's mission took him ever deeper into the urban Hellenistic Gentile world. Among Paul's letters, 1 and 2 Corinthians may be regarded as representing the typical emphases, concerns, and problems of the mission to the Gentiles: the impact of Hellenistic forms of religious wisdom and spiritual phenomena on the Christian understanding of the possession of the Spirit; ethical questions posed by Christians of non-Jewish background; difficulties with the doctrines of the resurrection of Jesus and the future resurrection of the believer; and the tendency to think of Jesus and his most immediate representatives, the apostles, as "divine men."

A major shift that occurs in Pauline Christianity, and in sharp contrast with Palestinian Christianity, is the *form* of his material. Paul does not stress sayings of Jesus or stories about him. In 1 Thessalonians, for example, we are very close to ideas found in the Q group: The Thessalonian community awaits and prepares itself for the coming of Jesus from heaven as eschatological judge and redeemer (1 Thess 4:13–5:11). However, the titles are "Lord" and "Son of God," not "Son of Man," and the instruction is given in the form of general Christian instruction, not sayings of Jesus. True, there is enough left of the Palestinian emphasis for Paul to say, "we ask and urge you in the Lord Jesus" (1 Thess 4:1), but even when the instruction appears to be from traditions of the Q sort (1 Thess 5:2 = Q 12:39–40 par.), it no longer has the form of a saying of Jesus. Paul does quote a "word of the Lord" occasionally (1 Cor 7:10; 9:14; 11:23; 14:37), but he uses it to make a point. Neither his letters nor the tradition they represent show much interest in the story of Jesus as such, with two exceptions: the founding of the Lord's Supper (1 Cor 11:23–26) and the crucifixion and resurrection (1 Cor 15:3–6).

Between Palestinian and Pauline Christianity, sayings of Jesus and stories about him take a different course. They continue in the oral tradition and will turn up again incorporated in narratives of the gospels. Sayings are also preserved in "sayings gospels" like the *Gospel of Thomas,* and variants of them reappear in second-century writings. The focus in Paul, however, is on the message about the death and resurrection of Jesus.

The Jerusalem Conference and the Antioch Incident

A major event in which Paul played a leading part was the Jerusalem Conference. Our two accounts, one from Paul (Gal 2:1–10) and one in Acts (15:1–29), are both tendentious. Paul is fighting for his view of the faith and for the very existence of his mission in the Gentile world, and he is interpreting the event he describes. The author of Acts writes when the issues that occasioned the conference were dead and he constructs speeches, interpreting their significance for the present reader rather than recording what had been said. The assumption has to be that Acts 15 represents a reinterpretation of the conference for a later generation.

In the light of these factors and of our general knowledge of this period of Christian history, the most probable hypothesis is that the Jerusalem Conference grew out of the success of the Hellenistic Jewish Christian mission in a Gentile environment. This success was probably a surprise. The earliest Christians devoted their missionary activity toward their fellow and sister Jews. They expected that the Gentiles would be included at the End. However, the Christian mission to the Jews was largely a failure. In contrast, the mission to the Gentiles developed into an astonishing movement of vitality and power hardly anticipated. This success created a major problem, namely, how far the new Gentile Christians should also become Jews: Should it be demanded of them that they accept circumcision and Jewish dietary laws? As we have already said above, the Jerusalem leaders yielded to Paul on the circumcision issue. They struck a compromise, requesting that he remember the poor, and that there be a division in the mission: Paul and his followers would go to the Gentiles, Peter and other Jewish Christians would go to the Jews. We shall discuss the problems raised by this solution in Chapter Six.

The result of the Jerusalem Conference was not the Apostolic Decree about food taboos found in Acts 15:22–29, for the later history of Paul's work and correspondence shows that he knew of no such decree. Moreover, the decree reads like the kind of compromise reached in a later period when the question was not the legitimacy of the Gentile mission, but the relationship between Jews and Gentiles in well-established Christian churches.

This conclusion means that the Jerusalem agreement left unresolved the question of table fellowship between Jewish Christians who accepted the Jewish dietary laws and Gentile Christians who did not. Paul's account of the **Antioch Incident** between him and Peter indicates the problems that could and did arise. Paul chastised Peter for refusing to eat with Gentiles any longer when "men from James" came from Jerusalem (Gal 2:11–21). These problems were probably not resolved until the Jewish War of 66–70 C.E. effectively removed Jerusalem Christianity from the scene, and the compromise now represented by Acts 15:22–29 became possible.

Another problem was that not all members of either side lived up to the spirit of the agreement. Incidents arose such as the one that called forth Paul's letter to the Galatians. However, agreement was a major achievement and made possible the subsequent advances of the Christian movement in the two decades that separated the Jerusalem Conference (most probably 48 C.E.) from the catastrophe of the Jewish War and destruction of Jerusalem (66–70 C.E.), which changed forever the circumstances of New Testament Christianity.

Finally, Pauline Christianity reveals a movement in some respects still "sectarian," yet in other respects beginning the process of institutionalization and assimilation to the Gentile world. For example, traditional attire of women is defended where to Paul restraint seems necessary (1 Cor 11:2–16), yet the ideal in another context is a lack of male and female distinctions (Gal 3:28) and women having leadership roles in some of the Pauline churches (Rom 16:1–3). Again, while that leadership is still spiritual, rather loose, and undefined, Paul himself wields authority in his churches (for example, 1 Cor 5, 6) and the seeds for organization are beginning to surface (1 Cor 12:28; Phil 1:1).

Written Collections and Sayings Gospels

We have already covered these collections; it remains to recall that most of them probably came from this period. Parable collections, miracle collections, anecdotes, stories about Jesus' passion, and testimonia (collections of scriptural texts) were brought together from the oral tradition. Q is usually dated before 70 C.E., and some scholars are willing to push the *Gospel of Thomas* back into this period. These collections imply images of Jesus and the importance of his words and deeds in the groups that brought the materials together.

The Middle Period of New Testament Christianity

The Impact of the Fall of Jerusalem

The Jews revolted against Rome in 66 C.E., and they expected God to end the war in their favor. However, the war went the way of the Roman legions, and Jerusalem and the Temple fell in 70 C.E. The war deeply affected the Christian communities. To most Jews the Christians were unorthodox, but to most Romans they were Jews. Some Palestinian Christians probably fought in the war. The Pella tradition, that they fled Jerusalem before the wars broke out, is doubted by many historians. Nonetheless, the war contributed to a major shift in relations with

Jerusalem. With the effective disappearance of Jerusalem Christianity, Palestinian Christianity gradually lost much of its influence. The Christians in the Hellenistic world no longer had to deal with the influence of the conservatively minded authorities in Jerusalem. After 70 C.E., as Christianity became increasingly Gentile, internal conflicts over circumcision and table fellowship dwindled in most circles.

It is by now obvious that the New Testament documents say little about external historical events. Yet, there is enough indirect evidence to say something about "the middle period of New Testament history." This refers to the generation that followed the fall of Jerusalem. The period was characterized by the need for coming to terms with the catastrophe of 70 C.E. and the delay of the parousia. The churches became more conscious of continuing in time and of being distinct entities with traditions to preserve. Gospels were written. The Pauline School continued writing letters in Paul's name. The Johannine School developed. The letters of James, Hebrews, and 1 Peter probably came from this period. Conflicts with formative Judaism under the leadership of the Pharisees became sharper in some sectors of Christianity. The need for normalization with Greeks and Romans was clear in other sectors. In addition, the period began and ended with a resurgence of Christian apocalyptic.

The Resurgence of Christian Apocalyptic

Christian apocalyptic eschatology with its beliefs about the imminent end of the world pervaded most of the earliest Christian communities, some of which developed apocalyptic movements. With the shift of early Christianity to the Gentile world, the passage of time, and the failure of the End to arrive, other emphases developed. Yet, apocalyptic movements and ideas tended to flare up in response to a crisis, a tendency that has continued throughout Christian history. Thus, apocalypses are usually related to such crises.

One such crisis was the Jewish Rebellion or War (66–70 C.E.). To many Christians and Jews it was the beginning of the End, the beginning of the war that God would terminate by direct intervention in human history. There was a resurgence of apocalyptic expectation among Jews and Christians, and its literary monument in the New Testament is the Gospel of Mark. This gospel contains a "little apocalypse" (Mark 13), which gives it an apocalyptic flavor. It is probably a product of the resurgence of apocalyptic expectation occasioned by the Jewish War in 70 C.E. (Mark 13:14). There is also a high level of apocalyptic expectation preserved in the Gospel of Matthew.

Another context that brought about renewed apocalyptic movements and expectations was persecution of the church. It revitalized the belief that the end of history as known was near and that God was about to change everything. The believer had to simply hang on until the End, when the evil powers would get their just punishment. When Christians in Asia Minor experienced local persecutions for their failure to participate in emperor worship under the Roman emperor Domitian (81–96 C.E.), the one complete apocalypse in the New Testament, the book of Revelation, was produced. An analogous social situation of persecution is found in 1 Peter (1:3–21; 4:5–5:11): "The end of all things is near; therefore be serious and discipline yourselves for the sake of your prayers" (4:7). Thus, apocalyptic was renewed at the beginning and end of the middle period.

The Delay of the Parousia

Central to the apocalyptic ideas and movements was an expectation of the return of Jesus as eschatological judge and redeemer, the parousia of the Son of Man. However, if such beliefs were revitalized during the crises of the Roman wars and persecution of Christians in Asia Minor, there was also the attempt to come to terms with his failure to return, the "delay of the parousia."

Some documents are transitional in this respect. For example, the Gospel of Matthew retains strong apocalyptic expectations (compare 24:35–44), but the Parable of the Ten Virgins in Matthew 25:1–13 implies the delay of the bridegroom, an allegorical reference to the delay of Jesus' return (compare 24:22, 48). James 5:7a admonishes, "Be patient, therefore, beloved, until the coming of the Lord. The farmer waits for the precious crop from the earth, being patient with it until it receives the early and the late rains. *You also must be patient.*" The Gospel of Luke retains some apocalyptic (Luke 21), but Luke 9:23 deals with the passage of time in everyday life by giving continual, present significance to cross-bearing: "If any want to become my followers, let them deny themselves and take up their cross *daily* and follow me." Its author supports a new interest in time by writing the story of early Christianity in Acts. The Gospel of John changes the time orientation of salvation altogether. It has almost no eschatology and treats salvation as a matter of belief in Jesus in the present. In this respect, the Johannine literature may share a common environment with a movement called Gnosticism (see below). The letters of 2 and 3 John, as documents of the Johannine School, do not mention the parousia at all. Neither does Ephesians, a deutero-Pauline work from this period. The Letter to the Hebrews is also a noneschatological book. It sees all that was good in Judaism and the ancient Tabernacle having been superseded by Jesus.

The Continuing Influence of the Apostle Paul

An important aspect of Paul's work was that he trained people to work with and after him in the Gentile Christian churches. Though we have no direct reference to this training in the New Testament itself, it would have been natural. Jewish rabbis regularly trained disciples, and tradition has it that Paul himself was trained by Gamaliel (Acts 22:3). Thus, Paul's letters and the narrative of Acts are studded with references to fellow workers and "helpers," some of whom were women. Furthermore, evidence for the existence of a Pauline School is the existence of the deutero-Pauline letters, written in the name of Paul and close to his thinking, yet sufficiently different from the genuine letters to conclude that they were not written by the apostle himself. These letters, 2 Thessalonians, Colossians, and Ephesians, come from the middle period of New Testament Christianity.

Whereas 2 Thessalonians tries to maintain the hope for the parousia, Colossians and Ephesians represent the church's development of doctrines and settling down to the problems and opportunities of life in the Gentile world. A concrete social example is the role of women. The ideals of sexual equivalence represented in Galatians 3:28 ("neither male nor female") and female leadership (Rom 16:1–3) are muted in favor of assimilation to the Greco-Roman social ideal of the "household code," that is, wives being subject to their husbands, just as children are to parents and slaves are to masters, all supported by a Christian theology of authority (Col 3:18–25; Eph 5:21–6:9). These letters represent the continuing influence of the apostle a generation after his death, but there is a very noticeable shift.

The Heightened Encounter with "Formative Judaism"

The period 80–90 C.E. was the period of postwar Judaism led by the Pharisees at the Yavneh Academy. Thus, tensions between Jews and Christians were heightened in some locales. Especially illustrative of this conflict are the Gospel of Matthew, which portrays Jesus' opponents as the Pharisees, and the Gospel of John, which has Jesus continually confronted by a misunderstanding group the author labels impersonally as simply "the Jews." There were probably other local groups of Diaspora Jews that had to contend with new Christian factions.

The Development of Johannine Christianity

Five of the texts in the New Testament were regarded in church tradition as having been written by the apostle John: the fourth gospel, the three letters of John, and the book of Revelation. However, Revelation represents apocalyptic Christianity and is wholly different; only the remaining four belong together. They exhibit a unity of language, style, and content. Moreover, a comparison between the first three gospels and the Gospel of John will show that despite some obvious similarities in overall form and an occasional episode, there are many differences in vocabulary, style, order, topography, and content, many more than among the first three themselves (see further, Chapter Twelve). To move from the synoptic gospels to John's gospel is to move from one world to another. In John, the Christian faith is developed out of an independent Jesus tradition, one that probably has only a tangential relation to the synoptic gospels, and it comes to terms with the Hellenistic world as thoroughly and successfully as did the apostle Paul (but in a different way). Like the Gospel of Matthew, the Johannine gospel also has to define Christianity as it separates from Judaism. Indeed, its world-denying tendencies tend to give it a sectarian flavor, despite its distance from Palestinian apocalyptic origins. Johannine Christianity became a major influence on the Christian piety of subsequent centuries. How should this phenomenon be explained?

Modern critics have noted several odd features about the last chapter of the gospel, John 21. There are some differences between its Greek and that of chapters 1–20. The sons of Zebedee, known from the first three gospels, but missing in John 1–20, suddenly surface in John 21:2. The resurrection appearance of Jesus in chapter 20 is located in Jerusalem (compare Luke 24), but in chapter 21 it takes place in Galilee (compare Matt 28). When the last two verses of John 20 read like the original ending of the gospel (compare 20:30–31), the conclusion is that John 21 is an appendix added to the first twenty chapters. Who added it, and why?

One reason for the addition of John 21 was to identify the person responsible for the Johannine traditions and to indicate what Jesus had said about him. John 21:20–24 identifies the author of the gospel, or at least the one who "*caused these things to be written*," as "the disciple whom Jesus loved . . . ," that is, "the beloved disciple" (13:23–25; 19:26–27) who is also "the other disciple" (18:15–16;

20:2–8). It also says that Jesus never said this person would not die before he, Jesus, returned. The mysterious "beloved disciple" is never named in the gospel, but church tradition identified him as John, the son of Zebedee, one of the inner group of twelve disciples in the first three gospels (Irenaeus, *Against Heresies* 3.1.2, ca. 180 C.E.; compare Eusebius, *Ecclesiastical History* 5.24.2ff.). However, this tradition was not unanimous in the ancient world and its main source, a Church Father named Irenaeus, was not always correct about John (Eusebius, *Ecclesiastical History* 3.39.1–7). A related difficulty is that the author of the second and third letters of John identified himself only as the "presbyter" (or "elder," compare 2 John 1:1; 3 John 1:1) and there was a presbyter John, who was a shadowy figure in early Christian tradition (Eusebius, *Ecclesiastical History* 3.39.1–7). Thus, the traditional identity of the author(s) of the gospel and letters as John, son of Zebedee, is not usually accepted in modern study (see Chapter Twelve). If we ask *who* added chapter 21, a common answer among scholars is that some member(s) of a Johannine School did so, possibly the one who was responsible for the three Johannine letters.

The Johannine understanding of faith was hammered out somewhere in Palestine or Syria and perhaps Asia Minor during the middle period of the New Testament, most probably by a strong leader with a group of close followers. Thus, we owe the Johannine corpus to a Johannine School, as we owe the Pauline corpus to a Pauline School. Whether the leader's name was John does not matter; what matters is that the Johannine understanding of the Christian faith is a major achievement of the Middle Period.

Miscellaneous Works

Hebrews, with its themes of Jesus as the great high priest, sacrifice, and the Tabernacle, is difficult to locate in time and place, but most scholars favor a period about 80–90 C.E. 1 Peter, a pseudonymous work whose date is also debated, is most probably a developed baptismal homily or sermon from the end of the first century, reflecting the situation of the church under persecution in northern Asia Minor. James' letter, also pseudonymous, is Christian moral exhortation ("parenesis") in a style familiar to Hellenism and Hellenistic Judaism, and its view of faith as the acceptance of a doctrinal proposition (Jas 2:18–19) presupposes the Pauline School. It is probably from this period, though some interpreters place it later.

The Final Period: The New Testament Church on the Way to Becoming More Ordered

Early Christianity began as a set of groups of varying sorts responding to the life and teachings of Jesus. Most of the them became dominated by Jewish apocalyptic, expecting the imminent end of the world. However, by the end of the New Testament period Christianity was on the way to becoming an institution in the world. It developed a credal basis, a distinctive literature, and an organizational structure. The full establishment of these developments—a creed, a canon, and an episcopate—did not come until later, but the movement toward them is clear in the final stages of the New Testament history and literature, especially in the

Pastoral Epistles (1 and 2 Timothy and Titus). In these letters we have a third-generation Paulinist writing in the name of the illustrious apostle, but the language and thought are those of the church at the beginning of the second century. Sayings are worthy of acceptance if they are "faithful" (1 Tim 1:15; NRSV says, "sure"); we are on the way to a creed. The "office of a bishop" is "a noble task" (1 Tim 3:1); we are on the way to the episcopate. The church is "the pillar and the bulwark of the truth" (1 Tim 3:15); we are on the way to the church as an institution. An equally pseudonymous letter written in the name of an illustrious apostle, 2 Peter, speaks of the letters of Paul as a collection and equates them with "the other scriptures" (2 Pet 3:16); we are on the way to the New Testament canon.

Other literature in the New Testament belongs to this last period. Though we have placed 1, 2, and 3 John with the Johannine literature, they could have come from the early second century C.E. The letter of Jude develops a polemic against heretics not by setting out a positive theological standpoint in opposition to the heresy, but simply by appealing to the authority of tradition. These texts represent, therefore, the church on the way to becoming an institution in the world with a creed, a canon, and an episcopate: needing and using baptismal and moral homilies, viewing faith as the acceptance of doctrinal propositions, and appealing to an authoritative tradition against what is considered heresy. We call this the period of the emerging institutional church, and its literature is the literature of the emerging institutional church.

Gnostic Christianity

You will recall from our discussion in Chapter Three that the term Gnosticism comes from the Greek word *gnōsis*, "knowledge," a revealed religious knowledge about human origins, existence, and destiny necessary for salvation. Gnostics believed that salvation is liberation from the evil world and matter created by an evil deity. Its myth sometimes included a Redeemer who descends from the world of light, disguises himself in human form, teaches *gnōsis*, and ascends again. Since the world is not home, Gnostics often totally renounced the body and its passions (asceticism) or allowed themselves the utmost freedom (libertinism). Either way, they experienced rebirth and considered themselves part of the privileged few.

Since Gnostics believed that the creation and the body are fundamentally evil, they were led to posit an evil creator god as distinct from, and almost as powerful as, the good god of Light. Some Gnostics influenced by Jewish and Christian ideas identified this God with the Jewish creator God of Genesis and therefore rejected the Jewish scriptures of the Jewish people (see "Canon" and Marcion's influence below). Such a worldview was sharply dualistic. Similarly, Gnostics who stressed that the world and body are evil were reluctant to think of a Redeemer who could assume human flesh, suffer, and die. This tendency conflicted with the view that Jesus of Nazareth was a divine being in the flesh ("incarnation"), which became normative for the majority of Christians. Thus, as the Christian majority settled on its canon and developed its orthodoxy in the late second to the fifth centuries C.E., Gnosticism was judged to be a heresy.

Did Gnosticism already exist in the first century C.E.? Was there a Redeemer myth? Was it known among Jews and early Christians? These are intriguing and

sharply debated questions. Undoubtedly the possibilities for such mythical thinking were current in Mediterranean antiquity, whether we label them "Gnostic"
or not. Discoveries in modern times (the Mandaean literature, the Manichaean
papyri, the Nag Hammadi texts [see Appendix]), combined with the previously
known Hermetic literature, have convinced many scholars that some Gnostic
themes originated in the East apart from Christianity and may also have been earlier than Christianity. There is still no consensus, however, on whether its most
essential ideas were current at the time of the rise of early Christianity. Did the
myth of the descending/ascending Gnostic Redeemer, despite the eventual
Christian judgment that its "otherworldliness" is heretical, already exist to influence the way some early Christians understood Jesus as a Divine Being come to
earth, as in the New Testament Christological hymns? Or did Christians, including Gnostic ones, develop their beliefs about the Redeemer with the help of more
general ideas about gods and saviors? The problem is that the Gnostic Redeemer
myth can be documented with certainty only in somewhat later Gnostic texts.

Nonetheless, some early type of early Gnostic thinking was probably in the air
during the first century C.E., and, on occasion, early Christians of the New Testament period, especially in the environment of the apostle Paul (1 Corinthians 1–4)
and the Fourth Gospel, were influenced by it. Thus, it is not surprising to learn
that second-century Gnostic Christians were quite fond of Paul's writings and the
Gospel of John. The deutero-Pauline literature and the Johannine letters imply
that a Gnostic interpretation of Paul and John existed—there were at least two
major streams of Christianity by this time—but they judged it to be false. From this
perspective, it becomes clear why they were included in the canon of the churches
that came to oppose Gnosticism, with which we conclude this chapter.

THE CANON OF THE NEW TESTAMENT

In Chapter Three we noted that religious groups usually distinguish between
what is holy or sacred, that is, people, places, times, objects, sounds, and the like
that they set aside as special and distinct from those that are polluted or profane, that is, common, ordinary, everyday. The term "canon" is used for holy or
sacred books. It is derived from a Greek word for "reed" (*kanōn*). In antiquity, a
reed was often used as a ruler, measuring rod, or "yardstick." Metaphorically it
can mean a rule, a standard, a model, a paradigm, and so on. Canon Law guides
the church; saints are "canonized" because they lead model lives; and a canon of
books consists of the sacred books used as a standard of measuring the beliefs and
practices of a religious group. Thus, there is the Buddhist canon; the Jewish
canon; and the Christian canon, that is the Old Testament canon plus the New
Testament canon.

The formation of a New Testament canon of twenty-seven books began in the
later first century C.E. and reached its climax in the late fourth century C.E. Many
books used by Christians from this period were rejected; some churches in the
Middle East still resist accepting some books that have been accepted in the western, or Roman churches. It should be emphasized that the development of the
canon paralleled the development of the western orthodox church, as the conflict
with Gnostic Christianity shows: The canon became—and still is—the orthodox

church's book. To study early Christianity historically and literarily, however, one must include books from the same period outside its canon. Hence we have stressed the importance of the environment in Chapter Three and included the *Gospel of Thomas* and a few of the earliest Church Fathers in this chapter.

The First Collections of Pauline Letters

Some sort of collection of letters attributed to Paul, the earliest writer in the New Testament, must have existed by the end of the first century C.E. Ephesians, now thought to have been composed by a Paul admirer *who knew the other Pauline letters*, was in existence by then, and the Acts of the Apostles, which features Paul as a hero (see Chapters Six and Eleven), is usually dated about 85–90 C.E. ("the middle period" above). Moreover, in about 95 C.E. a formal letter sent from Rome to Corinth, called *1 Clement*, contains references not only to the Romans, but to 1 Corinthians (*1 Clement* 47.2–4), and perhaps also the letter to the Hebrews (*1 Clement* 17.1–6; 36.1–6). Similar evidence about collections can be found about 115 C.E. (Ignatius, *Ephesians* 12.2: "all his letters") and slightly later (*Letter of Polycarp* 3.2). 2 Peter, perhaps from about 100–125, mentions "all his (Paul's) letters" as an addition to "scripture" (2 Peter 3:15–16).

We may surmise that one such Pauline collection consisted of ten letters, that is, nine (1, 2 Thessalonians; 1, 2 Corinthians; Romans; Galatians; Philippians; Colossians; Philemon) plus Ephesians as a cover letter, since that collection was known in the middle of the second century and four other Pauline letters eventually included in the canon are not listed as such before about 200 C.E. (see below).

The First Acceptance of Gospels

The fate of the gospels is more difficult to track. The Two-Source Theory implies that at least the second gospel and other sources, such as collections of Jesus' sayings (Q), were known and used by the authors of Matthew and Luke, and the latter writer explicitly notes other gospels (Luke 1:1–4). However, oral tradition continued and the four gospels were probably not known by name before the middle of the second century (see Chapter One, Historical Criticism).

The earliest testimony to gospels as "scripture" comes from the early second century (*2 Clement* 2:4 [Matthew 9:13 = Mark 2:17; compare Luke 5:32]). Somewhat later, a Church Father named Justin Martyr, writing about what is read in worship, speaks of the gospels as "the memoirs of *the apostles*" alongside the prophets (Justin, *Apology* 66, 67).

The Influence of Marcion and Gnosticism

Marcion flourished in the middle of the second century. Marcion was influenced by Gnosticism. Since for Gnostics the creation was evil, and for the Gnostic Marcion the creator deity was also the God of the Old Testament, and since

Jesus had revealed the supreme God, the God of love, previously unknown, Marcion flatly rejected the Old Testament for Christians. He further believed that the revelation by Jesus had been hopelessly corrupted by the Twelve but preserved by the one true apostle, Paul. To support his teaching Marcion depended on the ten-letter collection of the Pauline corpus and an edited version of the Gospel of Luke which he believed was Paul's gospel, and written by Paul's companion (see Chapter Eleven). Marcion apparently edited his text of Luke, and perhaps also that of the Pauline letters, to bring them into accord with his own understanding of the revelation of God by Jesus. In the process something new occurred: a set of authoritative writings distinct from the Jewish scriptures, consisting of two parts, the "gospel" and the "apostle." Although condemned as a heretic by the emerging orthodox churches, Marcion attracted a wide following.

By the late second century Gnosticism had become more developed and very influential. Marcion had limited his canon, but most Gnostic Christians used a greater number of books (see below, the New Testament Apocrypha). The orthodox churches struggled to define their canon, expanding it in their fight against Marcion, limiting it in relation to other Gnostic groups. In this struggle, they appealed (as did the Gnostics!) to "apostolic" writings, that is, writings thought to have been written by apostles (see above), but also used in public worship in churches thought to have been founded by apostles, and believed to support "apostolic" or orthodox ideas. In this same period (ca. 140–150 C.E.) Papias, bishop of Hierapolis, was the first to write about Matthew and Mark (see "Historical Criticism," Chapter One).

Other Pauline Letters

The three "pastoral letters" (1 Timothy, 2 Timothy, Titus) and Hebrews were added to the ten-letter collection sometime in the second half of the second century C.E. The Pastorals were undoubtedly more easily accepted because of their opposition to Gnosticism. The **Muratorian Canon** (named for its discoverer) was an official list of the books of the New Testament, perhaps written at Rome toward the end of the second century (see below), and opposed to Gnosticism. It accepts the Pastorals, but not Hebrews. Yet, Origen, head of the Catechetical School in Alexandria in 203, reports that Hebrews was accepted everywhere. Although he had doubts about Pauline authorship, he justified its acceptance because he believed that its thought was Pauline.

Though other letters circulated in Paul's name, the Pauline part of the canon (fourteen letters) was complete. The Muratorian Canon refers to several "which cannot be received into the catholic church, for gold ought not to be mixed with honey."

The *Diatessaron* and the Four-Fold Gospel

There were many gospels produced and in use in early Christianity (see The New Testament Apocrypha below). About 170 C.E. a Syrian Christian by the name of Tatian wove four gospels—those that were eventually accepted into the canon—into a single narrative called the *Diatessaron*. This shows that these four gospels had been initially accepted in the East; yet, the popularity of the *Diatessaron* in Syria for more than three centuries was a clear challenge to the acceptance of four separate gospels, which eventually came with the *Peshitta*. In the West, about 185, Irenaeus, bishop of Lyons (modern France), refers to the "fourfold gospel" (Greek: *tetraeuangelion*) and makes the following comment:

> And it is impossible that the gospels can be either more in number or, on the other hand, less than they are. For since there are four zones of the world in which we are, and also four principal winds, and [since] the church is scattered throughout the whole world, and since the pillar and support of the church is the gospel and the Spirit of life, it is natural that she should have four pillars breathing out immortality all over the rekindling of people.
>
> (Irenaeus, *Against Heresies* 3.11.8)

The Muratorian Canon

The Muratorian Canon, an official list of books perhaps from Rome toward the end of the second century, is anti-Marcionite in tone. It speaks of a letter "to the Laodiceans, another to the Alexandrians, forged in Paul's name for the sect of Marcion." This canon lists the four gospels, Matthew, Mark, Luke, John; the Acts of the Apostles; thirteen letters of Paul (omitting Hebrews); Jude; 1 and 2 John; the Wisdom of Solomon from the Old Testament Apocrypha; and two apocalypses (Revelation and the "apocalypse" of Peter).

From this point forward the orthodox church in the West maintained only the four gospels as canonical. Acts also had a firm place in the canon, as did the thirteen letters attributed to Paul. The other books mentioned remained in dispute for some time. Some were dropped and others added. However, the tendency was to accept more and more of the literature of emergent Catholicism, an understandable tendency because of orthodox characteristics.

The Canon in the Third Century

In the third century, Tertullian (about 160–220), writing in Latin (not Greek), is the first writer to speak of the "New Testament," and compared with the Muratorian Canon, he omits 2 John, the apocalypse of Peter, and the Wisdom of Solomon, but adds 1 Peter. Origen (185–254), who wrote in Greek in the East, mainly in Alexandria, distinguishes between twenty-two "acknowledged" books (four gospels, all fourteen letters attributed to Paul [adding Hebrews], Acts, 1 John, 1 Peter, and Revelation) and five often "disputed" (James [mentioned for the first time], Jude, 2 Peter, 2 and 3 John). These are all the books that finally constituted the canon of the New Testament.

A feature of the later third century in the East was a dispute about the book of Revelation. It was rejected in Alexandria and Antioch, and although it was eventually restored to the canon it never achieved the same status as the other books in Greek-speaking Christianity, and it has never achieved canonical status in the Syrian churches.

The Canon in the Fourth Century

About 325 Eusebius of Caesarea completed his famous *Ecclesiastical History*. In it he reports on the state of the New Testament canon in the Greek-speaking churches of the eastern Mediterranean. He is the first writer to speak of a distinct group of the "seven so-called Catholic epistles" (1, 2, 3 John; 1, 2 Peter; James; Jude) but he agrees with Origen that James, Jude, 2 Peter and 2, 3 John are "disputed." He is ambiguous about Revelation, and he notes that because Hebrews is not accepted as Pauline at Rome, some also reject it.

The most important event in the fourth century in the East was, however, **the *Festal Letter* of Athanasius,** bishop of Alexandria, that was circulated among the churches under his charge in 367. In it, he listed as "scriptures of the New Testament" precisely these twenty-seven books, with none "disputed." When Jerome made his Latin translation in the latter part of the fourth century, he followed the Athanasian canon of the New Testament, though in a letter to Paulinus written about 385, he acknowledged the difficulties some had with Hebrews and Revelation.

Further History of the New Testament Canon

The *Festal Letter* of Athanasius in the East and the work of Jerome in the West mark the formation of the New Testament canon as we know it. This canon gradually became accepted everywhere except Syria, where the *Diatessaron*, Acts, and fifteen letters of Paul (including a third letter to Corinth) prevailed. In the early fifth century, however, the four separate gospels replaced the *Diatessaron*, 3 Corinthians was omitted, and James, 1 Peter, and 1 John were accepted. Thus, the Syrian church agreed with the remainder of the church except Jude, 2 Peter, 2 and 3 John (four of Origen's five "disputed" books) and Revelation. The accommodation would doubtless have gone further, but in the fifth century fierce controversies about the doctrine of Christ split the Syrian church and separated it from the rest of the church. Thus, these five books were never fully accepted in Syrian Christianity.

The only other factor that needs mention here is that for some time other books were accepted in some places. The Church Fathers noted above were very influential in some circles. For example, fifth-century Codex Alexandrinus includes *1* and *2 Clement* in its New Testament. Besides Syria, however, the twenty-seven-book canon gained general acceptance. The acceptance was by common consent rather than by formal pronouncement of general church council.

EXTRACANONICAL EARLY CHRISTIAN LITERATURE

In Chapter One, we noted **Patristic citations** as part of the evidence for reconstructing the original text of the New Testament. Above we briefly noted an important set of writings, the **Patristic Literature,** also known as the **Church Fathers** (or Apostolic Fathers). Several of the early Church Fathers hovered on the edge of acceptance into the canon of the New Testament, for example, *1* and *2 Clement,* the *Shepherd of Hermas,* the *Epistle of Barnabas,* and the *Didachē·* Although these were finally rejected, they continued to exercise considerable influence in early Christian history, and we have therefore considered them above.

A large quantity of other early Christian literature, some but not all of it Gnostic in character, was once in use by early Christians, but was eventually rejected by the orthodox churches. This included many other gospels, letters attributed to Paul and others, acts of various apostles, and apocalypses. These are known as the **New Testament Apocrypha.** In this connection we must also mention again the Nag Hammadi Library noted in Chapter One under archeological discoveries of manuscripts (see Appendix). It logically belongs with the New Testament Apocrypha, though it is normally discussed separately because it is a single discovery. It contains the *Gospel of Thomas* considered above. Some scholars also value very highly the *Gospel of Peter* (an account of Jesus' resurrection), the Secret Gospel of Mark (probably a longer version of Mark, passages of which are purported to have been discovered in 1957), and Egerton Papyrus 2 (a few variant passages of the gospel stories).

Finally, there are various isolated sayings of Jesus found here and there, for example, in Acts 20:35 ("To give is more blessed than to receive"), in other manuscripts of New Testament books (Manuscript D of Luke 6:34), or in various other early Christian documents. These are called **Agrapha.**

FURTHER READING

This chapter attempts to present the history of earliest Christianity as it appears in the light of historical criticism, source criticism, form criticism, redaction criticism, and the social history of Palestinian and Hellenistic Christianity. The idea for distinguishing various phases in pre-Pauline Christianity was put forth by W. Heitmüller, part of whose important article is found in English as "Hellenistic Christianity Before Paul" (German original 1912) in W. Meeks, *The Writings of St. Paul* , pp. 308–19. Heitmüller argued that Paul learned about early Christianity not from the Aramaic-speaking Jerusalem church leaders, but from the Greek-speaking Hellenistic Jewish Christians at Damascus and Antioch. By "Hellenistic Christianity" he meant a mission Christianity carried on by Hellenistic Jews like Stephen, but in the Diaspora. The development was: Jesus—primitive church—Hellenistic Christianity—Paul. A similar conception was developed by W. Bousset in *Kyrios Christos* (1970; original German 1913), and carried on by R. Bultmann, *Theology of New Testament,* and H. Conzelmann, *History of Primitive Christianity,* wherein the term "Hellenistic" was used.

In the 1960s F. Hahn, *The Titles of Jesus in Christology,* followed by R. Fuller, *The Foundations of New Testament Christology,* further distinguished Hellenistic Jewish from Hellenistic Gentile Christianity. Thus one gained a general impression of the development: Jesus—Palestinian Aramaic-speaking Jewish Christianity—Greek-speaking Hellenistic Jewish (mission) Christianity—Greek-speaking Hellenistic Gentile Christianity—Paul. Though such developments in the first generation of early Christianity were not considered strictly successive in the chronological sense, that is, they could be parallel, there was nonetheless a quite natural tendency to think in terms of a temporal-geographical progression.

One of the major reorientations of more recent study is to acknowledge the Hellenization of Palestine, especially its cities. This perspective is typified by M. Hengel, *Judaism and Hellenism.* "Palestinian Jewish" and "Hellenistic Jewish" in the classical Hahn-Fuller christological studies has been modified toward the viewpoint that much of Palestinian Judaism, already known to be widely diversified in the pre-70 C.E. period, was indeed Hellenistic. This third edition has attempted to take such developments into account, though we separated Hellenism from Judaism in Chapter Three for pedagogical reasons.

A second, related development is that social-historical studies have placed less emphasis on precise development and more upon the transition from Aramaic-speaking, rural, agrarian, charismatic, and apocalyptic Palestinian Christianity to Greek-speaking, urban, commercial, Hellenistic-cultural Christianity. We have sought to include these features in both method and reconstruction. A cautious, but nonetheless helpful, survey of some of social-historical and sociological results of the period from 1970 to 1990 in this can be found in B. Holmberg, *Sociology and the New Testament.* The bibliography below emphasizes these developments.

For further bibliography on the attempt to relate the methods in Chapter One to early Christian history, see below.

History and Sociology of Early Palestinian Christianity

ABD: "Art and Architecture, Early Christian Art" (G. F. Snyder); "Christianity, Early Jewish" (G. Schille); "Christianity in Asia Minor" (R. E. Oster, Jr.); "Christianity in Egypt" (B. A. Pearson); "Christianity in Greece" (L. M. McDonald); "Christianity in Rome" (G. F. Snyder); "Chronology, New Testament" (K. P. Donfried); "Cities, Greco-Roman" (J. M. Stambaugh); "Community, New Testament *Koinōnia*" (R. W. Wall); "Early Christian Apocalypticism" (P. D. Hanson); "Eschatology, Early Christian" (D. E. Aune); "Hellenist" (T. W. Martin); "Heresy and Orthodoxy in the New Testament" (H. D. Betz); "Jews in the New Testament" (B. Chilton); "Pella" (R. H. Smith); "Persecution of the Early Church" (D. S. Potter); "Poor, Poverty" (T. D. Hanks); "Rome, Early Christian Attitudes to" (L. C. A. Alexander); "Travel and Communication (NT World)" (F. F. Bruce).

R. Brown, *The Community of the Beloved Disciple.*

R. Brown and J. P. Meier, *Antioch and Rome.*

S. Freyne, *Galilee, Jesus, and the Gospels.*

R. A. Horsley, *Jesus and the Spiral of Violence.*

———, *Sociology and the Jesus Movement.*

B. M. Mack, *A Myth of Innocence. Mark and Christian Origins.*

B. J. Malina, *The New Testament World. Insights from Cultural Anthropology.*

E. M. Meyers and James F. Strange, *Archeology, The Rabbis, and Early Christianity.*

J. M. Robinson and H. Koester, *Trajectories Through Early Christianity.*

C. Rowland, *Christian Origins: An Account of the Setting and Character of the Most Important Messianic Sect of Judaism.*

E. Schüssler Fiorenza, *In Memory of Her. A Feminist Theological Reconstruction of Christian Origins.*

J. E. Stambaugh and D. L. Balch, *The New Testament in Its Social Environment.*

G. Theissen, *Sociology of Early Palestinian Christianity* (British title: *The First Followers of Jesus*).

Source Criticism (See Further Reading, Chapter One)

Q (see Further Reading, Chapter Five)

IDB Suppl.: "Q" (F. Neirynck).

R. A. Horsley, "Questions About Redactional Strata and the Social Relations Reflected in Q," *Seminar Papers, SBL* (1989), pp. 186–203.

B. M. Mack, "The Kingdom That Didn't Come: A Social History of the Q Tradents," *Seminar Papers, SBL* (1988), pp. 608–635.

J. Kloppenborg, *The Formation of Q: Trajectories in Ancient Wisdom Collections.*

———, "*The Formation of Q* Revisited: A Response to Richard Horsley," *Seminar Papers, SBL* (1989), pp. 204–215.

———, "Tradition and Redaction in the Synoptic Sayings Source," *Catholic Biblical Quarterly* 46 (1984), pp. 34–62.

H. Koester, *Ancient Christian Gospels.*

J. M. Robinson and H. Koester, *Trajectories Through Early Christianity.*

The *Gospel of Thomas* (see Further Reading, Chapter Five)

ABD: "Thomas, Gospel of" (R. Cameron); "Nag Hammadi" (B. A. Pearson).

R. Cameron, "The Gospel of Thomas: A *Forschungsbericht* [Research Report] and Analysis," *Aufstieg und Niedergang der Römischen Welt* II 25.6 (New York: De Gruyter, 1988), pp. 4213–4224.

J. D. Crossan, *Four Other Gospels. Shadows on the Contours of Canon.*

H. Koester, "The Gospel of Thomas (II,2)," pp. 124–318 in J. M. Robinson, The *Nag Hammadi Library,* 3d ed. (English translation and introduction).

———, *Ancient Christian Gospels.*

S. J. Patterson and M. W. Meyer, "The Gospel of Thomas," pp. 75–159 in J. S. Kloppenborg, M. W. Meyer, S. J. Patterson, and M. G. Steinhouse, *Q Thomas Reader* (introduction, text, translation, notes).

J. M. Robinson, "On Bridging the Gulf from Q to the Gospel of Thomas (or Vice Versa)," pp. 127–175 in C. W. Hedrick and R. Hodgson, Jr., *Nag Hammadi, Gnosticism, and Early Christianity.*

Form Criticism (See Further Reading, Chapter One)

ABD: "Homily Form (Hellenistic and Early Christian)" (J. A. Overman); "Oral Tradition" (W. H. Kelber); "Preaching" (F. B. Craddock).

Aphorisms and Anecdotes

ABD: "Logia" (S. J. Patterson).

J. D. Crossan, *In Fragments. The Aphorisms of Jesus.*

B. M. Mack and V. K. Robbins, *Patterns of Persuasion in the Gospels.*

R. C. Tannehill, ed. *Semeia 20. Pronouncement Stories.*

Miracles and Miracles Sources

ADB: "Miracle (NT)" (H. E. Remus).

P. J. Achtemeier, "The Origin and Function of the Pre-Marcan Miracle Catenae," *Journal of Biblical Literature* 91 (1972), pp. 198–221.

———, "Toward the Isolation of Pre-Markan Miracle Catenae," *Journal of Biblical Literature* 89 (1970), pp. 265–291.

R. T. Fortna, *The Fourth Gospel and Its Predecessor.*

————, *The Gospel of Signs: A Reconstruction of the Narrative Source Underlying the Fourth Gospel.*

J. Hills, "Tradition, Redaction, and Intertextuality: Miracle Lists in Apocryphal Acts," *Seminar Papers 29, SBL* (1990), pp. 375–390.

G. Theissen, *The Miracle Stories of the Early Christian Tradition.*

U. C. von Wahlde, *The Signs in John: Recovering the First Edition of the Johannine Gospel.*

Passion Stories

W. H. Kelber, ed., *The Passion in Mark.*

G. Nickelsburg, "Genre and Function of the Markan Passion Narrative," *Harvard Theological Review* 73 (1980), pp. 153–184.

Paul (see Further Reading, Chapters Six and Seven)

R. Banks, *Paul's Idea of Community: The Early House Churches and Their Historical Setting.*

M. Y. MacDonald, *The Pauline Churches. A Socio-historical Study of Institutionalization in the Pauline and Deutero-Pauline Writings.*

W. Meeks, *The First Urban Christians. The Social World of the Apostle Paul.*

J. H. Neyrey, *Paul in Other Words. A Cultural Reading of His Letters.*

G. Theissen, *The Social Setting of Pauline Christianity. Essays on Corinth.*

Redaction Criticism (see Further Reading, Chapter One)

Sociology of Gospels (see Chapters on the Gospels)

P. F. Esler, *Community and Gospel in Luke-Acts.*

H. Kee, *The Community of the New Age: Studies in Mark's Gospel.*

B. M. Mack, *A Myth of Innocence. Mark and Christian Origins.*

B. J. Malina and J. H. Neyrey, *Calling Jesus Names. The Social Value of Labels in Matthew.*

H. Moxnes, *The Economy of the Kingdom. Social Conflict and Economic Relations in Luke's Gospel.*

J. Neyrey, ed. *The Social World of Luke-Acts.*

H. C. Waetjen, *A Reordering of Power. A Socio-Political Reading of Mark's Gospel.*

Formative Judaism

ABD: "Jewish-Christian Relations, 70–170 C.E." (S. G. Wilson).

S. Cohen, "The Significance of Yavneh: Pharisees, Rabbis and the End of Jewish Sectarianism," *Hebrew Union College Annual* 55 (1984), pp. 27–53.

J. L. Martyn, *History and Theology in the Fourth Gospel.*

J. Neusner, "The Formation of Rabbinic Judaism: Yavneh from A.D. 70–100," *Aufstieg und Niedergang der Römischen Welt* II.19.2, pp. 3–42.

A. Overman, *Matthew's Gospel and Formative Judaism. The Social World of the Matthean Community.*

J. B. Tyson, ed., *Luke-Acts and the Jewish People. Eight Critical Perspectives.*

History of the Jonannine Group

R. Brown, *The Community of the Beloved Disciple.*

E. Haenchen, "History and Interpretation in the Johannine Passion Narrative," *Interpretation* 24 (1970), pp. 198–219.

R. Kysar, "The Gospel of John in Current Research." *Religions Studies Review* 9 (1983), pp. 314–323.

Gnosticism

ABD: "Gnosticism" (K. Rudolph).

IDB Suppl.: "Gnosticism" (E. Pagels).

H. Jonas, *The Gnostic Religion.*

B. Layton, *The Gnostic Scriptures.*

E. Pagels, *The Gnostic Paul.*

————, The Johannine Gospel in Gnostic Exegesis.

J. M. Robinson, *The Nag Hammadi Library,* 3d ed.

K. Rudolph, *Gnosis. The Nature and History of Gnosticism.*

Canon, Apocrypha, Pseudepigrapha, Church Fathers

ABD: "Agrapha" (W. D. Stroker); "Apocrypha, New Testament" (S. J. Patterson); "Barnabas, Epistle of" (J. C. Treat); "Canon (NT" (H. Y. Gamble); "Clement, First Epistle of"; "Clementines, Pseudo-" (F. S. Jones); "Didachē" (R. Kraft); "Egerton Papyrus 2" (H. Y. Gamble); "Literature, Early Christian" (F. F. Bruce); "Marcion, Gospel of" (R. M. Grant); "Mark, Secret Gospel of" (M. W. Meyer).

IDB: "O. T. Canon" (R. H. Pfeiffer); "N. T. Canon" (F. W. Beare); "Apocrypha" (M. S. Enslin).

IDB Suppl.: "O. T. Canon" (D. N. Freedman); "N. T. Canon" (A. C. Sundberg, Jr.); "Apocrypha" (R. McL. Wilson); "Muratorian Fragment" (A.C. Sundburg, Jr.).

NJBC, pp. 1034–1043 (O. T. Canon: R. E. Brown [with R. F. Collins]); pp. 1043–1051 (N. T. Canon and Enduring Problems: R. E. Brown [with R. F. Collins]); pp. 1055–1082 (Apocrypha; Dead Sea Scrolls; Other Jewish Literature: R. E. Brown; P. Perkins; A. J. Saldarini).

H. Y. Gamble, *The New Testament Canon.*

E. Hennecke and W. Schneemelcher, *New Testament Apocrypha* (2 volumes). (Compare J. Jeremias, "Isolated Sayings of the Lord," Vol. 1, pp. 85–90).

B. M. Metzger, *The Canon of the New Testament.*

Library of Christian Classics (Church Fathers).

The Miracle of Loaves and Fishes mosaic, Sancta Apollinare Nuovo, Ravenna, Italy, ca. 520 C.E. Gatherings at meals were common in early Christianity, and the miracle story on which this mosaic is based (Mark 6:30–44 and 8:1–10 and parallels; John 6:1–15) contains language reflecting not only traditional Jewish and Christian meals, but Jesus' last meal with his disciples. See the Eucharistic Meal mural at the beginning of Chapter Fourteen.

CHAPTER FIVE

THE EARLIEST NON-PAULINE CHRISTIANS

In our last chapter we said that Christianity began as a series of responses to the life and teachings of Jesus. One response was to preserve his sayings and parables, to make collections of them, to apply them, to find interpretations of them, and to apply them to life. A related response was to tell stories about him. Still another was to continue his life-style. In the process, there were preserved traditions, interpretations, and new creations of Jesus material in a variety of Jesus movements.

In this chapter, we shall begin with the larger social context and narrow down to a few specific group contexts for the preservation of Jesus materials, such as meals, the Lord's Supper, and baptism. Next we shall note some of the traditions from Jesus and about Jesus. These include sayings, parables, anecdotes, miracle stories, and accounts of the passion, death, and resurrection. We shall also focus on three of the most important kinds of sayings material: wisdom, prophecy, apocalyptic. Finally, we shall note some early "Christological hymns." Though we shall draw on some traditions used by the apostle Paul, we shall reserve our discussion of Paul himself for the following two chapters.

THE LARGER SOCIAL CONTEXT: SOCIAL STRATIFICATION IN PALESTINIAN SOCIETY

Recall from Chapter Two that in an advanced agrarian society like the Greco-Roman society, social status was based on honor and came as a result of birth, grant by persons of higher status, or acquisition in social competition with equals. Shame meant a decline in social status, for the reverse reasons. Recall also that there was no dominant middle class. Rather, at the top was a tiny aristocratic class and at the bottom a large body of peasants, slaves, men and women set free from slavery, and people considered to be expendable (see p. 49). We adjusted this model of vertical social stratification for a regional context, Herodian Palestine under Roman colonialism (see p. 55). The major difference is that Roman governors of the lower (equestrian) rank (called prefects, such as Pontius Pilate) and native client kings (such as the Herodians), usually supported by priests and their representatives (retainers), are intermediate local authorities. This revised model helped us understand the Jesus movements of Palestine in the earliest period of Christianity.

We can now observe a few facts from the perspective of this vertical social hierarchy. Jesus was an artisan, and like many artisans he may have had peasant roots. His disciples included fishermen, a tax collector, and both male and female members of the peasant class. While some of Jesus' larger circle may have included those of means, including women, most of his followers were village peasants, that is, freeholders, tenant farmers who worked the land and had to give most of their surplus to the ruling classes, and perhaps some slaves. The majority of those who heard Jesus' teachings and were the beneficiaries of his exorcisms and cures in the villages were of the same lower classes, including some expendables. In short, Jesus' activity was primarily among the social have-nots, and much, though not all, of early Palestinian Christianity had its roots there. This view of the larger social system needs to be qualified by some view of the early Christian groups and their leaders.

THE EARLIEST CHRISTIAN GROUPS

If we critically sift the sources, we see that the earliest Christian groups came from, or lived in, the towns and villages of Galilee and in the city of Jerusalem. The gospel sources show that some early Galilean leaders were "apostles" sent out on a mission, or missionaries. They abandoned their homes, families, possessions, and security, and wandered from village to village begging, proclaiming the good news of the Kingdom of God, prophesying, and working miracles (Mark 3:13–14 and parallels; 6:7; Q 14:26). Like Jesus and the Cynic philosophers, they had nowhere to lay their heads (Q 9:57–60). When compared to traditional Jewish beliefs, norms, and practices, these missionaries were radical. The writings of Paul, Acts, and the *Didachē* (10:7–13:7) indicate that such missionaries continued to be active in various areas of early Christianity.

We can also see from Acts that some from this group remained in Jerusalem. The Jerusalem Christians met in homes for meals and social activities. It may be that they shared their goods in common, that they practiced a sort of ancient "voluntary communalism" (Acts 2:43–47), as did the Essenes at Qumran. Initially Peter the Galilean fisherman assumed a leadership role in Jerusalem, and probably he organized "the Twelve" (1 Cor 15:5; compare Luke 24:34; Acts 1:15–26). We do not know what happened to all of them. When Paul told the story of his return to Jerusalem for the first time, he says he met only Peter and James, Jesus' brother (Gal 1:19; compare Mark 6:3). At the Jerusalem Conference only the acknowledged leaders, Peter, James (Jesus' brother), and John appeared (Gal 2:1–10; compare Acts 15:13). Did at least some of them continue the mission to the Palestinian Jews or even to Diaspora Jews? Acts states that Philip went to Samaria (Acts 8:4–25), that he later resided in Caesarea (Acts 21:8), and that Peter went to Lydda, Joppa, and Caesarea (Acts 9:36–10:48). Peter also went to Antioch and so did "people from James," Jesus' brother (Gal 2:11–12) who had remained in Jerusalem (Acts 21:18). Possibly Peter or his followers went to Corinth (1 Cor 1:12; 9:4). Early church tradition indicates that Peter was martyred at Rome (1 Clement 5:2–7; compare Ignatius, *To the Romans* 4:3). Certain portions of Paul's letters (esp. Galatians 2; 2 Cor 10–13) also point to rival Jewish "apostles," or missionaries, who held positions about Jesus very different from those of Paul (see below, miracles; Chapter Six). The accounts of the Hellenists in Acts indicate that they were run out of Jerusalem (8:1) and that they went to Cyprus, Phoenicia, and Antioch (11:19). They are credited with establishing Christianity at Antioch (11:19–26), and they may have been responsible for establishing Christianity at places such as Damascus, as well (compare 9:10–25).

Many of the Jesus traditions must have been preserved and reformulated by the people who lived in Galilee and Jerusalem, especially by their itinerant and local leaders.

COMMUNAL GATHERINGS

Meals

Gathering for meals was a widespread social practice in the Hellenistic world in general and Judaism in particular. Festive meals were held in all sorts of voluntary associations in the Greco-Roman world and there were rather clear patterns of etiquette involving procuring of banquet halls, advance invitations, reclining at meal by rank, conversation, and the like (see D. E. Smith). There were also meal customs in Judaism, for example, Passover, or the gatherings of religious sectaries, such as the special meals of the Pharisees or the "messianic banquet" of the Essenes. Jewish meals normally began and ended with a blessing. During the Essene meal, for example, the priest during the meal was said to utter "a blessing over the first portion of the bread and wine, and [stretch out] his hand over the bread first of all" (1QS 6:4–5).

A more specific social context for creative interpretation of Christian teachings and traditions, then, would have been meals in homes where Christians gathered ("house-churches"; compare 1 Cor 11:23–26; 10:14–22; compare Acts 2:43–47). Acts 2:46–47a idealizes this custom when it says, "Day by day, as they spent much time together in the temple, they broke bread at home [or from house to house] and ate their food with glad and generous hearts, praising God and having the goodwill of all the people."

Elsewhere in the New Testament, meal traditions reflect religious and social relations. Jesus' meals with "tax collectors and sinners" were recalled (Mark 2:13–17; Q 7:24–35), and thus came the charge by opponents that Jesus was "a glutton and a drunkard, a friend of tax collectors and sinners" (Q 7:34). This saying implies a persistent justification of meal practices that included people who were judged by the most strict religious persons to be unclean and by persons of high status to be of lower status. Sayings about meals in the Jesus tradition reinforce this perspective. "Blessed are you that hunger now, for you shall be satisfied" (Q 6:21a; GTh 69:2) implies poverty, whether voluntary or involuntary. "And I tell you, many will come from east and west and sit at table with Abraham, Isaac, and Jacob in the kingdom of heaven" (Q 13:29, according to Matthew

8:11), points to an expectation for a "messianic banquet" (compare Isa 25:6–8 [see below on Isa 24–27]; Exodus Rabbah 25.8; the Dead Sea Scrolls [1Qsa 2.11–22; compare 1 QS 6.4–5]) that probably included all sorts of people. So initially Jesus' and early Christian meals were not marked by the usual rank and segmentation. We may recall that the parable of the Great Banquet concludes by sending invitations to "street people" (Q 14:16b–23; GTh 64).

There are also a number of sayings and controversy dialogues that combat rigorous, separatist Jewish food laws (Mark 7; *GTh* 14:3; Mark 8:15; Q 11:39–41; *GTh* 89). Nonetheless, as the Antioch Incident shows, "certain people from James" pressured Peter into adhering to stricter Jewish meal practices (Gal 2:11–14; see Chapter Four). Also, religious and social distinctions created problems for Paul in the house churches at Corinth (1 Cor 11:17–34; 8; 10; see Chapter Seven).

Accounts of Jesus' meals with the Pharisees were probably created by the Lukan author a few decades later (Luke 7:36; 11:37; 14:1), and thus we may exclude them from the earliest period. However, meal scenes of Jesus and a narrower group of disciples probably reflect early practice (Mark 14:3–9; Matt 26:6–13; Luke 7:36–50; John 12:1–8 [anointing at Bethany]; compare Luke 10:38–42 [Mary and Martha]). A specific example is what Christianity has come to know as the "Last Supper" or the "Lord's Supper," elements of which came from the first generation of disciples (see below; 1 Cor 11:23; Chapter Seven).

In short, early Christian gatherings for meals would have been ideally suited for "table talk" of just the sort in which the Jesus tradition was transmitted, interpreted, and enlarged, and in which early Christian beliefs about Jesus began to flourish.

Early Christian Worship

Information about Christian gatherings for worship in the very early churches is somewhat sparse and scattered. We have noted that the letter writers quoted hymns, confessions, creeds, benedictions, and other elements from early Christian liturgies of the New Testament churches (see Chapter Four), and we shall have occasion to say more about such matters (see below; Chapter Six). Paul probably reflects traditional liturgical practice when he says: "when you *come together,* each one has a hymn, a lesson, a revelation, a tongue, or an interpretation" (1 Cor 14:26). The word translated "a hymn" is literally "a psalm"; it could also mean an antiphonal chant, as existed in the Jewish synagogues, or a Christian song (compare Col 3:16; Eph 5:19), less probably a Christological hymn (see below; Chapter Four). "A lesson" is a teaching (*didachē*) and it is likely that some teachings included "words of the Lord," as well as beliefs about his death and resurrection (see below; Chapter Six). "A revelation" (*apocalypsis*) probably refers to the spiritual gift of apocalyptic prophecy (compare 1 Cor 14). "A tongue" is the spiritual gift of unintelligible guttural utterances by a person in a state of spiritual ecstasy (*glossolalia,* or "speaking in tongues"), for which virtually no ancient analogies have survived, though modern parallels exist. "Interpretation" refers to the gift of interpreting such utterances. The gift of "tongues" is potentially divisive (1 Cor 12–14), and therefore given low priority by Paul: "and God has appointed in the church first apostles, second prophets, third teachers; then deeds of power, then gifts of healing, forms of assistance, forms of leadership, various kinds of tongues" (1 Cor 12:28; compare Rom 12:6). For Paul, the apostle's function was "proclamation" or "preaching" (*kerygma;* compare 1 Cor 1).

Other spiritual gifts that might be associated with worship are utterances of wisdom, utterances of knowledge, faith, healing, other miracle working, and discernment of spirits (1 Cor 12:8–11). In the same contexts Paul speaks of prayer (1 Cor 14:13, 15). We also have some information about meals, baptism, and various liturgical terms connected to early Christian worship, for example, the Jewish expressions "Amen" and "Hosanna," and the Aramaic cry for the return of Jesus, *Maranatha,* "Our Lord, come!"

It is clear from all this that Jewish practices such as readings from the Scripture, sermons, singing of hymns, antiphonal recitations, and prayers had a strong influence (see Chapter Three). Hellenistic influences were also present, for example, meal traditions and spiritual phenomena. In such contexts, the Jesus tradition would have been preserved, discussed, and reinterpreted.

Jesus' Last Meal (The Lord's Supper)

An example of a more solemn, formal religious meal is the Lord's Supper (1 Cor 11:23–25; Mark 14:22–26; Matt 26:17–30; Luke 22:7–39; John 13:1–30). The apostle Paul had judged that the celebration of the meal at Corinth was being abused by Gentile Christians accustomed to more raucous Hellenistic-style banquets and separation of groups from different strata of society. His attempt to correct the Corinthian practice (1 Cor 11:17–34) led him to recall a tradition about Jesus' words at the meal. Such formal, liturgical traditions can often be spotted by form critics who note some or all of the following:

1. interruptions of an author's general line of argument to make a point;
2. commonly used terms for transmitting traditions [for example, "received" and "handed on," technical terms for handing on tradition in Judaism; see *Sayings of the Fathers* 1:1];
3. introductory words, such as "that" or "who";
4. poetic or hymnic style;
5. basic ideas about Jesus not typical of the author; and
6. terms and phrases not typical of the author.

On the basis of such principles, we observe what is probably the earliest tradition about Jesus' words at his last meal with the disciples:

> For I *received* from the Lord what I also *handed on* to you,
>
> that the Lord Jesus on the night when he was betrayed took a loaf of bread, and when he had given thanks, he broke it, and said, "This is my body that is for you. Do this in remembrance of me." In the same way he took the cup also, *after supper,* saying, "This cup is the new covenant in my blood. Do this, as often as you drink it, in remembrance of me."
> (1 Cor 11:23–25)

Note that this tradition of Jesus' words was still being connected with a "supper" or meal. A generation later, in the Gospels of Mark, Matthew, and Luke, the meal was interpreted as the Jewish Passover (Mark 14:22–25 = Matt 26:26–29 = Luke 22:15–20). Indeed, certain Jewish Christians in Asia Minor, the Quartodecimanians, continued to celebrate it at the same time as the Jewish Passover (*Epistula Apostolorum* 15 [140–170 C.E.]), which varied according to the lunar calendar, rather than the Thursday night before Easter. However, the meal was not a Passover meal in the Gospel of John (John 13:1–30), and not directly associated with the Passover in Paul, either. Some accounts refer to "breaking of bread," which sounds like a fixed expression for a common meal or supper (Acts 20:7, 11; 2:42, 46; compare Luke 24:30). Thus, the Lord's Supper probably grew out of common meals described above. Probably the whole meal would have included taking bread, giving thanks, a supper, and passing the cup (1 Cor 11:23–25; *Didachē* 9–10; 14:1–3; compare Acts 2:46). Hints of the practice are found elsewhere, including the language of the miraculous feeding stories (Mark 6:41 parallels; John 6:11; compare Luke 24:30). We shall say more about Jesus' meals in Chapter Fifteen. Paul's recommendation that the Corinthians first eat at home if they are hungry undoubtedly contributed to separating the ritual practice from the common meal (1 Cor 11:33–34).

Baptism

Christians would have passed on their traditions at other special occasions, notably baptism. The Essenes had an initiatory baptism and, like other Jews of the period, practiced ceremonial washings for purity. As far as we are aware, Christians did not practice ceremonial washings. Baptism, derived from the practice of John the Baptist (Mark 1:2–11; Q 7:18–20, 22–23, 24–35; John 1:15, 35–51), became an initiation rite. It probably involved some preliminary instruction and in some circles it broke the religious and social boundaries of separation. This inclusiveness is reflected in a baptismal formula that says that "in Christ Jesus" there should be no distinction between Jew and Greek, male and female, slave and free (Gal 3:28; Rom 6:1–6; compare Col 4:11). At the same time, there was undoubtedly an emphasis on a new kind of Christian separation from worldly values, norms, and practices, as the act of removing one's old clothing and putting on new clothing, or the symbolism of dying and rising with Christ to a new life, indicates (especially Rom 6). Thus, baptismal rituals reinforced cultural critique implied in the Jesus movements of Palestine.

Other Early Christian Gatherings

There must have been many other occasions for early Christian gatherings. Jewish Christians would have come together for circumcisions. We know a little about wedding customs (Matt 25:1–13 [parable of the Ten Bridesmaids]; John 2 [wedding at Cana]), and "mixed marriages" between Christians and non-Christians became an important issue (1 Cor 7). Anointing the sick with oil (compare Jas 5:14), death, contact with corpses (Luke 10:31–32), preparation of bodies and embalming, burial, cemeteries, tombs, burial inscriptions, mourning, memorial meals, reburial practices, the afterlife, and the like were immensely important in antiquity. Indeed, there were burial associations or clubs in Greco-Roman society. We have almost no information about early Christian funeral practices and rituals apart from the passion story of Jesus (Mark 15:42–16:2) and Paul's mysterious statement about "baptism for the dead" (1 Cor 15:29). Certainly, there was concern about the departed dead in connection with hopes for an imminent parousia (1 Thess 4:13–5:11). Otherwise, we may speculate that Christians gathered for such occasions, followed local customs, had meals, and discussed matters related to sayings of Jesus about marriage, life, and death.

Summarizing, we have attempted to be more specific about some of the religious and social groups for the transmission of sayings, stories, practices, and beliefs of earliest Christianity. We have singled out missions and meals, key ritual contexts such as the Lord's Supper and baptism, and other social and religious settings such as weddings and funerals. We now turn to some important early Christian teachings.

CHRISTIAN WISDOM, PROPHECY, AND APOCALYPTIC

In Chapters Three and Four we indicated that there were two orientations to Jewish and early Christian wisdom, the Wisdom myth, with its focus on descent and ascent, and wisdom sayings about everyday life. We shall treat the Wisdom myth below; in this section, the focus will be on sayings, though they will be of a special kind. We also indicated that prophecy was revitalized in early Christianity, that apocalypses were produced in Judaism and early Christianity from about 250 B.C.E. to 250 C.E., and that apocalyptic thought and apocalyptic movements were the most common contexts for such activity. We shall now explore these three areas in more detail, using the hypothetical Q document as our basis for discussion.

The Q Source

You will recall that the majority of modern scholars accept the Two-Source Theory as a solution to the Synoptic Problem. This solution requires that the non-Markan passages in Matthew and Luke that have the same or very similar wording come from a lost source, of which more than 235 verses survive. It is designated "Q" (German: *Quelle*, "source"). Since the Lukan writer preserves the order of Q better, Q passages are cited by scholars with the same chapter and verse as the Lukan gospel, but prefaced by the letter Q. The almost unanimous conviction of scholars is that most of its material came from the first generation of Jewish Christianity, that it was preserved in Galilee (or perhaps southern Syria), that its author was anonymous, that it was put in writing at least by the second generation, 50–70 C.E.

Below we list the Q passages from J. Kloppenborg's chart of Q in his *Q Parallels*. Note several points. Materials of *uncertain but probable* origin in Q are marked with parentheses, transitions that *might* have been in Q but are unrecoverable are marked with angle brackets, and materials of *improbable* origins are put in Q with brackets. Second, we have added H. Kee's somewhat oversimplified forms in Q listed in his second edition of *Jesus in History:*

Narratives	Na
Parables	Pa
Oracles	Or
Beatitudes	Be
Prophetic Pronouncements	PP
Wisdom Words	WW
Exhortations	Ex

Third, asterisks after the formal abbreviations indicate that the section contains what J. D. Crossan has identified as "aphorisms," that is, short proverbial-type sayings that go against conventional proverbial wisdom. Fourth, because Q and the *Gospel of Thomas* are similar in genre, another column indicates passages they share in common. Fifth, certain blocks of material are highlighted with boldface type (Nos. 7–14; Nos. 21–28; Nos. 35–42; Nos. 50–57). The highlighted and non-highlighted sections indicate what some scholars (especially Kloppenborg) think are two different layers in Q. We shall discuss this feature further below.

FORM AND CONTENTS OF THE Q SOURCE
( ) = probably originated in Q; [ ] = probably did not originate in Q
* = saying is, or unit contains, aphorism(s) [Crossan]

SECTION AND NAME	FORM	Q TEXT	MATTHEW	LUKE	GTh
Incipit & The Preaching of John					
1. Incipit		\<Incipit\>	[no text]	[no text]	
2. [The Coming of John the Baptist]		[3:2–4]	3:1–6	3:1–4	
3. John's Preaching of Repentance	PP	3:7–9,[10–14]	3:7–10	3:7–9,10–14	
4. John's Preaching of the Coming One	PP	3:16b–17	3:11–12	3:15,16–17	
5. [The Baptism of Jesus]		[3:21–22]	3:13–17	3:21–22	
The Temptations of Jesus					
6. The Temptations of Jesus	Na	4:1–13	4:1–11	4:1–13	
Jesus' Inaugural Sermon					
7. Introduction		\<6:20a\>	5:1–2	6:12,17,20a	
8. Blessing and Woes	Be*(****)	6:20b–23,(24–26)	5:3–12	6:20b–26	54,69b, 68,69a
9. On Retaliation	WW****(*)	6:27–33,(34–35b), 35c(Q/Matt 5:4)	5:38–47;7:12	6:27–35	95,6b
10. On Judging	WW**	6:36–37b;(Q/Matt 7:2a); (6:37c–38b),38c	5:48;7:1–2	6:36–38	
11. Blind Guides, Teachers and Pupils	WW**	6:39b–40	15:13–14;10:24–25	6:39–40	
12. On Hypocrisy	WW*	6:41–42	7:3–5	6:41–42	26
13. Good and Evil Men	Pa*****	6:43–45	7:15–20;12:33–35	6:43–45	43b,45a,b,c,d
14. The Parable of the Builders	Pa*	6:46–49	7:21–27	6:46–49	

SECTION AND NAME	FORM	Q TEXT	MATTHEW	LUKE	GTh
John, Jesus and This Generation					
15. The Centurion's Son	Na	7:1a,1b–2,(3–5),6–10	8:5–13	7:1–10	
16. John's Inquiry	PP	7:18–19,(20),22–23	11:2–6	7:18–23	
17. Jesus' Eulogy of John	PP*	7:24–28	11:7–11	7:24–28	78,45
18. The Kingdom Suffers Violence	PP*	16:16	11:12–15	16:16	
19. John and the Tax Collectors	PP	[7:29–30]	21:28–32	7:29–30	
20. The Children in the Agora [Marketplace]	Pa	7:31–35	11:16–19	7:31–35	
Discipleship and Mission					
21. Three followers of Jesus	PP*(*)	9:57–60(61–62)	8:18–22	9:57–62	86
22. The Mission Speech	PP*****	10:2–12	9:36–38;10:1–16	10:1–12	73,14b
23. Woes on the Galilean Towns	Or*	10:13–15(Q/Matt 11:23b–24)	11:20–24	10:13–15	
24. The Authority of Missionaries	PP*	10:16,[18–20]	10:40	10:16–20	
25. Thanksgiving for Revelation	PP*	10:21–22	11:25–27	10:21–22	
26. Blessing on the Eyewitnesses	Be*	10:23b–24	13:16–17	10:23–24	
On Prayer					
27. The Lord's Prayer	Ex*(4a)	11:2–4	6:7–13	11:1–4	2,92,94
28. Confidence in Prayer	WW**	11:[5–8],9–13	7:7–11	11:5–1	
Controversies with This Generation					
29. The Beelzebul Accusation	PP**	11:14–18a,19–20,(21–22),23	12:22–30;9:32–34	11:14–23	
30. The Return of the Evil Spirit	Or*	11:24–26	12:43–45	11:24–26	
31. True Blessedness	Be	(11:27–28)	[no parallel]	11:27–28	
32. The Sign of Jonah	PP*	11:16,29–32	12:38–42	11:16,29–32	
33. The Lamp and the Eye	Pa**	11:33–35,(36)	5:14–16,6.22–23	11:33–36	33b
34. Woes Against the Pharisees	Or*********	11:39b–44,46–52	23:1–39;13:34–35	11:37–54;13:34–35	39a,102,89
On Anxiety					
35. Hidden and Revealed	PP**	12:[1],2–3	10:26–27	12:1–3	5b,6b,33a
36. Appropriate Fear	Or/Pa***	12:4–7	10:28–31	12:4–7	
37. On Confessing Jesus	PP*	12:8–9	10:32–33	12:8–9	
38. Blasphemy of the Spirit	PP*	12:10	12:31–32	12:10	44
39. The Spirit's Assistance	PP*	12:11–12[Q/Matt 10:23]	10:17–20,23	12:11–12	
40. Foolish Possessions		(12:13–14,16–21)	[no parallel]	12:13–21	
41. Earthly Cares	Pa***	12:22–31	6:25–34	12:22–32,	36, OxyP 655
42. Heavenly Treasure	Pa**	12:33–34	6:19–21	**12:33–34**	**76b**
Sayings on the Coming Judgment					
43. Watchful Servants		[12:35–38]	[no parallel]	12:35–38	
44. The Householder and the Thief	Pa**	12:39–40	24:42–44	12:39–40	21c,103
45. Faithful and Unfaithful Servants	Pa*	12:42b–46	24:45–51	12:41–48	
46. Fire and Division on Earth	PP(*)*	12:(49),51–53	10:34–36	12:49–53	10,16
47. Signs of the Times	Pa*	12:54–56	16:2–3	12:54–56	91
48. Agreeing with One's Accuser	Pa*	12:57–59	5:25–26	12:57–59	
Two Parables of Growth					
49. The Mustard and the Leaven	Pa		13:18–21	13:31–33	13:18–21

SECTION AND NAME	FORM	Q TEXT	MATTHEW	LUKE	GTh
The Two Ways					
50. The Narrow Gate and the Closed Door	WW*(*)*	13:24,(25),26–27	7:13–14,22–23	13:22–27	
51. Gentiles in the Kingdom	Pa***	13:28–30	8:11–12;20:16	13:28–30	4b
52. Lament over Jerusalem	PP*	13:34–35	23:37–39	13:31–35	
53. Livestock in a Pit		[14:5]	12:11–12	14:1–6	
54. Exalting the Humble		14:11/18:14b	23:6–12	14:7–12;18:14	
55. The Great Supper	Pa	14:16–24	22:1–10	14:15–24	
56. Being My Disciple	PP**	14:26–27;17:33	10:37–39	14:25–27;17:33	55a,101a,55b
57. Savorless Salt	PP*	14:34–35	5:13	14:34–35	
Miscellaneous Sayings					
58. The Lost Sheep	Pa	15:4–7	18:10,12–14	15:1–2,3–7	
59. The Lost Coin	Pa	(15:8–10)	[no parallel]	15:8–10	
60. God and Mammon	WW*	16:13	6:24	16:13	47a
61. The Kingdom, the Law and Divorce	PP/WW/**	16:16–18	11:12–13;5:18,32	16:16–18	
62. On Scandals	*	17:1b–2	18:6–7	17:1–2	
63 Forgiveness	Ex**	17:3b–4	18:15–17,21–22	17:3–4	
64. On Faith	Ex*	17:6b	17:19–20	17:5–6	
The Eschatological Discourse					
65. The Presence of the Kingdom		[17:20b–21]	[no parallel]	17:20–21	
66. The Coming of the Son of Man	Or****	17:23–24,26–27,(28–29)	24:23–28,37–42	17:22–37	3a,(22b,46b), 51,113,61a
	**	30:34–35,37b			
67. The Parable of the Talents	Pa*	19:12–13,15b–26	25:14–30	19:11–27	41
68. Judging Israel	Or	22:28–30	19:27–29	22:24–30	

According to formal classification there are only two narratives (Nos. 6, 15). The point is that Q contains mostly sayings of Jesus. There are virtually no chronological or geographical connections, though there is evidence of clustering around themes. Note in this connection the total absence of a "passion story," that is, a narrative about Jesus' arrest, trial, suffering, and crucifixion, so important for the final genre of the four narrative (canonical) gospels. Analogies to sayings collections like Q have been sought in Old Testament collections of prophetic sayings and wisdom sayings, in Jewish wisdom collections like the *Sayings of the Fathers,* and in early Christian sayings collections such as the *Didachē* and, again, the *Gospel of Thomas.* All this suggests there were early Christians interested in collecting the sayings of Jesus as the words of a sage or wise man. The form of Q, a "sayings gospel," is important for attempting to understand its significance, and we shall return to this observation.

Recent study of Q emphasizes that it contains two main types of sayings material, wisdom and apocalyptic, the **boldface** clusters being "wisdom speeches" and the remaining (except No. 6) being apocalyptic sections that emphasize judgment against "this generation." We begin with the wisdom speeches. This stratum contains wisdom words, beatitudes, exhortations, and some oracles. With regard to *content,* the wisdom material has a strong stress on poverty, for example, "blessed are you who are poor" (Q 6:20b). Perhaps poverty is voluntary (12:13–14, 33–34; 16:13), at least in the case of itinerant missionary leaders (10:4). Thus, God provides for life's necessities (11:3, 9–13; 12:22b–31). Another ethical ideal is "turning the other cheek" (6:29), that is, nonviolence. It is based on forgiveness and mercy, as God forgives and extends mercy (6:27–29, 32–38). Thus, discipleship is radical (13:24). It includes rejection of family (59–62; 14:26) and includes being prepared for poverty, homelessness, and even martyrdom (9:57–58; 12:4–7, 13–14, 22b–31, 33–34; 14:27; 17:33; 16:13). Again, these teachings reflect God's mercy and generosity (6:27–30, 32–39) for the elect, as well as "following," "coming to," or "listening to" Jesus (6:40, 46–49; 9:57–62; 14–27). There is little sympathy for Gentiles (6:33; 12:30), despite some looseness about food laws (10:8). A key element is the belief that the Kingdom of God is dawning (6:20b; 9:62; 10:9; 11:2; 12:2, 29–31; 13:18–21). Note also that some Son of Man sayings stress that Jesus is the Son of Man already in the present, for example, in the saying about homelessness: "Foxes have holes, and birds of the sky have nests; but the Son of Man has nowhere to lay his head" (Q 9:58; compare 7:34; 12:10).

The second main type of material in Q is apocalyptic, which, as we have noted, is something of an extension of, and advance on, ancient prophecy. Typical *forms* in this section are prophetic judgment sayings and apocalyptic words (Q 3:7b–9, 16–17; 11:19b, 31–32, 47–51; 12:39–40, 49, 51–53, 54–56, 58–59; 17:34–35) and other sayings that give expression to a warning or threat to those who fail to respond to the message of the Kingdom of God (11:20 [a kingdom saying], 23–26 [proverb + demonological instruction], 33–36 [exhortation about preaching and warning about lucid moral discernment]; 12:39 [a hortatory parable], 54–55 [a weather proverb], 57–58 [a wisdom admonition]; 17:37b [wisdom saying]). A number of sayings in the apocalyptic group are now embedded in, or connected with, short narrative anecdotes (3:16–17; 7:24–28; 11:19–26; 11:30–36). There is also a miracle story that is somewhat anecdotal (7:1–10).

With regard to the *content* of this prophetic-apocalyptic stratum, the material is dominated by judgment of "this generation," the basis of which is the lack of response to John the Baptist, Jesus, and the missionaries of the group (7:31–35; 11:19–20, 24–26, 29–36, 49–51; 12:57–59). Thus, "this generation" is blind, stubborn, a "brood of vipers" (3:7); it follows Satan; it is an "evil generation" (7:31–34; 11:29); and the coming Kingdom will be accompanied by violence. Judgment will be soon (3:9, 17; 11:51b; 12:51–53, 54–56) and the parousia of the Son of Man will be universal, visible, sudden, and without warning (17:24, 37b; 12:39–40; 17:26–30, 34–35). There is also expression of forgiveness for the insiders (for example, 17:3b–4) and openness to the Gentiles (7:1–10), all the more proof of judgment on Israel. A number of scholars argue that many apocalyptic sayings attributed to Jesus, such as these, were spoken by early Christian prophets "in the Spirit." For example, sayings about the Son of Man coming from heaven, based on Daniel 7:13–14, were probably created by prophets within the Q community (11:30; 12:40; 17:24, 26–27, 28–30; see Chapter Three).

Some recent Q experts have concluded from the two major orientations in Q that there are two different layers, one superimposed on the other, that is, *successive redactional stages.* One theory is that the earliest layer was mildly apocalyptic prophecy that became more sharply apocalyptic and then attracted wisdom materials. This theory has often been connected to a widespread view that the historical Jesus was an eschatological prophet. Its most important argument is that the wisdom stratum looks more Hellenistic.

However, a growing position is the reverse: the wisdom layer is earlier. However, it is not traditional wisdom. Many sayings are aphoristic, that is, like cultural proverbs in form, but counterproverbial in effect. These sayings criticize acceptable cultural beliefs, norms, and values in a manner sharper than Cynic wisdom. This wisdom is subversive, and in that regard it *approaches* prophecy. It is sometimes put forward that its origin lies in the teaching of the historical Jesus who was not an apocalyptically oriented eschatological prophet, but a sage analogous to the Cynic sages (see Chapter Fifteen). From this perspective, the wisdom stratum has been "apocalypticized" by a secondary stratum that came to dominate the collection as a whole. A check of the chart above will show that most (though not all) of Crossan's aphorisms fall in the highlighted wisdom clusters. Perhaps most striking, the wisdom layer is like the *Gospel of Thomas* in that it has little eschatology and does not portray Jesus as the apocalyptic Son of Man, the most important title in the Q materials; thus, both are less apocalyptic and more aphoristic. There is a social aspect to this argument: As opposition to the Jesus movement from "this generation" increased, the sayings became increasingly judgmental. In other words, the Q group was developing an apocalyptic sectarian consciousness that emphasized salvation for the insiders and proclaimed judgment on opponents who persecuted them.

Apocalyptic came to dominate Q. Wisdom and exhortation for insiders was overcome by judgment and condemnation of outsiders. The Q community expected the return of Jesus from heaven as Son of Man with power to execute eschatological judgment (Q 12:8–9). He would come suddenly and unexpectedly, but he would most certainly come (Q 12:40). Faced with the need to give form and content to this expectation, prophets in the community reached back into the past history of the Jews and claimed that it would be like Jonah's coming to the Ninevites (Q 11:30), like lightning striking (Q 17:24), or like the judgmental catastrophes associated with Noah and Lot (Q 17:26, 30). In characteristic fashion, eschatological hopes in a time of alienation drew on prophetic and apocalyptic ideas and images from the other apocalyptic and prophetic literature.

It is clear from our interpretation of the Son of Man that the Q community was eventually led, at least in part, by Spirit-filled, eschatological prophets who spoke for the now departed, but soon to return, Jesus. Prophecy, then, was one of the chief characteristics of the emergent community, a conclusion that is supported by allusions to Old Testament prophetic and apocalyptic literature, explicit references to prophets, and various expressions of eschatological prophecy, such as warnings about impending judgment by John the Baptist and especially Jesus. A wisdom oracle about prophets condemned Jerusalem:

> "Jerusalem, Jerusalem, the city that kills the prophets and stones those who are sent to it! How often have I desired to gather your children together as a hen gathers her brood under her wings, and you were not willing! See, your house is left to you. And I tell you, you will not see me until the time comes when you say, 'Blessed is the one who comes in the name of the Lord.'"
> (Q 13:34–35)

A woe that preserved wisdom, but came from the apocalyptic stratum, condemned the Jewish "fathers" and "this generation" in an environment of persecution:

> "Woe to you! For you build the tombs of the prophets whom your ancestors killed. So you are witnesses and approve of the deeds of your ancestors; for they killed them, and you build their tombs. Therefore also the Wisdom of God said, 'I will send them prophets and apostles, some of whom they will kill and persecute,' so that this generation may be charged with the blood of all the prophets shed since the foundation of the world, from the blood of Abel to the blood of Zechariah, who perished between the altar and the sanctuary. Yes, I tell you, it shall be charged against this generation."
>   (Q 11:47–51)

Similar condemnations were especially directed at the Pharisees, who were leaders of "this generation," for example:

> "But woe to you Pharisees! For you tithe mint and rue and herbs of all kinds, and neglect justice and the love of God; it is these you ought to have practiced, without neglecting the others."
>   (Q 11:42)

In these passages, we see that in the view of the emergent Q group the problem was the attitude of some Jews, specifically "this generation," "Jerusalem," and Pharisaic leaders toward prophecy. Q, in contrast, appears to have been directed to a larger community of the righteous who, it was thought, would be invited to the joyous "messianic banquet" in the near future: "And people will come from east and west, and from north and south, and will eat in the Kingdom of God" (13:29).

Given this apocalyptic view of the world, what does it take to be a Christian before the End comes? The beatitudes (6:20–23) possibly hint at the social class of some members of that Q community when they affirm that in the future human values will be reversed: the poor, the hungry, those who weep—all will be vindicated in the future Kingdom, and those who will yet be hated on account of the Son of Man will be happy. The stress is on the near future. Prophets have been persecuted before, and prophets and (presumably) disciples are being persecuted now; but "in that day," they, and those who love their enemies, will receive a great reward (6:35). In parables, we discover that a tree is known by its fruit (6:43–44), and that it is important to build one's house on a rock (6:46–49). Attachment to riches is also problematic, for one cannot serve God and mammon (16:13). In short, the loving and well-grounded disciple, though perhaps poor and hungry, though persecuted, though hated because of the Son of Man, will receive a reward in the coming Kingdom.

Discipleship, then, is no easy task. Unlike the animals and birds, the Son of Man has no home (Q 9:57); so those who proclaim the kingdom cannot stop to do what for a Jew is an absolute requirement, burying the dead (Q 9:60). Disciples may be sent out like lambs in the midst of wolves, living off those who will take them in, healing the sick (Q 10:2–20) as Jesus healed (Q 7:22) and exorcising the demons (Q 11:20); the true disciple of the Kingdom should not even go back and say goodbye to his family (Q 9:62); in fact, following Jesus is bound to lead to family divisions (Q 12:51–53).

> "Whoever comes to me and does not hate father and mother, wife and children, brothers and sisters, yes, and even life itself, cannot be my disciple."
> (Q 14:26–27)

If we attempt to bring together the results of this all too brief description of Q and the community that preserved it, we gain the following impression. Q is almost exclusively a collection of sayings and discourses, almost exclusively attributed to Jesus. It is not a "gospel" in the usual sense, for it lacks the narrative structure, specifically notations of time and place, characteristic of the four gospels. Most importantly, it lacks a passion story. This means that its focus is not on the suffering, death, and resurrection of Jesus, but on his teaching and on his imminent return as apocalyptic Son of Man who will bring salvation to his true followers, the elect, and judgment on this evil generation and its leaders, who most certainly include the Pharisees. Jesus is apparently God's Wisdom, not in a mythical sense, but in the sense that he inspires prophets who speak in his behalf, and who, like himself, give wise teachings to sustain the community until he returns. Hence Q has a special interest in prophets and prophetic forms as well as wisdom and wisdom forms. Such teachings, which are often exhortations of a practical sort, sustain the apocalyptic community, perhaps composed of the poor and disinherited. The disciples of Jesus are persecuted now, but they expect their reward in the future. They may, like the earthly Son of Man, have no real home, for their allegiances are to the Son of Man to the extent that, if necessary, they break ties with their families. But they are sustained by a morality strongly rooted in love, even love of enemies; moreover, they have a mission to Gentiles, and, like Jesus, are expected to heal.

If one recalls the attempt to give the social context of Galilean Jewish Christianity in Chapter Four, it is clear that Q provides much of the data from which this description emerges. We may imagine that the prophets of the Q community were wandering charismatic prophets who lacked home, close family ties, wealth, and security. They would have provided some of the authority structure for the movement, with local leaders and many sympathetic disciples in the villages. In this case, one might think not only of a Q community, but also of related communities. In them, the model for the alienated Christian who awaits the End is the alienated Son of Man who has no home, and the hope of the alienated Christian is the hope for the Son of Man who will come as judge and savior.

PARABLES AND PARABLE COLLECTIONS

One special form of wisdom is the **parable.** C. H. Dodd has offered a classic definition of parable that will serve as a starting point:

> At its simplest the parable is a metaphor or simile drawn from nature or common life, arresting the hearer by its vividness or strangeness, and leaving the mind in sufficient doubt about its precise application to tease it into active thought.
> (C. H. Dodd, *The Parables of the Kingdom,* p. 5.)

A **metaphor** compares two kinds of reality that are different at a literal level. Some metaphors are familiar ("You're a tiger"; "You're a pussy cat"; "You dirty rat!"; "A mighty fortress is our God"). Metaphors, especially new ones, shock the imagination, or as Dodd says, "tease it into active thought" ("You're a chocolate chip cookie"). Thus, metaphors create participation in that to which they refer; they "draw you in." A **simile** has a comparison word, "like" or "as" ("You have a memory *like* an elephant"; "My love is *like* a red, red rose"). Parables extend these figures of speech into short stories. They are "secular" stories, not "religious" stories, like myths, though occasionally religious figures are in them ("a priest passed by. . ."). They speak about real, everyday persons, places, and things ("nature": seeds, bushes, trees; "common life": farmers, merchants, women baking bread). They are nonetheless imaginary—we would say fictional—and therefore not literal ("any resemblance to persons living or dead is purely coincidental"). Moreover, they point beyond themselves to a reality not crystal clear. Parables are therefore "open-ended," that is, they can, within limits, have several possible meanings and they invite nuanced interpretations. They are verbal symbols and they are often paradoxical. Thus, they engage the hearer (or reader), like a good film whose story provokes discussion or disagreement. This quality they share with their shorter companions, the aphorisms.

Parable is often contrasted with **allegory.** Though parables are open ended, they tend to have one central focus; allegories intentionally exploit many points of comparison with people or things in the story. Parables challenge in a concrete context; the numerous points of comparison in allegories each refer to hidden meanings outside the narrative. The open-ended quality of parables is not characteristic of allegories; they are closed, the referents are often the same from allegory to allegory, and the interpreter must know their secret meanings, the keys that will unlock them. Only if they are known will their mysterious meanings become clear. Finally, in modern fiction stories can be *composed* as allegories (for example, *Pilgrim's Progress*); among the Greeks, however, it had become common to read difficult stories that were not intended to be allegories as allegories, that is, to give them deeper symbolic meanings. For example, characters in ancient Greek myths could be interpreted as symbolizing virtues or vices, such as love, justice, hate, and the like. The Hellenistic Jew Philo of Alexandria interpreted the Biblical (that is, Old Testament) epics allegorically. As we shall see, early Christians interpreted Jesus' parables allegorically.

It is generally agreed by modern scholars that Jesus' most original utterances are, or lie embedded in, parables (see Chapter Fifteen), many of which were later understood by early Christians as allegories. In his classic work *The Parables of Jesus*, J. Jeremias, after a hundred pages of analysis, summarized how the parables changed as they were passed on in early Christianity. Here are his ten "laws of transformation":

1. The *translation* of the parables in Greek [from Aramaic] involved an inevitable change in their meaning.
2. For the same reason *representational material* [building techniques, legal procedures, horticulture, landscape] is occasionally "*translated*" (from Palestinian Aramaic terms to the Greek terms of different meaning in the larger Mediterranean world).
3. Pleasure in the *embellishment* of the parables is noticeable at an early date (an entertainment feature).

4. Occasionally passages of (Jewish) Scripture and folk-story themes have influenced the shaping of the material.

5. Parables which were originally addressed to *opponents* or to the crowd have in many cases been applied by the primitive Church to the Christian community.

6. This led to an increasing *shift of emphasis to the hortatory aspect* (moral instruction), especially from the eschatological to the hortatory.

7. *The primitive Church related the parables to its own actual situation,* whose chief features were the missionary motive and the delay of the Parousia; it interpreted and expanded them with these factors in view.

8. To an increasing degree the primitive Church interpreted the parables allegorically with a view to their *hortatory use.*

9. The primitive Church made *collections of parables,* and *fusion of parables took place.*

10. The primitive Church provided the parables with a setting, and this often produced a change in the meaning; in particular, by the addition of *generalizing conclusion,* many parables acquired universal meaning. (J. Jeremias, *The Parables of Jesus,* pp. 113–14)

We shall now illustrate these principles, especially numbers three to nine, with the parable collection in Mark 4.

In Chapter Four we isolated a parable cluster centering on "seed" in Mark 4:1–34. Here we outline the cluster again but add parallels in the *Gospel of Thomas:*

4:3–8	The Parable of the *Sower*	GTh 9
4:14–20	Allegorical Explanation of the Parable of the *Sower*	
4:26–29	The Parable of the *Seed Growing Secretly*	GTh 21:4
4:30–32	The Parable of the *Mustard Seed*	GTh 20

We shall now take up the four parts of the cluster. First, here are the versions of the Sower:

Matthew 13:3–8	Mark 4:3–8	Luke 8:5–8a	GTh
"Listen! A sower went out to sow. And as he sowed, some seeds fell on the path,	"Listen! A sower went out to sow. And as he sowed, some seed fell on the path,	"A sower went out to sow his seed; and as he sowed, some fell along the path, and was trampled on, and the birds of the air ate it up.	Behold, the sower went out, took a handful (of seeds), and scattered them. Some fell on the road; the birds came and gathered them up.
and the birds came and ate them up. Other seeds fell on rocky ground, where they did not have much soil, and they sprang up quickly, since they had no depth of soil. But when the sun rose, they were scorched; and since they had no root, they withered away. Other seeds fell among thorns,	and the birds came and ate it up. Other seed fell on rocky ground, where it did not have much soil, and it sprang up quickly, since it had no depth of soil. And when the sun rose, it was scorched; and since it had no root, it withered away. Other seed fell among thorns, and the thorns	Some fell on the rock; and as it grew up, it withered for lack of moisture. Some fell among the thorns, and the thorns grew with it and choked it.	Others fell on the rock, did not take root in the soil, and did not produce ears. And others fell on the thorns; they choked the seed(s), and worms ate them. And others
and the thorns grew up and choked them. Other seeds fell on good soil and brought forth grain, some a hundredfold, some sixty, some thirty.	grew up and choked it, and it yielded no grain. Other seed fell into good soil and brought forth grain, growing up and increasing and yielding thirty and sixty and a hundredfold."	Some fell into good soil and grew, and when it grew it produced a hundredfold."	fell on the good earth and it produced good fruit; it bore sixty per measure and a hundred and twenty per measure.

Probably the original parable stressed the mystery of unexpected acceptance of the Kingdom of God preaching despite much failure. Jesus may have told the parable in connection with his own activity as parable teller! Whatever Jesus' original point, the Lukan and Thomas versions are shorter and more compact. This suggests that the Markan version was already expanded in the retelling of the story ("not much soil...no depth of soil...no root in it").

More important, the *explanation* (Mark 4:14–20) interprets the Sower as an allegory that contains multiple, deeper meanings. The meanings are explained like this:

sower	= speaker of the word
seed	= word, with potential to "take root" and "bear fruit"
path	= hearers who are susceptible of evil
birds	= Satan (evil) who takes away the word sown in them
rocky ground	= hearers who are without conviction and courage, that is, who temporarily accept word with joy, but do not have "root in themselves," and fall away when tribulation or persecution comes
thorns	= hearers who are consumed with secular matters, wealth, and materialism, which choke the word so it cannot bear fruit
good soil	= hearers who accept the word and bear fruit

The allegory says that *Jesus himself* interpreted the parable for his inner circle. However, scholars have concluded that Jesus spoke parables, not allegories, and that allegories were *later* interpretations of his parables in the early church for new, concrete situations. In this instance the conclusion is supported by an analysis of language.

1. "The word" (4:14) as a technical term for what is preached (the gospel), joyfully received, results in persecution, "grows," bears fruit, and the like is found in the *primitive church,* but *not in the teaching of Jesus* (for example, Mark 2:2 [redactional]; 4:33 [redactional]; Luke 1:2; Acts 4:4; 6:4; 8:4; 10:36, 44; 11:19; 14:25; 16:6; 17:11; 18:5; Gal 6:6; Col 4:3; 1 Thess 1:6).

2. Many terms in the allegory do not occur elsewhere in the first three gospels, and for that reason also not in the teaching of Jesus. They do occur in other parts of the New Testament, especially Paul:

    a.   "sow" with the sense of "preach" (1 Cor 9:11; compare John 4:36);

    b.   "root" with the meaning of inward stability (Col 2:7; Eph 3:17);

    c.   "endures for a while" (2 Cor 4:18; Heb 11:25);

    d.   "delight" [in riches] (Eph 4:22; Col 2:8; 2 Pet 2:13; 2 Thess 2:10; Heb 3:13; 2 Pet 2:13);

    e.   "riches" (nineteen times, fifteen in Paul);

    f.   "unfruitful" (1 Cor 14:14; Eph 5:11; Titus 3:14; 2 Pet 1:8; Jude 12);

    g.   "accept" the word (Acts 15:4; 16:21; 22:18; 1 Tim 5:19; Heb 12:6);

    h.   "bear fruit" metaphorically (Rom 7:4–5; Col 1:6, 10); and

    i.   many other words that occur only once.

3. Two of the three parables, and the conclusion of the third, are found in the *Gospel of Thomas* (above outline), but the allegorical interpretation is not. This confirms that the allegory was added to interpret the sower.

In short, the allegory detailed the various kinds of soils = people who heard the gospel in the churches: Most people rejected it, but some accepted it.

The second seed parable in the cluster is the so-called Seed Growing Secretly (Mark 4:26–29; *GTh* 21:4). It is really about a patient sower:

> "The Kingdom of God is as if someone would scatter seed on the ground, and would sleep and rise night and day, and the seed would sprout and grow, he does not know how. The earth produces of itself, first the stalk, then the head, then the full grain in the head. But when the grain is ripe, at once he goes in with his sickle, because the harvest has come."

Patience before the harvest may have originally meant patience not to take up arms against oppression (yet?), as the revolutionaries did. *The Gospel of Thomas* 21:4 has a parallel only to the last sentence and then it adds the "ears to hear" aphorism: "When the grain ripened, he came quickly with his sickle in his hand and reaped it. Whoever has ears to hear, let him hear." Both statements were "free floating"; if so, we have an example of combining a parable and aphorisms. Clearly the harvest metaphor has potential for eventual apocalyptic interpretation, especially when it echoes Joel 3:13, "Put in the sickle for the harvest is ripe," an allusion to judgment.

Finally, here is the Mustard Seed in its four versions.

Matthew 13:31–32	Mark 4:30–32	Luke 13:18–19	GTh 20
"The kingdom of heaven is like	"With what can we compare the kingdom of God, or what parable will we use for it?	"What is the kingdom of God like? And to what should I compare it?	The disciples said to Jesus, "Tell us what the kingdom of heaven is like."
a mustard seed that someone took and sowed in his field; it is the smallest of all the seeds, but when it has grown it is the greatest of shrubs and becomes a tree, so that	It is like a mustard seed, which, when sown upon the ground, is the smallest seed of all the seeds on earth; yet when it is sown it grows up and becomes the greatest of all shrubs, and puts forth large branches, so that	It is like a mustard seed which someone took and sowed in the garden; it grew and became a tree, and	He said to them, "It is like a mustard seed: It is the smallest of all seeds. But when it falls on tilled soil, it produces a great plant and becomes a shelter
the birds of the air come and make nests in its branches."	the birds of the air can make nests in its shade."	the birds of the air made nests in its branches."	for birds of the sky."

In Mark and the *Gospel of Thomas* the mustard seed becomes a great shrub and the birds find shelter in its shade. The "tree" in Luke, also added to Matthew, is an example of law No. 4, the addition of a theme from scripture. Ezekiel 17:23 speaks of a tree that symbolizes the future reign of God and Daniel 4:10 tells about birds flocking to the tree to build nests in its branches. These allusions show the tendency to apocalypticize the parables.

Reference to the three "seed" parables *separately* in the *Gospel of Thomas* suggests that the parables originally circulated independently and were only subsequently clustered together on the basis of the theme sower/seed. Perhaps the allegorical interpretation was also added at that time. In any case, the whole section points to the activity of interpreting and gathering together parables around a common theme in early Christianity. First, the Sower itself has received some elaboration in the repetitions of the soil on rocky ground. Second, some of the parables have been combined with aphorisms, received additions from scripture, and apocalyptic interpretations. Third, the allegorical interpretation is much more precise in relation to the various responses and has a theology of "the word," Satan, and attitudes toward the world, materialism, and the like. Fourth, the allegorical interpretation stresses conflict and persecution in the early churches. Finally, the allegorical interpretation continued to have an effect on the section in Matthew and Luke: the emphasis on the four types of soils (hearers) is stronger and has blunted the contrast between the bad and good seeds in Mark. Probably the collection as a whole was intended to instruct Christians about the failures and successes of the early Christian mission.

ANECDOTES

A number of Jesus' witty, figurative, or argumentative sayings generated brief narratives that provided them with a living context; others were connected with a brief narrative context from the beginning. Sometimes the climax to such stories was an action of Jesus, such as a controversial healing, or a saying plus an action. These "Pronouncement Stories" or "Anecdotes" (Greek *chreiai*) could offer a teaching in response to a question by friend, neutral listener, or foe; illustrate a conflict about the Torah or early church teaching or practice; or simply give a biographical snapshot of some event in Jesus' life. While some of the sayings in the anecdotes may actually have gone back to Jesus, the narrative stories are usually scenes *typical* of what happened in Jesus' life, whether they happened precisely that way or not. As such they illustrate anecdotes formed by the early Christians.

Consider the following list.

Mark	Passage	Form
2:1–12	**The Healing of the Paralytic**	**Conflict anecdote**
2:13–14	Call of Levi	Biographical anecdote
2:15–17	**Tax Collectors and Sinners**	**Conflict anecdote**
2:18–20	**Question of Fasting**	**Teaching/Conflict anecdote**
2:21–22	Old and New	Aphorisms
2:23–28	**Disciples pluck grain on Sabbath**	**Conflict anecdote**
3:1–6	Sabbath Healing	Conflict anecdote

The first story is a miracle story made into a conflict about the ability of the Son of Man to forgive sins like God forgives sins (2:5b–10). Jesus' call of Levi sitting at the tax office stresses Jesus' authority ("Follow me!") and sets the stage for a meal controversy about Jesus' eating with tax collectors and sinners. It leads up to the saying, "Those who are well have no need of a physician, but those who are sick. I have come to call not the righteous but sinners" (2:17). The question about fasting is raised by those who fast, John's disciples and the Pharisees; the saying that the wedding guests will fast when the bridegroom is taken away reflects a context when Jesus is no longer alive. Aphorisms about the old not being able to contain the new (patch; wineskins) follow. Then comes the disciples' plucking grain on the Sabbath, which went against the Sabbath Law, and "The Son of Man is Lord also of the Sabbath" (2:28). Finally, Jesus heals a man with a withered hand on the Sabbath, provoking a controversy.

This section is a unity in the Gospel of Mark, especially if the Call of Levi and Tax Collectors and Sinners are combined into a single conflict anecdote (Levi is a tax collector), and the old and new aphorisms are linked with Jesus' words about fasting, which break the fasting custom. The whole section turns on conflict, with its climax in 3:6: "The Pharisees went out and immediately conspired with the Herodians against him, how to destroy him." Clearly, the hand of the Markan author is present.

At least part of the collection predated Mark. One possibility is represented by the boldface stories in the list. That these anecdotes go back to the early Palestinian groups is suggested by the issues of conflict: Jewish Sabbath, fasting, and meal practices. A radical solution to the conflicts is attempted by appealing to the sayings or precedent of Jesus, that is, Christology.

Here is a second example, a list of anecdotes.

Mark	Passage	Form
12:13–17	Taxes to Caesar	Conflict anecdote
12:18–27	The Resurrection	Conflict anecdote
12:28–34	The First Commandment	Teaching anecdote
12:35–37	The Son of David Question	Conflict anecdote

The present location of these four stories in the Gospel of Mark is the Jerusalem Temple. In the first story Pharisees and Herodians attempt to trap Jesus by asking whether taxes should be paid to Rome. After examining a coin with Caesar's image on it, Jesus says, "Give to the emperor the things that are the emperor's, and to God the things that are God's." The question about the resurrection is another trap question posed by Sadducees, who do not believe in it. According to Jewish Levirate Law a widow should marry the next of kin and bear children to perpetuate the family name. If a woman married seven brothers in succession, the Sadducees say, "In the resurrection whose wife will she be?" Again Jesus eludes the opponents by claiming there is no marriage in the resurrection and God is the God of the living. The question of the scribe about the First Commandment is a neutral question in Mark, but Matthew and Luke have made it into a conflict anecdote by omitting the praise of the scribe (Matt 22:34–40; Luke 10:25–28). Finally, Jesus himself poses a question about how the scribes can say that the Messiah can be the Son of David; the question implies that the title, or at least the usual meaning of the title, is insufficient.

These anecdotes form a unit in the synoptic gospels, but it is likely that they were already clustered in the pre-Markan tradition. It was typical for four types of question to be raised to the rabbi, and these questions represent those types. Thus, four traditional types of question were asked in a conflict context typical of Jesus' debates and discussions with opponents and others.

We have hardly mentioned the biographical type, for example, stories about Jesus' birth, family, youth, baptism, rejection at Nazareth, conflict with Herod, cleansing of the Temple, and the like. But enough has been said to indicate that

Jesus was certainly in conflict with the religious leaders over reform of basic Jewish beliefs and practices; this conflict persisted in early Christianity.

EARLY MIRACLE STORIES AND MIRACLE COLLECTIONS

Miracles were unusual in the ancient world, but they were certainly not considered unique. Miracle stories were recorded about the prophets Elijah and Elisha. Moses and Solomon took on the aura of famous magicians and miracle workers. Fascinating miracle stories were told about the famous Galilean Holy Men, Honi the Circle Drawer and Hanina ben Dosa. In the larger Hellenistic world, where Jews were thought by Gentiles to practice magic, miracle stories about the so-called heroes and heroines—physicians, philosophers, political leaders, generals, athletes, and the like—were told to demonstrate their powers (see Chapter Three). It is not surprising, then, that Jesus of Nazareth was remembered as a miracle worker, and that stories of his exorcisms, healings, miraculous feedings, resuscitations from the dead, and control over nature were told to entertain and demonstrate his divine power.

Those interested in propagating Christianity collected miracle stories. There have been two major attempts to isolate such collections, one in the Gospel of Mark, the other in the Gospel of John. Most of the same techniques are used as in isolating creeds, confessions, hymns, and the like, namely, intrusions into the text such as introductory words (*aporias*), differences from the context in vocabulary, style, or ideas. In addition, one can search for relations between scattered materials, which point to the possibility that they have been severed from some earlier connected source.

P. Achtemeier has attempted to isolate an early miracle collection behind Mark 4:35–8:26. In this section of Mark, there are ten miracles. Achtemeier theorizes that the Markan author rearranged two of them, the Woman with a Hemorrhage (5:24–34), and the Blind Man of Bethsaida (8:22–26). By placing both of them back in their original sequence, Achtemeier arrives at two parallel miracle cycles, as follows:

Cycle One (Mark 4:35–6:44)	Cycle Two (Mark 6:45–8:26)
4:35–41 Stilling of the Storm	6:45–51 Jesus Walks on the Sea
5:1–20 Gerasene Demoniac	**8:22–26 Blind Man of Bethsaida**
5:25–34 Woman with a Hemorrhage	7:24b–30 Syrophoenician Woman
5:21–23,35–43 Jairus' Daughter	7:32–37 Deaf Mute
6:34–44, 53 Feeding of 5000	8:1–10 Feeding of 4000

In other words, each of the cycles originally had the order:

1. Nature Miracle (Sea Miracle)
2. Healing (or exorcism)
3. Healing

4. Healing (resuscitation?)
5. Feeding Miracle

While this order has not turned up in any other known miracle collection, it is worth noting that the most important miracles Moses is reported to have performed were a sea miracle and a feeding (Exod 13–17), the types that begin and end both these cycles. In any case, the collection displays Jesus' divine power as a miracle worker. Because in the climactic feeding stories there are clear reminiscences of the breaking of bread (compare Mark 6:41 and 8:6 with 14:22 and 1 Cor 11:24), Jesus' meals may have been the context in which the stories were told.

A similar type of Christian group probably collected is taken up by the author of the Gospel of John. In general, this gospel contains three complexes of material:

1. miracle stories;
2. long discourses centered around great symbolic themes; and
3. a passion, death, and resurrection story.

An earlier generation of scholars thought that these complexes might represent three sources. The Discourse Source, however, has not stood the test of time because the discourses are most representative of the author's thought and often depend on the miracle stories. We shall consider a Passion Source below. Here we consider only the Miracle Source. Since miracles in the Fourth Gospel are called "signs," this source is known as the Signs Source.

If one removes occasional redactional elements, Robert Fortna's Signs Source emerges. It includes an opening unit about John the Baptist and the first disciples. Then come seven signs (seven is a number of completeness, see Chapter Thirteen). Fortna rearranges the source to conform to a geographical order moving from Galilee to Jerusalem:

Unit	Passage
The Opening	
1. John's Testimony	1:6–7,19–23,26b–27,[33d],29–34
2. First Disciples Find the Messiah	1:35,37,(38a),38b,39–42,43b–47,49
The Signs of Jesus	
Galilee	
3. Water to Wine	2:1–3a,5b–11a,(11b[himself]),11c
4. The Official's Son Restored to Life	2:12a; 4:46b,(47),49b,50ac,51–52,(53),54
5. The Catch of Fish	21:(1),2–4,6–7,8b,11,14
6. Feeding the Multitude	6:1,(3),5,7–11,(12–13a),13b–14,15c,17–20,21b,(22,25)
Jerusalem	
7. Lazarus Resuscitated from Death	11:1,2c–3,7,11,15c,17,32–34,38–39a,41,43b–45
8. A Blind Man Sees	9:1,6–7,(8)
9. A Crippled Man Walks	5:2–3,5–9

These two possible miracle sources behind the Gospels of Mark and John, which share a few stories (Mark 6:33–52 and John 6:1–21; compare Secret Gospel of Mark and John 11:1–57), suggest that there were early Christians who came together and told stories about Jesus as a powerful miracle-working Holy Man in the way that some Jews looked at Solomon, Moses, Honi, or Hanina ben Dosa. Hellenists would have transferred motifs to these collections related to the hero or heroine (see Chapter Three). In other words, miracle stories originally demonstrated Jesus' authority and power. Curiously, a group of missionaries who challenged the apostle Paul's authority at Corinth (2 Cor 3:7–8; 10–13) appear to have stressed Jesus' power and claimed that Paul's emphasis on the humility ("weakness") of the cross and resurrection was misplaced. Most other early Christians, as we shall see, came to the reverse position: Neither sayings collections nor miracle collections were sufficient without the story of Jesus' suffering in the passion, his death, and his resurrection.

JESUS' PASSION, DEATH, AND RESURRECTION IN THE LIGHT OF SACRED TEXTS

Using the principles mentioned above in connection with the Lord's Supper, scholars have isolated what appears to be the earliest New Testament tradition about Jesus' death and resurrection in 1 Corinthians 15:3–9.

For *I handed on* to you as of first importance what I in turn had *received,*

that Christ died for our sins
                                   in accordance with the scriptures, and
that he was buried, and
that he was raised on the third day
                                   in accordance with the scriptures, and
that he appeared to Cephas, then to the twelve.

Then he appeared to more than five hundred brothers and sisters [Greek: brothers] at one time, most of whom are still alive, though some have died. Then he appeared to James, then to all the apostles. Last of all, as to one untimely born, he appeared also to me. For I am the least of the apostles, unfit to be called an apostle, because I persecuted the church of God.

Scholars see in the four "that-clauses" a traditional "creed" quoted by Paul. This judgment is supported not only by its formal qualities and Paul's tendency to quote traditions to make a point, but by the terms "delivered" and "received," the technical terms for handing on tradition in Judaism (*Sayings of the Fathers* 1:1) and used by Paul to recall the Lord's Supper tradition to the Corinthians (1 Cor 11:23; see above). Moreover, the passage contains a number of terms and phrases not characteristic of Paul:

1. the plural "sins" in the expression "for our sins";
2. "according to the scriptures";
3. the Greek tense (perfect passive) of "was raised" (compare 2 Tim 2:8);
4. "on the third day" and its form in Greek;
5. "the Twelve."

Some scholars also argue that these phrases contain "Semitisms," or Greek words that reflect Hebrew/Aramaic idiom. If so, the tradition may have gone back to early Palestinian Christianity, perhaps Jerusalem, where Cephas (Peter), the

Twelve, and Paul's addition of James and "all the apostles" had some authority. In any case, the creed was formed in the generation prior to the writing of 1 Corinthians (ca. 54 C.E.). It stresses Jesus' death, resurrection, and early appearances, and we shall now consider them.

The death and resurrection clauses in the creed are balanced by the expression "according to the scriptures." Jesus' suffering and death on the cross was a shameful event. Nonbelieving Jews responded, "Cursed is everyone who hangs on a tree [= also a cross]" (Gal 3:13). This sort of execution, reserved primarily for political criminals, demanded interpretation. Also, Jesus' rejection by the majority of the Jews also needed some sort of explanation. One solution was found in early Christian interpretations of scripture where God's plan was found.

In retelling stories from Jesus' passion, details were picked up from the fourth "messianic" song about Yahweh's Servant who suffered and died (Isa 52:13–53:12), especially that "He was despised and 'rejected' (*exoudenō*) by men" (Isa 53:3) and "His soul was 'delivered up' (*parradothē*) death" (Isa 53:12). Thus, Mark 9:12 says that it is written of the Son of Man that he will suffer many things and "be treated with contempt" (*exoudenēthē*) and the verb "I deliver up" (*paradidomi*) is used as a description of what happens to the betrayal of the Son of Man in Mark (9:31; 10:33; 14:21). While Markan redaction is present in all these passages, they also suggest that early Christian reflection about the suffering and death of the Servant in Isaiah was a way to explain Jesus' tragic suffering and death. Similarly, the Psalms, regarded in the first century as prophecies by David, were related to the Suffering Servant motif. The famous "rejected stone" that becomes the chief cornerstone from Psalm 118:22 (Mark 12:10), an important psalm for Jewish worship (the so-called Hallel), concludes the allegorical parable about the slaying of the vineyard owner's beloved son. The implication is clear: The suffering and death of the "beloved son" of the baptism and transfiguration (Mark 1:11 parallels; Mark 9:7 parallels) leads the Markan author to add the "rejected stone" testimony.

The details of the betrayal, the agony in the Garden of Gethsemane, and most especially the crucifixion show a great deal of reflection on the Psalms. The following chart will illustrate some of the more prominent allusions (there are others), especially the "Suffering Psalms" 22 and 69:

Mark	Psalm	Psalm Reference (NRSV)
14:18	41:9	"Even my bosom friend in whom I trusted, *who ate of my bread, has lifted the heel against me.*
14:34	42:6,11; 43:5	"*Why are you cast down, O my soul . . . ?*"
15:23	69:21	They gave me poison for food, and for my thirst they gave me *vinegar to drink.*"
15:24	22:18	". . .*they divide my clothes among themselves, and for my clothing they cast lots.*
15:29	22:7; 109:25	All who see me mock at me; they make mouths at me, they *shake their heads;*
15:34	22:1a	"*My God, my God, why have you forsaken me?*"
15:36	69:21	"They gave me poison for food, and for my thirst they gave me *vinegar to drink.*"

Christian groups were not alone in using sacred texts as prophecies for their own groups in their own time. For example, scribes at Qumran quoted passages of Scripture and interrupted them by brief interpretations beginning with the word *pishrō* ("its interpretation [is]") to show that the prophecies referred specifically to them. For example, they believed that the true messianic "Son of David"/"Son of God" of 2 Samuel 7:14 is also the messianic "Shoot of David" (Jer 23:5; 33:15: Zech 3:8; 6:12) or, in similar terms, the "Branch of David" that is fallen (Amos 9:11). He will arise at the End to sit on the throne of Mount Zion with the founder of the Qumran community, the Seeker of the Law!

With a slightly different method, early Christians used this very same scripture, combined with others, as a prophecy about Jesus who will also "arise," that is, be raised from the dead. It is certainly implied in Romans 1:3–4, an important fact since this passage contains one of those early pre-Pauline creeds. This one is about the "gospel concerning his [God's] son" Jesus:

> who was descended from David
>   according to the flesh
> and was declared to be Son of God with power
>   according to the spirit of holiness by resurrection from the dead.

This creed suggests the enthronement of the Davidic king as Son of God, a well-known theme in the Hebrew Scriptures. The difference is that the king is Jesus and the enthronement explicitly takes place in the heavens as a result of his resurrection. The parallelism of descent from David and Son of God shows reflection not only on 2 Samuel 7, but also Psalms 2, 89, 110, and 132, the so-called enthronement Psalms. Similar, but more complex, parallels are found in Acts 2 and 13:16b–41. The Qumran scribes interpreted the 2 Samuel 7 text as a prophecy about the "Messiah of Israel" ("Shoot of David") *yet to come;* the author of Acts incorporates and further interprets an interpretation of it as a prophecy already fulfilled in the resurrection of Jesus to become Lord and Christ, that is, the Messiah *recently come* (compare also Luke 1:32). What is behind all of this interpretative labor is the belief that not only Jesus' tragic death on the cross was the fulfillment of God's plan as foretold in the Scriptures, but his vindication in the resurrection.

The fourth element, or "that-clause," in the pre-Pauline creed in I Corinthians 15 (cited above) stresses appearances to Peter and "the Twelve," to which Paul adds five hundred brethren at one time (most of whom are still alive), James, "all the apostles," and Paul himself. The term "appeared" here comes from the verb "to see." Paul does not describe these experiences, though he associates a revelation of "the Son" with his call to become apostle to the Gentiles (Gal 1:12, 15–16; see Chapter Six). In Acts Paul's "Damascus road conversion" is described three times, but these stories are heavily overlaid with the author's interpretation (compare Acts 9:1–19a; 22:6–16; 26:12–18). Similarly, in the gospels no actual *narrative description* of Jesus' resurrection survives (see, however, the fragmentary, apocryphal Gospel of Peter). Rather, we have empty tomb, promise-of-appearance, and appearance stories, sometimes combined. On the one hand, these stories emphasize what we would call spiritual (rather than physical) elements: lack of recognition (Matt 28:17; Luke 24:16; John 20:14; 21:4), seeing a spirit (Luke 24:37), forbidding touch (John 20:17), sudden appearances, even behind closed doors (Luke 24:31; John 20:19, 26). Yet, Jesus' resurrection is clearly bodily, especially in Luke and John. From all the evidence, it is clear that appearance traditions played a stronger role in belief in Jesus' resurrection than the empty tomb. In the earliest traditions the honor of having "seen" Jesus first fell to Peter (1 Cor 15:5; Luke 24:34), though in other traditions it fell to one or more of the women.

The longer story about Jesus' last days in Jerusalem (Mark 11–15 parallels; John 13–19) contains a number of features common to all four gospels:

1. The entry to Jerusalem (Mark 11:1–10 parallels; John 12:12–19).
2. The Cleansing of the Temple (Mark 11:15–17 parallels; compare John 2:13–17).
3. A conspiracy by Jewish authorities at the time of Passover (Mark 14:1–2 parallels; John 11:47–12:1a).
4. The symbolic anointing of Jesus at Bethany (Mark 14:3–9 parallels; John 12:1b–8).
5. Betrayal by Judas (Mark 14:10–11; John 13:2, 27; 6:70–71).
6. Jesus' last supper with the disciples on the evening when he was arrested (Mark 14:12–25 parallels; John 13:1–30).
7. Retreat to Gethsemane, arrest by authorities accompanied by Judas, a scuffle, and loss of ear of slave of the high priest (Mark 14;32–52 parallels; John 18:1–12).
8. Jesus' hearing at night before Jewish authorities (Mark 14:53–65 parallels; John 18:13–24).
9. Peter's denial (Mark 14:26–31, 53–65; John 13:36–38; 18:13–24).
10. Appearance before the Roman governor, Pontius Pilate, the next morning (Mark 15:1–5; John 18:28–38).
11. Release of Barabbas (Mark 15:6–15 parallels; John 18:39–40).
12. Crucifixion on a Roman cross as "King of the Jews" between two others (Mark 15:22–32 parallels; John 19:17b–27).
13. The vinegar (Mark 15:36 parallels; John 19:28–29).
14. Women witness the crucifixion (Mark 15:40–41 parallels; John 19:25–27).
15. Burial by Joseph of Arimathea; the linen shroud (Mark 15:42–47; John 19:38–42).

Such overlaps between the synoptic gospels and John, a quite different gospel, raise the question: Did a longer "passion story source" that described Jesus' last days in Jerusalem circulate in the early church prior to the writing of gospels?

Three answers have been given to this question. Form critics have argued that there once existed a connected passion story in the *oral tradition* of the early church. A second view has arisen because of difficulties with this oral tradition theory. It is based on three observations. First, there are *exact verbal parallels* between the Gospels of Mark and John in the passion story:

Mark	John	Words or Phrases
14:3	12:3	ointment of pure nard
14:5	12:5	300 denarii [*denarius* = coin, about a day's wage]
14:54, 67	18:18, 25	Peter warming [*thermainomenos*] himself
14:54	18:15	Peter goes "into" the courtyard
15:14	19:15	the cry "crucify him" in the Greek imperative case
15:17	19:2, 5	the purple cloak
15:42	19:15	mention of the Day of Preparation

Second, the order of the Gospel of John is most distinctive where the Johannine author wants to develop his own point of view (for example, 18:4–9, 14; 18:28–19:16). Third, a special Markan literary technique is the placing of one account inside another ("sandwiching"; "intercalation"; see, for example, 3:20–35; 5:22–43; 6:7–30; 11:12–25; 14:53–72). The author of John appears to be following this Markan technique in the "trial" scene (18:19–24):

	Mark	John
Peter's denial	14:54	18:15–18
Trial	14:55–65	18:19–24
Peter's denial	14:66–72	18: 25–27

These points have led to the view that the author of *the Gospel of John had at some time read the Gospel of Mark,* but simply preferred his own presentation. Some scholars have tried to make a similar argument with the Gospels of Luke and John.

The third theory is that the synoptic gospels and the gospel of John are indebted to a *written* passion source. One suggestion is based on the analysis of the Fourth Gospel. We noted above that in the theory of three possible sources behind this gospel-miracle stories, discourses, and passion story—a miracle-story source has retained plausibility. R. Fortna goes further and argues that before the Johannine gospel was written, a passion source was added to the Signs Source to make a narrative Signs Gospel, somewhat analogous to Mark's balancing the miracle stories with a focus on Jesus' passion, suffering, and death. Here we outline what he considers to be in the pre-Johannine passion story, before it was added to the Signs Source, picking up the numbers that followed the Signs Source in the Signs Gospel (see above).

Unit	Passage
The Culmination of the Signs	
10. Jesus Restores the Temple	2:14–16,(17),18–19
11. The Officials' Conspiracy	11:47ac,48,49ab,50bc,53;12:37–40
12. Jesus Is Anointed at Bethany	12:1–5,7,(8)
13. The Messiah Enters Jerusalem	12:12–15
14. The Last Supper	Redaction; unrecoverable
The Passion	
15. Jesus Is Arrested	18:1–3,4c–5,10–12
16. With Peter at the High Priest's House	18:13,[24],15,16a,19a,(19b–21a),[21b],22[16b–18],25b–27
17. Jesus Is Tried by Pilate	18:28a–29a,[29b],33,[37b],38c–40[];19:6ac,13,14a,[1–3],16a
18. Jesus Is Executed and Buried	19:16b,(17a),17b–18,19b,20c,23–25a,28–30,[25b],31–34,36–38,40b–42
19. The Empty Tomb; Jesus Appears	20:1–3,6b,9–13a,15a–20,22
20. The Author's Summary	20:30–31

On the basis of linguistic arguments, lack of concern about Torah questions, and knowledge of Palestinian traditions, customs, and geography, Fortna thinks that the Signs Gospel arose in Jewish Christianity.

A second suggestion about a precanonical passion source has been suggested by J. D. Crossan, namely, passages from a *written "Cross Gospel" lie behind all four canonical gospels and the apocryphal Gospel of Peter.* Part of the *Gospel of Peter* was discovered in 1886–1887 and two fragments of it were unearthed in 1972. The latter have been dated to the late second or early third century C.E., suggesting a date of surviving manuscripts from the late second century C.E. and an original sometime earlier.

The *Gospel of Peter* is fragmentary, but can be outlined as follows:

Unit	Narrative Content	Passage
GP 1	**Crucifixion and Deposition**	**1:1–6:22**
GP 2	Joseph and Burial	6:23–24
GP 3	**Tomb and Guards**	**7:25–9:34**
GP 4	**Resurrection and Confession**	**9:35–11:49**
GP 5	Women and Youth	12:50–13:57
GP 6	Disciples and(?) Apparition	14:58–60

The following illustrates the parallels with the four gospels in only the first section of the *Gospel of Peter:*

Literary Elements	GPet	Matthew	Mark	Luke	John
Unit 1: Crucifixion and Deposition					
1. Hand Washing	1:1	27:24a	—	—	—
2. Herod's Role	1:1, 2	—	—	23:6–12	—
3. Jesus Handed Over	2:5b	27:26b	15:15b	23:25b	19:16
4. Eve of Passover	2:5b	—	—	—	19:14
5. Mockery	3:6–9	27:27–31	15:16–20	—	19:2–3
6. Between Criminals	4:10	27:38	15:27	23:33b	19:18
7. Superscription	4:11	27:37	15:26	23:38	19:19
8. Garments by Lot	4:12	27:35	15:24	23:34b	—
9. Criminal Confess.	4:13	—	—	23:39–43	—
10. Legs Unbroken	4:14	—	—	19:31–37	—
11. Darkness Starts	5:15	27:45a	15:33a	23:44a	—
12. Gall & Vinegar	5:16–17	27:34	15:23	—	—
	—	27:48	15:36	23:36	19:28–29
13. Darkness Stays	5:18	—	—	—	—
14. Cry of Jesus	5:19a	27:46	15:34	—	—
15. Jesus Dies	5:19b	27:50	15:37	23:46	19:30
16. Temple Veil Rent	5:20	27:51a	15:38	—	—
17. Deposition, Quake	6:21	27:51b	—	—	—
18. Darkness Ends	6:22	27:45b	15:33b	23:44b	—

We cannot go into all of Crossan's arguments, but close parallels in this section plus two others in boldface type from previous outline above (Units 3, 4) suggests to him that in these sections all four gospels and the *Gospel of Peter* were dependent on a lost source. The reconstruction of this source is limited to overlaps with the *Gospel of Peter* that begin only with the crucifixion in Mark 15. Yet, if the theory stands the test of criticism, it will be suggestive for a possible pre-Markan passion-resurrection *written* account that would explain the verbal similarities between the synoptic gospels and the Gospel of John.

THE APOCALYPTIC DISCOURSE: MARK 13

We come near to the literary form of a little apocalypse in Mark 13 and its paral-lels in Matthew 24 and Luke 21. Apocalyptic discourses, or speeches detailing the events to be expected when the End actually comes, are a feature of apocalyptic literature in general. There are examples in the Assumption of Moses 10; 1 Enoch 1:3–9; 1 Enoch 46:1–8; 4 Ezra 6:13–28. These discourses follow the pattern of apocalyptic expectation concerning the End, with variations depending on the particular form of the expectation held by the writer. There is usually a descrip-tion of the "woes," the climactic catastrophes marking the death throes of human history as now known. This is followed by an account of the form of God's escha-tological intervention, either directly or through an eschatological redeemer figure. Then there is an account of the final judgment itself and a description of the punishment of the wicked and the eternal blessedness of the people of God that will follow.

Such discourses were written in a certain way. The particular form of the apoca-lyptic hope held by the writer gave the overall pattern, but the actual content came from two sources: the Scriptures, that is, the writings held by the writer to be sacred, and the experience of the writer and the group he represented. The Scriptures themselves appeared in two ways: Either the author directly quoted or only alluded to them. Sometimes the writer wished to reinterpret an existing text; sometimes the writer made a connection between texts by association of ideas, of words, or even of the sounds of words (in the ancient world reading usually meant reading aloud, even to oneself, as in Acts 8:30 when Philip hears the Ethiopian reading Isaiah 53). So an apocalyptic discourse was usually a mosaic of scriptural quotations and allu-sions, together perhaps with some references to the experience of the writer and his community, generally couched in scriptural language.

The Christian apocalyptic discourses vary from this general pattern in that they include sections of parenesis in which the writer exhorts the readers directly. In this respect the discourses follow the Christian practice of combining parene-sis with proclamation.

Mark 13 has often been thought to rest on an earlier, perhaps Jewish, apoca-lyptic discourse. We now offer an analysis of Mark 13 following in the main that offered by Lars Hartman in *Prophecy Interpreted*.

13:1–5a An *introduction* to the discourse, composed by the evangelist Mark to give the discourse its present setting in the gospel as a whole.

13:5b–8 *The first section of the discourse proper.* It quotes Daniel 2:28–29, 45 (LXX: "this must take place"), 2 Chronicles 15:6; Isaiah 19:2 (the refer-ences to nation against nation and Kingdom against Kingdom), and alludes to Daniel 7:21; 9:26; 11:4–27; and perhaps 2:40 at various places.

13:9–13 *The first parenetical section.* It couches references to the actual and anticipated sufferings of Christians in language deliberately reminiscent of the sufferings of Jesus during his passion but also alluding of various scrip-tural passages (Dan 7:25; Ps 119:46; Dan 6:13–24). Verse 11b hints at Exo-dus 4:11–17, and verse 12 quotes Micah 7:2, 6.

13:14–20 *The second section of the discourse.* It quotes and reinterprets Daniel 11:31 and 12:11 in the reference to the "desolating sacrilege" (in Daniel this is the altar to Zeus set up in the Jerusalem Temple by the Syrians; in 2 Thessalonians 2:1–12 it might have referred to the emperor Caligula in an earlier period). Many modern commentators suggest Mark could have had in mind the events surrounding the defeat of the Jews and the destruction of Jerusalem and the Temple in 70, thus giving a clue as to the date of Mark. The command to "flee to the mountains" is a quote from Genesis 19:16, as is the command for the man in the field not to turn back in verse 16. In verse 19 the description of the tribulation quotes Daniel 12:1.

13:21–23 *The second parenetical section.* The reference to the false prophets uses language taken from Deuteronomy 13:1–5, but the whole addresses itself to concrete problems faced by the Christian church in a period of intense apocalyptic expectation.

13:24–27 *The third section of the discourse.* Here the quotations are frequent. Verse 24 quotes Joel 2:10 (the sun being darkened) and Isaiah 13:10 (the moon not giving its light). Verse 25 has the stars falling and the powers of heaven being shaken (from Isaiah 34:4). The Son of Man reference in verse 26 is from Daniel 7:13, and verse 27 is a mosaic of Deuteronomy 30:3–4 and Zechoriah 2:10 (in the LXX version). There are allusions to Isaiah 11:10–12; 27:13; and Daniel 7:14 at various places.

Verse 27 ends the apocalyptic discourse proper. The remaining verses 28–37 form a loose-knit, final parenetical section that does not contain a single scriptural quotation but does show a good deal of Christian traditional material. It was almost certainly added to the original discourse by Mark himself.

If this discourse existed prior to the Gospel of Mark, what its precise form and original date might have been is impossible to say. It is the nature of apocalyptic writers to interpret and reinterpret texts, even their own, so that any discourse text we have represents the version of it that came from the hand of the particular evangelist concerned.

NEW TESTAMENT CHRISTOLOGICAL HYMNS

"Christological hymns" are isolated by form critics on the basis of the six critical principles noted above in connection with Jesus' Last Meal (the Lord's Prayer). They portray Jesus as a divine Christ being who comes to earth and returns. They are called Christological hymns because in the early second century C.E. a Roman governor wrote that Christians were known to "recite a hymn antiphonally to Christ, as to a god" (for the full text, see the correspondence between Pliny, governor of Bithynia in Northern Asia Minor, and the emperor Trajan, see Chapter Thirteen).

Philippians 2:6–11

Who, though he was in the form of God,
    did not regard equality with God
    as something to be exploited,

But emptied himself,
    taking the form of a slave,
    being born in human likeness.
And being found in human form,
    he humbled himself,
    and became obedient to the point of death—
        [even death on a cross.]

Therefore God also highly exalted him
    and gave him the name
    that is above every name,
So that at the name of Jesus
    every knee should bend,
    in heaven and on earth and under earth,
And every tongue confess,
    that Jesus Christ is Lord,
    to the glory of God the Father.

Colossians 1:15–20 (Slightly rearranged)

He [Who] is the image of
    the invisible God,
    first born of all
    creation;
for in him all things
    in heaven and on earth
    were created . . .

All things have been created
through him and for him

Who is the beginning,
the firstborn from
the dead.

For in him all the
fullness of God was
pleased to dwell,
and through him God was
pleased to
reconcile to himself
all things.

    He himself is before all things,
    and in him all things hold together
    He is the head of the body (the church).

1 Peter 3:18–19, 22

He was put to death
    in the flesh,
But made alive
    in the spirit,

In which also he went
    and made a proclamation
    to the spirits in prison.

Who has gone into heaven,
and is at the right hand of God,
with angels, authorities,
and powers made subject to him.

1 Timothy 3:16

Was manifested in the flesh,
Was vindicated by the spirit,
Was seen by angels,
Was proclaimed among the
    nations,
Was believed on in the world,
Was taken up into glory.

Hebrews 1:3

He (Who) is the reflection of God's glory
and the exact imprint of God's very being,
and he sustains all things by his powerful word.

When he had made purification for sins,
He sat down at the right hand of the Majesty on high,
Having become . . . superior to the angels . . . .

As we stated in Chapter Four, these hymns portray the pattern of a Redeemer who descends to the earth from a higher sphere, achieves his redemptive purpose on earth, and ascends to the higher, heavenly sphere. The pattern reflects the Wisdom myth (see Chapter Three), but it also occurs where Christianity has come in contact with Gentiles. The Q materials, early Johannine strata, and the book of Acts show that Greeks were admitted to Christianity at a relatively early date.

SUMMARY

In this chapter we have attempted to look at the some of earliest Christian communities apart from Paul and their beliefs and practices. Because the book of Acts is from a later time and highly interpreted, we have used critical reconstructions of various types of sayings and narratives, as well as the pregospel tendency to group them. The social level of earliest Christianity in Palestine was predominantly from the peasant classes. Christians from these classes continued to meet in houses on special occasions, such as common meals and religious celebrations. At such times, the Jesus traditions were transmitted, supplemented, and interpreted.

Some of those traditions were sayings of Jesus and early Christian prophets that gave guidance to the groups that preserved them. Typical were wisdom sayings, parables, and prophetic sayings, all of which became increasingly apocalyptic as the early Christian groups encountered opposition. Other traditions were narratives, such as miracle stories that demonstrated Jesus' power and anecdotes about his life and controversies. There were also traditions about his suffering, death, and resurrection as fulfillment of prophecy, and stories about his last days in Jerusalem. Finally, we can see the emergence of apocalypses about judgment of evil persons and salvation of good persons and Christological hymns that give Jesus the highest possible evaluation as one descended from God.

Not all early Christians accepted all of these traditions; rather, they tended to represent various kinds of groups. Some of them, of course, converged and were incorporated in the canonical gospels. Others were taken up by the apostle Paul, and to his life and thought we now turn.

FURTHER READING

Social Structures and Groups

ABD: "Call Stories" (A. J. Droge); "Poor, Poverty" (T. D. Hanks); "Worship, Early Christian" (D. E. Aune).

G. and J. Lenski, *Human Societies*. 5th ed.

D. Fiensy, *The Land Is Mine. The Social History of Palestine in the Herodian Period.*

J. D. Crossan, *The Historical Jesus. The Life of a Mediterranean Jewish Peasant.*

R. Horsley, *Sociology and the Jesus Movement.*

B. Mack, *A Myth of Innocence. Mark and Christian Origins.*

D. Oakman, *Jesus and the Economic Questions of His Day.*

G. Theissen, *Sociology of Early Palestinian Christianity.*

W. Meeks, *The First Urban Christians. The Social World of the Apostle Paul.*

Baptism; Early Christian Meals; The Lord's Supper

ABD: "Agape Meal" (E. Ferguson); "Baptism" (L. Hartman); "Last Supper" (R. F. O'Toole); "Lord's Supper" (H. J. Klauck, trans. D. Ewert); "Meal Customs (Greco-Roman)" (D. E. Smith); "Meal Customs (Sacred Meals)" (D. E. Smith); "Messianic Banquet" (D. E. Smith).

G. Freely-Harnik, *Lord's Table: Eucharist and Passover in Early Christianity.*

J. Jeremias, *The Eucharistic Words of Jesus.*

W. Meeks, *The First Urban Christians. The Social World of the Apostle Paul.*

N. Perrin, *Rediscovering the Teaching of Jesus.*

D. E. Smith, "The Historical Jesus at Table," *Seminar Papers SBL 1989,* pp. 466–486.

Parables and Early Christian Parable Interpretation; Preaching

ABD: "Parable" (J. D. Crossan); "Preaching" (F. B. Craddock).

J. D. Crossan, *In Parables. The Challenge of the Historical Jesus.*

R. W. Funk, B. B. Scott, and J. R. Butts, *The Parables of Jesus.*

J. Jeremias, *The Parables of Jesus.*

J. W. Miller, *Step by Step Through the Parables.*

B. B. Scott, *Hear Then the Parable. A Commentary on the Parables of Jesus.*

Early Christian Wisdom

ABD: "Sayings of Jesus (Oxyrhynchus)" (S. K. Brown).

D. Crossan, *In Fragments. The Aphorisms of Jesus.*

J. Kloppenborg, *The Formation of Q: Trajectories in Ancient Wisdom Sources.*

J. M. Robinson and H. Koester, *Trajectories Through Early Christianity.*

B. Mack, *A Myth of Innocence.*

R. A. Piper, *Wisdom in the Q-tradition. The Aphoristic Teaching of Jesus.*

Early Christian Prophecy

ABD: "Prophecy (Early Christian)" (M. E. Boring).

IDB Suppl: "Prophecy in Ancient Israel" (M. J. Buss); "Prophecy in the Ancient Near East" (H. B. Huffmon); "Prophecy in the Early Church" (E. E. Ellis).

D. Aune, *Prophecy in Early Christianity and the Ancient Mediterranean World.*

M. E. Boring, *Sayings of the Risen Jesus. Christian Prophecy in the Synoptic Tradition.*

D. Hill, *New Testament Prophecy.*

G. Theissen, *The Sociology of Early Palestinian Christianity.*

Early Christian Apocalyptic

ABD: "Early Christian Apocalypticism" (A. Yarbro Collins); "Eschatology (Early Christian)" (D. E. Aune); "False Apostles" (D. T. Watson); "False Christs" (D. T. Watson); "Gospels, Little Apocalypse in the" (G. R. Beasley–Murray).

IDB: "Apocalypticism" (M. Rist).

IDB Suppl.: pp. 28–34, "Apocalypticism" (P. D. Hanson).

P. Hanson, *The Dawn of Apocalyptic.*

L. Hartman, *Prophecy Interpreted: The Formation of Some Jewish Apocalyptic Texts and of the Eschatological Discourse Mark 13 par.*

K. Koch, *The Rediscovery of Apocalyptic.*

Journal for Theology and the Church, vol. 6, Apocalypticism, R. Funk, ed.

W. Schmithals, *The Apocalyptic Movement: Introduction.*

Interpretation, vol. 25, no. 4 (October 1971).

The Catholic Biblical Quarterly, vol. 39 (1977).

Early Christian Miracles and Miracle Collections

ABD: "Medicine and Healing" (H. C. Kee); "Miracle (NT)" (H. E. Remus); "Signs/Semeia Source" (R. T. Fortna).

P. J. Achtemeier, "Toward the Isolation of Pre–Markan Miracle Catenae," *Journal of Biblical Literature* 89 (1970), pp. 265–91.

————, "The Origin and Function of the Pre–Marcan Miracle Catenae," *Journal of Biblical Literature* 91 (1972) pp. 198–221.

————, *The Gospel of Signs.*

————, R. T. Fortna, *The Fourth Gospel and Its Predecessor. From Narrative Source to Present Gospel.*

H. C. Kee, *Medicine, Miracle, and Magic in the New Testament.*

R. Kysar, *John, the Maverick Gospel.*

D. M. Smith, "The Setting and Shape of a Johannine Narrative Source," *Journal of Biblical Literature* 95 (1976), pp. 231–41.

G. Theissen, *The Miracle Stories of the Early Christian Tradition.*

Anecdotes

ABD: "Apophthegm" (V. K. Robbins).

R. Bultmann, *History of the Synoptic Tradition.*

D. Daube, *The New Testament and Rabbinic Judaism.*

J. Dewey, "The Literary Structure of the Controversy Stories in Mark 2:1–3:6," *Journal of Biblical Literature* 92 (1973), pp. 394–401.

B. Mack and V. Robbins, *Patterns of Persuasion in the Gospels.*

V. Robbins, "The Chreia." Pp. 1–23 in *Greco–Roman Literature and the New Testament: Selected Forms and Genres.*

R. Tannehill, "Introduction: The Pronouncement Story and Its Types," *Semeia* 21 (1981), pp. 1–13.

Q

ABD: "Q (Gospel Source)" (C. M. Tuckett).

H. Kee, *Jesus in History*, pp. 76–120.

R. A. Edwards, "An Approach to the Theology of Q," *Journal of Religion*, 51 (1971), pp. 247–69.

————, *A Theology of Q*.

A. Jacobson, *The First Gospel. An Introduction to Q*.

J. Kloppenborg, *The Formation of Q*.

Passion, Death, and Resurrection Accounts; Scripture Fulfillment

ABD: "Christ, Death of" (F. J. Matera); "New Testament, OT Quotations in the" (H. Hübner); "Passion Narratives" (G. W. E. Nickelsburg); "Trial of Jesus" (T. Pendergast).

J. D. Crossan, *Four Other Gospels*.

————, *The Cross That Spoke. The Origins of the Passion Narrative*.

R. T. Fortna, *The Fourth Gospel and Its Predecessor. From Narrative Source to Present Gospel*.

E. Lohse, *History of the Suffering and Death of Jesus Christ*.

New Testament Christological Hymns, Creeds, Confessions, Prayers

ABD: "Christ" (M. De Jonge); "Christology (NT)" (J. D. G. Dunn); "Hymns, Early Christian" (M. A. Bichsel); "Jesus, Worship of" (R. Bauckham); "Prayer in Early Judaism" (J. H. Charlesworth).

D. Duling, *Jesus Christ Through History*, pp. 43–52.

A. M. Hunter, *Paul and His Predecessors*.

L. Hurtado, *One God, One Lord*.

C. Roetzel, *The Letters of Paul*.

J. T. Sanders, *The New Testament Christological Hymns*.

The Apostle Paul as portrayed in a mosaic medallion in the Chapel of St. Andrew in the Archbishop's Palace, Ravenna, Italy. An imaginative description of Paul in the apocryphal *Acts of Paul (and Thecla)* (second century C.E.) reads: "…a man small of stature, with a bald head and crooked legs, in a good state of body, with eyebrows meeting and nose somewhat hooked, full of friendliness; for now he appeared like a man, and now he had the face of an angel" (W. Schneemelcher in E. Hennecke and W. Schneemelcher, *New Testament Apocrypha*, trans. R. McL. Wilson, vol. 2, p. 354).

CHAPTER SIX

PAUL: APOSTLE TO THE GENTILES

Paul is a major figure in early Christianity. His letters, plus those the later church believed he wrote, make up over one-fourth of the New Testament, and over one-half of the lengthy Acts of the Apostles (twenty-eight chapters) is given over to the life, journeys, and speeches of this leading New Testament missionary. In terms of sheer bulk of material, Paul literally dominates the New Testament. Moreover, he hammered out an understanding of the Christian faith that is one of the great foundations for Christian theological history. At the same time, some things in his writings, as the author of 2 Peter knew, are "hard to understand" (2 Pet 3:16), and they have always been, like Paul himself, the occasion of controversy. While he inspired many of the church's greatest thinkers and reformers, Augustine, Luther, Calvin, and Wesley, he has also been accused in more recent times of distorting Jesus' simple message, of laying the groundwork for Christian anti-Judaism, and of perpetuating chauvinistic attitudes about race, politics, sex, and the status of women! A study of Paul and his letters can be as exasperating as it is interesting and challenging, but it can hardly be doubted that one is in the presence of a religious genius.

In this chapter we shall attempt to lay some groundwork for the study of Paul's letters. Our first objective will be to evaluate the sources for his life and thought, especially his undisputed letters in relation to the Acts of the Apostles. Then we shall attempt to establish a relative chronology for his career and give a sketch of his life stressing his background, his "conversion" and call, and his activity as a missionary. In addition, we shall discuss Paul's basis for authority both in relation to the church at Jerusalem and to the mission churches he founded, taking into account his opponents and the general social world of Pauline mission communities. Finally, we shall present the structure of his letters in comparison to the letters of antiquity and indicate some of the early Christian traditions that he incorporated.

SOURCES FOR THE LIFE AND THOUGHT OF PAUL

In order to develop a chronology for the outline of Paul's life and thought, it will be helpful first to reconstruct the sequence of his undisputed letters and parts of letters in them. This reconstruction can be compared to autobiographical comments that Paul makes in the letters and the stories about Paul in Acts. Only then will it be possible to develop a chronology.

The church came to believe that Paul wrote fourteen letters, thirteen of which bear his name (The Letter to the Hebrews excepted). It also came to believe that the Acts of the Apostles portrayed the course of his life from his first encounter with Christianity up to his imprisonment in Rome. Both of these assumptions can be briefly reviewed.

You will recall from Chapter Four that modern scholars do not think that Paul wrote (or dictated to his secretary) all fourteen letters attributed to him. This is evidence for the phenomenon of pseudonymity. On the basis of language, style, and content, the letters can be ranked on an ascending scale of probability, from the least likely to have been written by Paul to those which are undisputed. Our conclusions about those letters were:

Pauline (50s)	Pauline School (70–90)	Pauline School (100–125)	Non-Pauline (80–90)
1 Thessalonians	2 Thessalonians	1 Timothy	Hebrews
1 Corinthians	Colossians	2 Timothy	
2 Corinthians	Ephesians	Titus	
Philippians			
Philemon			
Galatians			
Romans			

The Letter to the Hebrews is almost universally rejected as Paul's letter, especially because its dominant theme, the heavenly high priesthood of Christ, is not found in the rest of the letters. Indeed, the letter is not really a letter and does not bear Paul's name. We may safely exclude it from the authentic Pauline letters; we shall take it up separately in Chapter Eight.

Only slightly more debatable are the three "Pastoral Letters," 1 Timothy, 2 Timothy, and Titus. In addition to serious problems of language and style, these letters testify to a highly developed church organization not found in the others, but similar to that found in Church Fathers from the turn of the first century. They are supposed to have been written by Paul as pastoral advice to his coworkers, Timothy in Ephesus (1 Tim 1:3) and Titus on the island of Crete (Titus 1:5), but especially the latter cannot be coordinated with what is otherwise known about Paul's life unless we accept the unproven theory that he was released from prison in Rome to carry out a further mission. Most contemporary scholars think they date from the early second century.

Finally, we note 2 Thessalonians, Colossians, and Ephesians. Beginning with the last, Ephesians contains many differences from the undisputed letters in language, style, and content. It also lacks Paul's usual personal touch, and the reference to Ephesus in 1:1 is not present in our earliest manuscripts. Moreover, as we demonstrated in Chapter Four, Ephesians is literarily dependent on Colossians.

Many scholars would accept the second book, Colossians, despite its distinctive vocabulary and ideas in comparison with the undisputed letters. As for 2 Thessalonians, we are clearly close to Paul and many hold it to be Paul's letter. The difficulty is that it seems to imitate 1 Thessalonians and at the same time it has a slightly different eschatology. Thus, those who do not accept these six letters as coming from Paul suggest that they may well emanate from a Pauline School, and they call them "deutero [secondary]-Pauline letters." We shall give more evidence in Chapters Eight and Fourteen.

Seven of the fourteen letters—Hebrews, 1 Timothy, 2 Timothy, Titus, Ephesians, Colossians, and 2 Thessalonians—will *not* be used as sources for the life and thought of Paul himself. Seven undisputed letters remain:

1. 1 Thessalonians
2. 1 Corinthians
3. 2 Corinthians
4. Philippians
5. Philemon
6. Galatians
7. Romans

Six of these letters are written to congregations in Asia Minor (Galatia), Macedonia or northern Greece (Thessalonica, Philippi), Achaia or southern Greece (Corinth), and Italy (Rome). Philemon purports to be written to a person, though it is clearly intended to be read to a congregation (Phlm 2, 3; "you" in verse 3 is plural).

We have removed seven letters from Paul. The remaining seven are actually more than seven, because at least one of them (2 Corinthians), probably another (Philippians), and possibly a third (Romans), are thought to contain fragments from other Pauline letters. The hypothesis about letter fragments and their sequence in relation to the letters themselves is very important for establishing a chronology for Paul's life and thought. Before attempting to summarize the relative sequence of letters and letter fragments, let us illustrate the problem briefly.

The most striking features about Paul's letters are radical interruptions in the flow of thought. Some of these can be explained by his own deviations in the course of his argument. In a very few instances, there are later insertions by a student of Paul (or perhaps even a later scribe), for example, the attitude that women should keep silent in the churches (1 Cor 14:33b–36; compare 1 Tim 2:11–15). Still others show signs of being parts of letters that are accidentally misplaced. In these cases, one can pick up the flow of thought a few verses, or even chapters, later. Note, for example, how the flow of thought in 2 Corinthians 6:11–13 picks up again in 2 Corinthians 7:2–4:

2 Cor 6:11–13: Our mouth is open to you, Corinthians; our heart is wide. You are not restricted by us, but you are restricted in your affections. In return—I speak as to children—widen your hearts also.

2 Cor 7:2–4: Open your hearts to us; we have wronged no one, we have corrupted no one, we have taken advantage of no one. I do not say this to condemn you, for I said before that you are in our hearts, to die together and to live together. I have great confidence in you; I have great pride in you; I am filled with comfort. With all our affliction, I am overjoyed.

In placing these passages after each other, we have left out 2 Corinthians 6:14–7:1. This omitted section contains language and ideas characteristic of the Dead Sea Scrolls, but very uncharacteristic of Paul:

1. "Belial" [Greek: Beliar] is a name for the Prince of Demons;
2. light-darkness dualism;
3. the particular way that the term "righteousness" is used;
4. Christian separation from unbelievers.

Many scholars conclude that it is a non-Pauline fragment that found its way into the letter when all of Paul's letters were brought together as a collection at the end of the first century (see Chapter Four, the canon of the New Testament). If we omit these few verses and read the text continuously as above, we can observe that it flows quite naturally as a discussion about Paul's relations with the Corinthians.

Another example of the same type is the following:

2 Cor 2:12–13: When I came to Troas to preach the gospel of Christ, a door was opened for me in the Lord; but my mind could not rest because I did not find my brother Titus there. So I took leave of them and went on to *Macedonia.*

2 Cor 7:5–6: For even when we came into *Macedonia,* our bodies had no rest but we were afflicted at every turn—fighting without and fear within. But God, who comforts the downcast, comforted us by the coming of Titus. . . .

Here we have omitted a rather long section, 2 Corinthians 2:14–7:4, which already incorporates the non-Pauline, Qumran-type fragment just discussed (6:14–7:1). In this longer section, the Corinthians are still loyal to Paul, but relations are deteriorating. If we read from 2 Corinthians 2:12–13 on to 2 Corinthians 7:5–7, again the flow of thought progresses quite naturally. In this flow, relations between Paul and the Corinthians are being patched up.

We also find mentioned a "tearful letter" illustrating angry comments by Paul (compare 2 Cor 2:3–4; 7:8). Many scholars identify this letter with Paul's angry self-defense against opponents who hold a different view of Jesus in 2 Cor 10–13 (see Chapter Five, "Miracles and Miracle Collections").

To these three letter fragments, we add 2 Corinthians 8, which takes up a new theme, the collection of money for the poor among the saints at Jerusalem, and 2 Corinthians 9, which discusses the collection as though it had not been mentioned in chapter 8! We can be fairly sure of the logical sequence of Paul's references to the gathering the collection for the poor among the saints in Jerusalem, and thus of the sequence of chapters 8 and 9:

1 Corinthians 16:1–4
2 Corinthians 8
2 Corinthians 9
Romans 15:25–29

The fragments of 2 Corinthians can now be rearranged in chronological sequence:

Five Letter Fragments in 2 Corinthians

1. 2:14–7:4 (minus 6:14–7:1)   deteriorating relations
2. 10–13, a "tearful letter"   hostile relations
3. 1:1–2:13 and 7:5–17   reconciling relations
4. 8   a collection note
5. 9   another collection note

If we attempt to place the remaining parts of the Corinthian letters and these five letter fragments in a sequence with at least two other letters to the Corinthians mentioned by Paul, but lost, and then combine them with what we know about the movements of Paul and his coworkers, we can get a picture of Paul's relations with the Corinthian Christians (leaving out the non-Pauline fragment, 2 Cor 6:14–7:1):

1. Paul leaves Corinth and resides in Ephesus (1 Cor 16:8); eventually he writes the "previous letter" (1 Cor 5:9), which is lost.	Letter I (lost)
2. There comes back an oral report from 'Chloe's people" about factions at Corinth (1 Cor 1:11).	
3. There also arrives a letter asking Paul about problems at Corinth (1 Cor 7:1), perhaps brought by Fortunatus, Stephanus, and Achaicus (1 Cor 16:17).	A Letter From Corinth
4. Paul responds with 1 Corinthians (minus a later addition, 1 Cor 14:33b–36). Timothy's visit is announced (1 Cor 4:17; 16:10; compare Acts 19:22). Paul also gives instructions about the collection (1 Cor 16:1–4).	Letter II (1 Cor)
5. Paul sends Titus to hurry up the collection (2 Cor 8:5–6, 10; 9:2; 12:18).	
6. Paul learns (from Timothy or Titus?) that Jewish Christian missionaries come to Corinth, challenge Paul's authority, and say that he lacks charisma (3:1; 11:4–5, 13, 22; 12:11).	
7. Paul writes 2 Corinthians 2:14–7:4 (minus 6:14–7:1); the church is still loyal, but relations are deteriorating.	Letter III (2 Cor 2:14– 6:13; 7:2-4)
8. Paul now makes a "painful visit" (2 Cor 2:1; 12:14; 12:21; 13:1), which includes an attack against him by a member of the church (2:5; 7:12).	
9. Paul returns to Ephesus and writes the "tearful letter" defending himself against the Jewish Christian missionaries (2 Cor 2:3–4; 7:8). This was probably 2 Cor 10–13 and may have been delivered by Titus (2 Cor 2:12–13; 7:5–7).	Letter IV (2 Cor 10–13)

10. Paul was apparently imprisoned in Ephesus at this time (2 Cor 1:8–11), and it was probably from there that he wrote three letters to Philippi (Phil 4:10–20; Phil 1:1–3:1; Phil 3:2–4:9) and another to Philemon at Colossae.

    (four letters not written to Corinth)

11. Paul is released from prison, heads north to Troas then to Macedonia to meet Titus, who reports that the situation at Corinth has much improved (2:12–13; 7:5–16).

12. Paul writes 2 Corinthians 1:1–2:13; 7:5–16, a letter of reconciliation that clarifies why Paul has not yet visited them on his way to Macedonia, and what to do about the person who had so offended Paul (2 Cor 1:15–2:4; 2:5–11).

    Letter V (2 Cor 1:1–2:13; 7:5–16)

13. Paul now writes 2 Corinthians 8 (about the collection) which he sends with Titus from Macedonia.

    Letter VI (2 Cor 8)

14. Leaving Macedonia, Paul writes 2 Corinthians 9 about the collection to all the Christians of Achaia (Greece).

    Letter VII (2 Cor 9)

15. Paul visits Corinth (compare Acts 20:2–3).

The final step in this reconstructive process is to add in the other Pauline letters in a hypothetical sequence. Based on the general conviction that 1 Thessalonians is Paul's earliest letter because of its apocalyptic orientation, that Paul wrote letters (letter fragments) to the Philippians and to Philemon while imprisoned at Ephesus (probably not later, at Caesarea or Rome; compare 2 Cor 1:8–11; Phil 1:12–26), and that Galatians is relatively late because of its similarity to Romans, his last letter (Rom 15:24–29), we may place Paul's letters and letter fragments in the following tentative order:

Letter	Origin
1. 1 Thessalonians (minus 2:13–16?)	Corinth: (2:2; 3:1, 6)
2. "Previous letter" to Corinth (1 Cor 5:9)	Ephesus?
3. 1 Corinthians (minus 14:33b–36)	Ephesus (16:8)
4. 2 Corinthians 2:14–6:13; 7:2–4 (minus 6:14–7:1)	Ephesus?
5. "Tearful letter"=2 Cor 10–13	Ephesus?
6. Philippians 4:10–20	Ephesus
7. Philippians 1:1–3:1 (4:4–7? 4:21–23?)	Ephesus

8. Philippians 3:2–4:9	Ephesus (perhaps earliest Phil fragment)
9. Philemon	Ephesus
10. 2 Corinthians 1:1–2:13; 7:5–16	Macedonia (7:5)
11. 2 Corinthians 8	Macedonia (8:1)
12. 2 Corinthians 9 (to Cenchreae near Corinth?)	Macedonia (9:2,4)
13. Galatians (to north Galatia? compare 4:13)	Macedonia?
14. Romans 1–15	Corinth? (15:25–26)
15. Romans 16 (to Ephesus? compare 16:3; 1 Cor 116:19)	Corinth?

We are finally in a position to attempt a reconstruction of the chronology of Paul's life based on the sequence of his letters, his occasional autobiographical comments, and the Acts of the Apostles. As we demonstrated in Chapter Four, Acts alone cannot be used, because some sections are legendary and because Paul's speeches there are free compositions of the author, as was customary in ancient historical writing. Yet, Acts can be used as a secondary source for various aspects of Paul's life, if interpreted with critical caution.

THE LIFE OF PAUL

Having attempted to evaluate and reorganize the sources for Paul's life into a sequence, we can now attempt to be more precise about the course of his career. Given the nature of our sources, it is important to anchor the chronology of the life of Paul as best possible in world history.

A Possible Chronology of Paul's Career

You will recall from Chapter Four that according to Acts 18:11, Paul had been in Corinth eighteen months when, as a result of Jewish opposition, he was taken before the proconsular governor Gallio. Scholarly evaluation of the **Gallio Inscription** places the period of Gallio's office most probably from about July 1, 51, to July 1, 52. Paul would have arrived in Corinth, then, sometime in *49 or 50 C.E.* This date seems to be confirmed by the Roman historian Suetonius in his *Life of Claudius* 25, for he speaks of **the expulsion of "the Jews" from Rome,** an event that can be dated in 49 **(Edict of Claudius)**. Acts 18:2, just prior to Paul's going before Gallio, states that Aquila and his wife, Priscilla, Jewish Christians, had recently come to Corinth because of Claudius' expulsion of the Jews from Rome.

To these two pieces of evidence we can now add a third. In 2 Corinthians 11:32 Paul mentions that he escaped from the governor of Damascus under King Aretas. This refers to **King Aretas IV of Nabatea,** a monarch who ruled a powerful kingdom of Arabs to the east and south of Palestine (Josephus *Antiquities* 1.12.4; 16.9.4; 18.5.1–2), with its capital at Petra (in modern Jordan, the location of the final scenes of *Indiana Jones and the Last Crusade*). Paul's conversion and call took place in Aretas' kingdom (compare Gal 1:17–18). Since the reign of Aretas IV was 9 to 40 C.E., Paul was in the region of Damascus after the death of Jesus, but prior to 40.

According to Paul's autobiographical statements in Galatians, after his "conversion" (see below) he had been in Damascus three years (or by Jewish reckoning at least two) and in Syria and Cilicia fourteen years (or by Jewish reckoning at least thirteen), a total of seventeen (or at least fifteen)—if the three is not to be included in the fourteen (Gal 1:17–18; 2:1). Then he went to the Jerusalem Conference, next to Antioch, and eventually to Macedonia and Achaia (modern Greece). If he arrived at Corinth about 49/50 C.E., his conversion and call occurred in the early thirties, fourteen to seventeen years earlier. A chronology of Paul's life would look like this:

Event	Approximate Date
Paul's date of birth	unknown (probably about the beginning of the century)
Crucifixion of Jesus	ca. 30?
Conversion and call	ca. 32 (perhaps as late as 36)
Jerusalem Conference	48(49?)
Paul first in Corinth	49/50 (winter) until summer of 51 about 1½ years (Acts 18:11-12)
Paul in Ephesus	probably 52–55
Last stay in Macedonia and Greece	(Acts 19:1, 10, 22)
Journey to Jerusalem and arrest	probably winter of 55/56
Taken prisoner to Rome	spring of 56
Two years' imprisonment in Rome	probably 58
	probably 58–60 (compare Acts 28–30)
Martyrdom under Nero	60–64?

This chronology is tentative; there are other, somewhat similar reconstructions. Also, it should be realized that its final dates are based on comments in the book of Acts and an early church tradition that Paul was martyred in Rome (*1 Clement* 5:7; 6:1). Finally, the chronology assumes that Paul was not released to carry on a mission in Spain and did not write the "Pastoral Epistles" (above; see Chapter Four).

A Brief Sketch of Paul's Life

Having evaluated the sources for Paul's life and attempted something of a chronology, we shall now fill in the gaps and present a general sketch of his life. Again, the letters will be primary sources, but occasional details can be furnished where the data of Acts will permit.

Background

Paul was a person of three interacting worlds. He was born, reared, and active in a strongly Hellenistic *Greek* urban environment. He was the son of a proud *Jewish* family living in the Diaspora and probably had some formal education in Jerusalem. He became a *Christian* when, as he said, God revealed his Son to him and called him to preach the good news of Jesus Christ to the Gentiles (Gal 1:15–16). In other words, he was a Hellenist, a Jew, and a Christian all at once—a Hellenistic Jewish Christian—a combination that made him especially suited for his important role as apostle to the Gentiles.

According to Acts, Paul was born in **Tarsus,** the capital of Cilicia in Asia Minor. Tarsus was a flourishing commercial city and contained many of the religions prevalent throughout the Greco-Roman world. It also had a well-known Stoic philosophical school. In fact, Tarsus rivaled Athens and Rome as an educational center. Paul's letters show that he had a formal Greek education, for he writes (and dictates) Greek well and displays a knowledge of Greek rhetorical devices especially characteristic of Cynic-Stoic preachers of the period. In some of his ethical discussions, Paul cites lists of virtues and vices of the type known in Cynic-Stoic schools. He also accepts from tradition, perpetuates, and develops views of Jesus Christ that would ring familiar to almost any person living in the broader Greco-Roman world. Anyone who knew the mystery religions would not be surprised to hear of dying and rising with Christ (Rom 6:5). Others would find the tradition that Jesus Christ was in the form of God, took the form of a servant, and was highly exalted by God (Phil 2:6–11) a congenial way of thinking not unlike the notion of descending-ascending redeemers widely known. In the light of this orientation, it is no surprise that Paul himself uses the Greek form of his name, Paul, not the Hebrew form, Saul (contrast Acts 9:4, 17; 13:9; 22:7, 13; 26:14).

If Paul was deeply indebted to his Hellenistic background, he was no less proud of his Jewish heritage. His most elaborate comment about it occurs in Philippians 3:5–6: "circumcised on the eighth day, of the people of Israel, of the tribe of Benjamin, a Hebrew born of Hebrews; as to the law a Pharisee, as to zeal a persecutor of the church, as to righteousness under the law blameless" (compare 2 Cor 11:22; Rom 9:3–5; 11:1). This important statement says a great deal about what Paul thought of his Jewishness: He considered himself a very good Jew. In this connection Acts comments that he was brought up in the city of Jerusalem and educated "at the feet of Gamaliel" (22:3), a famous Jerusalem rabbi of the period. How are these comments to be related to the "Paul of Tarsus" tradition? Clearly we can perceive the tendency of Luke-Acts to orient Paul to Jerusalem Judaism.

Is there any evidence in Paul's letters that would reflect a formal Jewish academic, or "rabbinic," training, especially with regard to his view of the Torah or, more generally, Scripture and its interpretation? Would Paul have passed his final exams at the rabbinical college? This issue has been hotly debated. Some have said "no," arguing that Paul had no formal education, that his interpretation of Scripture does not adhere to the text enough to be rabbinic, and that the Gamaliel tradition is another example of romantic historicizing and tendentiousness on the part of the author of Luke-Acts. Others, however, have argued that Paul's indebtedness to rabbinic-type Biblical interpretation is quite strong, and that he was in the main rabbinic, despite his view of Torah. The question is complicated by the problem that most of our sources for understanding rabbinic interpretation are later than the New Testament; moreover, one may well ask difficult questions such as the way a Diaspora Pharisee might interpret the Septuagint to make arguments to largely, but not exclusively, Greek Christians. Certainly, Paul was heavily influenced by his Greek background and education; but there is also evidence for connections with at least an early form of rabbinic Judaism and, indeed, certain aspects of Paul's thought can be illuminated by what are known to be Palestinian Jewish sources. Most important in this regard is the strong apocalyptic orientation in much of Paul's writing. It is safe to say, therefore, that one component in Paul's thought can be rooted in his Jewish background and education.

Before leaving Paul's background, there is one practical factor that will become important for his mission: his trade. Paul was an artisan. He worked with his hands (1 Cor 4:12). The author of Luke-Acts identifies his trade as a **tentmaker** (Acts 18:3), that is, a leather worker who made tents and other leather products. Paul probably learned his trade from his father as was characteristic in the Greco-Roman world, and this apprenticeship might have been given an impetus by the rabbinical ideal of combining learning with a worldly occupation. In Paul's society, the life of an artisan was not easy. One recent author has concluded, "Stigmatized as slavish, uneducated, and often useless, artisans, to judge from scattered references, were frequently reviled or abused, often victimized, seldom if ever invited to dinner, never accorded status, and even excluded from one Stoic utopia. Paul's own statements accord well this general description" (R. Hock, *Tentmaking*, p. 36). Such a life would have been relieved by the hospitality of those with whom he stayed and the intellectual discussions shared on journeys with traveling companions, in inns, homes, and possibly the workshop, as was the custom among the Cynics. As we shall see, Paul's desire to support himself led to a particular view of his role as missionary, one that was not without conflict at Corinth.

"Conversion" and Call

The combination of background and education in both Judaism and Hellenism particularly equipped Paul to assume leadership of the Christian movement as it moved out of Palestinian Judaism into the larger Hellenistic world. But there was more to his leadership than this background; there was his "conversion" to Christianity and his call to become an apostle to the Gentiles. The word "conversion" is controversial, and Paul's shift to Christianity has many complexities (hence, the quotation marks). How did this take place?

According to Acts, Paul entered the early Christian scene as a bystander at the martyrdom of Stephen (Acts 7:58). Subsequently, he became a persecutor of the fledgling Christian community in **Damascus** (Acts 9:1–2). Paul himself did not mention the former incident, but the latter was clearly an unforgettable memory for him, as we can see from three comments. In his statement about his Jewish background, Paul wrote, "as to zeal a persecutor of the church" (Phil 3:6). In citing Jesus' appearance to him, he remarked, "For I am the least of the apostles, unfit to be called an apostle, because I persecuted the church of God" (1 Cor 15:9). Still another reference of this sort is made to the congregation at Galatia in Asia Minor: "For you have heard of my former life in Judaism, how I persecuted the church of God violently and tried to destroy it; and I advanced in Judaism beyond many of my own age among my people, so extremely zealous was I for the traditions of my fathers" (Gal 1:13–14). As far as can be determined, widespread systematic Jewish persecution of Christians did not take place. Yet, there were sporadic local persecutions, and, since Paul was clearly involved, it will be helpful to make a hypothesis about this feature of Paul's past.

Hellenistic Judaism supported a missionary movement. We saw in Chapters Two and Three that certain ethical teachings of the Jewish religion were very attractive to outsiders, and that the synagogues had their groups of what the Lukan writer (Acts) calls "God-fearers" attracted to Judaism but resisting full proselytization because they were reluctant to accept circumcision and the dietary laws. In Galatians 5:11 Paul wrote rhetorically, "But if I, brethren, still preach circumcision, why am I still persecuted?" This leads us to conclude that at one time he had "preached circumcision," that is, he had been an active missionary for Judaism in the Hellenistic world.

If the supposition that Paul had been a missionary for the Jewish religion is correct, it is possible that he had come into conflict with Christian missionaries on the mission field. Remember that churches outside Jerusalem and the surrounding areas had been founded by Christian missionaries and that the Hellenists had gone a step beyond what even Hellenistic Jews could tolerate: a strong critique of the Temple and Jewish Law (Acts 6:14). Indeed, eventually they developed a view of Jesus that drew on many of the ideas current in the Hellenistic world at large. At any rate, it appears that such Hellenistic Jewish Christian missionaries had been driven from Jerusalem by persecution (Acts 8:1b–3), while the more conservative Jewish Christians were permitted to remain. Presumably such Hellenistic Christian missionaries would have attracted the "God-fearers" precisely because they were critical of those very aspects of Judaism that the "God-fearer" found to be stumbling blocks to full proselytization, especially circumcision. Such "God-fearers" were also the object of Jewish Christian missions. It is therefore likely that Paul came into conflict with the Hellenistic Jewish Christian missionaries and persecuted them—though one day he would join their ranks.

A discussion of Paul's persecution of the Christians leads to what he frequently links with it, his "conversion" and call (Gal 1:11–17; 1 Cor 15:9; Phil 3:6–7). The subject of Paul's "conversion" has been the occasion of much discussion because it raises fundamental issues such as his attitude toward Judaism, his conception of Torah and covenant, his view of the gospel, and the meaning and significance of his religious experience in later Christendom. We cannot discuss all of Paul's important theological ideas at this point, but a few remarks should be made about this central event. Not surprisingly, any interpretation of it is in part a question of which sources are most important, and what they mean; in part, it is a question of what is meant by the word "conversion."

As mentioned, Paul linked his persecution of the Christians, his experience of a revelation of Christ, and his call to be a missionary, or in his own words, an "apostle" (Greek *apostolos*, "one who is sent out"). In the letter to the Galatians in which Paul defended the truth of his gospel and thus of his apostleship, he began, "Paul an apostle—not from men nor through man, but through Jesus Christ and God the Father . . ." (Gal 1:1). All the evidence points to the probability that Paul had never known Jesus of Nazareth, which was apparently a necessary component for being an "apostle" for the author of Luke-Acts (Acts

1:20–26). Paul argued that his apostleship was not of human origin, an idea he developed in Galatians 1:11–17. In typical rhetorical style, he reminded the Galatians, "For I want you to know, brothers and sisters, that the gospel that was proclaimed by me is not of human origin. For I did not receive it from a human source, nor was I taught it, but I received it through a revelation *(apocalypsis)* of Jesus Christ" (v. 11). After telling of his formerly persecuting the Christians, Paul continued,

> But when God, who had set me apart before I was born and called me through his grace, was pleased to reveal his Son to me (literally "in me"), so that I might proclaim him among the Gentiles, I did not confer with any human being, nor did I go up to Jerusalem to those who were apostles before me, but I went away at once into Arabia (Nabatea), and afterwards I returned to Damascus.

The stress in this passage is not so much on changing from one religion (Judaism) to another religion (Christianity) in the usual sense of "conversion" as it is on a special call to be apostle to the Gentiles through direct revelation.

A striking pattern for this call is found in the Old Testament prophets Isaiah and Jeremiah, who were set apart while they were still in the womb (Isa 49:1; Jer 1:5); like them, Paul felt predestined to his vocation ("before I was born"). This conclusion does not deny that Paul had an intense religious experience. He says that God revealed his Son "in him" and that the Son, Jesus Christ, revealed the gospel Paul preached. This is, in the first place, a "vision" of the Son. In 1 Corinthians 9:1, Paul says, "Am I not free? Am I not an apostle? Have I not *seen* Jesus, our Lord?" and in 1 Corinthians 15:8 after noting resurrection appearances to Cephas, the twelve, five hundred brethren, James, and "all the apostles," he states, "Last of all, as to one untimely born, he *appeared* also to me" and again mentions his apostleship and persecution of the church (15:9). In the second place, it is implied that Paul also heard a voice; elsewhere he mentions his "visions and revelations of the Lord" in which one might hear things (2 Cor 12:1–5).

In these texts, Paul's focus combines two things: the revelation of Jesus and call to be an apostle to the Gentiles. He relates these two items to his persecution of the church, and speaks of a change from his "former life." As we shall see, he also has difficulties accepting the Law as sufficient for maintaining a relationship with God (see Rom 7), and he does not require circumcision as a prerequisite for becoming a Christian. Yet, his pride in his Jewishness suggests that Paul is not plagued with a guilty conscience for what he has done, and this raises the question whether the term "conversion" is the appropriate one. Another text, Philippians 3:4–9, reinforces this interpretation. Paul's Jewish background is, he says, reason for "confidence in the flesh" (verse 4). After giving his most important statement about his Jewishness (verses 5–6), he concludes, "But whatever *gains* I had, these I have come to regard as loss because of Christ. More than that I regard everything as loss because of the surpassing value of knowing Christ Jesus my Lord" (verses 7–8). It is this that leads him on to state the major theme of much of his writing, "the righteousness of God based on faith" (verse 9; see Chapter Seven).

The author of the Acts of the Apostles lays great weight on Paul's "Damascus road experience," for he relates the story three times (9:1–19a; 22:1–15; 26:4–20).

In fact, his stress on the intensity of the experience has probably contributed to its interpretation as an emotional conversion experience in the evangelical Christian traditions. There is, however, a constant element in all three of the accounts in Acts that is in accord with Paul's, and that is the central dialogue between Paul and the risen Jesus:

> "Saul, Saul, why do you persecute me?"
> "Who are you, Lord?"
> "I am Jesus, whom you are persecuting."

Furthermore, in this kind of traditional material the central dialogue is the oldest part, the nucleus around which the other details cluster as the tradition is transmitted. Whether the detail of the vision of light, which is also a constant in all three stories, was connected to the dialogue, is worth considering; at least it would accord with the notion of a vision. Enshrined in the Acts conversion stories are elements that are not inconsistent with what Paul himself says: a visual revelation of Jesus Christ that included some verbal communication.

However one evaluates Paul's "conversion," it is clear that a revelation of Christ is rooted deeply in his experience, and his letters reflect the vitality and power of one who is driven to accomplish what he believes is God's will for his life.

In summary, it is possible to say that Paul associated his persecution of the church with two interrelated facts: a *revelation of Jesus Christ, God's Son, and a prophetic call to become apostle to the Gentiles.* In Paul's statements, there is no emphasis on what has usually been associated with a "conversion," namely, a guilty conscience about his persecuting activities. Rather, his statements indicate that he had thought of himself as a loyal Jew, confident in the "flesh." The accent in these accounts falls rather on his call to become apostle to the Gentiles. The revelation itself had visionary and auditory elements, a fact that seems to be further supported in Acts. Acts, however, elaborates the stories with legend and theological interpretation related to Paul's connections with Jerusalem.

Paul's Early Activity as a Christian Missionary

After his conversion, which probably took place in 32 or 33 (though perhaps as late as 36), Paul spent three years in Arabia (Nabatea), the Gentile district east of the Jordan River, and **Damascus** (Gal 1:7–18). We do not know what he was doing there, but considering his character, it is most likely that he was already working as a Christian missionary. If he was, his missionary activity must have been unsuccessful, though it apparently aroused enough hostility that he had to flee Damascus (2 Cor 11:32–33; Acts 9:23–25; see above, p. 191).

Paul left Damascus and paid a brief visit to Peter, the primary leader of the Christian movement, in **Jerusalem** (Gal 1:18). Paul always referred to Peter by his Aramaic name, Cephas; perhaps they talked to each other in Aramaic. We would give a great deal to know about the content of their conversation, but it was obviously not only about the weather. In view of Paul's vehemence about his gospel not coming from human agency (Gal 1:12), it is unlikely that the visit was to take part in "a crash course in missionary work with Peter." Perhaps Paul learned of some Jesus traditions, for example, Jesus' teaching on marriage and divorce (1 Cor 7:10), or the Last Supper (1 Cor 11:23–25), or Jesus' death and resurrection "according to the scriptures" and appearances (1 Cor 15:3b–9).

Paul then went back to his own native district of **Cilicia** (the region of his home-town, Tarsus) to carry on missionary activity (Gal 1:21–23). Sometime during the next fourteen years, Barnabas, a leader of the church in Antioch, brought him to Antioch to help in the Hellenistic Jewish Christian missionary activity in Syria.

At **Antioch on the Orontes,** the third city in the Roman Empire after Rome and Alexandria, the cultural crosscurrents of the Hellenistic world came sharply into contact. Antioch, the capital of the Roman province of Syria, was located on the best land route between Asia Minor and Syria and Palestine, and hence between East and West. Here Greek civilization and philosophy interacted with oriental culture and religion more directly and on more equal terms than almost anywhere else, and the establishment of a Christian community here was there-fore an event of the greatest possible importance for the growth and develop-ment of the New Testament church. The New Testament itself says that "in Antioch the disciples were for the first time called Christians" (Acts 11:26).

Paul's coming to Antioch marked the beginning of the most important phase of his life and work as a Christian. Now he had the active support of a strategically located and missionary-minded Christian church. With its support Paul began the missionary work that is the major theme of the Acts of the Apostles. Acts 13:3–14:26 reports a first missionary journey that took him and his companions to Cyprus and the southern part of Galatia (in Asia Minor). No trace of this jour-ney is preserved in Paul's letters, and we do not know whether it took place before or after the Jerusalem Conference. Acts has it before and sees the Conference as a direct consequence of the success of this journey. But Acts also has it immedi-ately following a visit to Jerusalem by Barnabas and Paul, "the famine visit" (Acts 11:27–30; 12:25). That visit is not mentioned in Galatians, even though Paul is telling under oath the story of his relationship with Jerusalem down to the con-ference. It is probable, therefore, that the Jerusalem Conference was made nec-essary not by the success of the first missionary journey, but by the success of the work in Antioch itself, and that the missionary journey of Acts 13 and 14 was a *result* of the decision to authorize Paul and Barnabas to go into the Gentile world. If so, the conference was prior to the first missions westward to Asia Minor, not (as Acts has it) afterwards.

The Jerusalem Conference

As noted in Chapter Four, the Jerusalem Conference (Gal 2:1–10; compare Acts 15) was a major event in early Christianity. Dated about 48 C.E., Paul says that he went to the conference with Barnabas and that he took Titus with him. Acts is undoubtedly on target in saying that the conference was occasioned by Judean Christians who came to Antioch demanding that Christians be circumcised, for Paul states that Titus, a Greek, was not compelled to be circumcised (Gal 2:3). The central issue was adherence to Law and covenant and how they were related to the influx of Gentiles into the Christian movement. To what extent, if at all, did a Gentile have to become a "law-abiding" Jew to become a Christian (Gal 2:3, 7; Acts 15:1, 5–6)?

There appear to have been three parties to the debate: a group of conserva-tive Jewish Christians who, quite naturally, considered that the Torah was still in effect and that circumcision was necessary (in Gal 2:4 Paul calls them "false brethren" to whom he did not yield); the Jerusalem leaders, James, Peter, and John; and Paul, Barnabas, and Titus. What lay in the balance was the mission to the Gentiles, the heart of Paul's mission and, presumably, the Antioch church. If we take Paul seriously, the first group lost the debates and a compromise was reached between the second and third groups: Peter was entrusted with the "apostleship" to the circumcised, and Paul was entrusted with preaching to the uncircumcised Gentiles (Gal 2:7). Yet, Paul's language makes it unclear whether he was granted the status of *apostle* at that time, and there is the lingering doubt that Paul was as independent as he claimed some years later. If Paul was not a full apostle at the time, but something more like a delegate from Antioch with Barnabas, the situation was ripe for a challenge to his apostleship from the conservative party. Galatians itself shows that this challenge eventually came, for Paul writes that later he had to defend his freedom at Antioch when "certain men from James," whom Paul calls "the circumcision party," caused Peter to withdraw and not eat with the Gentiles (Gal 2:11–14). This was the **Antioch Incident** (see Chapter Four). We also know that other Jewish Christian missionaries questioned Paul's credentials (2 Cor 10–13; see further below).

What did it mean that the "pillars" James, Peter, and John gave Paul and Barnabas "the right hand of fellowship" (Gal 2:9) in apparent victory over the conservatives? How was this compromise solution viewed? Why was Peter so inconsistent? Did James change his position and become more conservative? And did Paul himself abide by the decision, "we should go to the Gentiles, and they to the circumcised" (Gal 2:9)? In 1 Corinthians 9:20, he states: "To the Jews I became as a Jew, in order to win Jews. To those under the law I became as one under the law (though I myself am not under the law) so that I might win those under the law." Again, it should be said that we are at the heart of the relationship of early Christianity with Judaism, and at the heart of the message of Paul. If the Jerusalem Conference compromise did not hold, and if Paul's status as apostle at that time was not absolutely clear, the Jewish Christian conservatives had a legitimate case against him. Indeed, it is not impossible that Paul lost out at Antioch, for eventually he seems to have centered his activity at Ephesus in "Asia" (western Turkey).

The second major decision of the conference was "They (Peter, James, and John) asked only one thing, that we remember the poor, which was actually what I was eager to do" (Gal 2:10). This refers to Paul's gathering a **collection** of money from members of the Gentile mission churches for "the poor" at Jerusalem, which at least included actual poor persons (Rom 15:27). This collection is mentioned several times in Paul's letters (1 Cor 16:1–4; 2 Cor 8; 9; Rom 15:25–29; see above). We can understand how it was gathered from 1 Corinthians 16:1–4:

> Now concerning the collection for the saints: you should follow the directions I gave to the churches of Galatia. On the first day of every week, each of you is to put aside and save whatever extra you earn, so that collections need not be taken when I come. And when I arrive, I will send any whom you approve with letters to take your gift to Jerusalem. If it seems advisable that I should go also, they will accompany me.

He elsewhere encouraged giving and complimented the generosity of those who contributed (2 Cor 8; 9). The importance of this collection to Paul is illustrated by his willingness to take it to Jerusalem, a potential danger to his own life. Romans 15:25–28a states:

> At present, however, I am going to Jerusalem in a ministry to the saints; for Macedonia and Achaia have been pleased to share their resources with the poor among the saints at Jerusalem. They were pleased to do this, and indeed they owe it to them; for if the Gentiles have come to share in their spiritual blessings, they ought also to be of service to them in material things. So, when I have completed this, and have delivered to them what has been collected, I will set out. . . .

Thus, Paul kept the promise made at the Jerusalem Conference and took the collection to Jerusalem despite his anticipation of harm from unbelieving Jews and his fear that the collection might not be accepted (Rom 15:30–31). We shall note the collection again in relation to his opponents.

The Mission in Galatia (central Turkey), Macedonia, Achaia, and "Asia" (western Turkey)

Paul began the most active phase of his missionary work, deliberately going out into the Gentile world from his base, the mission church in Antioch. Acts portrays Paul as carrying out three missionary journeys, one to Cyprus and southern Galatia (central Asia Minor or Turkey; 13:3–14:26); one through northern Galatia to Macedonia and Achaia (Greece), concluding at Ephesus in "Asia" or western Turkey (15:40–18:22); and a third in generally the same region (18:23–21:17). Three missionary journeys sounds very neat, suggesting an ordering by the author of Acts; nonetheless, the general picture of the regions to which Paul went is probably correct. Paul would have begun this phase of his work on the **island of Cyprus** and in **southern Galatia,** readily accessible from his base in Antioch. He must have then moved west, following the overland route from Antioch to the west through **northern Galatia.** The author of Acts writes a mission speech for Paul at this point in another Antioch, Antioch of Pisidia (Acts 13:13–52). Paul made the momentous decision to go further west into **Macedonia and Achaia** (Greece) rather than to turn south to the west coastal region of **Asia,** whose churches are the concern of the book of Revelation, or northeast to the area of Bithynia and the Black Sea, where other missionaries went (1 Peter; Pliny-Trajan Correspondence in Chapter Thirteen). Acts 16:6–10 presents this decision as a result of a direct revelation to Paul.

Paul's letters and Acts agree for a time on the essentials of Paul's itinerary in Macedonia and Achaia (Greece):

Philippi	1 Thess 2:2; Acts 16:11–40
Thessalonica	the letter to the Thessalonians itself; Acts 17:1–9
Athens	1 Thess 3:1; Acts 17:16–34
Corinth	1 Thess 1:1; 3:6; Acts 18:1–17

Letters to three of these four locations (Philippi, Thessalonica, Corinth) survive. It appears that Paul now shifted his center of activity from Antioch to Ephesus. Was this because of opposition and conflict at Antioch (the Antioch Incident)?

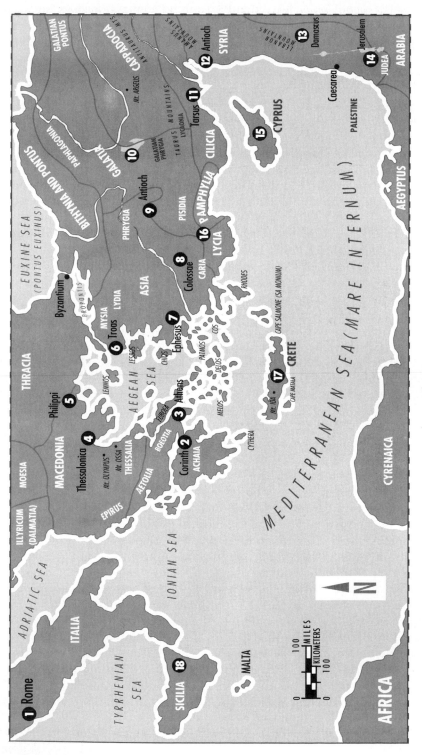

Major cities and regions of Paul's missionary activity.

In 1 Thessalonians we learn that Paul and his companions had "suffered and been shamefully treated at **Philippi**" (1 Thess 2:2), a comment that seems to receive some support from Acts 16:19–24, where they were whipped by command of city officials and thrown into prison, an account that is otherwise expanded with miracle stories. Paul later wrote the Philippians thanking them for their financial support when he was in Thessalonica; this support was unusual because Paul was normally proud that he supported himself as an artisan (Phil 4:15–16; compare 2 Cor 11:8–9). Paul displayed a deep affection for the Philippians. After leaving them, he probably followed the main highway westward across Macedonia (the Via Egnatia; see map, photo at beginning of Chapter Four) as far as **Thessalonica,** a seaport and the capital city of Macedonia (modern Salonika). In 1 Thessalonians, Paul encouraged the Thessalonians, among whom he had worked so hard (2:9), for their steadfast faith in the face of persecution by their countrymen (2:14), that is, they had become Christian from a Gentile background (1:9; contrast Acts 17:1–9). In the letter, which has a strong dose of apocalyptic eschatology, he mentions that Timothy had been dispatched to Thessalonica from **Athens** (3:1), and had returned (3:6), probably to Corinth (Acts 18:1, 18; compare Acts 17:10–15). We have no letter to the Athenians, but the author of the Acts of the Apostles presents us with one of the most magnificent Hellenistic Jewish mission sermons in the mouth of Paul at Athens (Acts 17).

Paul then went to **Corinth,** a thriving cosmopolitan seaport and capital of Greece. As we noted in connection with the Gallio Inscription, Paul arrived there in 49 or 50 C.E. and stayed about eighteen months (Acts 18:11). There he established (at the house of Stephanas? 1 Cor 1:16; 16:15) a lively house-church of mainly Gentile Christians. It was nurtured by Apollos (1 Cor 1:12; 3:5–6), whom Acts claims had been an Alexandrian Jew and an eloquent man well versed in the Scriptures (18:24–28). Probably Paul wrote 1 Thessalonians at this time. We have illustrated Paul's seesawing correspondence with the Corinthians. It indicates many problems related to the Greek background of the Corinthians. We have also noted his conflict with other apostles who challenged his authority. We shall say much more about these subjects below.

From Corinth Paul went to **Ephesus,** also a major port city (in antiquity) across the Aegean Sea. The Acts itinerary takes him from Ephesus to Palestine and up to Antioch, from which he retraced his steps through Asia Minor back to Ephesus (Acts 18:18–23; 19:1), thus launching a third missionary journey (down to 21:17). Though this account is full of legendary material, it is undoubtedly accurate in placing Paul at Ephesus for a long period of time, perhaps two and a half years (Acts 19:8, 10). 1 Corinthians was written there (1 Cor 16:8), as well as parts of 2 Corinthians, and if Paul was imprisoned there, as many believe (2 Cor 1:8–11), perhaps also the "prison letters" Philippians and Philemon were written there. He appears to have made a quick trip to **Corinth** from Ephesus (2 Cor 2:1; 12:14; 12:21; 13:1); eventually he left on a journey through Macedonia, where he continued his correspondence with the Corinthians (2 Cor 1:8–10, 15–16; 2:12–13; 7:5; 9:2). He may also have written Galatians about this time, though some scholars put it earlier.

Finally, Paul made his third and final trip to **Corinth** (2 Cor 13:1). Above, we stressed his interest in the collection of the Corinthians for "the poor" among the Christians at Jerusalem (1 Cor 16:1–4; 2 Cor 8; 9; Rom 15:25–28). At Corinth Paul showed the same interest when he wrote his most mature letter, Romans. Despite the dangers involved (Rom 15:31), he clearly indicated his intent to fulfill his promise to take the collection to Jurusalem.

Perhaps Paul's anxiety about the "unbelievers in Judea" (Rom 15:31) was correct. The author of Luke-Acts tells the story that Jews from Asia in **Jerusalem** claimed that Paul spoke against the Law and the Temple, that he was arrested, and that there was even a plot on his life. According to Acts, Paul appealed his case to Caesar, which was the right of every Roman citizen (Acts 21:1–18:16).

The journey to **Rome** was begun probably in either 56 or 58 C.E. Paul was taken as a prisoner. According to the conclusion of Acts, Paul spent two years in Rome under house arrest, nonetheless preaching "quite openly and unhindered." As we shall see in our discussion of Luke-Acts, this statement reflects the views of the author. Yet, it probably is true that Paul was an active missionary even while a prisoner.

Our New Testament knowledge of Paul ends at this point, since Acts ends here and no undisputed letters are preserved from this or any later period; possibly Philippians and Philemon were written during the Roman captivity, though we have preferred to situate them in connection with the imprisonment in Ephesus. Ecclesiastical tradition has it that Paul was released from his captivity, visited Spain, and returned to Rome a second time as a prisoner. But the tradition may well be only a historicization of the plans Paul details in Romans 15:24–29, and it seems most probable that Paul's first imprisonment in Rome ended with his death, probably as a martyr (*1 Clement* 5–6).

THE AUTHORITY OF PAUL AS APOSTLE

It is clear from Paul's letters and Acts that he encountered delicate problems in his claim to be an apostle to the Gentiles. He had never known Jesus. He had been a persecutor of the church. In many ways he was dependent on various traditions of the Jerusalem and Hellenistic Jewish churches. Yet, Paul said that his call originated in divine revelation. Though it was confirmed by the leaders of the Jerusalem church, he claimed that it was independent of any human agency. Moreover, the Gentile churches Paul founded had a special relationship with him. It should come as no surprise, then, that there were those who constantly challenged his authority as an apostle.

The issues surrounding Paul's authority and opposition to it have generated a great deal of discussion, partly because they are related to a number of classical questions about early Christianity, such as whether its spirit and vitality can be contained within the institutional church. Where do Paul and "his" churches fit within a spectrum of possibilities from a sect wrestling with its relation to the world and its origins in Judaism to a more independent, rational-legal institution accommodating itself to Hellenistic society? Degrees of religious assimilation can provoke strong emotions, both in favor and in opposition, and eventual religious factions within a group. Consider, for example, the Jewish experience in the United States.

In taking up such important questions, we shall highlight three issues: Paul's relationship to the Jerusalem church, his authority in the Gentile churches, and the opposition that developed against him on the mission field.

Paul and the Church at Jerusalem

Paul's relationship to the church at Jerusalem developed in the main from the results of the **Jerusalem Conference** (Gal 2:1–10; compare Acts 15). We suggested above that Paul appears to have launched his mission westward into Asia Minor and Macedonia-Greece after the conference. Yet, his precise relationship to the Jerusalem group has been highly debated. It is affected by the relative weight put on Galatians and Acts, the interpretation of Paul's emotional statements in Galatians, and the way one interprets the Jerusalem church's willingness to accept the collection.

Paul declares that he went to Jerusalem to meet with the pillars "by revelation" (Gal 2:2). However one interprets this term—clearly it implies he was not summoned or sent—we can see from Paul's version that he considered himself to be the dominant figure at the conference. In Acts, however, it is claimed that Barnabas and Paul were *sent* as delegates from the church at Antioch, and that the conference was dominated by James and especially Peter. Though Galatians was written some years after the conference, though Paul is writing in the heat of controversy, Galatians is, as we have stressed (see Chapter Four), the primary source. Paul did not report in to his "superiors."

Yet, we know that Paul received several Jesus traditions and creeds that he quotes from time to time (see Chapter Five), and he undoubtedly learned at least some of them from the Jerusalem group. Moreover, there is the collection for the poor for which Paul was willing to risk his life in going back to Jerusalem (Rom 15:25–32; see above). How should this collection be interpreted in connection with Paul's relation to the Jerusalem church?

Some have suggested that the collection was like a tax, in analogy with the collection of the Temple tax on all Jews. If so, it implies that Paul was indeed a representative of the Jerusalem "mother church," and submissive to it. However, there are a number of features about the collection—its limitation to Paul's "Gentile" churches, its one-time (not annual) occasion, and its destination for "the poor" in a literal sense that make the Jewish Temple tax an inappropriate analogy. Yet, the collection was more than *only* an act of charity; it was for Paul also an act of gratitude, an indication of the independence of the Gentile churches, and—despite Paul's defense of his apostleship in Galatians—a sign of the unity of the church. In short, Paul did not submit to the Jerusalem church, but neither did he wish to offend it.

Paul's Authority in the Gentile Churches

In the communities Paul "fathers," he is obviously an authority figure, even though he generates opposition and has occasion to warn against this attitude (for example, 1 Cor 1:10–17; 3:5–14). He counsels those in his communities to imitate him (1 Thess 1:6; Phil 3:17; 1 Cor 4:16; 11:1). His letters, as we shall see, are full of parenesis: exhorting, comforting, rebuking, making all sorts of value judgments about what Christians should be and should do. He has many coworkers, some of whom are clearly subordinate to him. We have seen that in one instance, he ranks persons with certain spiritual gifts (1 Cor 12:28; see Chapter Four). He places his one self-designation, "apostle," at the top (1 Cor

12:28; compare Eph 4:11) and those who are causing problems, "speakers in various kinds of tongues," at the bottom. In another instance, he mentions "bishops" (or "overseers") and "deacons" (Phil 1:1). Was Paul rebelling against the authority of the Jerusalem church while at the same time establishing his own "power structure"? At first glance it might seem so, but the issues are more complicated.

The exhortation to imitate Paul should be seen in the context of Paul's view that the gospel is a gospel of lowliness exemplified by the Cross of Christ, and that the apostle's difficult life "imitates Christ": "Be imitators of me, *as I am of Christ*" (1 Cor 11:1; compare Phil 3:17–18). Paul puts this in terms of a theological paradox with social and political implications: God's power lies in weakness (1 Cor 1:10–4:21). As we shall see, he will cite this form of power against certain kinds of boasting opponents. This power also expresses itself in love, and behind his parenesis is the one who loves his churches and wants to see them grow. "Knowledge (*gnōsis*) puffs up, but love (*agapē*) builds up." Thus, Paul believes that as an apostle "of Christ" and "in Christ" he could *command* Philemon to release his slave Onesimus, but he appeals to him "for love's sake" (Phlm 8), giving him the free will to make his own decision (Phlm 14). It is true that he views some of his coworkers as subordinate; but the relationship is an intimate, personal one, characterized by such terms as "faithful," "trusted," "beloved." His ranking of spiritual gifts needs to be seen in context. The stress of 1 Corinthians 12 as a whole is on the *unity* of the church, which was being torn apart by social and religious conflict. Paul recognizes that people have different functions in the congregation, and that each of them is necessary, but he wants to avoid the claim of those who think of *glossolalia* as superior. Finally, we may catch a glimpse of certain persons with authority at Philippi who are referred to as "bishop" and "deacon," but these terms are scarcely very distinct until a later time, and are sometimes equivalent to "presbyters" or "elders." Indeed, Paul thinks of his apostleship as being that of "minister" (2 Cor 11:23, *diakonoi* = "ministers" [NRSV]).

Paul did hold authority in his churches, but not in the sense of an official of the church today. It was rather the authority of "charisma," that is, his communities responded to him not as any ordinary person but as one who was in a special way in touch with the Divine, whom he believed was a loving, self-sacrificing God. He used this recognition to challenge the *status quo* in the name of what he believed to be the gospel of Jesus Christ and Christian freedom. Others, of course, could challenge him or claim greater "charisma" and oppose him.

Paul's Opponents

Paul clearly had authority in his churches, but there were also those who denied that authority. These were his opponents. This is also an area of much discussion. It is difficult to identify the opponents precisely, because it is necessary to reconstruct what they were saying about him from what *he* says about them. Moreover, what he says about them was usually based on hearsay from coworkers who traveled back and forth between him and the churches, or from letters. In addition, there is the problem of interpreting Paul's comments because they were often phrased in the style of ancient rhetoric. Finally, there is the everpresent tendency of Acts to smooth over Paul's conflicts with the Jerusalem church.

These problems have contributed to several different theories about the opponents. Some interpreters have attempted to view them as the same everywhere, often suggesting that they followed him from place to place. Others maintain that the opponents differ from place to place, and even that there are different types of opponents at the same place at different periods. One interpreter argues that Paul is not usually sufficiently informed to know who they are, and so we cannot know either. Nevertheless, the attempt to identify them is important because it sheds light on the diversity of early Christianity and, most important in this context, Paul's own point of view in countering them. Since Philemon is a personal letter to an individual (at Colossae? compare Colossians 4:9) read publicly, it does not reflect opposition to Paul by opponents in a church; therefore we shall move on to the other major locations.

Jerusalem

We have noted above that there was a debate at Jerusalem about Paul's mission to the Gentiles, that Paul seems to have had the edge initially at the Jerusalem Conference, but that subsequently conservatives, including "men from James," opposed him at Antioch. How would the Jerusalem conservatives who believed in the importance of the Law have responded to Paul's return to Jerusalem with the collection? Or anyone who believed that circumcision was the mark of God's people? Given that there is reason to doubt that not all accepted Paul's status as an apostle at Jerusalem, it becomes clear why Paul had to defend it and why the collection was of such great importance to him. Yet, if the conservatives, with some support from James, won out against Paul at Jerusalem, we cannot even be sure that the collection was accepted at Jerusalem; at any rate, it is never mentioned in connection with Paul's final visits to Jerusalem in Acts 21. One recent study concludes:

> from the time of the conference, at the latest, the Jerusalem church assumed a preponderately anti-Pauline attitude. Their rejection of the collection, which only a few years before had been a bond of unity between the two churches, was a clear public indication of the hostility to Paul of the Jerusalem church, from which James cannot be excluded.
> (Lüdemann, *Opposition to Paul*, 62–63)

Antioch

Paul's first mission center was the city of Antioch. We took up the Antioch Incident in some detail in Chapter Four and above, so at this point we simply reiterate that when conservative "men from James" came to Antioch, Peter withdrew from his practice of eating with Gentiles. Paul claims that he challenged Peter on this point. Thereafter, Ephesus seems to have become a major center of Paul's activity. It is sometimes argued, therefore, that the group backed by Peter and perhaps also the more conservative James ultimately won at Antioch.

Thessalonica

In 1 Thessalonians 2:1–12 Paul defends the manner in which he had presented the gospel to the Thessalonians. He says that he and his companions *were without* error, uncleanness, guile, without seeking to please men, to use words of flattery, to cover their greed, without attempting to gain glory from men. Were there opponents who, in Paul's view, did just that? Since Paul is not specific, and his style in this passage is typical of ancient rhetoric, perhaps there was no actual group of opponents at Thessalonica.

Philippi

In Philippians 3:2–3, Paul writes, "Beware of the dogs, beware of the evil workers, beware of those who mutilate the flesh (*katatomē.*) For it is we who are the circumcision (*peritomē.*), who worship in the Spirit of God and boast in Christ Jesus and have no confidence in the flesh." This is one of Paul's "cutting remarks"! It contains a pun on the terms "incision" (*katatomē.*) and "circumcision" (*peritomē.*). Paul is warning the Philippians against those who stress circumcision. Probably they were Christians of Jewish background, though that is not absolutely necessary. Yet, it is unlikely that these are the conservative Jerusalem Christians because they seem to think of the Law and circumcision as a means of attaining spiritual perfection. Spiritual perfectionism makes them closest to the *Gentile* opponents *internal* to the congregation at Corinth (1 Cor 9; 15). We shall indicate that they may have been influenced by outsiders, however. As in 1 Corinthians, Paul counters their arrogance with the humility of the crucified Christ (Phil 3:18–21). They may have held views of perfection that were eventually developed in second-century Gnosticism.

Corinth

At Corinth, the problem of opponents shifts as we move from 1 Corinthians to 2 Corinthians and, with regard to the latter, it is related to finding the correct sequence of letter fragments discussed above.

There is clearly some influence from *outsiders* in 1 Corinthians. In 1 Corinthians 9 Paul emphatically defends his and Barnabas' right and authority to be accompanied by a wife and to be supported by the Corinthians (though he renounces the latter). Other apostles, including the brothers of Jesus (especially James?) and Peter, did so, because there is a tradition about a command of Jesus that wandering missionaries (and their wives?) should live by the gospel (Q 10:7b), a tradition that Paul cites (9:14). Was Peter being used as an exemplary apostle over against Paul? Was this in any way related to the divisive faction that claimed, "I belong to Peter," with accompanying baptism (compare 1 Cor 1:12 and the discussion below)? Had they been influenced by Peter himself? Or by those representing Peter? In any case, Paul claims that he has chosen not to use his apostolic rights. This decision implies that Paul's credentials as an apostle were being questioned because he was unlike other apostles in supporting himself by his trade. Thus, Paul has renounced his apostolic rights, and he gives a reason: that he should not boast but exemplify "weakness," and that the gospel should be free of charge (9:18). A similar opposition to Paul may be implied in 1 Corinthians 15, where he defends his apostleship by having seen the Lord, as others—Peter, the Twelve, the 500, James, all from Jerusalem—have.

More difficult to relate to outside opposition is 1 Corinthians 1–4. Clearly the enthusiasts who stressed wisdom were not outsiders, for they had carried Paul's views of freedom to an extreme. Yet, they may have been influenced by outsiders. Paul had learned from "Chloe's people" (?) that there was quarreling at Corinth and that various factions were proud of their special relationships with their "spiritual fathers," that is, those who baptized them or those in whose name they were baptized: Paul, Apollos, and Peter (1:10–17). Later, only Apollos is judged positively by Paul; Peter is not mentioned (3:6; 4:6). Whether a Peter party is meant or not, these groups boasted of special human wisdom (1:26–30; 3:18–23; 4:6–7) and bragged about their special knowledge (*gnōsis*, compare 8:1–3) and their unique spiritual gifts (2:12), especially in the ability to speak in tongues, an ecstatic spiritual phenomenon. It appears that claims were being made for a kind of religious perfection, for some of the Corinthians believed that they were living the life of resurrection *already* (15) and that the community was a redeemed heavenly body (11–12). Others interpreted their freedom to mean they were "strong," not "weak" (8–10).

These views led to various ethical problems. One braggart boasted of living with his father's (second) wife, a legally incestuous act (I Cor 5:1–8). Others were going to houses of prostitution (6:12–20). Still others were refraining from intercourse altogether (7:1). The "strong" disturbed the "weak" by eating meat sacrificed to pagan gods (8; 10). The place of women in worship had become a problem (11:2–16). The rich abused the Lord's Supper by eating all the food and getting drunk before the poor arrived (11:17–34). In general, the church was in a state of crisis. It is likely that the Corinthians interpreted Paul's view of freedom from the Law and special Christian wisdom in terms of Hellenistic religious fervor and either libertine or ascetic attitudes toward sexuality. For Hellenists religion was a manifestation of the power of the Deity, of the ability to work miracles, of the experience of various kinds of ecstatic phenomena, of superior knowledge. Perhaps Paul had encouraged the Corinthians' fervor as a sign of spiritual vitality. However, the developments in Corinth were getting out of hand and were destroying the social and religious unity of the church. Moreover, sexual liberation was being taken to its radical extremes. All of this may point to an early form of Gnostic thinking *within* the congregation (4:18–21).

In 2 Corinthians we can observe opposition to Paul from at least one insider, the man who had done an injustice to Paul (2 Cor 1;23; 2:4–5). The Corinthians, after receiving Paul's "tearful letter" (perhaps 2 Cor 10–13), punished the offender, whereupon Paul counseled Christian love (2:6–8). There was also some criticism that through the collection Paul had taken advantage of the Corinthians (2 Cor 7:2; 8:20–24).

More prominent were the outside agitators that seem to have influenced the insiders. There came to Corinth those whom Paul labels sarcastically "**superlative apostles**" (2 Cor 3:1; 11:4–5, 11). They were really "false apostles" and, like witches, Paul accused them of being "deceitful workers, disguising themselves as apostles of Christ" (11:13). Clearly they, too, claimed to be apostles, and thus competitors for leadership at Corinth. They were envoys of Jewish background (11:22), were complimentary to each other (10:12, 18), and bore "letters of recommendation" (3:1–3). Paul says they preached "another Jesus"—probably Jesus as a hero (see Chapters Three, Four)—and had "a different spirit" (11:4). They also performed miracles. They attacked Paul by saying "his letters are weighty and strong, but his bodily presence is weak, and his speech contemptible" (10:10; compare 11:6). As in 1 Corinthians 9, they attacked Paul for supporting himself by his trade, that is, for not accepting the support of the church, but at the same time taking advantage of them with the collection (11:7–9; 12:6, 13). For them, Paul was not a true charismatic and lacked the proper authority to be an apostle.

Much of Paul's defense centered on a *"boasting"* theme, that is, he could also boast like a fool, but he boasted about his trials as an apostle, making comparisons between his supposed "weakness" and his conviction that God demonstrates his power through weakness exemplified in the Cross (13:4; compare 1 Cor 9). Paul went on to say that he, too, had "visions and revelations of the Lord" (12:1); that the signs of a true apostle were performed "in all patience" when he was among them, that is, "signs, wonders, and mighty works." Miracles, then, were being performed by the "superlative apostles," and Paul's response was that he, too, was a miracle worker.

Paul seems to have made some headway with the Corinthians, for in 2 Corinthians the letter fragments indicate reconciliation (2 Cor 1:1–2:13; 7:5–16) and Paul finally made his awaited visit in behalf of the collection (2 Cor 8, 9).

Galatia

After Paul had established a congregation at Galatia and moved on, there appeared a group among the Galatians that unsettled the church. They preached a "different gospel" than Paul's, suggesting that they were Christian, but they probably had a Jewish background, since the heart of their message was a stress on the Law and they pressured the Galatians to accept circumcision. They attacked Paul's version of the gospel and accused him of dispensing with circumcision to "please people" (1:10). Paul does not clearly identify them; he nonetheless attacks them sharply, saying that they "want to make a good showing *in the flesh*" (compare 6:12), probably another cutting remark that puns on their boasting in relation to circumcision. Yet, Paul also charges that they do not keep the Law, and that they stress circumcision to avoid being persecuted "for the cross of Christ" (6:11–16). In good rhetorical style, Paul knifes those who have "bewitched" (3:1) the Galatians with one of his sharpest cutting remarks, "I wish those who unsettle you would castrate themselves" (5:12).

Who were these Jewish Christian "Judaizers"? In the past some scholars have suggested that they were the Jerusalem conservatives (possibly Christians of a Pharisaic origin, compare Acts 15:1, 5) who followed Paul wherever he went. There is a certain cogency to this view, since Paul defends his apostleship in Galatians by recounting the stories of the opposition of the "false brethren" who wanted circumcision for Titus at the Jerusalem Conference (2:3–4) and by the Antioch Incident, in which Peter separated himself from the Gentiles in the face of "certain men from James," that is, "the circumcision party" (2:11–12).

A possible problem for this view is that Paul fears that the Galatians will again become slaves to the "elemental spirits," which are probably demonic powers (angels or stars, or both) believed to control "this evil age" (Gal 4:3, 9). Paul links such beliefs with the comment that the Galatians are observing days, and months, and seasons, and years, that is, calendrical observations characteristic of astrology (4:10). Such "syncretistic" views were widespread in the Hellenistic world. Were these also the views of the "Judaizers"? It appears so. If they were, would the Jerusalem conservatives have held such views? It is not impossible, though they are not typical of the Pharisees known from later Jewish literature. One also wonders if the Judaizers have not charged that he is too dependent on the Jerusalem Christians (chapters 1–2), which does not sound like Jerusalem Judaizers.

These problems have led to other alternatives. Some have suggested that there were two sets of opponents, the Jerusalem conservatives and the more syncretistic group; the problem with this view is that Paul does not explicitly identify two groups. Others have proposed a group of recently circumcised *Gentile* Christians within the church, or a group of *Jewish* Gnostic Christians.

Still another view modifies this theory to suggest that they were *Jewish Christian missionaries* rooted in a form of *syncretistic Judaism* found in Asia Minor (compare the Corinthian opponents, 2 Cor 10-13). If so, they did not follow the precise position of the Jerusalem conservatives, though from Paul's point of view, they were at one with them in the essential issue: They stressed circumcision and the Law. This theory is widely held today. If we accept it, it is necessary to explain Paul's references to the Jerusalem Conference and the Antioch Incident as Paul's way of viewing *what the Jerusalem conservatives and the opponents held in common and what, to Paul, was the major threat to his gospel: the demand for circumcision and adherence to the Law.*

Rome and Ephesus

The problem of identifying possible opponents at Rome is also difficult. It centers on the meaning of the admonitions to the Romans in 14:1–15:13, whether these admonitions have any relation to opponents mentioned in Romans 16:17–20, and whether Romans 16 was even part of the letter. We shall discuss these texts.

In 14:1–15:13, in relation to food practices and observances of special days, Paul admonishes "the weak" and "the strong" not to despise or pass judgment on each other. Paul has not yet been to Rome and the groups are not clearly identified. Are these actual groups? Or do his comments simply sum up his past experiences with factions? Recall that Paul had to counter other opponents on food matters and special observances (compare Gal 2:12; 4:10), and there had been differences about food between "the weak" and "the strong" at Corinth (1 Cor 8; 10). If the form of Paul's letter to the Romans is a "letter-essay," it is possible that Paul is doing both: discussing what he has learned about Rome from others (particular problems), and doing so in the light of his previous, painful experiences (general exhortation). Even if this compromise solution is accepted, it is still difficult to identify specific groups with precision. Those who have made the attempt suggest a conflict between more "conservative," perhaps Jewish, or at least more ascetically oriented, Christians and less ascetic Greek Christians influenced by Hellenistic enthusiasm and spiritual freedom. If the conflict is one of "Jew and Greek" in relation to Christianity, it can be integrated into the whole of Romans more easily.

The compromise solution to Romans 14:1–15:3 is complicated by its relation to Romans 16:17–20. This passage refers to *outside* opponents. Moreover, that is only part of the problem. There are also questions about (a) whether these verses are added to chapter 16 and (b) whether chapter 16 itself is an addition to the book of Romans!

In 16:17–20 Paul recommends that "the brethren" avoid those who oppose "the doctrine which you have been taught," thereby creating dissensions and difficulties. "For such persons do not serve the Lord Christ, but their own belly, and by fair and flattering words they deceive the hearts of the simple-minded" (16:18). Then comes a commendation for the Romans' obedience followed by a typical letter-closing benediction (verse 20). These verses seem to interrupt their context. Furthermore, there seem to be other independent sections to chapter 16. At the beginning comes a "letter of recommendation" for Phoebe, "a deacon of the church at Cenchreae" (the eastern harbor area of Corinth; 16:1–3). Second, there are greetings to twenty-six persons who are named and others in families and house-churches who are not named (16:4-16). If Paul has not been to Rome, how does he know them? Third, these verses contain a concluding benediction (16:20), but it does not conclude; greetings from seven friends and coworkers and the secretary follow (16:21–24). Finally, there is a very un-Pauline-sounding "doxology." To make matters worse, in some manuscripts this doxology is absent from chapter 16, but found at the end of chapter 14, and in the earliest Romans manuscript, at the end of chapter 15! All of this looks very suspicious. Was, then, the opponents section originally part of chapter 16? If it was, did the highly unusual chapter belong to the letter to the Romans? How does Paul know so many people there? How do these concrete references comport with the fact that he writes a general "letter-essay" to this church? Do chapter 16 and its attack give the "letter-essay" a more concrete situation that would, in turn, illumine the admonitions in 14:1–15:13?

Most modern critics have argued that because chapter 16 contains many greetings, because it includes greetings to Aquila and Priscilla who had been expelled from Rome at the time of the Edict of Claudius (49 C.E.), because they had subsequently moved to Corinth and then to Ephesus (1 Cor 16:19; Acts 18:2), and because it also contains a greeting to Epaenetus, "the first fruits" (= convert) of *Asia* (16:5) where Ephesus was located, the "letter of recommendation" accompanied by greetings (16:1–20) was sent to Ephesus where Paul was well acquainted. In other words, chapter 16 was a separate letter fragment. This theory is given some added weight by the fact that the final, "floating" doxology (16:25–27) occurs at the end of chapter 15 in some manuscripts (15:33). Some argue that Romans 16 could have been attached to a copy of the Romans letter and dispatched with Phoebe to Ephesus as Paul's statement to the churches of Asia, especially since he was headed for Jerusalem and had written to Rome, other key centers. If this is correct, and if 16:17–20 was part of chapter 16, we have evidence of opponents in *Ephesus,* not Rome.

Nonetheless, it has also been argued that Paul could have had acquaintances in the Roman church, since Nero had rescinded the Edict of Claudius in 54 C.E. (see Chapters Two, Four) and many of those Jews and Jewish Christians who had been expelled were able to return to Rome. If 16:17–20 is not seen as an interruption, Romans 16:1–24 could have been sent to Rome. It would then be possible to correlate the opponents passage with 14:1–15:13 and so explain the tensions between "the weak" and "the strong" by the recently returned Jewish Christians, especially in connection with food (verse 18: "such persons serve their own belly"). In this connection, we may recall that the opponents at Philippi are accused with "their god is the belly" (Phil 3:19).

Still, can the problems of 14:1–15:13 be equated with the *outside* opponents in 16:17–20? In the former passage, Paul recommends unity, harmony, and love; in the latter, he counsels separation from the agitators. Moreover, what of the final benediction in Rom 15:33? Whether in Ephesus or Rome, and we lean toward the former, it is clear that the opponents are viewed by Paul in language reminiscent of opponents in other areas, especially Philippi and Corinth. It is thus difficult to be specific about Roman opponents.

Concluding the opponents discussion, was continual opposition to Paul simply the story of Jews versus Gentiles and of typical group conflict? In large measure, yes. But it was also the story of a religious genius, a man of "charisma," who felt called and who carried out his call, despite amazing hardships. Again, in response to his opponents, Paul boasted of his weakness in terms of his trials:

> But whatever any one dares to boast of—I am speaking as a fool—I also dare to boast of that. Are they Hebrews? So am I. Are they Israelites? So am I. Are they descendants of Abraham? So am I. Are they servants of Christ? I am a better one—I am talking like a madman—with far greater labors, far more imprisonments, with countless beatings, and often near death . . . (here follows a catalogue of dangers). Who is weak, and I am not weak? Who is made to fall, and I am not indignant? . . . And to keep me from being too elated by the abundance of revelations, a thorn was given me in the flesh, a messenger of Satan, to harass me to keep me from being too elated. Three times I besought the Lord about this, that it should leave me; but he said to me, "My grace is sufficient for you, for my power is made perfect in weakness." I will all the more gladly boast of my weaknesses, that the power of Christ may rest upon me. For the sake of Christ, then, I am content with weaknesses, insults, hardships, persecutions, and calamities; for when I am weak, then I am strong.
> (2 Cor 11:21b–29; 12:7–10)

PAUL'S URBAN COMMUNITIES

Mark, Q, and especially Jesus' parables reflect a village or agrarian setting in (Syria-)Palestine. In contrast, Paul's letters reflect the urban culture of Hellenized cities in the eastern provinces of the Roman Empire. The commercial and political language of such cities was Greek. Paul, who was a Jew reared and, at least partially, educated in Tarsus, traveled the Roman roads appealing to Greek-speaking Gentiles, some of whom were undoubtedly on the fringes of Diaspora synagogues (in Luke and Acts, "God-fearers"). Thus, Pauline mission Christianity was an urban phenomenon.

Within the Greco-Roman cities, the Christians met in **house-churches** (compare 1 Cor 16:19; Phlm 2; Rom 16) where they worshipped, discussed, had communal meals, and in general carried on their common life, including the reading of letters from apostles. Such houses had to be large enough for a number of Christians to meet. Indeed, the "household" itself was not just a single family but included relatives, household slaves, hired hands, and occasionally professional or trade partners and tenants. Whole households were sometimes baptized into Christianity (1 Cor 1:16). This undoubtedly created some conflict, since a typical household was hierarchically organized from the head of the household (*pater-familias*) down; yet, as Christians, they were supposed to be of equal status. The house-churches were local; but Paul reminded them that they were linked to a larger group in their own geographical areas (2 Cor 1:1) and, indeed, to the "church of God" itself (1 Cor 1:2), an idea that the later Pauline School developed. For Paul himself, this unity is implied in the collection.

What kinds of people became Christians? This question has been extensively studied, especially in relation to Corinth. In the past it was argued that as a whole Christianity was a lower-class social movement. It is certainly true that the Jesus movement and Pauline Christianity attracted adherents from the lower classes. It included people who because of their status (artisans, freed persons, slaves, the poor) were alienated from social and political power. Yet, it also attracted *some* members of the upper classes, and they usually provided leadership.

The "house-church" was a phenomenon that required a house large enough for a number of Christians to assemble. Paul implied that at Corinth there were some of "noble birth," and perhaps also some "wise" and "powerful" in the worldly sense (1 Cor 1:26). A study of particular individuals in Paul's churches, some of whom had political positions or offered special services or could afford to travel, bears this out. We know, for example, of the Lord's Supper controversy at Corinth, where it appears the wealthy thought of the supper as a Hellenistic banquet, or as a dinner party at one of the clubs. They ate their own meals and got drunk while others remained hungry (11:21). In this situation, "those who have nothing" were humiliated (1 Cor 11:17-34). Paul's solution was that they should wait for one another, or if the wealthy are hungry, they should eat at home (11:33-34).

Although conflicts arose inside the Pauline communities, the members strove to maintain a united front before others so that Christianity might be positively perceived by "outsiders" or "nonbelievers." This attitude had some precedent among Diaspora Jews, but the language of Paul also suggests something of a sectarian movement. The Christians called themselves "chosen," "beloved," and "holy ones," and used the language of family, that is, "father," "children," "brothers," and "sisters." Pauline Christianity had rituals of entrance (baptism, Rom 6) and perpetuation (the Lord's Supper, 1 Cor 10:16–17; 11:23–25). Paul thought of ethical behavior in terms of "imitation": his "children" were to imitate him as he imitated Christ (1 Cor 11:1). There was also exclusion of the radical nonconformist (1 Cor 5:2, 11). Thus, Paul was developing a new sense of "clean" and "unclean," "insiders" and "outsiders," that is, he was creating and maintaining group boundaries.

Nevertheless, the communities were not totally withdrawn and exclusivist. For Paul, the new era meant abolishment of the distinctions between Jew and Gentile, slave and free, male and female (Gal 3:28). Christians were not asked to break off all relations with outsiders (1 Cor 5:9–13); they were permitted to be entertained at the homes of non-Christians and even to eat "meat offered to (pagan) idols," *if* the practice did not offend the conscience of another Christian (1 Cor 8; 10:23–30). Were these communities "sectarian?" Yes—and no. W. Meeks writes:

In the letters we see Paul and his followers wrestling with a fundamental ambiguity in their conception of the social character of the church. On the one hand, it is formed as an eschatological sect, with a strong sense of group boundaries, reinforced by images of a dualistic tendency and by foundation stories of a crucified Messiah raised from the dead as the root symbol of the way God's action in the world is to be perceived and followed. On the other hand, it is an open sect, concerned not to offend "those outside" but to attract them to its message and if possible to its membership. It has other forms of self-description and basic symbols which point toward universality and comprehensiveness: it is the people of the one God, including both Jew and Gentile. Indeed, Christ is the "last Adam," the "new anthropos ['man']," the image of God and therefore the restoration of humanity to its created unity. (Meeks, "Since Then You Would Need to Go Out of the World," p. 41).

In short, understanding of the authority of Paul the apostle and his opposition on the mission field is complex; it therefore should take account of the following points:

1. the diverse nature of the sources of Galatians and Acts in connection with Paul's relation to Jerusalem;
2. evaluation of possible fragments and benedictions within Romans;
3. Paul's emphasis on his "conversion" and call;
4. the possibility that not all Jewish Christians interpreted the Jerusalem Conference as Paul did;
5. the role of the collection as *at least* a symbol of unity in the church;
6. Paul's opposition to any group that sought to require circumcision and the Law as a prerequisite to becoming a Christian, for this was a hindrance to Christian freedom;
7. the probability that in the Hellenistic churches conflicts arose because Paul's opposition to such a prerequisite was interpreted to mean that the Christian was superior in his wisdom and newfound freedom, a superiority that was fostered by Hellenistic religious fervor; and
8. the fostering of this fervor by other Hellenistic Jewish Christian missionaries who came to Paul's churches and contributed to discord by attacking his authority on "charismatic" grounds. When this opposition occurred, Paul's response was to claim that his own authority was rooted in a different sort of "charisma," namely, the power of a loving God who acts through weakness. And the foundation for this claim was the Cross of Christ. In this way, Paul sought to put limitations on the misinterpretation of the freedom he himself had preached against slavery to circumcision and the Law. In this manner, he hoped to maintain Christian unity.

PAUL'S CONTINUING COMMUNICATION WITH HIS CHURCHES: THE PAULINE LETTER

When Paul was prevented from visiting a community for a period of time, he could not, of course, schedule a telephone conference call. Rather, he continued a dialogue with it by means of oral reports from travelers, coworkers, or delegations, and the letters they delivered. Thus, his communication continued, the oral reports supplementing the letters and vice versa.

As implied above, Paul's letters were normally dictated to a secretary (Latin, *amanuensis,* "of the hand"). Romans 16:22 says, "I, Tertius, writer of this letter, greet you in the Lord." Yet, Paul would sometimes give his stamp of authority to a letter by composing the last lines (Phlm 19; 1 Cor 16:21; Gal 6:11; compare 2 Thess 3:17; Col 4:18). The letters were usually written to the whole community or communities in a specific geographical area. Even Paul's most personal letter to Philemon was read publicly to those gathered in the house-church. In 1 Thessalonians 5:27, he stressed that his letter be read publicly, and as we shall see, this tradition was carried on in his name by his school (2 Thess 3:14–15).

How do Paul's letters compare with other letters of the period? This is an important question because letters have a particular social function and because an understanding of the medium in which he writes will be an important aid in understanding his message in a particular social-historical context. We are fortunate to have access not only to more "literary" types of letters from classical literature, including the "letter-essay," but to a large number of "nonliterary" papyrus letters discovered by archaeologists. These include personal letters to friends and relatives, business letters, and various kinds of governmental, military, diplomatic, and legal correspondence. The writers of these personal letters represent what is typical, for example, friendly, cordial relationships (*philophronesis*) between themselves and their recipients, just as Paul does in his letters (esp. 2 Cor 1:1–2:13; 7:5–16; Phil 1:3–3:1a; 4:1–20). Thus, they especially reveal typical role relationships within the Christian groups related to Paul's authority, local authorities, and opponents. Furthermore it is clear that Greco-Roman letter writers follow a rather set pattern, or form, and that Paul modifies it. That will be our concern here.

To illustrate the letter form, we offer as an example a typical personal letter from the papyri and compare it to Paul's most personal letter, the letter to Philemon.

Apion's Letter to His Father Epimachus

Apion to Epimachus his father and lord, many greetings. Before all things I pray that you are in health, and that you prosper and fare well continually together with my sister and her daughter and my brother. I thank the lord Serapis that when I was in peril on the sea he saved me immediately. When I came to Miseni, I received as viaticum (journey money) from the Caesar three pieces of gold. And it is well with me but I urge you, my lord father, to write me a little letter: first, about your welfare; second, about my brother and sister; third, so that I may do obeisance to your hand, because you have taught me well and I have hopes therefore of advancing quickly, if the gods are willing. Greet Capito much and my brother and sister and Serenilla and my friends. By Euctemon I am sending you a little picture of myself. Furthermore, my name is (now) Antonis Maximus. Be well, I pray. Centuris Athenonica (my military unit). The following send their greetings: Serenus the son of Agathus Daemon, and . . . the son of. . . and Turbo the son of Gallonius and . . . the son of . . . (Farewell!)

[On the back]
To Philadelphis for Epimaxus from Apion his son
Give this to the first cohort of the Apamenians to (?)
                              Julianus An ...
the Liblarios, from Apion   so that he may convey it to
                              Epimachus his father.

The Letter to Philemon as a Comparison

Behind the letter of Philemon was a story related to the ancient legal system and practice of slavery. Paul was in prison (probably in Ephesus) and there he met a runaway slave, Onesimus ("Useful"), whom he converted to Christianity. According to Roman law, runaway slaves had to be returned to their masters and were liable to severe punishment, even death; anyone who helped a slave was liable to his master for damages. Thus, Paul was sending Onesimus back to Philemon. In this instance, however, Onesimus' master, Philemon, was a Christian, that is, the problem centered on a Christian slave owner and a Christian runaway slave. Philemon also owed his "life" to Paul, and reciprocity was due. So Paul (in his letter) carefully blended punctilious observance of the slave law with shrewdly conceived appeals to Philemon.

Philemon is addressed as a "beloved fellow worker" and commended for his love and faith. Paul assures him that as an apostle, he could command him to do his duty, but prefers to appeal to his free will. In passing Paul puns that Onesimus has been "useless" to Philemon, but now he is "useful" to both of them (verse 11). Paul then offers to pay any damages incurred. He again makes a pun in writing that he "wants some benefit" (*onaimēn*) from Onesimus (verse 20) and adds that he is confident of Philemon's obedience. He asks him to prepare for his coming and he concludes with greetings and a benediction.

We may now compare the letter to Epimachus and the letter to Philemon to illustrate the extent to which Paul uses conventional letter-writing forms.

Paul follows the customary Greek letter form, making three interesting changes. First, Paul changes the simple "greetings" (*chairein*) to the similar Greek term "grace" (*charis*), which is one of Paul's key terms, referring to God's gift of salvation in Jesus Christ. Second, Paul adds to it the typical Jewish greeting, "Peace" (*Shalōm*), but Christianizes it with "peace from ... our Lord Jesus Christ." The greeting formula, "*Grace* to you and *peace* from God our father and the Lord Jesus Christ ..." is highly characteristic of Paul's letters. Finally, whereas the Greek letter usually has a simple "farewell" as a closing, Paul's letter has a religious benediction. Other letters of Paul have several common "closing" elements (see following page).

All of Paul's letters have this overall structure, though he modifies it to fit special circumstances. 1 Thessalonians is full of thanksgivings for the Thessalonians' persevering under persecution. In the letter to the Galatians, where Paul is angry, he omits the "thanksgiving," normally a highly complimentary section to the recipients, and his initial salutation becomes a defense of his apostleship. Romans has an analogous adaptation; since Paul has not been to Rome, the salu-

A. Introduction	Papyrus Letter	Philemon
I. Salutation		
1. Sender	Apion	Paul; Timothy;
2. Recipient	Epimachus	Philemon; Apphia;
		Archippus; his household
3. Greeting	greetings	Grace to you and peace from God our Father and the Lord Jesus Christ
II. Thanksgiving & prayer	Prays for their well-being and thanks God for a safe journey	I thank God always when I remember you in my prayers
B. Central Section		
III. Body	Statement about wages; hopes for advancement	Paul asks Philemon to "accept" the slave Onesimus
IV. Parenesis or other commands	Urges father to write to him about the family	Receive him as you would me... Charge that to my account. Refresh my heart in Christ. Prepare a guest room for me.
C. Conclusion		
V. Greetings to . . .	Capito; my brother; my sister; Serenilla; my friends	Absent but present in other letters; implicit in "you" (=recipients)
Greetings from . . .	Serenus; -?-; Turbo; -?-	Epaphras; Mark; Aristarchus; Demas; Luke; my fellow workers
VI. Closing or benediction	Absent due to text mutilation; usually, "Farewell"	The grace of the Lord Jesus Christ be with your spirit.

[(Based on C.J. Roetzel, *The Letters of Paul*, 2d ed. (1982), p. 40 (John Knox)]

tation contains a long summary of his gospel and defines his apostolic mission (1:1–7). Although Paul's salutations usually speak to the specific situation of the recipients, he sometimes alters them with materials from the liturgical tradition.

The central section contains the body and the parenesis. The body of the letter covers the major themes of the letter. Paul usually begins with some formula of request ("I beseech you . . .") or disclosure ("I would not have you ignorant . . .") and closes with some statement about his itinerary. He omits this only in Galatians because he has no intention to return, and so he refers to his previous visit (Gal 4:12–15).

The two examples above have very little parenesis in the central section, in part because they are so short. Usually Paul has a longer ethical exhortation section or homily ("sermonette") at this point. This does not mean that he omits parenetic exhortations in the body of his letters. Shorter clusters of moral maxims about Christian virtues or virtue and vice lists common in the Hellenistic schools may crop up almost anywhere. Yet, the lengthier parenetic sections normally occur after the body of the letter and before the conclusion.

There are various possibilities for the conclusion of Paul's letters: the "peace wish," the kiss, an apostolic command, and a benediction are often found. The "peace wish," like the term "peace" in the greeting, reflects the Hebrew *Shalōm*, that is, well-wishing for one's health, though Paul sometimes uses it as an occasion for recalling a major theme in the letter (1 Thess 4:9). Then come greetings and often another reference to "grace." Thus, as Paul opens with "grace" and "peace," so he closes with "peace" and "grace." As in Hellenistic letters, a prayer request may be added (1 Thess 5:25; Rom 15:30).

"The kiss" that follows sometimes has been thought to be a liturgical sign, that is, that after the reading of the letter the Christians would celebrate the liturgy. It is more likely a sign of affection within the Christian family. Exhortations often follow. Finally comes the benediction with its word of grace occasionally related to a threat (1 Cor 16:23; compare 1 Thess 5:27; Gal 6:17), or perhaps an apocalyptic cry, probably from the eucharistic liturgy (1 Cor 16:22: "Our Lord, come!" compare Rev 22:20).

Our model of comparison has been Paul's most personal letter. Even that letter, however, has its public side, since it was intended to be read to those gathered in the house-church (Phlm 2), probably at Colossae (compare Col 4:9). Moreover, this is not the only type of letter in the Pauline corpus. We find a letter of recommendation for Phoebe (Rom 16:1–2) and a reference to the opponents' letters of recommendation (compare 2 Cor 3:1–3). As noted, some letters stress thanksgiving (1 Thess 1:2–3:10; compare Phil 1:3–3:1a; 4:10–20). One contains responses to questions in a letter sent to Paul (1 Cor 7–15). Galatians is largely an apologetic letter, also containing advice. 1 Thessalonians is mostly a parenetic letter of exhortation. Romans 1–15 is a long letter-essay. All are all well-known letter types in the Greco-Roman world.

As we have said it was essential for Paul to stay in touch with his communities in order to continue his conversations with the believers and to challenge the views of the opponents. These letters employed the conventional forms of the day, modified in the direction of Christian faith and practice. As such, Paul's letters were an expression of his role as apostle to the Gentiles.

TRADITIONS IN PAUL'S LETTERS

Though Paul claimed that he was not *taught* his gospel, he remained at Damascus and Arabia (among Christians?) three years, visited Peter and James at Jerusalem for a little over two weeks, associated with Christians in the areas of Syria and Cilicia, and noted that his gospel was recognized at the Jerusalem Conference (Gal 1:11–2:10). At these locations, he undoubtedly became acquainted with Christological confessions and hymns, liturgical formulas, and traditions of "words of the Lord." Moreover, he was deeply immersed in the Scriptures and argued from them in ways he learned from his Pharisaic background. He was also educated in the Greek traditions, as his use of rhetorical devices, literary conventions, and parenetic traditions show.

As we have seen in Chapter Five, there are ways of recognizing and isolating traditions. They often interrupt Paul's line of argument, are sometimes introduced by well-known terms for transmitting traditions, and have a certain poetic or hymnic style; they contain basic Christological ideas (not always Paul's), and have a number of atypical terms and phrases. Here we shall summarize a few typical examples.

OUTLINE OF LETTER STRUCTURE

		1 Thessalonians	1 Corinthians	2 Corinthians	Galatians	Philippians	Romans
INTRODUCTION	I. SALUTATION						
	A. Sender	1:1a	1:1	1:1a	1:1–2a	1:1	1:1–6
	B. Recipient	1:1b	1:2	1:1b	1:2b	1:1	1:7a
	C. Greeting	1:1c	1:3	1:2	1:3–5	1:2	1:7b
	II. THANKSGIVING	1:2–10 2:13 3:9–10	1:4–9	1:3–7	None!	1:3–11	1:8–17
CENTRAL SECTION	III. BODY	2:1–3:8 (possibly 3:11–13)	1:10–4:21	1:8–9:15 (letter fragments) 10:1–13:10 (letter fragment)	1:6–4:31	1:12–2:11 3:2–4:1 4:10–20	1:18–11:36
	IV. ETHICAL EXHORTATION AND INSTRUCTIONS	4:1–5:22	5:1–16:12 16:13–18 (closing parenesis)	13:11a (summary)	5:1–6:10 6:11–15 (letter summary)	2:12–3:1 4:2–6	12:1–15:13 15:14–32 (travel plans and closing parenesis)
CONCLUSION	V. CLOSING						
	A. Peace Wish	5:23–24	—	13:11b	6:16	4:7–9	15:33
	B. Greetings	—	16:19–20a	13:13	—	4:21–22	16:3–15(?)
	C. Kiss	5:26	16:20b	13:12	—	—	16:16(?)
	Apostolic Command	5:27	16:22	—	6:17	—	—
	D. Benediction	5:28	16:23–24	13:14	6:18	4:23	16:20(?)

Reprinted from *The Letters of Paul: Conversations in Context*, 2d edition, by Calvin J. Roetzel, p. 40 (slightly modified). Copyright John Knox Press 1982. Used by permission.

A *death-resurrection-appearance tradition* is recognizable by technical terms for transmitting oral traditions ("delivered...received"), by a formal pattern, and a number of atypical terms and phrases (1 Cor 15:3–5; see Chapter Five).

A *Christological confession:*

...if you confess with your lips that Jesus is Lord and believe in your heart that God raised him from the dead, you will be saved. (Rom 10:9)

A *Christological creed* that does not accord precisely with Paul's views of Jesus as the preexistent Son of God (Rom 1:3–4; see Chapter Five).

A *Christological hymn* in Phil 2:6–11 (see Chapter Five).

A *Lord's Supper tradition* with the technical terms for transmitting tradition (see Chapter Five).

A *baptismal liturgy:*

(For as many of you as were baptized into Christ have put on Christ.)

There is neither Jew nor Greek,

There is neither slave nor free,

There is neither male nor female;

For you are all one in Christ Jesus. (Gal 3:27–28; compare 1 Cor 12:13; Col 3:11; Chapter Five)

A *prayer doxology:*

Thanks be to God through Jesus Christ our Lord. (Rom 7:25)

A *"word of the Lord"* (that is, a Jesus tradition):

To the married I give this command—not I but the Lord—that the wife should not separate from her husband...and that the husband should not divorce his wife. (1 Cor 7:10–11; see Mark 10:2–9)

A *catalogue of vices and virtues,* commonly used by Hellenistic moral philosophers: (Now the works of the flesh are plain:) immorality, impurity, licentiousness, idolatry, sorcery, enmity, strife, jealousy, anger, selfishness, dissension, party spirit, envy, drunkenness, carousing, and the like... (But the fruit of the Spirit is) love, joy, peace, patience, kindness, goodness, faithfulness, gentleness, self-control... (Gal 5:19–23; compare 1 Cor 6:9–11)

A *proverb:*

Bad company ruins good morals. (1 Cor 15:33)

We conclude by noting that Paul was immersed in the Scriptures and frequently used them as a source to buttress his arguments. Most of his allusions and quotations come from the Greek Septuagint, but many of his arguments rely on methods that, however strange to modern ears, were known among the Jewish scholars of his day. We cite two examples:

A *known Jewish "midrash" (scriptural interpretation)* given Christian meaning: (In speaking of the Israelites' wilderness wanderings after the Exodus from Egypt, Paul refers to the Rock.)

> I do not want you to be unaware, brothers and sisters, that our ancestors were all under a cloud, and all passed through the sea, and all were baptized into Moses in the cloud and in the sea, and all ate the same spiritual food [for example, manna, compare Exod 16:4–35], and all drank the same spiritual drink (Exod 17:6; Num 20:2–13). For they drank from the spiritual rock that followed them, *and the rock was Christ.* Nevertheless, God was not pleased with most of them,

and they were struck down in the wilderness. Now these things occurred as examples for us, so that we might not desire evil as they did.... (1 Cor 10:1–6; compare Tosefta, *Sukkah* 3:11)

An association between two meanings of a single Greek word *diathēkē*, "will" and "covenant," combined with an interpretation of the collective (plural meaning) noun *sperma*, "seed," meaning "offspring," in its grammatically singular sense.

Brothers and sisters, I give an example from daily life: once a person's *will* (*diathēkē*,) has been ratified, no one adds to it or annuls it. Now the promises were made to Abraham and to his *offspring (sperma:* "seed"); it does not say, "And to offsprings *(spermata:* "seeds")," as of many; but it says, "And to your offspring *(sperma)*" (Gen 12:7), *that is, to one person, who is Christ.* My point is this: the law (of Moses), which came four hundred thirty years later, does not annul a *covenant ([diathēkē]* with Abraham) previously ratified by God (like a *will*), so as to nullify the promise. For if the (willed) inheritance comes from the law, it no longer comes from the promise; but God granted it to Abraham through the promise. Why then the law? It was added because of transgressions, *until the offspring ("seed") would come to whom the promise had been made. . .* (Gal 3:15–19a)

In our interpretations of Paul's letters in the following chapter, we shall occasionally identify such traditional elements.

SUMMARY

In this chapter, we evaluated the sources for the life and thought of Paul and set forth a chronology of his career. We developed a brief sketch of Paul's life, including his background, "conversion" and call, and his activity as a Christian missionary. Along the way we highlighted the Jerusalem Conference and noted again the Antioch Incident. We briefly visited each of the major cities where Paul established a group of Christians. Then, we discussed Paul's authority as an apostle, indicating his relationship to the Jerusalem "mother" church, his authority in the Gentile churches he "fathered," and his conflicts with more conservative Christians at Jerusalem and on the mission field. Other opponents arose within his Gentile congregations. Some of them seem to have interpreted Paul's teachings in the light of the mystery cults and early forms of Gnosticism, as well as general Hellenistic religious fervor. Competitors challenged Paul's credentials as an apostle, apparently some on the basis that Jesus was a heroic miracle worker. We also noted the "class" divisions in Paul's urban house-churches. Finally, we indicated that Paul continued his conversations with his churches by means of the letter. We indicated its general structure in relation to Hellenistic letters, noting some Christian changes and his use of traditions and scripture.

Having used Philemon as a model, and noted some sources in Paul's undisputed letters, in the following chapter we shall interpret the letters by means of brief interpretative outlines.

FURTHER READING

(See Further Reading, Chapter Seven)

The literature on Paul is extensive. We shall give a general bibliography plus some works that have special relevance to the subjects discussed. General introductions to the New Testament often have discussions of isolated topics such as sources, Pauline chronology, the life of Paul, letter forms, and the like. Further bibliography will be given in the following chapter, and the student is advised to consult both.

For Bibliography:
NJBC: "Paul," pp. 1329–1337 (J. A. Fitzmyer).

General Books
J. Beker, *Paul the Apostle: The Triumph of God in Life and Thought.*
G. Bornkamm, *Paul.*
W. D. Davies, *Paul and Rabbinic Judaism.*
M. Dibelius, and W. G. Kümmel, *Paul.*
E. Käsemann, *Perspectives on Paul.*
J. Knox, *Chapters in a Life of Paul.*
W. Meeks, *The Writings of St. Paul.*
A. D. Nock, *Saint Paul.*
E. P. Sanders, *Paul and Palestinian Judaism.*
———, *Paul, the Law, and the Jewish People.*
S. Sandmel, *The Genius of Paul.*
H. J. Schoeps, *Paul: The Theology of the Apostle in the Light of Jewish Religious History.*
V. Wimbush, *Paul: The Worldly Ascetic.*
General Articles
ABD: "Paul" (H. D. Betz).

IDB: "Paul the Apostle" (A. C. Purdy).

Sources: Letters and Acts as Sources (see Chronology)
E. Haenchen, "The Book of Acts as Source Material for the History of Early Christianity," in L. Keck and J. L. Martyn, *Studies in Luke-Acts,* pp. 279–289.

M. Hengel, *Acts and the History of Earliest Christianity.*
J. Knox, "Acts and the Pauline Letter Corpus," in Keck and Martyn, *Studies,* pp. 258–278.

A. J. Mattill, "The Value of Acts as a Source for the Study of Paul,' in C. Talbert, ed. *Perspectives on Luke-Acts,* pp. 76–98.

P. Vielhauer, "On the 'Paulinism' of Acts," in Keck and Martyn, *Studies,* pp. 33–50.

Sources: Pauline Letter Fragments (see Chronology)
ABD: "Corinthians, Second Epistle to the" (H. D. Betz); "Philippians, Epistle to the" (J. T. Fitzgerald).

IDB Suppl.: "Corinthians, Second" (D. Georgi); "Philippians, Letter to the" (H. Koester); "Romans, Letter to the" (G. Klein).

H. D. Betz, "2 Cor. 6:14–7:1: An Anti-Pauline Fragment?" *Journal of Biblical Literature* 92 (1973), pp. 88–108.

K. P. Donfried, "A Short Note on Romans 16" in Donfried, ed., *The Romans Debate,* pp. 50–60.

———, "False Presuppositions in the Study of Romans," *Catholic Biblical Quarterly* 36 (1974), pp. 332–355.

J. A. Fitzmyer, "Qumran and the Interpolated Paragraph in 2 Cor. 6:14–7:1," *Catholic Biblical Quarterly* 23 (1961), pp. 271–280.

H. Y. Gamble, *The Textual History of the Letter to the Romans.*

D. E. Garland, "The Composition and Unity of Philippians," *Novum Testamentum* 27 (1985), pp. 141–173.

D. Georgi, *The Opponents of Paul in Second Corinthians: A Study of Religious Propaganda in Late Antiquity.*

J. Gnilka, "2 Cor. 6:14–7:1 in the Light of the Qumran Texts and the Testaments of the Twelve Patriarchs," in J. Murphy-O'Connor, *Paul and Qumran,* pp. 46–68.

R. Jewett, "The Epistolary Thanksgiving and the Integrity of Philippians," *Novum Testamentum* 12 (1970), pp. 40–53.

J. I. H. McDonald, "Was Romans XVI a Separate Letter?" *New Testament Studies* 16 (1969–1970), pp. 369–372.

J. Murphy-O'Connor, "Relating 2 Cor 6:14–7:1 to Its Context," *New Testament Studies* 33 (1987), pp. 272–275.

T. E. Pollard, "The Integrity of Philippians," *New Testament Studies* 13 (1966-1967), pp. 57–66.

B. D. Rahtjen, "The Three Letters of Paul to the Phillippians," *New Testament Studies* 6 (1959–1960), pp. 167–173.

D. Rendsberger, "2 Corinthians 6:14–7:1: A Fresh Examination," *Studia Biblica et Theologica* 8 (1978), pp. 25–49.

J. Reumann, "Philippians 3:20–21—A Hymnic Fragment?" *New Testament Studies* 30 (1984), pp. 593–609.

M. E. Thrall, "The Problem of 2 Cor 6:14–7:1 in Some Recent Discussion," *New Testament Studies* 24 (1977–1978), pp. 132–148.

———, "The Problem of II Cor VI.14–VII.1 in Some Recent Discussion," *New Testament Studies* 24 (1977–1978), pp.132–148.

Sources: Apocrypha

ABD: "Epistles (Apocryphal)" (D. A. Thomason); "Laodiceans, Epistle to the" (C. P. Anderson); "Paul and Seneca, Epistles of" (D. A. Thomason); "Paul, Acts of" (P. Sellew); "Paul, Apocalypse of" (P. Perkins); "Paul, Martyrdom of" (P. Sellew); "Paul, Prayer of the Apostle" (H. W. Attridge); "Peter and Paul, Acts of" (R. F. Stoops, Jr.); "Peter and Paul, Passion of" (R. F. Stoops, Jr.).

The Acts of Paul and Thecla in E. Hennecke and W. Schneemelcher, *New Testament Apocrypha,* Vol. 2, pp. 353–364.

The Acts of Paul and Thecla in W. Meeks, *The Writings of St. Paul,* pp. 199–207.

Chronology and Life of Paul (see Sources)

ADB: "Gallio" (K. Haacker); "Mark, John" (C. N. Jefford); "Peter" (K. P. Donfried); "Saul" (D. E. Edelman).

IDB Suppl.: "Chronology, Pauline" (J. C. Hurd); "Paul the Apostle" (J. C. Hurd).

NJBC: "Paul" (J. Fitzmyer), pp. 1329–1337 (text of Delphi [Gallio] Inscription).

G. Bornkamm, *Paul* (Part I).

R. Brown and J. P. Meier, *Antioch and Rome.*

T. H. Campbell, "Paul's Missionary Journeys as Reflected in His Letters," *Journal of Biblical Literature* 74 (1955), pp. 80–87.

J. Knox, *Chapters in a Life of Paul.*

G. Lüdemann, *Paul, Apostle to the Gentiles: Studies in Chronology.*

D. R. MacDonald, *The Legend and the Apostle: The Battle for Paul in Story and Canon.*

J. Murphy-O'Connor, "Pauline Missions Before the Jerusalem Conference," *Revue Biblique* 89 (1982), pp. 71–91.

G. Ogg, *The Chronology of the Life of Paul.*

Background

E. P. Sanders, *Paul and Palestinian Judaism.*

——, *Paul, the Law, and the Jewish People.*

Paul as Artisan (see below, Society and Culture)

Paul's Call and "Conversion"

J. G. Gager, "Some Notes on Paul's Conversion," *New Testament Studies* 27 (1981), pp. 697–704.

H. Räisänen, "Paul's Conversion and the Development of His View of the Law," *New Testament Studies* 33 (1987), pp. 404–419.

K. Stendahl, "The Apostle Paul and the Introspective Conscience of the West," reprinted in W. Meeks, *The Writings of St. Paul,* pp. 422–423, and *Paul Among Jews and Gentiles,* pp. 78–96.

Response: E. Käsemann, "Justification and Salvation History in the Epistle to the Romans," *Perspectives on Paul,* pp. 60–78; Stendahl replied, pp. 129–133.

Jerusalem Conference

ABD: "Jerusalem, Council of" (C. B. Cousar).

S. G. Wilson,. *Luke and the Law.*

Missions and Cities (see Chronology; Social and Cultural Environment).

ABD: "Antioch of Syria" (F. W. Norris); "Cities (Greco-Roman)" (J. M. Stambaugh); "Ephesus" (R. E. Oster, Jr.); "Athens" (H. M. Martin, Jr.); "Cities, Greco-Roman" (G. Downey); "Corinth" (J. Murphy-O'Connor); "Ephesus" (R. E. Oster, Jr.); "Philippi" (H. L. Hendrix); "Rome" (J. F. Hall); "Rome, Christian Monuments at" (G. F. Snyder); "Sardis" (J. G. Pedley); "Thessalonica" (H. L. Hendrix).

R. K. Harrison, ed. *Major Cities of the Biblical World.*

S. E. Johnson, *Paul the Apostle and His Cities.*

A. H. M. Jones, *The Cities of the Eastern Roman Provinces.* 2d ed., revised by Michael Avi-Yonah, *et al.*

J. Murphy-O'Connor, *St. Paul's Corinth: Texts and Archeology.*

Paul's Authority and Opponents (see Social and Cultural Environment)

ABD: "Apostle" (H. D. Betz).

G. Bornkamm, *Paul,* pp. 18–22, 32–35, 82–84, 174–176.

J. D. G. Dunn, "The Relationship Between Paul and Jerusalem According to Galatians 1 and 2," *New Testament Studies* 28 (1982), pp. 461–478.

——, "The Incident at Antioch (Gal 2:11–18)," *Journal for the Study of the New Testament* 18 (1983), pp. 3–57.

C. Forbes, "Comparison, Self-Praise, and Irony: Paul's Boasting and the Conventions of Hellenistic Rhetoric," *New Testament Studies* 32 (1986), pp. 1–30.

L. Gaston, "Paul and Jerusalem," in *From Paul to Jesus,* pp. 61–72.

G. Lüdemann, *Opposition to Paul in Jewish Christianity.*

K. F. Nickle, *The Collection: A Study in Paul's Strategy.*

W. Schmithals, *Paul and the Gnostics.*

1 Corinthians

C. Forbes, "Early Christian Inspired Speech and Hellenistic Popular Religion," *Novum Testamentum* 28 (1986), pp. 257–270.

R. A. Horsley, "Wisdom of Word and Words of Wisdom in Corinth," *Catholic Biblical Quarterly* 39 (1977), pp. 224–239.

———, "'How Can Some of You Say That There Is No Resurrection of the Dead?' Spiritual Elitism in Corinth," *Novum Testamentum* 20 (1978), pp. 203–231.

B. Pearson, *The Pneumatikos-Psychikos Terminology in 1 Corinthians: A Study in the Theology of the Corinthians Opponents of Paul in Relation to Gnosticism.*

2 Corinthians

IDB Suppl.: "Corinthians, Second Letter to the" (D. Georgi).

C. K. Barrett, "Paul's Opponents in II Corinthians," *New Testament Studies* 17 (1970-1971), pp. 233–254.

J. N. Collins, "Georgi's 'Envoys' in 2 Cor 11:23," *Journal of Biblical Literature* 93 (1974), pp. 88–96.

D. Georgi, *The Opponents of Paul in Second Corinthians: A Study of Religious Propaganda in Late Antiquity.*

D. Kee, "Who Were the 'Super-Apostles' of 2 Corinthians?" *Restoration Quarterly* 23 (1980), pp. 65–76.

S. E. McClelland, "Super-Apostles, Servants of Christ, Servants of Satan: A Response," *Journal for the Study of the New Testament* 14 (1982), pp. 82–87.

J. Neyrey, "Witchcraft Accusations in 2 Corinthians 10-13: Paul in Social Science Perspective," *Listening. Journal of Religion and Culture* 21 (1986), pp. 160–170.

M. E. Thrall, "Super-Apostles, Servants of Christ, and Servants of Satan," *Journal for the Study of the New Testament* 6 (1980), pp. 42–57.

Romans

K. P. Donfried, ed., *The Romans Debate.*

Galatians

B. H. Brinsmead, *Galatians—Dialogical Response to Opponents.*

G. Howard, *Paul: Crisis in Galatia.*

R. Jewett, "The Agitators and the Galatian Congregation," *New Testament Studies* 17 (1971), pp. 198–212.

———, "The Agitators and the Galatian Community," *New Testament Studies* 17 (1970), pp. 198–212.

J. Tyson, "Paul's Opponents in Galatia," *Novum Testamentum* 10 (1968), pp. 241–264.

Philippians

R. Jewett, "Conflicting Movements in the Early Church as Reflected in Philippians," *Novum Testamentum* 12 (1970), pp. 361–390.

A. F. J. Klijn, "Paul's Opponents in Phil 3," *Novum Testamentum* 7 (1964–1965), pp. 278–284.

H. Koester, "The Purpose of the Polemic of a Pauline Fragment (Phil III)," *New Testament Studies* 8 (1961–1962), pp. 317–332.

Social and Cultural Environment (See Paul's Authority, Cities)

ABD: "Aretas" (D. F. Graf); "Athens" (H. M. Martin, Jr.); "Christianity in Asia Minor" (R. E. Oster, Jr.); "Christianity in Greece" (L. M. McDonald); "Christianity in Rome" (G. F. Snyder); "Christianity in Syria" (D. Bundy); "Cilicia" (J. D. Bing); "Circumcision" (R. G. Hall); "Citizenship" (F. F. Bruce); "Contribution for the Saints" (B. R. Gaventa); "Education (Greco-Roman Period)" (J. T. Townsend); "Family (New Testament)" (C. J. H. Wright); "Festus, Porcias" (J. B. Green); "Gallio" (K. Haacker); "Gamaliel" (B. Chilton); "Greece" (J. R. McRay); "Prisca" (P. Lampe).

R. Banks, *Paul's Idea of Community: The Early House Churches in Their Historical Setting.*

R. F. Hock, "Paul's Tentmaking and the Problem of His Social Class," *Journal of Biblical Literature* 97 (1978), pp. 555–564.

———, "The Workshop as a Social Setting for Paul's Missionary Preaching," *Catholic Biblical Quarterly* 41 (1979), pp. 438–450.

———, *The Social Context of Paul's Ministry: Tentmaking and Apostleship.*

B. Holmberg, *Paul and Power.*

E. A. Judge, *The Social Pattern of Christian Groups in the First Century.*

M. Y. MacDonald, *The Pauline Churches. A Socio-Historical Study of Institutionalization in the Pauline and Deutero-Pauline Writings.*

A. J. Malherbe, *Social Aspects of Early Christianity.*

W. Meeks, "'Since Then You Would Need to Go Out of the World': Group Boundaries in Pauline Christianity," in T. J. Ryan, ed., *Critical History and Biblical Faith. New Testament Perspectives*, pp. 4–29.

———, *The First Urban Christians.*

J. Neyrey, *Paul, in Other Words.*

N. Petersen, *Rediscovering Paul: Philemon and the Sociology of Paul's Narrative World.*

J. H. Schütz, *Paul and the Anatomy of Apostolic Authority.*

G. Theissen, *The Social Setting of Pauline Christianity.* (Corinth)

F. Watson, *Paul, Judaism and the Gentiles. A Sociological Approach.*

Letters

ABD: "Letters (Greek and Latin)" (S. Stowers); "Kiss (NT)" (W. Klassen); "Thanksgiving" (C. Wolff, trans. R. H. Fuller).

IDB Suppl.: "Letter" (N. A. Dahl).

NJBC: "Introduction to the New Testament Epistles," pp. 768–771 (J. A. Fitzmeyer).

F. F. Church, "Rhetorical Structure and Design in Paul's Letter to Philemon," *Harvard Theological Review* 71 (1978), pp. 17–33.

W. Doty, *Letters in Primitive Christianity.*

R. Funk, *Language, Hermeneutic, and Word of God,* "Language as It Occurs in the New Testament: Letter," pp. 224–274.

N. Petersen, *Rediscovering Paul: Philemon and the Sociology of Paul's Narrative World.*

C. Roetzel, *The Letters of Paul.* 2d ed. (ch. 2).

K. H. Schelke, "The Letters of Paul," in K. Rahner, *Sacramentum Mundi,* vol. 4, pp. 198–203.

M. L. Stirnewalt, "The Form and Function of the Greek Letter-Essay," in C. P. Donfried, *The Romans Debate,* pp. 175–206.

S. K. Stowers, *Letter Writing in Greco-Roman Antiquity.*

J. L. White, ed., *Studies in Ancient Letter Writing. Semeia 22.*

J. L. White, *Light from Ancient Letters.*

Pre-Pauline Traditions (see Chapters Four, Five)

G. Bornkamm, "On Understanding the Christ-Hymn, Phil 2:6–11," *Early Christian Experience* (New York: Harper & Row), pp.112–122.

D. Duling, *Jesus Christ Through History*, pp. 43–52.

A. M. Hunter, *Paul and His Predecessors*.

R. P. Martin, *Carmen Christi: Philippians ii 5–11 in Recent Interpretation and in the Setting of Early Christian Worship*.

J. Murphy-O'Connor, "Tradition and Redaction in 1 Cor 15:3–7," *Catholic Biblical Quarterly* 43 (1981), pp. 582–589.

J. Neyrey, *Christ Is Community. The Christologies of the New Testament*. Part II.

C. Roetzel, *The Letters of Paul*. 2d ed. (ch. 3).

Additions to the Letters ("Interpolations") (See the bibliography on 2 Cor 6:14–7:1 above).

B. A. Pearson, "1 Thessalonians 2:13–16: A Deutero-Pauline Interpolation," *Harvard Theological Review* 64 (1971), pp. 79–94.

D. Schmidt, "I Thess 2:13–16: Linguistic Evidence for an Interpolation," *Journal of Biblical Literature* 102 (1983), pp. 269–279.

R. Scroggs, "Paul and the Eschatological Woman," *Journal of the American Academy of Religion* 40 (1972), pp. 283–303.

A beautiful young woman from a fresco originally in the city of Pompeii, Italy (destroyed by lava from the eruption of Mount Vesuvius in 79 C.E.), now in the National Museum, Naples, Italy. Her apparel shows that she was of the upper social strata. She was presumably educated (she muses over a book). In Paul's churches women of means held authority and seem to have been patrons (e.g., Rom 16:1–3). Paul's ideal was "…no longer male and female…in Christ Jesus" (Gal 3:28); see the summary of Paul's view of women on pp.252–253.

CHAPTER SEVEN

PAUL'S LETTERS: HISTORICAL CONTEXT, SOCIAL CONTEXT, AND THEOLOGY

Paul of Tarsus, educated in the Greek tradition, a Diaspora Jew with Pharisaic training, of the tribe of Benjamin, former persecutor of the Christian church, had a "religious experience": he received a revelation of Jesus Christ that he associated with his call to become apostle to the Gentiles. He became a Christian missionary who was especially equipped by his background and training to communicate his gospel to the non-Jewish inhabitants of the Roman Empire. He planted house-churches with zeal in the major urban centers of Asia Minor and Macedonia-Greece. With the exception of Antioch and Ephesus, he would stay at these locations for only short periods, and then leave to start a new house-church in a new city. Thus, we usually catch glimpses of Paul as he established a small community where none had existed, or on his travels. He normally supported himself as a tentmaker. Often he encountered opposition from political authorities and religious opponents. Continally he communicated by letters with the churches he had established.

We have set the stage for understanding Paul and his strategy. Now we shall read his correspondence with the aid of interpretative outlines, concentrating especially on 1 Corinthians, Galatians, and Romans. The following outlines are no substitute for reading Paul himself; the student should use them merely as a guide to some of the major points of Paul's thinking in his ancient historical and social context. The chapter will conclude with a brief summary of some of Paul's main theological ideas and his approach to ethical problems.

FIRST THESSALONIANS

Background

According to our reconstructed itinerary in Chapter Six, Paul entered Macedonia, or northern Greece, and established his first European house-church in

Philippi. He then traveled the major Roman highway, the Egnatian Way, westward across Macedonia to Thessalonica. This city, named for the sister of Alexander the Great, was the chief seaport and capital of Macedonia, and its most populous city. Here he established another congregation. While there Paul and his companions worked hard to support themselves, but they were treated shabbily (1 Thess 2:2). In this instance, we have a classic divergence between Acts and Paul's letters. Acts suggests that the major opposition came from *Jews* who resented Paul's preaching in the synagogue and who were jealous of the conversion of "God-fearers" to Christianity. They incited the rabble to riot. Jason, whose house was the center of activity, along with some of the brethren, were brought before the city authorities and charged with treason against Caesar because of their messianic beliefs. However, if 1 Thessalonians 2:13–16 is not an interpolation from a later Paulinist—Paul is not usually so harsh in condemning his Jewish compatriots—the converts and the opposition came directly from *Gentiles* (1 Thess 2:14). The small band of missionaries were there for some time (but Acts 17:2 says only three weeks).

According to Acts, Paul and his companions were sent on to Beroea by night (Acts 17:10), and when they were pursued, Paul himself was urged on to Athens, presumably joined by his companions later. They wanted to return to Thessalonica but, as Paul says, "Satan blocked our way" (1 Thess 2:18); so he sent Timothy from Athens (1 Thess 3:1–2) and went on to Corinth. He arrived there about 49 C.E. (the Gallio Inscription) and stayed about eighteen months (Acts 18:11). In lieu of his return to Thessalonica, Paul wrote 1 Thessalonians probably from Corinth about 51 C.E.

The first sections of 1 Thessalonians are dominated by Paul's **thanksgiving** for the Thessalonians' perseverance under persecution, apparently by their own countrymen (2:13–16). However, the primary teaching of 1 Thessalonians is in the area of **eschatology**. Paul presents the Christian faith as essentially a matter of believing that Jesus is God's Son, that God has raised him from the dead, and that the risen Jesus will shortly return as judge and redeemer. He presents the Christian life as essentially a matter of preparing oneself for the coming of Jesus as judge and redeemer, and he gives form and content to the expectation of the coming of Jesus, the parousia. The synoptic gospel source Q has a similar understanding of the Christian faith and the Christian life. It also has the same concern to give form and content to the expectation of the **parousia.** However, though 1 Thessalonians is in many respects close to Q and to the characteristic theology of earliest Christianity, it is also distinctively Pauline. In 5:9–10 we find a first statement of themes that were to become characteristic of the Pauline theology: the concept of Jesus offering to human beings salvation from the wrath of God, and that of Jesus dying "for us, so that . . . we may live with him." With respect to the letter's form, there is an unusually long thanksgiving for the Thessalonians' steadfastness in the face of persecution (1:2–3:13).

EXEGETICAL SURVEY OF FIRST THESSALONIANS

1:1 CHARACTERISTIC CHRISTIANIZED SALUTATION.

1:2–3:13 THANKSGIVING.

Paul normally uses this to set the tone of the whole letter and to express his understanding of the situation he is addressing.

> **1:2–10** is a more customary thanksgiving. 1:3 contains Paul's famous combination of faith, love, and hope (1 Cor 13). 1:10 is a formulalaic representation of the essence of Hellenistic Jewish Mission Christianity.

> **2:1–16 Recollection and interpretation** of Paul's work in Thessalonica. 2:1–12 may imply Gentile opponents who thought of Jesus as a hero (see Chapter Three), but could also be rhetorical. It contains two of Paul's more intimate analogies for his relationship with the Thessalonians, that he was "gentle . . . like a nurse" (2:7) and encouraging "like a father with his children" (2:11). 2:9 mentions Paul's pride in supporting himself as an artisan. 2:13–16 is possibly a later addition, a second thanksgiving.

> **2:17–3:13 An expression of Paul's affection and concern** for the Thessalonian Christians.

4:1–12 PARENESIS.

An exhortation to holiness and love.

4:13–5:11 INSTRUCTION WITH REGARD TO THE COMING OF THE PAROUSIA.

This section is the real concern of the letter. In traditional apocalyptic language—the cry of command, the archangel's call, and the sound of God's trumpet—it reiterates the common early Christian apocalyptic hope that Jesus will return "like a thief in the night" (5:2; see Matt 24.43). However, it uses "Lord" rather than the "Son of Man" of Daniel for Jesus as apocalyptic judge and redeemer. It goes into physical details not found in the words of the Christian prophets of Q or in the apocalyptic discourses of the synoptic gospels. Paul expects the parousia to come in his own lifetime (4:17), and he uses the belief to comfort the Thessalonians who are concerned about what will happen to their departed dead. As noted, 5:9–10 is important as a first statement of the themes that came to be characteristic of the Pauline theology.

5:12–22 FINAL PARENESIS.

A hint at some form of organization in 5:12 is followed by a stress on work and a *cautious* encouragement about charismatic gifts (compare 1 Cor 12, 14).

5:23–28 CONCLUSION.

The peace wish, request for prayer, kiss, command for letter to be read, and benediction.

THE CORINTHIAN CORRESPONDENCE

The city of Corinth in Achaia (southern Greece) is strategically situated on a narrow isthmus "between two seas" (Gulf of Corinth; Saronic Gulf) that joins the Peloponnesus, a large peninsula, to the Greek mainland. Destroyed by Rome in 146 B.C., it was rebuilt by Julius Caesar in 44 B.C.E., and became a Roman colony. It rapidly grew and Caesar Augustus made it the capital of Greece in 27 B.C.E.

Corinth was a natural seaport. Its eastern harbor area was called Cenchreae and its western harbor area Lechaeum. It became a center for shipbuilding, commerce, industry, and government. It was also a sports center, one of the four major locations for the Isthmian games held every two years. The bustling seaport was highly cosmopolitan, populated with Roman officials, merchants, people in business, soldiers, and sailors. It naturally gained a notorious reputation as a "city of sin" in ancient literature, so that the verb *korinthiazesthai*, "to live like a Corinthian," took on the connotation "to fornicate," and *korinthia korē*, "a Corinthian girl," became synonymous with a prostitute. Strabo, a writer from the latter first century B.C.E. who exaggerates the city's sinfulness, quotes the proverb, "Not everyman's concern is a trip to Corinth."

The city also had a religious life typical of a Hellenistic city. The temple of Aphrodite Pandemos, a goddess of love, stood above the city on a massive rock. Strabo speaks of this famous temple, and says it had a thousand temple prostitutes, though the comment is probably from his imagination. Sanctuaries of Demeter (of the Eleusinian mysteries not far away; see Chapter Three), Asklepios (the mystery god of healing), and Poseidon (the god of the sea, in connection with the games), have been preserved. Columns of the Temple of Apollo, the sun god, still stand. There were also sanctuaries to the Egyptian goddess Isis and god Serapis and to the Asian Mother of the gods. Moreover, there has been discovered on the Lechaeum Road leading into Corinth a damaged marble slab that preserves a partial inscription in Greek letters, which might be rendered "... **GOGEBR**...," that is, "[SYNA]**GOG[UE OF THE H]EBR**[EWS]." Though its writing style shows that it comes from a time centuries later than Paul, such buildings were continually built on traditional sites. Also, there are many remains of dining rooms where religious banquets were held; these are very important in light of the Corinthian excesses at the Lord's Supper (see below). Finally, in the center of the market place is the famous *bēma*, or "tribunal," a high raised platform where speeches and judicial pronouncements were made. No doubt Paul was brought before Gallio here (compare Acts 18:12–17).

The apostle Paul reached Corinth from Athens about 49 or 50 C.E. and stayed about eighteen months (the Gallio Inscription; Acts 18:1–11). There he established a Christian community with at least one major house-church. As we have seen in our discussions above, the apostle returned to Corinth twice (2 Cor 13:1) and wrote at least seven letters to the Corinthians. They reveal the Corinthians' tendencies to quarrel with each other, to lapse into their pre-Christian ways (especially into Hellenistic fervor), and to become influenced by Hellenistic Jewish missionaries who challenged Paul's authority as an apostle. Since we have discussed these problems in some detail, we shall proceed to our exegetical outline of 1 Corinthians, written from Ephesus (compare 1 Cor 16:8), perhaps about 53 or 54 C.E.

Exegetical Survey of First Corinthians

The body of the letter falls naturally into two parts, the first dealing with matters reported to Paul in Ephesus by messengers from "Chloe's people" (1:10–6:20), and the second with questions raised in a letter to him from the Corinthian community (7:1–15:58). The root of both sets of problems lies in the Corinthian religious fervor and the tendency for it to bring about disunity among the Corinthian Christians. Thus, Paul must challenge internal opponents.

1:1–3 CHRISTIANIZED SALUTATION FROM PAUL AND (AN UNKNOWN) SOSTHENES (COMPARE ACTS 18:17).

1:4–9 THANKSGIVING.

Characteristically setting the tone of the letter, noting an apocalyptic hope, the spiritual gifts of the Corinthians (note!), and their call to Christian fellowship.

1:10–6:20 PART I: THE MATTERS REPORTED TO PAUL BY "CHLOE'S PEOPLE" (1:11) IN EPHESUS.

This section of the letter has four main parts.

1. The factions in Corinth (1:10–4:21);
2. incest and sexual sins in general (5:1–13);
3. litigation before pagan courts (6:1–11); and
4. sexual morality: the claim of the enthusiasts that "all things are lawful for me" (6:12–20).

1:10–4:21 The factions in Corinth. The basic problem in the Corinthian church was factionalism brought about by religious fervor or "enthusiasm." The Corinthian Christian opponents developed a view of baptism in which the baptized persons identified themselves with the prominent person who baptized them, or someone who was identified with that person. Evidently they regarded baptism as a kind of mystery rite by which they came to share the power they attributed to the person whom they associated with their baptism. Moreover, once baptized they felt themselves to be "spiritual" in a way other people were not, to possess a special "wisdom" or "knowledge" *(gnōsis)* in a way other people did not. The quarrels between them were, therefore, quarrels among a spiritual and wise elite, all of whom claimed their distinctiveness from the rest of the world. Many interpreters see in the views an early form of Christian Gnosticism.

Paul's argument against this view results in one of his most important themes, the **"theology of the cross"** (1:18–25). It is stated in terms of a paradox. The wisdom of the world is folly to God and what the world would count folly ("Christ crucified, a stumbling block [*skandalon*] to Jews and foolishness to Gentiles," 1:23) is in fact the power and wisdom of God. The focus is on Christ's *humility and weakness.* Paul applies this theme socially to the Corinthians. *Most* of the Corinthians were from the lower classes (compare 6:11), that is, not wise, powerful, or of noble birth in the eyes of the world (1:26–31). Yet, God chose them. Presumably a *few* of them did have such status—for example, the leaders of the congregations in whose houses they met—and some of the problems at Corinth betray tensions between these social strata.

Paul nonetheless allows for a special kind of Christian wisdom for those who understand the crucifixion; in fact, if the Corinthians had understood this Christian wisdom, and not been immature children who were still in need of receiving baby's milk, they would not have split into factions. The theme of the "weakness" of God, that is, the Cross, as the basis for unity, will be a constant theme in the letter as Paul attempts to build up the church. Paul will also claim to imitate Christ's weakness in defense against enthusiastic opponents who claim he is weak.

5:1–13 Incest and sexual sins in general. Corinth was notorious for its sexual immorality (Greek *porneia*), and for Paul the Christian congregation was too tolerant in its view of the man who committed legal incest. Paul recommends that the community assemble and perform an exclusion ritual for the sexual offender, just as leaven must be excluded from the house during Passover; group purity must be maintained. The reference in 5:3–5 is a formula referring to God's final judgment. 5:9 mentions the "previous letter," lost to us (see Chapter Six). Paul's recommendations are not to avoid outsiders, "since you would then need to go out of the world" (5:10); yet, Paul is concerned with morality *within* the house-churches.

6:1–11 Litigation before pagan courts. Christians will participate in Christ's final judgment of the world, including its magistrates. They must, therefore, fittingly settle their disputes out of court, *within* their own group. Verses 9–11 contain a "catalogue of vices" (see Chapter Six; below on homosexuality).

6:12–20 Sexual morality: the claim of the enthusiast opponents that "all things are lawful." As truly "spiritual" people, the Corinthian enthusiasts are indifferent to things of the body. One form of this indifference is sexual libertinism, including the freedom to visit Corinth's brothels. The Corinthian opponents have slogans to legitimate their behavior. Against this Paul argues that the physical body must maintain purity for the social body to maintain purity.

7:1–15:58 PART II: THE QUESTIONS RAISED BY THE CORINTHIANS IN THEIR LETTER TO PAUL.

The Corinthian Christians had written to Paul asking for guidance on a number of practical problems (7:1). Paul responded as a pastor to his people, and the result is a fascinating account of an early Christian attempt to face social and religious problems—and perhaps also an illustration of the adage, "The more things change, the more they remain the same." Six important topics are treated:

1. marriage and celibacy (7);
2. Christian freedom and the problems of idolatry (8:1–11:1);
3. the dress and status of women in Christian worship (11:2–16; [compare 14:33b–36, probably an interpolation]);
4. practice of the Lord's Supper in worship (11:17–34);
5. spiritual gifts and the gift of love (12–14); and
6. the future resurrection of the dead (15).

Paul frequently introduces a new subject with the words, "now concerning" (7:1, 25; 8:1; 12:1; compare 16:1, 12).

7:1–40 Marriage and celibacy. Paul wrestles with all the dimensions of marital and sexual relationships. Here the moral position opposite to libertinism appears: religious asceticism in which newly converted Christians denied their wives and husbands sexual relations. Thus, on the one hand visiting prostitutes (6:12–20); here, sexual asceticism. Both extremes are also found in later Gnosticism, and perhaps here we have a glimpse of such Christian Gnostic thinking in its infancy (see wisdom and *gnōsis,* 1:10–4:21).

To understand Paul, it is important to note the perspective from which the advice is given: eschatology, or the imminent end of the world (verses 26–31). The Corinthians should keep the status quo because "the appointed time has grown very short" (verse 29) and the Christian mission will be better served. With this orientation, Paul clearly prefers that the Corinthians remain single, as he is (7:1, 7, 8), though the background for his nonmarried state is not clear (had he been married?). He considers this state a gift. However, he acknowledges, for some this state could easily lead to more sexual immorality (at the brothels? fornication?). So, he says, "it is better to marry than to be aflame with passion" (7:9).

Nonetheless, given marriage, he strongly recommends that the partners fulfill their mutual sexual obligations (7:3–5), separating only for prayer (found also in Jewish custom). Here he draws on a "word of the Lord" forbidding the woman to separate from her husband and the man to divorce his wife (compare Mark 10:1–12; Matt 5:32; 19:9; Luke 16:18). Yet, in the case of mixed marriages that follows, he gives his own advice. Neither the believing husband nor wife should divorce the unbelieving partner, again revealing equality. For Paul, the believing partner "consecrates" the unbelieving partner and makes "holy" their children. Paul suggests, however, that the unbelieving partner may "separate"—presumably meaning divorce—a modification of the "saying of the Lord" in new Christian circumstances. Nothing is said of the Torah command to produce children (Gen 1:28); presumably the apocalyptic situation makes this unnecessary.

Paul finally turns to the question of "the virgins." Traditionally this passage has been interpreted to mean a father's "daughter," that is, the refusal of fathers to offer their daughters' hands in marriage. However, in verses 25–35, he refers to the betrothed, and the same meaning is probable for verses 36–38.

8:1–11:1 Christian freedom and Christian love: the problem of eating meat sacrificed to other gods. As a newly baptized member of a tiny religious group living in Greco-Roman society, many problems faced the Christian. For example, if you went out to dinner at a "pagan" friend's house, you might be served meat from the marketplace that had been previously sacrificed to "pagan" gods and subsequently sold, a common practice in Hellenistic cities. This would usually imply worship at the god's table, or at least an acknowledgment of the god. Such meat would be forbidden to strict Jews and, as the Apostolic Decree in Acts shows, within some circles in Christianity as well (compare Acts 15:28). Or you might be invited to dinner at one of the many pagan sanctuary dining rooms where you would be offered a succulent menu of roast pork, just sacrificed. Clearly, no Jew could eat this either! Could the Christian? This was a crucial question at Corinth, and Paul had to deal with it as one of the questions posed to him. Moreover, the passage is complicated. Chapter 9, a defense of Paul's apostleship (see Chapter Six), seems to break the trend of thought, giving rise to letter-fragment theories. We shall consider it as a unity.

Still further problems exist. In 8:1–13, 10:23–11:1, Paul seems to agree with the Corinthian enthusiasts when he says (a) "we know that all of us possess knowledge (*gnōsis*)" (8:1) (b) that idols do not really exist (8:1, 4–6), and (c) that therefore it is permissible to eat food offered to "idols" in the name of Christian freedom (8:8; 10:26–27, 29b–30). This is the position of Christian wisdom. However, (d) he is concerned that "the weak" might be troubled in conscience if they see a Christian brother or sister "at table in an idol's temple" (8:10) or if someone (non-Christian?) informs a Christian at a non-Christian's house (or temple) that the meat has been (purchased in the marketplace and) offered in sacrifice (10:28). In these cases, the Christian will be concerned for the "weak" Christian's conscience. Paul is wrestling with a dilemma: He concedes a superior Christian *gnōsis* but "the stronger" Christian should back off because of the conscience of "the weaker" brother or sister.

The course of Paul's argument here is important. His orientation is stated at the beginning: " 'Knowledge' puffs up, but love builds up," suggesting that "we know that all of us possess knowledge" is a slogan of the enthusiasts. Paul grants a certain kind of knowledge, represented by the folly of the Cross. In ordinary terms, however, love is superior to knowledge, and Christian freedom operates out of love for one's brother or sister. Paul may not have been totally clear in his statements about the existence of idols, but he is consistent in his opposition to a freedom that leads to superior knowledge without love. That is the danger of "enthusiasm," and it tramples on the free conscience of the Christian brother or sister, a basic moral dilemma (see conclusion to this chapter).

We should understand that Paul is also engaged in an issue related to social status. Apart from occasional festivals, the poor do not normally eat meat; it is the "caviar" of the ancient world. Paul is grappling with a problem that engages the upper-class Christians, but impinges on not only those with religious scruples, but also the lower classes. We shall see this social class issue again in the troubles about banqueting in relation to the Last Supper observance (1 Cor 11:17–34).

In the midst of the "meat-offered-to-idols" discussion, Paul defends his apostleship (9:1–27), first on the grounds that he has had a vision of the Lord, and second, that his missionary activity has been successful. He also repudiates the argument that he is not really an apostle because he earns his own living rather than living off the results of his missionary labors, as did the propagandists of religion and philosophy generally in Hellenistic society. We have seen that Paul defended his self-support also in 1 Thessalonians (2:9).

11:2–34 The regulation of Christian worship. The apostle now turns to a series of problems connected with Christian worship: the dress and status of women (11:2–16); abuses of the Lord's Supper (11:17–34); and *glossolalia*, or "speaking in tongues" (12–14).

The first problem is whether a woman should have her head covered in worship. The passage contains several interesting and mystifying comments and is very difficult to interpret. The term "head" has both literal and figurative meanings. What does it mean to "dishonor one's head" by shaving it (verse 5b)? What does it mean that a woman ought to have a "symbol of authority" on her head because of the angels (verse 10)? It is immediately noticeable how ill at ease Paul becomes in discussing this question. Paul's argument falters, and in the end he falls back on a "church rule" (verse 16). We shall discuss this passage in more detail below.

The second passage deals with the observance of the "Lord's Supper" (11:17–34). At Corinth the Christian sacred meal took place in connection with a communal meal that was in danger of becoming just another Hellenistic banquet. Moreover, there was a social problem: The rich were eating and getting drunk and were thus humiliating those who had nothing. Paul recalls the tradition of the Lord's Supper (verses 23–25) to indicate the solemnity of the sacred part of the meal in connection with Jesus' death (see Chapter Six). Satiation and sacrament are thereby separated.

12:1–14:40 The true nature of spiritual gifts. A major feature of Corinthian religious enthusiasm was the proliferation of religious phenomena connected with religious ecstasy: utterances of wisdom and knowledge, faith, gifts of healing, working miracles, prophecy, "distinguishing between spirits," speaking in tongues, and interpretation of tongues (12:8–10). This in itself would not be extraordinary, since other religions in the Hellenistic world exhibited some of the same phenomena. Indeed, Paul states that these are spiritual gifts. What is interesting is Paul's perspective. As with the previous section, the middle chapter (13) is somewhat of an interruption in so far as it is a self-contained "poetic" section similar to Hellenistic and Jewish wisdom poetry of the period, and it is only loosely connected with chapters 12 and 14 (12:31; 14:1). In this case, the material comes from Paul. A second passage on denying women the right to speak at house-church meetings (14:33b–36) also interrupts the context; it does not represent Paul's views elsewhere (especially 11:2–16), and is similar to comments from the later Pastoral Letters (1 Tim 2:11–15). We shall consider it below. In the meantime, chapters 12 and 14 can be considered together.

In chapter 12 Paul's remarks show that in general he accepts (had encouraged) various spiritual phenomena, but he denies that a Christian can say "Jesus be cursed!" (an ecstatic cry of the enthusiasts marking a contrast with "Jesus as Lord" statement or perhaps a spontaneous comment by Paul to contrast with the latter). He draws on the general Hellenistic political notion (especially in Stoicism) of the body politic and its members to stress the unity of the church. Again, the physical body symbolizes the corporate body.

In chapter 14 it is clear that some of the Corinthians consider the highest gift to be speaking in tongues. Paul has prepared for this by giving his own ranking of charismatic gifts (12:27–30) with *glossolalia* and its interpretation last (12:27–30). In chapter 14, he states that incommunicable ecstatic experiences like *glossolalia* are gifts, but he sets limitations: only two or three should make such utterances, each in turn, to be followed by an interpretation (14:27–28). Otherwise, they do not contribute to the "upbuilding" or "edification" of the church as a whole, as does the communicable act of prophecy, which he much prefers. Paul stresses, then, the higher gifts (12:31: apostles, prophets, and teachers come first, compare 12:28).

In a "love hymn" of three stanzas Paul indicates that the highest gift of all is love (chapter 13). Not only speaking in tongues, but prophecy and many other gifts and virtues—knowledge of God, working miracles, giving one's possessions to the poor, and martyrdom—are nothing without love (13:1–3). In beautiful and active language containing fifteen verbs, Paul next describes the nature of love (*agapē*) and its power (13:4–7), and concludes with the eschatological theme that while the other gifts will pass away, love is indestructible (13:8–13).

14:33b–36 is usually held to be an interpolation. It interrupts the context, does not easily correspond to women who do speak in church in 1 Corinthians 11:2–16, appeals to the Law in an atypical way for Paul, and sounds very much like an opinion taken from a work of the Pauline School, 1 Timothy 2:11–15.

15:1–58 The future resurrection of the dead. A major problem for Paul in Corinth was that the Christian enthusiasts there believed that at their baptism they already began to share the resurrection life. Paul has to argue carefully for a future resurrection of the dead. A second problem was that for a Greek it was natural to think of the immortal soul as one's true self, but not of the resurrection of the body. Plato, for example, saw the body as the "prison of the soul." Thus, Paul has to argue for a future resurrection of the body.

We have already discussed a most interesting passage in this section, verses 3b–5, where Paul quotes an early liturgical formula, or confession, concerning the death and resurrection of Jesus (see Chapters Five, Six). He apparently understands his "conversion" in relation to his own vision of Jesus as a resurrection appearance, in part a defense of his apostleship.

Chapter 15 contains one of Paul's most famous Christological statements about Christ as the "new (last) Adam" who reversed the sin of the "old (first) Adam" (15:20–28). He will take it up again in Romans 5. He also mentions the mysterious practice of baptism on behalf of the dead (15:29). The chapter becomes increasingly dynamic as it concludes with the victory of Christ over death.

16:1–18 SOME FURTHER MATTERS.

Paul concludes his letter by discussing the arrangements he was making concerning the collection for the Christians in Jerusalem and his own future itinerary (see Chapter Six). Chapter 16:13–18 is parenetic.

16:19–24 HIS CLOSING.

This section includes greetings from Asia by his own hand, the kiss, a curse, the *Maranatha* ("Our Lord, come!"), which is an Aramaic prayer going back to the earliest days of Palestinian Christianity, and a final benediction.

Exegetical Survey of Second Corinthians

As we stated in Chapter Six, this letter is not a unity but rather a collection of fragments and larger remnants of a whole correspondence between Paul and the church at Corinth. Between the writing of 1 Corinthians and 2 Corinthians a group of **"superlative apostles"** affected the Corinthian Christians. The various parts were probably put together when the apostle's letters were circulated as a group toward the end of the first century. They were originally written over a period of time shortly after the writing of 1 Corinthians, around 55 C.E. The first two parts were probably written in Ephesus:

1. 2:14–6:13 and 7:2–4 [minus 6:14–7:1]. Relations deteriorating. (A "painful visit" (2 Cor 2:1; 12:14; 12:21; 13:1); Paul is attacked by a member of the church [2:5; 7:12].)
2. 10–13 (the "tearful letter" (2:3–4; 7:8). Paul defends himself. (If Paul's "prison letters" were written in Ephesus, the Philippians letter-fragments and Philemon ("prison letters") were probably written next. Then the rest of the 2 Corinthians fragments were composed, probably in Macedonia):
3. 1:1–2:13 plus 7:5–16 (compare 7:5). A letter of reconciliation.
4. 8 (compare 8:1). The collection.
5. 9 (compare 9:2). The collection.

The remnants of five Pauline letters (plus a non-Pauline fragment, 6:14–7:1) are in this collection. To read the first three fragments in their proper order is to become caught up in a very dramatic struggle.

2:14–6:13; 7:2–4 PAUL'S FIRST LETTER OF DEFENSE AGAINST HIS NEW OPPONENTS.

This is part of a letter that Paul wrote to defend himself and his authority against opponents who came to Corinth bearing letters of recommendation from Christian communities in which they had previously worked (3:1), and who rapidly assumed positions of authority in the Corinthian Christian community. Paul calls them "peddlers of God's word" (2:17) and offers in his own behalf a moving account of the humility and reconciliation of the true ambassador for Christ, for which the sufferings of Jesus are the model. Apocalyptic ideas of present/future and final judgment are combined with Hellenistic ideas of the inner and outer person.

10:1–13:14 THE "TEARFUL LETTER" (COMPARE 2:3–4; 7:8).

Apparently Paul's first letter of defense against his new opponents failed in its desired effect, and he paid a flying visit to Corinth where, however, he found the church in open rebellion against him. One opponent was even able to humiliate him publicly (2:5; 7:12; see Chapter Six). He returned to Ephesus and wrote a further letter to Corinth "out of much affliction and anguish of heart and with many tears" (2:4). This is traditionally known as the "tearful letter," and 2 Corinthians 10–13 is probably part of it (this section does not actually mention the humiliation of 2:5; 7:12).

In these chapters a picture of Paul's opponents takes shape as he parodies and attacks them (see Chapter Six). They represent a Jewish form of Christianity in which they boast of their achievements in the name of Christ, and they boast of their Jewish heritage. The "superlative apostles" are given visions and revelations as a special sign of their status. They offer "signs and wonders and mighty works" as proof that Christ speaks through them. Against all this Paul offers the "foolishness" of his own boasting. He appeals to the original effectiveness of the gospel he preached in Corinth, to the fact that he supported himself in Corinth so as not to be a burden on his converts, and alludes to his own Jewish heritage and his sufferings as a servant of Christ. Above all, he appeals to the Corinthian Christian's own sense of what they owe him and his gospel and to the example of Christ himself who was "crucified *in weakness*" (13:4, a deliberately ironic contrast to the power in Christ his opponents claim) but who lives by the power of God.

1:1–2:13; 7:5–16 THE LETTER OF RECONCILIATION.

Paul sent the "tearful letter" to Corinth by the hand of his trusted companion Titus, whom he must have charged with the task of attempting to restore the situation there. The letter and Titus' visit were successful—the Corinthian Christians were probably appalled by the realization of what they had done to the apostle to whom they owed so much—and Paul wrote a letter rejoicing in the resumption of good relations between him and the Corinthian Christian community. In short, Paul's authority at Corinth was confirmed. This and the following two letters were probably written in Macedonia.

8:1–24 PART OF A LETTER OF RECOMMENDATION FOR TITUS ABOUT THE COLLECTION.

This is part of a letter of recommendation for Titus as organizer of the collection for the saints in Jerusalem.

9:1–15 PART OF A LETTER CONCERNING THE COLLECTION FOR THE SAINTS IN JERUSALEM.

This is part of a letter concerning the collection for the saints.

6:14–7:1 A NON-PAULINE FRAGMENT.

Neither in terms of ideas nor vocabulary does this have any claim to come from the apostle Paul. It appears, rather, to reflect the influence of ideas characteristic of the Qumran community. We have no precise idea how it came to be included in a collection of Paul's letters to the Christians in Corinth.

PHILEMON

In Chapter Six, we used the little letter of Philemon to demonstrate the Christianized letter form developed by Paul. There we gave the background, outline, and content of the letter. Here, we should recall, first, that this little letter falls within Paul's "prison letters," probably written in Ephesus, perhaps about 56 C.E., probably to Colossae (see Col 4:9), both cities in Asia Minor. Second, there were various forms of slavery in Greco-Roman society. Many slaves were educated and held responsible positions (see Chapter Three). Third, the typical role relationships between slave owner and runaway slave were made very complex when both had been converted by Paul.

Note the language of authority, slavery, and fictive kinship in this letter. In Greco-Roman legal arrangements, the slave was to be returned, and debts were to be paid to slave owners for harboring slaves. In the church, however, Jesus was metaphorically a slave/servant who paradoxically had become the Lord and master (for example, the Philippians hymn, Phil 2:5–11). Moreover, Paul viewed

Christians metaphorically as slaves of Christ (for example, 1 Cor 7:17–24). At the same time, in the new Christian family Christians achieved a higher status: brothers and sisters. The ideal was "no longer slave or free" in Christ Jesus (Gal 3:28). Thus, Paul—literally a "prisoner of Christ" (verse 1)—made his shrewd appeals to his "brother" Philemon (verses 7, 20), a "beloved fellow worker" (verse 1), and a man of high social status who ran a household, about his "child" Onesimus (verse 10). He stressed Philemon's freedom of choice, not his obedience, and apparently attempted to humor him with puns on Onesimus' name ("useful" [see verse 11] or "beneficial" [see verse 20]). Paul hoped that Philemon would at least accept Onesimus back into his household, with Paul paying damages, since Philemon actually owed Paul the true debt, his own "self." Further, he hoped that Onesimus would be accepted as more than a slave, that is, as "a beloved brother." Finally, Paul hoped that Philemon would "do even more than I say" (verse 21). The precise meaning of this comment is not clear, but it appears that Paul was hinting at manumission, and perhaps even that Onesimus return to him as a "fellow worker."

PHILIPPIANS

Philippi, named for Philip II of Macedon (father of Alexander the Great), was located on the Egnatian Way, eight miles north of the seaport of Neapolis. It was the site of Paul's first European congregation, established in the period before Paul went on to Thessalonica, Athens, and Corinth about 49 C.E. Acts emphasizes the importance of Paul's entering Europe by recording that Paul went to Macedonia in response to a vision (Acts 16:9–10).

The author of Luke-Acts tells about the Philippi mission by recording, first, the story of the conversion of Lydia and the baptism of her household; and second, Paul's exorcism of a demon from the slave girl who supported her masters by practicing divination. Acts says that as a result of the latter event Paul and Silas were dragged before the city magistrates and charged by the Jews with being anti-Roman, for which they were imprisoned. According to the Acts dramatization, they did not take the opportunity to escape during an earthquake, but converted their jailer and baptized him and his family. Paul was finally released and demanded an apology because of his Roman citizenship (Acts 16:12–40).

Although the exorcism and earthquake episodes have clear legendary features, some of the account is credible. In any case, we know from the letter about four converts (Phil 2:25–30, Epaphroditus; 4:2–3, Euodia, Syntyche, and Clement), and other fellow-workers "whose names are in the book of life" (4:3). The community was basically Gentile (3:3) and there was some local organization (1:1: "bishops" and "deacons," though not yet in the sense of official offices). There is no assurance that Paul visited Philippi again, although it is highly likely he did (Phil 2:24; compare 2 Cor 13:1; Acts 20:1–6).

Philippians probably contains three letter fragments. Chapter 3:1a ("Finally, my brethren, rejoice in the Lord") appears to be a final statement or at least near the end of a letter. However, 3:2 launches off into a defense against opponents. Also, 4:10–20, which occurs rather late in the letter, is a thanksgiving for a gift.

Exegetical Survey of Philippians

4:10–20 PART OF A LETTER OF THANKS TO THE PHILIPPIANS.
Paul thanks the Philippians for the revival of their concern for him and the gifts sent to him at the hands of Epaphroditus. Paul notes that he accepted money from the Philippians while he was at Thessalonica, thus breaking his usual pattern (4:15). Paul appears to be at the beginning of an imprisonment, for he expects acquittal at an upcoming trial (1:25,26; 2:24).

1:1–3:1 A FURTHER LETTER OF THANKS.
Paul is grateful for the concern the Philippians have expressed for him; he is now enduring a considerable period of imprisonment. Epaphroditus has been very ill, but is now recovered and will be rejoining the Philippians shortly. There are hints of opponents in 1:17. The letter characteristically combines thanksgiving and parenesis. This fragment of Philippians includes some of the most moving passages in the Pauline correspondence, including the great Philippians hymn to Christ in 2:5b–11. As noted in Chapters Four and Five, the hymn portrays the descending-ascending redeemer figure, that is, the redeemer has a pre-earthly existence ("in the form of God"; "to be equal with God"), descends to take on an earthly existence ("empties himself"; "in the likeness of men"; "in fashion like a man"; "taking the form of a slave [or servant]"), dies, and is exalted to a postearthly existence where he is glorified and worshipped as a god. If the basics of the hymn were "pre-Christian," Paul himself probably added "the death on the cross" (verse 8b). This phrase breaks the rhythm of the hymn, and the theology of the Cross is one of Paul's favorite emphases (see 1 Cor 1:18–25).

3:2–4:9 THE REMNANT OF A SHARPLY POLEMICAL LETTER WARNING THE PHILIPPIANS OF THE DANGERS OF AN ENTHUSIASTIC "CIRCUMCISION" PARTY.
The opponents have traits reminiscent of those of both Galatia (circumcision) and Corinth (enthusiasm). As in Galatians and 2 Corinthians, Paul combats them with an autobiographical statement (3:4-11, esp. 3:5). The characteristic apocalyptic hope is still present (3:20-21). This letter clearly does not belong with the others and must have been written either before or after them. The attitude of thanksgiving for dangers passed and harmony achieved, which the others breathe, leads us to conjecture that this one was written earlier.

4:21–23 CONCLUSION.
The conclusion as a whole mentions "Caesar's household" (4:22). 1:13 mentions the "praetorian guard." The former refers to imperial administration throughout the empire and the latter can refer to the bodyguard of a governor, as well as of Caesar himself.

The second of these letters was certainly written in prison, and the first probably was also. The only imprisonment reported in Acts is that in Palestine and Rome, but we have already concluded that Acts is not always a trustworthy source for historical detail concerning Paul or the early church. The letters themselves assume constant intercourse between the imprisoned Paul and the church in Philippi, a factor difficult to imagine if the distance was that between Philippi and

Rome, and the letters breathe the same kind of atmosphere as that of Galatians and the Corinthian correspondence. For these reasons modern scholarship tends to assume that Paul was imprisoned in Ephesus during his long stay there and that this correspondence originated there. Paul himself speaks of facing death in Asia (2 Cor 1:8–10; compare his figurative comment in 1 Cor 15:30–32), and the letters date, therefore, from about 56 C.E.

GALATIANS

Paul addresses this letter to "the churches of Galatia" (Gal 1:2). There are two possibilities for this location: *(a)* the central plateau region of Asia Minor around modern-day Ankara, Turkey; or *(b)* the southern coastal region of east central Asia Minor, also in modern-day Turkey. Those who defend the former possibility (the North Galatian theory) take Galatia in its ethnic sense to refer to the Indo-Aryan Celts or Gauls *(Galloi/Galatai)* who settled there early in the third century B.C.E. Those who defend the latter possibility (the South Galatian theory) take Galatia in its Roman provincial sense, for Rome added the southern regions to Galatia in 25 C.E.

There are good arguments for each location. The South Galatian theory has in its favor the fact that in Acts (13–14) Paul is said to have visited the cities in this region (Perga, Pisidian Antioch, Iconium, Lystra, Derbe) on his "first missionary journey" (compare also 16:1–5). If this theory is correct, the letter was probably written rather early in Paul's career. The South Galatian theory has against it a number of speculative arguments based on a problematic chronology in Acts that conflicts at points with Galatians. In favor of the North Galatian theory is the probability that Paul will not return (Gal 4:20), which suggests that Paul wrote this letter late in his career. This theory also tends to be confirmed by his references in 2 Corinthians about opponents and especially by similar theological themes in Galatians and Romans, his last letter. If the churches of Galatia were in the north he may have written from Ephesus, Corinth, or as suggested above, from Macedonia, where the latest portions of 2 Corinthians were written, but before Paul reached Corinth, where Romans was written. We suggest that he wrote from Macedonia about 56 C.E.

We have already sketched out the occasion for this letter, the disturbances created by opponents coming into Galatia. They may be called "Judaizers," but probably not in the sense that they are conservative Pharisaic Christians from Jerusalem. Like the Jerusalem conservatives, they demanded circumcision and the Law; but they also had highly syncretistic views, and seem to have believed Paul was not really so independent of Jerusalem (Gal 1–2). Whoever they were, they irritated the apostle so much that he launched into one of his most heated apologies to defend himself. In fact, the genre of the letter itself might be called an "apologetic letter." Not only does Paul defend himself, but he also curses his opponents at the beginning (1:8–9) and defends his supporters at the end (6:16), making it something of a "magical letter," while at the same time employing all kinds of rhetorical arguments to this end. In accord with his anger, the structure of this letter is most unusual in its omission of any "thanksgiving."

The letter to the Galatians is Paul's defense of his gospel, and hence his apostleship. The heart of that gospel is the message of "freedom," freedom from that which represses one religiously, racially, nationally, socially, and sexually. It is a spiritual phenomenon, a position of faith in Jesus Christ "who gave himself for our sins to deliver us from the present evil age according to the will of our God and Father" (1:4). Paradoxically, Paul attempts to defend this freedom with a kind of rhetorical logic that draws on human experience, scriptural proof, liturgical tradition, past friendship, indeed the Torah itself. But ultimately freedom speaks for itself.

1:1–5 SALUTATION.
In the greeting Paul launches into his argument against his opponents in Galatia. He defends the divine origin of his apostleship and gives a terse summary of the gospel that he intends to defend.

1:6–10 AMAZEMENT, ANATHEMA, AND TRANSITION.
At this point in his letters Paul normally offers a thanksgiving for the faith of those he is addressing, but here he plunges immediately into polemic, expressing amazement at the state of affairs in the churches of Galatia and cursing the preachers of a false gospel.

1:11–2:14 A PERSONAL AND HISTORICAL DEFENSE OF PAUL'S GOSPEL.
In the first major section of the letter Paul defines and defends his understanding of the gospel against that of his opponents. The section has three parts.

1:11–24 The divine origin of Paul's gospel. This is an invaluable autobiographical account of Paul's conversion, call, and early activity as a Christian missionary (see Chapter Six). Paul roots his gospel in a revelation of God's Son and in traditional prophetic fashion, a call to become apostle to the Gentiles. He tells of his brief visit to Peter and James in Jerusalem after three years.

2:1–10 The approval of Paul's gospel by the leaders of the Jerusalem Christian community. After fourteen years Paul attends the Jerusalem Conference with Barnabas, taking Titus, who is not compelled to be circumcised. The conservative party loses to Paul and Barnabas when James, Peter, and John agree that Paul and Barnabas will direct their mission to the Gentiles, while they go to the circumcised. The collection for the poor in Jerusalem is agreed upon. Paul is concerned with defining his mission to the uncircumcised Gentiles who, because of the decision reached in Jerusalem, are free from the need to accept circumcision as they become Christians. His opponents apparently are arguing the opposite, namely, that Gentiles who become Christians have also to become Jews by accepting circumcision.

2:11–14 The Antioch Incident. We indicated in our review of the history of New Testament Christianity that major problems following the success of the Christian mission to the Gentiles centered on meals involving Christians who accepted Jewish dietary laws and Christians who did not. Apparently Peter wavered on this issue under pressure from envoys from James, but Paul did not. In reflecting on this incident and its significance, Paul comes to one of his great statements on the nature of Christian faith.

2:15–21 PAUL'S GOSPEL.

The heart of Paul's gospel was "justification by faith," which essentially involves a sinful person's standing before the judgment seat of God and being acquitted. Paul came to believe that obedience to the Law ("works") could not earn this approval; it is possible only through God's free gift, faith in Christ.

3:1–4:31 A DEFENSE OF PAUL'S GOSPEL ON THE BASIS OF GOD'S PLAN IN THE JEWISH SCRIPTURES: FAITH, NOT THE TORAH, IS THE BASIS FOR THE SALVATION OF HUMANITY.

Paul's opponents in Galatia were Judaizers, who strongly emphasized the Jewish Law. Paul now turns to an argument based on that Law and on the Scriptures as a whole, no doubt not only to meet his opponents on their own grounds, but also to satisfy himself of the viability of his own position. This second major section of the letter may be divided into six parts, which are basically six "proofs" for Paul's position.

3:1–5 The gift of the spirit in the group. Paul appeals to the very features of Hellenistic religious enthusiasm manifested by Christians in the Hellenistic environment that became a major problem for him in Corinth. Here they are a validation of the gospel he preached in Galatia.

3:6–26 Abraham as the prototypical father: justification by faith and freedom from the Law in the new family. In Jewish tradition Abraham believed God's promises and kept God's Law; he kept the covenant. Genesis says that he would be rewarded by becoming *the father of "many ethnē,"* or *"nations" (Gen 2:3)*. In Greek, *ethnē* also means "Gentiles" (the "nations" were, of course, also "Gentiles"), and Paul capitalizes on this dual meaning (Gal 3:8). Genesis also says that Abraham *"believed* God and it was reckoned to him as *righteousness"* (Gen 15:6; Gal 3:6). Paul also quotes this text and argues that Abraham's act of belief was *before* the giving of the Law to Moses on Mount Sinai (Exod 20). So justification by faith takes precedence over justification by works of the Law, if indeed the latter is held to be possible at all. Proceeding by a typically Jewish method of argument from Scripture, Paul strings together a series of quotes to show that anyone who relies on the Law and does not do all that the Law commands is under a curse. As Habakkuk 2:4, a favorite text, says, "the *righteous* shall live by *faith"* (compare Rom 1:17).

The Genesis covenant passages not only stress Abraham's becoming the "father" of many nations/Gentiles. Genesis 12:7 says, "To your descendants I will give this land." Paul makes nothing of the promise of the land, but he has a great deal to say about "descendants." In the Hebrew Old Testament the word "descendants" or "sons" is the collective noun "seed"; it is gramatically singular, just as it is in English (Greek *sperma*). Paul argues that singular "seed" refers to a single person, not a whole people: the true "seed" or "son" of Abraham is Christ. This is reminiscent of the argument about the "seed of David" = the messianic "Shoot of David"/"Branch of David" in the Dead Sea Scrolls (see Chapter Five). Paul then argues that Law—referring to the giving of the Torah on Mt. Sinai—came 130 years after the covenant with Abraham. Since no one annuls a ratified will (= covenant), Abraham's covenant based on promise that Abraham believed has not been annulled by the Mosaic covenant of Law and is still in effect.

The point at issue between Paul and his opponents was the Jewish Law. Paul did not dispose of it; he considered that between the time of Moses and of Christ it had fulfilled its function as a "custodian" (*paidagōgos*), that is, a slave who watches over and protects schoolboys until they reach puberty. With the coming of Christ, however, it has been superseded: mature Christians no longer need a guardian.

3:27–29 Baptism into the new family. This proof includes a traditional formula that expresses an important Christian social ideal: "There is neither Jew nor Greek, there is neither slave nor free, there is neither male nor female; for you are all one in Christ Jesus" (3:28).

4:1–11 Kinship with God ("Sons of God"). This is a magnificent celebration of the new family relation with God that Christ made possible for the believers. In his use of " '*Abbā'!* Father!" (verse 6) Paul is aware of the significance of the mode of address that Jesus taught his disciples to use in prayer, and the whole passage is an impassioned plea to the reader not to abandon that which Christ has made possible. A return to the Law, to the "weak and beggarly elemental spirits" (verse 9: probably a reference to stars and planets personified and understood as forces controlling one's life) and to the observance of a calendar of festivals (verse 10) would be such an abandonment. This passage is our clearest indication that Paul's opponents in Galatia were Judaizers who advocated observance of the Jewish Law and festivals together with a typically Hellenistic admixture of astrology.

4:12–20 Kinship with Paul. In this section Paul speaks of the Galatians as his children.

4:21–31 The allegory of Sarah and Hagar: kinship, law, and freedom. Abraham had two sons, one by Sarah's slave woman, Hagar, when Sarah was barren (Ishmael), another by Sarah according to the promise of God, despite Sarah's old age and barrenness (Isaac). The promise was fulfilled in Isaac, the very one whom according to God's command Abraham was willing to sacrifice, and thus risk cutting off God's promise. Paul says Hagar represents the covenant of law, "the present Jerusalem," and slavery; Sarah represents the covenant of promise, "the Jerusalem above," and freedom. Christians are *children of promise, of the free woman.*

5:1–6:10 Parenesis. Paul now exhorts his readers to preserve and to use correctly the freedom they have in Christ. He attacks his opponents as turning the Galatians back to a "yoke of slavery" (5:1–12). In 5:19–24 he uses typical vice and virtue lists, coordinating them with the contrast between the spirit with the flesh (see Chapter Six).

6:11–18 Closing. Paul takes the pen from his secretary and writes with large letters. Even here he cannot avoid a parting shot against his opponents. With a remark about the rigors of his apostleship, he ends with his benediction.

ROMANS   239

ROMANS

The letter to the church at Rome is unquestionably the most important for the religious thought of Paul, and it is to many Christians the most important text in the New Testament itself. Historically, it has been highly influential in some of the major religious and cultural revolutions in western civilization. To read Romans is to read not only an occasional letter, but a penetrating essay that wrestles with some of the most profound religious ideas of Western Christendom.

The church at Rome was not founded by Paul; in fact, its precise origins are a mystery. All roads led to Rome, and there were those professing all kinds of religion on them, including Judaism and Christianity. The tradition that Peter was martyred in Rome may be accurate, but there is no evidence that he was the first to take Christianity there.

It is known from reports and inscriptions that early first-century Rome contained a large number of Jewish synagogues, mainly Greek-speaking, and that from time to time anti-Judaism ran high. From the Roman historian Suetonius (*Life of Claudius* 25.4) we learn that in 49 C.E. Claudius expelled the Jews from Rome because of a disturbance that Suetonius believed was instigated by a certain "Chrestus." The probable cause, however, was a dispute over Christus, that is, a dispute between Jews and Jewish Christians. Perhaps, then, the church in Rome arose among Diaspora Jews there. At any rate, Acts 18:2 claims that the Jewish *Christian* Aquila and his wife, Priscilla, were among the expelled Jews (see Chapter Four, the Edict of Claudius).

By the time Paul wrote his letter to the Romans there was a sizable Christian congregation there. The general orientation of the letter suggests that the majority, though certainly not all, were Gentile (for example, 1:5–6, 13–15; 11:13; 15:15–33). Since the letter was written about two or three years after the Edict of Claudius was rescinded by the emperor Nero in 54 C.E., we may suppose that some Jews and Jewish Christians had returned to Rome. If chapter 16 was part of the letter, which we view with some suspicion, but which is held in some quarters, Aquila and Prisca (Priscilla) were among them (16:3; see Chapter Six). In any case, by the mid-50s Paul wrote to an established church at Rome; it consisted of a majority of Gentiles and a minority of Jewish Christians, the latter having perhaps recently returned from exile.

Why did Paul write his letter to the Romans? Some scholars have used the return of Jews and Jewish Christians after 54 C.E. to suggest that the tension developing between "the weak" and "the strong" (Rom 14:1–15:13) was directly related to friction between Jewish and Gentile Christians. In this theory "the strong" represented the Gentile Christian majority, and "the weak" represented the Jewish Christian minority. The primary dispute was about eating practices (14:20–21), and the dispute gave occasion to the letter. There is a certain plausibility in this theory because of Paul's concern with Jews and Gentiles in the letter as a whole.

Other interpreters derive the purpose of Paul's letter from several statements he makes in passing. In the thanksgiving Paul says he wishes to impart to the Roman Christians some spiritual gift to strengthen them, but quickly adds—cautiously, no doubt—"that we may be mutually encouraged by each other's faith, both yours and mine" (1:12). His general rule has always been not to preach the gospel in anyone else's mission territory (15:20; compare 1 Cor 3:10; 2 Cor 10:13–17), but he can also say, " . . . I am eager to preach the gospel to you also who are in Rome" (1:15). Yet, Paul certainly does not think of Rome as *his* mission territory; rather, he wishes to see the Romans "in passing" as he goes on to Spain, and to receive their encouragement (15:24). If he gets their approval Rome will then be something of a mission center from which he can move on, as Antioch and later Ephesus have been. Some interpreters, indeed, have seen this desire for acceptance at Rome as the major purpose of the document since Paul is aware that the controversies in which he has been embroiled are well known to the Roman Jews and Christians and might lead to a false impression of him and his gospel.

However, still other scholars believe that the letter is not intended to be read by the Christians only at Rome. One view is that it is in part a draft of what Paul actually wants to say in defense of himself at Jerusalem. More common is the theory that it is a circular letter to several churches. An extension of these theories is the suggestion that Romans is Paul's "last will and testament," which grew out of both Paul's anxiety in the face of the dangers that faced him at Jerusalem and his views as he had developed them from his conflicts with Judaizers and enthusiasts (Bornkamm). His polemical passages may thus be part of the Cynic-Stoic diatribe *style,* not directed only to specific opponents at Rome. This view tends to be reinforced by parallels in Romans with his views in Galatians, Philippians, and Corinthians, as follows:

Justification by faith alone and not by works of the Law (Gal 3 and 4; Phil 3; Rom 1–4; 9:30–10:4).

Abraham as the type of justification by faith (Gal 3; Rom 4).

Adam as the mythical embodiment of the fall of humanity and Christ as the head of the new humanity (1 Cor 15:22–28; Rom 5:12–21).

Natural humanity subject to Law, sin, and death (1 Cor 15:56–57; Rom 7:7–25).

The sending of the Son of God in the flesh for our redemption and the testimony of the Spirit that we are the children of God (Gal 4:4–7; Rom 8).

The unity of the church described as one body with many members (1 Cor 12; Rom 12:4–8).

The conflict of "weak" and "strong" over food matters (1 Cor 8,10; Rom 14:1–15:13).

The suggestion that Romans is Paul's last will and testament also gains some support from comparison with other ancient letters. The theory is that it is a letter-essay. As such, it is an actual letter sent to specific persons about specific subjects, but *at the same time* it is " . . . supplementary in some way to another writing usually by the same author or substitute for a work projected by him, and the idea of instruction is presented in the author's purpose to clarify, abridge, aid in memorizing, defend his thesis, recount history" (Stirnewalt, 176–177). In other words, Romans could have been written *both* to a specific situation of which Paul had some knowledge *and* at the same time have summed up his major ideas on the basis of his other letters. One scholar who has studied the letter-essay makes this conclusion:

This great document, which summarizes and develops the most important themes and thoughts of the Pauline message and theology and which elevates his theology above the moment of definite situations and conflicts into the sphere of the eternally and universally valid, this letter to the Romans is the last will and testament of the Apostle Paul.

(Stirnewalt, 206)

Exegetical Survey of Paul's Letter to the Romans

1:1–7 SALUTATION.
Paul extends this conventional salutation to include a definition of the gospel, which contains a traditional Christological formula (1:3–4; see Chapter Six).

1:8–15 THANKSGIVING.
This sets the tone and indicates the purpose of the whole letter, as it so often does. Paul's caution is clear. He hopes for mutual exchange of faith and the opportunity to preach the gospel.

1:16–17 SUMMARY STATEMENT OF PAUL'S UNDERSTANDING OF THE GOSPEL.
The righteousness of God is an active concept, with God as the acting subject. It refers to the power of God to act in accordance with his own true nature as creator and redeemer, to establish human beings as righteous before him. This state of acceptance in God's sight is God's own gift; it cannot be achieved by works of the Law, it is accessible only to one act, the act of faith. This is the climactic statement of Paul's characteristic doctrine of justification by faith, and one should compare the earlier statement of it in Galatians 3:10–11 and Philippians 3:9.

1:18–3:20 FIRST MAJOR SECTION: THE WORLD'S NEED FOR JUSTIFICATION BY FAITH.

1:18–32 The judgment of God is revealed against the sin of man. Gentiles have sinned and are without excuse; God's power and deity have been revealed to them in his creation. Their sin is clear from their homosexuality (1:24–27; see below). Paul associates their actions with vices in a typical vice list (1:28–32; see Chapter Six).

2:1–11 The Jews are just as much under the judgment of God as are the Gentiles. However, if they "do good," they will also have glory and peace. In both instances, Paul states, "The Jew first and also the Greek" (2:9, 10), on which see 1:16 and chapters 9–11.

2:12–29 God judges the Jews by the standards of the Law of Moses, and the Gentiles by the "law" of their conscience. But the Jew may not rely on outward observances; true circumcision is a circumcision of the heart.

3:1–8 The Jews nonetheless have an advantage. God has directly revealed his will and purpose to them in their Scriptures.

3:9–20 But all people, Jews and Gentiles alike, have fallen under the power of sin. Ultimately, then, the Jews are not any better off.

3:21–4:25 SECOND MAJOR SECTION: THE NATURE OF GOD'S SAVING ACT IN CHRIST, AND OF HUMAN APPROPRIATION OF THAT ACT.

3:21–26 Restatement of justification by faith. Having established that the whole world, Jewish and Gentile, needs justification by faith because it is estranged from God by its sin, Paul now restates justification to include the Cross of Christ. Paul's emphasis on the redemptive power of the Cross of Christ is a major feature of his "theology." The crucifixion of Jesus was a "stumbling block" (*skandalon*) to the Christian claim that Jesus was the Messiah, the Son of God. How could it be that the Messiah, the Son of God, had been allowed by God to suffer a criminal's death on a cross, subject to the power of the Jewish and Roman authorities? The word of his mouth should have had the power to blast them from the face of the earth.

Paul must have had this difficulty many times in his years of attempting to convince his fellow Hellenistic Jews that the crucified Jesus was the Christ. He must have spoken out of personal experience when he said, "We preach Christ crucified, a stumbling block to Jews and folly to Gentiles" (1 Cor 1:23). A crucified redeemer figure was "folly" to the Gentile, because the characteristic redeemers in that society were either heroes/heroines of the mystery cults or Divine Men. Mission Christianity met this problem by transforming Jesus into a Divine Man, an apotheosis. In a Jewish environment the Christians developed a "passion apologetic," that is, an attempt to show that the passion and Cross of Jesus was in accord with the will and purpose of God as revealed in the Scriptures. But as time went by, the Christians came more and more to accept the Cross as a fact and to develop an understanding of its meaning rather than an apologetic for its necessity. They moved from a passion apologetic to an emphasis on the Cross as symbol of God's act of salvation on behalf of humanity.

Paul played a major role in the development of this "soteriology of the Cross" (Greek *sōtēria* = "salvation"; soteriology, "how one is saved"). He sought to understand how the Cross of Christ changes forever the relationship between God and humans. The Jews, and early Christians in general, expected the relationship to be changed by the eschatological act of God. Among Christians the form of this expectation was the return of Jesus from heaven as apocalyptic judge and redeemer. Then the relationship between God and human beings would be forever changed. In Paul's thinking, this change had already taken place in the Cross of Christ. The whole world, Jewish and Gentile, was estranged from God by its sin, but the estrangement was not to be eradicated by an act of God in the future. It had already been eradicated by an act of God in the past: the Cross of Christ.

Paul never tires of this theme. The world is estranged from God by reason of sin, but God has done something about it. This "something" is the Cross of Christ, and Paul constantly tries to find ways of explaining how the Cross of Christ eradicates the estrangement of human beings from God created by their sins. Thus, in Romans 3:25 he turns to the word *hilastērion*. In the Septuagint, this unusual term refers to a *place* in the Holy of Holies of the Jerusalem Temple, that is, the lid of the Ark of the Covenant on which the blood of sacrifice was sprinkled on the Day of

Atonement, sometimes translated the "mercy seat" (Exod 25:16ff.; Lev 16:2, 11–17; see Chapter Three). Paul, a Greek-speaking Jew, seems to say that the Cross of Christ is the place where human sin meets the forgiveness of God. *Hilastērion* can also refer to the *gift* to the angry Deity that brings about God's appeasement. The fact is that we are at a point where language fails us, as the many translations show ("propitiation"; "expiation"; "sacrifice of atonement," and so forth). Paul's fundamental convictions are that *(a)* people are estranged from God and doomed for all eternity because of sin; and *(b)* God has changed this situation through the sacrificial Cross of Christ. The need of human beings is met by God in the sacrifice of Jesus on the cross.

The act of God that will eradicate human estrangement is "effective through faith" (NEB; NRSV). Paul reaches this view through reflection and as a result of his controversy with the Judaizers in Galatia and elsewhere. Whatever God has done in the Cross of Christ, it is effective for any person only insofar as that person responds to it by the act of faith. "Faith" is difficult to describe; it implies "belief," "trust," "obedience": Just as Jesus gives himself totally to God and humanity by accepting the necessity for the Cross, so must human beings give themselves totally to God-as-revealed-in-Jesus in order to appropriate for themselves the power of that Cross.

A final point is the meaning of a word group in Greek (*dikaio-*) related to the English terms "just" and "right," namely, the verb "to judge," "to justify" or "to make right" (*dikaioō*) the noun "justification" or "righteousness" (*dikaiosunē*) and the adjective "made just," or "righteous" (*dikaios*). These terms are derived from the law court, and the reference is to an act of judgment. God has given humans a standard by which to live—to Jews a Torah, and to Gentiles a conscience, or the law written on the heart—and ultimately they must stand before God and be judged by that standard. If a person has achieved it that person will be declared "righteous," and the divine act of declaring one righteous is the act of justification: God justifies the person who is righteous in God's sight. Paul's whole argument is that no one can achieve the necessary righteousness, and so God has established a new possibility: a person will be justified by God—that is, declared "righteous"—if that person has faith in Jesus, and this is a possibility for Jew and Gentile alike. The Jew has failed to live up to the Law and the Gentile to the conscience in his or her heart, but God nonetheless declares them "righteous" because of the "righteousness" of Jesus (who more than fulfilled all norms), which they appropriate to themselves by the act of faith.

3:27–31 It is faith and not works that matters. Paul's constant controversy with the Judaizers led him to the acute antithesis: *either* gladly accept by the act of faith what God has done in Christ *or* justify yourself before God by the quality of your own life. It is easy enough to say that it should have been in some respects a question of "both . . . and," but in the heat of controversy contrasting emphases become sharpened to radical opposites. Paul's argument is that justification must be by faith and not by Law. The Jews have the Law, but the purpose of God must be the justification of all. Everyone is capable of the act of faith.

4:1–25 Abraham himself was justified by faith and thus is the "father" of all who believe in the God who raised Jesus from the dead. Paul's position turns on the fact that in Genesis 15 it is said of Abraham, "he *believed* the Lord, and he (the Lord) reckoned it to him as *righteousness*" (Gen 15:6). Not until Genesis 17 is the requirement of circumcision laid on him as on his descendants (Gen 17:11). Faith is anterior and hence superior to circumcision as a means of being justified before God. This is a typically rabbinic method of argument. For his earlier formulation in relation to the new family, see Galatians 3.

5:1–8:39 THIRD MAJOR SECTION: THE NEW LIFE IN CHRIST.

5:1–5 The consequence of justification by faith: peace with God and joy in life.

5:6–11 The grounds for the possibility of justification by faith: the Cross of Christ. In one of his most lyrical passages, Paul expresses his fundamental convictions by using two images: the image of *justification,* taken from the language of the law court, and the image of *reconciliation,* taken from the language of personal relationships (compare 2 Cor 5:16–21). Both are ways of talking about the plight of human beings before God—the need for justification, the need for reconciliation—and both are ways of talking about the Cross of Christ—the means by which God has changed the plight of human beings. One is "justified by his blood" or "reconciled by his death." Two further notes are sounded: *(a)* the whole work of justification or of reconciliation is a work of God and hence an outpouring of God's love of humanity; and *(b)* the person who is justified or reconciled by the death of Jesus is further "saved" by Jesus' life.

This latter point is Paul's version of the claim of the Corinthian enthusiasts that they know already the power of the risen Lord, that their life in Christ is already the resurrection life. Paul does not deny this; he is willing to claim that Christians in this life share in the power of Jesus' resurrection and that their lives are already transformed by the power of that resurrection. But there is always for Paul what modern scholars tend to call an "eschatological reservation." However much a person now knows of the power and quality of the resurrection life in the present, there is still the final resurrection to come. However much one is now justified or reconciled, one still needs to be "saved from the wrath to come," that is, from the still outstanding, final, eschatological judgment of God. There is in Paul an inevitable element of tension between his ability as a Hellenist to interpret the Christian faith in terms of Greek religious enthusiasm and his necessity as a Jew to think in terms of a Last Judgment. We can understand Paul correctly only if we recognize that for all his enthusiasm for the effectiveness of the Cross of Christ, for all his glorying in the present experience of Christ's risen life, he nonetheless never loses touch with the typical early Christian apocalyptic hope for a second coming of Christ as judge and redeemer. So in this passage, although we are *already* "reconciled," we *still* need to be "saved." Logically it is inconsistent, but religious experience is not always logical. This view has fed the piety of centuries because it has been found to correspond to the reality of Christian religious experience.

5:12–21 The myths of Adam and Christ. In our discussion of the early Christian apocalyptic hope, we said that a reason for its enduring power was the correspondence between the myth explaining the existence of evil in the world as the result of the wrongdoing of a primal human ancestor and the myth explaining the removal of evil from the world as an activity of another human or humanlike figure. Paul now develops this correspondence of myths more exactly by claiming that just as the wrongdoing of the one man, Adam, led to the existence of sin and evil, and finally death, so also the righteousness of the one man, Jesus Christ, results in the possibility of the removal of sin and evil, and finally true life. For Paul's previous statement of the Adam/Christ myth, see 1 Corinthians 15:22–28.

6:1–14 Dying and rising with Christ. In Gentile environments where Paul preached, it was natural to think of sharing the power and destiny of a cult hero such as Serapis or Mithras. In responding to the imagined protest of an opponent with whom he is in dialogue—a characteristic Hellenistic literary device—Paul interprets the Christian initiatory rite of baptism as a sharing in the death of Christ. He then states the Christian *shall* be united with Christ in a resurrection like his, maintaining the "eschatological reservation." Paul then interjects a parenetic passage of exhortation (verses 12–14).

6:15–7:6 The two analogies: slavery and marriage. To drive home his point, Paul turns to two analogies: slavery and marriage. A slave is totally responsible to one master, but only to one. Similarly, a wife is totally responsible to her husband, but only as long as he lives. So Christians were once slaves to sin and married to the Law, but now they are slaves of righteousness, and the Law is dead for them.

7:7–25 The meaning and function of the Mosaic Law. As a Jew Paul inherited the understanding of the Law of God as given through Moses as the supreme gift of God's grace, given to humanity that he might know and do the will of God in the world and so inherit the blessings of all eternity. As a Christian he had come to see that under the Law Jesus himself stood condemned, since according to the Law, "cursed be every one who hangs on a tree" (Deut 21:23, quoted in Gal 3:13), that is, in his crucifixion Jesus was, according to the Law, cursed. Paul must have maintained this argument in his days of opposition to Jesus and to faith in Jesus. But he revised the meaning in Galatians to show that Christ took the curse of the Law upon himself in behalf of the Christian (Gal 3:13). Moreover, according to God's direct revelation to Paul, Jesus was God's own Son. Thus, Paul must have begun to question the validity of the Law.

In his days as a Christian preacher Paul was forced into controversy with his Judaizing opponents in Galatia and Philippi, and no doubt elsewhere, where the question at issue was the validity of the Law. Underlying this issue was Paul's gospel and the freedom of the Christian mission to be *Christian* (as Paul had come to understand the meaning of that term), and not simply Jewish. So Paul was again forced to question the validity of the Mosaic Law, and indeed to deny its enduring significance for Christians. Now in this passage from Romans, he brings his reflections together, and out of his own experience of the crucified Christ and of the Judaizing controversy fashions his classic statement on the ultimate significance of the Law given by God to the Jewish people as the supreme gift of God's grace. Sin brings about death. The Law in and of itself is not sin; it is "holy and just and good" (7:12). Yet, one knows sin through the Law. Only when one is forbidden to do something by the Law does one become aware that what he does is forbidden. "Apart from the Law sin lies dead . . . but when the commandment came, sin revived and I died" (7:8, 9). So, though the Law was intended to help, it did not; it became a tool of sin. The Law is spiritual, but humans are carnal. They are "sold under sin." So Paul says,

> I do not understand my own actions. For I do not do what I
> want, but I do the very thing that I hate. . . . Now if I do what
> I do not want, it is no longer I that do it, but sin which dwells
> within me.
>
> (7:14–15, 20)

It is sometimes supposed that this passage is autobiographical and that Paul was reflecting on his own soul-searching when he had attempted to fulfill the Law as a Pharisee. However, it seems more likely that the use of the first-person singular is a literary device. While we have no evidence that Paul thought this way about the Law before his vision of the risen Christ, who should have been cursed by God but was in fact vindicated by God, or before his conflicts with the Judaizers, the literary device makes it a powerful passage. The experience depicted corresponds to the reality of the experience of countless people who have conscientiously attempted to fulfill an established code of conduct. "The good that I would I do not: but the evil which I would not, that I do" (Rom 7:19, KJV) is a cry from the heart of conscientious humanity.

8:1–39 The new life in Christ and its details. Paul has paused to give his apology for the Law (7:7–25). Now in what is probably the greatest sustained passage from his letters, Paul depicts the details of the possibilities of the new life in Christ. These are life in the Spirit, life as free children of God, life as eschatological hope and love. Christ has accomplished what for Paul the Law is not able to do: Christians are no longer condemned, slaves to sin in the flesh and to die; Christians are free spiritual beings who live with the promise that nothing—none of the world's powers—can separate them from the love of God.

9:1–11:36 FOURTH MAJOR SECTION: THE PLACE OF ISRAEL IN GOD'S PLAN FOR THE SALVATION OF ALL HUMANITY ("SALVATION HISTORY")

Nothing disturbed Paul personally more than the problems posed by his Jewish heritage. He had grown up proudly as a member of the people of God, the "chosen people," to whom God's will and purpose had been revealed directly in the Law. Yet, Paul had come to think that the people of God had rejected God's own Son. Paul spent much of his life as a Christian arguing with his own people that Jesus was God's own Son because his life, death, and resurrection had been foretold in the Scriptures. Paul also tried to explain to Gentiles how it was that his own people, the chosen people of God, had not recognized the Son of God. Now he was proudly preaching a gospel that claimed a Gentile could be justified on the basis of responsiveness to the dictates of his conscience.

What, then, remained of the special calling of the Jewish people to become God's chosen people, the "light of the world"? The most natural answer would have been, "Nothing!", especially when facing the problems created by the conservative Jewish-Christian party at Jerusalem, or Judaizers who demanded circumcision and adherence to the Law. Since most of the Jews had rejected Jesus, the answer could even have been sharper, "Less than nothing!" Nonetheless, Paul continued to wrestle with the problem and came up with an answer scholars normally discuss under the rubric of the German word *Heilsgeschichte*.

Heilsgeschichte means literally "the story of salvation" and is usually translated "salvation history." The term is used to designate God's revealing and saving action in history. It is not simply secular history, but God working out a plan *through* secular history, at crucial points intersecting with secular history. Thus, secular history becomes the stage on which the religious story of God's relation with the people of Israel is told.

Paul is at a crucial point in his argument. Here we do not find parallels in his earlier letters, though he has come close in his discussion of Abraham as the Christian's true "father" (Rom 4; compare Gal 3), and in his comments about "to the Jew first and also to the Greek" (Rom 1:16; 2:8–9). The problem is this: If God now justifies each *individual* sinner—Jew or Gentile—on the basis of *faith* in Christ, what about his promises to Israel as a group? Paul has thus to relate justification by grace through faith to God's plan in history, and specifically to the rejection of God's Son and Messiah by most of Israel. Paul argues that everything that has happened has been in accordance with the will and purpose of God, and that purpose is the salvation of all humanity, Jews and the Gentiles. Except for a remnant, however, Israel has failed to recognize that righteousness is ultimately attained only by faith. Israel as a "nation" has remained obdurate in its insistence on a righteousness attainable by obedience to an external Law, "and seeking to establish their own, they did not submit to God's righteousness" (10:3).

Yet, God has not rejected the people of Israel, and the Gentiles should not feel superior to them. If God can break off some of the branches (the Jews who do not believe) of a cultivated olive tree and graft on branches of a wild olive shoot (Jewish and *Gentile* Christians), God can just as easily break off the wild branches and graft in old branches—if they believe—especially since they are natural branches. The rejection of God's Son by "the rest" of Israel has the consequence that the Gentiles have an opportunity to hear the gospel (11:11–12). The word of God to Israel has not failed—after all, the promise to Abraham means that his *true* descendants are those who believe, which includes the "nations"/"Gentiles." To be sure, this is not "Israel" as a whole, as a nation, but it is an "Israel." What then of Israel as a whole? Paul argues that there is an eschatological mystery here: while the full number of Gentiles come in, part of Israel will remain outside; nonetheless, in the end, he hopes, all Israel will be saved.

All this is argued in detail and with copious references to Scripture. Yet, the modern reader cannot help but feel that there is something very strained about the whole argument. The theme of Romans 1–8 is one theme; the theme of Romans 9–11 quite another. Romans 9–11 is a testimony to the agony of the spirit of a conscientious Jew who has come to believe that God's own people *as a whole* have rejected God's own Son as well as God's own gospel. Romans 9–11 is Paul's attempt to accept and to understand this reality. Whether its argument is fully convincing or not, it should be read with understanding for the agony of the human spirit that gave rise to it.

12:1–15:33 FIFTH MAJOR SECTION: PARENESIS.

Romans 12–15 is in the main the parenetical section of the letter. In Romans 12, we hear echoes of the "body politic" metaphor in 1 Corinthians 12, that is, though there are many members with differing spiritual gifts, there is one body (12:3–8). This is followed by a series of general exhortations about behavior, both with respect to life within the community and in relation to those outside (12:9–21). Chapter 13 contains Paul's most famous political statement, a recommendation to be subject to the governing authorities (see below) and the gospel tradition about love. Romans 14:1–15:13, discussed above in relation to the Romans debate about chapter 16, takes up the relation of "the weak" to "the strong." Romans 15:14–33 speaks of Paul's pride in his mission; it concludes with an itinerary where Paul expresses the hope of going on to Spain and relays his anxiety about taking the collection to Jerusalem. The closing contains an appeal to prayer on Paul's behalf and a benediction (15:33).

Romans 16

We have already discussed this passage as a possible addition to Romans 1–15. It contains a letter of recommendation for Phoebe (16:1–2), greetings to twenty-five people by name and others, and "the kiss" (16:16). Then comes a startling comment about opponents (17–20) that includes another benediction (verse 20), greetings from Paul and his companions (21–23), and finally an un-Pauline doxology (25–27).

PAUL'S THEOLOGY AND ETHICS: A SUMMARY

From our brief exegetical outlines of Paul's undisputed letters, it will now be helpful to put together a summary of some of his basic ideas.

As far as we know, Paul never met the historical Jesus. Yet, as a result of a religious experience in which he believed he had seen the crucified and risen Christ, the persecutor of Christians abandoned his former life and carried out his "call" to preach the "good news" as apostle to the Gentiles. As recovered from his surviving letters, the heart of this good news was not the perpetuation of the teaching of Jesus, telling stories about Jesus' power as a miracle worker, or having a "Christlike" moral life in the sense of following in the steps of Jesus of Nazareth, though Paul had his own emphasis on Christlike parenesis; rather, the center was "the Christ-event," that is, Jesus' death on the Cross and his resurrection from the dead.

For Paul, the "Christ-event" opens up the whole meaning of the divine plan and purpose of the one true God of Israel, and therefore the whole meaning and purpose of human existence. When properly understood, the Christ-event fulfills God's ancient promises, namely, that salvation is not only for those who are, and become part of, God's chosen covenant people as a national entity "Israel," with its religious heritage grounded in the Torah; it is rather for the whole human race and predicated on belief in the Christ-event itself. Salvation is good news about God, God's purposes, God's relation to humankind, the nature and destiny of humanity, human freedom and ethical responsibility, faith, hope, and love—in short, all of reality. The "Christ-event" is a "foundational myth," a creative act that gives meaning and purpose to human existence. This mystery of the Cross-resurrection is not understood by the wisdom of the world. For Paul, this event is a *powerful* event, signaling that the final period of history has begun, that the End is imminent. It is therefore an eschatological event. Paradoxically, however, God's power is manifested in weakness: It is power present both in manifestations of the Spirit of God through spiritual gifts, and in the self-giving love of God who commands that believers respond in the same way. For the Christian, then, spiritual enthusiasm and weakness are to be held in balance: Enthusiasm without the Cross leads to self-seeking pride and "knowledge"; yet, the new life in Christ is already manifested by spiritual security and gifts of the spirit.

At the same time, the "Christ-event" is a gift of God's grace. For Paul, the total self ("body") contains within a struggle between the "spirit," the higher self, and the "flesh," the self subject to attack by sin, a power Paul frequently personifies. It is sin in the flesh that leads the self to rebel against God, and this rebellion manifests itself in all forms of wickedness and vice. The self cannot overcome this evil power by itself; it therefore cannot overcome evil by good works—including those prescribed by the Torah. In fact, an angry God would be justified in rendering the verdict of "guilty" on sinful humanity. But God has not done so for those who believe in his act of power. In other words, "the righteousness of God" is the powerful movement of God toward human beings in which by his free gift of grace—the Christ-event—sinners are made just, or "justified," that is, acquitted on the basis of a trusting belief. The good news is the "power of God for salvation for everyone who has faith" (Rom 1:16). By this faith the believer departs from an old humanity, symbolized by Adam, and enters a new community, symbolized by Christ. The Christian becomes part of a new family, one of the true children of Abraham, who is the prototype of faith. The ritual of baptism means that the believer shares in Christ's death by dying to the old self and is offered the promise of participating in Christ's resurrection, the new self. This new life in the Spirit is sustained in the group by worship, especially in the common meal, the Lord's Supper, which commemorates Christ's death. It is also manifested by charismatic gifts and can be characterized as "life" and "peace." Vices associated with the flesh are rejected and virtues associated with the Spirit are fostered within the new body. By God's action "in Christ," then, the whole world and everyone in it is offered reconciliation with the Creator.

Much more could be added to this brief statement but it is obvious that Paul's view of the good news about Jesus Christ led him into conflict with his own Jewish religious traditions at the crucial point: the understanding of the Torah and its function among God's elect, covenant people, Israel. It is highly debated whether Paul, as a Hellenistic Jew of the Diaspora, fully appreciated his full religious tradition about the Torah when he spoke of it in terms of "works of the Law." Whether he did or not, it is clear that if the sign of God's covenant people is circumcision as stated in the Law, Paul's view that Gentiles could become part of the new community without circumcision, and his perspective that Christ is the "end of the Law," led toward a different idea of the community. Once the gospel was preached to the Gentiles on this basis, the conflict with those who upheld the more traditional view of the Torah was inevitable. Although the mature Paul could cite the baptismal formula, "neither Jew nor Greek . . . in Christ Jesus" (Gal 3:28), and hope for the ultimate inclusion of the mother, Israel, who had given birth to her children, the Christians (Rom 11), the way was prepared for the eventual emergence of a separate and distinct institution, the Christian church.

No matter how one evaluates Paul's theology, Paul will certainly be seen as a profound religious thinker. What, then, about his practical, ethical advice? We cannot enter into a full discussion of his ethical teachings at this point; we can, however, indicate his general orientation to ethical issues and cite a few concrete examples.

Much of Paul's advice is drawn from conventional morality in his time. Christians, like Jews, should settle their disputes outside the pagan courts (1 Cor 6); lists of vices and virtues reflect popular Hellenistic morality. There are also sources for authority such as the Old Testament (for example, 1 Cor 10), Christian tradition (1 Cor 11:23–25 on the Lord's Supper; 1 Cor 15:3b–5 on the resurrection), and more concrete "words of the Lord" on issues like divorce (1 Cor 7:10–11) and the apostolic right to financial support (1 Cor 9:14). His views of slavery, women, and homosexuality (see below) will not be accepted as such by modern, western, liberated people. Conventional, time-bound morality and the appeal to tradition, along with Paul's eschatological orientation toward the end of the world and his tendency to put parenetic sections at the end of his letters, have led some interpreters to suggest that Paul's ethical teachings are ancient and time-bound, and ultimately a subsidiary, even irrelevant, part of his thinking.

Others have concluded that whatever one may think of Paul's ethical views on specific subjects, it would be inaccurate to isolate them from his theological arguments. The form of the letter is sufficiently flexible to permit moral exhortation to occur at almost any place. Indeed, 1 Thessalonians might be called a "parenetic letter" and 1 Corinthians is dominated by responses to practical, ethical concerns of the Corinthian church. For Paul himself, at least, the parenesis is finally inseparable from his gospel proclamation. Ethics grows out of the Christ-event. As some New Testament theologians put it, the moral "imperative"—what believers ought to do—is rooted in, and therefore inseparable from, the theological "indicative"—what God has already done for believers. Thus, while Paul often draws on authority and conventional morality, some of which has a clearly time-bound quality, Paul's theology contains impulses for ethical reflection that go beyond what is typical of his contemporaries.

If Paul's ethical statements are in the service of his gospel, then they must be coordinated with his view of God's eschatological act of power and grace in the Christ-event. The final period of history has begun, but the consummation still lies in the future. Meanwhile, Christians have received a taste of the future in the activity of the Spirit (Rom 8:23), both in the individual and in the community. This is expressed in *Christian freedom within the bounds of love.* When freedom is threatened, especially by strict adherence to the Law, Paul rushes to defend the gospel; at the same time, he checks the abuse of freedom by appeals to love as the highest spiritual gift for interaction within the community, to weakness as true strength, and to the "eschatological reservation": Christians are not yet perfected. To be sure, Paul is willing to be accommodating (1 Cor 9:19–23), though he is cautious about this principle. More important, we see him struggling with the issue of freedom and love in his willingness to admit that there is a special wisdom for "the strong." Nonetheless, maturity should never be the occasion for causing "the weak" to stumble (1 Cor 8, 10; Rom 14–15). Finally, though the goal might not actually have been met, it finds one of its best expressions in the traditional baptismal formula of Galatians 3:28:

> There is neither Jew nor Greek,
> there is neither slave nor free,
> there is neither male nor female;
> for you are all one in Christ Jesus.

We are now in a position to look at some of Paul's highly debated, concrete cases.

1. Sex, marriage, and divorce. At Corinth, Paul had to counter two extremes: the enthusiasts who championed a libertine ethic with the slogan, "All things are lawful" (1 Cor 6:12; 10:23), and the ascetics who fought the evil of physical desire with the slogan, "It is well for a man not to touch a woman" (1 Cor 7:1). Paul responded to specific questions about sex, marriage, and divorce in 1 Corinthians 7 by taking a middle ground, and by defending the view that the Corinthians remain as they are because the End is near, a practical solution geared to Christian service without anxiety. He clearly preferred celibacy, but as a "gift" (verse 7), not as proof of superior moral status. Yet, he recognized the power of strong sexual desire and did not put marriage down. Drawing on his Pharisaic heritage, he declared that sex belongs in marriage with one partner; otherwise, sexual immorality *(porneia)* results. He said nothing of the other major rabbinic argument, that marriage is necessary for the propagation of the race (compare Gen 1:28). Paul argued that sex is a mutual responsibility of husband and wife as equal partners, conceding the possibility of temporary abstinence for prayer, again a rabbinic recommendation, again by mutual agreement (verse 6).

What, then, of divorce? In Roman law, either partner could divorce the other, and divorce was common. In Judaism, the Law of Moses permitted divorce only by the husband if the wife ". . . finds no favor in his eyes because he has found some indecency in her. . . ." (Deut 24:1). In the first century C.E., the conservative school of Shammai interpreted this to mean that adultery was the only basis for divorce, but the liberal school of Hillel said it meant for "any cause." Paul drew upon a "word of the Lord" forbidding divorce altogether, perhaps as a protection for the woman (Mark 10:2–12; Luke 16:18; contrast Matthew's "except for unchastity" [Matt 5:32; 19:9], perhaps a reflection of the Shammai position). Yet, Paul did not hold the Jesus word sacrosanct, for in an aside (if it was not interpolated by a scribe), he admitted "separations" would occur, that there should not be second marriages, and that if reconciliation between marriage partners is impossible, the wife (and the husband?) should maintain a single status. If an already married partner *becomes* a Christian (nothing is said of a Christian marrying a non-Christian!), Paul recommended that the couple stay together, for marriage is holy, and so the children of holy marriages are holy. Perhaps the non-Christian partner of a marriage would become Christian; yet, if the unbelieving partner wants to separate, the Christian partner is not bound to the marriage. In all of this we observe the apostle accommodating his own preference for celibacy, yet maintaining a position between the poles of libertine and ascetic ethics, and doing so in the light of his eschatology.

2. Attitudes toward women. In assessing Paul's view of women, it should be recalled that the religious and cultural background out of which he came was patriarchal. A woman was subordinate to her father before marriage and to her husband after marriage. In Judaism, the woman's main functions were childbearing (preferably a son) and child rearing, being a wife and sexual partner, cook and housekeeper. A second point to recall is that in looking at Paul's views one must exclude works of the Pauline School (especially Colossians and Ephesians) and especially the much later Pastorals (1, 2 Timothy, Titus). This is an important point since these later letters accommodate Paul's views to the patriarchal tradition of subordination in both Judaism and Hellenism (Col 3:18; Eph 5:24; 1 Tim 2:9–15). 1 Timothy, in fact, argues that women are not to teach or have authority over men (women are to remain silent) because Eve, not Adam, was deceived; indeed, she ". . . will be saved through bearing children, if she continues in faith and love and holiness, with modesty" (2:15). Another passage that shares this general perspective is 1 Corinthians 14:33b–36. This passage, as we have seen, interrupts the context in such a way that modern critics believe it is an interpolation by a later scribe, perhaps a member of Paul's school who produced the Pastorals.

This last passage is the strongest indication of subordination in Paul's undisputed letters, but it does not come from Paul. Five important passages remain. We have seen that in Galatians 3:28, Paul cites in the baptism formula, "neither male nor female . . . in Christ Jesus," clearly indicating that in the new community old distinctions shall not pertain. We have also seen that in 1 Corinthians 7, Paul balances evenly the roles of men and women in marriage (7:2, 3, 4, 10–11, 12–13, 33–34 [twice]). None of this sounds like the dominant patriarchal tradition. Furthermore, there are clear references to women who have achieved prominence as leaders in the churches. Paul says that Euodia and Syntyche "labored side by side" with him at Philippi (Phil 4:2–3). In Romans 16:1 Paul commends "our sister Phoebe, a deacon of the church at Cenchreae (the eastern port at Corinth)." The masculine term "deacon" *(diakonos)* implies at least a functional position in the church (Phil 1:1), and elsewhere Paul uses it of his own role as "servant" or "minister." She is also called a "helper" *(prostatis),* which in Hellenistic literature and inscriptions is clearly a term of authority ranging in meaning from "benefactor" or "patron" to "presiding officer" of a religious cult. Does this one use of the term in the New Testament have the same overtones? Perhaps. In any case, there follows the long list of greetings to persons among whom are Prisca (Priscilla) and Aquila who are given preeminence, Prisca now being mentioned first (compare 1 Cor 16:19, where Aquila is mentioned first, though greetings are given from the church in "their house" in Ephesus). The order of names clearly indicates her importance insofar as it departs from the usual practice of the day (compare Acts 18:26). Although there is a good deal of speculation as to how to interpret these passages, it is clear that while Paul is not liberated in the modern, western sense, women in Paul's communities are not customarily viewed in traditional patriarchal fashion, that in fact they can be seen on a par with men, and that they hold positions of status, and even authority.

We come, then, to what appears to be Paul's most "chauvinistic" passage, 1 Corinthians 11:2–16, a passage that is exceedingly difficult to interpret. Here Paul insists that women should wear a head covering when they pray and prophesy in church, and he gives several arguments to support this view. First, he appears to establish a hierarchy of subordination: God is the "head" *(kephalē)* of Christ, Christ is the "head" of man/husband, and man/husband is the "head" of woman/wife. Paul uses a play on words: "Any man who prays or prophesies with his head covered dishonors his head (= Christ), but any woman who prays or prophesies with her head unveiled dishonors her head (= man/husband)." In part he has the creation story of Genesis in mind, for in verses 7–9 he states that a man may worship with a bare head because he is "the image and glory of God" (Gen 1:26). The woman, however, should be veiled because she is the glory (image is absent) of man according to the order of creation (Gen 2:18–23). Does "head" refer to a subordinationist hierarchy, or is it simply a metaphor for the order of creation? If the latter view holds, Paul does not appear quite as "chauvinistic" as he might be otherwise, though he does not sound as liberated as he does elsewhere.

These problems of interpretation are compounded by another: the woman should wear a veil "because of the angels" (1 Cor 11:10). What does this mean? Demonic angels who lust for human women (compare Gen 6:2, the basis for the Jewish tradition of the fall of the angels)? Angels who also participate in worship? No one knows. But the following comment is clear: "In the Lord" men and women have equal status for if originally woman came from man, man is now born from woman, "and all things are from God" (verses 11–12). This comment sounds a good deal more like Paul's balancing of the sexes in 1 Corinthians 7. In chapter 11, his final comments on the issue of veils indicate his frustration: For a woman to pray without her head covered is improper, against nature, and against Paul's rule in the churches! What lies behind this contrived argument appears to be this: Equal status at Corinth has led to a denial of sexual differentiation, that is, for Paul freedom has led to potential abuse. In the process we learn that Paul attempts to reassert his Galatians 3:28 point of view (verses 11–12, "neither male nor female") and that women do speak in church insofar as they pray and prophesy. Paul's ethical premise of freedom within the bounds of love prevails, despite the difficulties it creates for him at Corinth.

3. Slavery. Slavery was an accepted institution in Greco-Roman society. Slaves could be procured through defeat in war, kidnapping, debt, sale of one's self or children, and breeding of female slaves. While slaves were often permitted common law marriages, they could not be legally married, and they had no legal rights or obligations over their spouses or children. Neither could they participate in local government. They could, however, join a social or burial club, and they were exempt from paying taxes and military conscription. A slave could be manumitted, that is, become a freedman/woman. This took place either formally (usually a master's legal will or by a magistrate, if eligible) or informally (by letter, permission to recline at table with one's master, the witnessing of friends, or by asking one's heir to manumit slaves at one's death). The freed person gained certain civil rights and the possibility of becoming a Roman citizen, but he/she owed his/her former master, also his/her patron, certain continuing obligations such as labor and professional services. Due to manumission and subsequent marrying, some scholars estimate that by the end of the first century five-sixths of the population of Rome was servile or had a servile background.

From this cultural perspective, it is not surprising that slavery is an accepted institution in the New Testament. A number of well-known "pet" names for slaves occur, one of which is Onesimus ("Useful"). The "master"/"slave" terminology is frequently found, both literally and metaphorically. Paul, who clearly understands the slave system, writes, for example:

> Were you a (real) slave when called? Do not be concerned about it. Even if you can gain your (real) freedom, make use of your present condition now more than ever (this clause could be translated as "by all means, [as a freedman/woman] live according to [God's calling]"). For whoever was called in the Lord as a (real) slave is (symbolically) a freed person belonging to the Lord, just as whoever was (really) free when called is (symbolically) a slave of Christ. (As a real slave is bought with a price so) you were (symbolically) bought with a price; do not (symbolically) become slaves of human masters.
> (1 Cor 7:21–23)

As we saw in the case of Philemon and Onesimus, Paul did not attempt to overturn the actual institution of slavery; he did, however, appeal to Philemon to accept back, and perhaps to manumit Onesimus, or even to return him to Paul. The final appeal, however, was directed to Philemon's Christian freedom.

4. Homosexuality. Once again, the Hellenistic cultural background should be kept in mind. Greco-Roman society, and especially public life, was dominated by men. Males sought out other males for companionship and intellectual stimulation. Nudity in athletics was the norm. The ideal of beauty was physical and youthful, and female-looking boys were in Hellenistic times considered very attractive. Bisexual relationships were common (see Scroggs).

With these aesthetic values in place, "voluntary" pederasty ("love of boys") became socially acceptable in many circles. Sometimes such relationships were physical, the older partner normally taking the active sexual role. Sometimes the relationships were not sexual, at least explicitly. Some philosophers came to distinguish between noble pederasty and base pederasty. Noble pederasty was considered masculine, served to aid military education, and fostered the teacher-pupil relationship as the pupil moved down the road to wisdom. Plato considered pederasty a higher form of love (Platonic love; the Platonic relationship). While pederasty was most common, similar relationships could be admired among women and girls. Sappho, a sixth-century B.C.E. poet, was head of a community of girls on the island of Lesbos, from which the term "lesbian" derives.

These supposedly voluntary homosexual relationships were distinguished from involuntary homosexual relationships. Slave boys were made to perform sexual favors for their masters and their companions. Slave boy prostitutes populated the brothels. Some were castrated to preserve their "effeminate" appearances. In Rome homosexual prostitutes were taxed and boy prostitutes were given a legal holiday.

Both voluntary and involuntary pederasty was distinguished from those who practiced as effeminate call boys, that is, boys who freely *sold* their sexual services. These practices were especially condemned. Moreover, there emerged a counter philosophical point of view that opposed pederasty as seductive, effeminate, domineering, impermanent, productive of jealousy, not as pleasurable as male–female relationships, associated with lust and debauchery, and *contrary to nature*. In the middle of the first century, the Roman philosopher Seneca deplored the exploitation of boy slaves. Slightly later, Plutarch and Dio Chrysostom had similar warnings. Laws against rape and abuse were enacted, and there were regulations to protect boys at school.

In the Jewish Torah, male homosexuality was seen as a practice typical of foreigners, or Gentiles. Within Israel, it was considered unholy, and both partners were to be punished by death (Lev 20:13; compare 18:22). The famous story of Sodom (Gen 19), however, was not about homosexuality, but homosexual *rape*. At the time of the New Testament, homosexuality was not condoned in Jewish society; indeed, it was viewed as a revolting Gentile vice and contrary to nature (Josephus *Jewish Antiquities* 15.2.6 particularly 27–29; *Against Apion* 2.199; Philo, *On Abraham* 135–36). The Rabbinic literature extends the Torah prohibition to female homosexual practices. None of this literature, of course, is aware of modern views of "sexual preference."

Paul does not appear preoccupied with homosexuality, but what he does say is in line with his Jewish background and the sort of Hellenistic moral philosophy that condemned abuses. In his attempts to preserve the purity of the group, Paul denounces same sex practices and sexual abuse. In 1 Corinthians 6:9 the difficult term *malakoi,* (those who are) "soft," "weak," "effeminate," occurs in a traditional "catalogue of vices" (see Chapter Six). Because that list includes other sexual sins ("adulterers"), it is probably a term of innuendo referring to pederasty, and would conjure up an image of the call boys. The second term in the list is *arsenokoitai,* which comes from two words, *arsen,* "male," and *koitē,* "bed" (English "coitus"). Since the word *arsenokoitai* is so rare, it may be Paul's translation of the Torah expression in the above noted prohibition against homosexuality, *mishkav zakur,* "lying with a male" (referring to the active, rather than the passive, partner). In short, these terms in the catalogue of vices seem to refer to the active and passive partners in pederasty.

A second passage is Romans 1:26–27. Here both male and female homosexual practices are viewed as the consequential activity of those who refused to acknowledge the one true God. Such practices are associated with idolatry. Since we know of no certain instance of homosexuality in Paul's churches, we gain no impression of how he would have related a specific case to his ethic of freedom within the bounds of love. The theological context of Romans as a whole shows his major point: *All*—Jews and Gentiles—have sinned and are in need of the gift of God's grace and salvation (Rom 1:16–3:31).

5. The state. Romans 13:1–7 is Paul's chief comment about the state, and it has been the source of much church-state reflection down through the centuries. In this passage God has instituted the governing authorities, and every person should be subject to them. Usually this view has been interpreted in a quietistic sense. This interpretation seems reinforced by Paul's appeal to conscience (verse 5). Nonetheless, the total context points to a specific issue—paying taxes—and it should be recalled that a little Christian movement that had as yet had no major conflict with mighty Rome would naturally pick up this Hellenistic Jewish position in relation to the Empire.

THE IMPACT OF THE APOSTLE PAUL

It is impossible to overestimate the importance of the apostle Paul to the New Testament and to Christendom in general. His vision of the nature of Christian faith came at the crucial moment when circumstances were transforming Christianity from an apocalyptic sect within Judaism into a missionary cult within Greco-Roman society, and beyond that into a world religion. In this process Paul came to play a major part, not only because he was a leader in the missionary movement, but even more because his view of the nature of Christian faith blended together the three aspects of its heritage—Judaism, Hellenism, and a distinctive Christian experience—into a new whole. Paul's vision of the nature of Christian faith became normative. He trained followers who not only served the church during his lifetime, but who also lived to provide leadership in the next generation. The very existence of 2 Thessalonians, Colossians, Ephesians, and the Pastorals, not to mention Gnostic interpreters of Paul, is eloquent testimony to his continuing influence. Though difficult to understand, as the author of 2 Peter knew (2 Pet 3:15–16), he had a tremendous influence on later thinkers such as Augustine, Luther, Calvin, and Wesley.

Finally, Paul's letter writing provided the impetus toward the formation of the New Testament itself. The first step in establishing the New Testament as a distinctive body of literature was taken when his letters to individual churches were recognized as being important to all churches and were copied and circulated. For Paul himself, "Scripture" was what we would call the Old Testament, but it is in no small part because of him that there is now a New Testament.

FURTHER READING

General studies, works pertaining to the life of Paul and his churches, and introductions, are cited in **Further Reading** at the end of Chapter Six.

General Studies of Paul's Life and Thought:

A. Deissmann, *Paul: A Study in Social and Religious History*, 2d ed.
M. Dibelius and W. G. Kümmel, *Paul.*
C. H. Dodd, *The Meaning of Paul for Today.*
L. E. Keck, *Paul and His Letters.*
L. E. Keck and V. P. Furnish, *The Pauline Letters.*
W. G. Kümmel, *The Theology of the New Testament*, pp. 250–350.
S. B. Marrow, *Paul: His Letters and His Theology.*
A. D. Nock, *St. Paul.*
H. Ridderbos, *Paul.*
R. Rubenstein, *My Brother Paul.*
E. P. Sanders, *Paul and Palestinian Judaism.*
S. Sandmel, *The Genius of Paul.*
H. J. Schoeps, *Paul.*
R. Scroggs, *Paul for a New Day.*

Paul's Historical and Social Context (see Further Reading, Chapter Six)

Paul's Theology:

ABD: "Atonement in the New Testament" (C. M. Tuckett); "Body" (R. E. Schweizer); "Bread" (S. A. Reed); "Christ, Body of" (A. B. Luter, Jr.); "Circumcision" (R. G. Hall); "Conscience" (R. W. Wall); "Forgiveness" (G. S. Shogren); "Freedom" (F. Stanley Jones); "Gifts, Spirit" (R. P. Martin); "Grace (NT)" (G. S. Shogren); "Healing, Gifts of" (M. D. Ham); "Holy Spirit" (F. W. Horn, trans. D. M. Elliott); "Hope (NT)" (T. Prendergast); "Incarnation" (J. D. G. Dunn); "Law" (S. Greengus); "Love (NT and Early Jewish)" (W. Klassen); "Parousia" (C. Rowland); "Redemption (NT)" (G. Shogren); "Righteousness (NT)" (J. Reumann); "Resurrection" (G. W. E. Nickelsburg); "Salvation" (G. G. O'Collins); "Sin, Sinner (NT)" (E. P. Sanders); "Tongues, Gift of" (L. T. Johnson); "Wrath of God (NT)" (S. T. Travis).

NJBC, pp. 1382–1416 (J. Fitzmyer) = J. Fitzmyer, *Pauline Theology: A Brief Sketch,* 2d ed.

 F. Amiot, *The Key Concepts of St. Paul.*

 C. K. Barrett, *From First Adam to Last: A Study in Pauline Theology.*

 G. Bornkamm, *Paul,* Part 2.

 R. Bultmann, *Theology of the New Testament,* vol. 1

 L. Cerfaux, *Christ in the Theology of St. Paul.*

 ———, *The Church in the Theology of St. Paul.*

 H. Conzelmann, *An Outline of the Theology of the New Testament,* pp. 155–282.

 D. H. Whitely, *The Theology of St. Paul.*

Collected Studies:

 C. K. Barrett, *Essays on Paul.*

 C. K. Barrett, *Freedom and Obligation: A Study of the Epistle to the Galatians.*

 G. Bornkamm, *Early Christian Experience.*

 N. A. Dahl, *Studies in Paul.*

 M. D. Hooker and S. G. Wilson, eds., *Paul and Paulinism.*

 E. Käsemann, *Essays on New Testament Themes.*

 ———, *New Testament Questions of Today.*

 ———, *Perspectives on Paul.*

 W. Meeks, *The Writings of St. Paul,* Part 2.

 K. Stendahl, *Paul Among Jews and Gentiles.*

Studies of Paul's ethics:

ADB: "Ethics (NT)" (P. Perkins); "Sex and Sexuality" (T. Frymer-Kensky); "Slavery (Greco-Roman)" (S. S. Bartchy); "Parenesis and Protreptic" (B. Fiore); "War in the NT" "(B. Witherington, III); "Women (NT)" (B. Witherington, III).

IDB Suppl.: "Ethics in the NT" (W. Schrage); "Woman in the Ancient Near East" (R. Harris); "Woman in the OT" (P. Trible); "Woman in the NT" (R. Scroggs); "Homosexuality" (M. Pope); "Rome, Early Christian Attitudes toward" (G. Krodel); "Slavery in the NT" (W. G. Rollins).

 B. Byrne, *Paul and the Christian Woman.*

 V. P. Furnish, *Theology and Ethics in Paul.*

 ———, *The Moral Teaching of Paul,* 2d edition.

 J. L. Houlden, *Ethics and the New Testament.*

 W. Meeks, *The Moral World of the First Christians.*

 P. Richardson, *Paul's Ethic of Freedom.*

 J. Sanders, *Ethics in the New Testament,* ch. 3.

 R. Schnackenburg, *The Moral Teaching of the New Testament.*

 R. Scroggs, *The New Testament and Homosexuality.*

 L. W. Countryman, *Dirt, Greed, and Sex. Sexual Ethics in the New Testament and Their Implications for Today.*

Commentaries and Studies by Individual Books (see also Further Reading, Chapter Six)

1 Thessalonians

ABD: "Thessalonians, First and Second Epistles to the" (E. Krentz).

IDB: "Thessalonians, First Letter to the" (F. W. Beare).

IDB Suppl.: "Thessalonians, First Letter to the" (J. Hurd).

NJBC, pp. 772–779 (R. F. Collins).

E. Best, *A Commentary on the First and Second Epistles to the Thessalonians.* (Harpers New Testament Commentaries).

F. F. Bruce, *1 & 2 Thessalonians.* (Word, No. 42).

R. Jewett, *The Thessalonian Correspondence: Pauline Rhetoric and Millenarian Piety.*

W. Meeks, *Writings,* pp. 3–10.

1 Corinthians

ABD: "Corinthians, First Epistle of" (H. D. Betz; M. Mitchell).

IDB: "Corinthians, First Letter to the " (S. M. Gilmour).

IDB Suppl.: "Corinthians, First Letter to the" (D. Georgi).

NJBC, pp. 798–815 (J. Murphy-O'Connor).

C. K. Barrett, *A Commentary on the First Epistle to the Corinthians.* (Harpers New Testament Commentaries).

H. Conzelmann, *1 Corinthians.* (Hermeneia).

W. Meeks, *Writings,* pp. 22–48.

W. Schmithals, *Gnostics in Corinth.*

2 Corinthians

ABD: "Corinthians, Second Epistle to the" (H. D. Betz).

IDB Suppl.: "Corinthians, Second Letter to the"(D. Georgi).

NJBC, pp. 816–29 (J. Murphy-O'Connor).

C. K. Barrett, *The Second Epistle to the Corinthians.* (Harper's).

F. T. Fallon, *2 Corinthians.* (New Testament Message).

V. P. Furnish. *II Corinthians.* (Anchor Bible).

W. Meeks, *Writings,* pp. 48–66.

Phillippians

JBC: pp. 247–253 (J. A. Fitzmyer).

IDB: "Philippians, Letter to the" (B. S. Duncan).

IDB Suppl.: "Philippians, Letter to the" (H. Koester).

F. W. Beare, *A Commentary on the Epistle to the Philippians.* (Harper's).

M. E. Getty, *Philippians and Philemon.* (New Testament Message).

W. Meeks, *Writings,* pp. 94–101.

Philemon

NJBC, pp. 869–70 (J. A. Fitzmyer).

IDB: "Philemon, Letter to" (M.E. Lyman).

IDB Suppl.: "Philemon, Letter to" (W.G. Rollins).

E. Lohse, *Colossians and Philemon.* (Hermeneia).

M. E. Getty, *Philippians and Philemon.* (New Testament Message).

P. T. O'Brian, *Colossians, Philemon.* (Word, No. 44).

W. Meeks, *Writings,* pp. 101–104.

Galatians

NJBC, pp. 780–790 (J. A. Fitzmyer).

IDB: "Galatians, Letter to the" (J. Knox).

IDB Suppl.: "Galatians, Letter to the" (H. D. Betz).

H. D. Betz, *Galatians.* (Hermeneia).
C. B. Cousar, *Galatians.* (Interpretation).
W. Meeks, *Writings,* pp. 10–22.

Romans

ABD: "Romans, Epistle to the" (C. D. Myers, Jr.).

NJBC: pp. 830–868 (J. A. Fitzmyer).

IDB: "Romans, Letter to the" (F. W. Beare).

IDB Suppl.: "Romans, Letter to the" (G. Klein).

P. J. Achtemeier, *Romans.* (Interpretation).
C. K. Barrett, *A Commentary on the Epistle to the Romans.* (Harper's).
C. E. B. Cranfield, *A Critical and Exegetical Commentary on the Epistle to the Romans.* (International Critical Commentary).
E. Käsemann, *Commentary on Romans.*
W. Meeks, *Writings,* pp. 66–94.

Acts

ABD: "Luke-Acts, Book of" (L. T. Johnson).

E. Haenchen, *The Acts of the Apostles.*

Title page of the book *Thomas the Contender*, one of the texts discovered at Nag Hammadi, Egypt, most of which are Gnostic. Especially important for New Testament study is the *Gospel of Thomas* from Nag Hammadi (see Chapter Five, Appendix).

CHAPTER EIGHT

EARLY DEUTERO-PAULINE CHRISTIANITY AND THE LETTER TO THE HEBREWS

Pseudonymity (from *pseudonymous:* under a "false name") is the attachment of a famous name to a book, either by the author or some other person, such as a manuscript copyist. It was a common phenomenon among the ancients, who apparently had not developed the modern notion of "intellectual property." Pseudonymity was fostered by writers in groups that revered or venerated the persons who bore these names; it was therefore both individual and social. We have already seen that Jewish apocalypses written in the period before, during, and just after the rise of Christianity were attributed to ancient ancestors, for example, Abraham, Moses, Daniel, and Ezra (Chapter Three). These pseudonymous works are collected mostly in the "pseudepigrapha" (*pseud:* "false"; *epigraphos:* "superscription"). The phenomenon was shared by the early Christians. We have seen, for example, that the Gospel of Matthew was composed by some anonymous person and later attributed to "Matthew," presumably the tax collector and disciple named Matthew (Chapter One). New Testament apocryphal writings such as the *Gospel of Thomas* and the *Gospel of Peter,* as their names show, were attributed to disciples. We also know of works written in Paul's name, for example, the letters to the Laodiceans (compare Col 4:16) and to the Alexandrians (see the Muratorian Canon [Chapter Four]). Finally, we suggested that there were various reasons for the phenomenon: Books were associated with an author's *opinion,* books were *believed* to have been written by an author, and books were named with the *conscious intention to give them authority.* In some cases it is difficult to be sure which reasons apply. Indeed, all three reasons could simultaneously apply: conscious attribution of an author, belief that the author wrote, and association with the author's opinions. In short, pseudonymity was a common early Christian phenomenon, and we shall have much more to say about it later (see especially Chapter Fourteen and the Excursis there).

Six letters attributed to Paul in the New Testament—Hebrews is not so attributed; it became associated with him only in later Christian tradition—are an example of the phenomenon of pseudonymity. Modern New Testament scholarship is divided on several of these letters. The Pastorals—1 Timothy, 2 Timothy, Titus—are judged by almost all scholars to be pseudonymous, Ephesians by most, and Colossians and 2 Thessalonians by some. While there is difference of opinion, especially on 2 Thessalonians, we are satisfied that all six are pseudonymous, and we proceed on the basis of this opinion, giving arguments for the opinion as each letter is discussed.

That letters were written in the name of the apostle Paul, and that quite elaborate steps were taken to claim his name—2 Thessalonians exactly imitates the greetings from Paul in 1 Thessalonians—speaks volumes for the influence of the apostle. The writers of some of these letters were most probably pupils of the apostle who consciously imitated their teacher, wrote in his name, and identified themselves with him. This means that we are in the presence of a Pauline School similar to the many schools of learning that existed in the Greco-Roman world, from the rabbis to the Stoics (see Chapter Three). It is well known, for example, that members of Platonic schools who imitated the life-style of Plato wrote works now called pseudo-Socratic and pseudo-Platonic.

The six canonical letters fall into two groups because of their concerns and probable dates. 2 Thessalonians, Colossians, and Ephesians probably date from the 70s or 80s of the first century of the Common era. They reflect the concerns of the generation immediately following the death of the apostle. The Pastorals were probably written a generation later, about 100–125 C.E., and reflect the church at the beginning of the second century. Here we give again the basic chart for these letters.

Pauline (50s)	Pauline School (70–90)	Pauline School (100–125)	Non-Pauline (80–90)
1 Thessalonians	2 Thessalonians	1 Timothy	Hebrews
1 Corinthians	Colossians	2 Timothy	
2 Corinthians	Ephesians	Titus	
Philippians			
Philemon			
Galatians			
Romans			

In this chapter, we shall take up only the deutero-Pauline letters 2 Thessalonians, Colossians, and Ephesians, adding to them the Letter to the Hebrews, but only because it is difficult to place Hebrews with any other literature and it comes from the same general period. We are leaving the Pastorals until a later chapter, largely because of content and chronology (see Chapter Fourteen).

SECOND THESSALONIANS

Historical Criticism of 2 Thessalonians

You will recall that 1 Thessalonians was Paul's earliest, most apocalyptic letter. It was written to give thanks and encouragement to the persecuted Christians at the port city of Thessalonica, the capital of Macedonia. 2 Thessalonians is very much like 1 Thessalonians, but it is also different. Verbal similarities begin with the first verse and continue throughout; the same is true of stylistic peculiarities. Both letters are structurally alike. Both letters deal with the theme of apocalyptic eschatology. These facts, plus the claim that Paul himself signed the letter in 2 Thessalonians 3:17 (compare 1 Cor 16:21; Gal 6:11), lead some scholars to conclude with church tradition that Paul himself wrote it. Occasionally a scholar argues that 2 Thessalonians was written *before* 1 Thessalonians, or to another place, such as Philippi.

Nonetheless, there are very real differences between the two letters. At the level of vocabulary and style, 2 Thessalonians contains many un-Pauline clichés and phrases and omits Paul's characteristic tendency to state matters in threes. The similarities, yet differences, suggest direct reliance on 1 Thessalonians. Indeed, the similarity in structure, including a second thanksgiving (1 Thessalonians 2:13–16, which some scholars think is interpolated), leads to the theory of imitation. As for the claim that Paul signed a greeting in his own hand, Colossians also contains one (Col 4:18) and Colossians, we shall argue, is also deutero-Pauline. Thus, such a claim can also be an imitation of Pauline style.

Even more important are theological differences between the two letters. The most important is the eschatological perspective. In 1 Thessalonians the parousia, or coming of Jesus from heaven as apocalyptic judge and redeemer, is *imminent*. When Paul speaks of "we who are alive, who are left until the coming of the Lord" (1 Thess 4:15; compare 4:17; 5:1–15), he clearly expects the event in his own lifetime. However, 2 Thessalonians 2:1–12 sets out an elaborate apocalyptic scenario of what must first happen *before* that event can occur. In addition, nowhere else does Paul speak of the Antichrist, the apostasy, and "what restrains." Not only has the apocalyptic imagery changed, but the whole tenor and content of the expectation is different: *The End is no longer imminent.* Yet, Paul's *later* correspondence, especially 1 Corinthians, maintains the eschatological perspective of imminence found in 1 Thessalonians.

A notably *non-Pauline* feature of the letter is the idea that the judgment of God will result in a reward for the persecuted Christians and punishment for the persecutors (1:5–10). To be sure, the idea is common in apocalyptic; for example, it is poetically expressed in Revelation 16:5–7 and 19:2. Yet, it is not typical of Paul. Furthermore, 2 Thessalonians ascribes to Jesus attributes and functions that Paul himself reserves for God. This tendency was a natural result of a developing Christology. Thus, Paul says, "Now may our God and Father himself and our Lord Jesus direct our way to you. And may the Lord make you increase and abound in love to one another . . . so that he may establish your hearts unblamable in holiness before our God and Father . . ." (1 Thess 3:11–13). In 2 Thessalonians Jesus Christ is put first. We read of "our Lord Jesus Christ himself and God our Father, who loved us and through grace gave us . . ." (2:16). We also find the prayer, "May the Lord direct your hearts to the love of God and to the steadfastness of Christ" (3:5). The two types of statements are close enough together to be related, but in 2 Thessalonians the Christology represents a slight advance in the importance of Jesus. While the latest possible date for 2 Thessalonians is about 110 C.E. when Polycarp, bishop of Smyrna, quotes it (Polycarp, *Letter to the Philippians* 11:4), more likely it comes from the generation after Paul.

We also read about an oral report and another letter purporting to be from Paul (2:2, 15; compare 3:14, 17) saying that the parousia has *already* come. Since such a letter cannot be 1 Thessalonians, it must represent opponents who believe in a kind of apocalyptic enthusiasm. Perhaps they have interpreted the persecutions that the Thessalonians are suffering as the "day of the Lord" (2:2). Some of the Thessalonians have stopped working and are living in idleness. Do the letter and the oral report come from an alternative, rival Pauline school? In any case, a Paulinist writes 2 Thessalonians using 1 Thessalonians as a model. *The best understanding of 2 Thessalonians, therefore, is to see it as a deliberate imitation of 1 Thessalonians by a member of a Pauline School.*

Exegetical Survey of Second Thessalonians

The Paulinist exhorts the community to keep the Pauline traditions, warning against opponents who teach a kind of apocalyptic enthusiasm. He admonishes certain members of the church not to be idle and tells them to work and to earn their own living. In so doing, the author stresses a delay of the parousia in a way that goes beyond anything Paul himself envisages. He reveals a situation of persecution and the response to it reaching the stage we know from the book of Revelation, a text from near the end of the first Christian century. His Christology is somewhat advanced from, though clearly related to, that in 1 Thessalonians. The letter is apocalyptic, and like other apocalyptic, is meant to be a source of encouragement and hope for those who are in crisis and who suffer persecution. However, the persecution context fits the generation after Paul better (see 2:1–12 below).

1:1–2 SALUTATION.
This is an imitation of 1 Thessalonians 1:1.

1:3–12 THANKSGIVING.
Thanksgiving is offered with the awareness of persecution and the expectation that God will reward the persecuted and punish the persecutors. Paul's "faith, hope, and love" (1 Thess 1:3; 1 Cor 13) is missing.

2:1–12 THE PROBLEM OF THE DELAY OF THE PAROUSIA.
The delay of the parousia is dealt with by developing what must come first: "the rebellion," the revelation of "the lawless one, . . . the one destined for destruction. He opposes and exalts himself above every so-called god or object of worship, so that he takes his seat in the temple of God, declaring himself to be God" (2:4). Satan will be involved, but someone or something "restrains" him (compare Rev 20:1–3), and there will be feigned signs and wonders. Such references sound like a recollection of events associated with the destruction of Jerusalem and the Temple in 70 C.E., on which see the discussions in Chapters Two, Five (Mark 13), and Nine. See also Revelation 13.

2:13–3:5 THANKSGIVING AND PARENESIS.
The church must hold fast to the Pauline traditions ("the things that we command," 3:4.) The pattern of thanksgiving, admonition, and benediction occurs twice (2:13–16; 3:1–5).

3:6–16 CLOSING APPEALS, REBUKES, AND PRAYER.
Considering the delayed parousia, the Paulinist warns: "Anyone unwilling to work should not eat."

3:17–18 AUTOGRAPHIC CONCLUSION.
In itself an argument for pseudonymity, this note is based on the genuine note in Galatians 6:11. See also 1 Corinthians 16:21; Colossians 4:18.

COLOSSIANS

Church Tradition about Colossians

Statements within the Letter to the Colossians claim that the apostle Paul wrote it (1:1; 4:18) to a Greek-speaking church (1:2, 21; 2:13) while he was in prison (4:3, 18; compare 1:24) with several companions, namely, Epaphras (4:12; 1:7), Aristarchus (4:10), Mark (4:10), Luke (4:14), and Demas (4:14; compare Phlm 23). Tradition as early as Marcion, about 150 C.E., included Colossians as one of Paul's ten letters, and by the time of the Mutatorian Canon, about 200, it was in the canonical lists.

Historical Criticism

Among modern scholars the authorship of the letter to the Colossians is much debated. Many who review the evidence and arguments decide for authenticity; many decide against authenticity. The data on which the issue has to be decided is not in dispute; only the interpretation of that data is in dispute. The data and the questions they raise may be summarized as follows:

1. Language and Style

The vocabulary of Colossians is not homogeneous with the seven undisputed Pauline letters. There are twenty-five words not found elsewhere in Paul and thirty-four not found elsewhere in the New Testament; so the vocabulary is, to say the least, distinctive. Its awkward style is very unlike Paul's. The author overloads sentences with words, dependent clauses, and various other Greek constructions, and heaps up synonyms together. For example, Colossians 1:9–20—twelve verses—is one sentence (compare also 2:9–15)! On the other hand, several expressions and stylistic peculiarities in Colossians are found elsewhere in the New Testament only in the genuine Pauline letters. Some argue that this non-Pauline language and style is due to an intentional use of the opponents' vocabulary (see below).

Another important variable is the very extensive use in this letter of traditional material—hymns, confessions, lists of virtues, household codes, and the like. If these factors are determinative, the non-Pauline language and style would not be indications of pseudonymity. Yet, such an extensive use of traditional material is not typically Pauline. In Philippians 2:6–11 Paul does quote a hymn, and in Romans 1:3–4 he cites a traditional liturgical formula, and so on, but never does he quote such material to the extent that we find in Colossians. So the argument from language and style seesaws back and forth and by itself is inconclusive.

2. The Absence of Typical Pauline Concepts

Several of the important concepts particularly characteristic of Paul—right-eousness, justification, law, salvation, revelation, Christians as brothers and sisters (besides the greeting)—are noticeably absent from Colossians. Of course, some of them are missing from any of the undisputed Pauline letters; nevertheless, the absence of these central Pauline themes in Colossians is particularly high.

3. The Presence of Central Ideas Not Found in the Earlier Letters

Colossians has a whole series of concepts that are either new in the Pauline corpus or a significant development over anything in the earlier letters. The most important of these are the following.

a. *Christology.* The Christology of Colossians 1:15–23 is an advance on anything found earlier. In 2 Corinthians 4:4 (NEB), Christ is the "image" of God, and in Romans 8:29, God predestines Christians "to be conformed to the image of his Son, in order that he might be the first born among many brethren." However, in Colossians 1:15 "He is the image of the invisible God, the firstborn of all creation." No longer does Christ reflect a likeness to which others can be conformed, but he is now seen as a true representation of God, making visible what was invisible. He is no longer the first born among the believers who in part share that new birth at their baptism and will share it completely at their resurrection, but rather the first born of *all creation.* In 1 Corinthians 8:6, *God* is the goal of creation, "from whom are all things and for whom *we exist.*" In Colossians, *Christ* is now the goal of all creation, "all things have been created through him and for him" (Col 1:16). In the undisputed letters Paul never reaches the pan-cosmic thinking of Colossians, even though in Romans 8:19–23 he is on the way to it. If we argue that these developments in Colossians occur because the author is quoting a Christological hymn, as indeed he is, it is still a fact that he is identifying himself with what he quotes, and the differences between Colossians and Romans or the Corinthian correspondence remain.

b. *The church as the body of Christ.* In Colossians 1:18 Christ is the head of the body, the church, where the "body" is a cosmic reality (1:18, 24; 2:19; 3:15), but in Romans 7:4, 12:5, and in 1 Corinthians 12:12–31, it is a metaphorical way of expressing mutual interdependence of Christians in the church. Again, he quotes a hymn, but accepts its distinctive view.

c. *"Reconciliation."* A further development from the earlier letters applies both to Colossians and to Ephesians: It is the verb in both letters that expresses the activity of Christ in reconciliation. "In Christ God was reconciling the world to himself" (2 Cor 5:19) is the starting point for the developments in Colossians 1:19–20 ("to reconcile to himself all things") and in Ephesians 2:16 ("reconcile us both [Jew and Gentile] to God in one body through the cross"). However, 2 Corinthians 5:19 uses *katallassein* for "to reconcile," as the earlier letters uniformly do. In contrast, Colossians and Ephesians uniformly use *apokatallassein*. There is a small, yet significant, difference between the two terms.

d. *Eschatology.* When Paul speaks of baptism in Romans 6, he emphasizes what we have called the eschatological reservation, that is, the final resurrection of the dead will be future. For Paul, the Christian does not yet share the full benefits of the resurrected state.

we have been   united with him in a death like his,
we *will certainly be united with him in a resurrection like his.*
                    (Romans 6:5)

Contrast Colossians 2:12–13:

you were   buried with him in baptism in which
you *were also raised with him* through faith in the power of God,
    who raised him from the dead. 13) And when you
    were dead in trespasses and the uncircumcision of your flesh,
God *made you alive together with him,*
    when he forgave us all our trespasses. . . .

A similar statement occurs in Colossians 3:1: "If then you *have been raised* with Christ, seek the things that are above, where Christ is, seated at the right hand of God." Here, a subtle shift has occurred: those who have faith and have been baptized have been incorporated into a new community with its attendant benefits: resurrection to new life (see below).

4. Ethics

In Galatians Paul's ethical ideal is expressed:

neither Jew nor Greek,
neither slave nor free,
neither male nor female.
                    (Galatians 3:28)

Though he does not always maintain these norms in specific situations, Paul hints that the Christian slave Onesimus should be set free (Phlm). He also balances the mutual relationship between men and women in marriage (1 Cor 7) and supports women of authority in his churches (Phil 4:2–3; Rom 16:1–3). In contrast, Colossians 3:18–4:1 draws on a "household code," an ancient social norm for family arrangements believed necessary to preserve a stable social order:

wives subject to husbands,
children subject to parents,
slaves subject to masters.

In Christianity such household codes are typical of literature that is written in the late first and early second centuries, that is, in the generations after Paul (Eph 5:22–6:9; 1 Pet 2:13–3:7; Titus 2:1–10; *1 Clement* 21:6–9; Polycarp's *Letter to the Philippians* 4:1–6:3; Ignatius's *Letter to Polycarp* 4:1–6:1; *Didachē* 4:9–11; *Barnabas* 19:5–7).

5. Steps Toward the Church as an Organized Social Institution

The most important developments in Colossians are not so much those *from* as those *toward:* developments toward the kind of thinking characteristic of the church becoming a structured social institution rather than of the freer, more charismatic days reflected in the undisputed Pauline letters.

1. *The diakonos.* This term first occurs in references to Epaphras as "a faithful minister of Christ on our behalf," to the gospel "of which I, Paul, became a minister," and to Paul's ministry as "a divine office" (1:7, 23, 25). These references are a significant step beyond the use of the same Greek word, *diakonos,* in any undisputed Pauline letter. In Philippians 1:1 ("deacons") and Romans 16:1 ("deacon") a specific office is not clearly indicated. In Romans 13:4, 5, the word is used of the worldly "governing authorities," in Romans 15:8, of Christ as a "servant" to the circumcision, and in 1 Corinthians 3:5, 2 Corinthians 6:4, 11:23, it is used of Paul and others as "servants" of God or of Christ. In two of these last three instances, the New Revised Standard Version uniformly uses the English word "servant" rather than "minister." Yet, only in 2 Corinthians 3:6, which the Revised Standard Version translates, "[God] who has made us competent to be ministers of a new covenant," do we come even near to the usage in Colossians. Yet, even here there is a significant difference. A glance at the word in 1 Timothy 4:6, "If you put these instructions before the brothers and sisters (Greek: brothers), you will be a good minister of Christ Jesus," shows us where the difference lies: The use in Colossians is a move *from* the earlier Pauline letters *toward* the use in the early second-century Pastorals.

2. *Authoritative tradition.* A further step from the earlier letters toward the Pastorals is the understanding of "Christ Jesus" as the subject of the authoritative tradition the believer "receives" and in which he or she "walks" (Col 2:6). Here there is an understanding of Christian faith as accepting authoritative tradition being the basis for Christian living. All this is characteristic of the literature of the emergent institutional church but is foreign to Paul himself. Paul accepts this role of tradition only in connection with the details of Christian living (1 Cor 7:10) or the liturgical practice of the churches (1 Cor 11:23–26), *never* as providing the essence of Christian faith.

3. *Baptism.* In Colossians 2:11 baptism is the Christian equivalent of Jewish circumcision: It is the formal signification of membership in the community. In the undisputed Pauline letters circumcision is a Jewish rite now abandoned by Christians (Rom 2:25–29; 3:1; 3:30; 4:9–12), and baptism is the dynamic means of entrance into a new and different life (Rom 6:3–11). Though Colossians 2:11–14 uses the baptismal language of Romans 6:3–5, baptism has become more formal and does not have the "eschatological reservation" of

Paul. In Colossians we are on the way toward 1 Peter, which says, "Baptism . . . *now* saves you, not as a removal of dirt from the body but as an appeal to God for a clear conscience, through the resurrection of Jesus Christ" (1 Pet 3:21). We should also note that the baptismal formula in Galatians 3:28, "There is no longer Jew or Greek, there is no longer slave or free, *there is no longer male and female* . . ." looks different in Colossians: it does not have the last pairing (see Col 3:11), and thus it conforms to the sharper male dominance of the household codes of the post-Pauline period.

Each scholar evaluates the data differently, but for us the cumulative weight of the evidence indicates pseudonymity, and the new concepts developed in Colossians provide the decisive impulse for that conclusion.

The Opponents at Colossae

Colossae was located in the Lycus River Valley in Phrygia, in the interior of western Asia Minor about 100 miles east of Ephesus. It was not far from Laodicea and Hierapolis, where there were also churches (Col 4:13–17). As far as we know, Paul himself had never been there, although it was in his general area of missionizing. From the letter we may state that the church at Colossae was a Gentile church (1:21, 27; 2:13).

The letter to the Colossians shows that there are certain opponents there who hold a "philosophy" (especially 2:8,16–23). This philosophy is very different from the belief based on the crucified Lord who reigns over all the "principalities and powers" (1:16; 2:15). It accepts the "elements of the universe" (compare Gal 4:3; Greek *stoicheia*) who demand "worship of angels" and Jewish cultic practices (food, drink, festivals, new moons, and sabbaths). These are only a shadow of what is to come. It also stresses ascetic rigor of devotion, self-abasement and severity of the body, and regulations such as "Do not handle, Do not taste, Do not touch." We also hear of "wisdom" and "knowledge" (2:3).

Who held this "philosophy"? Who are the Colossian opponents? What is this so-called Colossians heresy? To complicate matters, there is a difficult phrase in Colossians 2:18 that might be translated "taking his (the opponent's) stand on visions" (RSV). This difficult phrase can also be read "which he has seen, upon entering." The Apollo shrine at Claros, which has the same language, was not far from Colossae, and the term "entering" here has frequently been held to refer to entering the secret sanctuary of a mystery cult. If this is right, the initiate might have had an ecstatic vision of the cosmos during the rite of initiation, having already been instructed in proper beliefs, especially angel worship. Another theory is that "worship of angels" refers to what some would call an "out-of-body" experience, a revelatory vision of entering into heaven in a mystical trance state. In other words, the initiate would experience participating in heaven by worshiping with the angels.

In view of such difficulties, it is not surprising to find a number of theories about the identity of the Colossian opponents. Some have suggested that the cultic regulations point to a sectarian Judaism like that at Qumran. Others, probably more accurately, have noted parallels in Hellenistic Judaism, especially "Wisdom" speculation and Pythagorean philosophy (see Chapter Three). A very widespread view based on language ("wisdom," "knowledge," "fullness"), the boasting and arrogance of adherents, and the connection with the redeemer myth in Colossians 1:15–20 is that the "philosophy" is an early form of Gnosticism (see Chapter Three). You will recall that the Gnostic despaired of this world, since it is under control of evil and hostile powers that have imprisoned one's true spiritual self in a material body. The Gnostic sought release in the form of a true "knowledge." This enabled the Gnostic to "know" of his or her origins from the God of Light, his or her status as an alien in this world, and his or her destiny in returning to the world from which he or she came. Later Gnosticism developed a Gnostic redeemer myth that stated that the redeemer brought the knowledge necessary for salvation; this, however, cannot be proved for New Testament times. In any case, it will be illuminating to point to some passages from a second-century Gnostic text, the *Gospel of Truth:*

> The Gospel of Truth is joy for those who have received from the Father of Truth the grace of knowing Him through the power of the Word, which has come forth from the Plēroma, (the Word) which is in the thought and mind of the Father (and) which is he whom they call "the Savior," for that is the name of the work which he is to accomplish for the salvation of those who were ignorant of the Father; for this name "the Gospel" is the revelation of hope, since it is a discovery for those who seek Him.

> Therefore if anyone possesses knowledge, he receives that which is his own and draws it back to himself. For he who is ignorant is deficient, and it is a great thing which he lacks, since he lacks what will make him perfect. Since the perfection of the All is in the Father, it is necessary that the All ascend to Him, and that each one receive that which is his own, (the things) which He has written down beforehand, having prepared them to be given to those who came forth from Him.

> If anyone possesses knowledge, he is a being from on high. If he is called, he hears, replies, and turns towards Him who calls him in order to ascend to Him, and he knows in what way he is called. Since he knows, he performs the will of Him who called him. He desires to please Him (and) receives rest.

> He will speak about the place from which each one has come, and (each) will hasten to return once more to the region from which he derived his true condition, and to be delivered from that place, the place wherein he has been, since he tastes of that place and receives nourishment and growth (therein).

> (*Gospel of Truth,* Hennecke-Schneemelcher, vol. 1, pp. 523, 525, 530)

The primitive Gnosticism at Colossae was a form that had borrowed widely from Judaism, for example, dietary laws and observances of religious festivals and the Sabbath (Col 2:16–17). It also accepted the idea of "elemental spirits (Greek *stoicheia*) of the universe." These were considered supernatural intermediaries between God and the world. They had to be pacified because they controlled the world and human destiny. One had to know what days were favorable or unfavorable; what was under the control of malevolent supernatural beings and hence taboo; and what was under the control of beneficent beings and hence permitted to the person of "knowledge" (Col 2:20–23).

The author of Colossians meets the problem by claiming that Christianity is superior to any form of Gnosticism. Christ is superior to the supernatural beings, because the salvation he offers is superior to that offered by Gnostic knowledge. The author rebukes those falling into the heresy for disqualifying themselves from enjoying the true riches available in Christ. In doing this, the author interprets both Christ and the Christian faith very much in Gnostic terms, and the letter is an interesting blend of Pauline and Gnostic ideas.

Exegetical Survey of Colossians

1:1–2 SALUTATION.
Somewhat shorter than usual.

1:3–14 THANKSGIVING AND INTERCESSION.
In Paul's letters, and now in the Pauline School, the Thanksgiving often anticipates the concerns of the letter. In verse 7 Epaphras is strongly and emphatically supported in his position in the Colossian church. Nowhere in the undisputed letters does Paul show such esteem for a fellow or sister worker as is here exhibited for Epaphras. The Intercession fades over into the Hymn to Christ (1:15–20). For all the periods and paragraphs in the English translations, in the Greek 1:9–20 is one long sentence.

1:15–23 CHRISTOLOGY AND PARENESIS.
1:15–20 The Christological hymn.
We have already given an analysis of the structure of this hymn (see Chapter Five). There is a strong case for the hypothesis that originally it was not a hymn to Christ at all but to another redeemer figure from the Hellenistic world. The language is characteristic of an ancient Wisdom myth that was further developed in later Gnosticism. One theory is that we have here an early form of the Gnostic myth of the redeemer (see Chapter Three). This does not mean that the language and ideas are any less Christian. It simply means that early Christianity was as eclectic as any other religious movement in the Hellenistic world. Thus, it adopted material offered to it by its cultural environment. The social setting of this hymn is suggested by verses 12–14. They contain reminiscences of the baptism of Jesus ("beloved Son," Mark 1:11) and of texts relating to baptism elsewhere in the New Testament. The dynamics of New Testament Christianity in its middle period are illustrated by a church that adapts a known hymn to a redeemer to express faith in Christ as *the* Redeemer and uses it in baptismal rites. Then the author of Colossians, wishing to focus attention on Christ as *the* Redeemer, takes it up and uses it in his letter.

1:21–23 Parenesis. The Christological hymn is followed by an exhortation to the readers based on it. This concludes on the note of Paul as a "servant of this gospel," which leads into the next section.

1:24–2:5 THE APOSTOLIC OFFICE.

Colossians has a more advanced concept of the office of "minister" than we find in the undisputed Pauline Letters (see above). This indicates a higher level of formal church organization. In this section the Paulinist is more formal than Paul, but he has learned from him a preparedness to suffer in and for the ministry of the church (compare 2 Cor 1:5–6; 4:10). Moreover, the Christian message takes on more Hellenistic emphases. The word of God is the hidden "mystery" now made manifest; the Christian knows "the riches of the glory of this mystery" (1:27), is warned "in wisdom," and becomes "mature." Though "mystery" turns up in the Dead Sea Scrolls, it is characteristic of Hellenistic religion in general. Yet, Jewish or specifically Christian emphases are also to be found: "the word of God," "the energy that he (Christ) powerfully inspires within me," "faith in Christ." This passage is a good example of how different religious traditions came together in Hellenistic Christianity after Paul.

2:6–23 WARNING AGAINST THE FALSE TEACHING.

2:6–7 The nature of Christian faith. In Colossians 2:6, the Paulinist takes up a Jewish technical term, the verb *"to walk," "to go."* This is the Hebrew verb from which the Jewish scribes took their term for legally binding decisions, *halachah.* Paul is using a technical term when he says, "As you therefore have received Christ Jesus the Lord, so *walk* (NRSV note *l*) in him." "Christ Jesus" has become the subject of tradition handed on formally in the church and received as authoritative by the church member. We are moving from the notion of tradition found in the undisputed Pauline Letters (1 Cor 11:23; 15:3: "receiving," "delivering") to the notion of Christian faith as the acceptance of the authoritative tradition about Jesus Christ, and of response as how the Christian should "walk."

2:8–15 Warning against the false teaching as doctrine. The central element in true Christian faith is "Christ Jesus" as the subject of authoritative tradition. Thus, the Paulinist must claim that Christ Jesus as understood in orthodox Christian tradition is superior to the spiritual powers and beings who figure so prominently in various Hellenistic religions. This he does by contrasting the "human tradition" concerning "elemental spirits of the universe" with the Christian concept of Christ as the supreme spiritual being. In Christ "the whole fullness (*plērōma*) of the deity dwells bodily." He "is the head of every ruler and authority." He has made available to those who believe in him a salvation infinitely superior to anything offered by the "rulers and authorities" over whom Christ triumphed on his Cross.

An interesting aspect of this section is the dynamic blend of developments of Pauline ideas (which the author clearly knows well) with ideas taken from Hellenistic religions. The term *plērōma,* a key word in the Christology of this passage, is a technical term in later Gnosticism (see *Gospel of Truth* above). Furthermore, Colossians 2:11–14 must be compared to Romans 6:4–11. The differences in the two passages are sufficiently great for us to regard the Colossians passage as written by a

Paulinist rather than by Paul himself. Yet, the author has understood Paul and is legitimately developing his insights to meet the needs of a later generation. Similarly, Colossians 2:15 develops for still another situation a metaphor Paul uses in 2 Corinthians 2:14.

2:16–23 Warning against the false teaching as practice. The Paulinist now argues against the religious and ethical practices encouraged by the false teaching at Colossae. He contests the Jewish dietary laws and festival and Sabbath-day observances that the false teaching encourages: "These are only a shadow of what is to come, but the substance belongs to Christ" (2:17). This statement is not only telling; it is also a further example of the eclectic blending of Hellenistic and Jewish-Christian ideas in deutero-Pauline Christianity. The distinction between shadow and substance (with the worldly being the shadow and the eternal the substance) is Hellenistic, and indeed Platonic. However, the reality to come in the future is a note from Jewish-Christian eschatology. The Paulinist further argues against "visions" and the "worship of angels" by claiming that they are not proper to the church that is the body of Christ and wholly dependent on its head. Here the church's need for an integrated structure and a disciplined organization come to the fore and necessarily push out the charismatic freedom of an earlier day typified by Paul and his revelatory visions. Finally, in this section the author again takes his point of departure from the Pauline idea of dying with Christ in baptism. He holds that this idea sets the Christian free from an asceticism that would be a form of service to those very elemental spirits to which he died in baptism. This argument applies to a later and different set of circumstances a view that Paul expressed in Galatians 2:19–21 and in Romans 6, namely, that in baptism the believer "died to" the Jewish Law and its demands.

3:1–4:6 PARENESIS.

There now follows a long parenetical section. Colossians 3:1–4 accepts the claim characteristic of Hellenistic Christian religious enthusiasm (and apparently a part of the false teaching at Colossae), namely, that *already in the present* the Christian enjoys the power of the resurrection life. The Paulinist accepts this, where Paul himself had rejected it (1 Cor 15; Rom 6:5: the eschatological reservation). Yet, he maintains that there is still something that will only be known in the future: "When Christ who is your life is revealed, then you also will be revealed with him in glory" (3:4). A similar note of traditional Pauline eschatology is sounded in 3:6, "the wrath of God (the final judgment) is coming."

Colossians 3:18–4:1 is the first example in the Pauline corpus of a household code (see above), a literary form typical in Hellenistic moral instruction. Such codes were widely used in the Hellenistic world. They are a feature of the deutero-Pauline literature and the emergent institutional church in the New Testament, but not of the genuine Pauline letters. Except for the references to "the Lord" and the "Master in heaven," this code in Colossians 3:18–4:1 has no specifically Christian elements. What we have here is most probably the Christianization of a previously existing household code.

4:7–18 FINAL GREETINGS AND BENEDICTION.

Note the references to Onesimus (Philemon), Mark (4:10), and "Luke the beloved physician" (4:14).

EPHESIANS

Historical Criticism

Scholars debate the data about Pauline authorship of 2 Thessalonians and Colossians. We have maintained that Pauline authorship is less likely than pseudonymity. Thus, we have placed these two letters among the deutero-Pauline writings. Ephesians is also clearly attributed to Paul (Eph 1:1). In this case, however, the difficulties with Pauline authorship are widely acknowledged. We shall now summarize them.

1. *Language and Style.* More than ninety words in Ephesians do not occur elsewhere in the Pauline corpus. Many of them appear in later New Testament writings and in the Christian literature immediately following the New Testament period. Where typical Pauline terms do appear, they are often used in different combinations and with different shades of meaning than in the undisputed Pauline letters. Further, synonyms are clustered together in an absolutely non-Pauline manner. Ephesians 1:19, for example, has four separate words for "power." There is also a passion for long, involved sentences, going far beyond anything even in Colossians. Examples are Ephesians 1:15–23 (nine verses); 3:1–7 (seven verses); and 4:11–16 (six verses). They are so complex that some modern English translations have broken up the sentences as an (admittedly necessary) aid to translating them. In general, the style of Ephesians is not terse, but slow and somewhat tedious.

2. *Relationship to Colossians.* A glance at the margin of any annotated text that cites parallels shows that Ephesians constantly quotes and develops Colossians. About one-third of the words in Colossians are found in Ephesians. Of 155 verses in Ephesians, 73 have verbal parallels in Colossians. Only short connected passages from Ephesians have no parallel in Colossians (for example, Eph 2:6–9; 4:5–13; 5:29–33). We illustrated one example of Colossians as a source for Ephesians, Colossians 4:7–8 and Ephesians 6:21–22, in Chapter Four. Here are two other examples:

Colossians 3:12–13	Ephesians 4:1–2
As God's chosen ones, holy and beloved, clothe yourselves with compassion, kindness, *humility, meekness,* and *patience,* 13) *bearing with one another* and, if anyone has a complaint against another, forgive each other; ...	I therefore, the prisoner in the Lord, beg you to lead a life worthy of the calling to which you have been called, 2) with all *humility* and *meekness,* with *patience, bearing with one another* in love ...

Colossians 3:16–17	Ephesians 5:19–20
Let the word of Christ dwell in you richly; teach and admonish *one another in* all wisdom, and with gratitude *in your hearts* sing *psalms and hymns and spritual songs*	... addressing *one another in* *psalms and hymns and spiritual songs,* singing and making melody *to* the Lord *in your hearts,*
to God. 17) And whatever you do, in word or deed, do *everything in the name of* the *Lord Jesus, giving thanks to God the Father* through him.	20) *giving thanks to God the Father.* at all times and for *everything in the name of* our *Lord Jesus* Christ

This dependence on a previous letter is unparalleled in the Pauline corpus. As an argument for pseudonymity it is reinforced by observing that Ephesians depends verbally on other Pauline letters, except 2 Thessalonians (see below). The same person could have written both Colossians and Ephesians in much the same language within a short time; this is the usual way of arguing for the Pauline authorship of Ephesians. However, it is unlikely that Paul would have reached back into his memory for constant reminiscences of earlier letters written to meet quite different needs.

3. *Theology.* Ephesians contains the Pauline theme of justification by faith (2:5, 8–9). In many respects, however, the theology of Ephesians is simply non-Pauline. That is so even if Colossians were to be counted among the genuine Pauline letters, a position we have rejected.

    a. Ephesians 2:19–22, where Christians are "members of the household of God, built upon the foundation of the apostles and prophets, with Christ Jesus himself as the cornerstone," is inconceivable as a statement of the apostle, even if Colossians 2:7 were to be included among the Pauline letters, and much more so if it is not.

    b. The reference to the "holy apostles" as recipients of special insights into "the mystery of Christ" in Ephesians 3:4–5 is not Pauline. Paul never distinguishes apostles in this way and never regards them as "holy" in a way other Christians are not.

    c. Ephesians uses the word "church" (*ekklēsia*) for the *universal* church (Eph 1:22; 3:10, 21; 5:24,25,27). In the undisputed Pauline letters and even in Colossians (4:16), the term is used for the local congregation. Indeed, in Ephesians there is a striking movement toward understanding the church as the "Great Church" characteristic of later centuries, but not typical of Paul.

    d. In Ephesians 3:4–6 the "mystery of Christ" is the unity of Jews and Gentiles in the body of Christ. In the undisputed letters Paul was still fighting for this synthesis. Moreover, the idea of "church" engulfs the view of Christ; in other words, ecclesiology swallows Christology. Paul does not think this way in the undisputed letters.

e. In Ephesians 2:16 *Christ* is the subject of the verb "to reconcile," whereas in Colossians 1:20 *God* is the subject. In Ephesians 4:11 *Christ* appoints the apostles and prophets, whereas in 1 Corinthians 12:28 *God* does this. In general, Paul's emphasis on the death of Christ is not central; what replaces it is an emphasis on the exalted Christ.

f. Eschatology: Ephesians never mentions the parousia of Jesus or final judgment, as does Paul, and Christians are, as in Colossians 3:1, already resurrected (2:6), in contrast to Paul (Rom 6:1–5; 1 Cor 15).

4. *Literary Character of Ephesians.* One last point to be made is that Ephesians is not really a letter at all. If we observe a distinction made in our discussion of "Paul as a writer of letters"—that the letters are written because of some particular conflict, set of problems, or at least an occasion in Paul's life (Romans)—then Ephesians is not a letter by Paul. All of the localized features are missing, even though Paul had clearly made Ephesus a kind of "mission headquarters" and had spent considerable time there.

Much more could be said—see also the lack of address below—but we have suggested enough to show why on literary, source, and theological grounds even scholars who accept Colossians as Pauline regard Ephesians as pseudonymous. For those who accept Colossians as pseudonymous, this conclusion is all the more convincing.

The Occasion for the Writing of Ephesians

If Ephesians was not a letter in the more usual Pauline sense, it must now be determined, if possible, why it was written. Two factors related to pseudonymity are very important.

1. *The Lack of an Address.* Though the opening salutation parallels the Pauline letters, the oldest and best manuscripts (P^{46}, B, and others) and the text of Marcion and some of the late second-century Fathers *omit any reference to Ephesus.* The conclusion of textual critics is that "at Ephesus" was added by a scribe later in the transmission of the text. Thus, all modern critical Greek texts and most translations omit it. Since titles of the letters such as "To the Romans" or "To the Ephesians" come from the period when Paul's letters were collected, these titles (superscriptions) cannot be used to argue for the destinations of the letters. The address read simply, "To the saints who are also faithful in Christ Jesus." Another possibility is that since "who are" in Paul's letters is normally followed by a place name, the Paulinist wrote, "To the saints who are . . . and faithful in Christ Jesus" ("and" is ambiguous in Greek; without a place name it could mean "also"). The reader could have filled in the place name. In short, we have a letterlike document with no address. This oddity suggests that it was an open letter addressed to the church at large.

2. *Relationship of Ephesians to Other Letters Attributed to Paul.* We have already indicated how Ephesians knows and makes extensive use of Colossians. In addition, Ephesians shows familiarity with all the other letters attributed to Paul except 2 Thessalonians. Particularly interesting parallels are:

Ephesians 1:4–5 = Romans 8:29
Ephesians 1:10 = Galatians 4:4
Ephesians 1:11 = Romans 8:28
Ephesians 1:13 = 2 Corinthians 1:22 (compare also Eph 4:30)
Ephesians 3:81 = 1 Corinthians 15:9–10
Ephesians 4:11 = 1 Corinthians 12:28
Ephesians 4:28 = 1 Corinthians 4:12
Ephesians 5:2 = Galatians 2:20 (compare also Eph 5:25)
Ephesians 5:51 = 1 Corinthians 6:9–10
Ephesians 5:23 = 1 Corinthians 11:3

These parallels—there are many more—suggest a theory that Ephesians was written as a general introduction to Paul's letters when they were first brought together into a collection. This would have happened sometime in the last quarter of the first century. While the theory is not always accepted, it gets some reinforcement by three facts: The other letter elements in Ephesians are very formal, not personal; this letter contains no greetings to or from individuals; and there are statements that sound as if the writing was not written to people who knew Paul personally (1:15: "I have heard of your faith . . ."; 3:2: " . . . for surely you have already heard . . ."). The theory of a circular letter that introduces Paul's views should not be ruled out. In any case, Ephesians is hardly a letter written by Paul to a location that had become his headquarters.

Exegetical Survey of Ephesians

1:1–23 SALUTATION, THANKSGIVING, AND INTERCESSION.

1:1–2 Open salutation. This is typically Pauline, but it lacks a specific addressee (see above).

1:3–14 Blessing. In Greek this whole section is one long sentence with an amazing conglomeration of interesting expressions, all of which results in a great variety of English translations. Yet, the Thanksgiving does make clear the general concern of the "letter," the unity of the whole cosmos in Christ, an anticipation of which is the Christian group.

1:15–23 Thanksgiving. Everyone everywhere should grasp the magnitude of the hope that awaits them in the church of which Christ is the head. The myth of the world as the body of the "cosmic man" has been transferred to the body of the church, with the resurrected Christ in heaven as the head.

2:1–3:21 THE GLORY OF THE ONE HOLY CHURCH.

2:1–10 By grace Christians are saved through faith. The basis for the glory of the church is that all persons, including the writer and his readers, are brought into it because they are saved by grace through faith. As in Colossians (3:1), Christians already participate in the resurrection.

2:11–22 Jew and Gentile are reconciled in Christ. The readers were once Gentiles, "without Christ, being aliens from the commonwealth of Israel, and strangers to the covenants of promise, having no hope and without God in the world," but now they are included. The rhetoric of this section, which develops the idea that Christians are citizens in a great city-state, the church, is magnificent. They have been reconciled and brought into the one body of the church by the work of Christ.

In this section there is probably a Christological hymn that has been reworked. A possible translation is:

[For]
he is our peace,
Who has made both one
And has broken down the dividing wall of the fence
[the enmity],
In order to make the two into one new man in him
[making peace]
And to reconcile both in one body to God
[through the Cross].

The strophic arrangement has been lost in the text itself because the author is both quoting and interpreting. One interpretation is that the words we have put in brackets were added. This method of interpretation by addition is also found in Paul. For example, he interprets the "became obedient unto death" of the hymn in Philippians 2 by adding "even death on a cross" (see Chapter Five). It is possible that the hymn in Ephesians 2 originally had a first stanza celebrating the redeemer's participation in creation as does the hymn in Colossians 1:15–20. The stanza that is in fact quoted deals with reconciliation, a major theme in deutero-Pauline Christianity. Christ has broken down the dividing wall between Jews and Christians (the wall that separates Jews and Gentiles in the Temple precincts at Jerusalem? The proto-Gnostic barrier between heaven and earth?) Here it refers to the Law. Thus, one man is created out of two. In a series of images the church is viewed as a holy temple of the Spirit.

3:1–21 Intercession and doxology. The basic structure of this passage is a prayer-style intercession (interceding with God for people) begun in 3:1, broken off at 3:2, resumed in 3:14–19. The intercession is a prayer for the Gentile members of the church, that they may know all the riches belonging to a Christian group offers the believer. Ephesians 3:2–13 is a parenthetical interruption concerning Paul's mission to the Gentiles, and it testifies to the importance of Paul's work among the Gentiles to a later generation, as the Acts of the Apostles also does. The section concludes with a doxology, or concluding praise of God, in 3:20–21.

4:1–6:20 PARENESIS.

Now comes the characteristic element of exhortation.

4:1–16 The unity of the faith and of the church. As in 1 Corinthians 12 and Romans 12, there is mention of gifts of the Spirit in the church; however, the church is again viewed as the body of which Christ is the head (compare 1:22–23).

4:17–32 The necessity to put off the old and to put on the new.

5:1–20 **Instruction to shun immorality and impurity.** This section develops negatively from a "vice catalogue" (verses 3–7) and then positively from a "virtue catalogue" (verses 8–20). Such lists of vices and virtues are, like the household codes, characteristic of Hellenistic moral philosophy (see Chapter Five; see Gal 5:19–23; 1 Cor 6:9–11).

5:21–6:9 **The household code.** This is a further and more developed Christianization of a household code such as that found in Colossians 3:18–4:6. Ephesians 5:31–33 develops the image of the church as the bride of Christ.

6:10–20 **The "panoply passage"**: the armor of God and the warfare of the Christian.

6:21–24 CLOSING REFERENCE TO TYCHICUS AND BENEDICTION.

SOCIAL-HISTORICAL FACTORS: DEUTERO-PAULINE CHRISTIANITY AS A MOVEMENT

Deutero-Pauline Christianity shows the continuing influence of the apostle in the churches he founded. These first Paulinists were probably taught by Paul. They possessed and meditated on his letters, developed some of his ideas, carefully and conscientiously attempted to meet in his spirit the challenges and needs of the churches, and wrote formally in his name. They were probably responsible for collecting Paul's letters and for their circulation as a corpus. The literature they left behind represents the authority and influence of Paul and his ideas a generation or so after his death. It gives us valuable insights into the nature of one type of Pauline Christianity in the latter first century.

The problems of the Paulinists in what we have called this "middle period" of New Testament Christianity are engrossing, and so are the ways they were solved. From 2 Thessalonians we learn that a major difficulty was the *delay of the parousia.* Jesus should have already come on the clouds of heaven to judge the world, but he had not done so. The Paulinist who wrote 2 Thessalonians met this problem as his teacher had. He virtually repeated 1 Thessalonians, which he clearly knew well and obviously regarded as a tract for his own time and as an answer to the problems he and his group were facing. Yet there are subtle differences between the two letters. Paul himself had expected the parousia in a very short time, whereas the Paulinist knew that a considerable time had passed and the parousia was still delayed. So in presenting the scenario for the parousia, the Paulinist tried to make sense of this delay.

A second problem faced by Hellenistic Christianity after Paul came to the fore in Colossians, namely, *the increasing challenge of ideas that became characteristic of second-century Gnosticism.* At this stage the church freely adapted such ideas and terms and met the challenge by an "anything you can do we can do better" claim. Later it grew more intense, and the church developed several responses. First, it gathered an authoritative body of literature from which Gnostic texts and Gnostic interpretations of them were excluded. Thus emerged a *canon.* Second, it formulated an authoritative statement of faith that the Gnostics could not accept, that is, a *creed.* Finally, it claimed that its authoritative leaders were real descendants of the apostles and the similar claim of the Gnostics was false. These leaders became the source of authority in the church, *an "episcopate"* (from Greek *episkopos*, "bishop"). Some sort of tighter institutional structures would have developed even without the threat of Gnosticism, but the life and death struggle with that movement encouraged and speeded up the process. We see in the post-Pauline period the beginnings of these developments.

A further insight into the situation of Hellenistic Christianity a generation after Paul also can be gained from 2 Thessalonians: The church had to come to terms with *the increasing possibility of persecution.* Historically, the first major persecution of Christians occurred at Rome under the emperor Nero, in 64 C.E. Christianity faced other threats, real and imagined, down to the period of its legitimation in the early fourth century C.E. We catch a glimpse of this already in 2 Thessalonians.

Another insight is that through this middle period of New Testament Christianity, reflection about *the more-than-human nature of Jesus, or Christology, is developing.* The author of 2 Thessalonians attributes to Jesus what the previous generation had attributed only to God. The author of Colossians moves Christological thinking a long step forward by taking insights about the nature and function of a redeemer and applying them to his understanding of Christ. He develops particularly the idea of Christ as active in creation, as embodying in himself the fullness (*plērōma*) of the godhead, and as reconciling everything unto himself as the head of the body, the church. The Paulinist of Ephesians, whose special concern is the single universal church in which Jew and Gentile are one, develops further the theme of Christ as reconciler and head of the body, the church.

Christ as reconciler is a major theme of Colossians and Ephesians. It is already a major theme in Paul's letters, that is, Romans 5:10 and 2 Corinthians 5:18–19. The statement in 2 Corinthians 5:19, "in Christ God was reconciling the world to himself, not counting their trespasses against them," is the point of departure for what happens in Colossians and Ephesians. Colossians 1:19–20 says, "For in him all the fullness of God was pleased to dwell, and through him to reconcile to himself all things, whether on earth or in heaven . . ." Ephesians 2:16 states, "[that he] might reconcile us both to God in one body through the cross." Colossians and Ephesians even use a different form of the verbal root, *apokatallassein,* a verb found only in Christian writers; Paul uses *katallassein,* a verb used in secular Greek to denote human reconciliation. It is so used by Paul in 1 Corinthians 7:11. The difference is small but significant. Paul always uses the verb metaphorically, one metaphor among others (that is, justification, redemption, or sacrifical ideas like propitiation or expiation) used to portray the saving work of God in Christ. *In Colossians and Ephesians the reconciliation is an expression of reality and no longer a metaphor.*

A similar development takes place with *Christ as the head of the body, the church.* Paul himself never speaks of Christ as the head of the body, the church. When he speaks of the church as the body of Christ (Rom 12:5; 1 Cor 12:12–26), the expression is a metaphor for the mutual interdependence of Christians in the church. In contrast, when Colossians 1:18 and Ephesians 1:23 and 5:23 claim that the church is the body of Christ, it is a "cosmic" reality. Christ as its *head* is what gives it life, power, and direction. These are developments that take their departure from Paul, but nevertheless go beyond him.

Another feature of deutero-Pauline Christianity, and of Hellenistic Christianity after Paul, is the increasing adaptation of Hellenistic religious and philosophical literary material. Paul himself uses Hellenistic literary forms and metaphors. Yet, the hymn in Philippians 2 is a Christian literary product, not a hymn about the Gnostic redeemer made Christian. *In Colossians and Ephesians, the influence of Hellenistic religious myth is more pervasive.*

There is also a difference in ethical orientation. Paul's statements about slaves and women often do not correspond to the usual cultural norms. Paul's undisputed letters never cite a household code with its model of husband/father/master dominance, the accepted basis for political stability in the larger Greco-Roman society. In contrast, both Colossians and Ephesians have such codes. Thus, *Christianity as typified by Colossians and Ephesians has become "acculturated."* It is settling down in the Hellenistic world and making increasing use of material presented to it by the cultural environment to which it is increasingly integrated.

The theme of reconciliation in deutero-Pauline Christianity leads naturally to the major theme of Ephesians: *the unity of Jew and Gentile in the one body of Christ.* Paul normally uses the word "church" to refer to a house-church at a particular place; only secondarily is it linked to churches at other locations. In his Corinthian correspondence he addresses "the church of God that is in Corinth . . . together with all those who in every place call on the name of our Lord Jesus Christ" (1 Cor 1:2; compare 2 Cor 1:1). For the author of Ephesians, "church" refers primarily to the *one universal church.* This is an important development of New Testament Christianity. The local Christian congregation gathered in a house, Paul's usage, is one manifestation of the broader movement of "those who call on the name of the Lord Jesus." In contrast, Ephesians speaks of " . . . the church, which is his body, the fullness (*plērōma*) of him who fills all in all" (1:22–23). It also speaks of "God who created all things; so that through the church the wisdom of God in its rich variety might now be made known to the rulers and authorities in the heavenly places" (3:9–10). Finally, it uses the benediction "to him be glory in the church and in Christ Jesus to all generations" (3:21). Christianity is no longer perceived as small sectarian groups meeting at house-churches within a broader movement, but the one all-encompassing unit that represents God to all peoples, and by means of which people come to God. It is when we come to Ephesians in the New Testament that we hear about the Christian Church, with a capital C, rather than Christian churches. A major theme of Ephesians is the Church Universal, the One Body of Christ. We have now approached the self-understanding that was to characterize and sustain the Christian Church through the long centuries of the Middle Ages.

Our discussion of Ephesians called attention to the rhetoric of Ephesians 2:11–22. The rhetoric is magnificent not so much because the author has polished his phrases, but because he is here at the heart of his concern: the unity of Jew and Gentile in the Church of God. Jerusalem has now fallen to the Romans, the Temple is no more, there is no longer a Jerusalem church from which emissaries can come arguing that the Christian must also be a Jew. The circumstances that led to Paul's battles in Galatia, Philippi, and elsewhere are no more, and the author of Ephesians can celebrate in sonorous phrases the unity of Jew and Gentile in the One Church of God. Yet, even here we catch a glimpse of a major concern of New Testament Christianity in its middle period: *the necessity to come to terms with the destruction of the Jerusalem Temple.* The section concludes:

> So then you are no longer strangers and aliens, but you are citizens
> with the saints and also members of the household of God, built upon
> the foundation of the apostles and prophets, with Christ Jesus himself as
> the cornerstone. In him the whole structure is joined together and grows
> into a holy temple in the Lord; in whom you also are built together in the
> Spirit into a dwelling place for God.
>   (Eph 2:19–22)

This passage shows the church getting prepared for its own future. *The church is
"built upon the foundation of the apostles and prophets."* Christ Jesus is "the cornerstone." The days of the free, charismatic enthusiasm that provided the dynamism
for the beginning of the churches are past. We have the first glimpse of the firm
and careful structure that enabled the church to survive and, indeed, to mold the
centuries that were to come.

THE LETTER TO THE HEBREWS

You will recall that there are seven undisputed letters of Paul (1 Thessalonians,
1 Corinthians, 2 Corinthians, Philippians, Philemon, Galatians, Romans), three
early deutero-Pauline letters (2 Thessalonians, Colossians, Ephesians), and the
three Pastorals (1 Timothy, 2 Timothy, Titus), for a total of thirteen. We have
studied the seven undisputed letters and the early deutero-Pauline letters. The
Pastorals are also from the Pauline School, but because they are usually dated in
the early second century and show further institutional development, we shall
consider them in Chapter Fourteen. The fourteenth and final "letter" that
church tradition came to associate with Paul was called simply "To the Hebrews,"
but, as we shall soon see, it was not a letter at all and was probably not sent simply "to the Hebrews," or Jewish Christians. Thus, "Hebrews," as it is often called,
cannot be fit into any survey of the New Testament. Like the Scriptural figure
Melchizedek of whom it speaks, it is "without father, without mother, without
genealogy" (Heb 7:3; compare Ps 110:4), and we would be tempted to add also
"without offspring." In the New Testament it has neither antecedents nor descendants and is not part of any other known movement; yet, it is a text of great excel-
lence and, when finally associated with Paul, it eventually made its way into the
canon of the New Testament.

Early Christian Tradition about Hebrews

The earliest traditions about "To the Hebrews" come from the very late second
and early third centuries C.E. Clement of Alexandria (ca. 150–215 C.E.), who was
head of a catechetical school in Alexandria, Egypt, argued that Paul wrote "To
the Hebrews" in the Hebrew language but failed to mention his own name
because its recipients, the conservative Jewish Christians, were hostile to the apostle to the Gentiles. He proposed that Luke translated Hebrews and published it in
Greek for the Greeks, thus giving it its fine, Lukan-like Greek style (Eusebius *Ecclesiastical History* 6.14.2–4). The second Alexandrian authority, Origen (185–253
C.E.), perhaps head of the same catechetical school, argued that the thought of

Hebrews was Pauline, but also acknowledged that its style and composition were more "Greeklike" than Paul's, noting that some critics said it was written by another Clement, a bishop at Rome, who first quotes it (see *1 Clement* below), while other ancient writers said it was written by Luke. Origen offered what has become the most famous statement about Hebrews from antiquity, "But who wrote the letter, God really knows" (compare Eusebius *Ecclesiastical History* 6.25.11–14). Despite the hesitation of these great Alexandrian theologians, however, Pauline authorship gradually gained ground in the churches of the East. Thus, Hebrews is found after Romans in the important third-century Egyptian papyrus of Paul's letters, P^{46}. When Bishop Athanasius of Alexandria circulated his famous Easter Letter of 367 C.E. (see Chapter Four), he included Hebrews among the twenty-seven books of the New Testament canon.

Meanwhile, Church Fathers in the West remained sceptical. Hebrews was not included in New Testament lists of Irenaeus of Lyons and the Roman presbyter Gaius. It was also missing from the list of books used in worship at Rome about 200 C.E., the Muratorian Canon. At Carthage in North Africa, Tertullian (155–220 C.E.), the "father of (western) Latin theology," suggested that it was written by Paul's early companion, Barnabas (Tertullian *On Modesty* 20). It did not begin to be generally accepted as Paul's until the late fourth century, when the great Augustine supported the canon of the eastern bishop Athanasius and the famous Vulgate translator Jerome added his assent. In the following century Pope Innocent I concurred (405 C.E.). In short, the battle for Hebrews was won in the West only after three centuries of doubt. Once established, the common opinion of East and West persisted until the sixteenth century, at which time Martin Luther surmised that it might have been written by the learned Alexandrian apostle Apollos (1 Cor 1:12; 3:4–6, 21; Acts 18:24–28), a view that has been attractive to some modern scholars.

General Historical Criticism about Hebrews: Author, Date, Place

As the ancients discerned, there are many reasons to doubt that Paul wrote this book. Some of the points made by modern critics are these: First, the author is never mentioned by name within the book, which is not at all typical of Paul or even deutero-Pauline letters. The work does mention "our brother Timothy," but Timothy is a common name and it occurs in a closing that makes the book look more letterlike (13:22–25), so much so that it has sometimes been considered an addition to the book. Second, as the ancients realized, the carefully composed and studied Greek of Hebrews is not Paul's spontaneous, volatile, contextual Greek. Third, Hebrews is not formally a letter. Though it does close like a letter, as just mentioned, it has no salutation, greeting, or thanksgiving; rather, it alternates theological and ethical exhortation in a manner quite unlike Paul. Fourth, the author of Hebrews considers himself the recipient of apostolic tradition in a way Paul scarcely would have done (2:3). Fifth, and most important, the content of Hebrews is totally different from the content of Paul's letters. It not only lacks ideas of Paul's such as justification, the body of Christ, and the like; its major theme, Jesus as the great heavenly High Priest who himself is a sacrifice, is never found in Paul. Indeed, it is unique to the whole New Testament. In short, the ancient Alexandrian Origen was correct: The person who wrote Hebrews is known only to God. We thus consider it to be anonymous.

Anything else we know about the person or persons from whom the book was sent or those to whom the book was addressed must be inferred from the book itself, and there are many theories about these matters. The writer of Hebrews speaks frequently of the Jewish sacrificial system; yet he thinks about it in terms of substance and shadow, of reality and copy of reality, thoroughly Greek ideas stemming ultimately from Plato and highly characteristic of a first-century Hellenistic Jew, Philo of Alexandria. For example, Hebrews 9:1–5 describes the "earthly sanctuary . . . a tent," but 9:11 says that "the greater and more perfect tent not made with hands, that is, not of this creation," appears with Christ. Hebrews 9:23–24 speaks of "the heavenly things" and the "sketches of the heavenly things," of "a sanctuary made by human hands, a mere copy of the true one." Such ideas suggest that the author of Hebrews has to be regarded as a product of Hellenistic Judaism; he is probably a Jew of the Diaspora, like Philo, but converted to the Christian faith. Apparently his Greek way of thinking about his Jewish heritage has prepared him to interpret that faith as the revelation of the reality of which Judaism was always a copy.

The letterlike conclusion to Hebrews contains greetings from "those from Italy" (13:24). Some interpreters have concluded that the book was written *from* Italy and, since it also contains material about the Jerusalem Temple, that it was written to Jerusalem. Yet, it has often been concluded that "those from Italy" refers to Italians who were living someplace else and were writing home, in which case Hebrews was written *to* Italy, perhaps Rome, from some unknown location. This solution gains some support from the fact that Clement of Rome wrote a letter from Rome to the church in Corinth in 96 C.E. and in it he cited passages from Hebrews (*1 Clement* 17:1 [Heb 11:37]; 36:2–5 [Heb 1:3, 4, 5]). Yet, we also recall that this book had great problems at Rome being accepted as having been written by Paul. Did the Romans have a tradition that it was not Paul's work?

We said that the title "To the Hebrews" was present when P[46] was copied in the third century; thus, it was current by about 200 C.E. While the term "Hebrews" was the old term for Jews who spoke Hebrew (or Aramaic?), the book was clearly written to Christians (6:1–3) who practiced baptism (10:22), and who were thought to be in danger of falling away from their faith (for example, 6:1–12; 10:23–32). "Hebrews" could have meant Hebrew- or Aramaic-speaking Jewish Christians who remained loyal to worship in the Jerusalem Temple. This meaning would correspond with the "Hebrews" in Acts 6 who came into conflict with the more radical Hellenists, as well as Paul's use of the term Hebrews in Philippians 3:5 and 2 Corinthians 11:22. Correspondingly, two main attempts to explain the use of the title for this book are current. The first is that it was soon added to the anonymous book because a Hellenist Christian like Stephen sought to correct certain Hebrew Christian beliefs (compare, for example, 2:1), in which case the book might well have been written to exhort more traditional Jewish Christians. This view is interesting because there are certain themes in Hebrews that parallel Stephen's ideas as portrayed by the author of Acts, notably the wandering people of God (Acts 6–7). The other view is that, given the likelihood that the recipients of "To the Hebrews" included Gentiles, the title was added in the early church because the subject matter of the book is concerned throughout with Jewish ritual. The latter seems to us more likely, but either way, the title was added to the book.

As for **date,** Hebrews must have been written before 96 C.E. because in that year Clement, bishop of Rome, referred to passages from it. The other end of the temporal spectrum has been debated. Some scholars have argued that Hebrews must have been written before 70 C.E. because its theme of the sacrificial cultus implies that the Temple of Jerusalem was still intact. While this suggestion would push it closer to Paul, it nonetheless seems unlikely in the light of internal evidence in the text. Hebrews 2:3 speaks of the message of salvation as being "declared at first through the Lord, and . . . attested to us by those who heard him," and Hebrews 13:7–8 implies that "those who spoke the word of God to you " had died some time ago. Such references, which are similar to those found in Luke 1:1–4, suggest that the writer belongs at least to the generation of the author of Luke-Acts, about 85–90 C.E.

Other internal factors reinforce this view. At some earlier time the recipients had experienced persecution (10:32–35; compare 12:3–13), perhaps—if it was written to Rome—a reference to the Neronian persecution in 64 C.E. Moreover, the references to the sacrificial cultus are not to the *actual* Jerusalem Temple, but to its very ancient predecessor, the tent sanctuary, or tabernacle, of the time of Moses (compare Exod 25:9; 33:7). In fact, the author's argument might have been derived wholly from Scripture, not a knowledge of the actual Jerusalem Temple still standing in his own day. Moreover, as we noted above, the discussion of the tent sanctuary is in terms of a heavenly reality and of an earthly copy of that reality, of heavenly substance and earthly shadow, as we mentioned (9:1–5, 11). This kind of thinking is characteristic of Hebrews altogether, and it shows that the author is not concerned with the physical fact, but with the spiritual reality of which the Old Testament tabernacle was always only a shadow and copy. We have indicated the Platonic and Philonic associations of these ideas. In short, it is likely that Hebrews should be dated sometime between 70 and 96 C.E.., or about 80–90 C.E.

We may conclude that "To the Hebrews" was an anonymous writing by a Hellenistic Jewish Christian probably written to a community that contained both Jewish and non-Jewish Christians, perhaps at Rome, its aim being to correct some of the views of that community. It its likely that the book was written in the Middle Period of Christianity sometime after 70, but before 96 C.E., or about 80–90 C.E.

Social-Historical Context of Hebrews

The social historical context of Hebrews is difficult to determine, and we gain only vague impressions. The Christian recipients of Hebrews can recall earlier preaching; some of their leaders have died; thus, they seem to have been Christians for some time (2:4; 13:7). In days gone by, the community was marked by love and charismatic miracle working (2:4). It has also suffered and some are still in prison (10:32–34), though there have been no martyrs (12:4). Yet, the Christians appear to be in danger of tiring of their faith (5:11–14; 12:3). They are tempted to unbelief (3:2–14), and some appear to have renounced their faith altogether (6:4–6; 10:26–31; 12:15–17). They are clearly in need of exhortation, guidance, and comfort, and that is precisely what they receive:

"Take care, brothers and sisters, that none of you may have an evil, unbelieving heart that turns away from the living God. But exhort one another every day . . ." (3:12).

" . . .let us go on toward perfection . . ." (6:1).

"Let us hold fast to the confession of our hope without wavering . . ." (10:23).

" . . .let us consider how to provoke one another to love and good deeds, not neglecting to meet together, as is the habit of some, but
   encouraging one another . . ." (10:24).

" . . .be made perfect" (11:40b).

"Endure trials for the sake of discipline" (12:7).

"Pursue peace with everyone, and the holiness without which no one will see the Lord" (12:14).

"Let mutual love continue" (13:1).

"Do not neglect to show hospitality to strangers . . ." (13:2).

"Remember those who are in prison, as though you were in prison with them; those who are being tortured, as though you yourselves were being tortured" (13:3).

"Let marriage be held in honor by all, and let the marriage bed be kept undefiled . . ." (13:4).

"Keep yourselves free from the love of money, and be content with what you have . . ." (13:5).

"Remember your leaders . . .and imitate their faith" (13:7).

"Do not be carried away by all kinds of strange teachings . . .by regulations about food" (13:9).

"Obey your leaders and submit to them . . ." (13:17).

Such sayings represent general parenesis backed by the ideal of Christ's purity or perfection. Thus, as Christ is perfect, and the leaders have faith to be imitated, so the followers are encouraged to go on to perfection. Clearly, there is also a group dimension to the sayings, especially those that exhort the community to peace, love, good deeds, and hospitality. Finally, as in many early Christian communities, the tendency to desire riches is decried.

Language, Style, and Form of Hebrews

Hebrews is known as a letter, but, as already indicated, its only characteristic of a letter is its conclusion, which contains a benediction, final remarks, and greeting (13:22–25). Hebrews is better understood as a homily or sermon deeply rooted in Scripture. Some recent study has suggested that it might be a "homiletic midrash" (a special Jewish sermonic interpretation) on the Old Testament Psalm 110, for this psalm contains one of the two instances where the High Priest Melchizedek, a key figure in the book, is mentioned in the Scriptures (Ps 110:4; compare Gen 14:17–20; see below). While this midrash theory may go too far, it is nonetheless a provocative suggestion because an eschatological midrash on

Leviticus 5:9–13 that uses the Melchizedek theme has been discovered among the Dead Sea Scrolls, and there Melchizedek, "the priest of the Most High," is represented as a heavenly angelic being (11QMelch). In Hebrews, the sermon is a mixture of proclamation and parenesis, and it represents the kind of discourse the Christian church was developing to meet the needs of its members. It is not a missionary sermon designed to convert non-Christians; it is directed to believers who are in need of exhortation, guidance, and comfort.

Intellectual Environment and Theology of Hebrews

Hebrews uses the Greek Septuagint, though it contains some variants from the Septuagints that we know, some of which may have come from a different form of the Septuagint that has disappeared. The book contains many explicit quotations, especially from the psalms, and above all, Psalms 110, 2, and 8. It also alludes to Scripture frequently. All of this is done without great concern for the original contexts of the passages; what counts is the author's new interpretations. We may also note the famous "praise" passage in chapter 11, which refers to many heroes from Scripture. We shall note further uses of Scripture below.

The importance of Scripture, especially ideas about the tabernacle and the priesthood and sacrifice, points to Judaism; yet, on the other hand, it uses the Septuagint, and its notion of heavenly pattern and earthly example sound very Platonic, and thus Greek. A wide variety of opinion exists about its intellectual environment. Following the Jewish route, some scholars suggest that the heavenly/earthly dualism of Hebrews, along with its Melchizedek theme, is reminiscent of the Dead Sea Scrolls, which has the midrash on Melchizedek; others have gone in the direction of the philosophy of Plato. Still others have looked at the very Platonically-oriented Hellenistic Jewish philosopher, Philo of Alexandria, and still others have gone further and seen in Hebrews an early form of Gnosticism. One area of connection is the Acts view of the Hellenists who, as represented by Stephen, held that the ancient nomadic Hebrews worshiped a God who could be moved about in a tent or tabernacle, who therefore should not be confined to a Temple "made with human hands" (Acts 6–7). Still others have noted that the opposition to the Jerusalem Temple and certain other themes point to connections with the Samaritans.

There is no simple explanation to the intellectual environment of Hebrews. Ideas about dualism and Melchizedek are similar to those in the Dead Sea Scrolls, but many other features of belief in the scrolls are not present in Hebrews. Platonic and Philonic ideas are clearly present but do not easily fit with Hebrews' eschatology. Contacts with Samaritan and Hellenistic Jewish Christian themes of the "Stephen" type are present, as well. What becomes obvious is that, as with the Johannine literature, we are again in the environment of a very syncretistic Hellenistic Jewish Christianity, but one very different from that found in the Johannine literature.

The heart of the theology of Hebrews is its fascinating Christology. Jesus is the preexistent, exalted Son, and also the great heavenly High Priest according to the priesthood of Melchizedek, one who is "without father, without mother, without genealogy" (Heb 7:3; compare Ps 110:4). This Christology is not always systematic and logical. Hebrews 1 opens with the affirmation that the Son of God is preexistent, the divine agent in the creation of the earth. The passage proceeds with what is probably a traditional "Christological hymn" (1:3; see Chapter Five):

> Who, being the reflection of God's glory and
>   the exact imprint of God's very being,
> Sustaining all things by his powerful word,
>   Having made purification for sins,
> Sat down on the right hand of the
>   Majesty on high. (RSV)

The hymn is based in part on the widespread Hellenistic Jewish myth of the descent from heaven to earth and reascent to heaven of God's divine Wisdom (see Chapter Five). Thus, terms like "reflection" and "exact imprint" are known from other Wisdom literature and from Philo of Alexandria; they describe Wisdom's, or the Son's, or the Logos' close relation to the Deity (for example, Wisd 7:26; Philo *On Special Laws* 3.161; compare John 1:1–16; Phil 2:5–11, and elsewhere). The "purification for sins" describes the work of Christ in Hebrews 9 and 10 and is so closely related to the dominant sacrificial themes and the heavenly High Priest in the book that some scholars think that this theme might have been added to the hymn by the author of Hebrews.

The one who sits at the right hand of God describes Christ's exaltation and is derived from Psalm 110:1:

> The Lord says to my lord,
>   Sit at my right hand,
>   Until I make your enemies your footstool.

This verse is quoted in 1:13 at the end of a string of Scriptural quotations (1:5–13). Psalm 110:1 in most passages of the New Testament (contrast Mark 12:35–37 = Matt 22:41–46 = Luke 20:41–44) provides the imagery for the position of power of the resurrected and exalted Messiah/Son/Lord: sitting at God's right hand (for example, Mark 14:62; Acts 2:34–36). Its imagery is implied again in 8:1, 10:12–13, and 12:2, and in every instance the author of Hebrews links it with Jesus' preceding death on the cross (12:2), which is interpreted as a sacrificial purification for sins (8:1; 10:12).

Verse four of this same psalm is one of two Scriptural sources for Hebrews' central theme that Christ is the great heavenly High Priest after the order of Melchizedek:

> The Lord has sworn and will not change his mind,
> "You are a priest forever according to the order of Melchizedek."

In Genesis 14:17–24, the second place Melchizedek is mentioned in the Hebrew Scriptures, he appears to Abraham "the Hebrew" (Gen 14:13). He is also called "king of Salem" and priest of the "Most High" (Hebrew = *ēl-elyōn*, now known to have been a name for a Canaanite deity). Abraham has been victorious in regaining the possessions of Lot in war; so Melchizedek produces bread and wine and blesses Abraham, whereupon Abraham gives him a tenth of the possessions. Melchizedek says he does not want the possessions, but only the people. Abraham then swears an oath to God, now also called by Melchizedek's God's name, "Most High," and says that he does not want the tenth either, lest Melchizedek think that he is greedy.

Six points are important for understanding Hebrews' interpretation of this figure. First, the name "Melchizedek" in the Hebrew language means "My king is righteous" or alternatively "King of Righteousness." Second, the consonants of Salem, which in Hebrew are *Sh-l-m*, can also spell *Shālōm*, "peace" (the Hebrew vowels were not yet written in this period of history); thus, as the author Hebrews points out, the "King of Righteousness" is also the "King of Peace" (7:2). Third, even though it is absolutely imperative in Judaism for the priest's parentage and genealogy to be known—purity has to be maintained (see Chapter Three)—nothing is said in the two Melchizedek passages of the Hebrew Scriptures about genealogy; Melchizedek suddenly appears and disappears. This point is also not lost. Fourth, you will recall that a major function of priests is to sacrifice for the atonement of the sins of the people. Fifth, in 11QMelch of the Dead Sea Scrolls, Melchizedek is presented as the heavenly eschatological Redeemer Figure, a warrior who is chief of the heavenly armies, and who will execute final judgment, one who protects the faithful people of God and opposes the chief demon Beliel; as such, his role parallels the role of the archangel Michael. Finally, there are expressions of Melchizedek as a heavenly figure in other ancient Jewish texts (especially 2 Enoch 71–72), a Christianized Nag Hammadi text called *Melchizedek* (*NHC* 9,1), and it continues in Jewish and Christian traditions.

Though the parallels are not exact, the author of Hebrews is clearly knowledgeable about Melchizedek themes and puts many of them together in a special way. In chapter 1 messianic passages are cited to show that Jesus is God's Son, who is higher than the angels. Psalm 2:7 ("You are my Son . . .") comes first (1:5a). This psalm verse is found in the synoptic gospels where it is cited as God's words to Jesus identifying him as his Son at the baptism and transfiguration (compare Mark 1:11; 9:7). Psalm 2:7 is also combined with 2 Samuel 7:14 ("I will be his father and he will be my son"), Hebrews' second quotation (1:5b), in another text of the Dead Sea Scrolls (4QFlor). Both Psalm 2:7 and 2 Samuel 7:14 are further combined with Psalm 110:1, Hebrew's last quotation (1:13), in Luke-Acts; there the passages also identify the resurrected and exalted Son to God's right hand in heaven (compare Acts 2:33–35; 13:33). The third passage, Deuteronomy 32:43, is cited to show that the angels worship the Son (1:6). The fourth, the Septuagint of Psalm 104:4, shows the impermanence of the angels, in contrast to the fifth, Psalm 45:7–8, which shows the permanence of *God's* throne, thus implying an identification of the Father with the Son (1:8–9). The sixth, Psalm 102:26–28, stresses that the creation is impermanent in contrast to the creator, again implying the Son's agency in creation. The seventh returns to Psalm 110:1, quoted in full. Thus, the Son is superior to all the angels and all the heavenly beings must serve him.

In Hebrews 2 the argument is continued with Psalm 8: The Son of Man was temporarily made lower than the angels (Ps 8:6a), but was then crowned with glory (Ps 8:6b). Thus, he became like "his brothers" and was tested by the devil, but he defeated him (compare Melchizedek's defeat of Beliel in 11QMelch). Then, he became the merciful and faithful high priest before God "to make a sacrifice of atonement for the sins of the people" (2:17). This theme is developed in Hebrews 4:14–5:10 by reference, again, to Psalm 2:7, Psalm 110:1, and Melchizedek, but the climactic passage is Hebrews 7, where the main elements of the Genesis 14 account are given, including the meanings of his name, "righteous king," and "king of peace." With hints of Psalm 110:4 in the last line, Hebrews 7:3 reads like a hymn about Melchizedek:

Without father, without mother, without genealogy,
having neither beginning of days nor end of life,
but resembling the Son of God,
he remains a priest forever (7:3).

His permanence is highlighted; because of it, this new priesthood is superior to
the old Levitical and Aaronic priesthoods, as well as the Moses who in Philo is also
a High Priest (compare 3:1–6). According to Psalm 110:4, God has sworn it by
an oath (7:17, 20). Moreover, as heavenly Son of God, he is superior also to
Melchizedek, who was a type of the Christ, but not yet the Christ himself. It is
this priest whose sacrificial death and purifying blood are "once for all" (7:27;
9:12, 26; 10), yet he perpetually atones for the sins of humankind. He does so in
the heavenly temple. It establishes a new and lasting covenant between God and
his people (Heb 8–10; compare Jer 31:31).

The Structure of Hebrews

A feature of Hebrews is the careful alternation of proclamation and parenesis that
gives it its distinctively sermonic form. It has no introduction, but plunges immediately into proclamation. A simplified structure is as follows:

Proclamation:	Jesus as Son of God and Savior, 1:1–3:6
Parenesis:	3:7–4:13
Proclamation:	Jesus as High Priest, first statement of the theme, 4:14–5:10
Parenesis:	Christian maturity, 5:11–6:20
Proclamation:	Jesus as High Priest, development of the theme, 7:1–10:18
Parenesis:	10:19–39
Proclamation:	Jesus as the pioneer and perfecter of faith, 11:1–39
Parenesis:	12:1–13:17

Closing benediction and greetings: 13:18–25

Exegetical Survey of Hebrews

1:1–3:6 FIRST ASPECT OF THE PROCLAMATION: JESUS AS SON OF GOD AND SAVIOR OF ALL.

The preacher dwells on Jesus as Son of God and as savior of all, and, further, as
the merciful and faithful High Priest who has expiated the sins of the people. Yet,
human beings are flesh and blood, and so Jesus had to share their nature. Sharing human nature and sufferings, he has not only redeemed human beings, but
he can also help them since he understands their temptations.

Thus, we have a major feature of Hebrews, its Christology (see above). On the
one hand, Jesus is the "heavenly" High Priest, making the true sacrifice for the
sins of the people; on the other hand, he is of the same flesh and blood as those
he sanctifies (2:5–18). In a later generation this was to contribute the Christology of the great creeds, where Jesus is declared to be both truly God and human.

In Judaism, the High Priest represented the people before God, and this he could do because he was one with them. Yet, he also represented God before the people, and in doing this came to be thought of as partaking in some way in the aura of divinity, especially when he came out of the Holy of Holies, which he and he alone might enter and even then only one day in the year. Against this background it is easy to see how the writer of Hebrews, who regards Jesus as fulfilling both functions perfectly as compared to the imperfect fulfillment in the person of the Jewish High Priest, came to use the language that he does.

Hebrews 2:1–4 contains a short section of exhortation. Note also the warning against falling away from the faith in 2:1, a theme repeated many times in Hebrews. Hebrews 2:3–4 implies that the author is not from the first generation of Christians.

3:7–4:13 FIRST MAJOR SECTION OF PARENESIS.

This section is built around Psalm 95:7b–11. Verses 7b–10 are concerned with the journey of the Israelites through the wilderness, or what has been called by modern scholars "the wandering people of God." The section interprets it as God testing his people. The people failed this testing by rebelling against Moses, hence their failure to reach the perfect "rest" of God (verse 11). The Christians must not similarly fail, and if they can but endure, if they persist in their belief, they will inherit the promised "rest," in which they will share the glory of God's own Sabbath when God rested after the creation (compare Genesis 1:1–2:4). The priesthood of Melchizedek in Psalm 110:4 is cited in 5:6, 10.

4:14–5:10 SECOND ASPECT OF THE PROCLAMATION: JESUS AS HIGH PRIEST.

(first major statement of the theme).

5:11–6:20 SECOND SECTION OF PARENESIS: CHRISTIAN MATURITY.

Chapter 6 may be based on a traditional Christian catechism.

7:1–10:18 THIRD ASPECT OF THE PROCLAMATION: JESUS AS HIGH PRIEST.

(the major development of the theme). The major Christological theme of Jesus as High Priest is now developed in various ways, each designed to exhibit the superiority of the high priesthood of Jesus over what it superseded.

7:1–28 Jesus is High Priest after the order of Melchizedek. The shadowy figure of the priest-king Melchizedek blesses Abraham the father of the Jewish people in Genesis 14, and this is interpreted as indicating that his order is superior to that of any Jewish priesthood. A special emphasis is on God's oath in Psalm 110:4 (see above).

8:1–6 Jesus has made the one perfect sacrifice. It is eternal and takes place in the heavenly sanctuary.

8:7–13 He is the mediator of the new covenant that replaces the old, obsolete one.

9:1–14 The priesthood of Jesus is the pure perfection of which the Jewish Levitical priesthood had only been the promise. The Day of Atonement ritual is mentioned in verse 7, thus leading to the sacrificial blood of Christ (9:11–14, especially verse 12).

9:15–22 The new covenant is superior to the old, since the death that ratified it is a death redeeming human beings from their transgressions under the old.

9:23–10:18 Shadow and substance in regard to the sanctuary and the sacrifice.

10:19–39 THIRD SECTION OF PARENESIS.

Because of Christ, Christians can enter the Holy Place purified, and should encourage each other to love and good works.

11:1–39 FOURTH ASPECT OF THE PROCLAMATION: JESUS AS THE PIONEER AND PERFECTER OF FAITH.

The writer's definition of faith indicates his Hellenistic Jewish heritage. Faith as "the assurance of things hoped for" reflects the Jewish model of promise and fulfillment, and faith as "the conviction of things not seen" reflects the Greek model of appearance and reality. The idea of listing the heroes of the faith is Jewish. In ben Sira 44:1 we read, "Let us now praise famous men, and our fathers in their generations," and there follows a list from Enoch to Simon the High Priest (Sir 44:16–50:21). The heroes listed in Hebrews 11 were all faithful to God, but they did not receive the promise. God had reserved the promise for Christians.

12:1–13:17 FOURTH SECTION OF PARENESIS.

13:18–25 BENEDICTION AND GREETINGS.

FURTHER READING

General (See Further Reading on letter, Chapter Six; Excursís and Further Reading on Pseudonymity, Chapter Fourteen)

R. F. Collins, *Letters That Paul Did Not Write.*

2 Thessalonians

ABD: "Thessalonians, First and Second" (E. M. Krentz); "Thessalonica" (H. L. Hendrix); "Parousia" (C. Rowland).

IDB: "Thessalonians, Second Letter to the " (F. W. Beare).

IDB Suppl.: "Thessalonians, Second Letter to the" (J. C. Hurd).

NJBC, pp. 871–875 (C. H. Giblin).

R. Aus, *II Thessalonians.* Part II of A. J. Hultgren and R. Aus, *I–II Timothy, Titus; II Thessalonians.* (Augsburg Commentary on the New Testament).

E. Best, *A Commentary on the First and Second Epistles to the Thessalonians.* (Harpers).

G. Krodel, "2 Thessalonians," in G. Krodel, ed., *Ephesians, Colossians, 2 Thessalonians, The Pastoral Epistles* (Proclamation Commentaries), pp. 73–96

Colossians

ABD: "Colossae" (C. E. Arnold); "Colossians, Epistle to the" (V. P. Furnish); "Christ" (M. De Jonge); "Christology (NT)" (J. D. G. Dunn); "Hymns, Early Christian" (M. A. Bichsel); "Jesus, Worship of" (R. Bauckham); "Principalities and Powers" (C. E. Arnold).

IDB: "Colossae" (M. J. Mellink); "Colossians, Letter to the" (G. Johnston).

IDB Suppl.: "Colossians, Letter to the" (F. O. Francis).

NJBC, pp. 876–882 (M. P. Horgan).

J. Burgess, "The Letter to the Colossians," in G. Krodel, ed., *Ephesians; Colossians; 2 Thessalonians; The Pastoral Epistles.* (Proclamation Commentaries), pp. 41–47.

F. O. Francis and W. Meeks, *Conflict at Colossae.*

E. Lohse, *Colossians and Philemon.* (Hermeneia).

P. T. O'Brian, *Colossians, Philemon.* (Word).

J. T. Sanders, *The New Testament Christological Hymns.*

E. Schweizer, *The Letter to the Colossians.*

D. C. Verner, *The Household of God.*

Ephesians (See Further Reading, Colossians)

ABD: "Ephesians, Epistle to the" (V. P. Furnish); "Ephesus" (H. M. Martin, Jr.).

IDB: "Ephesians, Letter to the" (G. Johnston).

IDB Suppl.: "Ephesians, Letter to the" (N. A. Dahl).

NJBC, pp. 883–890 (P. J. Kobelski).

J. P. Samply, "The Letter to the Ephesians," in G. Krodel, ed., *Ephesians, Colossians, 2 Thessalonians, The Pastoral Epistles* (Proclamation Commentaries), pp. 9–39.

C. E. Arnold, *Ephesians: Power and Magic.*

C. L. Mitton, *Ephesians.*

Hebrews

The section on Hebrews in this edition is especially indebted to the commentaries of Harold Attridge and Robert Smith.

ABD: "Hebrews, Epistle to the" (H. W. Attridge); "Melchizedek (Person)" (M. C. Astour); "Melchizedek (11QMelch)" (G. J. Brooke); "Melchizedek (NHC IX,1)" (B. A. Pearson).

IDB: "Hebrews, Letter to the" (E. Dinkler).

IDB Suppl.: "Hebrews, Letter to the" (F. F. Bruce).

NJBC, pp. 920–941 (M. M. Bourke).

H. Attridge, *Hebrews.* (Hermeneia).

F. F. Bruce, *The Epistle to the Hebrews.*

G. W. Buchanan *To the Hebrews.* (Anchor Bible).

M. Delcor, "Melchizedek from Genesis to the Qumran Texts and the Epistle to the Hebrews," *Journal for the Study of Judaism* 2 (1971), pp. 115–135.

J. A. Fitzmyer, "Now This Melchizedek (Hebr 7:1)," *Catholic Biblical Quarterly* 25 (1963), pp. 305–321. Reprinted in *Essays on the Semitic Background of the New Testament,* pp. 221–244.

R. H. Fuller, "Hebrews," pp. 1–27. R. H. Fuller, et al., *Hebrews, James, 1 and 2 Peter, Jude, Revelation.* (Proclamation Commentaries.)

D. A. Hagner, *Hebrews.* (Good News Commentaries).

R. Jewett, *Letter to Pilgrims: A Commentary on the Epistle to the Hebrews.*

W. G. Johnson, "The Pilgrimage Motif in the Book of Hebrews," *Journal of Biblical Literature* 97 (1978), 239–251.

M. de Jonge and A. S. van der Woude, "11Q Melchizedek and the New Testament," *New Testament Studies* 12 (1966), pp. 301–326.

J. P. Meier, "Symmetry and Theology in the Old Testament Citations of Heb 1,5–14," *Biblica* 66 (1985), 504–533.

H. Montefiore, *A Commentary on the Epistle to the Hebrews.* (Harpers).

R. H. Smith, *Hebrews.* (Augsburg Commentary on the New Testament).

R. Williamson, *Philo and the Epistle to the Hebrews.*

Y. Yadin, "The Dead Sea Scrolls and the Epistle to the Hebrews," *Scripta Hierosolymitana* 4 (1958), pp. 36–55.

The Wailing Wall in Jerusalem. The larger stones remain from the western wall of the first-century Herodian Temple; the smaller stones come from Moslem additions beginning in the seventh century. It is so named because Jews return to this site to mourn its destruction by the Romans in 70 C.E. and pray for its restoration (note the separation of men and women). The synoptic gospels, including the Gospel of Mark, are usually dated in part by the Roman destruction of the Temple (Mark 13:14; see also Matt 24:15; 22:7; Luke 21:20, 24b; 19:43-44). The mount above is a holy site for Jews, Christians and Moslems. For Ritmeyer's reconstruction of the Herodian Temple, see p. xx; for its floor plan, see p.xxi.

CHAPTER NINE

THE GOSPEL
OF MARK
A Mysterious Apocalyptic Drama

In Chapter One we observed that there are in general four kinds of books, or literary genres, in the New Testament: gospels, letters, a chronicle (Acts), and an apocalypse (Revelation). We have discussed letters in connection with Pauline writings. In this chapter we shall take up the first type, "the gospel."

The word "gospel" (Hebrew: *basrāh*; Greek: *euangelion*; Latin: *evangelium*; Old English: *godspell*) means literally "good news," its verbal form being "to proclaim good news" (Hebrew: *bāsar*; Greek: *euangelizesthai*). In the Hebrew Scriptures, the verb refers to the oral proclamation of good news about Yahweh's liberating rule of peace (Isa 40:9; 52:7; compare Rom 10:15). Not long before the birth of Jesus, the term also occurs in Roman imperial inscriptions, where it means the proclamation of good news about peace brought by the rule of the emperor, inaugurating a new age (especially the Calendar Inscription of Priene [in Asia Minor], 9 B.C.E.). Thus, the term "gospel" has a well attested cultural background in antiquity.

In the New Testament, the term "gospel" refers primarily to the oral proclamation of the good news of salvation. Its core is usually Jesus' death and resurrection (Paul) or Jesus' own message of salvation (especially Matthew). The only *writing* that begins with a reference to "gospel" is the Gospel of Mark: "the beginning of the good news (gospel) of Jesus Christ, Son of God" (Mark 1:1). There is a continuing debate about whether this verse refers to the whole written gospel or simply the opening Baptist story that begins the good news about Jesus' passion, death, and resurrection. Recent scholarship tends toward the latter view. Indeed, it has even been argued that originally the term might not have been in the Markan gospel, that is, that Mark's initial verse might have been added by a later copyist to mark off Mark's story from other material in the manuscript! This argument tends to gain some credibility from the fact that no other New Testament gospel is explicitly called a "gospel" and, indeed, the term "gospel" cannot be otherwise documented as a title for Christian writings before the latter half of the second century C.E. Thus, it is possible that "gospel" was not the title for a document in earliest Christianity.

Whatever we call the four narrative stories at the beginning of the New Testament—we continue to call them gospels—we are dealing with a narrative form, or genre. Three of the genres mentioned above—letters, chronicles, and apocalypses—were clearly Christian variants of well-known genres in antiquity. We have observed, for example, how Paul "Christianized" the letter form, and we shall offer similar discussions of the chronicle and apocalypse. The gospel, however, presents us with some special problems. Though the ancients did not write "biographies" in the modern sense, they did compose stories of various sorts about gods and heroes. Does the gospel correspond to some known genre in antiquity? Or was it, in contrast to the other three, distinctive enough to be unique? Whether such a judgment is possible or not, the question of genre has generated a sizable literature, and the question has become especially acute with respect to the gospel thought by most to have been written first, the Gospel of Mark. We shall say much more about the genre of Mark later. For now, we shall begin by considering some general historical questions.

EARLY CHRISTIAN TRADITION ABOUT THE GOSPEL OF MARK

Early Christian tradition about the Gospel of Mark is preserved in the writings of a fourth-century church historian named Eusebius. Eusebius records that a certain Bishop Papias of Hierapolis in Asia Minor, who wrote in the first half of the second century, claimed that he had received an oral tradition about "Mark" from a certain, otherwise unidentifiable presbyter, or elder. Papias is reported by Eusebius to have recalled,

> And this the Presbyter used to say: Mark indeed, since he was the interpreter (*hermēneutēs*) of Peter, wrote accurately, but not in order, the things either said or done by the Lord, as much as he remembered. For he neither heard the Lord nor followed Him, but afterwards, as I have said, [heard and followed] Peter, who fitted his discourses to the needs [of his hearers] but not as if making a narrative of the Lord's sayings; consequently, Mark, writing some things just as he remembered, erred in nothing; for he was careful of one thing—not to omit anything of the things he had heard or to falsify anything in them.
> (Eusebius, *Ecclesiastical History*, 3.39.15)

The core of this tradition affirms that "Mark" was the interpreter, or perhaps translator (Greek *hermēneutēs*), of Peter. Furthermore, the gospel is reported to have been based on what Mark remembered about what Peter said, to not have been in order, but nonetheless to have been accurate. This so-called Papias tradition needs to be examined further and then evaluated.

Though the name "Mark" was common in the ancient world, Papias was most likely referring to the New Testament Mark, who is also called "John Mark" in the Acts of the Apostles. Acts says that early Christians met in Mark's mother's house in Jerusalem, that Mark accompanied Paul and Barnabas on the first missionary journey to Asia Minor but left them and returned to Jerusalem, that he was not welcomed by Paul on Paul's next missionary journey, and that he afterwards accompanied Barnabas on a mission to Cyprus (Acts 12:12, 25; 13:5, 13; 15:37–40). Second, Mark is mentioned in the Pauline literature. Paul's letter to Philemon states that when Paul was in prison (Ephesus? Rome?) he sent greetings from "Mark" (Phlm 24). If the Mark of Acts was meant, a reconciliation between Paul and Mark must have taken place. Third, a second-generation Paulinist from the latter third of the first century also connected Mark with Paul (Col 4:10) and a third-generation Paulinist probably from the early second century placed Paul and Mark together in prison, apparently Rome (2 Tim 4:11; 1:17). In short, three kinds of references—Acts, a Pauline letter, and letters from Paulinists—connected Mark with Paul and, less securely, Rome. This is the dominant New Testament tradition.

A fourth type of New Testament reference is found in the book called 1 Peter, a pseudonymous writing probably from the late first century C.E., subsequently attributed to Peter. 1 Peter concludes with greetings from its author and "my son Mark" (1 Pet 5:13). In other words, *Peter*, not Paul, is being associated with Mark, as in Papias. A possible similarity with the Pauline traditions, however, is that the greetings in 1 Peter are sent from "Babylon" (1 Pet 5:13). In Christian apocalyptic literature beginning in the late first century, "Babylon" is symbolic for *Rome* since both are remembered for destroying Jerusalem (587 B.C.E. [Babylon]; 70 C.E. [Rome]). In short, a *Peter*-Mark-Rome connection in 1 Peter parallels the *Paul*-Mark-Rome connection in the Pauline and Acts materials. In this connection, we note that there was a tradition circulating in the late first century and early second century that both Peter and Paul were martyred at Rome (John 21:18–19?; Rev 11:3–4?; compare *1 Clem* 5; Ignatius, *To the Romans* 4:3; compare also the Secret Gospel of Mark).

In short, sometime in the first half of the second century C.E., certain circles of early Christianity accepted that the shortest "gospel" was written by "(John) Mark," who from time to time had been a follower of Paul and an interpreter (translator?) of Peter. The place of composition was widely thought to have been Rome, the location where Peter and Paul were believed to have been martyred. By the latter second century, such conclusions were taken for granted (for example, Irenaeus, *Against Heresies*, 3.1.1).

GENERAL HISTORICAL CRITICISM: AUTHOR, DATE, PLACE

According to general historical criticism, which attempts to evaluate documents on the basis of external events and internal analysis (see Chapter One), it is possible to argue that the Papias tradition contains a kernel of truth. First, if Mark was chosen by second-century Christians only to give the gospel authority, why did they choose a follower of Paul rather than an immediate disciple of Jesus, especially when there are ample illustrations of "disciple attribution" of books in early Christianity, for example, Matthew. Second, there are details in the Markan story that might be related to Peter. Clearly, Peter is the most prominent disciple in the gospel (for example, 1:16–18, 29–31; 8:27–9:1; 9:2–8; 14). Third, although written in Greek, Mark contains a number of "Latinisms," or words derived from Latin, the language of native Romans (for example, 4:21; 5:9, 15), and Aramaic language terms and phrases are explained (5:41; 7:34; 10:46; 14:36; 15:34). Fourth, Mark also reckons time in the Roman style (6:48; 13:35). Fifth, Jewish customs are interpreted (7:3–4; 10:12), sometimes inaccurately (14:1). Sixth, the gospel is imprecise about Palestinian geography (for example, 5:1; 6:45, 53; 7:31). These considerations might suggest composition by someone at Rome, though the gospel's geographical imprecision about Palestine seems odd if the author was the Jerusalem-based John Mark of Acts (even if geography is only symbolic). If Rome is correct, the "desolating sacrilege" (13:14; see below) might have symbolized that famous persecutor of Christians at Rome, the emperor Nero. Thus, modern scholars who have accepted the Papias tradition have usually dated the gospel to about the time of the Neronian persecution of Christians at Rome, 64 C.E., or soon thereafter.

Yet, there are many problems with the Papias tradition. The description of "Mark" in Papias sounds suspiciously defensive, as though there is an attempt to give the gospel authority ("accurately"; "erred in nothing"; "not to omit... or falsify," although these phrases might have been additions to Papias by Eusebius). Moreover, though Mark is not a disciple, he is connected with a disciple, for there is a "chain" of tradition established: Jesus ——> Peter (disciple/apostle) ——> Mark (disciple of disciple/apostle). Suspicions about the Papias tradition combined with no explicit statement in Mark about its composition have led scholars to comb the gospel for the slightest hints about matters of authorship and time and place of writing (internal evidence). They have usually turned to a verse in the apocalyptic speech attributed to Jesus, Mark 13:14: "But when you see the 'desolating sacrilege' standing where *he* ought not to be (let the *reader* understand), then let those who are in Judea flee to the mountains..." In Chapter One we noted that the expression "desolating sacrilege" in the Matthean parallel (Matt 24:15) was derived from the "abomination that makes desolate" in the apocalyptic book Daniel (11:31; 12:11; compare 9:27; 8:13–14; compare 1 Macc 1:54), where it referred to setting up an altar to the Greek god Zeus in the Jerusalem Temple by Seleucid Greeks in 168 B.C.E. (for the history, see Chapter Two). This act was considered terrible, offensive, disgusting, an act of pollution, and in the first century it probably symbolized the polluting presence of the Roman general Titus in the Temple in 70 C.E. (the masculine "he" is present in Mark's Greek). Titus' presence in the Temple in 70 C.E. not only defiled it (an abomination or sacrilege), but also accompanied its awful destruction (a desolation).

The identification of this allusion has widespread scholarly backing and gains some further support from the prophecy of the destruction of the Temple earlier in Mark 13:2: Either that tragic event is about to happen or it has just happened. While there is no certainty, we lean toward "has just," that is, shortly after the destruction in 70 C.E., especially because apocalyptic writers often portray their characters as predicting events that had happened (on Mark as an apocalyptic writer, see below).

The most important reason for questioning the Papias tradition, however, is the modern critical theory about the gradual way the gospels were formed. The Papias view of a chain of tradition one step removed from Jesus does not easily fit the commonly held form critical view that the gospel authors modified *anony-*

mous traditions that *gradually developed,* as well as written sources, to create their own individualized accounts (Chapter One: "Redaction Criticism"; see Chapter Four). Thus, most modern study of the gospels simply does not allow us to think of them as personal reminiscences of Peter to Mark.

If an unknown writer composed the gospel shortly after the destruction of Jerusalem and the Temple in 70 C.E., was it nonetheless composed at Rome? As noted above, Rome seems to fit some of the internal evidence. Yet, a location in some eastern Roman province is also possible. The Greek of this gospel is unsophisticated, and, though it contains Latinisms, it also contains Semitic (Hebrew or Aramaic) language influences. The work's Jewish flavor, its accuracy about matters such as housing and taxation, and its interest in peasant, village, and rural agricultural life might suggest Galilee. The problem with Galilee is always that the gospel is inaccurate about its geography. Even if Jesus' Galilean movements have mainly symbolic meaning, it is difficult to imagine that the author of the Markan gospel was intimately familiar with Galilee. Thus, some scholars have settled on the region north of Galilee, rural Syria.

In short, the evidence about Mark is mixed and difficult to establish critically. We cautiously conclude that the gospel is pseudonymous and that a date soon after the destruction of the Temple in 70 C.E. is most likely. Southern Syria is possible for a place of composition, but Rome cannot be ruled out. For the sake of convenience, we shall continue to call the author of this gospel Mark.

SOCIAL-HISTORICAL CONTEXT

The precise groups from whom and to whom Mark wrote are also very difficult to determine. From time to time in the gospel, the author seems to hint at something about his intended readers. Many interpreters think that "disciples" in Mark shade off into any disciples, including the intended readers. For example, Jesus' words stating that he would "lead" (the verb translated "go before" in the NRSV actually means "to lead") the "disciples" back to Galilee after his death (Mark 14:28) imply that the readers, like the women at the tomb to whom they were spoken in the story (16:7), also live after his death and wait for the parousia (compare also 9:9). However, such an observation is helpful only in a very limited and general way.

More important for the question of the writer and his recipients is the apocalyptic discourse, Mark 13:3–37, which contains the phrase used to date the gospel ("desolating sacrilege," 13:14), but also has an aside, "Let the *reader* understand" (13:14). If this phrase was not added later (there is no textual evidence for an addition), it implies that the discourse is addressed not only to those in the story, Jesus' twelve disciples, but to Mark's intended *readers* at the time of *writing.* As the context puts it, "the disciples" are being led astray by false Christs (verses 5–7); they are undergoing tribulation and persecution (verses 8–13); and they are seeing "the desolating sacrilege set up where he ought not to be" (verse 14), which has led to more tribulation and to an increase in the activity of false Christs and false prophets (verses 19–23). Yet, the End is near, the Son of Man will soon be seen "coming in clouds with great power and glory" (verse 26); one must now "Take heed, watch" (verses 33–37). If the "desolating sacrilege" in Mark 13:14

refers to destruction of the Temple by the Roman Titus in 70 C.E., this shattering event would have brought apocalyptic fervor and expectation to a fever pitch. Such an event *had to* be the beginning of the End. Mark wrote to support this view, to encourage his readers to wait and hope, and to instruct them that as Jesus himself had to go through his passion to his glory, they had to be prepared for discipleship that involves suffering.

In short, Mark and the readers of this gospel are living in a state of heightened apocalyptic expectation: The parousia is believed to be imminent and the readers are being led astray by "false Christs" and "false prophets." We do not know who these charlatans were, but 13:5b–6 suggests that some were claiming to be the risen Jesus himself, that is, that he had returned.

Was, then, the Gospel of Mark directed to *Palestinian* readers? Again, this conclusion, which some interpreters connect with the question about the place of composition, is only possible. To be sure, there is a very strong emphasis on Galilee in the gospel. Not only is rural and peasant Galilee the scene of Jesus' early activity—gathering of disciples, exorcisms, healings, and the like—it is the location for the awaited parousia (14:28; 16:7). The major problem with Galilee, however, is that in Jewish thinking "Galilee," itself a district of marked ethnic mixing, could be a symbol for the work of God in the *whole world*. In Ezekiel 47:1–12 the river of life flows from Jerusalem toward Galilee. Matthew 4:15 says that God will pour forth the light of his salvation on "Galilee of the Gentiles." Thus, we cannot be certain that the emphasis on Galilee in the gospel means that it was intended for literal Galileans.

The opposite argument can be made: Because Galilee is symbolic and Mark has a strong concern for the conversion of Gentiles, the gospel was *not* written to people in Palestine. Certainly the Markan emphasis on a mission to the Gentiles cannot be denied. The Jews reject Jesus "the son" and the gospel goes to "others" (12:9–11); "the gospel must first be preached to all nations" (13:10); the elect are "from the ends of the earth" (13:27); "the good news is preached in the whole world" (14:9). There are also many references to Gentiles in the miracle stories in chapters 5 and 7. Finally, in the climactic crucifixion scene a Gentile centurion is the only human to confess Jesus as Son of God (15:39). Yet, a Gentile emphasis would not exclude Palestinian recipients, for there were many Gentiles in Palestine. Moreover, Jews are not excluded from receiving the message in the Markan Gospel. Both are included. Archeological evidence also indicates that in later times Jews and Christians lived side by side in Galilee. Thus, an emphasis on the Gentile mission does not rule out Palestine.

Finally, we may note that in Mark 13:14 there is the comment, "let those who are in Judea flee to the mountains." We have dated the gospel in connection with the crisis of 70 C.E. when Jerusalem and the Temple were destroyed. Do these factors have some geographical import? If they do, the false prophets and false Messiahs are in Judea and the author is warning Judean Christians and offering hope that while the End is not yet, still it is not far off. As a result of these possibilities, some critics have concluded that the old tradition that the Jerusalem Christians fled to Pella across the Jordan at the outbreak of the war with Rome (compare Eusebius *Ecclesiastical History* 3.5.3) is not accurate (see Chapters Two and Four).

In short, Palestine, especially Judea, remains a real possibility for the recipients, but there can be no absolute certainty. Much more certain is that Mark writes apocalyptically and gives warning and hope to those under oppression and persecution.

Our discussion of historical background has shown that the Markan gospel is a document produced at a time of crisis and that it is dominated by apocalyptic eschatology. Apocalyptic movements emerged among Jews and early Christians who were alienated from dominant social and religious structures, especially in times of catastrophe and persecution. Mark is apocalyptic when it warns readers to beware of false prophecy, encourages them to hold on to their hope in the imminent parousia, and teaches them that discipleship may involve suffering in the face of persecution.

More specifically, Mark came out of and wrote for an early Christian apocalyptic "sect." In his story Jesus appears as something of an apocalyptic prophet, preacher, and healer. Similarly, the disciples are called to become preachers and healers (1:39; 3:14–15; 6:13). They are somewhat like the Cynic-Stoic wandering philosophers. They abandon everything (10:28) and take on their mission only the bare essentials (6:8–9: "a staff; no bread, no bag, no money . . . sandals . . . ," one tunic). Throughout the Markan gospel the field of activity is not in the cities, but in the villages. Furthermore, the disciples must be prepared to be rejected by (6:4), and to abandon their families and villages (6:1–6) and join together with true mother, brothers, and sisters (3:20–21, 31–35). This new family seems to be composed primarily of "marginal" people. It includes women (1:31; 10:30; 15:41) and children (9:33–37; 10:13, 16), the unclean and dispossessed, and the poor and outcast (6:34–41; 8:2). Riches can be an obstacle (10:17–27). Both Jews and Gentiles are welcome (4:35–8:21; compare 15:39). Jesus' proclamation of the Kingdom brought into being an apocalyptically oriented community for which John and Jesus are models: As they "preach" and are "delivered up," so the followers "preach" and are "delivered up." But discipleship in the eschatological community, for all its trials and sufferings, at least for those who understand and are faithful, has its reward: eternal life in the age to come (10:31).

THE TRADITIONAL MATERIAL USED BY MARK

You will recall that the Synoptic Problem is solved for the majority of New Testament scholars by the Two-Source Theory, that is, Mark and Q are written sources for Matthew and Luke. A by-product of this theory is the "priority of Mark," the theory that Mark comes chronologically first. We have just seen that the probable date of the Markan gospel is soon after the destruction in 70 C.E. You will also recall that form critics argue that the author had at his disposal traditional material in the form of sayings of Jesus and stories about him, some created by early Christian prophets and story tellers. A number of these sayings and stories were gathered into collections and put into writing. Here we shall briefly note again some important pre-Markan materials, especially collections (see Chapters Four, Five).

Many scholars in the past thought that the most extensive unit was a connected passion narrative, that is, an account of the arrest, trial, and crucifixion of Jesus in Jerusalem. The most important reasons for this theory were that this story is linked by numerous and specific references to time (the days of "Holy

Week" or the hours of the day of crucifixion) and place (specific sites in and about Jerusalem), giving it the impression of realism. More recent studies of the passion story in Mark's gospel, however, have tried to argue that *Mark* put the passion story together out of a number of isolated oral traditions. Yet, those who hold this view do not deny that many of the individual episodes were rooted in early tradition.

Other suggestions for collections of sayings and stories have been proposed. Mark 2:1–3:6 contains a healing story and a cycle of anecdotes revolving around Jesus' controversies with opponents about forgiveness of sins, eating with tax collectors and sinners, fasting, and keeping the Sabbath. Since these anecdotes are not clearly linked by specifically Markan literary traits for joining together isolated traditions, Mark may well have inherited a version of them as a unit. Jesus' controversies with Jewish leaders in the Temple precincts in Jerusalem may also have been a pre-Markan controversy collection placed at this location to heighten the conflicts leading to his death (compare Mark 12:13–37a).

It is very likely that Mark received some sort of collection of parables from the oral tradition around the theme "seed" (Mark 4:3–8 [Sower], 26–29 [Seed Growing Secretly], 30–32 [Mustard Seed]). These seem to have been put in written form when the Sower was interpreted by an allegory (4:13–20). If so, Mark has added some miscellaneous sayings (4:21–25), added the secrecy motif of verses (4:10–12), and fitted the whole into a Galilean seaside context (4:1–2, 33–35).

Other possible units of pre-Markan tradition are parallel "cycles" of miracle stories:

Cycle One (Mark 4:35–6:44)	Cycle Two (Mark 6:45–8:26)
4:35–41 Stilling of the Storm	6:45–51 Jesus Walks on the Sea
5:1–20 Gerasene Demoniac	**8:22–26 Blind Man of Bethsaida**
5:25–34 Woman with a Hemorrhage	7:24b–30 Syrophoenician Woman
5:21–23,35–43 Jairus' Daughter	7:32–37 Deaf Mute
6:34–44, 53 Feeding of 5000	8:1–10 Feeding of 4000

These miracle stories portray Jesus as exhibiting the powerful traits of a Jewish hero and especially a Hellenistic "Divine Man" (see Chapter Three). They suggest that some group in early Christianity who admired Jesus in this way collected them. After the feeding, the sequence continues with (*a*) a crossing of the lake, (*b*) a controversy with Pharisees, and (*c*) teaching concerning bread:

6:34–44 Feeding of 5000	8:1–10 Feeding of 4000
6:45–56 Crossing of the lake	8:10 Crossing the lake
7:1–13 Dispute with Pharisees	8:11–13 Dispute with Pharisees
7:14–23 Discourse about food and defilement	8:14–21 Incident of "no bread" and discourse about the leaven of the Pharisees

What is more remarkable is that the Gospel of John, normally so different from the synoptic gospels, has a cycle of tradition similar to this latter sequence:

6:1–14	Feeding of 5000
6:15	Attempt to make Jesus a king
6:16–21	Crossing of the sea
6:22–51	Coming of the people and discourse on bread

Possibly Mark inherited two versions of the same cycle of tradition—the feeding of the 5000 and 4000 are especially symmetrical—and some of this sequence was recalled in relation to a miracle tradition that came to the author of John (the "Signs Source"). If so, Mark has transposed the story of the Blind Man to 8:22–26 in order to introduce the theme of blindness (8:22–10:56; see below).

Finally, as noted above, the apocalyptic discourse now in Mark 13 may have been developed from pre-Markan apocalyptic materials from earliest Christianity. If so, Mark has totally reworked the discourse. This is especially clear not only from Markan vocabulary and style (compare especially 13:5b–27), but also from specific historical allusions (13:5b–6, 14, 21–22; compare 13:2).

Several scholars add other items to the list of pre-Markan collections we have given, and others argue against some of them. Nonetheless, it is generally agreed that some such list of collected traditions came to Mark. Apart from these, there are the small or isolated units of oral tradition. Thus, the organization of the traditional material into an integrated whole with a structure is something the Markan author himself has done. The structure of the Gospel of Mark is the work of the evangelist, and it is very important for an understanding of what he was trying to do and say. It should be noted in this regard that collections of Jesus' sayings (Q), miracles, and anecdotes did not survive the dominating influence of the passion story in the canonical gospels. One example of the preservation of a "sayings gospel" outside the New Testament is the now-famous *Gospel of Thomas* from Nag Hammadi (see Chapter Four).

Before attempting to determine Mark's structure, we need to look at several other emphases and techniques that contribute to isolating this structure.

STYLISTIC, LITERARY, AND STRUCTURAL FEATURES OF MARK

Literary critics, many of them less interested in pre-Markan source questions, attempt to analyze how Mark's story is told, that is, its "rhetoric." For example, the story is not told from the perspective of one of its characters, but by a third party, one who takes a position outside and above the story. The storyteller is able to move his readers imaginatively from one place to another in space and over time, or tell what will happen (an "omniscient narrator"). He has a particular ideological "point of view" from which he directs his readers, like a movie director. He leads them to make judgments about events and tells them what the characters are thinking. This unstated perspective is occasionally interrupted when Mark speaks directly to his anticipated reader (asides), for example, "let the reader understand" (13:14).

With this orientation, the narrator with a "hidden" perspective tells the story in the third person in simple, terse, pictorial, and imaginative language. The story moves rapidly from scene to scene. Action dominates. A dramatic sense of urgency is present. The author also uses a number of stereotypical words and phrases. If you read through the story, you will see heavy use of "and" (Greek *kai*) and "immediately" (Greek *euthus*), sometimes in combination, to link sections. An especially well-known example is "And he said to them..." This narrative style helps readers to spot places where Mark links together his sayings or narratives, and thus to see him at work in structuring his narrative.

If one combines such observations with the author's use of oral traditions and written sources, it is noteworthy that such stereotypical words and phrases are often found in the little introductions and conclusions to the smaller units of oral tradition, and on linguistic grounds many of these links give every indication of having been composed by the evangelist himself. In considering his overall structure, we shall note especially the introductions to the apocalyptic discourse and the passion narrative (13:1–5a and 14:1–2, 10–12).

The introductions and conclusions to Mark's episodes also contain local settings for his story, though some may have come to Mark embedded in the oral and written traditions. In the gospel, they often take on some symbolic significance. Thus, the Sea of Galilee is a place where Jesus teaches; the wilderness represents a place of temptation; a house is often a place for private teaching to the disciples; the synagogue and temple are places of opposition; the mountain and sea are places of revelation; and Gentile areas are regions where Jesus' compassion to outsiders is demonstrated. Such places are usually filled with complications or conflicts, and move the plot along.

The author of the Markan gospel also uses a number of structuring techniques. For example, there is a tendency to put things in a series of three, such as three people (for example, 3:35: brother, sister, mother; 5:37, 9:2, 14:33: Peter, James, and John; 8:31, 11:27, 14:43, 14:53, 15:1: chief priests, scribes, and elders), three passion predictions (8:31; 9:31; 10:33–34), three times when the disciples fall asleep and are rebuked by Jesus (14:32–42), or three denials by Peter that he knows Jesus (14:66–72). In many instances, the author develops his account by units of three, each building on those that have gone before (three-step progression; see V. Robbins).

Another well-known Markan technique is called the "sandwich" or "intercalation," that is, one story is placed inside another story. For example, Jesus' identity as Son of Man with authority to forgive sins (Mark 2:5b–10) is inserted into a miracle story, the healing of the paralytic (Mark 2:1–5a, 11–12). The interruption is marked by "he said to the paralytic" (2:5a), which is then repeated when the healing story resumes (2:10b), thus breaking the syntax of the sentence (the latter is usually marked by dashes in English translations). Another example is the insertion of the cleansing of the Temple (11:15–19) into the cursing of the fig tree and its meaning (11:12–14, 20–25). Still another is the woman with a hemorrhage (5:25–34) sandwiched into the healing of Jairus' daughter (5:21–24, 35–43). In some of these intercalations, one kind of material interprets the other, for example, the cursing of the fig tree and the cleansing of the Temple seem to interpret each other.

Very important for the structure of the gospel as a whole is something like a large "sandwich" in the middle of the gospel (8:22–10:52). A section in which Jesus tries to make his disciples see the necessity for his suffering and its significance for discipleship (8:27–10:45)—the section contains the three passion predictions (8:31, 9:31, 10:33–34)—is sandwiched between two stories about people being given their sight, the blind man at Bethsaida (8:22–26) and blind Bartimaeus (10:46–52). (We noted above that the former was displaced from its original sequence in a miracle collection.) These "giving-of-sight" stories clearly have a more-than-literal sense: Blind people with faith truly "see," but disciples who physically see remain blinded by their lack of understanding of Jesus' teaching and mission.

Finally, we come to two of the most important structural features of the Gospel, the overall geographical movement of the story and the summaries of Jesus' teaching and activity. The first feature revolves around Galilee in the first half of the gospel and Jerusalem in the second half of the gospel. More specifically, from 1:14 to 6:13 the story takes place in Galilee; from 6:14 to 8:26 beyond Galilee; from 8:27 to 10:52 moving from Caesarea Philippi to Jerusalem; and from 11:1 to 16:8 in Jerusalem. This movement from Galilee to Jerusalem gradually funnels the plot to the scene of ironic tragedy, Jesus' passion and death on the cross and his return to Galilee at the parousia (14:28; 16:7). If we had only the Galilean story, Jesus would appear primarily as a miracle worker who occasionally teaches.

The summary reports of Jesus' teaching and healing activity are generally recognized to occur at 1:14–15, 21–22, 39; 2:13; 3:7–12; 5:21; 6:6b, 12–13, 30–33, 53–56; 10:1. They mark transitions in the narrative, and thus point both backward and forward. If we observe the coincidence of a geographical shift plus a summary, we have the following natural divisions: 1:14–15; 3:7–12; 6:6b.

There is no clear consensus about the structure of the Markan gospel. Suggestions range from "clumsy construction" to geographical and place designations, to overlapping structures, to quite elaborate outlines. Our procedure will be to stress primarily the geographical outline and the summaries, occasionally adding other literary, stylistic, and structural features discussed above. This will give Mark's structure as follows:

1:1–13	**Introduction**
1:14–15	*Transitional Markan summary*
1:16–3:6	**First major section:** the authority of Jesus exhibited in word and deed
3:7–12	*Transitional Markan summary*
3:13–6:6a	**Second major section:** Jesus as Son of God and as rejected by his own people
6:6b	*Transitional Markan summary*
6:7–8:21	**Third major section:** Jesus as Son of God and as misunderstood by his own disciples
8:22–26	*Transitional giving-of-sight story*
8:27–10:45	**Fourth major section:** Christology and Christian discipleship in light of the passion
10:46-52	*Transitional giving-of-sight story*
11:1–12:44	**Fifth major section:** the days in Jerusalem prior to the passion
13:1–5a	*Introduction to the apocalyptic discourse*
13:5b–37	**Sixth major section:** Apocalyptic discourse
14:1–12	*Introduction to the passion narrative* with intercalation, verses 3–9
14:13–16:8	**Seventh major section:** Passion narrative

EXEGETICAL SURVEY OF THE GOSPEL OF MARK

1:1–13 INTRODUCTION.

The best manuscripts of Mark that we possess begin with the words, "the beginning of the good news (gospel) of Jesus Christ [the Son of God]" (1:1). If the author of Mark wrote these words and if they characterize the whole writing (see above and below, "Christology"; "What is a Gospel?"), he announces the "good news" of a divine human drama in which Jesus Christ as the Son of God is the chief protagonist. This drama begins with John the Baptist's preaching, continues with Jesus coming into Galilee preaching the Gospel of God. It will continue with the preaching of the gospel of Jesus Christ, the Son of God, by the church, including the evangelist Mark, and will shortly reach its climax when Jesus comes into "Galilee" again as Son of Man.

A necessary preliminary to the story, a kind of overture to the whole, is the mission of John the Baptist, interpreted as the returning prophet Elijah and relegated to the role of a forerunner of Jesus the Messiah, and the baptism of Jesus. Mark leads up to the moment of revelation when the status of Jesus as Son of God (compare 1:1) is revealed by the very voice of God from heaven at Jesus' baptism (1:11). The Temptation of Jesus by Satan—good versus evil—is brief (1:12–13).

1:14–15 TRANSITIONAL SUMMARY.

The drama begins. As John is arrested, literally "delivered up," so Jesus will be "delivered up." The summary stresses the "gospel" (compare 1:1) and points forward to Jesus' central Kingdom preaching (for example, Mark 4).

1:16–3:6 FIRST MAJOR SECTION: THE AUTHORITY OF JESUS EXHIBITED IN WORD AND DEED.

This section is dominated by the sheer authority of Jesus, as its two summaries emphasize (1:32–34, 39). Jesus calls fishermen Simon and Andrew, as well as James and John, who immediately leave their father, Zebedee, to follow him (1:16–20); he exhibits his authority in Capernaum in teaching and healing (1:21–34); he cleanses a leper (1:40–45); he heals a paralytic at Capernaum (2:1–12); he calls another disciple, who immediately leaves everything to follow him (2:13–14). Mark 2:15–3:6 is a series of anecdotes exhibiting the authority of Jesus in various ways: to deny convention by eating with the outcast "tax collectors and sinners"; to disregard fasting regulations; to abrogate the Sabbath law, in both working and healing on the Sabbath. The rubric for this section as provided by the evangelist himself is found in 1:27: "What is this? A new teaching! With authority he commands even the unclean spirits, and they obey him."

This section on the authority of Jesus includes two Son of Man sayings both emphasizing the earthly authority of Jesus as Son of Man to forgive sins (2:10) and to abrogate the Sabbath Law (2:28). It will be remembered that in 1:11 the divine voice at his baptism identified Jesus as Son of God. Now he is being identified in his full authority as Son of Man.

In this section there are also a number of miracle stories:

1:21–28	the man with an unclean spirit
1:29–31	Simon's mother-in-law

1:32–34	a summary report of many healings and exorcisms
1:39	a summary report of proclaiming and many exorcisms
1:40–45	the leper
2:1–12	the paralytic at Capernaum
3:1–5	the man with the withered hand

These stories have a definitive function: to exhibit the power and authority of Jesus in deeds, just as his teaching and his calling of disciples exhibit it in words.

The miracle stories also introduce a theme that will be developed throughout the gospel until it reaches a climax in 14:62, the theme of the Messianic Secret (see the special section on this theme below). This theme is introduced in a summary report, "he would not permit the demons to speak, because they knew him" (1:32–34). It is certainly written by Mark himself; so evidently the theme of the demons "knowing Jesus," that is, knowing the secret of his identity as Son of God (see 3:11–12) and being commanded to keep silent about it is Mark's concern. What he intends to achieve by it will become evident as we trace the theme through the gospel to its climax.

The section ends on a note anticipating the passion, the plot to destroy Jesus (3:6).

3:7–12 TRANSITIONAL SUMMARY.

This is the longest of the summary reports composed by the evangelist, and it marks the transition from the first to the second major section of the gospel. The summary points both backward and forward to familiar themes: the spread of Jesus' fame, Jesus' activity by the sea, miraculous exorcisms and healings, the designation of Jesus as Son of God, and the Messianic Secret.

3:13–6:6a SECOND MAJOR SECTION: JESUS AS SON OF GOD, AND AS REJECTED BY HIS OWN PEOPLE.

Two themes dominate this section. The first is the power of Jesus as Son of God exhibited through miracles, as in the following references.

4:35–41	"even wind and sea obey him"
5:1–20	the Gerasene demoniac: "What have you to do with me, Jesus, Son of the Most High God?"
5:21–24a, 35–43	Jairus' daughter: "they were overcome with amazement."
5:24b–34	the woman with the hemorrhage: "And Jesus, perceiving in himself that power had gone forth from him . . ."

The miracle stories are longer and more elaborate than in the first section of the gospel, and the emphasis on the supernatural in Jesus' power is more marked. He is shown as a charismatic healer and miracle working hero, with power over wind and sea and with power to raise the dead, as one who is openly confessed as Son of God, the touch of whose garments has the power to heal. There are major questions about the origin of these stories and about the use to which Mark is putting them. These are best discussed after we have reviewed the very similar stories in the next section of the gospel.

The second theme dominating this section is Jesus' being misunderstood and rejected. He is misunderstood by his friends (3:21); he is in tension with his family (3:31–35); and finally, he is rejected by the people of his own village

(6:1–6a). This final rejection anticipates the passion.

Mark inserts his parable chapter (4:1–34) in this section. It is inherited from the tradition of the church more or less as a unit, and Mark inserts it here because it enables him to begin a theme that becomes prominent in the next section (6:7–8:21) and dominant in the fourth (8:27–10:45): the theme of the disciples and discipleship.

The disciples appear originally in the first major section of the gospel, where their immediate response to Jesus' call is an aspect of the presentation of Jesus' authority. In this second section they figure more prominently, and characteristic Markan ideas and themes appear in connection with them. The section begins with an account of their formal appointment as a group (3:13–19), and in the parable chapter Mark makes a special point about them. They are among those privy to "the secret (Greek: *mystērion,* "mystery") of the Kingdom of God" and so are in an especially privileged position compared to "those outside." In a summary report (4:33–34), again composed by Mark, their privileged position is further emphasized: "...he explained everything in private to his disciples." Mark makes a great deal of the privileged position of the disciples and yet of their total failure to understand Jesus. The latter theme is developed more and more strongly in later sections of the gospel until it reaches a climax in the flight of the disciples (14:50) and the denial by Peter (14:66–72).

Note the use of Christological titles. The introduction established Jesus as Son of God (1:1 and 1:11), accompanied by the special revelatory circumstances of the heavens opening and the divine voice speaking. The first major section had two occurrences of Son of Man (2:10 and 2:28), and these are now balanced by two occurrences of Son of God (3:11 and 5:7). This placement of titles is one means whereby Mark presents his Christological teaching.

6:6b TRANSITIONAL SUMMARY.

This is the shortest of the transitional summaries in Mark's gospel, but the shift in emphasis between the second and third sections of the gospel is not great.

6:7–8:21 THIRD MAJOR SECTION: JESUS AS SON OF GOD, AND AS MISUNDERSTOOD BY HIS OWN DISCIPLES.

This section does not move as smoothly as do the others, probably because Mark is reproducing two versions of the same cycle of tradition and finding it difficult to fit them into the overall movement of his narrative. Nonetheless, the two overall themes of the section are clear; indeed, if we accept the thesis that Mark is using a duplicated cycle of tradition, the second, the misunderstanding of the disciples, becomes even clearer.

The first theme of this section is a continuation of the presentation of Jesus as Son of God by reason of his miracles:

6:30–44	The feeding of the 5000.
6:45–52	Jesus walks on the water, presumably enraptured—"He meant to pass them by" (verse 48).
6:54–56	A summary report emphasizing that Jesus' garments have the power to heal (compare 5:28).
7:24–30	The Syrophoenician woman's daughter, healed at a distance.
7:31–37	The deaf man with a speech impediment. This is much more

in the spirit of the stories in the first section (compare 7:37 with 1:27). But Mark can and does link the stories together in the various sections by returning to former emphases (compare 1:27 with 4:41 and 7:37).

8:1–9   The feeding of the 4000.

Although these stories continue the theme of Jesus as Son of God (for example, in the deliberate link between 6:56 and 5:28), the title Son of God does not occur. Having balanced the two "Son of Man" references in 2:10 and 28 with the "Son of God" references in 3:11 and 5:7, he does not use another title until the "Christ" of 8:29.

Mark clearly is reinterpreting the miracle stories he presents in these two sections of his gospel. In the form in which he inherited them from the tradition of the church they presented Jesus as a miracle working hero, and Mark preserves the traits by which they do this. But he then introduces the note of secrecy (3:11; 5:43; 7:36, but not in the story of the Gerasene demoniac, see 5:19). This element of secrecy would strike his readers as startling, because the purpose of such stories is normally precisely to proclaim the power and authority of the hero, a tendency that Mark preserves unaltered in the story of the Gerasene demoniac (5:1–20). Mark goes a step further by the careful balancing of the Christological titles, whereby Son of God is interpreted in terms of Son of Man, and still further in his narrative structure, which subordinates everything to the passion.

The second theme of this third major section of the gospel is that of the disciples and their misunderstanding of Jesus. The section begins with an account of the mission of the Twelve (6:7–13) and of their return (6:30), into which is sandwiched the account of the death of John the Baptist (6:14–29). Mark does not report this mission of the disciples as a success. He cannot do so, of course, because he is developing the theme of the misunderstanding and failure of the disciples that comes to a climax in chapter 8:

6:52   "they did not *understand*..., but their *hearts were hardened*"
7:18   "...are you also without *understanding?*"
8:15, 21   "Do you not yet perceive or *understand? Are your *hearts hardened?*"..."Do you not yet *understand?*"

8:22–26 TRANSITIONAL GIVING-OF-SIGHT STORY.

Mark moves from the third section to the fourth, as he does from the fourth to the fifth, with a story of Jesus giving sight to a blind man (8:22–26; 10:46–52). These stories enclose the fourth section of the gospel (8:27–10:45), in which Jesus attempts to lead his disciples to "sight" (that is understanding) and fails to do so.

8:27–10:45 FOURTH MAJOR SECTION: CHRISTOLOGY AND CHRISTIAN DISCIPLESHIP IN LIGHT OF THE PASSION.

This is the most homogeneous and carefully constructed of all the sections in the gospel. It begins geographically at Caesarea Philippi to the north of Galilee and has the external form of a journey from there to Jerusalem. The stages of the journey are clearly marked by further geographical references: 9:30: Galilee; 9:33: Capernaum; 10:1: Judea and beyond Jordan (10:1: is also a summary report, the last such in the gospel); 10:32: the road to Jerusalem. The section is built around three passion prediction units about the Son of Man, which have a fixed pattern: prediction of the passion and resurrection by Jesus, misunderstanding by the disciples, and teaching by Jesus concerning discipleship. Each of these occurs at a different geographical location. The section indicates that true discipleship means "following" Jesus "on the way" to the passion.

Geographical Reference	Suffering Son of Man Prediction	Disciples' Misunderstanding	Discipleship Teaching
8:27 (Caesarea Philippi)	8:31	8:32–33	8:34–9:1
9:30 (Galilee)	9:31	9:32, 33–34	9:35–37
10:32 (near Jerusalem)	10:33–34	10:35–41	10:42–45

The section as a whole has the following structure:

8:22–2   Bethsaida transitional giving-of-sight story
8:27   **Caesarea Philippi**
      8:27–30   Fundamental narrative of Peter's confession
8:31–9:1   **First Suffering Son of Man prediction unit**
         Prediction, 8:31
         Misunderstanding, 8:32–33
         Teaching about discipleship, 8:34–9:1
9:2   "After six days ..."
      9:2–8   Transfiguration
      9:9–13   Elijah as forerunner
      9:14–29   Appended incident and teaching on discipleship
         Disciples and boy with the dumb spirit, 9:14–27
         Teaching to disciples, 9:28–29
9:30   **Galilee** (9:33 **Capernaum**)
         9:30–37 Second Suffering Son of Man prediction unit
         Prediction, 9:31
         Misunderstanding, 9:32
         Teaching about discipleship, 9:33–37
      9:38–50   Appended incident and teaching on discipleship
         Nondisciple practicing exorcism, 9:38–40
         Teaching to disciples, 9:41–50
10:1   **Judea and beyond Jordan.** Intercalated units of incident and
         teaching to disciples
      10:2–12   Divorce
         The Pharisees and divorce, 10:2–9
         Teaching to disciples, 10:10–12
      10:13–16   Receiving the Kingdom of God
         The presentation of the children, 10:13
         Teaching to disciples, 10:14–16
      10:17–31   Entering the Kingdom of God
         The man with the question, 10:17–22
         Teaching to disciples, 10:23–31
10:32   **The road to Jerusalem**
         10:33–45 Third Suffering Son of Man prediction unit

> Prediction, 10:33–34
> Misunderstanding, 10:35–41
> Teaching about discipleship, 10:42–45
10:46–52   Jericho transitional giving-of-sight story

Taken together, the three prediction units are extraordinarily interesting. The first summarizes the divine necessity for the passion and is entirely in the present tense. The second provides a hinge in that the first part anticipates Jesus being delivered into the hands of men, but still uses the present tense, "is to be betrayed," and then puts the second half of the prediction into the future tense, "they will kill . . ." The third puts the whole prediction into the future and introduces specific references to Jerusalem and the details of the passion itself. This care in composition provides an element of movement to the plot of the gospel. In this central section we look back over what has happened to make the passion necessary (the plots, rejections, misunderstanding, all foreseen by God), we pause for these solemn moments of revelatory teaching, and then we move forward to Jerusalem and the passion itself.

The predictions and the prediction units provide the framework for this section of the gospel; they are also the main thrust of the teaching on Christology and Christian discipleship. The first prediction follows Peter's confession of Jesus as the Christ (8:29), and so follows the pattern of interpretation of Christology by coordinating titles as in the first and second sections of the gospel. Peter's confession is correct only if "the Christ" is understood as the Son of Man who "must suffer," and Peter's reaction indicates that his confession was in fact a false one (political?). The second and third prediction units continue the development of a true Christology by using "Son of Man," and they also implicitly continue the corrective reinterpretation of Peter's confession of Jesus as the Christ. These units provide the key elements to the teaching on discipleship in light of the necessity for the passion: As the Master went, so must the disciple be prepared to go. The first unit stresses the need to take up the Cross in following Jesus (8:34–37); the second, the necessity for servanthood (9:35); and the third defines servanthood in terms of the Cross (10:45). There is, further, more general teaching on discipleship between 10:1 and the third prediction unit, probably introduced here in a general context of teaching to disciples.

The first and second prediction units each have appended to them an incident and teaching to the disciples, and the incidents are curiously related. In the first (9:14–27) the disciples are failures as exorcists, while in the second (9:38–40) a nondisciple is successful as an exorcist using the name of Jesus. In this way Mark pursues dramatically his theme of the misunderstanding and failure of the disciples. The third prediction unit has no such appendix; the ransom saying in 10:45 is the climax of the whole section, in some respects its summary, and so its climax.

The one unit in the section we have not discussed is the Transfiguration-Elijah unit (9:2–13); it is linked to the first prediction unit by the "after six days" of 9:2, which contrasts with the "after three days" of the resurrection in 8:31 (and 9:31; 10:34). In Mark's gospel and purpose, the transfiguration is an anticipation of the parousia, especially in 9:9, the command to secrecy "until the Son of Man should be risen from the dead." This indicates that the event symbolized by the transfiguration will be of special importance after the resurrection, and hence this event is the parousia. The same point is made by the contrast between the "after three days" used of the resurrection (8:31; 9:31; 10:34) and the "after six days" used of the transfiguration (9:2). Here is an element of Mark's consistent thrust through the passion, including the resurrection, to the parousia.

The transfiguration is, then, an anticipation of the parousia, and its link to the first prediction of the passion and resurrection prepares the reader to appreciate his or her own position. Like the disciples, the reader now stands between the past passion and resurrection and the imminent parousia. The transfiguration unit also furthers Mark's Christological purpose by a characteristic juxtaposition of titles. Having presented a confession of Jesus as the Christ, Mark now reminds the reader that Jesus is also the Son of God (9:7), again in a special revelatory manner and with the implication that both need correction and interpretation by a use of Son of Man, a point he makes explicit at his Christological climax in 14:61–62.

The discussion of Elijah is added at this point (9:11–13) because of the reference to Elijah in 9:4. It is a convenient moment for Mark to present the early Christian understanding of John the Baptist as Elijah, the forerunner of the Messiah, an understanding of the role of the Baptist that he shares.

The motif of the Messianic Secret is continued through this section (8:30–9:9).

10:46–52 TRANSITIONAL GIVING-OF-SIGHT STORY.
Bartimaeus "sees" and follows "on the way."

11:1–12:44 FIFTH MAJOR SECTION: THE DAYS IN JERUSALEM PRIOR TO THE PASSION.
The entry (11:1–10) presents all kinds of problems at the level of the historical life of Jesus, but Mark's purpose in presenting the narrative is clear. Though not explicited quoted, it fulfills Zechariah 9:9:

> Lo, your king comes to you;
>   triumphant and victorious is he,
>   humble and riding on a donkey,
>   on a colt, the foal of a donkey.

In Jewish interpretation of scripture the irony of the king coming in such a humble fashion is apparent. The Babylonian Talmud preserves a traditional exegesis that claims that if Israel is worthy the Messiah will come in might "upon the clouds of heaven" (that is, in fulfillment of the coming of the Son of Man in Dan 7:13); if it is not worthy he will come "lowly, and riding on a donkey" (that is, in fulfillment of Zech 9:9). Mark implies that Israel was unworthy, and so the Messiah entered Jerusalem in this way.

Mark 11:11–25 contains the sandwich noted above. He interprets the cleansing of the Temple (11:15–19) by intercalating it into the account of the cursing of the fig tree (11:12–14, 20–25). Mark thus comes to terms with the catastrophe of the destruction of the Temple by understanding it as the judgment of God on a place become unworthy and by seeing the tradition of Jesus' cleansing the Temple as anticipating that judgment.

The remainder of the section offers a series of units relevant to the situation of Jesus in Jerusalem immediately before the passion: a parable interpreting the fate of Jesus (12:1–12); a series of three controversy anecdotes, the first two featuring adamantly hostile authorities and the third an individual who can be swayed and become sympathetic (12:13–17, 18–27, 28–34). The section may represent a source. Then there follow two incidents featuring scribes, a question whether Messiahship should be understood in terms of a Son of David (12:35–37), and a denunciation of scribes (12:38–40). The section closes on the widow's sacrifice, which anticipates the sacrifice of Jesus.

13:1–37 THE APOCALYPTIC DISCOURSE.

After 12:44 there are no more summaries and no more transitional units or stories. Rather, we are presented with two important sections, an apocalyptic discourse (Mark 13) and the passion narrative (Mark 14–16). Each has an introduction composed by Mark (13:1–5a; 14:1–2, 10–11).

We have already discussed the content of this discourse in Chapter Five and the situation of Mark's readers as reflected in this discourse above. Note further that the concluding parenesis (13:28–37) is most probably a Markan addition. Certainly this parenesis reflects a particular emphasis in Mark's message to his readers. Similarly, the parallel of the apocalyptic discourse and the passion narrative reflects Mark's desire to have his readers see their situation as they watch for the parousia as necessarily and profoundly affected by the passion of Jesus.

14:1–16:8 THE PASSION NARRATIVE.

We discuss this section of the gospel unit by unit.

14:1–11 The introduction. Mark takes a traditional account of an anointing of Jesus in Bethany and intercalates it into the introduction to the passion narrative. The intercalation has the ironic effect of juxtaposing the plots of the authorities and the connivance of Judas Iscariot with an anointing of Jesus as the Messiah ("anointed one").

14:12–25 Jesus' last meal with his disciples. The parallel in 1 Corinthians 11:23–26 indicates that Mark is using a traditional account of the Last Supper, but the emphasis on the betrayal is a characteristically Markan emphasis, as is the language in Mark 14:21 ("is betrayed" is *paradidotai* from *paradidonai*, the verb used in the passion predictions, 9:31 and 10:33). This language was used by early Christians of the passion of Jesus, but Mark develops it, especially in the predictions.

14:26–31 Prediction of the flight of the disciples and the betrayal by Peter. Again, Mark is moving his readers toward the climax of themes very important to him. Note also 14:28, the movement toward the anticipated parousia in "Galilee."

14:32–52 The betrayal and the arrest. This narrative represents Markan redaction of a traditional narrative and reflects the Markan emphasis on the disciples' failures: They do not watch as they were commanded to do (14:37, 38), and they flee from the scene of Jesus' arrest (14:50). In 14:41 it further reflects the traditional language used of the passion of Jesus, "the Son of Man *paradidotai*…"

14:53–72 The betrayal by Peter and an intercalated account of the night trial before the Sanhedrin. First there is the intercalated account of the night trial before the Sanhedrin (14:55–65). It is evident that Mark himself composed this narrative, and it brings his Christological concerns to a climax.

The high priest challenges Jesus as "the Messiah, the Son of the Blessed One," that is, Son of God (14:61), thus bringing together the two titles that have been separately juxtaposed with Son of Man earlier in the gospel. Jesus accepts the titles (14:62), thus formally abandoning the Messianic Secret by using "I am," which is a formula of self-identification for deities, heroes and heroines, and redeemers in the Hellenistic world, and indeed in the ancient Near East at a much earlier period (Exod 3:14–15). Jesus himself uses such a formula earlier in Mark (6:50; compare Mark 13:6). Then Jesus goes on to interpret both Christ and Son of God in terms of Son of Man, the last such reinterpretation in the gospel. The Messianic Secret is now revealed: Jesus is both Christ and Son of God, but as such has to be understood in light of the emphases associated with Son of Man.

The betrayal by Peter is also a climax, a climax to the presentation of Peter as representative disciple typifying in himself the promise and failure of discipleship as such: the confession (8:29); the misunderstanding (8:32); the leader at the Transfiguration (9:5); the responsible person at Gethsemane (14:37). Here he betrays Jesus, as had been predicted after the Last Supper (14:30–31) and then collapses (14:72) in a scene that Aristotle would have recognized as "cathartic."

15:1–47 The trial before Pilate and the crucifixion. This section is probably in the main pre-Markan tradition. It heavily quotes or alludes to the Hebrew Bible, especially in the crucifixion scene itself where 15:23 = Psa 69:21; 15:24 = Psa 22:18; 15:29 = Psa 22:7; 15:34 = Psa 22:1; 15:36 = Psa 69:21.

An incident of particular importance, in view of earlier elements in the gospel, is the rending of the curtain: "And the curtain of the temple was torn in two, from top to bottom" (15:38). The curtain separated the innermost part of the Jerusalem Temple, the Holy of Holies, which only the High Priest might enter and where God was particularly to be experienced, from the remainder of the Temple. Its tearing probably symbolizes in the church's tradition an interpretation of the death of Jesus as removing the last barrier between God and humanity. However, in Mark's gospel it picks up the interpretation of the cleansing of the Temple by means of the fig tree incident (11:13–25) and emphasizes that the Temple not only no longer exists, it is no longer needed. In other words, it is part of Mark's attempt to come to terms with the catastrophe of the destruction of the Temple.

The next verse (15:39) is also very important to Mark, for the centurion's confession of Jesus as Son of God is the climax of Mark's Christological interest. It is the first and only confession of Jesus by a human being in the gospel that is not immediately corrected or reinterpreted, and the reason is that after 14:62 the reinterpretation of a confession of Jesus as Christ or Son of God by a use of Son of Man is complete, the Messianic Secret is finally revealed, and such a correct confession is now possible. That a Roman centurion makes the confession symbolizes Mark's concern for the Gentiles, also to be seen in his reference to Galilee (14:28 and 16:7).

16:1–8 The Resurrection. We are again dealing with specially Markan material, and we saw earlier in 16:7 the movement to the parousia in "Galilee" and the situation of the women as ideal disciples. In this regard we may note that anecdotes about women in Mark's gospel serve as models of faith (5:24–34; 7:25–30; 12:41–44; 14:3–9). Furthermore, 16:7, "tell his disciples *and* Peter," must be read in the light of 14:72 as implying a restoration of Peter and expressing Mark's hope for a similar happy issue out of the problems afflicting the readers Peter represents in his narratives.

A problem in connection with 16:8 is whether it truly is the ending of the gospel. It seems abrupt, and we can see that the early church regarded it as insufficient, because in the course of transmitting the text of the gospel of Mark two endings were added: a shorter addition to verse 8 and a longer addition that the King James Version has as verses 9–20. One manuscript (W) also adds a verse to the longer ending; it is an attempt to explain the disciples' blindness as the work of the devil. All modern translations properly relegate these endings to the margin. Yet, 16:8 ends with a conjunction, *gar,* "for" (*kai ephobounto gar*), and this is a barbarism unlikely to be found at the end of any Greek book. It is difficult, however, to imagine that the text of the gospel could have been accidentally mutilated at a sufficiently early period for our best textual traditions to reflect it and not have had the mutilation repaired by the author himself or someone close to him who knew the original ending. This is an extraordinarily difficult issue, and commentators are equally divided. The ending as it stands in 16:8 is appropriate to the gospel as a whole with its consistent thrust through the passion to the parousia and its view of the readers as standing between those events. For this reason we are inclined to accept the gospel as ending at 16:8.

FURTHER OBSERVATIONS

Having completed our exegetical survey of Mark's gospel, we now make further observations on some of the points touched on in our earlier discussion.

Esoteric Secrecy and Mysterious Revelation: The Messianic Secret and the Markan Christology

As noted in the exegetical outline above, a major motif in the Gospel of Mark is the Messianic Secret. Jesus' identity as Messiah or Christ is dominant, but it is part of the more subtle motif about esoteric secrecy and mysterious revelation that pervades the Markan gospel as a whole. This motif, usually expressed in the words of Jesus in the narrative, is interpreted by scholars as the special and intentional emphasis of the evangelist. In other words, it is not a secret and self-revelation emanating from the historical Jesus, but *Mark's* motif about secrecy and revelation.

Here are some of the most explicit references about secrecy in Mark:

1. **The Kingdom of God:**

   4:11: "And [when he was alone] he said to them [the twelve disciples and a few others around him]: 'To you has been given the secret of the Kingdom of God, but for those outside everything is in parables; so that they may indeed see but not perceive, and may indeed hear but not understand; lest they should turn again and be forgiven.'"

2. **Exorcisms:**

1:34: "[Jesus] would not permit the demons to speak because they knew him."

3:12: "[Jesus] strictly ordered them [the demons] not to make him known."

3. **Healings:**

1:44: "See that you say nothing to anyone" (leper).

5:43: "And he [Jesus] strictly charged them [the people] that no one should know this" (ruler's daughter).

7:36: "And he charged them to tell no one; but the more he charged them, the more they zealously proclaimed it" (deaf man).

8:26: "And he sent him away to his home, saying, 'Do not enter the village'" (blind man).

4. **Disciples:**

8:30: "(Peter:) 'You are the Christ.' And he [Jesus] charged them to tell no one about him."

9:9: "...he charged them to tell no one what they had seen [on the Mount of Transfiguration], until the Son of Man should have risen from the dead."

The first category, Mark 4:11–12, shows that for Mark Jesus' parables were interpreted as riddles meant to be understood only by a select few. Parables told by Jesus to be open-ended disclosures of some aspect of reality became esoteric wisdom for insiders, especially the twelve disciples. However, their privileged position, as the rest of the story shows, was not maintained (see the "Blindness of the Disciples" below).

The other three categories focus on Jesus' hidden identity as Messiah. The author of the gospel apparently wishes to show that Jesus is not a messiah *simply* because he performs acts of miraculous power; he is not merely a miracle-working hero. Indeed, those who are healed already come to Jesus with faith. Nonetheless, that the miracles play a role is indicated by showing how the people sometimes do not heed his commands to remain silent about his identity. In the larger picture, however—and we readers sense it—Jesus' messianic identity is especially unveiled in mysterious and unexpected ways, especially through his suffering and death. This leads the author to redefine well-known traditional titles of social status and honor about messianic dignity, usually called "Christological titles."

We have studied Christological hymns in the Pauline literature and elsewhere as confessions about the identity of Jesus as "the Christ" (Chapters Four, Five). The whole story of Mark tells about the identity of Jesus; the gospel is a narrative Christology with a focus on the suffering and crucified one, as in Paul. Yet, within the story there are also particular messianic or Christological titles that capture images of a variety of messianic expectations in Judaism. Thus, like "president" or "governor" in our society, these titles identify and crystalize specific cultural roles of status and honor in antiquity: Son of David (Jewish king descended from David), Son of Man (heavenly apocalyptic figure), Son of God (Hellenistic emperor, Jewish king, and/or miracle worker), Lord (emperor; a title for God in the Scriptures), and Messiah ("anointed," usually in reference to kings). There are also other cultural roles less associated with titles: prophet, teacher, exorcist, healer, and martyr. Mark interprets and remolds these roles in relation to his portrayal of Jesus.

Jesus is identified as Son of God, a title for kings, emperors, and miracle workers, in key revelatory scenes: the baptism (1:11), the transfiguration (9:7), the trial (14:61–2), and the Cross (15:39). This is certainly an important role for Jesus. Thus, it probably occurred in the author's initial statement (1:1; see below, "What is a Gospel?"). However, the titles are also interpreted and interrelated. There are two occurrences of Daniel's title for the heavenly apocalyptic figure, Son of Man, in the first section (2:10, 28). They are balanced by two uses of Son of God in relation to Jesus' miracle working in the second (3:11; 5:7). The titles "Christ" and "Son of Man" are juxtaposed in the story of the confession of Peter at Caesarea Philippi (8:27–34) and are immediately followed by the use of Son of God at the Transfiguration (9:7). Further, Christ, Son of God, and Son of Man are juxtaposed at the trial before the Sanhedrin (14:55–65), and Son of God is the title in the climactic confession by the centurion (15:39). Thus, Mark seems to use Son of Man to correct and interpret an inadequate understanding of Christ and Son of God prevalent in the church for which he writes. Moreover, Son of Man has a threefold emphasis: authority on earth (2:10, 28), apocalyptic authority at the final judgment (8:38; 13:26), and necessary suffering (8:31; 9:31; 10:33–34, the passion predictions). Some interpreters think that the threefold Christological emphasis expressed by the use of Son of Man is Mark's answer to a false Christology he is combating, and that this emphasis is his great contribution to the development of New Testament Christology.

The "Blindness" of the Disciples

In Mark's parable interpretation (4:11–12) the disciples are insiders who receive special instruction in esoteric wisdom (compare 4:13–34). Outsiders see and hear, but do not *really* see and hear, that is, perceive and understand. Moreover, as Jesus' companions they should (like the true "disciples"/readers of this story!) begin to understand the mysterious Messiah. Yet, as Mark tells his story, the twelve disciples persistently, even increasingly, fail to understand. In contrast, outsiders are recipients of Jesus' compassion. Thus, the insiders look like outsiders and some outsiders look like insiders. Such role reversals are highlighted in the transitional section: Two blind men receive their sight (8:22–26; 10:46–52), but ironically the disciples, who have already been described as having "hardened hearts" (6:52; 7:18; 8:15, 21), misunderstand Jesus and his mission as the suffering martyr/Son of Man, as well as the true nature of their discipleship (8:32–33; 9:32–34; 10:35–37). They will not really "follow" Jesus "on the way" to his passion and death. Ultimately, one of them betrays him, the rest abandon him, and at the end he is crucified alone. Interestingly, if anyone is consistently loyal in the story, it is the Galilean women who look on his crucifixion from a distance (15:40–41) and come to bury him (16:1–8). While burial of an unclean corpse would be "women's work," this role of the women seems consistent with anecdotes about women as models of faith earlier in the story (5:24–34; 7:25–30; 12:41–44; 14:3–9). Thus, as Mark would have it, the twelve (male) disciples never receive Jesus' final message that he would lead them back to Galilee, where the parousia will occur (16:8).

To what extent is Mark still thinking about "disciples" in general? Some modern interpreters argue that the "blindness of the disciples" theme in relation to Peter and the other disciples of Jesus should be seen as a polemic against "church authority" in *Mark's* day. In other words, Mark engages in "disciple bashing" because the church leaders in his time, symbolized by Peter and the other disciples, do not understand the real nature of Jesus and discipleship; that is the reason they do not get the final message of Jesus about Galilee (16:8). Why else would they be portrayed so negatively? Yet, other modern interpreters have argued that this theory about the Markan disciples has gone too far, that it is too negative, and that Mark is simply addressing the fact that any disciple who wishes to follow Jesus is in danger of not understanding the significance of Jesus and must be prepared to endure suffering and martyrdom. If these latter interpreters are correct, Mark would be warning about the potential misunderstanding of any disciple. While this position is more attractive in relation to other New Testament literature that portrays Peter and the disciples as important church leaders in the interim between Jesus' death and writing of the gospels, it cannot be denied that the Gospel of Mark is very hard on the disciples. Thus, we lean toward the former interpretation, but suggest that it does not totally cancel out the latter interpretation (see 16:7 above). In either case, as we shall see, the gospels of Matthew and Luke modify Mark by giving a more favorable impression of Peter and the disciples.

The Passion of Jesus

It has often been said that the Gospel of Mark is "a passion narrative with an extended introduction." In other words, the drive of the gospel is toward the passion: Jesus' suffering and martyrdom, with such a fate possible for those who follow him. Certainly the passion of Jesus looms large in Mark, and our structural analysis bears this out. Every major section of the gospel ends on a note looking toward the passion, and the central section, 8:27–10:45, is concerned with interpreting it:

3:6	the plot "to destroy" Jesus
6:6	the unbelief of the people of "his own country"
8:21	the misunderstanding of the disciples
10:45	the Cross as a "ransom for many"
12:44	the widow's sacrifice, which anticipates Jesus'

All through the gospel, the passion and the parousia of Jesus stand in a certain tension with each other. For example, our structural analysis shows that the apocalyptic discourse of Mark 13, in which the parousia is the central concern, is parallel to the passion narrative of 14:1–16:8. They both have introductions—neither one is subordinated to the other—and there is an element of carefully organized parallelism in that the events predicted for the Christians in 13:9 are exactly what happens to Jesus in the passion narrative. Furthermore, there appears to be a relationship between the uniform "after three days" of the prediction of the resurrection in 8:31 (and 9:31; 10:34) and the "after six days" of the transfiguration in 9:2. Since the transfiguration anticipates the parousia, the sequence would seem to be: after three days, the resurrection; after six days, the parousia. Moreover, 9:9 indicates that the event represented by the transfiguration comes after the resurrection and will be of concern to the disciples then: "he ordered them to tell no one what they had seen, until after the Son of Man had risen from the dead." Finally, there are the references to Galilee in 14:28, "*after* I am raised up, I will go before you into Galilee," and in 16:7, "he is ahead of you to Galilee; there you will see him, as he told you." These appear to be references to the anticipated parousia. They are, therefore, a final indication of a consistent movement in the gospel through the passion, including of course the resurrection, to the parousia. Mark is addressing people in a situation like that of the women at the tomb, aware of the resurrection and awaiting the parousia in "terror and amazement" (16:8).

WHAT IS A "GOSPEL"?

At the beginning of this chapter we said that the question about the gospel as a genre has generated much discussion. Having studied the Gospel of Mark in some detail, we are now in a somewhat better position to restate the genre question: "What is a gospel?"

The genre question has, first of all, a theoretical dimension. To what extent do any writings have enough similarity in structure, content, length, and emotional tone to be classified as a common type? Obviously, the more we speak in terms of what is common, the more likely we are to find a common form. Similarly, the more we speak about what is distinctive in a particular writing, the more it becomes impossible to speak of a common form. Genre vanishes. To be specific, the four canonical gospels are different from each other. Should they be classified together? Are they enough like some other texts in antiquity to be classified with them? Or is the gospel something different?

In addition to theory, the question of the gospel genre has a history. In the nineteenth and early twentieth centuries the Gospel of Mark was usually classified as an ancient biography. With the emergence of form criticism in the 1920s, however, it was judged to be primarily a loose collection of oral traditions ("pearls on a string") brought together to form a popular eschatological myth about the death and resurrection of an otherworldly divine being. From this perspective, its author was mainly a compiler who nonetheless had compiled something new, even unique. In the past few decades, however, it has been argued by redaction and literary critics that the authors of the gospels were creative literary artists. With respect to genre, some have maintained the uniqueness theory. However, the view has gained ground that gospel sources, including Mark, contained not only oral traditions, but written collections of materials that themselves represent various genres found in noncanonical texts (miracle accounts, sayings collections, infancy gospels and so forth). Moreover, if authors wrote in and for particular historical and social contexts, they had to have adapted *some* known forms of communication for their story in order to communicate (historical and social-science criticism). Thus, the quest for some ancient genre prototype for the gospel has resurfaced, and again, especially in relation to the Gospel of Mark.

What, then, might have served as a prototype for the *whole narrative story of Mark*? Some scholars have reexamined the ancient biographical literature. One suggestion is that Mark is an "aretalogy," defined as an account in which a hero is characterized by a life of virtue (Greek *aretē*), especially wise teachings, miracle working, and martyrdom at the hands of a tyrant. One problem with this model has to do with the genre: One prototype often cited has no miracle stories (Plato's life of Socrates), another no martyrdom (Philostratus's *Life of Apollonius of Tyana*). Did such a genre really exist? Another problem is that no ancient narrative text is called an aretalogy. If one restricts the discussion to an emphasis on miracle stories, clearly typical of many heroic miracle workers in antiquity, and an important feature of Mark, the prototype (if it existed) might come closer to miracle collections behind Mark. However, these are sources used by the Gospels of Mark and John (the "Signs Source"). Mark, as we have seen, incorporates the miracle working feature of Jesus' life into a larger narrative that emphasizes Jesus' passion, death, and secret messiahship.

Another theory goes back to Greek tragedy. We noted in our exegetical survey that the movement from Galilee to Jerusalem gradually funnels the Markan plot to the scene of ironic tragedy: Jesus' passion and death on the cross. Correspondingly, Greek tragedy, with its dramatic movement from complication (blindness of the disciples; conflict) to crisis (messiahship; opposition) to resolution (death; resurrection) has been proposed as a prototype. This proposal has the advantage of stressing a known genre and accenting action leading to tragic death. Yet, Mark's story of Jesus as a miracle working Jew who engages in dialogue and debate, as well as its tone, does not quite fit the Greek tragedy. Modification of this theory in the direction of tragicomedy, stressing the underlying structure of death and resurrection, has also been found wanting.

Another possibility returns to the Hellenistic biography (*bios*), this time with a special emphasis on praise (*encomium*) of the hero. This was a known genre, and because the gospels clearly praise their protagonist, it has much to commend it. The question is whether it addresses the issues originally raised by the form critics against the Hellenistic biographies as prototypes: the otherworldly, apocalyptic, mythical dimension of the Markan story of Jesus.

Other theories from Hellenistic literature have been tried, with perhaps less success. The Hellenistic "romance" novel, which mixes history and myth, is not quite suitable because it has weird and fanciful elements not characteristic of the gospel. Martyrologies, which contain aphorisms, speeches, and heroic contempt for death and Roman authority, seem to have a different tone from the gospels.

There have also been suggestions developed from special Hellenistic types of literature found in Judaism. One suggestion is that Mark was an interpretation of, or commentary on, Jewish sacred texts meant to serve as readings for part of the Jewish year. In other words, Mark is a *midrash*. Moreover, goes the theory, Matthew is a *midrash* on Mark, and Luke is a *midrash* on Matthew. This sophisticated theory is interesting, but not convincing in its details. It does not correspond with the prevailing Two-Source Theory. Moreover, the links of Mark with the Jewish calendar are difficult to demonstrate. Another recent theory suggests that Mark is developing a "biography of the prophets," perhaps with the aid of biographies about Roman officials ("office biography").

Two common, recent theories are Mark as parable and Mark as myth. The parabolic view of Mark has built on intensive discussions about the nature of parables in general and of Jesus in particular. Parables are considered to be stories about the natural world and everyday life (secular stories), but they are not literal, descriptive fact; rather, they are metaphorical, that is, imaginative glimpses about life in all its mystery, paradox, and subtlety. On the one hand, they are a challenge to well-established ways of viewing reality; on the other, they are open-ended, that is, open to a variety of interpretative possibilities. They are revolutionary. The parabolic nature of Mark resides in its mysterious revelation: The story is about the realistic, everyday life of a human being, but it is also about a person and a reality much more extravagant than everyday life, someone and something subtle, complex, paradoxical, ironic. Messianic titles are filled with new meaning, thus challenging the usual ways of viewing them; the Kingdom is not a king's kingdom in the usual geographical sense, but the Kingdom of God, without well-defined form or content; the disciples do not understand the reality with which they are faced; insiders become outsiders, and outsiders insiders, in a dramatic role reversal; the story ends "up in the air," allowing the possibility of multiple interpretations. Thus, in many respects Mark is like a parable. However, there are some problems with the parable analogy. *Is* the Markan story a parable? Is not its narrative framework too long? Is it not already an interpretation of Jesus' life? Does Mark's own view of parables as esoteric riddles fit the open-endedness of the modern parable theory? Does it not let the reader sense what the outcome *should* be, at least in the future? While Mark is in many respects parabolic, it is also apocalyptic, and this brings us to the final suggestion.

The form critics had suggested that Mark is something like a myth. Today, the suggestion has been renewed that the Markan gospel is an apocalyptically oriented myth. The term "myth" in this context does not mean something that is false. A myth is a narrative that expresses in symbolically rich language human experiences that resist expression in any objective, descriptive language. Fundamental human emotional experiences are articulated initially by spontaneous confessions expressed in symbolic language. Such language is opaque, that is, it points beyond itself to a situation of human beings that can take other forms of expression. For example, the feeling that it is not "my fault," or that I am worth something, can be couched in symbolic language about being clean and pure; innocence is articulated in the language of acquittal; or integration into reality is spoken with the language of being centered, saved from tragedy, or bought back out of slavery (redemption). When the symbolic language is taken up into a narrative form and placed in a time and place that cannot be precisely coordinated with actual historical times and places, it becomes myth. Sin and exile are expressed in the form of the Biblical story about the "fall of man" (Hebrew 'adām means literary "humankind") and the expulsion from the garden of Eden. Being saved from tragedy becomes the story of the exodus to freedom from slavery in Egypt (celebrated in the Passover) or the sacrifice of an innocent victim for the sin of humankind (celebrated in the Christian sacred meal). Most important here, we may note that there are also myths of hope about the future which are told in highly symbolic language. If they draw their symbolism from the realm of cosmic catastrophe, the end of the world as we know it, and the ultimate redemption of a repressed people, they are apocalyptic myths.

You will recall from Chapter Three that the word "apocalyptic" has come to be a useful, inclusive term for written apocalypses, apocalyptic thought, and apocalyptic movements. Apocalypses are written versions of visual and auditory revelations from an otherworldly medium such as God or an angel, sometimes in the form of dreams about the heavenly world, given to a human seer who "sees" in an ecstatic state (in the Spirit). Usually beginning and ending with a narrative, apocalypses stress *temporal matters* (the origin of the world, history, contemporary or future crises, resurrection of the dead, final judgment of sinners, salvation of the elect, the afterlife) and *spatial matters* (heavenly regions, heavenly beings [angelic or demonic], often revealed to one who takes a heavenly journey to one or several of seven heavens, where he is awestruck and receives assurance). The revelation is full of symbols. The writing usually concludes with the seer's return to a normal state and his reception of instructions about concealing or publishing the revelation. Yet, the author is normally identified with some venerable worthy from the remote past— Abraham, Moses, David—who is represented as prophesying the future.

The Gospel of Mark is not formally an apocalypse. However, as our above discussion shows, it does contain a "little apocalypse" (Mark 13) and, especially in the light of that chapter, it is dominated by apocalyptic thought. The author's writing implies a larger view of history. It contains language from the prophets of old, as do other Markan passages, recalling periods in the history of Israel long before the coming of John the Baptist and Jesus. It also points to the destruction of the Temple, which, as Mark writes, has recently taken place, and it refers to the coming of the Kingdom of God in power and the return of the Son of Man, which have not yet taken place, though such events are thought not to be far off. As preparation for the parousia, Mark seeks to instruct his readers in a correct understanding of Christology and a true understanding of Christian discipleship. This he does not by writing letters to churches and by telling of visions, as did John of Patmos, nor only by putting prophetic words on the lips of Jesus, as in the discourses, nor only by a mixture of remembering, interpreting, and creating Jesus tradition, as in the case of the source Q. Rather, Mark tells the story of Jesus so that the concerns of the risen Jesus for his church in the present come to the fore. For him the story of Jesus in the past in Galilee and Judea, the story of Jesus in the present in the churches for which Mark writes, and the story of Jesus that will begin in the future with his parousia in "Galilee," are all the same story and can all be treated together in a narrative in which past, present, and future flow together into the one apocalyptic time.

An aspect of Mark's presentation is that the story of Jesus and the future community in Mark is a drama in three acts. Each act involves people who "preach" and who are "delivered up." In Mark 1:7 John is described as "preaching" and in 1:14 he is "delivered up." Then Jesus comes "preaching the gospel of God" (1:14), and he is to be "delivered up" (9:31 RSV, "delivered into the hands of men"; 10:33 RSV, "delivered to the chief priests"). After Jesus is "delivered up" the Christians "preach" (for example, 13:10, where "the gospel must first be preached to all nations"; if 1:1 is Markan, it represents the author's "gospel" preaching). In their turn the Christians are to be "delivered up" (13:9–13). We may represent Mark's theme as follows:

1. John the Baptist "preaches" and is "delivered up."
2. Jesus "preaches" and is "delivered up."
3. The Christians "preach" and are to be "delivered up."

When the third act is complete, the drama will reach its climax in the coming of Jesus as Son of Man (13:26).

The author, like the author of Revelation, sees his readers standing between the passion and the parousia of Jesus, and he wants to prepare them for the imminent parousia. Like an apocalyptic seer, he views himself and his readers as caught up in a divine human drama, for him the divine human drama that began when John the Baptist "preached" and was "delivered up" and that entered its second act when Jesus came into Galilee preaching the gospel of God. This drama ended its second act when Jesus himself was "delivered up" and rose from the dead, and reached its third act when the church began to preach the gospel of Jesus Christ the Son of God. It is hurrying to the climax of the church being "delivered up" and of Jesus "coming on the clouds of heaven" to "Galilee."

Is, then, the Markan narrative an apocalyptic *myth*? In many respects, yes; the story expresses guilt, evil, sin, suffering, alienation, failure, hope, and much more in symbolically rich and meaningful ways and in narrative form. Yet, the Markan story is not rooted only in some dim and distant past or future; it is also rooted in recent history. If the Markan author was not clumsy (this theory has also been suggested!), we must conclude at this point that the Markan author used the literary techniques of apocalyptic writers, but that he nonetheless combined them with elements of other genres to create something distinctive: the gospel. Thus, it has elements of *bios*, aretalogy, encomium, and prophecy; yet, its heroic element is highly ironic and expresses the tragic, even though its hope can be simply seen; it interprets ancient texts, but is not simply a commentary on them; it is parabolic in its mystery and open-endedness, yet mythic in its significance for telling the truth and revealing the future for its readers. It is not an apocalypse, but it is nonetheless very apocalyptic.

Is, then, the Markan gospel unique? The word "unique" is too strong as a historical description, but the work is a distinctive mixture. This solution is less than satisfying at the formal level of genre, but perhaps the key to the genre of the Gospel of Mark has not yet been found. We shall have more to say about these questions when we consider the other canonical gospels.

THE INTERPRETATION OF THE GOSPEL OF MARK

From the very beginning, the Gospel of Mark presented problems to its interpreters because of tensions within the gospel itself: a tension between the purpose of the evangelist and the actual needs of the church within a generation of the writing, and a further tension between the evangelist's purpose and the literary form he chose to express that purpose.

The evangelist followed an apocalyptic purpose, writing within the circumstances of the resurgence of apocalyptic during and immediately after the Jewish War of 66–70. Nevertheless, for all the resurgence of apocalyptic at that time (and at subsequent times of persecution or catastrophe), apocalyptic itself was on the verge of an inevitable decline in the Christian churches. The early Christians were faced with the necessity not only of coming to terms with the delay of the parousia, but also with finding a way of living and working out their faith in a world that continued to exist despite all their hopes, expectations, and prayers to the contrary. In this context the Gospel of Mark received its first and perhaps its most dramatic reinterpretation when Matthew and Luke independently did essentially the same thing: they transformed the apocalyptic gospel of mysterious revelation into narratives approaching on the one hand a *bios* and on the other a foundation myth. They changed the apocalyptic time of Jesus (which Mark had merged with his own time and that of the nearing of the parousia) into a kind of Sacred Time of the past. They separated it from all other time by providing it with a beginning, the birth stories, and an ending, the resurrection-ascension (Luke) and the resurrection-commissioning of the church (Matthew). They also made it a Sacred Time by various literary devices that emphasized the element of the sacred and the miraculous in that time. Then they provided the reader with a structured means of relating to that Sacred Time and of living through its power and significance. Now the gospel story became the myth from which Christians lived, as the Jews lived from the myths of creation and the Exodus. The apocalyptic gospel became a foundation myth, and apocalyptic time became Sacred Time, meeting the needs of a generation later than Mark's, and indeed of a hundred generations to come.

The other element of tension was that between the purpose of the evangelist Mark and the literary form through which he expressed that purpose, between his apocalyptic purpose and his "realistic" story about Jesus. There is no doubt that the narratives of Mark sound literal. They are so realistic that as perceptive a modern literary critic as Erich Auerbach ascribes their realism to the personal reminiscence of an eyewitness and participant. However, our discussion has shown that the personal reminiscence is only an echo or shadow, if indeed there is any personal reminiscence at all, but there can be no doubt that the narratives sound realistic. With the dwindling of apocalyptic concern in some churches, the apocalyptic purpose of Mark came to be lost, and what remained was the realistic nature of the narratives. As Gnosticism grew and spread, it preferred gospels expressing its teaching in the words of Jesus, especially in secret words of Jesus to his disciples, or in post-resurrection revelatory discourses. The more orthodox churches combatted the Gnostic Christian movement by emphasizing the apostolic authority of *its* gospels, and under these circumstances a tradition developed that the Gospel of Mark was built up largely of the reminiscences of Peter, as we noted at the outset of this chapter.

This realism provides us with the first clue to the interpretation of Mark's gospel: The narratives are meant to be understood. The evangelist himself takes pains to help his readers by explaining the value of coins (12:42) and by giving the Roman equivalent for the name of a place (15:16). So we must welcome and use the patient work of historical scholarship that helps us understand the references and allusions in the narratives. We need to appreciate the significance of the charge of blasphemy in 2:7—the forgiveness of sins was not only reserved to God, it was reserved to God at the End Time—or the force of the plot in 3:6—Pharisees and Herodians were mortal enemies; and much more. We need to know enough about the references and allusions in these narratives for them to become realistic to us and not strange or foreign.

A second clue lies in the fact that narrative functions in a certain way: It draws its reader into the story as a participant. When the one who took up his cross challenges the disciples to be prepared to take up theirs (8:34), or as he who gave his life interprets the giving as a "ransom for many" (10:45), the reader is there, like a disciple similarly challenged. Similarly, in the dark hours of the passion when Peter protests that he is loyal (14:26–31) but ultimately abandons Jesus, the reader in part shares the catharsis of Peter's breakdown in the courtyard (14:72) and wonders whether he or she would also have abandoned the Messiah in a time of crisis. The natural function of narrative is to help the reader hear the voices, take part in the action, get involved in the plot, identify with the characters. The effectiveness of the evangelist Mark as a preacher is that he has cast his message in a realistic narrative rather than in the direct discourse of a letter or a homily. We appreciate once again the significance of the realism of Mark's narratives, for it enables the reader to be caught up into the narrative as a participant.

Now we can take the important step of recognizing the affinities and differences between Mark and John of Patmos, the author of an apocalypse, the book of Revelation. Both are living in a period of turmoil and an accompanying resurgence of apocalyptic; one because of the Jewish War and the other because of fears about a time of persecution for the church. Both address their readers directly out of their narrative: Mark by a parabolic discourse, sections of teaching on discipleship, an apocalyptic discourse, and so on; John of Patmos by letters to the churches and interpretations of his visions. Both have essentially the same purpose: to prepare their readers for the imminent parousia. But there is an extremely important difference between them. Mark's narratives are more realistic, John's more symbolic. The one captures the imagination of his readers by drawing them into his narrative as participants, the other by the sheer power of his symbols to challenge, evoke, and sustain.

We can now recognize that like all apocalyptic writings, the Gospel of Mark needs to be interpreted. The Jesus who comes on the clouds of heaven as Son of Man is probably for Mark already a symbol; certainly he is a symbol for modern readers. We must allow Mark to catch us up into his narratives as participants and to challenge us with the teaching and example of the Jesus these narratives portray, as well as by the example of another kind set by the disciples and opponents.

FURTHER READING

(See **Further Reading** on sources and oral traditions, Chapter Five)

Important Theories, Sketches, and Recent Bibliography

J. Dewey, "Recent Studies on Mark," *Religious Studies Review* 17/1 (1991), pp.12–16.

V. K. Robbins, "Text and Context in Recent Studies of the Gospel of Mark," *Religious Studies Review* 17/1 (1991), pp. 16–23.

One-Volume Commentaries and Dictionary Articles

ABD: "Biography, Ancient" (C. H. Talbert); "Caesarea Philippi" (J. Kutsko); "Capernaum" (V. C. Corbo); "Divorce" (R. W. Will); "Gospel Genre" (W. S. Vorster); "Gospels, Apocryphal" (S. J. Patterson); "Gospels, Little Apocalypse in the"; "Hosanna" (M. H. Pope); "John the Baptist" (P. W. Hollenbach); "Leprosy" (D. P. Wright); "Mark, Gospel of" (P. J. Achtemeier); "Mark, Secret Gospel of" (M. W. Meyer); "Marriage (NT)" (R. F. Collins); "Mary" (B. Witherington, III); "Messianic Secret" (C. M. Tuckett); "Miracle (NT)" (H. E. Remus); "New Commandment" (R. F. Collins); "Papias" (W. R. Schoedel); "Parable" (J. D. Crossan); "Parousia" (C. Rowland); "Peter" (K. P. Donfried); "Son of God" (J. Fossum); "Son of Man" (G. W. E. Nickelsburg); "Suffering" (D. J. Simundson); "Transfiguration" (B. Chilton); "Trial of Jesus" (T. Prendergast); "Twelve, the" (R. F. Collins).

IDB: "Mark, Gospel of" (C. E. B. Cranfield).

IDB Suppl.: "Mark, Gospel of" (N. Perrin); "Mark, Secret Gospel of" (V. P. Furnish).

NJBC, pp. 596–629 (D. J. Harrington).

Standard Studies (Mostly Redaction Critical)

P. J. Achtemeier, *Mark.* (Proclamation Commentaries).

E. Best, *Disciples and Discipleship: Studies in the Gospel According to Mark.*

G. G. Bilezikian, *The Liberated Gospel: A Comparison of the Gospel of Mark and Greek Tragedy.*

J. Donahue, *Are You the Christ? The Trial Narrative in the Gospel of Mark.*

———, *The Gospel in Parable.*

———, "Jesus as the Parable of God in the Gospel of Mark," *Interpretation* 32/4 (1978), pp. 369–386; reprinted in J. L. Mays, ed., *Interpreting the Gospels.*

D. Duling, "Interpreting the Markan Hodology [Thinking about 'the Way']," *Nexus* 17 (1974), pp. 2–11.

W. Kelber, *The Kingdom in Mark.*

———, ed., *The Passion in Mark.*

———, *Mark's Story of Jesus.*

W. Marxsen, *Mark the Evangelist.*

N. Perrin, "The Christology of Mark: A Study in Methodology," *Journal of Religion* 51 (1971), pp. 173–187.

———, *What Is Redaction Criticism?* pp. 40–63.

———, "Towards the Interpretation of the Gospel of Mark," *Christology and a Modern Pilgrimage: A Discussion with Norman Perrin,* pp. 1–78.

T. Weeden, *Mark—Traditions in Conflict.*

Among the many articles on Mark and its context, we may note:

P. J. Achtemeier, "The Origin and Function of the Pre-Marcan Miracle Catenae," *Journal of Biblical Literature* 91 (1972), pp. 198–221.

———, "Toward the Isolation of Pre-Markan Miracle Catenae," *Journal of Biblical Literature* 89 (1970), pp. 265–291.

J. Dewey, "Mark as Interwoven Tapestry: Forecasts and Echoes for a Listening Audience," *Catholic Biblical Quarterly* 53/2 (1991), pp. 221–236.

E. S. Malbon, "Fallible Followers: Women and Men in the Gospel of Mark, " *Semeia* 28 (1983), pp. 29–48.

Commentaries:

V. Taylor, *The Gospel According to St. Mark.*

H. C. Waetjen, *A Reordering of Power. A Socio-Political Reading of Mark's Gospel.*

Literary:

R. Fowler, *Loaves and Fishes. The Function of the Feeding Stories in the Gospel of Mark.*

F. Kermode, *The Genesis of Secrecy. On the Interpretation of Narrative.*

E. S. Malbon, *Narrative Space and Mythic Meaning in Mark.*

D. Rhoads and D. Michie, *Mark as Story. An Introduction to the Narrative of a Gospel.*

M. A. Tolbert, *Sowing the Gospel: Mark's World in Literary-Historical Perspective.*

A. Wilder, *The Language of the Gospel.*

Social-Historical and Social Scientific:

F. Belo, *A Materialist Reading of the Gospel of Mark.*

H. Kee, *Community of the New Age. Studies in Mark's Gospel.*

B. Mack, *A Myth of Innocence. Mark and Christian Origins.*

C. Myers, *Binding the Strong Man: A Political Reading of Mark's Story of Jesus.*

V. Robbins, *Jesus the Teacher. A Socio-Rhetorical Interpretation of Mark.*

Miscellaneous:

D. Dungan and D. R. Cartlidge, *Documents for the Study of the Gospels.*

M. Hadas and M. Smith, *Heroes and Gods. Spiritual Biographies in Antiquity.*

W. Kelber, *The Oral and Written Gospel.*

H. Koester, *Ancient Christian Gospels. Their History and Development.*

N. R. Petersen, *Literary Criticism for New Testament Critics.*

P. I. Shuler, *The Synoptic Gospels and the Problem of Genre.*

J. Z. Smith, *Drudgery Divine. On the Comparison of Early Christianities and the Religions of Late Antiquity.*

C. Talbert, *What Is a Gospel?*

C. Tuckett, ed., *The Messianic Secret.*

D. O. Via, *The Ethics of Mark's Gospel: In the Middle of Time.*

A scribe at work in a way that has not changed through the centuries. Only in the Gospel of Matthew does Jesus refer to a "scribe... trained for the kingdom of heaven" (13:52), usually considered by modern scholars to be an apt description of the anonymous author of this gospel. See the medieval scribe at the beginning of Chapter One.

CHAPTER TEN

THE GOSPEL OF MATTHEW

Christianity as Obedience to the New Revelation

The Gospel of Matthew was placed first among the four gospels because it was believed in the latter second century to have been the first gospel written (Irenaeus, *Against Heresies* 3.1.1–2). It had become influential in early Jewish Christianity and was fast becoming the most important of all the gospel texts for the emerging Christian church. Its stories about Jesus' miraculous birth, its representation of Jesus' moral discourses, its importance for liturgy (for example, the Lord's Prayer), its views of church discipline, law, discipleship, Jesus' presence with the Christians until his return—all made it destined to become the "church's gospel." By the third century C.E. it was used to defend the authority and primacy of the Roman bishop as pope, and thus it became special to the western, or Roman, branch of Christendom. In short, the Matthean gospel provided an understanding of the past, present, and future that made sense of the emerging church's ongoing life in the world.

EARLY CHRISTIAN TRADITION ABOUT THE GOSPEL OF MATTHEW

The earliest explicit Christian reference to Matthew outside the New Testament came from the same author who gave us the first reference about the Gospel of Mark, namely, **Papias,** bishop of Hierapolis in Asia Minor, who wrote in the first half of the second century C.E. As recorded by the fourth-century historian Eusebius, the Papias tradition about Matthew states:

> Then Matthew put together [variant: wrote] the sayings (*logia*) in the Hebrew (*Hebraiois*) dialect (*dialectō*) and each one translated (*hērmēneusen*: interpreted?) them as he was able.
>
> (Eusebius, *Ecclesiastical History* 3.39.16)

Just as we were uncertain about whether Papias meant "interpreter" or "translator" (*hermēneutēs*) in his statement about Mark, so we are uncertain about whether Papias meant "interpreted" or "translated" (*hērmēneusen*) in his statement about Matthew. In this case the problems are more complex since the words *logia*, "sayings," and even *Hebraiois* and *dialectō*, are also debated.

One recent theory is that Papias meant that Matthew wrote in the *Hebrew manner* (not dialect) and each *interpreted* (not translated) as he was able. This interpretation removes the difficult problem posed by the fact that our Matthew was not written in Hebrew or Aramaic, but Greek: Translation would not be necessary. However, the ancients understood Papias to mean language (Irenaeus *Against Heresies* 31.1–2; Eusebius *Ecclesiastical History* 3.24.5), and most modern critics think that Papias meant by "Hebrew" the *Aramaic* language, as in John 20:16 (compare also Acts 21:40; 22:2; 26:14).

Another problem is that Papias referred only to the *person* "Matthew." Was he then describing a gospel? Papias probably had the gospel in mind, since he had just described how the Gospel of Mark came to be written (see Chapter Nine). If he meant the gospel, and if he meant Aramaic, he must also have meant "translated" for *hērmēneusen*.

In short, the most common view is that Papias was referring to a Semitic-language document, probably Aramaic, that he was indeed referring to the gospel, and that *logia* meant "sayings," its usual meaning. Papias meant that Matthew wrote a gospel of sayings in Aramaic and that it had to be translated to be understood. Before evaluating this tradition historically, we need to recall some facts about "Matthew."

The Name Matthew

Though the name "Matthew" was not unusual in antiquity (Greek *Matthaios* from the Hebrew *Mattiyah*, "gift of Yahweh," or simply "gift of God"), this tradition and others based on it (for example, Irenaeus, *Against Heresies* 3.1.1) are no doubt referring to Jesus' disciple and apostle Matthew in the New Testament. There is some confusion about the name of this person in early Christianity. The name "Matthew" is found in all four of the lists of the twelve disciples/apostles (Mark 3:18; 10:3; Luke 6:15; Acts 1:13). In the Matthean list, and only here, Matthew is identified as the tax collector, or better, the "toll collector" (10:3: *telōnēs*). This identification refers back to the man sitting at the Capernaum "toll booth" (9:9: *telōnion*), whom Jesus called to be his disciple. However, the Gospels of Mark and Luke name this toll collector Levi (Mark 2:14; Luke 5:27), and for them he is not one of the twelve disciples. Further, Mark and the apocryphal *Gospel of Peter* identify Levi as the "son of Alphaeus" (Mark 2:14; *GPet* 60). To add to the confusion, the "son of Alphaeus" describes James in the disciple lists (Mark 3:18; Matt 10:3; Luke 6:15; Acts 1:13). Apparently this is the reason why a later copyist called Levi "*James* the son of Alphaeus" (Mark 2:14 variant). We may restate the problem like this:

| Levi | the son of Alphaeus | toll collector story in Mark 2:14 and Luke 5:27 |
| James | the son of Alphaeus | disciple in lists; text variant of Mark's toll collector story |

| *Matthew* | three disciple lists; *called toll collector* only in Matthew 9:9 |
| *Matthew* the toll collector | only so called in Matthew's disciple list (10:3) |

In other words, *only the Gospel of Matthew* identifies Matthew of the disciple/apostle lists as **the toll collector at the border checkpoint in Capernaum.**

Why did the Gospel of Matthew call the toll collector Matthew? An ancient view that became traditional is that Levi and Matthew were the same person (Jerome *Prologue to Matthew*). However, there is no evidence for such a name change (for example, like Simon was symbolically named "Peter," see below). The simplest explanation is that the author of Matthew, like the later Christian copyist of Mark, sought to replace an unknown person with a known disciple: the disciple Matthew became the toll collector in the Gospel of Matthew, just as the disciple James the son of Alphaeus became the toll collector in a text variant of Mark. Following the Two-Source Theory, Matthew changed Mark, not the reverse. "Levi" (Mark 2:14) became "Matthew" (9:9). Subsequently Matthew identified "Matthew" in his list as "Matthew the tax [toll] collector" (10:3). Luke simply retained Mark's "Levi" in the toll booth story.

Why did the author of Matthew choose Matthew and not some other disciple? There are several interesting theories. Perhaps the disciple Matthew was honored in the circles where the gospel was written; perhaps the word "disciple" (*mathētēs*) and the command "learn" (*mathete*) suggested the name *Matthias* as the true representative of learning and discipleship; perhaps the author considered that the name "Matthew" ("gift of Yahweh") symbolized God's acceptance of "toll collectors and sinners." Whatever the precise explanation—some combination is not impossible—only the Gospel of Matthew correlates the apostle Matthew in the lists with the Capernaum toll collector (9:9; 10:3). Papias undoubtedly meant this Matthew.

GENERAL HISTORICAL CRITICISM: AUTHOR, DATE, PLACE

Our translation and text critical solutions now leave us with a number of historical problems. The first is the Semitic language question. If we conclude that Papias is referring to a gospel, and if he is referring to a "Hebrew dialect," our Greek Gospel of Matthew would have to be a translation from Aramaic. However, while language experts recognize Semitic influences on the author's Greek, they do not think that our Matthew is a Greek translation. Also, the Gospel of Matthew extensively uses the *Greek* Gospel of Mark. We conclude that our Gospel of Matthew was not originally written in "Hebrew," but Greek, apparently by a bilingual, or even multilingual, person.

The second problem is that our Gospel of Matthew is not simply a collection of "sayings," the usual and natural meaning of *logia*. Indeed, Papias' description sounds more like an Aramaic form of Q. Was Papias referring to some tradition about Q and confusing it with Matthew? We do not know. The conclusion is inescapable that Papias' description does not describe our gospel.

Papias' statement about Matthew is also difficult to accept on the basis of other historical factors. Ancient writers who built on the Papias traditions concluded that Mark wrote down what he remembered of what Peter said after Peter's death (Irenaeus *Against Heresies* 3.1.1–2; compare Eusebius *Ecclesiastical History* 5.8.2), that is, sometime in the early 60s. Correspondingly they thought that Matthew, which they believed was written before Mark, was composed earlier than the 60s. However, we dated the gospel of Mark shortly after the destruction of Jerusalem and the Temple in 70 C.E. because the "Abomination of Desolation" referred to the Roman general Titus in the Temple—"let the reader understand" (Mark 13:14). We also indicated in Chapter One that the Gospel of Matthew might have understood Mark's reference this way (Matt 24:15–18; Luke 21:20; 19:13). Evidence for Matthew's interpretation is also found in the allegorical reference to the king (God) who destroyed the murderers (the Jewish people) and their city, Jerusalem (Matt 22:7). Combining these two internal references (Matt 24:15–18; 22:7; compare also Matt 21:41) with the Two-Source Theory, the Gospel of Matthew also must have been written some time after 70 C.E.

If 1 Peter comes from the late first century, the latest possible date for the Matthean gospel might be established by the possibility that 1 Peter knows the gospel (especially 1 Pet 2:12 [Matt 5:16]; 1 Pet 3:14 [Matt 5:10]. However, the date of 1 Peter is controversial (see Chapter Fourteen). More important, the references in this case might indicate only that Matthew and 1 Peter share common oral tradition, especially when it is observed that the parallels with 1 Peter are found only in the Special M stratum of Matthew (see Chapter One, the Two-Source Theory). Thus, the latest date has usually been established by the reference to the gospel by **Ignatius of Antioch** in Syria, an early Christian bishop and martyr. Modern critics place the period of Ignatius' letter writing some time between 105 and 135 C.E., probably earlier rather than later. This would accord with fourth-century Eusebius, who dated Ignatius' martyrdom in the reign of the Roman emperor Trajan, 98–117 C.E. (*Ecclesiastical History* 3.21–22).

There is no question about whether Ignatius was familiar with the kind of materials found in the Gospel of Matthew. The debated question is whether he referred to creedal-sounding oral traditions that also found their way into the Gospel of Matthew, as we suggested for 1 Peter, or to the written gospel itself. We think it probable in this case that Ignatius quoted the gospel itself. The most important reason is that in addition to Matthean traditions (mostly Special M) Ignatius quoted an expression redaction critics think was composed by the Matthean author himself (Matt 3:15: "that all righteousness might be fulfilled by him"; compare Ignatius, *To the Smyrnaeans* 1.1; compare also *To the Philadelphians* 3:1 [Matt 15:13]). On the basis that Ignatius quoted the gospel itself, the gospel would likely have been written before 110 C.E.

It is possible to be more precise about the time of composition between 70–110 C.E. Two factors are important. First, the Two-Source Theory would suggest the probability that the Gospel of Matthew was composed some years after the Gospel of Mark. One generation would place composition about midway between the outside limits, or about 90 C.E. Second, internal evidence from the gospel suggest that its composition was related to the type of Judaism that was emerging under the leadership of a coalition of Pharisees of the Yavneh Academy about 80–90 C.E. It will be important to say much more about this perspective in Matthew. For now, several considerations converge to conclude that **it was written about 85–90 C.E.** While it is not totally impossible that a toll collector who was Jesus' disciple wrote a gospel in his old age, this late date adds to the difficulties about translation from Aramaic and "sayings" form. We can only conclude that the Papias tradition about Matthew is highly unlikely.

Finally, *where* was Matthew written? The Church Fathers apparently deduced that the disciple who wrote this Jewish gospel in "Hebrew" wrote for his own people in Judea (Jerome, *Commentary on Matthew;* Monarchian Prologue to Matthew). A few recent interpreters have tried to make a case for Palestine, too. Since the gospel has hints of having been written in an urban area (see below), some city with Greek-speaking Jewish Christians is usually sought. One suggestion is Jerusalem, though it was not very suitable for Jews or Jewish Christians after 70 C.E. A case has also been made for the "Roman capital" of Palestine, Caesarea Maritima (see Chapter Two), which became an early Christian center. However, the Jews of Caesarea were massacred in 66 C.E., and apparently very few of those who escaped returned; also, the ancient Church Father Eusebius of Caesarea never mentions Matthew, which is surprising. Comments in the gospel that Galilee and Judea lie "beyond the Jordan" (Matt 19:1; 4:15) have suggested to some a city east of the Jordan River, for example, Pella. Other suggestions such as Alexandria, Egypt, or Edessa, Syria, have not won much acceptance. Some other city just north of Palestine is possible, but speculative. Most modern interpreters have therefore turned to Antioch in Syria. It was an important location from which Gentile missions were initially launched (see Chapters Four, Six, the "Antioch Incident"), but it also contained a sizable Jewish population. Syria was not far from Palestine, and Matthew's gospel contains definite links with Palestinian Christianity, especially Matthew's fondness for using the term Son of Man in the apocalyptic sense (10:23; 13:37–41; 16:28 [for Kingdom of God, Mark 9:1]; 19:28), and other Palestinian Christian traditions have been isolated by form critics (5:17–20; 7:22–23; 10:23; 10:41; 19:28–29; 23:8–10). Thus, a city in Syria meets the conditions of the gospel, and this suggestion is reinforced by the probability that Ignatius of Antioch referred to the gospel, as mentioned above in connection with its date. **Antioch** is as good a choice as any.

In summary, the gospel now attributed to Matthew was anonymous and first circulated anonymously. It was written about 85–90 C.E., perhaps in Antioch of Syria. The ascription of this gospel to Matthew, disciple of Jesus and eyewitness to his life, is probably a second-century attempt to give special authority to the most important gospel. It was called "According to Matthew" during the same period that the Papias tradition was written. For convenience we shall continue to call the author "Matthew."

SOCIAL-HISTORICAL CONTEXT

We noted in Chapter Four that the post-70 era was the middle period of Christianity and that during this period there were a number of Christian responses to the fall of Jerusalem and the Temple. To understand Matthew's response better, it will be helpful to discuss some major developments in Judaism.

You will recall that Palestine prior to 70 C.E. was a minor temple state, a colony subject to imperial Rome. The destruction of Jerusalem and its Temple in 70 was catastrophic. It meant the destruction of Palestinian Judaism as it had existed, as well as its social system, its political organization, and its economic order. Religiously, the Holy Temple and its worship were no longer available as a way of knowing God and the Holy City was no longer the center of pilgrimage for the great religious festivals, especially the Passover. There also emerged a shift in the balance of power, status, and influence of the various Jewish parties and sects active before the war. The Sadducees, the aristocratic ruling elite of Jerusalem (subject to Roman authority), were primarily concerned with the Temple, which they controlled, and with the organization of the Jewish state under the authority of the high priest. Now, however, there was no Temple. Along the shores of the Dead Sea at Qumran was another group (probably the Essenes), a priestly community that opposed the Sadducean priesthood and Temple at Jerusalem and interpreted the Scriptures eschatologically to refer to their own history and messianic hopes for the future. The Romans destroyed this Qumran Community. The various revolutionary groups took to the sword against their enemies and God's, and were prepared to kill and to die for their beliefs. They provided the backbone of the final resistance to Rome, their remnants holding out in the fortress at Masada after Jerusalem itself had fallen.

The **Pharisees** were the religious sect that attempted to extend the laws of Temple purity to everyday life in the home and at table. They were devoted to copying, studying, interpreting, and obeying the Torah, and applying the laws of purity to everyday life, especially Sabbath observance, festivals, oaths, lawful divorce, kosher food, prayer, almsgiving, and punctilious payment of tithes ("building a fence around the Torah"). Fundamentally, the Pharisaic sect understood the Law as revealing the will and purpose of God for humanity in the world, by obedience to which they achieved the blessing of God. Only the Pharisees survived the Roman-Jewish War.

The Pharisees had the resources for consolidating whatever Jewish factions remained after the holocaust in 70 and for forging a coalition that sought, and was gradually able, to extend its influence. They set up a new school at Yavneh, a town west of Jerusalem not far from the Mediterranean Sea coast. While the later Jewish traditions about the Yavneh Academy are legendary, it appears that the aim of the Pharisees was to form a united Judaism under their leadership, and thus to bring an end to whatever Jewish sectarianism remained. Archeological evidence shows that Palestinian synagogue buildings were built in the post-70 era. The Pharisees introduced into the synagogue prayers a new prayer, the **"Prayer Against the Heretics"** aimed at any sort of dissenters (not just Christians), and they increasingly banned schismatics from the synagogues (see Chapter Three). The process of settling the canon and text of the Hebrew Scriptures was probably begun. They were concerned particularly with the Torah, God's fundamental revelation of his will to his people, and its interpretation.

A word about their subsequent history is in order. The Pharisaic interpretations and applications of the Torah to everyday life ("building a fence around the Torah") were at first transmitted orally, repeated over and over, and thus committed to memory. The most important of them were called the **Mishnah** ("that which is learned by repetition"). By about 200 C.E. this law code was fixed in writing under the leadership of Rabbi Judah ha-Nasi. The Mishnah was in turn the basis for further discussion, interpretation, and application. The next development of the Mishnah became known as **the Gemara** ("completion"), and it was added to the Mishnah to make up **the Talmud** ("teaching"). The Palestinian version of the Talmud (known as the Jerusalem Talmud) was never completed. The Babylonian Talmud was finished about 550 C.E., and it became and remains the textbook of Judaism, the basis for Jewish life. It is an immense work, covering in encyclopedic fashion every aspect of life that could be imagined or discussed in the five centuries during which it was produced. It is divided into thirty-six tractates, or books, and it contains about 2,500,000 words. While the rabbinic literature is notoriously ahistorical and difficult to date, experts have found that parts of it can be useful for understanding certain aspects of Pharisaism, not to mention certain aspects of the New Testament. In short, Pharisaism developed into what is usually called Rabbinic Judaism, because its center was the authoritative interpretation of Torah by the rabbis, who now became its most authoritative teachers. It is the ancestor of the Judaism that has survived into modern times. Some scholars refer to this early phase of postwar Judaism as "formative Judaism" (see Chapter Two).

It is highly likely that Matthew wrote his gospel in the context of **formative Judaism.** The Matthean group was a struggling, marginal group, in conflict with outsiders and facing some internal disarray. A classic study of Jesus' famous miracle of stilling the storm in Matthew (Matt 8:23–27 = Mark 4:35–41 = Luke 8:22–25) shows that Matthew thought of the group as a "little ship" that is tossed back and forth on a stormy sea, with the disciples pleading, "Save, Lord, we are perishing!" (see exegetical survey on 8:23–9:8 below). Parables indicate that the church was thought to contain both good and evil until the judgment day (13:24–30; 22:1–14; 25:1–13), and statements about the Kingdom of the Son of Man make the same point about the "righteous" and "unrighteous" (13:41; 16:28). The group was apparently disturbed by false prophets (7:15–20) and antinomian Christians (5:17–20; 7:15–20), that is, Christians who were not following the Law, or Torah (antinomian, from Greek *nomos*, "law"). Apparently there was some internal discord about a Matthean faction called the "little ones" and those who caused them to sin (18:6).

In order to deal with outside opponents and inside factionalism, the Matthean writer stresses the Law. He is in sharp opposition to the particular developments going on at the Yavneh Academy. His opposition seems not to be with Yavneh directly, but rather with the Yavneh-influenced synagogue or synagogues in some Gentile city with a strong Jewish element in its population (perhaps Antioch). There are a number of reasons for this widely accepted conclusion. Extremely pertinent is the sharp condemnation of the "the scribes and Pharisees" in Matthew 23. They have correct teaching: "The scribes and the Pharisees sit on Moses' seat; so practice and observe whatever they tell you" (Matt 23:2–3). The passage continues, however, "But not what they do; for they preach, but do not practice." Six times comes the refrain: "Woe to you, scribes and Pharisees, hypocrites!" (23:13, 15, 23, 25, 27, 29) which is joined by "Woe to you blind guides" (23:16). Of them it is said, "So you also outwardly appear righteous to men, but within you are full of hypocrisy and iniquity" (23:28). In other words, Matthew honors the activity of scribes and Pharisees at Yavneh in interpreting the authoritative revelation; his

quarrel with them is about the details of their interpretation and their observance, especially its public display (6:1–18; see Chapter Three). Thus, the heart of
the matter lies in the revelation of the Torah and its authoritative interpretation
by "scribes and Pharisees." For Matthew, the Christian revelation is the Torah as
definitively interpreted by Jesus, and is, indeed, Jesus himself: There remains,
therefore, the further interpretation of this revelation by the Christian equivalent
of "scribes and Pharisees," those who teach.

The conflict with Yavneh-inspired Pharisaism also seems apparent from
Matthew 23:8–10. Here Matthew attributes to Jesus the communal ideal that
Christians in his community should not use the titles of honor known to have
increasing importance among the Pharisees (and some members of the Matthean
community?!) in the post-70 context:

> 8) ". . . you are not to be called rabbi, for you have one teacher and you are
> all students [Greek: brothers]. 9) And call no one your father on earth, for
> you have one Father—the one in heaven. 10) Nor are you to be called
> instructors, for you have one instructor, the Messiah."

We observe, then, the emergence of a distinct group that thinks of itself as being
in competition with the Pharisees, their leadership, and their interpretation of
the Torah.

It is clear that the Matthean objection to emergent Pharisaic leadership
is expressed chiefly in a clash over the right interpretation of the Torah and
its proper observance. For Matthew, Jesus is *the* instructor, *the* teacher, but
more: the very fulfillment of the Torah and the prophets. In a key passage,
most of which is found only in the Gospel of Matthew, 5:17–20, Matthew's
Jesus says,

> 17) "Do not think that I have come to abolish the law or the prophets; I
> have come not to abolish but to fulfill. 18) For truly I tell you, until heaven
> and earth pass away, not one letter, not one stroke of a letter, will pass
> from the law until all is accomplished. 19) Therefore, whoever breaks
> one of the least of these commandments, and teaches others to do the
> same, will be called least in the kingdom of heaven; but whoever does
> them and teaches them will be called great in the kingdom of heaven.
> 20) For I tell you, unless your righteousness exceeds that of the scribes and
> Pharisees, you will never enter the kingdom of heaven."

Matthew, in contrast to the Yavneh Pharisees, claims that the promises of Torah
are fulfilled in Jesus as a new revelation to be further interpreted. Thus, it is necessary to practice a "higher righteousness," that is, an obedience that exceeds that
of the scribes and Pharisees. So Jesus teaches the famous Sermon on the Mount
(Matt 5–7), from which this passage is taken.

Matthew 23:8–10 argues that no one should be called "rabbi," "father," and
"instructor"; it sounds as if there should be no fixed, formal titles of leadership
in the Matthean group. Yet, there were leadership roles with authority and status differentiation in the group. Prophecy and prophets are highly valued (for
example, 10:41; 23:34), and there are warnings against false prophets (7:15–23;
compare 24:11–12, 23–24; compare *Didachē* 11–13). The community had its

scribes (13:52; 23:34) and "wise men" (23:34). Perhaps "righteous men" were also a distinct group (especially 10:41–42; 13:17; 23:29).

In this connection, note that the Gospel of Matthew is the only one of the four gospels to use the word we have also seen in the Pauline writings, **"church"** (Greek: *ekklēsia*). It is found in two places. The first of them, 16:18, occurs in Matthew's version of the turning point in Mark's story, Peter's Confession and the first passion prediction at Caesarea Philippi. In Mark 8:27–9:1, as analyzed in Chapter Nine, we find a tightly structured incident. Following the Two-Source Theory, Matthew significantly alters it, first, by adding the title "Son of God" to Peter's confession that Jesus is "the Messiah" and then by inserting the "blessing of Peter" and the "church" saying, together called the "praise of Peter." The following chart highlights this insertion:

Mark	Matthew	Passage
8:27–29	16:13–16	Peter's confession
———	**16:17**	**Blessing of Peter**
———	**16:18–19**	**Commissioning of Peter as the rock of the church**
8:30	16:20	Command to secrecy
8:31	16:21	First passion prediction
8:32–33	16:22–23	Peter's misunderstanding and Jesus' rebuke
8:34–9:1	16:24–28	Teaching on discipleship

Matthew's insertion reads:

17) And Jesus answered him, "Blessed are you, Simon son of Jonah! For flesh and blood has not revealed this to you, but my Father in heaven.
18) And I tell you, you are "Peter" (Greek *Petros*), and on this rock (Greek *petra*) I will build my church, and the gates of Hades will not prevail against it.
19) I will give you the keys of the kingdom of heaven, and whatever you (sg.) bind on earth shall be bound in heaven, and whatever you (sg.) loose on earth shall be loosed in heaven.

This tradition singles out Simon son of Jonah, gives him a new name, Peter, and makes a play on the name (Greek: *Petros/petra;* also possible in Aramaic: *Kēphas/kēpha;* English: Rocky/rock). It then emphasizes the authority of the church on earth, and stresses that Jesus ascribes honor and authority to Peter (singular tense) in the church. Most critics have taken the power of the "keys" and the binding and loosing statements to refer to honor and authority as it is found in Scriptural (compare Isa 22:22b) and other Jewish, especially Rabbinic, texts. Several possible meanings can occur: authority to teach, to ban or excommunicate and readmit persons to the group, and also to forgive or not forgive sins (compare John 10:23). The passage thus offers clear evidence for a group that sharply defined its boundaries (an "in-group") and its leadership in contrast to the Pharisaic group and its leadership.

Matthew refers again to the word *ekklēsia* in the Jesus' discourse in 18:1–35, this time twice (18:17). The discourse has a core in Mark 9:42–50, but Matthew expands and develops it. Part of what he has added to the section, 18:17, reads:

17) If the member (the one who sins against, literally, "his brother," verse 15a) refuses to listen to them (two or three witnesses, verse 16), tell it to *the church*; and if the offender refuses to listen even to *the church*, let such a one be to you as a Gentile and a tax collector.

This section represents an embryonic order for regulating the life of the Christian group, perhaps to include or exclude "a brother" who has sinned. Matthew then adds a version of the binding and loosing saying found in the above Petrine passage, this time in the plural tense:

18) Truly I tell you (pl.), whatever you (pl.) bind on earth shall be bound in heaven, and whatever you (pl.) loose on earth shall be loosed in heaven.

In this case the plurals show that the authority to "bind" and "loose" previously invested in Peter is now given to the assembled group as a whole. Yet, the general point is similar: the community self-consciously defines itself, now in terms of certain moral norms (sin), and if the offender does not conform, he is banished. Thus, what appears to be a judicial process is in place. Again, hints at an emerging group structure go beyond anything we find in the Gospel of Mark.

There are other aspects of the Matthean community. Note that the above "Praise of Peter" in Matthew counterbalances the rebuke of Peter in Mark (Mark 8:32–33; Matt 16:22–23). This insertion about Peter corresponds to a major change in Matthew's attitude toward the disciples. Whereas in the Markan gospel they are without understanding, there are instances in Matthew where they do understand (for example, 13:51; compare the omission in 14:32 [Mark 6:52]; 17:23 [9:32]), even though they are of portrayed as "men of little faith" (6:30; 8:26; 14:31; 16:8).

Matthew's "rehabilitation" of the disciples is also found in the climax of the gospel. Whereas in Mark the disciples do not get the message of Jesus to return to Galilee, in Matthew we find a crucial passage called the Great Commission (28:16–20). Here the risen Jesus commands his disciples to "make disciples of all nations/Gentiles, teaching them all that I have commanded you" (28:19). Matthew has a deep concern for the mission of the church to the whole world (Greek *ethnē:* "nations" or "Gentiles"), and the disciples are to undertake it. Yet, there are points within the gospel where the Matthean Jesus states that his own mission is only to "the lost sheep of the house of Israel" (10:5; 15:24), that is, among the Jews. Was the Matthean author a Hellenistic Jew or a Gentile interested in Jewish matters? Did Matthew consider himself a Jewish Christian or a Christian Jew? Was his "church" still within the orbit of Judaism, in the process of breaking its ties with Judaism, or now separated from it as a distinctly Christian entity?

The conflicts with a Pharisee-led Judaism influenced by Yavneh, the close contact with Palestinian traditions, Greek as the gospel's original language, and the possibility that Antioch, Syria, is the place of origin, point to the probability that "Matthew" is a Hellenistic or Greek-speaking Jewish Christian. Other features pointed out below suggest that he may be a scribe who, like the scribe he describes, is "trained ['discipled'] for the Kingdom" and is "like a master of a household who brings out of his treasure what is new and what is old" (13:52). If so, he is a Christian scribe who opposes Pharisaic scribes. He also stands in the tradition of the Hellenistic Jewish Christian mission. The author of Luke-Acts also represents the Hellenistic Jewish Christian mission, but where he represents the movement into the Hellenistic world, the evangelist Matthew represents the continuing links with and concern for the Jewish element in the movement.

Was the Matthean "church" still part of Judaism (Christian Judaism), or had it separated from Judaism (Jewish Christianity)? It may be that "formative Judaism" and Matthean Christianity of the Middle Period make this an oversimplified question. It is nonetheless clear that the polemic against Jewish leaders is very strong (Matt 23). It is also clear that the Matthean writer speaks of "their synagogues" (4:23; 9:35; compare 10:7; 28:20). Finally, it is clear that the Matthean writer writes about the Gentile Pilate's confession of innocence (27:24) and follows it with a statement that has left an unspeakable mark on subsequent Jewish-Christian relations: "Then the people as a whole answered, 'His blood be on us and on our children!'" (27:25). While it is possible that such ideas can come from a context of factional disputes within Judaism, we lean toward the view that the Matthean "church" has separated from the synagogue (see below on The Kingdom of Heaven, ethics, and the church).

LANGUAGE, STYLE, AND LITERARY FEATURES OF MATTHEW

Matthew's Greek has been characterized as "synagogue Greek." It is a more polished Greek than the Semitic-sounding Greek of Mark or Q, but it is nonetheless "semitizing," that is, filled with Hebrew/Aramaic idioms characteristic of a bilingual context. Matthew likes parallelisms characteristic of Hebrew poetry, and he stresses the numbers two (for example, many instances of two versions of the same story ["doublets"]), three (temptations [4]; acts of piety [6:1–18]; dwellings [17:4]; denials [26:34,75]) four (four parables about the church [21:28–22:14]), and seven (3 × 14 names in genealogy [1:1–16]; seven parables [13]; seven "woes" [23]). He often repeats key words (for example, "angel of the Lord" [1:18–2:23]; "righteousness" [5–7]) and emphasizes key passages (law [5:17–20]; behavior [12:35–40]). Similarly, he lumps materials with a common theme together (ten miracles in 8–9; parables about Israel and the "church" in 21:28–22:14; the Pharisees in 23; see the five discourses below). Most of his quotations from (what were becoming) the Jewish Scriptures seem to be from the Septuagint, and it has influenced his language, though not his style. His style is meant for teaching: It is very tightly focused, and is characterized by formulas, leading words, leading and concluding verses or sections that frame his materials, and "chiasms" (for example, A, B, C, C ′, B ′, A ′, approximating the Greek letter *chi*, which looks like an "X"). As in the case of leading sentences, in general Matthew likes to anticipate themes that are only gradually developed (for example, 1–4: Jesus is Son of David, Son of God; righteousness; Galilee is the land of the Gentiles). "Framing," or "inclusion," that is, leading and concluding sentences that summarize the material that falls between them, also occur (see below on structure).

Formula Quotations

Matthew has many quotations and allusions to Scripture. Among them are a special series of **"formula quotations,"** usually addressed to the readers by the writer ("asides"; exceptional are 2:5–6, spoken by chief priests and scribes; 13:14–15, spoken by Jesus). These quotations from the Jewish Scriptures are always preceded by a formula, such as "all this took place to fulfill what the Lord had spoken by the prophet," or something similar, and always preceded or followed by the narration of an incident from the life of Jesus in which the Scripture is fulfilled. With exceptions where the formula quotation is cited by persons in the story, they could be removed and the narrative would flow quite nicely. These formula quotations are as follows:

Matthew	Jewish Scripture	Incident from the Life of Jesus
1:22–23	Isa 7:14	The virgin birth
(2:5–6)	Mic 5:1(2)	The birth in Bethlehem
	2 Sam 5:2	
2:15	Hos 11:1	The flight to Egypt
2:17–18	Jer 31:15	The massacre of the innocents
2:23	Unknown; Isa 11:1?	Jesus dwells in Nazareth
4:14–16	Isa 9:1–2	Jesus moves to Capernaum
8:17	Isa 53:4	The healing ministry of Jesus
12:17–21	Isa 42:1–4	The healing ministry of Jesus
13:14–15	Isa 6:9–10	Jesus' reason for parables
13:35	Psa 78:2	Jesus' teaching in parables
21:4–5	Isa 62:11	Jesus' entry into Jerusalem
	Zech 9:9	
27:9–10	Zech 11:12–13	The fate of Judas
	Jer 18:1–13	
	32:6–15	

While most of Matthew's quotations and allusions to Scripture appear to come from the Septuagint, most of the formula quotations do not seem to represent the Septuagint. This observation has led to the highly debated question whether they come from some special source; if so, they should be discussed in the following section on sources. Whatever the origin of the Scriptural quotations themselves, there is strong evidence from vocabulary and style that the Matthean author himself has created the opening formula and, at the very least, has worked over the quotations.

SOURCES AND STRUCTURE OF MATTHEW

Following the Two-Source Theory, much material in the gospel of Matthew comes from three sources: the Gospel of Mark, the sayings source Q, and other oral and written material (Special M). Much of this latter material, however, may have been composed by the author himself.

Many subsections of the gospel are clearly tightly structured. One of the most impressive uses the framing technique (RSV):

4:23:   *And* he *went about all* Galilee,
teaching *in their synagogues and* **preaching** *the gospel of the
kingdom, and* **healing** *every disease and every infirmity* among
the people.

5–7:   The Sermon on the Mount (**teaching and preaching**)
8–9:   the ten-miracle collection: (**healing**)

9:35:   *And* **Jesus** *went about all* the cities and villages,
teaching *in their synagogues and* **preaching** *the gospel of the
kingdom, and* **healing** *every disease and every infirmity.*

Most critics have argued that Matthew has created the Sermon on the Mount largely
from Q and Special M, and that he has created a collection of ten miracles from scattered stories in Mark, sometimes making doublets and creating his own miracle
account. His object may have been to hint at the ten plagues of Moses. Thus, he
has introduced and concluded his collections with essentially the same summary.

The structure of the Matthean gospel as a whole follows the structure of the
gospel of Mark, especially in chapters 3–4 and the second part of the gospel,
chapters 12–28. Thus, some have proposed a geographical outline for Matthew
similar to that found in Mark: After a prologue (1:1–2:23), he takes up the baptism and temptation (3:1–4:11), and then develops Jesus' ministry in Galilee
(4:12–13:58), around Galilee and toward Jerusalem (14:1–20:34), and
Jerusalem (21:1–28:20). Nonetheless, Matthew diverges from the Markan outline considerably. Not only are there additions of material such as the birth stories at the beginning (Matt 1–2) and the resurrection, appearance, and
commissioning scene at the end (Matt 28); there are great divergences in
chapters 5–11.

In addition to geography, one obvious way that Matthew orders his gospel is
in the creation of five major discourses, mainly from Q and Special M. He calls
attention to them by ending each discourse with a formula, "when Jesus finished
these sayings," or the like, as follows (RSV):

Matthew	Subject of Discourse	Formula Ending		
5:1–7:27	Sermon on the Mount	7:28	And when Jesus	finished these sayings
10:5–42	Missionary discourse	11:1	And when Jesus had finished instructing his twelve disciples	
13:1–52	Teaching in parables	13:53	And when Jesus had finished these parables	
18:1–35	Community regulations	19:1	Now when Jesus	finished these sayings
24:3–25:46	Apocalyptic discourse	26:1	When Jesus had finished all these sayings	

The creation of five discourses and their formula endings recalls the five books of
the Torah, and many scholars have accepted the hypothesis that Matthew's Jesus
offers a new Torah. For Matthew, the new revelation fulfills, yet supersedes, the
old. Perhaps he imagines that, as Moses was thought to have taught the old
Torah, Jesus is thought to have taught the new Torah. In any case, this structure
emphasizes Jesus as *the* teacher.

Matthew's creation of the five great discourses and his tendency to
develop **"chiastic" patterns** or **"ring structures"** (A B C B´ A´, and so forth)
have led to the well-known "five-book" structure (B.W. Bacon). It can be
simplified as follows:

Matthew		Content
1–2	A Prologue	Infancy
3–4	B Narrative	First appearance in Galilee
5–7	C *Discourse 1*	*Sermon on the Mount*
8–9	D Narrative	Ten miracle stories
10	E *Discourse 2*	*Mission of the Twelve*
11–12	F Narrative	Growing opposition
13	G *Discourse 3*	*Parables*
14–17	F' Narrative	Miracles and discipleship
18	E' *Discourse 4*	*Community order and discipline*
19–23	D' Narrative	Journey to, and first days in, Jerusalem
24–25	C' *Discourse 5*	*Little apocalypse*
26–27	B' Narrative	Passion story
28	A' Epilogue	Resurrection; Great Commission

This chiastic structure emphasizes alternating discourses, or speeches, and narratives, or stories. It is based on the Markan source by the addition of Q and Special M, it has concluding formulas clearly marking the speeches, and its construction is balanced—indeed, discourses 1 and 5 are longer, discourses 2 and 4 are shorter, almost the same in length. It does seem to highlight the new five-book Torah or Pentateuch and Jesus' role as teacher. It corresponds to many themes in the gospel and fits social historical context nicely. In short, it has much to commend it and has been widely held by scholars.

Yet, it has some problems. Matthew 11 and 23 are not really narratives, but discourses, and there are other minor speeches in narrative sections (for example, 12:25–45; 21:18–22:14). Also, while there are clearly some Moses parallels in Matthew—the slaying of the boy babies (2:16–18), ten miracles (8–9; ten plagues in Egypt), Jesus' exodus from Egypt (2:13–15), revelation on a mountain (5–7; compare Mount Sinai)—one wonders why the Moses typology is not more explicit.

Dissatisfaction with the dominant five-book hypothesis has led to alternative hypotheses. One structure is based on the saying, "from that time on, Jesus began. . ." in Matthew 4:17 and 16:21 (E. Krentz; J. Kingsbury). If the gospel is divided on the basis of this formula, it looks like this:

1. 1:1–4:16   The person of Jesus Messiah
2. 4:17–16:20   The proclamation of Jesus Messiah
3. 16:21–28:20   The suffering, death, and resurrection of Jesus Messiah

From this perspective, Matthew 1:1, "the book of the origin of Jesus Messiah" is a title to the first section, and "from that time on Jesus began . . ." is a title to the second and third sections. Correspondingly, chapters 1–2 (the infancy) are not a preface to the Markan-based story, but are continued directly into chapters 3–4 (baptism, temptation, first appearance in Galilee). The direct flow into chapters 3–4 means that the "Son of God" title in the baptism (3:17 [Mark 1:11]) and temptation stories (4:3, 6) is more dominant in the first section. The second section develops the proclamation about the Kingdom of Heaven, and the third section develops the passion.

This structure has gained a number of adherents. It is more congenial to Christology, Matthew's view of history (see below, "salvation history"), and a literary analysis of the gospel as a continuous, unified story, or narrative. A distinct weakness of the theory is that "from that time on Jesus began . . ." does not seem to make the crucial break that the structure demands. Also, if Matthew is a redaction of Mark, a gospel that has no infancy, it is difficult to deny that the Matthean author has prefaced a story about the adult Jesus with a quite distinct account of his infancy, thus producing a natural break between chapters 2 and 3.

The fact that Matthew follows Mark closely after chapter 12 and has many repetitive formulas (not only 4:17 and 16:21) without always making striking demarcations of divisions may mean that the connected narrative story itself, not a hypothetical outline, is most important. If the author did intend to present an overall structure, as he surely does in subdivisions, one can only conclude that he must have tired of making his structural rearrangements in the latter part of the story.

Given all the difficulties—and recognizing both the story quality of the gospel and at the same time its stress on Jesus as teaching the new revelation, indeed being the new revelation—we propose an outline whose subdivisions will attempt to account for several of the features noted above. A simplified view of this structure, which also has its problems, looks like this:

1. **Introduction, 1:1–4:16** The origins: Jesus as the new revelation of God.

2. **The ministry of Jesus to Israel, 4:17–13:58** As the new revelation of God, Jesus fulfills the old revelation and hence, fittingly comes first to the people of God, whose leaders nevertheless oppose him.

3. **The ministry of Jesus to his disciples, 14:1–20:34** In the face of opposition, Jesus continues to minister to Israel but turns his attention more and more to his disciples and prepares them for their work in the world.

4. **Jesus in Jerusalem, 21:1–25:46** The drama approaches its climax as Jesus confronts the Jewish leaders and teaches his disciples concerning the final judgment.

5. **The passion, resurrection, and Great Commission, 26:1–28:20** The drama reaches its climax in the passion and resurrection of Jesus and in his commissioning of his disciples. This mission, which is sporadically anticipated, is to all the nations.

EXEGETICAL SURVEY OF THE GOSPEL OF MATTHEW

Introduction, 1:1–4:16

1:1–17 GENEALOGY.

"An account of the genealogy of Jesus the Messiah, the son of David, the son of Abraham," is the superscription of the first section, but especially the genealogy (see Gen 5:1 LXX). In the Psalms of Solomon 17 (ca. 63 B.C.E.) and among the Jewish rabbis, Son of David became a favorite title for the expected Messiah. It emphasized the Messiah's descent from David and his coming as fulfilling God's promise to David in 2 Samuel 7. Matthew, in dialogue with formative Judaism, uses the title frequently of Jesus (1:1; 9:27; 12:23; 15:22; 20:30; 21:9, 15; 22:42, 45), strengthening the claim that Jesus is the Jewish Messiah, but doing so in relation to Jesus' miracle working. The genealogy traces the descent of Jesus back through the royal line of King David to Abraham, the father of the Jewish people, to whom was also given the promise of becoming the father of many nations (Gen 17:4). It is divided into three divisions of fourteen names (the numerical value of the Hebrew consonants of David's name is fourteen (D = 4; V = 6; D = 4). Matthew stresses Jesus' significance as the fulfillment of the Jewish heritage and anticipates the Great Commission of Jesus to the disciples to go to all nations (28:19).

1:18–2:23 THE BIRTH AND INFANCY OF JESUS.

Each sequence in the story fulfills Scripture, for example, virgin birth (LXX Isa 7:14); Bethlehem birth (Mic 5:2; 2 Sam 5:2); flight into and return from Egypt (Hos 11:1); weeping over slaying of infants (Jer 31:15); the residence in Nazareth ("He shall be called a Nazorean," a prophecy not explicitly found in the Jewish Scriptures; compare Isa 11:1; Judg 13). This is the heaviest concentration of "formula quotations" (five). Matthew's flight-to-Egypt story allows him to stress the exodus theme through a formula quotation: as Israel (= God's son) had come out of Egypt, so now Jesus as God's son (Hos 11:1; "Out of Egypt I have called my son"). The "Son of God" idea will be important in the upcoming baptism and temptation stories.

3:1–4:16 THE PRELUDE TO THE MINISTRY.

3:1–6 John the Baptist in the wilderness (= Mark 1:1–6; Q 3:2–4 [in part]?). Matthew brings John the Baptist into close contact with Jesus, giving him exactly the same message as Jesus (3:2 = 4:17) and making his ministry also a fulfillment of prophecy. As Jesus' immediate precursor, he shares in the act of fulfillment. He is portrayed in terms reminiscent of the description of Elijah in 2 Kings 1:8.

3:7–10 John's warning to Pharisees and Sadducees (= Q 3:7–9). Matthew depicts the leaders of Israel as a homogenous group, a united front opposed to Jesus; in this passage they are opposed to John, whom Matthew closely links with Jesus. John's language here is echoed by Jesus in 7:16—20 and 12:33.

3:11–12 John predicts the coming of Jesus (= Mark 1:7–8; Q 3:17). These verses reflect the Christians' belief that their baptism is superior to John's. The idea of the separation of the good from the evil at the last judgment is dominant in Jesus' eschatological teaching in Matthew 24–25. Matthew is further paralleling John the Baptist and Jesus. This part of John's message has no parallel in Mark.

3:13–17 The baptism of Jesus (= Mark 1:9–11; Q 3:21–22?). Although Matthew carefully parallels John the Baptist and Jesus in several ways, he also carefully subordinates John to Jesus by adding verses 14–15, which have no parallel in his source, the gospel of Mark. "Righteousness," a favorite term of Matthew's (compare especially 5:17–20), is introduced; the theme of Jesus' sonship is expressed through a combination of words from Psalm 2:7 and Isaiah 42:1.

4:1–11 **The temptation of Jesus** (= Mark 1:12–13). Mark 1:12–13 simply mentions the temptation of Jesus in the wilderness, while but both Matthew and Luke share a tradition (Q 4:1–13) in which Jesus meets the temptations by quoting Deuteronomy (Matt 4:4 = Q 4:4: Deut 8:3; Matt 4:7 = Q 4:12: Deut 6:16; Matt 4:10 = Q 4:8: Deut 6:13). The passages in Deuteronomy reflect the Jewish interpretation of their people's journey through the wilderness as a test by God to determine their fitness to inherit the Promised Land (Deut 8:2–3). Again, Jesus, like Israel before him, is identified as Son of God (4:3, 6).

4:12–16 **Jesus goes to Galilee and begins to preach** (= Mark 1:14). Verse 14 introduces Matthew's sixth formula quotation (Isa 9:1–2), which identifies Galilee as "Galilee of the Gentiles," apparently anticipating the church's mission to all nations (28:16–20). *The preliminaries are complete; the new revelation can now begin.*

The New Revelation: The Ministry of Jesus to Israel, 4:17–13:58

4:17 JESUS' CENTRAL KINGDOM PROCLAMATION AND REVELATION (= MARK 1:15).
"From that time on . . ." (RSV) marks a temporal division (16:21 RSV). Jesus takes up the message that John had proclaimed (3:2).

4:18–22 THE CALL OF THE FOUR FISHERMEN (= MARK 1:16–20).
The ministry begins with the challenge to "follow" Jesus, as it will end on the note of "Go therefore and make disciples . . ." (28:19). Note that Matthew does not call them "disciples" until 5:1 when they begin to listen to the teaching.

4:23–25 SUMMARY OF THE CHARACTERISTIC ACTIVITY OF THE MINISTRY (= MARK 1:39).
As noted above, verse 23 is a framing summary stressing teaching, preaching the good news of the kingdom, and healing every disease and infirmity; after a section on teaching (5–7) and healing (8–9), Matthew repeats essentially the same summary (9:35).

5:1–7:27 THE FIRST BOOK OF THE NEW REVELATION: THE SERMON ON THE MOUNT.
This takes place on a mountain, whereas the comparable discourse in Luke is on a plain (compare Luke 6:17, 20–49). Matthew is stressing the parallel to Moses receiving the Torah on a mountain, the previous revelation now being superseded (Exod 19:36). The first book of the new revelation concerns the personal aspects of Christian piety and behavior.

5:3–12 **The Beatitudes** (= Q 6:20b–23). "Blessed" in the sense used here refers to the fortunate, happy condition of a person blessed by God. The reference is to the blessed conditions that will obtain after Jesus has returned as Son of Man. These are eschatological blessings, and Matthew is using them to set the whole teaching in the context of eschatological expectation.

5:13–16 **Salt and light: the disciples' special status** (= Q 14:34–35; 11:33).

5:17–20 **The essential nature of Christian faith: obedience to the new revelation.** This is a key passage in Matthew's gospel (see above); it expresses the evangelist's understanding of the essence of Christian faith: obedience to the new revelation as it is interpreted by the Christian equivalent of "scribes and Pharisees." In Judaism, obedience to the revelation in the Torah was expressed by the concept of righteousness. Righteousness was the quality of obedience one must have achieved to be able to stand before God, and the righteous are those who have achieved it. For Matthew the quality of the Christian's obedience to the new revelation must exceed that of the scribes and Pharisees to the old. By this means they will "enter the Kingdom of Heaven," that is, enter into that state of blessedness Jesus will establish for the righteous when he comes as Son of Man.

5:21–48 The antitheses (partial parallels only in Mark and Luke; Q 6:27–38). In a series of six antitheses, Matthew expresses aspects of the new revelation in contrast to the old (" formula:") "You have heard that it was said [to those of ancient times], but I say to you . . . ." In each instance the new is either radicalizing (Nos. 1,2,6) or an annulment (Nos. 3,4,5) of the old.

6:1–18 Instruction on almsgiving, prayer, and fasting (Matt 6:9–13 = Q 11:2–4). Almsgiving, prayer, and fasting are forms of Jewish piety independent of the Temple. Even while the Temple stood the Pharisees emphasized them, and after its destruction they developed them still further. Matthew speaks here in dialogue with the developments going on at Yavneh, and his acrimonious tone indicates its intensity. Matthew is close enough to the Pharisees to quarrel violently with them and denounce them vigorously. Note his constant use of the epithet "hypocrites," which occurs as a refrain throughout the denunciation of the "scribes and Pharisees" in Matthew 23. For the Lord's Prayer (Matt 6:9–13 = Q 11:2–4), see Chapter One.

6:19–34 Various images describing the truly righteous person.

7:1–12 Various maxims illustrating the new righteousness.

7:13–27 Warnings designed to stress the necessity for obedience to the new revelation. These warnings constitute the ending to the Sermon. They end it on a note of eschatology, as the Beatitudes had begun it on a similar note.

7:28—29 CONTAINS THE FORMULA ENDING TO THE FIRST BOOK OF THE NEW REVELATION.

8:1–9:34 THE TEN MIRACLES OF JESUS.

Matthew characteristically arranges his material in blocks. He follows his first revelatory discourse with a block of ten miracle stories interwoven with teaching on discipleship. In 4:23 and 9:35 the summaries of the characteristic activity of Jesus' ministry stress healing, and nine of the ten miracles are healing miracles. The collection of ten miracles perhaps recalls the ten plagues of Moses in Egypt (Exodus 7:8–11:10). In general, Matthew transforms the miracles by omitting narrative detail and introducing or expanding dialogues.

8:1–17 The first three healings: the leper, the centurion's servant, and Peter's mother-in-law. In Matthew 8:17 the seventh formula quotation (Isa 53:4) stresses the healing focus of Jesus' ministry. The faith of the centurion, a Gentile, is emphasized.

8:18–22 First discipleship section: sayings on discipleship (Matt 8:19–21 = Q 9:57–59). "I will follow..." sets the stage for stilling the storm.

8:23–9:8 The second three miracles: the stilling of the storm, the healing of the demoniac, and the cure of the paralytic. The stilling of the storm deserves special comment because here we see Matthew's own understanding most clearly. Matthew's source is the account of the same miracle in Mark 4:35–41, and it is instructive to observe his redaction of that source. In Mark the story has the natural form of a miracle: Jesus and his disciples embark in a boat, accompanied by other boats; a great storm arises; the disciples appeal to Jesus, and he calms the storm. The following dialogue ends on a note of wonder. In Matthew there is no mention of any other boats; the context is the disciples' "following." The dialogue takes place *before* the storm is calmed, and Jesus is addressed as "Lord" (Mark: "teacher"); he in turn addresses the disciples as "men of little faith," a frequent reproach by Jesus in this gospel (6:30; 14:31; 16:8; 17:20), and only in this gospel. Matthew has redacted the traditional miracle story to make it an allegory of the church. The one boat is the little ship of the church, beset by the storms of persecution, and the disciples are the members of the church who follow but fail because of their "little faith" and need the presence of their Lord to help them, which presence they have.

9:9–17 Second section on discipleship: the call of Matthew, eating with "tax collectors and sinners," fasting. Eating with "tax collectors and sinners" is important in the Hellenistic Jewish Christian mission because in Palestine they were ostracized and treated as Gentiles. Since table fellowship between Jews and Gentiles was a major problem in the Christian mission, Jesus' attitude to "tax collectors and sinners" was for Matthew an important aspect of teaching on discipleship. Fasting was also important because it was a form of piety stressed by the Pharisees (compare 6:16–18).

9:18–34 The last four healings: the ruler's daughter and the woman with a hemorrhage, the two blind men, the dumb man. (Mark 5:21; 10:46–52; compare Matt 20:29–34).

9:35–38 SUMMARY OF THE CHARACTERISTIC ACTIVITY OF THE MINISTRY (9:37 = Q 10:2).

Matthew has inherited from Mark 6:6b–11 an account of a teaching journey by Jesus, followed by the commissioning of "the twelve" for a missionary journey. The teaching journey further summarizes the activities characteristic of Jesus' ministry—preaching, teaching, and healing (9:35; compare 4:23).

10:1–10:42 THE SECOND BOOK OF THE NEW REVELATION: THE MISSIONARY DISCOURSE.

The commissioning of "the Twelve" becomes the occasion for the second revelatory discourse. The discourse itself (10:5–42) contains originally disparate elements from Mark and mainly Q. Matthew 10:5–6 reflects the Christian mission to the Jews rather than the Hellenistic Jewish Christian mission. In 10:7 Matthew gives to the disciples the exact proclamation of Jesus (4:17) and John the Baptist (3:2). John the Baptist, Jesus, and now the Christian church are the succession of the new revelation. Notice, however, that the disciples are *not* commissioned to teach, as they are when the revelation is complete. Matthew 10:9–16 seems to be a development from some traditional handbook for the missionaries of the Hellenistic Jewish Christian mission, since Luke 10:4–12 has a similar set of instructions. They are similar to Cynic virtues.

11:1 CONTAINS THE FORMULA ENDING TO THE SECOND BOOK OF THE NEW REVELATION.

11:2–12:50 OPPOSITION BY LEADERS; THE PEOPLE'S LACK OF UNDERSTANDING.

Matthew ends his account of the mission of Jesus to Israel by focusing attention on Jesus himself, developing a Christology, and interweaving with it an account of the opposition by leaders and the people's lack of understanding. It is a skillful blend of Jesus as the Jewish Messiah and the difficulties he faced among the Jews themselves.

11:2–6 John the Baptist's question (= Q 7:18–23). Jesus is the Christ (Messiah), as his ministry testifies.

11:7–15 Jesus' testimony to John (= Q 7:24–28; 16:16). John is the Elijah expected by the Jews to come as the forerunner to the Messiah.

11:16–19 Parable of the Children in the Market Place (= Q 7:31–35). Neither John the Baptist nor Jesus has been recognized or accepted by "this generation" (compare 12:38–39).

11:20–24 Woes on the Galilean cities (= Q 10:13–15). The cities that have rejected Jesus will be judged accordingly.

11:25–30 The "thunderbolt from the Johannine sky" (= Q 10:21–22). These verses are astonishing, because their style is associated with the gospel of John rather than Matthew. Yet they represent a major Matthean christological statement: Jesus is the revealer of knowledge of God, a knowledge that he reveals to his intimates. "Yoke" is a metaphor much used by the Jewish rabbis of joyful but difficult obedience to the Law, the "yoke of the Torah." Matthew 11:25–30 therefore contrasts the burden of the old revelation to the ease and joy of the new.

12:1–14 Jesus in controversy with Pharisees (= Mark 2:23–28; 3:1–6). Matthew gives two stories of Jesus in controversy with Pharisees, taken from a collection of five such stories in Mark 2:1–3:6. He had given the three others earlier (9:1–8, 11–13, 16–17), interpreting them as dealing mainly with discipleship.

12:15–21 Jesus as servant of God. A further christological statement is made by the eighth formula quotation.

12:22–24 A healing and two reactions (= Mark 3:19b–22). A healing evokes two reactions: The crowd raises the question whether Jesus might not be the Son of David; the Pharisees denounce him as an emissary of Beelzebub.

12:25–37 Jesus denounces the Pharisees (= Mark 3:23–30). The opposition between Jesus and the Pharisees sharpens. Matthew expands and intensifies the tone of his Markan source.

12:38–42 The sign of Jonah (= Q 11:29–32). Jesus rejects a Pharisaic request for a sign that would vindicate his authority and denounces "this evil and adulterous generation." The sign will be the sign of Jonah; that is, Jesus' resurrection will be his vindication over "this generation" that rejected him.

12:43–45 Further denunciation of "this generation" (= Q 11:24–26).

12:46–50 The true family of Jesus (= Q 8:19–21). Matthew stresses, in contrast to the crowds' misunderstanding, that the true family of Jesus consists of those like the disciples who accepted him and his revelation.

13:1–52 THE THIRD BOOK OF THE NEW REVELATION: THE PARABLES OF THE KINGDOM.

Like Mark, Matthew has a collection of parables, but he increases their number and makes special use of them. He has just called attention to the true family of Jesus as those who accept his revelation. Now Jesus addresses the parables of the Sower, the Weeds, the Mustard Seed, and the Leaven to "the crowds" (13:1–33). Jesus then turns to the "disciples," the true family, and gives them the explanation of the Weeds and the parables of the Pearl and the Net.

13:1–35 The Sower, Weeds, Mustard Seed, and Leaven. The Sower (13:1–9) with its explanation (13:18–23 = Mark 4:19, 13–20) interprets the ministry of Jesus as rejection and acceptance. The intercalated verses (10–17 = Mark 4:10–12) contrast those who accept Jesus with those who reject him, and it adds the ninth formula quotation (Isa 6:9–10). The parable of the Weeds (13:24–30) continues the theme of acceptance and rejection, this time in the context of the coming "harvest," that is, final judgment of God. The parables of the Mustard Seed (13:31–32 = Mark 4:30–32 = Luke 13:18–19) and the Leaven (13:33 = Luke 13:20–21) in Matthew's context and use are means of interpreting the rejection of Jesus and of holding out the hope of ultimate acceptance, if not by all the Jews then certainly by the rest of the world at large. 13:34–35 contains the tenth formula quotation (Ps 78:12).

13:36–50 Interpretation of the Weeds; the Treasure in the Field, the Pearl, and the Net. Matthew 13:36 shifts from the crowds to the disciples. In this new context the parable of the Weeds is interpreted as an allegory of the earthly ministry of Jesus as Son of Man and of his coming apocalyptic judgment. Notice the Matthean promise of blessing to "the righteous" in verse 43, and compare it with 5:20. In Matthew, the parables of the Treasure in the Field and the Pearl refer to the blessing that awaits the righteous, those who accept Jesus' revelation and obey it. The parable of the Net is a restatement of Matthew's characteristic view of the judgment that will separate the evil from the righteous.

13:51–52 The Christian scribe. As a climax to his parable chapter, Matthew adds this description of the ideal of acceptance and obedience, the scribe "trained for the kingdom of heaven." This is a reasonably good description of the author of Matthew's gospel.

13:53 CONTAINS THE FORMULA ENDING OF THE THIRD BOOK OF THE NEW REVELATION.

13:54–58 THE CLIMACTIC REJECTION.
Matthew follows his third revelatory discourse with the theme that Jesus is not honored "in his own country and in his own house," and because of lack of belief, he is not able to work many miracles.

The New Revelation: Jesus Instructs His Disciples, 14:1–20:34

The ministry to Israel now having reached the climax in the inability of Jesus to find faith among "his own," Matthew turns to the second stage of the new revelation, which occurs in the relationship between Jesus and his disciples.

14:1–16:12 PRELIMINARY INSTRUCTION.

In this section Matthew is closely following his source, the gospel of Mark.

14:1–12 The death of John the Baptist (= Mark 6:14–29). Matthew abbreviates the story as it occurs in Mark, and he subordinates other elements in the story to his theme of John's death being the occasion for the withdrawal of Jesus with his disciples.

14:13–21 The withdrawal of Jesus and the feeding of the Five Thousand (= Mark 6:30–44). Matthew is still abbreviating Mark's narrative in the interest of his withdrawal theme. Jesus, having compassion on the crowds, heals them and feeds them. In Matthew 14:19 the disciples play more of an intermediary role than they do in Mark 6:41; they are becoming the church that mediates the sacraments.

14:22–33 The walking on the water (= Mark 6:45–52). Again Matthew is abbreviating Mark, in this instance to make room for the redactional insertion of the incident of Peter also walking on the water (Matt 14:28–31). Peter becomes a paradigm of the disciple who has "little faith" and so needs the help of his "Lord"; compare 8:23–27, another sea miracle. Matthew ends the account with a formal confession of Jesus as the Son of God (verse 33). In Matthew's thinking, the story has become a paradigm of the relationship between Jesus and his followers in the Christian church, and so a formal confession is in place here.

14:34–36 Healings at Genneseret (= Mark 6:53–56).

15:1–20 Dispute with "scribes and Pharisees" about the tradition of the elders (= Mark 7:1–23). In the dispute with the scribes and Pharisees Matthew is following Mark, but he uses it as a starting point for instruction of the disciples.

15:21–39 A group of three miracles (= Mark 7:24–8:10) becomes two and a summary. Matthew is still following Mark closely, shortening somewhat as he goes. Jesus claims he was sent only to the lost sheep of the house of Israel (compare 10:6), but he nevertheless heals a Gentile woman because of her faith (compare 8:10, the centurion). The crowds glorify the God of Israel in response to Jesus' healing, that is, Matthew has created a summary (15:29–31) from Mark's healing of the deaf mute (7:31–37). Jesus has compassion on the crowds and feeds the Four Thousand, the disciples again acting as intermediaries (compare 14:13–21). The one real change is that a healing of a deaf mute in Mark 7:31–37 is generalized into a healing of many sick persons in Mathew 15:29–31.

16:1–4 The sign of Jonah (= Mark 8:11–13). This is another version of the pericope found earlier in the gospel (12:38–40). Matthew has added verses 2–3, taken from Q (Q 12:54–56), and the reference to Jonah. He also has the request coming from "Pharisees and Sadducees" (Mark: "Pharisees"), indicating further opposition from the Jewish leaders (compare 3:7).

16:5–12 Warning against the teaching of Pharisees and Sadducees (= Mark 8:14–21). Again from Mark, with "Pharisees and Sadducees" substituted for Mark's "Pharisees and Herod" (16:6; compare 16:11, 12; 16:1).

16:13–17:27 THIS SECTION IS MATTHEW'S EQUIVALENT OF MARK 8:27–9:32.

16:13–28 Caesarea Philippi (= Mark 8:27–9:1). We pointed out earlier that Matthew adds the blessing and commissioning of Peter to the narrative in Mark 8:27–9:1. Further changes are the addition of "and then he will repay everyone for what he has done" (verse 27) and the modification of Mark's "before they see the Kingdom of God come with power" to "before they see the Son of Man coming in his Kingdom." These changes transform the Markan understanding of discipleship as preparedness to accept suffering as one followed Jesus to his Cross and awaited the parousia, into the Matthean form of discipleship as living the life of obedience to the new revelation in the church until the coming of Jesus as Son of Man. Note the key temporal marker, "From that time on Jesus began . . ." (16:21) discussed above.

17:1–8 The transfiguration (= Mark 9:2–8). This reproduces Mark with the significant addition of verses 6–7, where Jesus reassures the disciples who are afraid. We saw in 8:23–27 and 14:22–33 that this is a very important theme to Matthew, representing his understanding of the reality of life in the church. Matthew keeps Mark's theme of Jesus' divine sonship.

17:9–13 The coming of Elijah (= Mark 9:9–13). Matthew adds his verse 13 to Mark's narrative, stressing the identification of John the Baptist and Elijah.

17:14–20 The healing of the epileptic boy (Mark 9:14–29). Matthew shortens Mark's narrative to make room for verse 20, which introduces another of his favorite themes, the disciple in the church as a man of little faith (see also 6:30; 8:26; 14:31; 16:8).

17:22–23 The second prediction (= Mark 9:30–32). Matthew abbreviates the prediction and then breaks up the highly structured Markan prediction unit by introducing his fourth revelatory discourse.

17:24–27 The temple tax. An early Christian legend, reproduced here by Matthew because it features the prominence of Peter, the foundation stone of the church, in verse 24.

18:1–35 THE FOURTH BOOK OF THE NEW REVELATION: CHRISTIAN COMMUNITY REGULATIONS.

In this discourse Matthew follows Mark where he can, but he adds material from Q and special material of his own to make the whole a revelatory discourse.

18:1–5 Greatness in the Kingdom (= Mark 9:33–36; 10:15; 9:37). Matthew uses the latter part of Mark's second prediction unit to introduce the discourse.

18:6–9 On temptations (= Mark 9:42–48).

18:10–14 The parable of the Lost Sheep. Matthew interprets the "little ones" of Mark 9:42 as members of the Christian community and then uses the parable of the Lost Sheep to reassure them that God will take care of them. The parable has a quite different application in Luke 15:3–7.

18:15–22 Two community regulations. In verses 15–20 Matthew greatly expands a saying from Q (Q 17:3) by adding references to the need for witnesses to the church, to the authority of the church (18:18 = 16:19), and to the promise of the presence of the risen Lord in the church. All told, 18:15–20 is a major Matthean statement about the church. In verses 21–22 Matthew reproduces a regulation concerning the necessity for reconciliation within the community from Q (Q 17:4).

18:23–35 The parable of the Unmerciful Servant. Matthew brings his discourse to a close by using the parable of the Unmerciful Servant to reinforce the regulation concerning the necessity for reconciliation within the Christian community. Note the characteristic emphasis on the eschatological judgment in verse 35.

(19:1a CONTAINS THE FORMULA ENDING OF THE FOURTH BOOK OF THE NEW REVELATION.)

19:1–20:34 THE JOURNEY TO JERUSALEM.

After concluding his revelatory discourse. Matthew resumes his close following of Mark as he portrays the journey of Jesus from Galilee to Jerusalem. As in Mark, the journey features teaching on discipleship, and the differences reflect the different understandings of discipleship by Matthew and Mark.

19:1–12 Marriage and divorce (= Mark 10:1–12; compare Matt 5:31–32). Matthew now gives his characteristic formula for ending a discourse and then goes on to shorten, then extend, a pericope from Mark as a community regulation on marriage and divorce. Note the addition of "except for unchastity" in verse 9, which seems to bring the teaching into line with that of the strictest Jewish rabbi of the period (Rabbi Shammai), and the addition of verses 10–12, introducing the note of "celibacy" into the life of the church.

19:13–15 The blessing of the children (= Mark 10:13–16).

19:16–30 The rich young man (= Mark 10:17–31). The Markan incident is made into a community regulation by the addition of verse 28, which introduces the eschatological promise for those who will accept the challenge to leave all for the sake of discipleship.

20:1–16 The parable of the Laborers in the Vineyard. Matthew inserts this parable into the Markan narrative to illustrate the theme of the reversal of values in the coming Kingdom of the Son of Man (verse 16; compare 19:30). But the parable fits that purpose uneasily, and it is an example steadfastly resisting an attempt to serve a later and different context.

20:17–28 The third prediction unit: prediction-misunderstanding-teaching (= Mark 10:32–45). This essentially reproduces Mark's third prediction unit. In our discussion of the gospel of Mark we saw how carefully structured were the three prediction units (Mark 8:27–9:1; 9:32–37; 10:32–45) with their constant theme of prediction-misunderstanding-teaching on discipleship. Matthew broke up the first two by various insertions, but he left the third practically intact. Even in Mark the third unit has what are to all intents and purposes Christian community regulations (Mark 10:42–44); so as it stands the narrative serves Matthew's particular purpose.

20:29–34 The healing at Jericho (= Mark 10:46–52). In Mark this is a transitional giving-of-sight pericope, but Matthew simply reproduces it with a characteristic doubling of the healing as blind Bartimaeus becomes two blind men. Matthew is fond of healings in pairs (8:28–34; 9:27–31). Note the address "Son of David."

Jesus in Jerusalem, 21:1–25:46

This section narrates Jesus' activity in Jerusalem before the beginning of the passion itself. For the most part Matthew follows Mark 11:1–13:37, but with some very significant changes and additions.

21:1–23:39 THE FINAL CLASH BETWEEN JESUS AND THE JEWISH LEADERS.

21:1–11 The entry (= Mark 11:1–10). Matthew follows Mark in the main, but he adds the eleventh formula quotation in verses 45 and changes one animal to two to make the narration agree exactly with his own understanding of the quotation.

21:12–17 Jesus in the Temple (= Mark 11:11a, 15–19, 11b). Mark intercalates the cleansing of the Temple into the fig tree incident to interpret the cleansing by means of the fig tree. Matthew has no such purpose; so he restores what must have been the original unity of the cleansing. Note that verses 14–16 have no parallel in Mark; they represent Matthew's characteristic emphasis on the healing ministry of Jesus. The children respond to Jesus' healing with the same cry as that found in the entry scene, "Hosanna to the Son of David!" This arouses official indignation.

21:18–22 The fig tree incident (= Mark 11:12–14, 20–25). What in Mark had been a testimony to the judgment of God on the Temple and a way of coming to terms with the fact of its destruction becomes in Matthew an example of the power of faith.

21:23–27 The question of Jesus' authority (= Mark 11:27–33). This follows Mark in narrating a clash between Jesus and the Jewish authorities.

21:28–32 The parable of the Two Sons. The true son of God is he who accepts Jesus as his revelation (Matt 21:31–32 = Q 7:29–30).

21:33–46 The parable of the Wicked Tenants (= Mark 12:1–12). In the main this follows Mark, but the addition of verse 43 stresses that the Christians and not the Jews are now the heirs of God.

22:1–14 The parable of the Marriage Feast (= Q 14:16–24). Matthew interprets the parable as testimony that after the Jews rejected Jesus and killed him, the heritage passed to the Christians. But even the Christian must have the wedding garment of true obedience. Note the allegorical reference to the destruction of Jerusalem in 70 C.E. (22:7).

22:15–46 Four questions in dispute between Jesus and his opponents (= Mark 12:13–37). Matthew now follows Mark in narrating four questions that cause disputes between Jesus and the Jewish leaders: tribute to Caesar, the resurrection, the Great Commandment, and David's son. In the first three, leaders challenge Jews to respond; in the last, Jesus challenges the lenders to respond. Since his source already had a strong element of conflict between Jesus and his Jewish opponents, Matthew engages in no extensive redaction, except that he omits the sympathetic answer of the scribe and Jesus' praise of him in Mark 12:32–34. He then places the concluding remark at the end of the question about David's Son (22:46) and thereby formally brings to an end all debate between Jesus and his opponents. The rejection is complete and the conflict over; there remains now only the working out of the consequences.

23:1–36 The woes against the Pharisees. Mark 12:38–40 has a warning against the scribes; in Matthew it becomes a carefully organized diatribe against his opponents, the scribes and Pharisees at Yavneh, and their influence. It is not their *function* he is against, very much to the contrary, but their practice.

23:37–39 The lament over Jerusalem (= Q 13:34–35). This is a Christian lament over Jerusalem that interprets its destruction as the judgment of God for its rejection of his emissaries and which anticipates a restoration at the parousia. A saying developed in the church to help Christians come to terms with the destruction of Jerusalem, it is used by both Matthew and Luke.

24:1–25:46 THE FIFTH BOOK OF THE NEW REVELATION: THE APOCALYPTIC DISCOURSE.

The apocalyptic discourse proper, Matthew 24:1–36, in the main follows Mark 13:1–32. But Matthew omits Mark's ending of the discourse and goes on to add apocalyptic teaching that he takes from Q (Matt 24:37–51 = Q 17:26–27, 34–35; 12:39–40, 42–46) and then a series of parables (the Ten Maidens [Special M], Talents [Q 19:12–27], Last Judgment [Special M]). All three imply the delay of the parousia. As Matthew interprets them, the first two are concerned with the coming of the Son of Man and his judgment (25:13, 29–30), and the third describes that judgment. The third parable, the Last Judgment, is the last element of the teaching of Jesus in the gospel, and it sums up many prominent themes: the need for "righteousness" to enter the Kingdom; righteousness consisting of an obedience expressed in deeds; the fact that the Son of Man will repay everyone according to his deeds; the need for mercy, especially to those who are weak. It is thus a fitting climax to Matthew's presentation of the teaching of Jesus.

(26:1 CONTAINS THE FORMULA ENDING OF THE FIFTH BOOK OF THE NEW REVELATION.)

The Passion, Resurrection, and Great Commission, 26:1–28:20

26:1–27:66 THE PASSION AND DEATH OF JESUS.

In his account of the passion and death of Jesus Matthew follows Mark closely, with only minor redactional changes. We follow our division of the Markan narrative.

> **26:1–16 The introduction (= Mark 14:1–11).** An important change here is the introduction of a fourth passion prediction in verse 2, which links the narrative more closely to the previous teaching of Jesus.
>
> **26:17–29 Jesus' last meal with his disciples (= Mark 14:12–25).** Mark does not identify the betrayer until the Gethsemane scene (14:43); Matthew indicates who it is here (26:25).
>
> **26:30–35 Prediction of the flight of the disciples and the betrayal by Peter (= Mark 14:26–31).**
>
> **26:36–56 The betrayal and the arrest (= Mark 14:32–52).** Matthew makes minor editorial changes that heighten the theme of the fulfillment of Scripture: adding verses 52–54 and rewriting verse 56 (= Mark 14:49b) to read, "But all this has taken place, so that the scriptures of the prophets may be fulfilled."
>
> **26:57–75 Betrayal by Peter and intercalated account of the night trial before the Sanhedrin (= Mark 14:53–72).** The only significant change is that Matthew edits the dialogue between Jesus and the High Priest to make it a formal statement of the person of Jesus before the spiritual head of Judaism: "I put you under oath before the living God, tell us . . . You have said so . . ." (verses 63–64).

27:1–2 Jesus is delivered to Pilate (= Mark 15:1).

27:3–10 The fate of Judas. Only Matthew has this narrative of the fate of Judas as fulfilling a formula quotation (Zech 11:12–13; compare Matt 26:15).

27:11–66 The trial before Pilate and the crucifixion (= Mark 15:2–47). Matthew introduces several editorial changes in this narrative. In verse 19 he emphasizes the innocence of Jesus, and hence by implication, the guilt of the Jews, and in verses 24–25 he makes the guilt of the Jews explicit. In verse 43 he uses Psalm 22:8 to add to a narrative already saturated with allusions to that psalm. Then in verses 52–53 he inserts a whole series of supernatural events, including a temporary resurrection of "the saints" to stress the fact that God is at work in these events and that new life will emerge from the death of Jesus. Finally, in verses 62–66 he adds the incident of the guard at the tomb. This is a late composition, very probably by Matthew himself, designed to forestall a possible claim that the resurrection was a lie because the disciples had stolen the body of Jesus.

28:1–20 THE RESURRECTION OF JESUS AND THE GREAT COMMISSION.

At this point Matthew begins to go beyond Mark, necessarily so since Mark has no account of the resurrection as such, only of the women at the tomb.

28:1–10 The empty tomb (= Mark 16:18). The main changes here are that additional verses 24 further emphasize the supernatural nature of these events, and in verses 9–10 Matthew goes beyond the Markan ending to provide an appearance of Jesus and an explicit command of the risen Lord himself for the disciples to go into Galilee.

28:11–15 The report of the guard. This is a narrative loaded with anti-Jewish polemic. See 27:62–66 above.

28:16–20 The Great Commission. This climax to the gospel of Matthew relates the intended reader to what the gospel has narrated. Jesus has given the new revelation to his disciples, and it is now their responsibility to go into the world and make new disciples. Thus the reader becomes a "disciple," heir to the new revelation and to the task of interpreting and obeying it, as well as making further disciples. In this way the reader appropriates the revelation to himself and locates his place in the scheme of things. There will be an extended interval between the passion and the parousia, and during this interval he is to accept, interpret, and obey the revelation, and at the same time persuade others to do the same. But he will not be alone in this task; always the risen Lord will be with him, to the close of the age.

The narrative is not so much a resurrection appearance as an account of the risen and exalted Lord commissioning the church and its members. Certainly it represents the message of the evangelist Matthew to his readers, as it reveals the convictions that inspired his writing of the gospel: Jesus as the medium of the new revelation that fulfills and decisively reinterprets the old; the disciple as recipient of the revelation he is to obey so that the quality of his obedience exceeds that of the scribes and Pharisees. These are the themes that have dominated the gospel, but new elements are added. In language recalling the Son of Man vision in Daniel 7:14, Jesus explicitly claims the authority that had before been his only implicitly (verse 18). Now, for the first time, the disciples are commissioned to teach, to interpret the revelation. Now also the church is given the baptismal confession that will separate it from the world and dedicate it to its Lord (verse 19). Finally, the gospel ends on a note sounded earlier (8:25–26; 14:27; 18:20): the distinguishing mark of the church and the source of its power and authority is the presence of the risen Lord in its midst.

FURTHER OBSERVATIONS

The Matthean View of Jesus: The New Revelation
Requiring Interpretation

Matthew's five major discourses, plus Jesus' temptation of forty days and forty nights and the first discourse delivered from a mountain, have often suggested to scholars that Matthew thinks of Jesus as a new Moses giving a new Torah. At the very least, Matthew presents the teaching of Jesus as the correct interpretation of "the Torah and the prophets" (5:17). This perspective leads to the recognition that for Matthew, as for the Pharisees at Yavneh, revelation requires authoritative interpretation with changing times and circumstances.

Matthew goes further: Jesus not only *teaches* the new revelation; he also *is* the new revelation, the very fulfillment of "the law and the prophets." The new revelation is, to be sure, related to the old revelation. Jesus is descended from Abraham, the father of the Jewish people, but also the one to whom a promise was given to the nations. He is descended also from the first great king of Israel, King David and his royal line, giving him the proper credentials to be a royal messianic king and he can enter Jerusalem as such (21:5, 9); Matthew further develops the Son of David theme in the miracle stories (9:27; 12:23; 15:22; 20:30; 21:9, 15; 22:42, 45), even healing the daughter of a Gentile woman who addresses Jesus as Son of David (15:22). Related to the Son of David is the Son of God, also a title for the messianic king of Israel (for example, Ps 2:7). We noted that one major attempt to see Matthew's overall structure stresses the expression "from that time on, Jesus began . . ." (4:17; 16:21) and the title Son of God. Certainly, Jesus' birth of the virgin Mary is exceptional; he is Immanuel, "God is with us" (1:23), and like Israel, he has been called out of Egypt as God's Son (2:15 [Hos 11:1]). As in Mark, God himself in the voice at the baptism and the transfiguration declares, "This is my son, the Beloved, with whom I am well pleased (listen to him)" (3:17; 17:5; compare Ps 2:7; Isa 42:1). As in Q he is tempted as the Son of God (4:3, 6). Peter's messianic confession also refers to Jesus as "Son of God" (16:16).

While the Moses themes and the titles Messiah, Son of David, and Son of God are important to relate the new revelation to the old, Matthew also emphasizes the titles "Son of Man" and "Lord." As in Mark and Q, the Son of Man title encompasses authority on earth (for example, 9:6; 12:8; 8:20), necessary suffering (16:21; 17:22; 20:18–19, the passion predictions), and apocalyptic authority at the final judgment (for example, 16:27; 24:27, 30). While, as in Mark, Son of God and Son of Man are coordinated, Matthew's particular interest is the apocalyptic category, to which he adds the most sayings (six). Thus, Matthew is primarily interested in Jesus as Son of Man at his parousia, where his role is particularly associated with judgment of outsiders, that is, Israel and the nations. Though delayed, he will suddenly come at the End with his angels on the clouds of heaven with power and glory; standing before the world as a king before his kingdom (13:37–38), he will judge (for example, 25:31–46).

Finally, we note that Jesus is "Lord." This can mean "sir," but often it has Christological meaning associated with worship, though not yet *the* Lord God of the Scriptures. Matthew employs the title not only in relation to the miracle working Son of David (see above; 22:41–46) and as one who is frequently addressed as such by the disciples who worship him (8:25; 17:4; 20:33), but especially in his return as Son of Man (compare 7:21–22; 24:42; 25:11, 37, 44).

The Disciples in Matthew

We noted above that in contrast to Mark who portrays the disciples as those who misunderstand Jesus, Matthew views them as sometimes being "men of little faith" but as nonetheless growing in understanding, ultimately to be entrusted with the new revelation. So when Matthew is thinking of disciples, he is probably thinking of a Christian equivalent to the Jewish "scribes and Pharisees." He does not object to the *function* of "scribes and Pharisees." On the contrary, at one point he applauds it: "The scribes and the Pharisees sit on Moses' seat; therefore, do whatever they teach you . . ." (23:2–3a). He also says, "Therefore every scribe who has been trained for the kingdom of heaven is like the master of a household who brings out of his treasure what is new and what is old" (Matt 13:52). In Matthew's view, the need is for scribes "trained for the kingdom of heaven" as official interpreters of the revelation as fulfilled in Jesus Christ. Certainly Peter is given a special role, and the Matthean disciples themselves are said to "understand."

An interesting aspect of his presentation is that he avoids any mention of the disciples of Jesus *teaching*. He regularly summarizes Jesus' activity as "proclaiming the Kingdom," "healing," and "teaching" (4:23; 9:35; compare 11:1), but when the disciples are commissioned by Jesus (10:1–7), they are to heal and to proclaim the Kingdom, *not* to teach. In the gospel of Matthew only Jesus teaches, and that teaching is the new Torah, the fulfilled revelation. But after the revelation is complete, and the situation has become such that the revelation now needs authoritative interpretation, *then* the disciples begin to teach. At the end of the gospel the resurrected Jesus says to the disciples: "Go therefore and make disciples of all nations, baptizing them . . .*teaching them to obey everything that I have commanded you;* and remember, I am with you always, to the end of the age" (Matt 28:19–20, the Great Commission). The commandment in italics sums up the major emphasis of the gospel of Matthew: the teaching of Jesus is the new revelation, and it requires the authoritative interpretation of disciples who have a special role in Matthew's "church."

The Kingdom of Heaven, Ethics, and the Church

Whereas the Gospel of Mark refers to Jesus' preaching the Kingdom of *God,* the Gospel of Matthew much prefers Jesus' preaching the Kingdom of *Heaven*, a way of speaking about God indirectly, though there are spatial overtones. Statistics indicate the importance of Matthew's Kingdom of Heaven: Mark has fourteen references and Q has at least nine references, but Matthew has a striking thirty-eight references plus sixteen references to "Kingdom," all attributed to Jesus but one (3:2: John the Baptist; compare 10:7). The "gospel of the Kingdom" is primarily what Jesus preaches in "their synagogues" (4:23; 9:35; compare 10:7; 28:20), but it implies for Matthew the presence of Jesus himself—"repent, for the Kingdom of Heaven is at hand" (4:17; compare 3:2)—and might even refer to what Matthew writes (13:19; compare 4:15).

For Matthew the Kingdom of Heaven is primarily future, and a number of sayings emphasize that "the righteous" will "enter" the Kingdom in the future (for example, 5:20; 7:21). Thus, there are implications for ethical activity in the present, as the repentance theme indicates. Those who are "righteous" are those who "bear fruit" (7:16–21), who are like children (18:3–4; 19:13–15), and though there are positive hints about the urban rich (5:3), "a rich person" will have difficulty entering (19:23–24). One gains the impression that for Matthew the Kingdom of Heaven is anticipated in his present "church," which, as some of the parables show (13:24–30; 22:1–14; 25:1–13), contains both good and evil until the final judgment. A parallel idea seems to be the Kingdom of the apocalyptic Son of Man (for example, 13:41; 16:28), a kind of provisional Kingdom of both righteous and unrighteous, ultimately to be replaced the Kingdom of the Father (13:41–43a), which will include only "the righteous."

The Idea of Salvation History

In Biblical literature, an author will sometimes think in temporal terms, that is, of past, present, and future. An apocalyptic writer writes with sights fixed on the present and near future; the ancient Biblical "historian" stresses the past and present. But the history the ancient Biblical writers see is not merely the factual recounting of events; their idea of history is a history of the world in which God may be known, a history that is both a history of a chosen people and their affairs and a history of God's affairs with his chosen people. As the history of God's affairs with people, of God's activity on behalf of people, it is "*salvation* history," the history of the salvation of humanity at the hand of God. There is then a world history, a history of people and their affairs in the world, and a salvation history, a history of God and his activity directed toward the salvation of his chosen people.

The New Testament writer who has most often been thought to have a concept of salvation history is the author of Luke-Acts (see also Rom 9–11). Yet, there are also indications that Matthew had an idea of salvation history. We have noted that one of the major structural analyses stresses the temporal division "from that time on" (4:17; 16:21). There are other temporal expressions in Matthew (for example, "then," some ninety times; "in those days," 3:1, compare 24:3, 19, 22 [twice], 29; "at that time," 11:25; 12:1; 14:1; ". . . to the close of the age," 28:20; compare 24:3). We have also noted that a major theme throughout Matthew is the fulfillment of "the old" by "the new," especially in the formula quotations. Further, Matthew's view of Jesus' limited the mission to the Jews, especially the "lost sheep of the house of Israel" (10:5; 15:24) in the course of Jesus' life; yet, the Great Commission of the resurrected Christ at the end of the gospel stresses a mission to "all nations/Gentiles" (28:19).

Clearly Matthew's view of the new revelation in Jesus Christ suggests a distinction between a "period of Israel" and a "period of Jesus" beginning with John the Baptist (compare the temporal references and Kingdom proclamation in 3:1 and 4:17). The difficult question is whether these two phases should be extended to three, that is, whether "period of Jesus" and "period of the church" can be distinguished and, if so, when the latter begins. It is clear that Matthew follows in the steps of Mark insofar as he lets the story of Jesus, the disciples, and their opponents speak to problems in his own day. This tends to blur the distinction between the period of Jesus and the period of the church and to suggest only a two-phase salvation history. Yet, he has gone beyond Mark when he thinks of the "church" as a distinct entity with its mission to the world, and he certainly places central significance on the Great Commission in that regard (28:16–20). The gospel ends with the promise of the risen Lord to the disciples: "and remember, I am with you always, to the end of the age" (28:20). Moreover, in the discourse on community regulations this same note is sounded: "For where two or three are gathered in my name, I am there among them" (18:20). Such passages would point to a three-phase salvation history: Israel—Jesus—the church. Thus, while Matthew has not yet developed a salvation history to the extent of Luke-Acts, what has been said above tends to favor a move toward a three-phase periodization, the period of Israel, the period of Jesus, and the period of the church.

THE GENRE OF MATTHEW

Matthew opens with "An account of the genealogy of Jesus Christ, the Son of David, the Son of Abraham" (Matt 1:1 NRSV). Since the term "account" is literally "book" (Greek *biblos*) and "of the genealogy" can mean "of the genesis" or "of the origin" (Greek *geneseōs*), some modern interpreters have wondered if Matthew is not referring to his whole composition. However, it is much more likely that he refers "an account of the genealogy," as the NRSV translation suggests. These same words refer to a genealogy in Gen 5:1 (NRSV of the Hebrew: "list of the generations"). Moreover, Matthew rarely uses "gospel" except when following Mark, and when he does develop the term it is usually what *Jesus* says (compare for example, 4:23; 9:35). Again, it is very unlikely that Matthew calls his whole work a "gospel," as might be thought in the case of Mark (Mark 1:1).

Mark's apocalyptic story collapses past, present, and future; he deliberately involves his readers in the story beginning with the adult Jesus and ending at the empty tomb awaiting the parousia in fear and trembling. Matthew's stress on Jesus as Son of Man, his parousia, and his role in the judgment maintains much of the Markan apocalyptic focus. Also, the role of Peter and the disciples has implications for the church and its leadership in Matthew's day, and thus the period of Jesus and the period of the church to a certain extent overlap. However, in contrast to Mark, Matthew's salvation history sets the time of Jesus off from all previous and subsequent time. For Matthew, the time of Jesus becomes a time in the past, a special time, the time of fulfillment and revelation, a Sacred Time. Moreover, the Christian "church" is constituted on the basis of this Sacred Time. The Sacred Time of Jesus is the time of Christian origins. It functions something like a "foundation myth," a myth of origins to which the group relates by careful study and interpretation. Matthew's concept of salvation history, his foundation myth, and a revelation to be interpreted go hand in hand.

Does the Gospel of Matthew conform to any known genre? In our previous chapter we claimed that despite its realistic narrative the Gospel of Mark was essentially apocalyptic revelation approximating a narrative myth, but we left the gospel genre question open. Following the Two-Source Theory, the Gospel of Matthew is an extensively revised edition of the Gospel of Mark. The story contains the addition of birth and infancy stories, the teaching about ethical norms is more explicit, and the moral example of Jesus for disciples is clearer. There is here a step toward salvation history and thus "pastness." All this suggests that the Gospel of Matthew moves a step closer to the genre of Hellenistic biography (*bios*). Thus, one scholar (Shuler) has called it an "*encomium* (praise) biography." Yet, its Jewish qualities—genealogies, references to Scripture, fulfillment, and the like—are distinctive. Thus, by a broad notion of genre, the Gospel of Matthew approximates something like a Jewish *bios;* by a narrower definition, it, too, does not quite fit any known genre.

THE INTERPRETATION OF THE
GOSPEL OF MATTHEW

The evangelist Matthew has distinctive ideas. The notion of the fulfillment of a previous promise, of a revelation authoritatively interpreted, of a carefully organized and structured community of believers—for all these Matthew is indebted to his Jewish heritage. One could, of course, find parallels in the varied religious communities in the Hellenistic world, but the fact is that Matthew inherited them from Judaism, and he developed them in debate and conflict with the formative Judaism symbolized by the innovations at the Yavneh Academy. Yet, Matthew's views are not simply those of Christianized Judaism. He is indebted to his distinctively Christian heritage at many points, especially for the concept of the risen Christ present in the church. Even though Jewish rabbis were to come to speak of the "presence" (*shekînāh*) of God wherever two or three gathered to study the Torah, the Matthean view of the risen Lord present in the church, helping, sustaining, and guiding the "disciples" has its roots in the Hellenistic Christian concept of the presence of the Lord in the cultic worship of the community. Matthew is in the tradition of the Hellenistic Jewish Christian mission.

By the intent of its author, the gospel of Matthew cries out for the interpretation it has in fact received through the centuries: as a text enshrining a revelation subject to authoritative interpretation within the Christian community. More than that, this is what happened to the whole of the New Testament of which Matthew became the first book. The centuries have treated it as the enshrinement of revelation and authoritatively interpreted it within the church, which would have delighted the evangelist himself. Even today, when a Christian claims, "the Bible says . . . !," expression is often being given to the stance and attitude of the evangelist Matthew.

FURTHER READING

Important Theories, Sketches, and Recent Bibliography

D. R. Bauer, "The Interpretation of Matthew's Gospel in the Twentieth Century," *Proceedings of the American Theological Library Association* 42 (1988), pp. 119–145.

W. D. Davies and D. C. Allison, *The Gospel According to Matthew.* (International Critical Commentary), Introduction.

D. France, "Matthew's Gospel in Recent Study," *Journal of Theological Studies* 14 (1989), pp. 41–46.

U. Luz, *Matthew 1–7. A Commentary.* Trans. W. C. Linss, Introduction.

D. Senior, *What Are They Saying about Matthew?*

G. Stanton, "The Origin and Purpose of Matthew's Gospel: Matthean Scholarship from 1945–1980," *Aufstieg und Niedergang der römischen Welt* II.25.3 (1985), pp. 1890–1951.

G. Stanton, ed. *The Interpretation of Matthew.* (Collected Articles).

One-Volume Commentaries and Dictionary Articles

ABD: "Adultery" (S. D. Ricks); "Antioch of Syria" (F. W. Norris); "Beatitudes" (R. F. Collins); "Didachē" (R. Kraft); "Divorce" (R. W. Wall); "Fast, Fasting" (J. Muddiman); "Genealogy" (R. W. Wilson); "Great Commission, the" (A. B. Luter, Jr.); "Hosanna" (M. H. Pope); "Ignatius, Epistles of" (W. R. Schoedel); "Infancy Narratives in the NT Gospels" (R. E. Brown); "Jewish-Christian Relations 70–170 C.E." (S. G. Wilson); "John the Baptist" (P. W. Hollenbach); "Joseph, Husband of Mary" (S. E. Porter); "Keys of the Kingdom" (R. F. Collins); "Lord's Prayer" (J. H. Houlden); "Marriage (NT)" (R. F. Collins); "Mary" (B. Witherington, III); "Mary, Mother of Jesus" (M. M. Pazdan); "Matthew (Disciple)" (D. C. Duling); "Matthew, Gospel of" (J. P. Meier); "Matthew, Hebrew Version of" (G. Howard); "New Testament, OT Quotation in the" (H. Hübner, trans. S. S. Schatzmann); "Papias" (W. R. Schoedel); "Parable" (J. D. Crossan); "Peacemaking, Peacemakers" (J. Beutler); "Peter" (K. P. Donfried); "Phylacteries" (R. S. Fagen); "Rabbinic Literature in the NT" (A. J. Saldarini); "Resurrection" (G. W. E. Nickelsburg); "Sermon on the Mount/Plain" (H. D. Betz); "Virgin" (J. J. Schmitt).

IDB: "Matthew, Gospel of" (F. C. Grant).

IDB Suppl.: "Matthew, Gospel of" (R. G. Hamerton-Kelly).

NJBC, pp. 62–114 (B. T. Viviano).

Historically Influential Studies

B. W. Bacon, *Studies in Matthew.*

Standard Studies (Mostly Redaction Critical)

G. Bornkamm, G. Barth, and H. J. Held, *Tradition and Interpretation in Matthew.*

R. Brown, *The Birth of the Messiah.* 2d ed.

L. Cope, *Matthew, A Scribe Trained for the Kingdom of Heaven.*

W. D. Davies, *The Sermon on the Mount.*

———, *The Setting of the Sermon on the Mount.*

J. Fenton, *The Gospel of St. Matthew.*

D. E. Garland, *The Intention of Matthew 23.*

M. Goulder, *Midrash and Lection in Matthew.*

Gundry, *The Use of the Old Testament in St. Matthew's Gospel.*

D. Hare, *The Theme of Jewish Persecution of Christians in the Gospel According to St. Matthew.*

D. Hill, *The Gospel of Matthew.* (New Century Bible).

M. Johnson, *The Purpose of the Biblical Genealogies with Special Reference to the Setting of the Genealogies of Jesus.*

G. D. Kilpatrick, *The Origins of the Gospel According to Matthew.*

J. D. Kingsbury, *Matthew.* (Proclamation Commentaries).

————, *Matthew: Structure, Christology, Kingdom.* 2d ed.

J. Meier, *Law and History in Matthew's Gospel.*

————, *The Vision of Matthew.*

J. Neusner, *Development of a Legend: Studies in the Traditions Concerning Yohanan ben Zakkai.*

E. Schweizer, *The Good News According to Matthew.* Trans. D. E. Green.

D. Senior, *The Passion Narrative According to Matthew.*

K. Stendahl, *The School of St. Matthew.*

J. Suggs, *Wisdom, Christology and Law in Matthew's Gospel.*

W. Thompson, *Matthew's Advice to a Divided Community.*

S. Van Tilborg, *The Jewish Leaders in Matthew.*

Among the many articles on Matthew and its context, we may note:

S. Cohen, "The Significance of Yavneh: Pharisees, Rabbis, and the End of Jewish Sectarianism," *HUCA* 55 (1984), pp. 27–53.

D. Duling, "Binding and Loosing: Matthew 16:19; Matthew 18:18; John 20:23," *Forum* 3/4 (1987), pp. 3–31.

————, "The Therapeutic Son of David: An Element in Matthew's Christological Apologetic," *New Testament Studies* 24 (1978), pp. 392–410.

————, "Matthew's Plurisignificant 'Son of David' in Social Science Perspective: Kinship, Kingship, Magic, and Miracle," *Biblical Theology Bulletin* 22 (1992), pp. 99–116.

R. A. Edwards, "Uncertain Faith: Matthew's Portrait of the Disciples," pp. 47–61 in F. F. Segovia, ed., *Discipleship in the New Testament* (1985).

W. R. Farmer, "The Post-Sectarian Character of Matthew and Its Post-War Setting in Antioch of Syria," *PRS* 3 (1976), pp. 235–247.

R. Kimelman, "*Birkat Ha-Minim* and the Lack of Evidence for an Anti-Christian Jewish Prayer in Late Antiquity," pp. 226–244, 391–403 in E. P. Sanders, ed., *Aspects of Judaism in the Greco-Roman Period* 2.

J. D. Kingsbury, "Reflections on 'The Reader' of Matthew's Gospel," *New Testament Studies* 34 (1988), pp. 442–460.

Listening. Journal of Religion and Culture 24/3 (Fall, 1989) (Articles by M. McVann, F. H. Gorman, F. J. Matera, R. A. Edwards, J. J. Pilch, G. R. O'Day, P. Perkins).

J. Neusner, "The Formation of Rabbinic Judaism: Yavneh from A.D. 70–100," *Aufstieg und Niedergang der römischen Welt* II.19.2, pp. 2–42.

D. Slingerland, "The Transjordanian Origin of St. Matthew's Gospel," *Journal for the Study of the New Testament* 3 (1979), pp. 18–28.

G. Strecker, "The Concept of History in Matthew," *Journal of the American Academy of Religion* 35 (1967), pp. 219–230.

G. Stanton, "Matthew," pp. 205–219 in D. A. Carson and H. G. M. Williamson, eds., *It Is Written: Scripture Citing Scripture.*

B. V. Viviano, "Social World and Community Leadership: The Case of Matthew 23:1–12, 34," *Journal for the Study of the New Testament* 39 (1990), pp. 3–21.

Commentaries:

W. D. Davies and D. C. Allison, *The Gospel According to Matthew.* (International Critical Commentary).

R. Gundry, *Matthew: A Commentary on His Literary and Theological Art.*

U. Luz, *Matthew 1–7. A Commentary.*

Literary:

R. A. Edwards, *Matthew's Story of Jesus.*

J. Kingsbury, *Matthew as Story.* 2d ed.

Social-Historical and Social Scientific:

D. L. Balch, ed., *Social History of the Matthean Community.* (Contributions by A. F. Segal, A. J. Saldarini, R. H. Gundry, D. L. Balch, A. C. Wire, P. Perkins, W. R. Schoedel, J. P. Meier, R. Stark, L. M. White, F. Norris, J. D. Kingsbury).

R. Horsley, *The Liberation of Christmas. The Infancy Narratives in Social Context.*

B. Malina and J. Neyrey, *Calling Jesus Names. The Social Value of Labels in Matthew.*

D. E. Orton, *The Understanding Scribe. Matthew and the Apocalyptic Ideal.*

J. A. Overman, *Matthew's Gospel and Formative Judaism. The Social World of the Matthean Community.*

A. J. Saldarini, *Pharisees, Scribes and Sadducees.*

P. L. Shuler, *A Genre for the Gospels: The Biographical Character of Matthew.*

Miscellaneous:

H. D. Betz, *Essays on the Sermon on the Mount.*

R. Brown and J. Meier, *Antioch and Rome.*

R. Guelich, *The Sermon on the Mount.*

J. Neusner, *Invitation to the Talmud.* 2d. ed.

D. Patte, *The Gospel According to Matthew: A Structural Commentary on Matthew's Faith.*

J. Schaberg, *The Illegitimacy of Jesus. A Feminist Theological Interpretation of the Infancy Narratives.*

G. Strecker, *The Sermon on the Mount. An Exegetical Commentary.*

Detail from *The Liberation of St. Peter* by Raphael (1483–1520), Vatican Stanze, Rome. Peter's cell is illuminated by the light of an angel who miraculously helps him to escape (Acts 12:1–10). The story is typical of the Lukan view that God guides his chosen people through history, or "salvation history."

CHAPTER ELEVEN

THE GOSPEL OF LUKE AND THE ACTS OF THE APOSTLES
The Idea and Ethics of Salvation History

It was a great disservice to readers of the Gospel of Luke and the Acts of the Apostles to separate them in the canon and modern editions of the Bible, since they were originally written to be read together as a single work in two volumes (Luke 1:3: ". . .to write an orderly account for you, most excellent Theophilus . . ."; Acts 1:1: "In the first book, Theophilus, I wrote about all that Jesus did and taught . . ."; compare comment in the exegesis on Luke 1:1–4 below). But when the New Testament texts were collected, the four gospels were put in a group separate from the remainder, and the Gospel of Luke was separated from the Acts of the Apostles. This separation led to the title "According to Luke" being given to the first volume and "Acts of the Apostles" to the second. As far as we know, the author did not title his two-volume work, though he does refer to it as "a *narrative* of the things which have been accomplished among us" and an "*orderly account*" (Luke 1:1). Here we treat the two-volume work as the unity it is intended to be and refer to it as Luke-Acts.

EARLY CHRISTIAN TRADITION ABOUT LUKE-ACTS

Christian writers in the latter second century identified the author of the third gospel, and therefore the Acts of the Apostles, as Luke, the follower of Paul. After offering comments about Matthew and Mark that sound like the Papias tradition, the Church Father Irenaeus, bishop of Lyons, from the late second century, is noted by fourth-century Eusebius to have said:

> Luke also, the follower of Paul, put down in a book (Greek: *biblō*) a gospel (Greek: *euangelion*) preached by that one.
>
> (Irenaeus *Against Heresies* 3.1.2 in Eusebius *Ecclesiastical History* 5.8.2.)

Of the Acts of the Apostles Irenaeus writes:

> Now, that this Luke, was inseparable from Paul, and his fellow-worker in the Gospel, he himself made clear, not vaunting, but guided by truth itself. For when both Barnabas and John, who was called Mark, had departed from Paul and had sailed to Cyprus (Acts 15:39), he says: "We arrived at Troas" (16:8, though the Greek says, "they went down to Troas"). And when Paul had seen a Macedonian man in a dream saying: "Come over into Macedonia and help us, Paul," he says: "Immediately we sought to proceed into Macedonia, knowing that the Lord had called us to proclaim the Gospel to them. So we set sail from Troas and steered our course toward Samothrace" (Acts 16:9–11). . . .
>
> (Irenaeus, Against Heresies 3.14.1)

Irenaeus continues with other examples, but enough is quoted to see that from certain passages in Acts in the first-person plural Irenaeus deduced that the narrator, whom he says was Luke, was referring to himself as a close traveling companion of Paul. These first-person plural statements are now called "we-passages" (see below).

A second tradition is found in a late second-century Greek prologue to the gospel, which some have thought was anti-Marcionite (for the "heretic" Marcion, see Chapter Four, the canon of the New Testament). This prologue reads:

> Luke was a Syrian of Antioch, a physician by profession, a disciple of the apostles, and later a follower of Paul until his martyrdom. He served the Lord without distraction, without a wife, and without children. He died at the age of eighty-four in Boeotia, full of the Holy Spirit.

The prologue continues by claiming that the gospel was composed in Achaia (southern Greece) for Gentile converts, and that Acts was composed after the gospel.

A third tradition is found in the Muratorian Canon (named for its discoverer), which contains a list of authoritative books and which almost all scholars think represents the views of the church at Rome in the late second century. It has the following statement:

> The third book of the Gospel [is that] according to Luke. Luke, the physician, after the ascension of Christ, when Paul had taken him with him as a companion of his traveling, [and after he had made] an investigation, wrote in his own name—but neither did he see the Lord in the flesh—and thus, as he was able to investigate (Luke 1:3), so he also begins to tell the story [starting] from the nativity of John.

These traditions are all from the late second century C.E. Our earliest, best manuscripts of the Third Gospel from the late third and fourth centuries C.E. follow this tradition when they call the gospel "According to Luke."

Luke in the New Testament

The late second-century tradition about the author of the Gospel of Luke and the Acts of the Apostles affirms that he is "Luke the beloved physician" and companion of Paul, who at an old age wrote the gospel for Gentiles in Greece and then wrote Acts. Luke is mentioned three times in the New Testament. In Paul's prison letter to the slave owner Philemon (see Chapters Six, Seven), Paul extends greetings from "Mark, Aristarchus, Demas, and *Luke,* my fellow workers" (Phlm 24). Colossians, probably deutero-Pauline, describes him as "the beloved physician" (Col 4:14) and implies that he was probably a Gentile (4:11: "of the circumcision"). In a deutero-Pauline letter called 1 Timothy the author states, "Only Luke is with me" (2 Tim 4:11).

GENERAL HISTORICAL CRITICISM: AUTHOR, DATE, PLACE

The second-century view that the author of Luke-Acts was Luke, the beloved physician and companion of Paul, has led to several major critical questions. First, is it possible to discern in Luke-Acts a specialized **medical language**?

In the late nineteenth century the answer to the question about medical language was a decisive "Yes!" Scholars pointed to expressions such as "suffering from a very high fever" (4:38) or "paralyzed" (5:18, 24). However, twentieth-century scholars have come to realize that Luke's supposed medical terms were in fact commonly used by educated writers of the times. A contemporary analogy might be that those who use Freudian psychiatric terms like "inferiority complex" or "paranoid" are not necessarily trained psychiatrists. Thus, it is now thought impossible to prove by analysis of language that Luke-Acts contains technical medical terms and was therefore written by an ancient physician.

Second, does the Acts' portrayal of **Paul's life** accord with what Paul says about his life in the letters? This question has already been answered in Chapter Four. Sometimes Acts accords with the letters, but often it does not. While valuable in some cases for the movements of Paul, Acts is often legendary and conflicts with what Paul says about himself on many points. Despite its importance, the dominant position today is that Acts can be used for constructing Paul's life only with great caution. This conclusion does not add to our confidence that its author was a close companion of Paul.

Third, do the **speeches of Paul** in Acts correspond with **Paul's thought** as known in the letters? Studies have shown that Paul's speeches in Acts differ in some important points from what is known about Paul's theological beliefs as expressed in the Pauline letters. In Paul's speech on the Areopagus hill near the Acropolis in Athens (Luke 17:22–31), for example, Paul tells his Gentile audience that they are very religious and attributes to them knowledge of God. Initially, the point sounds similar to Paul's remarks in Romans 1 that the Gentiles know God. However, in Romans the Gentiles' knowledge of God does not lead beyond idolatry and immorality, and thus their immoral acts are condemned as inexcusable and sinful (Rom 1:18–21). This sounds very different from the Acts speech, which emphasizes humanity's enlightened quest for, and natural kinship with, God (especially verses 26–31). Both Romans and Acts may be influenced by Stoicism, but the tone of Acts is much more philosophically open.

Another example is the speech attributed to Paul in Pisidian Antioch in Asia Minor (Acts 13:16–41). It is basically a speech about the story of Israel and the Jews' misunderstanding of the messianic prophecies about Jesus, and it sounds much like other speeches in Acts by Peter and Stephen (compare Acts 2; 4; 7). In these speeches in general, we fail to find the great Pauline themes: the emphasis on the cross, justification by faith, freedom from the Law, the expectation that Christ will soon return. Moreover, the ancient Greek, Roman, and Jewish historical writers (for example, Thycydides; Livy; Josephus) compose speeches for their heroes based on what they deem appropriate for the occasion. Most analysts conclude that the author of Acts composes the speeches for his hero, Paul (see below, Luke as a historian). Again, the differences between them and what Paul himself says do not lead us to conclude that their author was a close companion of Paul's.

Finally, did a companion of Paul's mentioned in the letters write sections of Acts in the first person plural as though he were present with Paul on his journeys? There are sections in Acts where the author suddenly drops into the first-person plural, the "**we-passages,**" already observed by second-century Irenaeus above (compare Acts 16:10–17; 20:5–15; 21:1–18; 27:1–28:16). Like Irenaeus, many interpreters have concluded that these passages come directly from a companion of Paul's, or at least from some diary-source of Paul's companion. This conclusion, if sustained, could support the Lukan authorship of Acts (though it might be argued that someone else used Luke's diary). Yet, again we face a complication. Each of these sudden first-person narratives occurs in connection with the beginning of a sea voyage. The study of ancient sea voyage narratives shows that it is typical for authors to drop into the first-person style. In other words, when one narrates a sea voyage, it is customary literary convention to say "we" did thus and so (Robbins). Such a literary practice means that it is impossible to conclude that the person writing was actually present on the voyage. In short, most critics conclude that the "we-passages" cannot prove that the author of Acts was present with Paul on his voyages.

Internal analysis—medical language, comparison of Paul's life and thought in the letters with details of his movements and the speeches in Acts, and the we-passages—does not support the church traditions that the author of Luke-Acts (who, by the way, does not see Paul as Paul sees himself, as an "apostle," compare Acts 1:21–22; but compare 14:4, 14) was Luke the physician, his loyal companion. Most critics today lean in the direction of pseudonymity. Again, we shall refer to "Luke." To find out who Luke is, it is necessary to look more closely at the two-volume work itself. First, however, the problems of date and place need to be examined.

As in the case of the Gospels of Mark and Matthew, **a date for Luke-Acts** must be fixed by external and internal evidence. Late second-century Christians clearly knew about the Third Gospel, as the above early church traditions of Irenaeus, the Greek Prologue, and the Muratorian Canon show. Probably Acts was cited by Dionysius of Corinth in a letter to Soter of Rome about 170 C.E. (Eusebius *Ecclesiastical History* 4.23.3). Earlier references from the middle of the second century are possible but debatable (for example, Justin Martyr *Dialogue With Trypho* 105 [Luke 23:46]), and Marcion seems to have known Luke or some version of Luke. Thus, the latest possible date of composition would be about 150 C.E.

At the other end of the dating spectrum, the author of the Gospel of Luke clearly states that other accounts were written before his, and implies that he is not from the first generation of Christians (1:1–4). Like Matthew, Luke knows and uses the Gospel of Mark, which we have dated shortly after 70 C.E. This conclusion is supported by Luke's interpretation of Mark's "desolating sacrilege" (Mark 13:14), probably referring to Titus in the Temple of Jerusalem, with the words, "When you see Jerusalem surrounded by armies . . ." (Luke 21:20). Luke 19:39–44 (compare verse 43: "when your enemies will set up ramparts around you and surround you") seems to confirm the point. In short, Luke-Acts must have been written sometime between 70 and 150 C.E. Since, as we shall see, Luke's view of the church and its faith shows movement toward the institutionalism and theology characteristic of the middle period of early Christianity, most interpreters date it in the generation following the fall of Jerusalem. So a date of about **80–90 C.E.,** about the time of the composition of Matthew, is appropriate.

The tradition above located **the place of composition** in Achaia, or southern Greece, and other ancients placed it in Boeotia, the traditional place of Luke's death, or Rome, where Acts' story of Paul ends (Acts 28). Luke's view of the geography of Palestine is not very good, suggesting some place outside of Palestine. Based on internal analysis, probably any city where Greek was spoken would be possible.

In summary, the gospel now attributed to Luke was anonymous and circulated anonymously. It was written about 80–90 C.E. probably in some city where Greek was spoken, Caesarea Maritima having often been suggested. The ascription of the gospel to Luke the physician and companion of Paul by the late second century cannot be demonstrated by internal analysis. Perhaps it was an inference from clear indications of its having been written by a well-educated Greek (see below).

SOCIAL-HISTORICAL CONTEXT

As noted at the beginning of this chapter, both volumes of Luke-Acts are addressed to **"Theophilus."** The name is Greek, though it is commonly found among both Jews and Greeks. It means "lover of God," and it is prefaced by "most excellent," meaning something like "your excellency." Since a person named Theophilus is otherwise unknown in early Christianity, these facts have led some interpreters to suggest that the address refers to *any* Greek-speaking/reading person of high rank and status, for example, members of ruling classes and the elite aristocracy. We think it likely that Luke addresses an actual person, unknown though he may be, perhaps a wealthy patron who has recently been initiated to Christianity. At the same time, his two volumes are intended to be read by a broader audience, perhaps those of higher status in Greco-Roman society.

We may illustrate Luke's broader interests and audiences by his boundary-breaking inclusiveness, often called his **universalism.** In the new family of God the old social, economic, ethnic, religious, and sexual barriers are broken down. Only in the Gospel of Luke does Jesus' genealogy extend back beyond Abraham to the first Son of God, the progenitor of the whole human race, Adam, whose very name in Hebrew means "humanity" (Luke 3:23–28). Only in the Gospel of Luke does Jesus send *seventy* disciples on a mission, the number seventy being symbolic for the number of nations of the world (Luke 10:1–20). Luke's second volume, Acts, shows how the gospel spreads by guidance of the Spirit from Jerusalem, through Judea, to Samaria, and Gentile lands. Luke's world is cosmopolitan. Thus, salvation is extended to everyone: women, sinners, the poor, Jews, Samaritans, Gentiles, and among the Gentiles, expressly the Romans. Let us expand on this point.

Women are very prominent in Luke's two volumes. Whereas in Matthew Joseph dominates the infancy story, in Luke's version Elizabeth, the mother of John of the Baptist, and Mary hold center stage (Luke 1–2). Only the Lukan Gospel contains the verses about the blessedness of Mary for bearing Jesus (11:27–28); the sinful woman who shows Jesus hospitality, and whom Jesus forgives (Luke 7:36–50); the women of means who support Jesus' ministry (Luke 8:1–3); the praise of a certain Mary, who sits at the feet of Jesus listening to Jesus' teaching, in contrast to her complaining sister Martha, who did the customary women's work (Luke 10:38–42); Jesus' healing the crippled woman (Luke 10:13–17); and the "great number" of women who were present at the crucifixion (Luke 23:27). In Acts, we find the wealthy purple-cloth merchant, Lydia, extending hospitality to Paul (16:11–15); the accounts of Priscilla and Aquila, who also extend Paul hospitality at Corinth (18:1–3, 18); and Philip's four daughters, who are prophetesses (21:9). When it is recalled that most women in antiquity were very subordinate to men, that Jewish women were unclean a good part of their lives, and that especially Palestinian Jewish women were near the bottom of the social ladder, Luke's accounts of women are truly remarkable, and the question has been raised whether the author is not a well-educated Gentile woman! In any case, there must have been many women converts in the Lukan community.

Luke also has a special concern for **sinners,** sometimes called "the lost." We have already noted the woman who was a sinner (7:36–50). The rich tax collector Zacchaeus is designated "a sinner" (19:7). In this gospel occurs the story of the tax collector who beats his breast, who cries out to God, "God, be merciful to me, a sinner!" and goes down to his house, justified (Luke 18:9–14). Here, too, the poor widow successfully importunes an unjust judge (Luke 18:1–8), and paradise is promised to the penitent thief on his cross (Luke 23:43). This theme is especially prevalent in Luke's well-known cluster of parables about "the lost": the Lost Sheep, the Lost Coin, and the Lost (or Prodigal) Son (Luke 15). Joy is expressed by God, most members of the family, and neighbors when the lost are found again.

Luke-Acts also shows a great interest in **the poor.** Jesus proclaims good news to the poor (4:16–20; 7:22), blesses the literal poor (6:20; contrast Matt 5:3), tells parables in behalf of the poor (for example, 12:13–21; 16:19–31), condemns the Pharisees as lovers of money (16:14), and says it is impossible to serve both God and mammon (16:13). Peter is poor (Acts 3:6), yet his miraculous powers are not for sale (Acts 8:18–24). Cornelius the Gentile convert is praised for his almsgiving (Acts 10:2) and Paul observes the same practice (24:17). Luke stresses, "one's life does not consist in the abundance of possessions" (Luke 12:15) and ". . .where your treasure is, there will your heart be also" (12:34). Thus, in a society of mainly peasants and urban poor living at a subsistence level, Luke stresses the honor code of the poor: hospitality, redistribution of the wealth, and almsgiving. It would appear that there are a number of rich among those to whom Luke writes; he suggests that if it is not in every case necessary to sell everything (19:8), the message of the Kingdom brings with it concern in the community for the poor. In other words, Luke tells his patron and others who may read his works that those in the upper strata of society—the rich, powerful, and prestigious—should support the lower strata, the peasants and other marginal people.

Luke's inclusivism or universalism includes many ethnic groups, which is illustrated especially by the historical enemies of the Jews in Palestine, the **Samaritans.**

Only the Gospel of Luke contains a parable in which a hated Samaritan is good (Luke 10:29–37). Luke also has the story of the healing of the ten lepers, only one of whom returns to thank him, and Luke emphasizes, "And he was a Samaritan" (Luke 17:11–19 [verse 16]). Luke also tells the story of the conversion of the Samaritans in Acts (8:4–8, 14–17). Thus, Luke states as the purpose of his second volume the attempt to show how the gospel moves from Jerusalem to "all Judea and Samaria. . ." (Acts 1:8).

For Luke, the Christian movement passed beyond Samaria to the "ends of the earth" (1:8), and Acts portrays its movement to Rome. In this regard Luke-Acts is very **pro-Roman.** To be sure, Luke does not present Jesus as subservient to Rome, nor does he always portray the Roman procurator Pontius Pilate as a sterling character (Luke 13:1–3); indeed, Pontius Pilate yields to the Jewish leaders' charges that Jesus stirs up and perverts the people (compare 23:2, 5, 14). Yet, Pilate accedes only after declaring three times that Jesus is innocent (Luke 23:4, 14–15, 22). Moreover, Luke has other pro-Roman passages. The Roman centurion who has a sick slave (Q 7:1–10) is commended by the elders of the Jews, ". . . he loves our nation, and it is he who built our synagogue for us" (Luke 7:5). The first Gentile to be converted to Christianity in Acts is the Roman centurion Cornelius (Acts 10:1–33). In Cyprus the proconsular governor "believes" on the basis of Paul's message (Acts 13:12); in Achaia (Greece), the proconsul Gallio takes Paul's side against the Jews (Acts 18:14–15); Paul is portrayed as a Roman citizen (Acts 16:37–38; 22:25–29; 23:27); and in general, Paul is treated with respect by Roman authorities.

Can this pro-Roman stance be explained? You will recall that in the middle period of Christianity many of the various Christian groups had to adjust to their growing success among the Gentiles. Part of this story was the everpresent possibility of, and fear about, persecution by the Romans (Chapter Four). Yet, the Christians also had to come to terms with their Jewish roots. In Luke-Acts the Christian movement is consistently represented as descended from Judaism, and indeed the proper fulfillment of Israelite prophecy, especially in the speeches in Acts (for examples, 13:16–41). Thus, one explanation for Luke's pro-Roman stance has been that he wanted the Christians to be able to share the Jews' special privileges in the Roman Empire, with its implications of toleration and freedom to practice their rites (see Chapter Two). If this explanation is valid, the author attempted to present the Christians as nonthreatening to Roman authorities and perhaps also Roman authority to Christians. Both were depicted in the best possible light in the hope of fostering good relations between them. This explanation may be related to the possibility that there were a number of Romans in the Lukan community (was Theophilus a Roman with a Greek name?) and that Luke wanted to show that, despite the crucifixion of Jesus in the Roman manner, which was usually a punishment for crimes against the state, being Christian and being Roman were not really mutually exclusive. All this would have been an attempt to legitimize Christianity politically.

There is a much debated question in this regard: does the pro-Gentile, and especially pro-Roman, emphasis in Luke-Acts continue to allow room for **the Jews** to be included in God's plan of salvation? This is not an easy question to answer for Luke-Acts (see Wills).

The early part of Acts claims that many Jews, literally, "were persuaded" of the truth of Christianity (for example, 4:4; 5:14; 6:1, 6; 9:26–28). Moreover, the theme of the inclusion of the Jews seems to continue (for example, 12:24; 13:43; 14:1; 17:10–12; 18:4, 8; 19:17, 20, 26) even down to this final scene at Rome where the imprisoned Paul is still attempting to prove to the Jewish leaders that Jesus is the Messiah. Thus, near the end of Acts, the Lukan Paul, referring to his appeal to Caesar and coming to Rome as a prisoner, says, "since it is for the sake of Israel that I am bound with this chain" (28:20; compare 26:7). *Some* of Jewish leaders were then "convinced," that is, "persuaded" (28:24).

Yet, the Christians' main difficulties do not stem from the hostility of Roman authorities, but the machinations of especially the Jewish leaders, who are said to have misunderstood the prophecies (Luke 22:66; 23:1–2; Acts 2:23; 13:28; 14:2, 19; 18:12, and so forth). Clearly the Jewish authorities, though not the Jewish people as a whole, are blamed for Jesus death. Also, there are recurring statements in Acts that Paul "turns to the Gentiles" when the Jews oppose him, become violent or incite violence, and reject his message about the "word of God" (for example, Acts 13:43–48; 18:6). Moreover, we have the volatile statements in the speech of Stephen, who is said to have been martyred by a Jewish mob in Jerusalem:

> You stiff-necked people, uncircumcised in heart and ears, you are forever opposing the Holy Spirit, just as your ancestors used to do. Which of the prophets did your ancestors not persecute? They killed those who foretold the coming of the Righteous One, and now you have become his betrayers and murderers. (Acts 7:51–52)

Such speeches are usually considered to represent the author's views in a very special way. Finally, at the end of Acts, Paul's further statement is added in reference to those Jewish leaders who were *not* "persuaded." Their lack of understanding is said to fulfill the Scriptures:

> "The Holy Spirit was right in saying to your ancestors through the
> prophet Isaiah,
>   'Go to this people and say,
>   You will indeed listen, but never understand,
>   and you will indeed look, but never perceive.
>   For this people's heart has grown dull,
>   and their ears are hard of hearing,
>   and they have shut their eyes;
>   so that they might not look with their eyes,
>   and listen with their ears,
>   and understand with their heart and turn—
>   and I would heal them.'"
>   (Acts 28:25–27 [Isa 6:9–10])

Then, Paul claims that salvation "has been sent to the Gentiles; they will listen" (28:28).

What, then, is Luke's position about the Jews? Luke's views that Christianity fulfills the Scriptures and that it is the true Israel, along with his universalism, suggest that despite their tragic rejection the door of salvation remains ajar, however slightly. If this is correct, it is probably because there are Jewish Christians in his community. Yet, it is difficult not to conclude that the constant opposition by the Jews, especially the Jewish leaders and mobs, combined with the reception of the Gentiles, especially the Romans, indicates that Lukan Christianity has now become virtually Gentile and that despite Luke's universalism, little hope is held out to the Jews.

Another social aspect of Lukan Christianity is portrayed especially in Acts, namely, a growing **institutionalization** of the church. Luke portrays a smooth and almost noncontroversial internal Christian movement from Jesus to Peter and the apostles, and then to Paul and his mission to the Jews and the Gentiles. Twelve apostles bear witness to the life of Jesus from the point of his baptism (1:21–26); Peter emerges as the leader of the Jerusalem church (2–5; 8–10; 15); people are now commanded and missionaries are sent; the Spirit is received by the "laying on of hands" (for example, 8:17; 9:17; 19:6); and the seven (6:1–6) and elders are appointed (for example, 14:23). "Apostles and elders" seem to be in charge, and Paul seems to entrust the elders of Ephesus with pastoral authority (20:28–35). Such passages might suggest "apostolic succession" is in its infancy, however undeveloped. While there is no concept of an institution so developed that it has a sacramental system and is itself the guarantor of the Spirit and of salvation, yet, there can be no doubt that there are those who wield some authority, and in portraying the church in this manner, Luke-Acts reflects its own period. We have noted this also in connection with the Jerusalem Conference.

We catch other glimpses of communal life in Luke-Acts; especially in house-churches. More than any other gospel, Luke has comments about **meals:** eating and drinking, meal parables, and Jesus banqueting with all sorts of people (for example, 11:37–41; 14:7–24; 15:1–2; 16:19–31; 22:14–38; Acts 6:1–6), especially "the poor, the maimed and blind and lame" (14:13, 21), and even distribution of food to widows (Acts 6:1). Some meals merge with liturgical life, as in the Last Supper (Luke 22:14–38). Eating together symbolizes the life of the group. Luke's Jesus is also the Jesus of **prayer.** In the gospel, Jesus is praying before every major event: the baptism (3:21), the choice of the Twelve (6:12), Peter's messianic confession (9:18), the transfiguration (9:28), the teaching about the Lord's Prayer (11:1), and Jesus' last hours in Jerusalem in the Garden of Gethsemane (22:4). **Baptism** is also a major motif throughout Luke-Acts, and it is often connected with the gift of the Holy Spirit (for example, Luke 3:16; Acts 1:5; 10:47; 11:16).

LANGUAGE, STYLE, AND LITERARY FEATURES OF LUKE-ACTS

Since antiquity Luke has been recognized as the best writer among the four evangelists. We have indicated that he composes speeches and writes Paul's sea voyages in the typical first-person plural style. We make four further points. First, the prologue of Luke-Acts (1:1–4) is written in an elegant and formal Greek style or "Atticistic Greek," that is, like the Greek of the classical Attic prose and poetry writers. Second, scholars have compiled lists of the numerous ways in which Luke improves the Greek of his sources, especially Mark, and of many terms not otherwise found in the New Testament. Often Luke's improved style is recognizable in English, for example, removal of Mark's repetitious sequences of "ands" ("parataxis") and replacing them with more complicated constructions with subordinate clauses. Third, Luke is fond of repeating words, but he varies their form and bunches them together in particular contexts. Finally, Luke likes to show how the events of his writings fulfill Scripture. His Bible is the Greek Septuagint. So imbued with the Septuagint is his thinking that he can imitate its Hebraicized style of Greek ("Septuagintisms"). We shall say a bit more about this phenomenon.

Luke's Use of Scripture

Luke does not stress formula quotations as does Matthew (see Chapter Ten), but he is nonetheless concerned to show that the events he portrays fulfill Scripture. He indicates this intent by his use of the Septuagint, especially at the beginning and end of his gospel and in the Acts speeches. For example, the famous song of Mary, called the "Magnificat" (Luke 1:46–55), is carefully modeled on the song of Hannah (1 Sam 2:1–10), and other poetic-type materials in the infancy story draw on words and phrases from the Greek Septuagint (for example, Luke 1:14–17, 32–34, 68–79; 2:29–32).

Extremely crucial for understanding Luke's use of Scripture is his view that God's foreordained plan is being carried out by the fulfillment of the prophecies, especially those in Isaiah. Two examples will suffice. First, in Luke 4:16–30 the scene of Jesus' first teaching in the synagogue at Nazareth has been moved forward from its location in the Markan outline (compare Mark 6:1–6), and thus has been put here as a kind of leitmotif for the image of Jesus in Luke's gospel. In Luke's version of this dramatic scene, Jesus fulfills the Isaianic prophecies about preaching good news to the poor and healing by an anointed, Spirit-filled prophet (Isa 61:1–2). The passage continues with an anticipation of rejection by the Jews and a movement toward the Gentiles, as reflected in the Scriptural stories about Elijah and Elisha. This theme, as we have seen, is interpreted at the end of Acts as a fulfillment of the words in Isaiah about the Jews' lack of understanding (Acts 28:25–28 [Isa 6:9–10]).

Second, it should be noted that in the Acts speeches it is common for the purported speaker to trace major events in the early history of Israel down to the time of David, then to cite prophecies about David and his descendant, and finally, by linking these to other prophecies by David himself in the Psalms (for example, Ps 2:7; 16:10; 89; 110:1; 132:10–12), to show how Jesus' life, death, resurrection, and ascension fulfills them (Acts 2:14–36; 7:1–53; 13:16–41).

SOURCES AND STRUCTURE OF LUKE-ACTS

According to the Two-Source Theory, the author of Luke-Acts uses the gospel of Mark, Q, and his special traditions, or Special L. However, Luke omits about three-tenths of the Gospel of Mark and includes a higher proportion of special source material, which is about one-third of the gospel. Moreover, whereas Matthew combines Q and Special M into large blocks that are periodically inserted into the Markan framework (the five major discourses), Luke combines Q and Special L into blocks that in general *tend to alternate* with Markan blocks something like this:

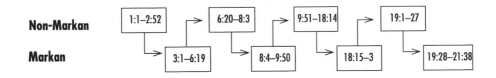

Non-Markan	1:1–2:52	6:20–8:3	9:51–18:14	19:1–27
Markan	3:1–6:19	8:4–9:50	18:15–3	19:28–21:38

This schema is somewhat oversimplified. There is non-Markan material in some Markan blocks (for example, 3:7–9 [Q]; 3:1–14, 23–38 [Special L]) and Luke 22:14–24:12 (not represented) mixes Mark with Special L. Luke occasionally omits a section from Mark, for example, the **Great Omission** at 9:17, apparently in part because it contains duplicate materials (Mark 6:30–44; 8:1–10; compare 8:14–21). He also transposes Mark, for example, by moving forward the synagogue scene at Nazareth (Mark 6:1–6; Luke 4:16–30). Luke also tends to clump most of his Q material in the second and third (non-Markan) blocks, Luke 6:20–8:3 (**the Lesser Insertion**) and Luke 9:51–18:14 (**the Greater Insertion**). Finally, Q and Special L occur together such that a few interpreters think that they were already combined in a source into which he inserted Mark, rather than the other way around. This source theory is called **Proto-Luke.** Some interpreters still think that Luke had a separate passion source. "Proto-Luke" seems to have fallen out of favor among scholars and we shall suggest below that Luke's distinctive passion story probably bears his own stamp.

In short, five major changes in relation to Mark's structure stand out:

1. **the infancy narrative** (1–2);
2. **the Lesser Insertion** (6:20–8:3), which includes Luke's Sermon on the Plain (6:20–49), almost all Q;
3. **the Great Omission** (at 9:17) of a portion of Mark (6:45–8:26), consisting primarily of miracles, parts of which are duplicated by Mark elsewhere;
4. **the Greater Insertion** (9:51–18:14), an extended journey to Jerusalem, with much Q and Special L;
5. **the resurrection and ascension** (24:13–53) accounts at the end.

We must say more about the Greater Insertion. It is a rambling **Travel Narrative to Jerusalem.** We noted above that Luke places much Q material in the Greater Insertion section and that about one-third of his gospel is Special L, much of which is also in this section. Thus, of five distinctive miracles, three are in the Travel Narrative (13:11–14; 14:2–4; 17:12–19). Even more impressive, of Luke's seventeen distinctive parables, sixteen are in the Travel Narrative. These parables stress many of the distinctive Lukan themes about rich and poor, lost and saved, women, and the like. Two of the most famous parables in the New Testament are among them, the Good Samaritan (10:30–37) and the Prodigal Son (15:11–32).

Two interlocking purposes stand out in relation to the Travel Narrative or Greater Insertion: (a) Jesus is the messianic prophet who will meet *a prophet's death at Jerusalem* where, (b) *in an event separate from the resurrection, his* **ascension** *to God's right hand in heaven will take place.* The following passages with Luke's words for the ascension in the left margin will illustrate the point:

exodon	Luke 9:31: "[Moses and Elijah] . . . were speaking of his *departure*, which he was about to accomplish at *Jerusalem*."
analēmseōs	Luke 9:51: "When the days drew near for him to be *taken up*, he set his face to go to *Jerusalem*."
	Luke 9:53: " . . . but they [the Samaritans] did not receive him, because his face was set toward *Jerusalem*."
	Luke 13:33b: " . . . because it is impossible for a *prophet* to be killed outside of *Jerusalem*" (compare Acts 7:52 quoted above: "Which of the *prophets* did your ancestors not persecute?")
anaphereto	Luke 24:51: "[at Jerusalem] . . . he withdrew from from them and was *carried up* into heaven."
analēmphthē	Acts 1:2: " . . . first book . . . all that Jesus did and taught until the day when he was *taken up* to heaven [at Jerusalem]"
epērthē	Acts 1:9: "[at Jerusalem] . . . he was *lifted up*, and a cloud took him out of their sight."

Jesus goes up to Jerusalem and there endures the passion, which climaxes in the ascension, the act of Jesus being taken up into heaven: "While he was blessing them, he withdrew from them and was carried up into heaven. And they worshipped him, and returned to Jerusalem with great joy; and they were continually in the temple blessing God" (24:51–53). Thus, the gospel anticipates the passion and ascension of its hero at Jerusalem.

Jerusalem is also an important structural and thematic feature in Acts. The story of the church begins in Jerusalem (Acts 1–7). Moreover, each of the three accounts of Paul's conversion (9:1–30; 22:3–21; 26:9–23) has him begin his witnessing in Jerusalem immediately after his conversion. Moreover, Acts exhibits the same compositional feature as Luke: It has a rambling travel narrative beginning with a statement of intent. Acts 19:21 reads, ". . . Paul resolved in the Spirit to go through Macedonia and Achaia, and then to go on to Jerusalem. He said, "After I have gone there, I must also see Rome!" and from that point the narrative is about Paul's journey to Jerusalem and Rome, ending with Paul preaching in Rome "with all boldness and without hindrance" (28:31). The narrative of Luke-Acts leads quite deliberately from Jerusalem, the place of Jesus' passion-ascension, to Rome. Thus, the author of Luke-Acts structurally places Jerusalem in the center of his two-volume work; indeed, he has a special spelling of the term (*Ierousalēm*, sixty-three times in Luke-Acts out of an approximate total of seventy-four New Testament uses; *Ierosolyma*, from Mark, occurs only twice, 13:22 [= Mark 10:32] and 19:28 [= Mark 11:1]). We shall note this feature again.

We should also observe that at critical moments in the geographical progression of the Acts narrative there are formulaic summaries of the action: 2:43–47; 5:42; 9:31; 12:24; 15:35; 19:20. Coming where they do in the plot of the narrative, they provide us with the clues to its structure. We shall note them further in our outline of Acts below.

Finally, of all the New Testament writings, Luke-Acts contains a set of episodes that are parallel in structure (see Tolbert). It might even be said that Luke-Acts is a work of art organized according to the "law of duality." The most obvious structural element is the addition of the Acts of the Apostles to the gospel. However, there are also many parallels between the gospel and Acts, for example, the parallel introductions to each volume (Luke 1:1–4; Acts 1:1–5), the parallelism of the baptism and descent of the Spirit in each volume, the parallelism between the healing activities of Jesus and the apostles (for example, Luke 8:40–42, 49–56; Acts 9:36–42), the parallelism of the journey motif of Jesus to Jerusalem and Paul to Rome, and the parallelism between the trials of Jesus and Paul (Luke 23:1–25; Acts 25–26). There are many other parallels of detail.

All of these structural features play a role in Luke-Acts and contribute to our understanding of his purpose. Before we note that purpose, we need to consider one other very dominant feature of Luke-Acts, the delay of the parousia.

THE DELAY OF THE PAROUSIA

Like all the authors of the middle period of New Testament history, the author of Luke-Acts wrestles with the delay of the parousia, Jesus' return on the clouds of heaven, which should have happened, but had not. To be sure, certain Lukan passages stress the near expectation of the parousia (compare Luke 3:9, 17; 10:9; 21:32), and the author even seems to add to them (Luke 10:11; 18:7–8). Yet, these passages should be interpreted in relation to what is clearly Luke's more dominant view: the parousia will take place in some *indefinite* future.

The author defers the time of the parousia by his treatment of certain key passages in the gospel of Mark, one of his sources. Mark 1:14–15 has Jesus coming into Galilee and proclaiming, "The time is fulfilled, and the Kingdom of God has come near," a proclamation intended to arouse a fervent expectation that the End is imminent. Luke 4:14 simply says, "Then Jesus, filled with the power of the Spirit, returned to Galilee . . ." and makes a comment about his growing fame. Then, Luke 4:15 says, "He began to teach in their synagogues and was praised by everyone." The key passage for Luke, his "leitmotif," as we have seen, is found in the next scene where Jesus is teaching in the synagogue at Nazareth (Luke 4:16–30). The theme is the fulfillment of Isaianic prophecies about preaching good news to the poor and healing by an anointed, Spirit-filled prophet, with an anticipation of rejection and a movement toward the Gentiles. Mark's significant apocalyptic theme has been replaced by Luke's equally significant non-apocalyptic theme in which the element of imminent expectation has been replaced neatly by a focus on the past ministry of Jesus as the savior of all.

Perhaps an even more important illustration of the delay of the parousia is Luke's reworking of the synoptic apocalypse (Mark 13 = Luke 21). For the gospel of Mark, the warning is made not to identify the End specifically with the coming of false prophets announcing the immediate parousia (which, for the gospel writer, occurs in connection with the destruction of Jerusalem, Mark 13:5b, 14 21–23), but it will, nonetheless, be soon thereafter (Mark 13:24: "But in those days, after that suffering . . ."). For Luke, the close proximity of the destruction of Jerusalem and the parousia has been severed. Luke makes the reference to the destruction of Jerusalem more specific (21:20, 24a), but he omits the reference to the false prophets at this point (compare 17:20–23) and adds a reference to an interim period, ". . . until the times of the Gentiles are fulfilled" (21:24b). Luke has thereby lengthened the time between the earthly signs in relation to the destruction (21:7–24) and the cosmic signs of the parousia of the Son of Man (21:25–28). Finally, Luke emphasizes things that must happen first (21:8–9, 32). Thus, Luke stresses that the parousia is indefinitely postponed.

The author of Luke-Acts also makes sense of the extended interim period; it is the period of the witness of the church, the story of which is told in Acts. This is very clear in the words of the resurrected Jesus to the disciples noted above: "You shall be my witnesses in Jerusalem and all Judea and Samaria and to the end of the earth" (Acts 1:8).

"SALVATION HISTORY" IN LUKE-ACTS

We have frequently observed the penchant of apocalyptic writers to portray historical epochs by means of symbols, and we have noted that several Biblical writers think in terms of the theme of salvation history. Among the evangelists, however, the one most dominated by the idea of salvation history is the author of Luke-Acts, who has sometimes been called "Luke the historian." To place Luke-Acts particular view of salvation history in proper perspective, it will be important to recall something of the nature of historical writing in antiquity.

Ancient Greek historians tended to focus on key events and personalities, especially from their own time, because they illustrated the human drama of political life, they were important for moral instruction or exhortation, they illustrated national aspirations, or because they were simply interesting or entertaining. Characteristically, these historians created speeches for their heroes in order to give an impression of some of the great ideas of the age.

Roman historians, writing in Greek and Latin not long after Luke-Acts, generally followed these precedents. Lucian of Samosata, in his *How to Write History*, stressed that the task of the historian is not entertainment, but description of things as they actually happened; yet, Lucian chose to describe only the very important matters, such as political events and wars, and the very important people, such as generals, politicians, or poets, and he freely placed programmatic speeches in their mouths on subjects that he considered appropriate for the occasion. Livy's *Annals of the Roman People*, tended to combine history and legend in the interest of writing "inspiring history." Indeed, Livy stated his rationale: to perpetuate the memory of "the first people in the world" and to hold before the reader models of moral behavior. Even Tacitus, one of the most accurate Roman historians of the period, chose his material with a political prejudice and freely wrote the speeches of the Roman emperors.

If we turn to Israelite and Jewish history writing, the Court History of David (2 Samuel 9:1–20:26; 1 Kings 1–2) appears to be almost eyewitness in character, but underlying it is the ideology of Deuteronomy that attempts to show how God is operating in human affairs to fulfill his promises to David (2 Samuel 7). Real history yields to "salvation history" (German: *Heilsgeschichte*). Closer to New Testament times 1 Maccabees develops fairly accurate Jewish history but inserts pious addresses and prayers into the mouths of its heroes. Finally, Josephus, a Jewish historian who is a contemporary of the author of Luke-Acts, writes to glorify his national heritage and to defend his participation in the Jewish wars with Rome. He follows the general practice of composing speeches appropriate to the occasion, reflecting the ideas he himself believed were important. One need only read the masterfully written speech of the revolutionary Eleazar atop Masada to grasp the point (see the exegetical survey on Luke 1:1–4).

If such were the general methods of writing history in that period, one further point should be mentioned: "Luke" was not only an ancient "historian"; he was also a religious writer and a gospel writer. Here it should be recalled that ancient Greco-Roman biography was not like modern biography, but ranged from rather loose collections of sayings and anecdotes, such as Diogenes Laertius' *Lives and Opinions of Famous Philosophers* to the Hellenistic romance calculated to evoke praise of the hero's virtues, such as Plutarch's *Lives* or Philostratus' sketch of the divinely begotten, miracle-working Apollonius of Tyana. With this observation, one is back to the controversial question as to what extent the gospels in general, and the third gospel in particular, can be seen in relation to ancient romantic biographies of especially endowed human beings (see Chapters Nine and Ten). Luke's version comes closest to the popular biographies of the period.

Thus, when thinking of Luke-Acts as historical writing, four points must be kept in mind: (1) the character of Hellenistic and Roman historical writing, especially in relation to the Acts of the Apostles; (2) the character and diversity of the Greco-Roman popular romance as a biographical form, especially in connection with the gospel of Luke; (3) the tradition of salvation historical writing in the Old Testament with prophecy and fulfillment as major themes; and (4) the actual modification by Luke of his source Mark, examples of which have been noted in connection with Luke's reorientation of Mark's understanding of the synoptic apocalypse.

As history, then, Luke-Acts is not modern history, but an example of Hellenistic-Roman historical writing ruled by a Biblical concept of salvation history. It is not a mere chronicle of events but a history that portrays God's activity in saving all people. As a salvation history, it is an account of a remote past, an immediate past, a present, an immediate future, and a remote future. It looks back to a remote past, the time of the creation of the first human (taking the genealogy of Jesus back to Adam, Luke 3:38), and toward the distant future, the time of the parousia, now delayed. The salvation history of God's activity on behalf of all people began before the creation of human beings and before the beginning of world history, and it will continue after the parousia has brought world history to an end. Within these outer limits lies world history. It is a history of everyday events, of emperors, governors, kings, and high priests, of taxation and censuses (Luke 2:1; 3:1–2). As in no other New Testament writing, Luke-Acts is concerned with locating its story in a particular time and with reference to particular locations. But this history is also a history in which the promises of God are made, the word of God is proclaimed, and the salvific message is made known to the world. In this history the Spirit of God is operating in Jesus and in the church. But salvation history is also beyond world history, for it is the history from which the Spirit comes and to which Jesus ascends after his resurrection.

Viewing history in the context of salvation history, the dominant view of much modern study of Luke-Acts is that its author thinks of history as divided into a series of three epochs. At least two of the three epochs are indicated by Luke 16:16: "The law and the prophets were in effect until John came; since then the good news of the kingdom of God is proclaimed, and everyone tries to enter it by force." The *first era* is the era of "the law and the prophets" down to the mission of John the Baptist, a transitional figure. Then comes an *interim period* represented by the birth and infancy stories of John and Jesus and the activity of John as forerunner. The *second era* is the era of "the proclamation of the Kingdom of God," the time of Jesus and of the church (Luke 16:16; Acts 28:31). This second era is further subdivided by the descent of the Spirit on Jesus at his baptism and at the Cross, where Jesus returns the Spirit to the Father (Luke 23:46), the adult life of Jesus. Then there follows an *interim period* in which Jesus is raised from the dead and reveals to the disciples the secret of the second part of the era of the Kingdom of God, an interim culminating in the ascension (Luke 24:51; Acts 1:1–11). This is followed by the *third era,* the period of the church, also inaugurated (according to the "law of duality") by the descent of the Spirit at Pentecost (which is a baptism, Acts 1:5) and epitomized by Paul preaching the Kingdom of God "with all boldness and without hindrance" in Rome (Acts 28:31). This era will end with the parousia (Luke 21:25–28), which will be at some indefinite point in the future (Luke 9:27; 17:20–21; 19:11; 21:8–9; compare Acts 1:7). The whole conception may be represented as follows:

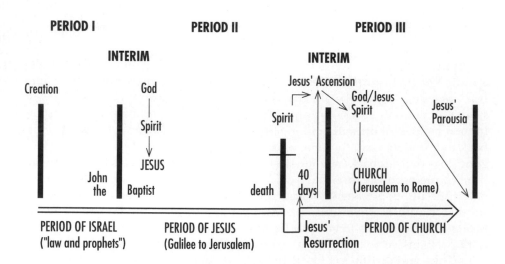

The Lukan Three-Stage Salvation History.

The Period of Jesus can be further subdivided and Jesus' journey from Galilee to Jerusalem paralleled to the journey of the church from Jerusalem to Rome:

The Lukan Journey Theme.

Luke's "salvation history" can be summarized as follows:

First era: The time of "the law and the prophets," from Adam to John the Baptist.

Interim period: The time of the birth and infancy of John and Jesus and of the ministry of the forerunner John.

Second era: The time of the proclamation of the Kingdom of God by Jesus, from the descent of the Spirit on Jesus to the return of the Spirit to the Father at the Cross.

Interim period: The time of the resurrection, revelatory teaching to the disciples by the risen Jesus, and the ascension.

Third era: The time of the proclamation of the Kingdom of God by the church, from the descent of the Spirit at Pentecost to the parousia.

We will now say something about each of these divisions.

The Time of "the Law and the Prophets"

The key to understanding this epoch is Luke 16:16: "The law and the prophets were in effect until John came; since then the good news of the kingdom of God is proclaimed, and everyone tries to enter it by force." The time of the law and the prophets, distinguished from the time of the preaching of the Kingdom of God (compare Acts 1:3; 19:8; 28:23), is most characterized by prophecy, which the author of Luke-Acts sees as fulfilled, as well as renewed, in the succeeding periods of Jesus and the church.

The Interim Period of the Birth and Infancy of John and Jesus and of the Ministry of the Forerunner John

The place of John the Baptist in Luke's schema ("since then") is difficult to determine. It may be that he is a transitional figure somewhat structurally analogous to a second interim period, that between Jesus and the church. On the one hand, John does not preach "the good news of the Kingdom of God" (contrast Matt 3:2) and the author of Luke-Acts brings forward the imprisonment of John to a time before Jesus' public ministry begins (3:20; compare Mark 6:17–18), thus stressing the tradition of John's subordination (3:15–16; Acts 13:25). On the other hand, Luke 1–2 shows a clear parallelism between the birth of John and the birth of Jesus. John's birth is announced in Old Testament prophetic fashion by the old age of his parents (1:7); he is called "prophet of the Most High" who will "prepare his ways" and "give knowledge of salvation to his people by the forgiveness of their sins" (1:76–77); and in Luke 3:18 John's exhortations are viewed as preaching the good news. Thus, Luke's ambiguous "since then" (16:16) seems to see John as a transition figure who, though clearly subordinate, prepares the way for the time of proclamation of the Kingdom of God by Jesus.

The Time of the Proclamation of the Kingdom of God by Jesus

The descent of the **Holy Spirit** on Jesus at his baptism (3:21–22) more clearly marks a time when "the good news of the Kingdom of God is proclaimed." This time will be continued in the third major epoch, the time of the church, which is also given the Spirit (at Pentecost, Acts 2). Thus, the coming of the Spirit on Jesus and then on the church, combined with the division between Book One and Book Two of the two-volume work, divides the period of preaching the Kingdom into two epochs. Luke stresses the activity of the Spirit in each epoch: Jesus is identified as God's son at the descent of the Holy Spirit; he is "full of the Holy Spirit" and "led by the Spirit" (4:1) when, as the Son of God, he is tested by Satan in the wilderness (4:3, 9). In the "power of the Spirit" Jesus returns to Galilee. Then comes the programmatic scene in the synagogue at Nazareth (4:16–30; compare Mark 6:1–6) where the author adds the crucial prophecy about the Spirit–filled Messiah who brings liberation and healing (Isa 61), which Jesus fulfills "today."

The author of Luke-Acts also emphasizes that after the temptation of Jesus the devil "departed from him until an opportune time" (Luke 4:13; compare Matt 4:11), and that opportune time does not come until Jesus is in Jerusalem, the place of his passion and death, where "Satan entered into Judas called Iscariot, who was one of the twelve" (Luke 22:3). Thus, during the time of Jesus, Jesus is not again directly hindered by Satan until the passion in Jerusalem, which also fulfills prophecy. To be sure, the activity of Satan lies behind the sick and possessed whom Jesus heals (compare 10:18; 11:16–18; 13:16); yet, Jesus himself is free from Satan's malevolent activity.

The time of Jesus presented by the author of Luke-Acts has been called **"the center of time."** It is the central time, the hinge of history, in which both the meaning of the past and the course of the future are revealed. The author recognizes that he and the people for whom he is writing are involved in the flow of history in the world, but in effect he is claiming that one epoch in that history, the time of Jesus, is also the decisive epoch in salvation history, the time when the good news of God's activity on behalf of human salvation is proclaimed in the world.

The Interim Period of Jesus' Resurrection, Revelatory Teaching to the Disciples, and Ascension

Between Jesus' act of committing his spirit to God at the Cross (Luke 23:46) and the return of the Spirit to the church at Pentecost (Acts 2), there is an interim period of resurrection, teaching, and ascension. Luke stresses the resurrection of Jesus more than either Mark or Matthew. Mark has no resurrection appearances at all (16:1–8), while Matthew has one (28:9–10) and then the commissioning scene (28:16–20). However, Luke has the appearance on the Emmaus road (24:13–35), the appearance in Jerusalem itself (24:36–43), and he also mentions an appearance to Peter (24:34). Further, Luke-Acts has a period in which the risen Jesus is with his disciples, teaching them (Luke 24:44–49; Acts 1:6–8), and then the ascension is an event separate from the resurrection (Luke 24:51; Acts 1:9). As far as we know, the author of Luke-Acts is the first person to conceive of the ascension as separate from the resurrection. Normally in the New Testament the resurrection–ascension is conceived of as one act. But Luke needs a separate ascension to have a place in his narrative for the revelatory teachings of the risen Jesus to his disciples. This teaching is very important. It is in Luke 24:44–49 and Acts 1:4–8 that the heart of the Lukan understanding of things is revealed. Here we find the necessity for repentance and forgiveness of sins to be preached by the disciples, who are "witnesses." Here we find, further, the "beginning from Jerusalem" and the moving "to the end of the earth," and finally the baptism with the Spirit that will make it all possible. These themes are crucial to the author of Luke-Acts, and they are all given in this interim period of revelatory teaching.

The Time of the Proclamation of the Kingdom of God by the Church, from Jerusalem to Rome

The *time of Jesus,* the center of time, is the time of the work of the Spirit through *Jesus,* the time of preaching the good news of the Kingdom of God, the time of witnessing from Galilee to Jerusalem. The *time of the church* is the time of the work of the Spirit through the *church,* the time of the proclamation of the Kingdom of God in the form of the church preaching repentance and the forgiveness of sins, the time of witnessing from Jerusalem to Rome. This time of the church will continue until the parousia, and it is the time of the author of Luke-Acts and his readers, and beyond.

THE STRUCTURE OF LUKE-ACTS

Drawing these themes together, the following structure emerges for the two-volume work:

Gospel of Luke

> Introduction to the two volumes, 1:1–4

Book One: The Ministry of the Spirit Through Jesus

> Introduction of the ministry of the Spirit through Jesus, 1:5–4:15
>
> The ministry in Galilee, 4:16–9:50
>
> The Journey of Jesus to Jerusalem, 9:51–19:27
>
> Jesus in Jerusalem 19:28–21:38
>
> The passion narrative, 22:1–23:49
>
> Burial, resurrection, ascension, 23:50–24:53

Acts of the Apostles

> Introduction to the second volume, 1:1–5

Book Two: The Ministry of the Spirit Through the Church

> Introduction to the ministry of the Spirit through the church, 1:6–26
>
> The descent of the Spirit on the church, 2:1–42

summary, 2:43–47

The church in Jerusalem, 3:1–5:41

summary, 5:42

The movement into Judea and Samaria, 6:1–9:30

summary, 9:31

The movement into the Gentile world, 9:32–12:23

summary, 12:24

To the End of the earth (1): Paul's first missionary journey and its conse quence, the Conference at Jerusalem, 12:25–15:33

summary, 15:35

To the End of the earth (2): Paul's second missionary journey, the movement into Europe and the decision to go to Rome, 15:36–19:19

summary, 19:20

The journey of Paul to Rome, 19:21–28:16

Paul in Rome, 28:17–31

EXEGETICAL SURVEY OF LUKE-ACTS

Because of the limitations of space it will not be possible in this interpretation to do more than indicate the outline and flow of the narrative and call attention to particular emphases and concerns of the author. We give the parallels to Mark or Matthew where the parallelism is close.

Introduction to the Two-Volume Work, Luke 1:1-4

The introduction is couched in the conventional language and style known from other, similar prologues in antiquity (for example, Josephus *Against Apion* 1.1. paragraph 1–3; compare Acts 1:1–2 and Josephus *Against Apion* 2.1 paragraph 1). It indicates that the author is deliberately attempting to compose a literary work. Note that he calls his work a "narrative" and wants to put matters into "an orderly account." But note also that his orderly account is a blending of secular history and salvation history.

Book One: The Ministry of the Spirit Through Jesus

Introduction to the Ministry of the Spirit Through Jesus, 1:5-4:13

1:5–80 THE BIRTH OF JOHN THE BAPTIST AND THE ANNOUNCEMENT OF THE BIRTH OF JESUS.
This introduction is written in Septuagint Greek. John's annunciation and birth (1:5–25, 57–80) are parallel in structure to Jesus' annunciation and birth

(1:26–38; 2:1–20), and the two are dovetailed by the pregnant Mary's visit to the pregnant Elizabeth (1:39–56). However, John is a prophet who is clearly subordinate (1:39–45); he will announce salvation and forgiveness of sins (1:77); he is of priestly descent, while Jesus will be called "Son of the Most High" (1:32), a clear reference to the King of David's royal line (2 Sam 7:13–16; Ps 89:26–29; compare Luke 3:23–28). Mary's role is highlighted in the anticipation of Jesus' supernatural birth (1:25–56).

2:1–52 THE BIRTH AND INFANCY OF JESUS.
Now salvation history and world history approach the point of intersection. Whereas Matthew concentrates in his infancy stories on the fulfillment of scriptural prophecy, Luke is concerned particularly with the promise that Jesus holds for the future, and his infancy stories are designed particularly to interpret the "center of time" of salvation history in advance (for example, 2:30–32, 34). Again the Spirit inspires prophecy (2:25–38). Luke balances the male prophet, Simeon, with a female prophet, Anna (2:22–38).

3:1–18 ACTIVITY OF JOHN THE BAPTIST (= MARK 1:1–8 = MATT 3:1–12).
This section first picks up the Markan order and is close to Mark and Matthew and hence in general is from Mark and Q. Luke extends the Isaiah quotation with its comment, "all flesh shall see the salvation of God," but omits its conclusion (3:6). He tones down the note of apocalyptic urgency in John's proclamation and adds the general ethical teaching of verses 10–14.

3:19–20 THE IMPRISONMENT OF THE BAPTIST.
This is a remarkable passage. In the service of his understanding of the periodization of salvation history, Luke has John shut up in prison *before* the baptism of Jesus.

3:21–22 THE DESCENT OF THE SPIRIT ON JESUS (= MARK 1:9–11; MATT 3:13–17).
What in the other gospels is the baptism of Jesus becomes in Luke the descent of the Spirit on him. Note the characteristic introduction of "and was praying" in verse 21. Luke places Jesus at prayer at critical turning points in his salvation history (3:21; 6:12; 9:18; 9:28; 11:1; 22:41); he is the master at prayer, teaching the church to pray (6:28; 10:2; 11:1–3; 18:1–8; 21:36).

3:23–28 THE GENEALOGY OF JESUS (= MATT 1:1–16).
Here the descent of Jesus is traced back to Adam, the first human, and not, as in Matthew, just to Abraham. Jesus is the Son of God; his salvation is for all.

4:1–13 THE TEMPTATION OF JESUS (= MARK 1:12–13; MATT 4:1–11).
Jesus, full of the Holy Spirit, is led by the spirit and tempted as the Son of God, material largely from Q. The devil, unsuccessful, departs "until an opportune time" (22:3).

The Ministry in Galilee, 4:14–9:50

4:14–15 THE FIRST PREACHING IN GALILEE (= MARK 1:14–15).
Luke omits the eschatological content of Jesus' Kingdom preaching.

4:16–30 THE SYNAGOGUE SCENE AT NAZARETH (= MARK 6:1–6).

What in Mark is an account of the rejection of Jesus by "his own" in Galilee
(Mark 6:1–6) becomes in Luke a staged introduction to the whole ministry of
Jesus. We have called it his leitmotif. Jesus reads the Isaianic prophecy about
the Spirit-filled Messiah who brings good news to the poor, release to the cap-
tives, healing of the blind, freedom of the oppressed, all at the time of "Year of
Jubilee," or "Year of Liberty," the fiftieth year, when in theory ancestral lands
were to be returned to the family and Jewish slaves were to be released (Isa 61).
Despite legislation, the Jubilee Year was not really practiced. Yet, Jesus claims
that the text is fulfilled "today." Moreover, when Jesus mentions two accounts
about Gentiles who receive such benefits, the Jews in his village want to kill him
by mob action (see above on Jews and Romans in Luke-Acts). With Elijah/Elisha
healing miracles he shows that Jesus is rejected because he implies that it is
God's will that his offer of salvation go to the Gentiles. The Nazareth scene deliberately presents the reader with an announcement ahead of time of events to follow, a typical literary technique of Luke and thereby an understanding of the
time of Jesus as a time when prophecy is fulfilled, specifically Isaiah 61:1–2 (compare also Isa 58:6). These themes dominate the presentation of the time of
Jesus in the Gospel of Luke (see above, the discussion of the social-historical context of Luke-Acts).

4:31–41 THE SABBATH DAY AT CAPERNAUM (= MARK 1:21–34).

Luke omits the call of the first disciples, thereby showing how Jesus' success at
Capernaum follows his rejection at Nazareth, but fulfills the programmatic intent
of the Nazareth scene. He follows Mark with only minor modifications.

4:42–44 A PREACHING JOURNEY (= MARK 1:35–39).

Verse 43 represents Luke's view of the ministry.

5:1–6:11 INCIDENTS OF THE MINISTRY IN GALILEE (= MARK 1:40–3:6).

With the exception of the miraculous catch of fish, which is a hint forward to
the worldwide mission of the church (5:1–11), Luke is with minor variations following Mark.

6:12–16 THE CALL OF THE TWELVE (= MARK 3:13–19).

This follows Mark in general, but note the characteristic Lukan emphasis on Jesus
spending the night in prayer before choosing the twelve.

6:17–19 JESUS HEALS THE MULTITUDES (= MARK 3:7–12).

6:20–49 THE SERMON ON THE PLAIN.

Luke 6:20–8:3 combines Q and Special L, deviating from the Markan order (**the
Lesser Insertion**). The Sermon on the Plain is Luke's equivalent of Matthew's Sermon on the Mount, though it lacks Matthew's characteristic understanding of it
as the first book of the new revelation. That both Matthew and Luke have such a
sermon indicates that the tradition of bringing together teaching material and
giving it a brief narrative setting was already a feature of the sayings source Q.
Like Matthew, Luke also gives the sermon an eschatological setting (the Beati-

tudes, 6:20–23), as Q must therefore have done. Luke, concerned for the poor and outcast, characteristically adds a series of woes on the rich and happy (6:24–26). The remainder of the sermon parallels various places in Matthew; it is Q material, and probably in the same order as Q.

7:1–8:3 FURTHER INCIDENTS OF THE MINISTRY IN GALILEE.
Now we have a series of incidents reflecting Luke's interests and concerns. The Centurion's Slave emphasizes the faith of a Gentile (7:1–10); the Widow's Son portrays Jesus' concern for a widow (7:11–17); the Baptist's Question (7:18–23) echoes the key note of the Nazareth synagogue scene; Jesus' testimony to John the Baptist stresses John's preparatory role in the history of salvation (7:24–35; compare 1:76–77; the quotation of Malachi 3:1 [Mark 1:2] was omitted in 3:4); the Woman with the Ointment highlights Jesus' concern for a sinner (7:36–50); and the Ministering Woman stresses his preparedness to help and be helped by women (8:1–3). Some parts have parallels in Matthew (Luke 7:18–35 = Matt 11:2–19), but the configuration and concerns are those of Luke and his gospel.

8:4–18 THE PARABLE OF THE SOWER AND THE PURPOSE OF PARABLES (= MARK 4:1–29).
Here Luke returns to the Markan order again. He follows Mark's parable chapter except that he omits Mark's parable of the Seed Growing Secretly and transposes the Mustard Seed to a different setting (Luke 13:18–19). Also, the three sayings in 8:16–18 are from Mark 4:21–25, but Luke has doublets of them at 11:33; 12:2; and 19:26, each time with a Matthean parallel. Clearly, different versions of these sayings were known to Mark and to the Q community. Luke 8:16 is particularly interesting. Mark 4:21 has a saying about a lamp being put on a stand. Matt 5:15 has a version in which the lamp "gives light to all in the house." The Lukan writer implies reform in Jewish life; normally in a Roman house, a lamp is put in the vestibule, so that people who enter can find their way by the light. The reinterpretation of traditional sayings in accordance with the interests and concerns of the evangelists is a complex and fascinating process.

8:19–21 JESUS' TRUE RELATIVES (= MARK 3:31–35).

8:22–25 THE STILLING OF THE STORM (= MARK 4:35–41).

8:26–39 THE GERASENE DEMONIAC (= MARK 5:1–20).

8:40–56 JAIRUS' DAUGHTER AND THE WOMAN WITH THE HEMORRHAGE (= MARK 5:21–43).

9:1–6 THE MISSION OF THE TWELVE (= MARK 6:6B–13).

9:7–9 HEROD THINKS JESUS IS JOHN, RISEN (= MARK 6:14–16).

9:10–17 THE RETURN OF THE TWELVE AND THE FEEDING OF THE FIVE THOUSAND (= MARK 6:30–44).
Luke is following Mark, with some transpositions of order, but he omits Mark's account of the fate of the Baptist (Mark 6:17–29), because he has John in prison before the baptism of Jesus.

9:18–27 CAESAREA PHILIPPI (= MARK 8:27–9:1).

Like Matthew, Luke omits the healing of the blind man at Bethsaida (Mark 8:22–26). But in Luke's case it is left out along with other material, the whole block being called the **Great Omission** (Mark 6:45–8:26). Luke's version of Mark's first prediction unit introduces a characteristic emphasis on Jesus at prayer (9:18), and he omits the misunderstanding and rebuke of Peter, most probably in the interest of honoring a hero of the church. Also, the eschatological note of Mark 9:1 is minimized in Luke 9:27 and the delay of the parousia is indicated in 9:23 ("daily").

9:28–36 THE TRANSFIGURATION (= MARK 9:2–8).

Luke follows Mark but omits the eschatological note of the reference to the coming of Elijah in Mark 9:9–13 and places Jesus at prayer for this major event in salvation history.

9:37–43a THE HEALING OF THE EPILEPTIC BOY (= MARK 9:14–29).

Luke omits Mark's identification of John the Baptist with Elijah (Mark 9:9–13; compare 7:24–35; 8:19–21) who was expected to return at the End, that is, he is consistent with his view that the parousia is delayed and that Elijah themes are related to Jesus himself. His special use of prayer will explain its omission in an exorcism (compare Mark 9:29).

9:43B–48 THE SECOND PREDICTION UNIT (= MARK 9:30–37).

Luke greatly abbreviates Mark at this point, almost obliterating the passion prediction. This is a consequence of his particular understanding of the passion, which we discuss later in connection with his passion narrative.

9:49–50 THE STRANGE EXORCIST (= MARK 9:38–41).

Again, an abbreviation of Mark.

The Journey to Jerusalem, 9:51–19:27

Luke begins this section with a key verse: "When the days drew near for him to be taken up, he set his face to go to Jerusalem" (9:51). The reference is to the ascension (see above) and from this point forward the gospel moves toward Jerusalem and the ascension. Luke 9:51–18:14 is a rambling section loosely organized around the journey to Jerusalem, until in 18:15 Luke rejoins Mark's narrative at Mark 10:13. The material in this section of Luke is his longest non-Markan block (the *Greater Insertion*), being derived partly from Q and partly from Luke's own special traditions. Sixteen of Luke's seventeen special parables are in this section. We will content ourselves with calling attention only to some features that particularly represent the characteristic concerns of this gospel.

10:1–20 THE MISSION OF THE SEVENTY.

Only Luke has this mission, probably a symbolic anticipation of the church's mission to the Gentiles, since in Jewish thinking seventy is the traditional number of the nations.

10:29–37 THE PARABLE OF THE GOOD SAMARITAN.

The parable reflects Luke's concern for the outcast, since the Jews regarded the

Samaritans with real hostility (compare 9:51–56). Luke has created an introduction to the parable from Mark 12:28–31 and Q (Matt 22:34–40).

10:38–42 MARY AND MARTHA.
The characteristic approach to women in Luke's gospel: The woman disciple is praised; the woman domestic is chided.

11:1-13 PRAYER.
Again Luke portrays Jesus at prayer (11:1) as a prelude to Jesus' teaching about prayer to the disciples (and to the church). The Lord's Prayer (11:1–4), which stresses the literal poor, is followed by a parable (11:5–7) and a series of sayings about persistence and God's willingness to give the Holy Spirit, all dealing with prayer. For further analysis, see Chapter One.

12:1–53 TEACHING TO THE DISCIPLES.
Jesus stresses the risks of discipleship and the importance of devotion to his way. Note especially the parable of the Rich Fool (12:13–21), the theme of the Holy Spirit (12:10, 12), and the notation about the delay of the parousia (12:45).

13:22, 31–35 JERUSALEM THEMES.
Luke reminds his readers of the journey to Jerusalem (13:22); in sayings of Jesus he stresses that a prophet should perish in Jerusalem (13:33) and gives the lament over Jerusalem (13:34–35).

14:7–24 LUKE'S BANQUET THEME AND TEACHING ON HUMILITY, PARABLE OF THE GREAT DINNER.
The characteristic stress on wealth and concern for the poor, which is associated with the Kingdom, stresses inviting the uninvited: "the poor, the crippled, the lame, and the blind" (14:13, 21).

15:1–32 THE LOST SHEEP, THE LOST COIN, AND THE LOST SON.
This is one of the great chapters in the New Testament. The banquet theme is picked up with Jesus' banquet with the outcast tax collectors and sinners (15:1). In three parables Luke presents what he believes to be Jesus' intense concern for the lost. The sheep is lost from the flock, the coin from the woman's meager store, the boy from the land and standards of his father. However, all are found again, and in this Luke sees a symbol of God's love and concern for the lost and the outcast as epitomized by Jesus and to be echoed by the believer.

16:1–31 RICHES AND THE KINGDOM.
The parable of the Unjust Judge, told to the disciples, becomes the occasion for sayings culminating in the theme, "You cannot serve God and wealth" (16:13). The Pharisees, who observed Jesus' banquet with sinners (15:2), are now accused as lovers of money (16:14–15). Luke 16:16 gives a clue to salvation history by contrasting the era of the law and prophets with the era of the proclamation of the good news of the Kingdom of God. The parable of the Rich Man and Lazarus (16:19–31) continues the theme of riches and concern for the poor.

17:11–19 THE FAITH OF THE SAMARITAN LEPER.

Ten lepers are cleansed "on the way to Jerusalem . . . between Samaria and Galilee." Only the Samaritan gives thanks. Jesus notes that the faith of "this foreigner" has healed him.

17:20–21 THE KINGDOM OF GOD AND THE DAY OF THE SON OF MAN.

The question "when" the Kingdom will come is answered with a denial of signs and denial of place; it is "in the midst of you." Luke 17:22–23 reflects the delay of the parousia.

18:1–14 THE PARABLES OF THE UNJUST JUDGE AND THE PUBLICAN.

Characteristic piety in the form of prayer, encouraged by the stories of a poor widow who successfully importunes an unjust judge and a tax collector who successfully prays for mercy.

18:15–43 JESUS DRAWS NEAR TO JERUSALEM (= MARK 10:13–52).

At 18:15, Luke rejoins Mark's narrative. The blessing of the children (18:15–17 = Mark 10:13–16) would obviously appeal to Luke, as would the story of the rich young man (18:18–30 = Mark 10:17–31). Mark's third prediction unit (Mark 10:32–45) is itself composite, since the teaching on discipleship was probably originally in a Eucharistic setting, where Luke has it (Luke 22:24–27). Luke 18:31–34 has the third prediction of the passion, and 18:35–43 the healing of the blind man with only minor variations from Mark.

19:1–27 ZACCHAEUS AND THE PARABLE OF THE POUNDS.

Luke 19:1–10 picks up the story of Zacchaeus (Special L), a tax collector; it is characteristic of Luke's concern for the ministry of Jesus to the outcast. The parable of the pounds from Q (19:11–27 = Matt 25:14–30) is told "because he was near Jerusalem, and because they [wrongly] supposed that the Kingdom of God was to appear immediately" (19:11).

Jesus in Jerusalem, 19:28–21:38

This section basically follows Mark 11:1–13:37. Luke 19:39–44 adds a prediction of the destruction of Jerusalem, which interprets that catastrophe as a judgment on the city, "because you did not recognize the time of your visitation from God" (19:44). Luke maintains the apocalyptic discourse of Mark 13 because he accepts the parousia (Luke 21:25–38). He even adds a note of his own (Luke 21:34–36) that stresses the universal nature of the event. He redacts the chapter to separate the destruction of Jerusalem (21:20–24) from the more remote parousia (21:25–36), the "times of the Gentiles" falling between (21:24; compare 21:8–9).

The Passion Narrative, 22:1–23:49

This is rather different from the account in Mark 14:1–16:8, and it has been suggested that Luke may be following another source. However, the general framework of his narrative is from Mark, and the divergences can probably be explained partly by his use of special material at some points and partly by a par-

ticular interpretation of the passion that causes him to undertake a rather extensive redaction of the Markan narrative in some places.

Luke understands the passion of Jesus as the legal murder of Jesus by the Jewish authorities joined by the Jewish people, achieved despite a favorable attitude to
Jesus by the Roman and Herodian authorities. The Jews and the Jews alone—especially the Jewish leaders—bear the guilt for the death of Jesus. A second major
deviation from Mark is that Luke does not regard the Cross as an atonement for
sin: The death of Jesus is not the basis for human salvation. In Luke's version of the
Last Supper, the Cross of Jesus is interpreted as an act of service, not as in Mark
10:45 as a "ransom for many." There is even doubt as to whether the words of interpretation of the bread and wine at the supper—a body "given for you" and blood
"poured out for you" belong in the original text of the gospel (Luke 22:19b–20).
The Lukan passion narrative has to be reviewed with some care.

22:1–2 THE CONSPIRACY AGAINST JESUS (= MARK 14:1–2).

22:3–6 SATAN RETURNS TO THE SCENE (= MARK 14:10–11).
This is Luke's account of Judas Iscariot's agreement to betray Jesus, with the spe-
cial note on the return of Satan, who was absent from Luke's narrative since the
Temptation (4:13).

22:7–13 PREPARATION FOR THE SUPPER (= MARK 14:12–16).

22:14–38 THE LAST SUPPER (= MARK 14:17–25, BUT WITH SIGNIFICANT VARIATIONS).
Luke begins his account of the supper with the institution of the Eucharist and follows it with the announcement of the traitor, an inversion of the order in Mark.
In itself this is of no great moment. More important is that Luke 22:15–16 has the
reference forward to eating in the Kingdom of God before the words of interpretation, 22:17–19a (?19b–20), whereas Mark has the reverse order. It is entirely possible that Luke is minimizing the impact of the words of interpretation by
deliberately preceding them with the reference to the future of the Kingdom of
God. Luke 22:24–27 is his version of Mark 10:42–45, and it is certainly independent of what Mark represented. The two versions of the teaching developed separately in the tradition of the church, and Luke apparently chooses this one
rather than what is in Mark because it avoids the ransom saying of Mark 10:45.
Verses 28–30 seem to be from Q; Matt 19:28 has the saying in a different context. Verses 31–34 and 35–38 are special Lukan tradition.

22:39–53 JESUS IN GETHSEMANE (= MARK 14:26–52).
A somewhat abbreviated version of Mark's narrative.

22:54–71 THE TRIAL BEFORE THE SANHEDRIN AND PETER'S DENIAL (= MARK 14:53–72).
Luke finishes the account of the denial before beginning the trial, whereas Mark
intercalates the trial into the denial story.

23:1–5 JESUS BEFORE PILATE (= MARK 15:1–5).
Luke develops Mark's account in accordance with his wish to stress the positive
attitude of Pilate to Jesus and the guilt of the Jews.

23:6–12 JESUS BEFORE HEROD.
A further demonstration of Luke's emphasis: the innocence of Jesus, the guilt of the Jews, the favor of the authorities toward Jesus.

23:13–25 THE SENTENCING OF JESUS (= MARK 15:6–15).
Luke adds verses 13–16 to Mark's narrative, reiterating his emphases.

23:26–32 THE ROAD TO GOLGOTHA.
Luke adds verses 27–31, the lamenting of the women of Jerusalem, to Mark 15:21.

23:33–43 THE CRUCIFIXION (= MARK 15:22–32).
Particular Lukan emphases are the prayer for forgiveness (verse 34), and the Penitent Thief (verses 39–43).

23:44–49 THE RETURN OF THE SPIRIT TO THE FATHER (= MARK 15:33–41).
Luke rewrites the account of the death of Jesus in accordance with his concept of the role of the spirit in salvation history. The centurion's confession becomes a declaration of the innocence of Jesus, not a confession of his status as Son of God, as it is in Mark 15:39.

Burial, Resurrection, Ascension, 23:50–24:53

23:50–24:11 THE BURIAL OF JESUS AND THE EMPTY TOMB.
Basically follows Mark 15:42–47; 16:1–8.

24:13–35 THE ROAD TO EMMAUS.
This is the first of the Lukan resurrection appearances, and verses 19–21 represent Luke's view of Jesus. It is located near Jerusalem (24:13). The story stresses that the preceding events fulfill Scripture.

24:36–49 THE RISEN CHRIST IN JERUSALEM.
This is the gospel version of the risen Jesus' teaching to his disciples. A further version is given in Acts 1:6–9, and Luke uses the opportunity of the repetition to develop slightly different emphases each time. These two sets of teaching are the key to the Lukan enterprise, and our overall interpretation of Luke-Acts builds heavily on them. Again, the prophecy-fulfillment theme is predominant.

24:50–53 THE ASCENSION.
In accordance with 9:51 the reference to the ascension should be read in verse 51b and not relegated to the margin.

Introduction to the Second Volume (Acts of the Apostles), Acts 1:1–5.

This introduction to Volume Two mentions the recipient Theophilus again, and recalls the introduction to Volume One (Luke 1:1–4). There are parallels in Josephus, see the comment on Luke 1:1–4 above.

Book Two: The Ministry of the Spirit Through the Church

Introduction to the Ministry of the Spirit Through the Church: the Risen Lord and His Disciples, 1:6–26.

1:6–11 THE RISEN LORD WITH HIS DISCIPLES.

This is Luke's second version of the interim period of special revelation. Note the emphasis on the empowering by the Spirit, the work of witnessing, and the geographical progression from Jerusalem to the end of the earth (Rome). This is a statement of the theme of Acts. Note further that the expectation of the parousia is still maintained (verse 11).

1:12–26 THE REPLACEMENT OF JUDAS.

The author of Luke-Acts is moving toward a view of the church as an more organized institution, and the fact that it is headed by a formal group of twelve apostles is important to him. Note the emphasis on prayer in verse 24, no doubt deliberately reminiscent of Jesus at prayer before the appointment of the twelve in the gospel.

The Descent of the Spirit on the Church, 2:1–42

This descent of the Spirit had already been interpreted as a baptism in 1:5 and so parallels the beginning of the ministry of Jesus. The gift of tongues symbolizes the worldwide mission of the church. Peter's speech in verses 14–36 and 38–39 has some similarity to methods of the interpretation of Scripture in the Dead Sea Scrolls. As it stands in its present context, the speech represents Luke's understanding of things. Note especially the emphasis on the humanity of Jesus (verse 22), the guilt of the Jews (verse 23), the death, resurrection, and present status of Jesus as the fulfillment of Scripture (Ps 16:8–11; 132:10–11; 110:1) and the witness of the church (verse 32), the subordination of Jesus as "Lord" and "Messiah" to God (verse 36), and repentance and the forgiveness of sins (verse 38).

The section closes with a summary, 2:43–47.

The Church in Jerusalem, 3:1–5:41

The witness of the church begins in Jerusalem, in accordance with the programmatic statement in 1:8. Luke may be drawing on early traditions about the church in Jerusalem, but he clearly stamps them with his own emphases and concerns, especially in the speeches: 3:12–26 (Peter at Solomon's Porch), 4:8–12 and 5:29–32 (Peter before the Sanhedrin). Here, for example, Jesus is understood as a prophet (3:22); there is also an emphasis on the resurrection (3:26; 5:30) and on the guilt of the Jews (4:11; 5:30). For the most part, however, the legends are about the early days of the church, developed in the church for the edification of the believers.

The section closes with a summary, 5:42.

The Movement into Judea and Samaria, 6:1–9:30

Following on the programmatic statement in 1:8, the witness now moves out-ward to Judea, the territory immediately surrounding Jerusalem, and Samaria. Here we begin to have some contact with the history of the early church as dis-tinct from myths and legends about it. Behind the narrative of the dispute between Hellenists and Hebrews in Jerusalem (6:1–6) and the persecution of the church in Jerusalem (8:1), there lies the reminiscence of a real division in the church and the persecution of one part of it and not another. This section of Acts echoes the historical origins of the Hellenistic Jewish Christian mission.

Stephen's speech (7:2–53) must be regarded as an example of the interpre-tation of Scripture and the interpretation of events by which Hellenistic Jewish Mission Christianity justified its break with Judaism. We noted earlier the parallels the author of Luke-Acts carefully draws between the passion of Stephen, the pro-tomartyr, and that of Jesus. In 8:1 Paul appears for the first time, and there can be no doubt that he did in fact persecute the church in some such manner as is here depicted. Luke 8:4–24 is a collection of legends about the origin of the Hellenis-tic Jewish Christian mission, remarkable in that it associates Peter firmly with that movement and presents both Philip and Peter as Hellenistic "heroes."

Acts 8:25 is a summary reflecting a division in the narrative, not major since it is not associated with a geographical shift, but a division nonetheless. It is followed by the incident of Philip and the Ethiopian Eunuch (8:26–39). Then comes a sum-mary of Philip's further activity (8:40), making it probable that the author of Luke–Acts has deliberately inserted this narrative here. It certainly represents two of the author's characteristic concerns. The eunuch was an outcast, since the Jews would not have accepted a mutilated man as a proselyte, and the quotation from the Suffering Servant passage in Isaiah 53 avoids any interpretation of the death of Jesus as an atonement for sin.

Acts 9:1–30 is the first of the three accounts of the conversion of Paul in Acts (see also 22:3–21; 26:9–23). That this event is narrated three times indicates its importance to the author of Luke-Acts and the Hellenistic Jewish Mission Chris-tianity he represents. We have already discussed the conversion of Paul, and here we need only note that the account is deliberately redacted in line with the programmatic statement of 1:8. Paul's witness did not begin in Jerusalem as all three accounts of his conversion insist it did, but the program announced in 1:8 is here dominant for our author. The myth is overtaking the history.

The section closes with a summary, 9:31.

The Movement into the Gentile World, 9:32–12:23

Still following the programmatic statement of 1:8, the narrative now moves to an account of the first Christian witness in the purely Gentile world. The author of Luke-Acts emphasizes the role of Peter in this movement, as he had previously emphasized the role of Peter in the beginning of Hellenistic Jewish Mission Chris-tianity. In part the author wants to bring Peter and Paul, the two great heroes of early Christianity, into essential agreement with each other. But that Peter did in fact take part in the Hellenistic Jewish Christian mission is attested by his appear-ance in Antioch and Paul's passionate altercation with him there (Gal 2:11–21).

Characteristically Lukan themes recur in Peter's speech (10:34–43) and the founding of the church at Antioch (11:19–21). The latter marks the true beginning of the Christian mission to the purely Gentile world, and the fact—and it probably is a fact—that "in Antioch the disciples were first called `Christians'" (11:26) is symbolic testimony to the importance of this moment in the history of New Testament Christianity.

The section closes with a summary, 12:24.

The Movement to the "Ends of the Earth" (1): Paul's First Missionary Journey and Its Consequence, the Conference at Jerusalem, 12:25–15:33

A feature of Acts is the presentation of Paul's missionary work in the form of three missionary journeys: 13:13–14:28; 15:36–18:21; 18:23–19:19. Clearly Paul must have undertaken missionary journeys; however, in view of the fondness of the author of Luke-Acts for the literary theme of "journeys" (Luke 9:51 and Jesus' journey to Jerusalem; Acts 19:21 and Paul's journey to Rome) these missionary journeys in Acts are probably a literary device around which the author organizes his presentation of Paul's work.

The first "missionary journey" features the first major speech by Paul in Acts, at Pisidian Antioch, 13:16–41. It rehearses themes characteristic of Luke-Acts: the guilt of the Jews, an emphasis on the resurrection, the witness of Christians, the proclamation of the forgiveness of sins as the heart of the Christian message, and so on. It represents the mind of the author of Luke-Acts far more than it does anything appropriate to the Paul of the New Testament letters (see above). The Jerusalem Conference was probably the start of Paul's missionary journeys into the world beyond Antioch, not after an initial journey. The "decree" of 15:29 represents a solution to a problem that arose as a consequence of Paul's work rather than during the course of it (see above). At the same time, the activity and experiences depicted here in connection with Paul and Barnabas must have been typical of Hellenistic Jewish Christian missionaries in general as known to the author of Luke-Acts.

This section ends with a summary, 15:35.

The Movement to the "Ends of the Earth" (2): Paul's Second Missionary Journey, the Movement into Europe and the Decision to Go to Rome, 15:36–19:19

This section of Acts is dominated by Paul's decision to carry the Christian witness from Asia into Europe, presented as a direct consequence of the activity of the Spirit, and it leads to Paul's decision to go to Rome (19:21), which in Acts structurally parallels Jesus' decision to go to Jerusalem in Luke 9:51. Paul's experiences as presented here must have been very like those of most Hellenistic Jewish Christian missionaries, as Paul's speech at Athens (17:22–31) no doubt represents typical Christian preaching to the Hellenistic world. Note also the characteristic themes of the favor of the Roman authorities toward the Christians and the guilt of the Jews (18:14–17). This section also contains the first of the we-passages (Acts 16:10–17).

The section ends with a summary, 19:20.

The Journey of Paul to Rome, 19:21–28:16

We now find in Acts the same rambling travel narrative beginning with the chief protagonist's resolve that is in the gospel of Luke beginning with 9:51. It is a literary device obviously dear to the author of Luke-Acts. The narrative has been composed of a mixture of traditions and legends about the work of the apostle Paul on which the author of Luke-Acts has imposed his own understanding of things—as, for example, in the second and third accounts of the conversion of Paul (22:3–21; 26:9–23), where Paul's Christian witness always begins in Jerusalem and moves toward Rome.

A feature of this section of Acts is long "we passages" (20:5–15; 21:1–18; 27:1–28:16).

Paul in Rome, 28:17–31

Luke-Acts ends with the establishment of Paul and his mission in Rome and the programmatic note of Paul preaching the gospel "with all boldness and without hindrance" there. It is the climax of the narrative as depicted in 1:8. We have already discussed the complex issue it raises for the position of Luke on the salvation of the Jews (see the discussion above).

FURTHER OBSERVATIONS

Jesus as the Prophet, Servant-Messiah, "Divine Man" Hero, and Benefactor of All Humanity

In Luke-Acts, Jesus is the "center of time." He is portrayed, on the one hand, as the fulfillment of Old Testament prophecies (16:29, 31), especially as the Spirit-filled, anointed Davidic Servant-Messiah and prophet who brings salvation to all, especially by preaching to the poor and outcast, by healing (Luke 4:16–43; 24:19, 27, 41). He also fulfills the prophecies when he is rejected by the Pharisees, is condemned by the Jews, and is martyred at Jerusalem, the city where the prophets have been killed (7:16, 39; 11:47–50; 13:34–35). Finally, he fulfills the prophets and the psalms when he is vindicated as Christ, Lord, and Son of God in his resurrection and ascension to God's side (Luke 24:25–26, 44–53; Acts 2:33, 36; 13:26–41).

On the other hand, Jesus is portrayed as a Son of God by a human mother and supernatural agency, as full of the Spirit, as a wandering teacher and healer whose ways of life, teaching, and healing were bequeathed to his disciple-followers, as a figure who appeared after death and ascended to heaven, and as a Savior who offered peace and salvation to the whole world. In this orientation, Luke's Jesus is the great benefactor of all humanity. Such an account read by any high-ranking Gentile or Gentile group would indicate that the Jewish Messiah who fulfilled the Scriptures shared much in common with all manner of Savior figures throughout the Eastern Mediterranean, from the miracle workers and wandering philosophers, whose disciples learned and passed on their teacher's teaching and total way of life, to the emperors whose inscriptions proclaimed peace and salvation to the world, to the gods themselves.

These overall views in Luke-Acts contrast sharply with dominant Son of God as Son of Man Christology in the Gospel of Mark. The evangelist Mark wants to present Jesus as Christ and Son of God and to interpret those designations by a careful and systematic use of Son of Man, leading up to the climactic interpretation of Jesus as Son of Man in 14:62 and the climactic confession of him as Son of God by the centurion in 15:39. In the gospel of Luke all this changes. The confession of the centurion becomes in Luke 23:47 simply a declaration, "Certainly this man was innocent," and the formal acceptance and reinterpretation of the titles "Christ" and "Son of God" by Jesus in Mark 14:61–62 is in Luke 22:67–70 an indiscriminate use without any sensitivity to the nuances of meaning attaching to these titles. The author of Luke-Acts does not have either the same Christology or the same christological concerns as the evangelist Mark.

It is also interesting to consider Luke's interpretation of Mark's predictions of the passion and resurrection (Mark 8:31; 9:31; 10:33–34) in Luke (Luke 9:22; 9:44; 18:31–33). In all the predictions Mark stresses the authority of Jesus in that Jesus is said to "rise again" or "rise." But in Luke 9:22 the verb goes into the passive voice, and it is said that Jesus will "be raised." Luke-Acts emphasizes the resurrection throughout but as the act of God on behalf of the man Jesus. The impact of the gospel of Mark is strong enough for Jesus simply to "rise" in Luke 18:33, but the concern of the author of Luke-Acts in general is to subordinate Jesus to God and to stress the resurrection as an act of God's power, for example, as in Acts 2:33,36; 4:10; 5:30, and elsewhere.

Examining Luke's interpretation of Mark's predictions of the passion and resurrection leads to Luke's understanding of Jesus' passion. For Mark, the passion and death of Jesus is the means of human salvation. Jesus comes "to give his life as a ransom for many" (Mark 10:45), and his Cross is a sacrifice in which his blood is "poured out for many" (Mark 14:24). None of this survives in Luke-Acts. For Luke the Cross is simply an act of service (Luke 22:27), not the means of human salvation. Similarly, Luke's account of the Last Supper omits the word of interpretation of the wine, Luke 22:19b–20 having little claim to being part of the original text of the gospel of Luke. Moreover, this understanding of the Cross of Jesus as determinative for human salvation was reached in early Christianity by interpreting that Cross in terms of the great suffering servant passage of Isaiah 53, to which Mark 10:45 and 14:24 certainly allude. But when this passage comes up in Acts 8:32–33, it is most emphatically not used to interpret the death of Jesus as an atonement for sin. The author of Luke-Acts simply does not understand the passion and death of Jesus in the same way as does the evangelist Mark.

In short, for Mark the death of Jesus is the means of human salvation, the gospel of Jesus Christ is the proclamation that the Cross of Christ has made possible this salvation. For the author of Luke-Acts the death of Jesus is an act of legal murder by the Jews, and the gospel as preached by Jesus and the church is a proclamation that if people will repent and turn to God they will receive the forgiveness of their sins. The death of Jesus does not have the role in Luke-Acts it has in the gospel of Mark, and in Luke-Acts Christian discipleship is a witnessing to the resurrection of Jesus rather than a following of Jesus in the way of his Cross. Indeed, there is a sense in which the Jesus of the gospel of Luke is the first Christian, living out of the power of the Spirit of God in the world. He is not the Jewish Messiah in the sense that his death ransoms people from the power of sin over them.

It is also interesting to compare the different and yet sometimes similar rein-terpretations of the Gospel of Mark by the evangelist Matthew and by the author of Luke-Acts. The similarity is that both separate the time of Jesus from all pre-ceding or succeeding times. Matthew does so by birth stories at the beginning and the commissioning scene at the end; Luke by the descent of the Spirit at the beginning and the ascension at the end. Moreover, the similarity continues in that both emphasize the special nature of the time of Jesus; for both the time of Jesus is the time of fulfillment. Matthew does this with his constant use of formula quotations; Luke with his insistence on the absence of Satan between the temp-tation of Jesus and the plot to betray him, and also with the various portrayals of the time of Jesus as the center of time. There is a sense, therefore, in which both Matthew and Luke transform what is essentially the apocalypse of Mark into a foundation myth of Christian origins, and this becomes most evident in the Lukan form of salvation history.

The Apostles and Apostleship in Luke-Acts

If Matthew and Luke both transform the apocalyptically oriented Mark into a foundation myth, they go very different ways in portraying how their readers may relate to this foundation myth. For Matthew, the means is an authoritative interpretation of the teaching that occurred in the Sacred Time of Jesus. For Luke, the means is an imitation of the Jesus of the Sacred Time, because for him Jesus is quite simply the first Christian. Luke sees Jesus as the primary example to be imitated, as he sees the heroes of the Christian church in Acts as secondary examples to be imitated. For him, Christian faith means essentially the imitation of Jesus and following the example of those heroes of the early church who did successfully imitate him.

Thus, a remarkable feature of the gospel of Luke is the way Jesus is presented as a model of Christian piety, and the way parallels are drawn between the prac-tice of Jesus in the gospel and that of the apostles in the Acts (again the "law of duality"). In presenting Peter as one whose rebuke can bring Ananias to death (Acts 5:3–5) and Simon to penitence (8:14–24), or Paul as one whose garments have the power to heal and whose name has power over demons (19:11–15), the author is reflecting the tendency of his movement to think of its heroes as espe-cially endowed human beings. In line with Hellenistic Jewish Mission Christianity, Luke claims Peter as its supporter, Paul as its hero, and Jesus as its Savior; all three have the aura of divinity, are human and yet more than human, and they are presented according to the conventions of the Hellenistic world.

One striking parallel between Jesus and the apostles is the one drawn between the passion of Jesus and the fate of Stephen, the first martyr. In his account of the trial of Jesus, Luke has no reference to the false witnesses found in Mark (Luke 22:66–71; compare Mark 14:56–64). However, in Acts 6:13–14, false witnesses appear at Stephen's trial with the testimony that Mark has them give at the trial of Jesus. At his stoning Stephen cries with a loud voice, "Lord, do not hold this sin against them" (Acts 7:60), just as Jesus had cried from his Cross, "Father, forgive them; for they do not know what they are doing" (Luke 23:34).

The many parallels between Jesus and the apostles are then extended by implication to the readers of Luke-Acts, and Luke hopes that the readers find themselves at one with Jesus, Peter, and Paul. For this reason he tones down the Christological emphases of his source, the Gospel of Mark, and also avoids any soteriological emphasis in connection with the Cross. Again, Jesus himself is a model, or example, of Christian piety. As Jesus and the apostles are empowered by the Spirit, so might be any believer, and as they pray and attend worship regularly, so should the believer. Again, the death of Jesus is not "a ransom for many," but Jesus is "one who serves" (Luke 22:27; compare Mark 10:45). Correspondingly, the author of Luke-Acts consistently plays down the differences between Jesus as the Christ and others. A good example is the reply to the question of the High Priest. In Mark 14:62, Jesus accepts the titles of "Christ" and "Son of the living God" by using the formula "I am." But in Luke 22:70, when Jesus is asked if he is the Son of God, he replies, "You say that I am."

The effect of these parallels between the time of Jesus and that of the church, and between Jesus and the apostles, is to make it possible for any believer—such as Theophilus and others like him—to relate directly to the time of Jesus and to Jesus himself. The author of Luke-Acts is providing his readers with an understanding of their place in salvation history and of their role in the world.

The Kingdom of God, Ethics, and the Church

In our discussions of salvation history, we have already elaborated the time of the proclamation of the Kingdom of God since the transitional time of John the Baptist, that is, during the time of Jesus and the time of the Church. It needs only to be reemphasized that the Kingdom in Luke-Acts mostly has not "come near," as in the future apocalyptic emphases of Mark and Matthew (compare Luke 4:43). To be sure, the future element of his sources is not totally abandoned by Luke (Luke 21:27 [Mark 13:24], 31–33; compare 11:2 [Q]; 9:26 [Mark 8:38]; 22:18 [Mark 14:25]). Nonetheless, striking statements say that the Kingdom is "among you" (17:21; compare 19:11), or present in Jesus' exorcisms (Luke 11:20), or near in Jesus' and the disciples healing (Luke 9:2, 11; 10:9). Other sayings stress "seeking" his Kingdom (12:31 [Q], or "receiving" or "entering" the Kingdom like a child (18:16 [Mark 10:14]; 18:24 [Mark 10:15].

Thus, the Kingdom points to the past time of Jesus and the present time of the church, and especially the ethical approach to life based on the models of the great heroes, Jesus, Peter, and Paul. It is no accident that the Gospel of Luke has functioned in historical Christianity as a basis for the "social gospel," and more recently as the gospel of political and social liberation. Luke's leitmotif passage (4:16–30) discussed at the outset stresses the inclusion of Gentiles, Romans, Samaritans, women, the poor, sinners, the sick, and the like. All point preeminently to the life of the church and its inclusive ethical ideals.

The Genre of Luke-Acts

As with the other gospels, there has been an extensive discussion about the the genre of the Gospel of Luke and the Acts of the Apostles. While there have been various proposals, our discussion of Jewish, Greek, and Roman history, and Luke as a historian and author of Salvation History naturally prejudices us in favor of a genre closely related to ancient history. To be sure, the Gospel of Luke of all the canonical gospels comes closest to the ancient *bios,* or biography. Given Luke's penchant for Isaiah and prophecy, much can be said for the story of Jesus as a "prophetic biography." Acts, too, features its heroes Peter and Paul, and in some ways it is like biography. Strong cases have also been made for Luke-Acts in relation to biographies of the philosopher and his school, or the historical romance. We lean toward ancient history, especially for Acts, with the gospel coming somewhat closer to the *bios.*

THE INTERPRETATION OF LUKE-ACTS

The author of Luke-Acts is the model of all presentations of the life of Jesus in which Jesus is an example to be imitated and the early church is a challenge to and exemplar of what is expected of Christians in the world and of what Christians may expect of their life in the world. He presents Jesus and the heroes of the early church as models of the challenge and possibilities of Christian existence in the world. Whereas the evangelist Matthew encouraged the interpretation of the gospel as a teaching to be authoritatively interpreted, the author of Luke-Acts encourages the interpretation of that gospel as an example to be followed in daily life. What Jesus, Peter, Stephen, and Paul did becomes the norm for all those who would follow in the way of Luke-Acts.

FURTHER READING

Important Theories, Sketches, and Recent Bibliography

F. Bovon, *Luke the Theologian: Thirty-three years of Research (1950–1983)*.

J. A. Fitzmyer, "The Current State of Lucan Studies," in *The Gospel According to Luke I–IX* and *The Gospel According to Luke X–XIV*.

W. W. Gasque, *A History of the Criticism of the Acts of the Apostles*.

I. H. Marshall, "The Present State of Lucan Studies," *Themelios* 14 (1989), pp. 52–56.

M. A. Powell, *What Are They Saying About Luke and Acts?*

———, "Are the Sands Still Shifting? An Update on Lukan Scholarship," *Trinity Lutheran Seminary* 11 (1989), pp. 5–22.

E. Richard, "Luke—Writer, Theologian, Historian: Research and Orientation of the 70's," *Biblical Theology Bulletin* 13 (1983), pp. 1–13.

C. Talbert, "Shifting Sands: The Recent Study of the Gospel of Luke," in *Studies in Luke-Acts*, edited by L. Keck and J. L. Martyn, pp. 197–213.

One-Volume Commentaries and Dictionary Articles

ABD: "Benedictus" (F. W. Danker); "Elizabeth" (Ben Witherington, III); "Emmaus" (J. F. Strange); "Genealogy" (R. R. Wilson); "Heaven, Ascent to" (J. D. Tabor); "Hellenist" (H. D. Betz); "Holy Spirit" (F. W. Hahn, trans. D. M. Elliott); "Infancy Narratives in the NT Gospels" (R. E. Brown); "James (Person)" (D. A. Hagner); "Lame, Lameness" (J. R. Mills); "Lazarus and Dives" (G. A. Yee); "Lord's Prayer" (J. L. Houlden); "Luke" (E. Plümacher, trans. D. Martin); "Luke-Acts, Book of" (L. T. Johnson); "Lydia" (B. K. McLauchlin); "Martyr, Martyrdom" (J. D. Tabor); "Mary" (B. Witherington, III); "Mary, Mother of Jesus" (M. M. Pazdan); "Matthias" (T. W. Martin); "Meal Customs (Greco-Roman)" (D. E. Smith); "Meal Customs (Sacred Meals)" (D. E. Smith); "Nicodemus" (J. Paulien); "Pentecost" (M. J. Olson); "Philippian Jailer" (R. F. O'Toole); "Sapphira" (R. F. O'Toole); "Theophilus" (R. F. O'Toole); "Virgin" (J. J. Schmitt).

IDB: "Luke, Gospel of" (V. Taylor); "Acts of the Apostles" (H. J. Cadbury).

IDB Suppl.: "Luke, Gospel of" (W. C. Robinson, Jr.); "Acts of the Apostles" (W. C. Robinson, Jr.).

NJBC, pp. 675–721 (R. J. Karris) and pp. 722–67 (R. J. Dillon).

Historically Influential Studies

H. Cadbury, *The Making of Luke-Acts*. 2d ed.

H. Conzelmann, *The Theology of St. Luke*.

M. Dibelius, *Studies in the Acts of the Apostles*.

E. Haenchen, *The Acts of the Apostles*.

Collected Essays:

L. E. Keck and J. L. Martyn, eds., *Studies in Luke-Acts*.

E. Richard, ed., *New Views on Luke and Acts*.

C. H. Talbert, ed., *Perspectives on Luke-Acts*.

———, ed., *Luke-Acts. New Perspectives from the Society of Biblical Literature*.

J. B. Tyson, ed., *Luke-Acts and the Jewish People. Eight Critical Perspectives*.

Among the many articles on Luke-Acts and its context, we may note:

D. Duling, "The Promises to David and Their Entrance into Christianity—Nailing Down a Likely Hypothesis," *New Testament Studies* 20 (1973–1974), pp. 55–77.

R. J. Karris, "Poor and Rich: The Lukan *Sitz im Leben*," in C. H. Talbert, *Perspectives on Luke-Acts*, pp. 112–125.

W. G. Kümmel, "Current Theological Accusations Against Luke," *Andover Newton Quarterly*

16 (1975), pp. 131–145.

P. Minear, "Luke's Use of the Birth Stories," in *Studies in Luke-Acts,* ed. by L. Keck and J. L. Martyn.

V. K. Robbins, "By Land and by Sea: The We-Passages and Ancient Sea Voyages," in C. H. Talbert, ed., *Perspectives on Luke-Acts,* pp. 215–45.

R. Tannehill, "The Mission of Jesus According to Luke IV 16–30," in E. Grässer, A. Strobel, and R. Tannehill, *Jesus in Nazareth.*

P. Vielhauer, "On the 'Paulinism' of Acts," in L. E. Keck and J. L. Martyn, *Studies in Luke-Acts,* pp. 35–50.

L. M. Wills, "The Depiction of the Jews in Acts," *Journal of Biblical Literature* 110/4 (1991), pp. 631–654.

Commentaries:

F. Danker, *Luke.* (Proclamation Commentaries).

————, *Jesus and the New Age. A Commentary on St. Luke's Gospel.* 2d ed.

J. Fitzmyer, *The Gospel According to Luke I–IX* and *The Gospel According to Luke X–XXIV.* (The Anchor Bible Commentary).

E. Schweizer, *The Good News According to Luke.* Trans. D. E. Green.

C. H. Talbert, *Reading Luke. A Literary and Theological Commentary on the Third Gospel.*

R. Tannehill, *The Narrative Unity of Luke-Acts. A Literary Interpretation.* 2 vols.

Other:

M. Hengel, *Acts and the History of Earliest Christianity.*

J. Jervell, *Luke and the People of God.*

D. Tiede, *Prophecy and History in Luke-Acts.*

Literary:

J. M. Dawsey, *The Lukan Voice. Confusion* and *Irony in the Gospel of Luke.*

O. C. Edwards, *Luke's Story of Jesus.*

L. T. Johnson, *The Literary Function of Possessions in Luke-Acts.*

R. Karris, *Luke: Artist and Theologian. Luke's Passion Account as Literature.*

C. H. Talbert, *Literary Patterns, Theological Themes, and the Genre of Luke-Acts.*

Social-Historical and Social Scientific:

K. E. Bailey, *Poet and Peasant: A Literary-Cultural Approach to the Parables in Luke* and *Luke Through Peasant Eyes: More Lucan Parables, Their Culture and Style.*

R. Cassidy, *Jesus, Politics, and Society: A Study of Luke's Gospel.*

R. Cassidy and P. J. Scharper, eds., *Political Issues in Luke-Acts.*

F. Danker, *Jesus and the New Age.*

P. Esler, *Community and Gospel in Luke-Acts.*

J. M. Ford, *My Enemy Is My Guest: Jesus and Violence in Luke-Acts.*

R. Horsley, *The Liberation of Christmas. The Infancy Narratives in Social Context.*

H. Moxnes, *The Economy of the Kingdom. Social Conflict and Economic Relations in Luke's Gospel.*

J. Neyrey, ed. *The Social World of Luke-Acts. Models for Interpretation.*

W. E. Pilgrim, *Good News to the Poor. Wealth and Poverty in Luke-Acts.*

D. Seccombe, *Possessions and the Poor in Luke-Acts.*

P. Walaskay, *"And So We Came to Rome." The Political Perspective of St. Luke.*

Miscellaneous:

S. R. Garrett, *The Demise of the Devil. Magic and the Demonic in Luke's Writings.*

G. Lüdemann, *Early Christianity According to the Traditions in Acts.*

J. Neyrey, *The Passion According to Luke. A Redaction Study of Luke's Soteriology.*

J. T. Sanders, *The Jews in Luke-Acts.*

M. L. Soards, *The Passion According to Luke.*

Rylands Greek Papyrus 457, a fragment of John 18. Known also as P[52], it is the oldest surviving New Testament text fragment, and shows that the Gospel of John could not been written later than its date (ca. 125–130 C.E.). For a discussion, see Chapter One and p. 409.

CHAPTER TWELVE

THE GOSPEL AND LETTERS OF JOHN

The Literature of the Johannine School

Traditionally, five of the texts in the New Testament are regarded as having been written by Jesus' disciple John: the Fourth Gospel, the three letters of John, and the book of Revelation. The last, however, has at best only a tenuous relationship to the others and is so representative of the style and thought of apocalyptic Christianity that it cannot easily claim a place in the Johannine corpus. We shall consider it in the following chapter. The four other texts, however, exhibit a unity of style and content that shows that they certainly belong together, whatever the details of their origins may turn out to have been.

The gospel and letters of John give the impression of carefully composed literary compositions, of being a response to the internal dynamics of the genius and vision of the author. As a consequence, it is difficult to answer historical questions about these works, and some recent interpreters have shifted to studies of the gospel as literature. At the same time, there has also been a good deal of progress in attempting to identify the traditions and sources behind the gospel and the history of the communities that transmitted them, as well as the contexts of the gospel and letters themselves. This progress will be reflected in what follows.

EARLY CHRISTIAN TRADITION ABOUT THE JOHANNINE LITERATURE

One of the earliest surviving traditions about the Gospel of John comes from Irenaeus of Lyons (125–202 C.E.) in the late second century, about 180 C.E. In a passage about the four gospels, he writes:

> Afterwards John, the disciple of the Lord who also leaned upon his chest, he too published a gospel while residing in Ephesus.
> (Irenaeus, *Against Heresies* 3.1.1)

The reference here is to John 13:23, where at the Last Supper a disciple "leaned upon his chest," that is, reclined in banquet style with his head close to Jesus' chest, the place of honor (NRSV: "was reclining next to him"). Elsewhere Irenaeus states that this John moved from Jerusalem to Ephesus, that he wrote all five Johannine writings there, that he lived to an old age and died in Ephesus, and that the gospel was written against certain Gnostics, especially Cerinthus (*Against Heresies* 3.3.4; 3.11.7; 5.33.4). A number of other Church Fathers from about the same time have some of these or similar traditions (for example, Bishop Polycrates of Ephesus, about 190 in Eusebius *Ecclesiastical History* 5.24.2–3; Latin anti-Marcionite Prologue, which some scholars date to about 200 C.E.). Clement of Alexandria (ca. 150–203 C.E.) adds in a now-famous statement that in contrast to the other three gospels, John wrote "a spiritual gospel" (Clement of Alexandria, *Outlines;* compare Eusebius, *Ecclesiastical History* 6.14.5). Finally, the first known canonical list of the New Testament, the Muratorian Canon, generally thought to have been published at Rome about 200 C.E., states that the Fourth Gospel was written by the disciple John from the revelation he received after fasting three days, and that the other apostles checked it.

In short, Christian tradition from the latter second century says that the Gospel of John was a spiritual gospel written by a disciple who in the Johannine account of the Last Supper "was reclining next to him [Jesus]" (John 13:23; see below), and that this person was "John." It also claims that the gospel was written in Ephesus, a major city on the coast of western Asia Minor also associated with Paul and the book of Revelation. No date is given, though it is considered to be the fourth of the four gospels, and written in John's old age.

Finally, we may add that Irenaeus attributes the letters of 1 and 2 John to this same John (*Against Heresies* 3.15.5, 8). Curiously, there is no mention of 3 John in the second century. By the third century, Origen says that John might have written a second and third letter, but not everybody admits that they are genuine (*In John* 5.3); by the fourth century, Eusebius is still putting 2 and 3 John in his list of "disputed books" (*Ecclesiastical History* 3.25.3), though he says that they may have been written by *another* John. In the fourth century Jerome builds on all these traditions, but identifies the author of 2 and 3 John with another John, "John the Presbyter" (see below), whom he says has a separate grave at Ephesus (Jerome, *Illustrious Men* 9). To complicate matters, the author of 2 John and 3 John identifies himself simply as "the presbyter" ("elder," compare 2 John 1:1; 3 John 1:1).

John in the New Testament

There are a number of persons with the common Jewish name "John" (Hebrew: *Yōhānān;* Greek: *Iōannēs)* in the New Testament: John the Baptist; John, the disciple of Jesus; John Mark, who followed Paul; John, the father of Peter (John 1:42; 21:15–17); even an unknown John (Acts 4:6).

It is highly likely that Irenaeus and the other second-century Christians meant to refer to the John who was Jesus' disciple. He is mentioned in the Gospels of Matthew, Mark, and Luke (but not the Gospel of John!) as the son of Zebedee and brother of James, all of whom were fishermen on the Sea of Galilee (Mark 1:19–20 = Matt 4:21–22). Luke adds that they were partners with Peter who was the brother of Andrew (Luke 5:10). At Jesus' call, all left their nets (James and John left their father!) and followed Jesus.

In the first three gospels John is often honored along with Peter and James, John's brother, as the inner circle of Jesus' disciples. They are not only found (along with Andrew, Peter's brother) first in the disciple lists (Mark 3:17 = Matt 10:2 = Luke 6:14), but they also occur together as those closest to Jesus (Mark 5:37 = Luke 8:51; Mark 9:2 = Matt 17:1 = Luke 9:28; Mark 14:33 = Matt 26:37). In one story John joins in rebuking a man who has been casting out demons in Jesus' name, for which he in turn is rebuked by Jesus (Mark 9:38; Luke 9:49). Mark says that John and his brother James requested that Jesus give them special positions of power in the future Kingdom (Mark 10:35–41; Matt 20:24 attributes the request to their mother!). The brothers were also nicknamed "Sons of Thunder" (Mark 3:17), perhaps—this is a guess—a reference to their stormy personalities.

John is also mentioned once in Paul and three times in the Acts of the Apostles. Paul considers him one of those "acknowledged pillars" at the Jerusalem Conference, the two others being Peter and James, the brother of Jesus (not the brother of John; compare Gal 2:9). In Acts, John follows Peter in the list of disciples (Acts 1:13). He accompanies Peter when Peter goes to the Jerusalem Temple and heals the lame beggar; the two are subsequently arrested and imprisoned, and then released (Acts 3–4). He also accompanies Peter on Peter's mission to Samaria (8:14–25). He is clearly subordinate to Peter here. While the martyrdom of John's brother James under Herod Agrippa I is recorded (Acts 12:2), which would have been prior to 44 C.E., a hint of John's death is given only by way of a prediction of Jesus that both brothers would be martyred (Mark 10:35–40; Matt 20:20–23). This prediction could have reflected a historical event after the fact, of course, since according to most prevailing critical theory Mark and Matthew were written well after 44 C.E.

GENERAL HISTORICAL CRITICISM OF THE GOSPEL: AUTHOR, DATE, PLACE

We have seen that Irenaeus and others outside the New Testament from the late second century state that the one who leaned on Jesus' chest at the Last Supper was John, probably meaning the disciple who in the first three gospels was one of Jesus' inner circle. Thus, it was thought, John the son of Zebedee, Jesus' disciple, was the author of the gospel, as well as the letters and Revelation. Here we shall focus on the gospel.

As you might expect, there are some problems with this traditional view. First, the notion that John wrote the Fourth Gospel was not unanimous in Christian antiquity. The "Alogoi," who opposed the Logos view of Jesus in John 1:1–18 (see below), said it was written by the Gnostic Cerinthus. While this could have been a prejudicial view of the Alogoi—John was indeed a favorite gospel of the Gnostics—the Cerinthus identification was also held by the Roman presbyter Gaius in the early third century.

Second, it is highly likely that our chief early witness, Irenaeus, was incorrect. Irenaeus claimed that he got his information from the old Polycarp "when I was still a boy" and that Polycarp had an "association with John and others who had seen the Lord" (Irenaeus, *Letter to Florinus*). This suggests a chain of tradition: Jesus

—> John (in his old age) —> Polycarp (in his old age) —> Irenaeus (still a boy). However, the ancient historian Eusebius was quick to point out that Irenaeus was not always a reliable witness. Irenaeus said that Papias was also a "hearer of John," but according to Eusebius Papias said only that he had questioned *followers* of the *presbyters* (or "elders"), who in turn were respected *disciples* of the *first disciples,* including John (Eusebius, *Ecclesiastical History* 3.39.1–7). In other words, there was a much longer chain of tradition: Jesus —> John —> presbyters —> followers of the presbyters —> Papias, who is still a couple of generations earlier than Irenaeus. One of those presbyters was also named John. To complicate matters, it will be recalled that the author of 2 John and 3 John identifies himself simply as the "presbyter" ("elder," compare 2 John 1:1; 3 John 1:1). If Irenaeus misconstrued what Papias, whom he apparently did not know, said about a certain presbyter John, it is also possible that Irenaeus' evidence about Polycarp was inaccurate, especially if John was martyred at an earlier age, as Jesus' prophecy in Mark 10:39 seems to imply, and Irenaeus' memory comes from his childhood.

Finally, the author of the Fourth Gospel is never explicitly identified as John in the gospel itself. Indeed, authorship by John appears to have been a logical deduction from comments both within and outside the gospel. Within the gospel, the one who "leaned on Jesus' chest" at Jesus' last meal is also called "the one whom Jesus loved," or simply the Beloved Disciple (13:23). This disciple is mentioned later in the story as one known to the high priest and present at Jesus' trial before him (18:15–16), as one to whom Jesus on the cross entrusted his mother (19:26–27), and as linked with Peter (18:15; 21:7), in fact as "the other disciple" who outran Peter to the tomb, but entered the tomb only after Peter (20:2–8). This interesting comment clearly implies that the author of the Fourth Gospel thinks of the Beloved Disciple as some kind of competitor with Peter (note the gospel traditions about Peter, James, and John above). Now John 21:20–24 says that the author of the gospel, or at least, rephrasing, "the one who caused these things to be written" is the "one who had reclined next to Jesus at the supper and had said, 'Lord, who is it that is going to betray you?'!" (21:20). This passage implies that the Beloved Disciple is dead, or perhaps near death, and its main point is to correct the false impression that Jesus had said that the disciple whom Jesus loved would still be alive at Jesus' parousia, that is, to forestall the view that Jesus had made a false prophecy about the time of his return. In the process, however, it comments about one who "caused these things to be written," and it is stated that "*his testimony is true*" (21:24). If 19:35 refers to him—"he who saw this has testified…and *his testimony is true*"—then he is also said to have been an eyewitness to Jesus' death. This identification of the author in chapter 21 was, as we shall see, added to the first twenty chapters of the gospel at a later date, but that would not have concerned second-century readers. Finally, there is also a mysterious, unnamed disciple present when the brothers Andrew and Peter, along with Philip and Nathaniel (the latter is not mentioned in the first three gospels), are called to become disciples (John 1:35–40). Since in the first three gospels James and John are called at the same time as Peter and Andrew, since in those gospels John was one of Jesus' inner circle among the Twelve, and since the Beloved Disciple leaned on Jesus' chest, the place of honor, it would have been logical to deduce that the unnamed disciple was also the Beloved Disciple and was John.

We summarize: In chapter 21 of the Fourth Gospel the Beloved Disciple—the one who in the first twenty chapters is so close to Jesus that Jesus entrusts his mother to him, who is a competitor of Peter's, who may have witnessed Jesus' death—is said to have written the gospel, or at least have caused it to be written. A natural inference would have been that this was the one who in the synoptic gospels was from Jesus' inner circle, namely, John. This would have been reinforced since the unknown disciple was, like John, called in the early part of the story (John 1:35–40) and because the mysterious disciple was in competition with Peter. Thus, it was probably deduced that John wrote the Fourth Gospel. Yet, the gospel does not identify him as such, and maintains the enigma. At the very least, then, both external and internal evidence pose a very knotty problem about the identity of the author(s) of the gospel. We shall attempt to deal with this problem in a variety of ways in what follows.

The latest possible **date** of the Fourth Gospel can be established by an interesting piece of external evidence. You will recall that the earliest manuscript fragment we have of any part of the New Testament is a papyrus fragment containing parts of John 18:31–33, 37–38, discovered in Egypt (P^{52}). Scholars consider it to have been written about 125 C.E. Since this fragment comes from a copy, the gospel must have been written early enough for it to have circulated in Egypt in the first decade or two of the second century. If it came from the region of Ephesus, which is not impossible (though the location may have been deduced by association with the author of the Apocalypse, John of Patmos, off the coast of Ephesus), the latest date was about 100 C.E.

As for the earliest possible date, we have noted in the case of the other gospels possible oblique references to the most important event of the first century, the destruction of Jerusalem in 70 C.E. John's gospel seems to make such a reference in the mouths of the chief priests and Pharisees: "If we let him go on like this (performing miracles), everyone will believe in him, and the Romans will come and destroy both our holy place and our nation" (11:48). Such a reference points to a date after the destruction of Jerusalem. Such a date would be possible if John wrote in his old age, but it does not correspond with the possibility that John was martyred before 44 C.E., as might be implied from Jesus' prophecy in Mark 10:39 and from Acts 12:2. The post-70 date is suggested by other internal factors, especially, as in the case of the Gospel of Matthew, the conflict with the Jewish synagogue (see below).

In short, the reference to the destruction of Jerusalem and the conflict of the Johannine Christians with the Jewish synagogue, on the one hand, and P^{52} on the other hand, point to a date in the late first century. It seems probable that the Gospel of John is to be dated about 90 C.E.

Finally, the **place** of composition in the second-century church traditions is Ephesus in Asia Minor. While that location is connected to the belief that the author of the Fourth Gospel was the same John who wrote Revelation on the Island of Patmos off the coast of Asia Minor, Asia Minor has remained a possibility for the location for the gospel. Nonetheless, many other suggestions have been offered, especially some city in Syria. We cannot be certain about the place of origin, but Ephesus is probably as good a place as any. We shall suggest that at least some of the Johannine materials have come from Palestine.

Questions of authorship, date, and place of the Johannine literature have often been correlated with certain source questions and the history of the Johannine community. To those we now turn.

TEXTUAL, ORAL-TRADITIONAL, AND SOURCE QUESTIONS IN THE GOSPEL OF JOHN

The Gospel of John has many fascinating literary puzzles, sometimes called "the Johannine riddle," and much effort and imagination have been spent trying to solve them. They result in part from interruptions in the flow of the narrative, for example, sudden shifts in geographical location, time, themes, language, or style. These "aporias," as they are called, plus various theories about oral traditions and written sources, have led to a variety of positions about the Johannine riddle. Here we can touch only on some of the more important problems and a few of the proposed solutions.

1. The Text of the Gospel: Chapter 21.

No extant, complete manuscript of the gospel omits chapter 21. Yet, as we suggested above, that chapter is all but universally recognized to have been a supplement to the original text of the gospel. There are several reasons for this consensus. First, the last verses in the *previous* chapter (20:30–31) read, among other things, like the original ending to the gospel. Second, there are important differences between the Greek of chapter 21 and that of chapters 1–20. Third, whereas in chapter 20 Jesus' resurrection appearances are located in Jerusalem, as in Luke-Acts, in chapter 21 they take place in Galilee, as in Matthew. The usual view is that someone wanted to supplement the Jerusalem appearance traditions with the Galilean resurrection appearances traditions. Finally, as noted above, John 21:24 seems designed to identify the Beloved Disciple as the author of what has been written. This remark could refer to everything up to that point, including 21:1–23, but most scholars conclude that it refers to chapter 1–20. Given these factors, it seems very probable that chapter 21 was added to the original chapters 1–20 of the gospel, but before the text of the gospel had actually circulated beyond those who were certifying it (21:24: "we").

Who added chapter 21 to the Gospel of John? In this connection, we should note that the famous account of the woman taken in adultery, the "let among you who is without sin be the first to throw a stone at her" story (7:53–8:11), is quite Johannine in style, but is not found in the earliest manuscripts. The usual view is that it has been added later. Some scholars have argued that there are other features that have been added to the gospel, thus creating some of the above-mentioned aporias. Thus, we may be dealing with member(s) of a Johannine School, which clearly affects our judgment about authorship. We shall consider this possibility later; at this point we shall note several other well-known aporias in the gospel that lead in this direction.

2. Geographical, Temporal, and Content Problems in John 1–20.

There seem to be a number of geographical, temporal, and content interruptions or dislocations in the flow of the gospel. We cannot cite all these aporias, but here are some of the more interesting ones. In chapter 5 Jesus is suddenly in Jerusalem, in chapter 6 back in Galilee, and in chapter 7 back in Jerusalem again; a more logical order would be chapters 6, 5, and 7. In chapter 3 Jesus is in Judea; yet, 3:22 says that he came into Judea. At the Last Supper Peter asks Jesus where he is going (13:36); yet, later, Jesus complains that no one has asked him that

(16:5). In 14:31, Jesus says, "Rise, let us be on our way," but they stay to hear Jesus' farewell discourse, which takes up three chapters. Jesus performs his first sign in Cana at 2:11 and 2:23 says he works many miracles there; yet, 4:54 says that his second miracle was at Cana as if no intervening miracles had taken place. John 7:3–5 speaks as if Jesus has performed no signs in Judea, but he has (5:1–9). There are also some clear interruptions about John the Baptist in the Prologue to the Gospel (1:1–18; see below). Finally, there seem to be two conclusions to Jesus' public activity (10:40–42; 12:37–43).

Many modern critics have claimed that either there was some accidental misplacement of manuscript pages or parts thereof, or more plausibly, that the writer or writers were loosely merging several traditions or sources, perhaps over a long period of time by a series of redactions.

3. Differences and likenesses between John and the synoptics.

Let us note some major differences and likeness between John and the synoptic gospels. This will help prepare us further for the problems about traditions and/or sources.

a. Differences:

1. The chronological and geographical framework of the Gospel of John is quite different from that of the synoptics. John envisages a ministry of Jesus beginning with the joint activity of Jesus with the Baptist and featuring several extended periods in Jerusalem; thus, for example, the cleansing of the Temple occurs already in chapter 2. The synoptics have Jesus begin his ministry only after John the Baptist is imprisoned, and it lasts one year and includes only one visit to Jerusalem. A quite specific example of a chronological difference is that the Last Supper in John takes place on the night before Passover, but in the synoptics it is a Passover meal. An interesting aside is that from the perspective of archeology and other data, specific Palestinian sites are more accurately placed than in the synoptics.

2. Differences in style and presentation between John and the synoptics are abundant. In the synoptics, Jesus teaches in aphorisms, parables, and short discourses; even Matthew's longer discourses are collections of these shorter forms. In John, however, there are long discourses on symbolic themes such as "light" and "life," and these evolve as complex monologues or dramatic dialogues. In addition, John has a very lengthy farewell discourse and prayer of Jesus not found in the synoptics (John 13–17).

3. John has many incidents unknown to the synoptics, for example:

1. the narrative concerning Nicodemus (3:1–21);
2. the narrative about the Samaritan woman (4:7–42);

These unique incidents include a number of miracle stories:

1. changing water into wine at the wedding at Cana (2:1–11);
2. the healing at the pool of Bethzatha (5:1–9);
3. the healing of the man born blind (9:1–12); and
4. the raising of Lazarus (11:1–44).

4. John does not contain the content and forms of Jesus' teachings that are so typical of the synoptics.
John has no Kingdom of God sayings and no developed parables, which are absolutely integral to the form of Jesus' expression in the synoptic gospels; instead we find the long discourses revolving around symbolic themes noted above. The difference in style and content of Jesus' teaching, as we shall see, has raised the question whether the author of the Fourth Gospel has access to a discourse source that has provided him with material very different from that found in the synoptics (see below).

5. John does not contain some forms of Jesus' activity that are so typical of the synoptics.
In this connection, John has no exorcisms, which are very central to the activity of Jesus in the synoptics. What we find are the miracle stories, some of which, as noted above, are unique.

6. Jesus' opponents in John are less differentiated.
Another striking difference is that the synoptics refer to Jesus' opponents as distinct groups, even though they are not always historically accurate (scribes, Pharisees, Sadducees). In contrast, John usually prefers an undifferentiated group called "the Jews."

b. Likenesses.

1. There are several incidents in John that have parallels in the synoptics:

1. a call of disciples (1:35–51);
2. Peter's confession (6:66–70);
3. the triumphal entry into Jerusalem (12:12–15);
4. the cleansing of the Temple (2:13–22);
5. the anointing at Bethany (12:1–8);
6. the Last Supper with a prophecy of betrayal (13:1–11); and
7. especially important, the general story of the passion itself.

2. John and the synoptics also share three miracle stories:

1. healing of the official's son (4:46–53);
2. a feeding (6:1–15); and
3. a sea miracle (6:16–21).

3. The Gospels of Mark and John contain a few rather exact verbal similarities:

Mark	John	Words or Phrases
2:11	5:8	"Stand up, take your mat and walk."
6:37	6:7	"two hundred denarii worth of bread"
		[*denarius* = coin, about a day's wage]
14:3	12:3	"costly perfume made of pure nard"
14:5	12:5	"300 denarii"
14:54, 67	18:18, 25	Peter "warming [*thermainomenos*] himself"
14:54	18:15	Peter goes "into" the courtyard
15:14	19:15	they cry "crucify him" in the Greek imperative case

| 15:17 | 19:2,5 | the purple cloak |
| 15:42 | 19:15 | mention of the Day of Preparation |

Three areas of discussion have arisen to help solve the these problems: 1) John's relation to the synoptic gospels; 2) John's special sources; and 3) the history of the Johannine community. We shall take them in order.

1. The Relation of the Gospel of John to the Synoptic Gospels.

Was the Gospel of John written with a knowledge of any or all of the synoptic gospels or is the relationship best seen as based on a common oral tradition? That difficult question has never been resolved by a consensus of scholarly opinion. In recent opinion, there is some tendency toward theories of indirect rather than direct dependence of John on the synoptic materials.

Many, perhaps most, scholars, have become convinced that the differences are so great, and the likeness so small, that John and the synoptics simply shared some of the same materials from the oral tradition. Thus, they argue that the few verbal parallels are precisely of the type that would be preserved in the oral tradition. Many scholars still hold this position, or at least combine it with source theories.

Others, however, say that the differences are not enough grounds for denying John's knowledge of one or more of the synoptic gospels, especially Mark. From this perspective, for example, the Johannine author simply does not want to follow the order of Mark. Down to 12:37–38 he is probably building around his Signs Source, which we shall discuss presently (see also Chapter Five); 13–17 are thematic discourses and a prayer; from 18:1 onward we have the passion narrative, which is closer to Mark and Luke. In this section, the order of the Gospel of John is most different from the order of the Gospel of Mark in passages where the Johannine author wants to develop his point of view (for example, 18:4–9, 14; 18:28–19:16). Finally—this is an impressive argument—the *Markan* author often places one account inside another (sandwiching; or intercalation; see, for example, 3:20–35; 5:22–43; 6:7–30; 11:12–25; 14:53–72). The author of John appears to be following this Markan gospel technique in placing the hearing of Jesus scene (18:19–24) inside the account of Peter's denial of Jesus like this:

	Mark	**John**
Peter's denial	14:54	18:15–18
Hearing	14:55–65	18:19–24
Peter's denial	14:66–72	18: 25–27

Such factors have led to the view that the author of the Gospel of John was using the Gospel of Mark and simply preferred his own order of presentation. If any of these views is correct, a relationship via oral tradition or sources becomes less compelling.

To illustrate the debate further, let us look at a single passage that is similar in John and the synoptics, John 12:25–26 and Mark 8:34–35.

John 12:25–26	**Mark 8:34–35**
He who loves his life	If any man would come
loses it, and he who hates	after me, let him deny
his life in this world will	himself and take up

keep it for eternal life.	his cross and follow me.
If anyone serves me he	For whoever would
must follow me; and where	save his life will lose
I am, there shall my servant	it; and whoever loses
be also; if any one serves me	his life for my sake and
the Father will honor him.	the gospel's will save it.

The parallels of the theme of following Jesus and losing and saving one's life indicate a relationship between the two. The problem is that in both of these examples, the differences are great enough that we might conclude that in each case the texts were not related to one another directly or by some written source, but came from a common oral tradition that had undergone independent development in different directions before each writer of the gospel used it.

Yet, those who defend dependence of John on one or more of the synoptics argue that the differences of language in similar sections is complicated by the fact that they represent the redactional interests of each author. Thus, Mark 8:34–35 contains characteristic Markan emphases on the passion and "the gospel." In John 12:25–26, these are absent, and what one finds are important Johannine themes: "hating life in this world"; "eternal life"; "where I am, there shall my servant be also"; "the Father will honor him." It is possible to argue that the Johannine material has gone through a considerable period and process of reflection and meditation. This process suggests that it is by no means evident that John 12:25–26 does not exhibit some knowledge or memory of Mark 8:34–35.

Defenders of dependence sometimes suggest that the few passages that share exact verbal similarities, as in the nine sections noted above, reinforce their view. Yet, it could also be argued either that these examples are just the sort of thing that might be remembered in oral tradition, or, because the first two examples occur in miracle stories and the last seven examples occur in the passion story, that they come from miracle and passion story sources behind Mark and John rather than *direct* dependence (see below).

With respect to the relationship of John and *Luke,* an important passage is the anointing story (John 12:3–8 = Luke 7:36–50; cf. Luke 10:38–42). All the names in John occur in Luke at various places, and John's version of the anointing (Mary anoints Jesus' feet and wipes them with her hair, itself a not very reasonable process) is explicable if John knew the Gospel of Luke, where the woman wipes Jesus' feet with her hair and then anoints them. In Mark 14:3–9 and Matthew 26:6–13, by contrast, the woman anoints Jesus' head, and there is no mention of her hair. Some conclude that the references to the woman anointing the feet and drying them with her hair that Luke and John have in common could indicate that John knew the Lukan account. Yet, it could also mean that they shared an oral tradition.

Another example occurs in the passion story.

Luke 22:67c–8b	John 18:23
If I tell you,	If I have spoken wrongly,
you will not believe;	bear witness to the wrong;
and if I ask you,	but if I have spoken rightly
you will not answer.	why do you strike me?

In both Luke and John Jesus gives an evasive answer to the high priest. Did John know Luke or did they draw on a common source? They are different enough that a strong case could also be made for oral tradition.

These are some of the considerations on which a decision as to whether the author of John knew one or another of the gospels must be based. Obviously, they do not point overwhelmingly in one direction or the other. Some scholars try to mediate by suggesting that the author of the Gospel of John had *at one time* read the Gospel of Mark, and perhaps also of the Gospel of Luke. Yet, there seems to be a growing opinion that John's knowledge of the synoptics is mediated or indirect knowledge, if not from common oral tradition, then perhaps through John's special sources that contained some of the same traditions, or some combination of the two. We now look more closely at the option of special written sources.

2. The Gospel of John and special written sources.

We indicated in Chapter Five that the Gospel of John contains three obvious complexes of material:

1. miracle stories;
2. long discourses centered around great symbolic themes; and
3. passion, death, and resurrection stories.

R. Bultmann is famous for arguing that these complexes represent three sources:

1. a miracle collection, or Signs Source;
2. a discourse source derived from Gnostic revelation discourses; and
3. a passion story source.

Bultmann argued that the author put these together and edited them, but then the whole was later worked over by an ecclesiastical redactor who added some more traditional points of view, for example, apocalyptic matters (5:28–29; 12:48) and sacramental themes (for example, 6:51–58).

Bultmann's second source, the Gnostic revelation discourse source, is the most difficult to establish. There are mainly three reasons. First, the discourses contain what is usually thought to be the most distinctive ideas of the author himself, making a previous source hard to isolate. Second, in the Johannine context many of the discourses are so closely connected to miracle stories that they often look like author's developments of them; as such, they are, again, extremely difficult to separate as coming from a previously existing source. A third, quite different, reason is that since the discovery of the Dead Sea Scrolls in 1947, increasing numbers of scholars have related the background of John to dualistic *Judaism; some* of these scholars are not convinced that this Judaism has been influenced by Gnosticism. Because of these difficulties, the theory of a discourse source related to Gnosticism has not received the same support as the miracles and passion sources.

Of Bultmann's three supposed sources, the first, or Signs Source, has received the most support (see Chapter Five). It derives its name from "sign" as the special Johannine term for miracles (2:11; 2:23; 4:54; 12:37; 20:30–31). In John 1–20 there are seven signs, the three mentioned above that are paralleled in the synoptics (4:46–53; 6:1–15; 6:16–21), and the four that are unique to John (2:1–11; 5:1–9; 9:1–12; and 11:1–14). In addition there is the miraculous catch of fish in the supplementary chapter (21:1–14). In Chapter Five, we cited Robert Fortna's attempt to reconstruct the Signs Source behind John. Fortna combined the two signs connected with the sea in John 6 and added the sign in John 21. This theory maintains a collection of seven, an astrological number (seven days of the week, and so forth) and the sacred number of wholeness and completeness (see Chapter Thirteen). Fortna then placed all the signs in a geographical sequence and prefaced the collection with John's testimony about Jesus and the first disciples' discovery of Jesus, which he believed on linguistic grounds was in the source. We cite the source again:

UNIT	PASSAGE
The Opening	
1. John's Testimony	1: 6–7, 19–23, 26b–27, [33d], 29–34
2. First Disciples Find the Messiah	1: 35, 37, (38a), 38b, 39–42, 43b–47, 49
The Signs of Jesus	
Galilee	
3. Water to Wine	2:1–3a, 5b–11a, (11b[himself]), 11c
4. The Official's Son Restored to Life	2:12a; 4:46b, (47), 49b, 50ac, 51–52, (53), 54
5. The Catch of Fish	21: (1), 2–4, 6–7, 8b, 11, 14
6. Feeding the Multitude	6:1, (3), 5, 7–11, (12–13a), 13b 14, 15c, 17–20, 21b, (22, 25)
Jerusalem	
7. Lazarus Resuscitated from Death	11:1, 2c–3, 7, 11, 15c, 17, 32–34, 38–39a, 41, 43b–45
8. A Blind Man Sees	9:1, 6–7, (8)
9. A Crippled Man Walks	5:2–3, 5–9

There has been some criticism of Fortna's placing the catch of fish miracle from chapter 21, which was added to the gospel later, with the signs that fall in the first half of the gospel. One alternative is to exclude the catch of fish (chapter 21) and keep the two miracles in chapter 6 as two separate miracles, maintaining the number seven. Either way, there is strong sentiment in some scholarly circles for the possibility of a Signs Source, and others have attempted to reconstruct it. There has also been a good deal of discussion about the interpretation of the Signs Source by the Johannine author. We shall consider this item below under "Signs and Faith."

Bultmann's third hypothesis, also discussed in Chapter Five, is that the synoptic gospels and the Gospel of John are indebted to a *written passion source*. This possibility has received mixed reviews. Fortna, for example, went on to suggest that *before* the Gospel of John was written this passion source had already been joined to the Signs Source to make a narrative gospel that he called the The *"Signs Gospel."* In other words, there existed a protogospel that, somewhat analogous to Mark, attempted to balance the miracle stories with a focus on Jesus' passion, suffering, and death. We have also noted another passion story theory in Chapter Five, that suggested by J. D. Crossan, namely, passages from a *written "Cross Gospel"* lie behind all four canonical gospels and the apocryphal Gospel of Peter. If such interesting theories have any validity, they would make it possible to explain many of the similarities between John and the synoptics, for example, the verbal similarities. Note that in the list above, the first two examples occur in the miracle stories and the last seven examples occur in passion accounts. Were they from miracles sources and passion sources, or the two combined in a Signs Gospel? If so, it would not be necessary to show John's direct dependence on one or another of the synoptics or on common oral traditions.

In short, of Bultmann's three source proposals, the Signs Source has received the most positive response, and there is also some support for a Signs Gospel. Yet, the problems of method and lack of unanimity have not led to any total consensus on oral tradition, sources, and knowledge by John of any of the gospels, not even approaching the majority opinion about the Two-Source Theory in synoptic studies. Thus, we turn to the third major option.

3. The History of the Johannine Communities.

The third option for dealing with the aporias and possible relationships of John with the synoptics and other possible sources attempts to read between the lines and see various stages of development in the history of the Johannine community. Some scholars stress pregospel oral stages in touch with presynoptic traditions and/or sources; others stress multiple editions of the gospel itself, for example, building on Fortna's Signs Gospel and showing how it went through several revisions. In either case, the Johannine literature is seen as coming out of a developing Christian community for the most part independent of the synoptic groups.

Here we shall draw primarily on the popular theory of the American scholar R. Brown, who sees in John a "two-level drama," one level being the story about Jesus, the other being the way the story reveals important problems of the author and his community. Brown projects a development scheme for the Johannine community in which its changing Christology brought it into conflict with certain Jewish groups. Brown see less conflict within the Johannine tradition itself, or between it and other Christian communities, which is much debated. In any case, the following six-stage development is based largely on Brown's reconstruction. The first three stages are prior to the writing of the gospel; the last two stages come after its composition.

1. The *first stage*, reflected in John 1:35–41, consisted of an original group of Palestinian Jews, including followers of John the Baptist, who held some views somewhat like those found in the Dead Sea Scrolls (dualism of light/darkness and so forth) and some rather traditional views about the Messiah, Jesus. According to this "low," or human Christology, Jesus was descended from David, fulfilled the Law and the prophets, and worked miracles, like Moses or Elijah. This group probably began to collect some synopticlike sayings and miracle stories, the latter that would emerge as the Signs Source. One of this original group was a disciple of Jesus (1:35–40), perhaps a former follower of the Baptist, who would eventually be known as the Beloved Disciple.

2. Jesus' journey through Samaria and encounter with the Samaritan woman in John 4:4–42 reflects a *second stage* of Johannine Christianity: Christians who oppose the Temple, like Stephen and the Hellenists (Acts 6–7), carry out a mission to, and conversion of, Samaritans (compare Acts 8). In the process they

absorb Samaritan ideas, especially that the Messiah was to be the new Moses, a new Law bringer, teacher, and revealer who would restore his people (the Taheb). Like Moses, then, Jesus is now thought of as having seen God and descended from him; indeed, he is called the "Savior of the world" (John 4:42). Thus, the inclusion of the Samaritans becomes the catalyst for a more divine, or "high," Christology. Such a Christology is not tolerated by more traditional Jewish monotheists, and perhaps also some of the first Jewish Christians, including former adherents of the Baptist; thus begin conflicts with traditionalists. In this phase, there is a reduction of the future expectation of the return of Jesus ("delay of the parousia"), leading ultimately to the Johannine focus on the presence of Jesus ("realized eschatology"; see below). The disciple who shepherds the community through this conflict is known as the Beloved Disciple.

3. The *third stage,* suggested by John 12:20–23, 37–42, is marked by the inclusion of the Gentiles and a more universalistic outlook. Perhaps at this time the Johannine Christians migrate from Palestine to the regions of Ephesus or some other city, perhaps in Syria (compare John 7:35). In any case, we begin to see that the Johannine Christians are being expelled from the synagogue for the same reasons (12:42; see below).

4. In the *fourth stage* the Johannine gospel is written, about 90 C.E. Seven groups can be distinguished; three groups of outsiders with whom the Johannine group has increasing conflict, three groups of sympathizers whose faith is nonetheless inadequate, and the Johannine Christians themselves. The *outsiders* are: *(a)* "the world" (for example, 9:39; 12:31, 35–36), a society more inclusive than, yet sometimes identified with *(b)* "the [undifferentiated] Jews," and among them especially "the chief priests and scribes" and the Pharisees at Yavneh, who are behind exclusion of Christians from the synagogues (see below); and *(c)* the continuing followers of John the Baptist (3:2–26). There are also sympathizers whose beliefs the Johannine author thinks are inadequate: *(a)* Jews who secretly believe in Jesus, but fear being expelled from the synagogues (9:28; 12:42–43); *(b)* Christians whose faith is inadequate (6:60–66; 7:3–5; 8:31; 10:12); and *(c)* believing Christians of other churches represented by Peter who is therefore portrayed as competing with the Beloved Disciple (6:60–69). Finally, there are *believing Johannine Christians themselves.*

5. The *fifth stage,* about 100 C.E., is the period of the writing of the Johannine letters, to which may be added at least John 21 and 7:53–8:11. The leaders of the community become something of a Johannine School. The letters stress that it is necessary both to believe that Jesus came "in the flesh" and to keep the commandments; those who do not so believe are said to be of the devil and the antichrist. Once again we find a factional conflict about the Christology. Some elements stress that the dominant "high" Christology means that the humanity of the Man from heaven is of little importance for salvation; others believe in the importance of maintaining Jesus' humanity ("the Word became flesh").

6. The *sixth stage.* The Johannine community splits into two groups: a majority that, like the former group, denies that the human Jesus "in the flesh" is indispensable for the symbolic message about "Christ," a view that sounds like Gnosticism, which will be judged by the orthodox Great Church to be heretical. A minority follows the interpretation found in 1 John, namely, that Johannine Christology is anti-Gnostic, thus paving the way for the acceptance of the gospel

into the canon in the late second century. Ironically, the same high Christology that leads to Gnosticism contributes heavily to the "high" Christology of the orthodox creedal confessions of the church.

THE GOSPEL, THE LETTERS, AND THE JOHANNINE SCHOOL

We now take up the question of the literary relationship between the gospel and the letters (Stage 5). Are they by the same author? You will recall that in Christian antiquity there was a good deal of doubt about 2 and 3 John, whose author was called simply the "presbyter." Jerome, for example, claimed that the author of the gospel and 1 John was not the author of 2 and 3 John. We may also complicate matters by noting that there is some evidence that 1 and 2 John were known and quoted in the late second century, but nothing survives about 3 John. Nonetheless, 2 and 3 John were gradually accepted as having been written by the same person who wrote the gospel and 1 John.

Analysis shows that in general the Johannine literature has a similar style, tone, and thought. That commonality seems to indicate they are by the same person, especially in the case of the letters and the discourses in the gospel. However, a closer examination reveals a poverty of vocabulary and style in the first letter compared to the gospel and some real differences in thought.

The latter aspect of the matter is particularly important since these differences concern especially eschatology and the sacraments. The author of the letter has a strong hope for the future, a version of the traditional Christian hope for the parousia (2:17, 18, 28; 3:2, 3; 4:17), and he has a great interest in the sacraments of the church (2:12, 20, 27; 3:9; 5:1, 6). In the Gospel of John the main thrust is toward a denial of the hope of the parousia, on the grounds that the first coming of Jesus was the decisive event and no further coming, no further judgment, is to be expected (for example, 3:16–21, 36). Yet, scattered through the gospel there are some individual sayings that express the more traditional Christian hope (5:27–29; 6:39–40, 44b, 54; 12:48). Similarly with the sacraments: the gospel as a whole puts its major emphasis on the idea that people are brought to faith by their response to the church's proclamation (3:31–36 and elsewhere); it has no particular concern for the sacraments. Yet, the words "water and" in 3:5 make that verse an unmistakable reference to baptism, where no such reference exists apart from those two words; 6:51b–58 makes the discourse on the bread of life sacramental, whereas without those verses it is not; and 19:34b–35 introduces an allusion to baptism as it interrupts the continuity of the narrative.

For some interpreters, notably Bultmann, these isolated verses suggest that the gospel has been redacted, that is, a future parousia hope and concern for the sacraments have been introduced into the gospel by the author of the first letter. If this is the case (and it is all very tentative), the main text of the gospel is by one author and the first letter by another. Is either of these authors the "presbyter" who wrote the second and third letters, especially when (as we shall see) only 2 and 3 John are real letters? Is this the person who added chapter 21 and perhaps the story of the woman taken into adultery? There are similarities of language and thought, yet there are small subtle differences. We simply do not know; the most we can say is that probably at least two authors are involved in the gospels and letters of John, and perhaps three.

All of this points to a Johannine School. As we noted in Chapter Three, schools were a common feature of the environment of the New Testament, from the rabbinical schools and schools of scribes such as those at Qumran to the many schools of the Greco-Roman world. Within Christianity itself there was the tradition of Jesus and his disciples, and in Chapter Eight we discussed the school of Paul and his followers. The existence of a Johannine School is most likely, and the literary features of the gospel and letters of John make it virtually certain.

SOCIAL-HISTORICAL CONTEXT

We are now in a better position to look at the social-historical context of the composition of the Gospel of John and the letters. We have suggested a probable date for the gospel and letters, about 90–100 C.E., the gospel probably being at the beginning of that decade, the letters near the end. Stage 4 in the above history of the community, the stage of the gospel's original composition, shows that a major conflict had developed between Johannine Christians and the world, which overlaps with those labeled "the Jews." Thus, the Fourth Gospel even more than the first suggests a break with the synagogue, and in this case the fundamental issue is the Johannine community's "high" Christology in conflict with Jewish monotheism.

This view is confirmed by three instances where the gospel refers to those who are put out of the synagogue (9:22, 34; 12:42; 16:2a). Perhaps the most illuminating example of the three is found in the story of the sabbath healing of the man born blind in chapter 9 (see J. L. Martyn, bibliography). When brought before the Pharisees, the man who now "sees" calls Jesus a prophet, and when he is reexamined, he claims that Jesus must be from God or Jesus cannot have healed him. He is promptly thrown out. In between the two examinations, we learn that his parents do not want to discuss the miraculous healing because "the Jews had already agreed that anyone who confessed Jesus to be the Messiah would be put out of the synagogue" (9:22). "The Jews" regard Jesus as a sinner, not one sent from God (9:24, 29). For the author of John the issue is Christology.

You will recall from previous chapters that by about 80–90 C.E., the Pharisees at the Yavneh Academy were attempting to consolidate Judaism under their authority and influence. According to Rabbinic tradition *(Berakoth* 28b) they introduced a benediction against the *Minîm* ("heretics") to the synagogue prayers. Part of it said: "may they perish immediately. Speedily may they be erased from the Book of the Life ..." This **"Prayer Against the Heretics"** *(Birkat Ha-Minîm)* was aimed at dissenters.

While there is reason for caution in making the precise connections between the new prayer and the ban—the Fourth Gospel does not explicitly link the two and, as we noted in connection with the Gospel of Matthew and the Yavneh Academy, the new prayer was not yet fixed and the explicit reference to Christians *(Nōzrîm)* in the prayer might not have been added at this early stage—the three references to exclusion from the synagogue are quite clear.

The Gospel of John's separation from "the world" that tends to darkness and its view that the nonbelieving Jews will ban believing Jews from the synagogue suggest that Johannine Christianity was a particular kind of Christianized Jewish "sect," a marginal group that had turned inward. W. Meeks argues that as the Jesus of this gospel is an enigma, a stranger to "the world" as especially represented by "the Jews," a man from heaven who returns to heaven, so John's gospel was a book for insiders, not outsiders, those who, as is emphasized, "love one another," thus reinforcing the community's largely negative social identity (see bibliography). Otherworldly Christology and otherworldly community mirror each other; those who are alienated believe in the Alien Man, and the Alien Man symbolizes those who are alienated. The Johannine community must live in the world, but is not of the world. While from Brown's perspective the Johannine community was not a sect and ultimately communed with the Great Church, it may be legitimately asked whether this very unique and different community had *always* been in direct contact with other Christian groups, as its view that there are those whose faith is not yet complete shows. Certainly this group was not a reformist apocalyptic-type sect, but it appears to have been an "introversionist sect" (B. Wilson). This accords with the view of some scholars who argue that the majority group of Johannine Christians that moved in the direction of Gnosticism followed the real heartbeat of the Johannine sectarians, despite the protestations of that Johannine group that stresses Jesus "in the flesh" and God's love for the world, so preparing the ground for the gospel's acceptance in the canon.

The Intellectual Environment of the Fourth Evangelist

As noted above, it is one of the interesting facts of Christian history that the Gospel of John became the favorite gospel of many Gnostic churches that were viewed as heretical by the Great Church, while at the same time the gospel became determinative for the Great Church's formulation of its official view of Jesus Christ in the fourth and fifth century creeds. It will be useful at this point to examine briefly the intellectual ambiance of the evangelist. By "evangelist," or Fourth Evangelist, we mean minimally the author of the Fourth Gospel apart from 7:53–8:11 (the story of the adulteress) and chapter 21.

We have concluded that the Fourth Gospel was written sometime near the end of the first Christian century in a place where some members of John's community had been excluded from the synagogue. This points to a Jewish environment. There are many other aspects of the gospel which suggest a Jewish atmosphere: parallels with Aramaic paraphrases of the Old Testament (the Targums); interpretation of the Old Testament typical of rabbinic midrash (for example, John 6); a Christology deeply indebted to the myth of a descending and ascending figure of Wisdom, as well as Jewish miracle-working figures such as Moses (the ten plagues, which in the Scriptures are "signs") and Elijah; influence of the Septuagint, with fourteen direct Scriptural quotations, seven from the prophets. We shall discuss the famous Johannine "I Am" sayings, which among other things, suggest Scriptural statements about Yahweh's self-identity (for example, Isa 45:18; Exod 3:14). There are also connections of John's dualism with the light and darkness dualism of the Dead Sea Scrolls. Yet, the gospel was written in Greek and apocalyptic is not a characteristic feature of the gospel. Moreover, there are other features that indicate contact with the far-flung Hellenistic mystery religions and a quasi-Gnostic dualism. These features point to a highly diversified and complex religious background.

Can one be more precise about late first-century Judaism? C. K. Barrett has studied this problem and concludes the following: *(a)* that this period—with some exceptions—was beginning to see the end of Jewish apocalyptic, for this expression of Jewish faith had fulfilled its purpose; *(b)* that early Gnostic concepts had already before 70 C.E. penetrated Judaism, as Qumran shows, but the gnosticizing of Judaism continued, particularly in those circles in which Judaism came into contact with Christianity (Ignatius); that *(c)* at the same time a new institutional development began, for after the destruction of the Temple increased emphasis was laid upon those observances whose execution was not bound to the Temple, and it was these that furthered the cohesiveness of the nation and strengthened it against the threat of heresy and disintegration. This latter point appears to be supported by recent information about the growth of the synagogue. Some scholars, partly in reaction against Bultmann, would reject the Gnostic background in point *(b)*. Others, however, still defend some connection with an early form of Gnosticism citing among other things the parallels in the newly discovered Coptic Gnostic texts from Nag Hammadi. Certainly no one would deny the diversified nature of John's Jewish environment, a milieu that may also include the influence of rabbinic-type interpretation of the Old Testament and Samaritan thinking about Moses. It seems all observers acknowledge a highly complex environment that might, for want of precise language, be called syncretistic Hellenistic Judaism.

JOHANNINE THEOLOGY

Within the context of syncretistic Hellenistic Judaism, the major Johannine theological ideas can be outlined as follows.

1. Christology.

The Gospel of John has a "high" Christology. Jesus fulfills all the Old Testament messianic expectations—Lamb of God, Chosen One of God, Messiah, King of Israel, the new Elijah—and in all of these, he is vastly superior to John the Baptist (1:19–51). However, the center of John's Christology is that Jesus is the mysterious "man from heaven," the Son of Man, or simply Son (of the Father). He is not the synoptics' apocalyptic Son of Man derived from Daniel; rather, he originates from his Father in heaven, *descends* to earth as one "sent" as an envoy from his Father (8:42) or as one who "came" from God, stays for a period (7:33), and *ascends* to his Father again (3:13–15; 6:62; 8:14; 16:28). He is as close to the Father as one can imagine (10:30) and yet he is subordinate to the Father (14:28) and is the Father's representative dispensing judgment (5:22, 27) and "eternal life" (3:13–15; 6:27; 6:53). He reveals God's "glory" (13:31). His ascent is also his being "lifted up," which is given a double meaning in terms of his being "lifted up" on the Cross (3:13–15; 8:28; 13:34–36). He is God's only son (3:16,18), and responding to Jesus is equivalent to responding to the Father. "The Jews" and a disciple do not understand his origins (6:41–42; 3:11–13). Ultimately, he is a stranger from another world (8:23).

It was noted above that the revelation discourses represent John's own theology. One of the central themes of the discourses is the statement "I Am," sometimes without a predicate, sometimes with an implied predicate, sometimes with an explicit predicate (6:35: "I am the bread of life"; 8:12: "I am the light of the world"; 10:11,14: "I am the good shepherd."). The sayings with no predicate seem to have a background in the Old Testament (Exod 3:14); those with a predicate are like those known in various Hellenistic religions (the Coptic Gnostic texts; the Hermetic literature; the Mandaean literature; the Isis mystery cult). One example comes from the Hermetic literature in connection with the revealer Poimandres:

> [The revealer appears to the speaker in a vision] "Who are you?" I said. "I am Poimandres," said he, "the Mind of the Sovereignty. I know what you wish, and I am with you everywhere.... Keep in mind the things you wish to learn and I will teach you."

Clearly, the "I Am" sayings are intended to signal the revelation of a god.

We must note the concept of the Logos, or "Word," the preexistent mythical Wisdom figure who participates in the act of creation, a figure from the realm of Light. This idea, well known in Hellenistic Judaism (see Chapter Three), will be discussed in connection with the Johannine prologue (1:1–18).

2. Dualism.

The Fourth Gospel is characterized by a set of symbolic opposites: light/darkness; life/death; God/Satan; above/below; heaven/earth; spirit/flesh; truth/falsehood; (true) Israel/"the Jews"; belief/unbelief. This dualism is not simply the *temporal,* or horizontal, dualism that contrasts "this world" and "the world to come" as known in Jewish apocalyptic; it may have roots in this type of thinking, but it has become much more cosmic (Greek *kosmos* = "world"), or *vertical,* a contrast between the heavenly world above and the earthly world below. But this dualism also has a human, personal dimension, that is, the way of the world is a sinful, inauthentic existence contrary to God's plan. In short, the world has become so corrupted by Satan (12:31) that it falls on the negative, earthly side of darkness (8:12), and is in need of redemption by a loving God who sends the man from another world (3:16), the world of light. Clearly, a document that is so negative to the world implies that it proceeds out of a community that has experienced alienation from the dominant political and religious structures, an observation that corresponds with the view that the Johannine Christians are a sect that has been expelled from the synagogue.

3. Signs and Faith.

Above, it was briefly suggested that the evangelist reinterprets a Signs Source that originally presents Jesus as a Divine Man whose miracles induce faith. They become the basis for the first part of his work (2:1–12:50), that is, they become actions around which his monologues and dialogues are constructed. With regard to specific miracles, it seems at first that the evangelist uses them in the same manner as the Signs Source, that is, they lead disciples and others to faith (compare 2:11, 25; 12:37; 20:30–31), and they prove his Messiahship (2:18). An example is 20:30–31: "Now Jesus did many other signs in the presence of the disciples, which are not written in this book. But these are written that you may come to believe..." This view is not the synoptic view of miracles, however. In the synoptic gospels the emphasis is on faith as a prerequisite for miracles (for example, Mark 6:5–6). However, the faith-inducing function of miracles also contrasts with the remainder of the gospel of John itself. In 2:23–25 as in 4:48, Jesus repudiates the kind of faith induced by signs. The conversation with Nicodemus contrasts such faith unfavorably with rebirth "from above" and "of the spirit" (3:2, 3, 5–6). These passages make it very probable that the author of the Gospel of John is using as a source a book of signs that presents Jesus as a Hellenistic Hero whose miracles induce faith, but that he *reinterprets the source by indicating that faith induced by miracles is not enough*. Yet, "seeing" a sign can mean *more* than understanding Jesus as a wonder-worker miraculously capable of providing basic needs, such as food (6:26); and others do *not* respond to signs with faith (12:37). These subtleties about the impact of signs seem to be reinforced by 4:48, where Jesus responds to the request of the Capernaum official's son for healing by what appears on the surface to be a negative statement: "Unless you see signs and wonders you will not believe" (4:48). Thus, the evangelist understands signs in a more complex manner: *(a)* not all who see signs *truly* "see" and believe; *(b)* some do "see" and believe, or perhaps "see" *because* they are open to faith; *(c)* some who "see" see more than the mere performance of a sign, that is, they "see" spiritually, beyond material needs; *(d)* and some may not need signs at all: "Blessed are those who have not seen and yet have come to believe" (20:29). There seem, then, to be different levels of perception of "signs," and some qualitative difference among them, suggesting to at least one scholar stages in the maturation of faith. Whether this is the case or not, John sees a multilevel, dynamic interaction between signs and faith, or to put it another way, between religious experience and religious knowledge. This view can be correlated with his subtle view of faith and knowledge throughout the gospel.

4. Eschatology.
The eschatology of the Fourth Evangelist is rooted in his Christology, that is, acts that are normally associated with the *future*—the coming of the Messiah, resurrection, judgment, eternal life—are already *present* for the believer in the encounter with Jesus. In contemporary scholarship, this is called "realized eschatology." It is one way of responding to the delay of the parousia. To be sure, futurist eschatology in John is not totally lacking (compare, for example, 5:28–29; 6:39–40, 44, 54; 12:48). There may also be a *type* of parousia that suggests Jesus will return and take the Christian to his heavenly home, perhaps at death (14:2–3). This, of course, is not the traditional apocalyptic view, but neither is it realized eschatology. In general, the futurist eschatology might have been preserved from the tradition or, as Bultmann suggested, it might have come from a member of a Johannine School who subsequently redacted the gospel to bring it more into line with traditional views. The evangelist's own view is characterized more by 5:24: "Very truly, I tell you, anyone who hears my word and believes in him who sent me has eternal life, and does not come under judgment, but has passed from death to life."

5. Spirit, Church, and Sacraments.
The stress on the present in John's eschatology is matched by his view of the presence of the Spirit among believers. The special term for the Spirit in John

14–16 is Paraclete (Greek *paraklētos,* compare 14:15–17, 25–26; 15:26–27; 16:5–11, 12–15). Literally, it means "the one called beside," but it can mean *(a)* "Advocate" or "Intercessor," that is, a defense attorney before God in behalf of the Christian; *(b)* "Comforter" or "Counselor" to the Christian; and *(c)* "Exhorter" or "Proclaimer." Like the Stranger from heaven, the Paraclete comes from the Father at the request of Jesus, or in Jesus' name after Jesus departs, or alternatively he is sent by the departed Jesus himself. He represents, then, the continued and recognized presence of Christ. He is a prophet teaching his believers and bearing witness and glorifying Christ, recalling all that Jesus said. In fact, Jesus is viewed as the first Paraclete in relation to "another Paraclete" (14:16). Like Jesus, the Paraclete is rejected by the world; it does not recognize him. However, the Paraclete convicts the world of sin because it does not believe in Jesus.

The Fourth Evangelist, unlike Matthew and Luke, seems to have no interest in the organized institutional church. He mentions no church officials and he normally refers simply to "the disciples." In fact, Peter's role (and the apostolic church related to him) is devalued in contrast to the role of the Beloved Disciple. John seems more concerned with believers in general. As Christ is one with the Father and manifests his glory, so believers are one in Christ and manifest his glory (17:22–23); as God loved the world and gave his Son (3:16), so the Son loves his followers and they are to love one another (15:17). It would appear that John shares an important characteristic with apocalyptic Christianity: its expulsion from the synagogue seems to have led to a somewhat sectarian, "free" association with regard to the church.

Finally, the Fourth Evangelist does not lay emphasis on the sacraments; true, we catch glimpses of *possible* sacramental language (3:5: "water and"; 6:51–58), but these are highly debated, and in any case they may be the product of a member of the Johannine school wishing to be more explicit about sacramental matters.

In summary, the major Johannine ideas may be stated: the world below has become dominated by sin so that God the Father in his love sends his preexistent Son who descends, works signs, reveals himself in revelatory discourses, undergoes a passion and ascends, his Spirit-Paraclete being an Advocate and Comforter of believers who, without necessity of ecclesiastical structures and sacraments, already experience resurrection and eternal life now, in the present.

VOCABULARY, STYLE, STRUCTURE, AND PLOT OF THE GOSPEL OF JOHN

The Greek of the Johannine literature is some of the easiest Greek in the New Testament. Its focus on symbolic themes and style, which returns to major themes again and again ("spiral structure"), often means the repetition of vocabulary and syntax. There are also many antitheses, sandwiches, chiasmas (ABCDC ′B ′A ′), and a special use of irony: various interlocutors, especially opponents of Jesus, do not understand who Jesus is, but the reader of the story does. Thus, the author and the reader share something of the mystery of Jesus' identity.

The approach of redaction criticism to determining the main emphases of a gospel writer relies in part on the ability to determine how an evangelist modifies and interprets sources. It also attempts to learn about the writer's intentions by the way the material is structured as a whole, and this becomes especially important when the sources used are more tentative. Such a commentary has now been attempted (Fortna, *The Fourth Gospel and Its Predecessor,* 1988). Yet, the problems with regard to structure are especially complicated in this particular instance because of the many possible displacements and sources. Moreover, in a text as reflective and meditative in character as the Gospel of John, narrative consistency is not to be expected, and if there are displacements within and sources behind the text, they do not affect our general understanding of it.

In this connection, we must make a comment about the plot of the gospel. The goal of the story is the glorification of Jesus at his "hour," a symbolic time when Jesus on the cross will be "lifted up," that is, will return to his Father. This theme is anticipated by Jesus' references to "the hour" ("My hour has not yet come" [2:4]; "an hour is coming..." [4:21, 23; 5:25, 28–29; 16:2, 25, 32] or "has come" [12:23; 17:1]; compare 12:27; 13:1). Thus, while Jesus periodically faces opposition and misunderstanding by outsiders and others, ultimately he arrives at this goal.

Given the analysis above, the Gospel of John falls naturally into five main parts:

1. **Introduction: Prologue and Testimony, 1:1–51.** In the prologue (1:1–18) a christological hymn is presented with comments, and then a series of incidents bring John the Baptist on the scene to give his testimony to Jesus, testimony confirmed by some of his disciples.
2. **The Book of Signs, 2:1–12:50.** Even before the general recognition of the use of a Signs Source in this part of the gospel, C. H. Dodd recognized the essential nature of these narratives by giving it this title (see bibliography).
3. **Farewell Discourses and Prayer for the Church, 13:1–17:26.** These discourses and the prayer are found in the context of the Lord's Supper (13:2; compare 1 Cor 11:20), and they meditate on the nature, meaning, and significance of the passion of Jesus.
4. **Passion Narrative, 18:1–20:30.**
5. **Epilogue: The Appearance in Galilee, 21:1–25.**

Dodd points out that there is a characteristic Johannine pattern of narration. It consists of the following elements, as seen in John, chapter 5:

Action ("sign"): 5:1–9 (healing at Bethzatha)

Dialogue: 5:10–18 (Sabbath healing)

Monologue: 5:19–40

Appendix: 5:41–47

Or it can be, as in chapter 6:

Action ("sign") and Dramatic Dialogue: 6:1–23 (feeding of the multitude)

Dialogue Tending to Monologue: 6:24–59 (bread of life)

Two Brief Concluding Dialogues: 6:60–65, 66–71

Or it can be, as in chapters 9 and 10:

Action ("sign"): 9:1–7 (healing at Siloam)

Dialogues: 9:8–41 (trial scene and two brief colloquies)

Monologue: 10:1–18

Brief Concluding Dialogue: 10:19–21

Appendix: 10:22–39

The farewell discourses and prayer follow this pattern, except that in this instance we have the action, the passion narrative, coming last and not first.

Opening Dramatic Scene: 13:1–30

Dialogue: 13:31–14:31 (on Christ's departure and return)

Monologue: 15:1–16:15 (on Christ and his Church)

Concluding Dialogue: 16:16–33

Appendix: 17:1–26 (the prayer for the Church)

Action: 18:1–20:31 (the passion narrative; anticipated in 13:1–3)

This is a very important structural observation, and we take it seriously as we attempt the following exegetical survey of the gospel, though at some points our analysis differs slightly from Dodd's; for example, our experience with the other gospels has led us to pay particular attention to transitional passages.

EXEGETICAL SURVEY OF THE GOSPEL OF JOHN

Introduction: Prologue and Testimony, 1:1–51

Prologue, 1:1–18

The prologue consists of a hymn with comments. As reconstructed and translated by R. E. Brown, the hymn reads as follows:

1	In the beginning was the Word;
	the Word was in God's presence,
	and the Word was God.
2	He was present with God in the beginning.
3	Through him all things came into being,
	and apart from him not a thing came to be.
4	That which had come to be in him was life,
	and this life was the light of men.
5	The light shines in darkness,
	for the darkness did not overcome it.
10	He was in the world,
	and the world was made by him;
	Yet the world did not recognize him.
11	To his own he came;
	Yet his own people did not accept him.
12	But all those who did accept him
	he empowered to become God's children.
14	And the Word became flesh

and made his dwelling among us.
And we have seen his glory,
the glory of an only Son coming from the Father,
filled with enduring love.
16   And of his fullness
we have all had a share—
love in place of love.

The interruptions in this hymn are the testimony of the Baptist (verses 6–9), the reference to being born "of God" (verse 13), further testimony of the Baptist (verse 15), and the evangelist's climactic summary (verses 17–18). These comments represent important themes to the evangelist, which are further developed in the gospel: the testimony of the Baptist (1:19–42); being born of God is the theme of the dialogue with Nicodemus (3:1–15); and verses 17–18, which are a summary of the whole gospel, not only of the prologue. The hymn itself presents features foreign to the rest of the gospel—except for the prologue Jesus is never called the Logos nor is the phrase "enduring love" (literally, "grace and truth") found again—but its presentation of Jesus as the preexistent redeemer who manifested his glory in the world matches well the major aspects of the gospel's presentation of Jesus. In its presentation of Jesus as the redeemer who descends to the world the hymn shares the emphasis of the other christological hymns we discussed in Chapter Five.

Testimony, 1:19–51; 3:22–30

The theme of testimony, prominent in the comments on the hymn in the prologue is now developed with regard to John the Baptist, and with regard to some of his disciples who become disciples of Jesus. Originally, 3:22–30 followed 1:51. It has been displaced.

The Book of Signs, 2:1-12:50

The first major section of the gospel, the Book of Signs, is built on the skeleton framework of seven miracle stories or signs. These are as follows:

Changing water into wine at Cana (2:1–11)

Curing the official's son at Cana (4:46–54)

Curing the paralytic at Bethzatha (5:1–15)

Miraculous feeding in Galilee (6:1–15)

Walking on the water (6:16–21)

Curing the blind man in Jerusalem (9)

Raising of Lazarus in Bethany (11)

In addition, there is a series of three consecutive thematic concerns:

1. From Cana to Cana—Jesus manifests his glory in various ways and elicits various responses (2:1–4:42)
2. Jesus and the principal feasts of the Jews (5:1–10:39)

3. Jesus moves toward the hour of his glorification (11:1–12:50)

With these observations as our starting point and with Dodd's compositional insight as our guide, we offer the following exegetical survey of the Book of Signs.

Manifestation and Response, 2:1–4:42

Action

The first sign: the miracle at Cana, 2:1–11. It is explicitly stated that this is the first of the signs through which Jesus manifested his glory, and that it elicited the response of faith (verse 11). Jesus' relationship with Mary is not without respect, but nevertheless distant (compare Mark 3:31–35).

Transition, 2:12.

The anticipation of the final sign: the cleansing of the Temple in Jerusalem, 2:13–22. The cleansing of the Temple is not itself a sign, but it anticipates the climactic sign, the resurrection. In turn, the resurrection elicits the response of faith (verse 22).

Transitional summary, 2:23–25.

Dialogue

Jesus and Nicodemus, 3:1–15. This dialogue is built on the theme of the new birth (compare the theme of being born "of God" in the prologue). It climaxes in a Son of Man saying (verses 14–15), which is itself a major statement of the Johannine theology of "the man from heaven."

Monologue

The power of the Son to give eternal life to the believer, 3:16–21. The evangelist now moves into a monologue developing the theme of the Son's power to give eternal life to the believer, stated in the preceding verse. The traditional Christian future eschatology has been replaced by an eschatology realized in the present (a realized eschatology): "This is the judgment..." (verse 19). The farewell discourses parallel the same theme (12:46–48), where, however, the traditional eschatology has been restored ("the word that I have spoken will be his judge on the last day," 12:48). An editor has apparently made the reference to baptism more explicit in 3:5.

A displaced section of monologue, 3:31–36. John 3:22–30 originally belonged after 1:51. But what about 3:31–36, obviously part of a monologue by the Johannine Jesus on the theme of witness, testimony, and belief? It does not fit well after 3:21; perhaps it originally belonged after 3:15, where it would certainly fit better, but we cannot be sure.

Action

Jesus moves to Samaria, 4:1–6.

Dialogue

Jesus with the woman, 4:7–21. The dialogue turns on two themes, "living water" and worship "in spirit and truth." Water is a universal symbol for life, and worship is a universal religious practice. John develops them in his characteristic dualism by contrasting "this" and "living" water, false worship and true.

Monologue

The coming of the true worship, 4:22–26. The second theme of the dialogue now develops in a short but characteristic monologue. It is significant that Jesus reveals himself as the Messiah the Samaritans expect (the Mosaic Taheb) to the strange Samaritan woman in the first "I Am" saying (4:25–26). The theme of living water is not further developed here; the evangelist will return to that later.

Appendix

Further dialogue and testimony in Samaria, 4:27–42. As a result of the woman's witness, the Samaritans accept Jesus as "Savior of the world" (4:41–42).
Transition to Galilee, 4:43–45.
The second sign: the official's son in Capernaum, 4:46–54. While in Cana, Jesus heals an official's son from a distance. This second sign in Cana marks the end of the first section of the Book of Signs. It ends as it had begun—in Cana and with a sign.

Jesus and the Jewish Festivals, 5:1–10:39

The second section of the Book of Signs explores the significance of Jesus as understood in the symbolism and meaning of the great Jewish religious festivals and observances.

Jesus and the Sabbath, 5:1–47. The Sabbath is a weekly observance, built on Genesis 2:3: "So God blessed the seventh day and hallowed it, because on it God rested from all his work which he had done in creation." The Jews kept, and still keep, this day of the week free from work for religious observance, to link themselves ever more closely with God. This observance led to the question of what was to be considered work on the Sabbath, which is the background for synoptic gospel controversy stories such as Mark 2:23–27, the Plucking of the Grain. In the Fourth Gospel, however, the aspect of controversy between Jesus and the Jews as to what work was lawful on the Sabbath has been transformed into a meditation on the fact that Jesus "works" as God "works," to give life to the dead and to judge.

Transitional verse, 5:1. This verse speaks of a feast, that is, a religious festival, but the term is used broadly, since the concern is not with an annual religious observance but with the Sabbath.

Action

Jesus heals a lame man on the Sabbath, 5:2–9. The exact parallelism between the command to this paralytic (5:8) and that to a paralytic in Capernaum in Mark 2:9 is striking; it is one of the bases for arguing that John knew the Gospel of Mark. But the meditative character of the Johannine narrative is such that it leaves in the dark how far and in what ways this story is related to Mark 2:1–12. All the narratives in the Book of Signs have been so transformed into vehicles for meditation on the significance of Jesus for the believer that historical questions about them are all but impossible to answer.

Dialogue

A series of dialogues between the Jews, the man, and Jesus, 5:10–18. By means of these dialogues, the evangelist introduces the theme of the relationship between Jesus and God. Jesus is the Son of the Father, and equal with God.

Monologue
Jesus relation to God, 5:19–47. This monologue explores the relationship of Jesus and God. Jesus is the Son of God, and as such his actions are identical with those of God: he judges, and he gives life to the dead.

Jesus and the Passover, 6:1–71. The passover celebrates the deliverance of the Jewish people from Egypt. It is observed annually by a meal in which the food eaten and the wine drunk symbolize this deliverance and anticipate the final eschatological deliverance. The Christian Eucharist is based on the Passover and uses much of the same symbolism. The evangelist John now explores the significance of Jesus in terms of Passover and Eucharistic symbols.

Action
The feeding of the multitude, 6:1–14. *Transitional verse,* 6:15.
The walking on the water, 6:16–21. The two incidents of a miraculous feeding and a sea miracle are in Mark in exactly the same sequence: Mark 6:30–44 (feeding); 45–51 (walking on the water). In John's gospel they both have parallels in the narrative of the deliverance from Egypt: the Jews miraculously crossed the sea (Exod 14:21–25) and were equally miraculously fed in the wilderness (Exod 16:13–16, "He gave them bread from heaven to eat" [6:31]. In Exod 16:31 this bread is called manna).

Dialogue
A dialogue between Jesus and the Jews on the bread that God gives to humans, 6:22–34. John follows his usual pattern of introducing the theme of the ensuing monologue by means of a dialogue. The theme is the "bread of life," and it evokes both the manna of the wilderness and the bread of the Eucharist.

Monologue
Jesus as the bread of life, 6:35–40.
Dialogue
The bread of life is the flesh of Jesus, the bread of the Eucharist, 6:41–59. The theme of Jesus as the "bread of life" is developed in a monologue, which in turn is followed by a dramatic dialogue. The manna the Jews ate in the wilderness has become a symbol of the life-giving power of God to his people, which is now fulfilled forever in Jesus. The life-giving power of Jesus is in turn symbolized in the bread of the Christian Eucharist.

Appendix
Jesus and his disciples, 6:60–70. In its theme, this passage is strikingly reminiscent of the misunderstanding and confession in Mark 8:14–21.
Transition to the Feast of Booths, 7:1–13. Jesus is now to be considered in light of the symbolism of a further major Jewish festival, the Feast of Booths.

Jesus and the Feast of Booths, 7:14–10:21. The Feast of Booths was held in the autumn. It was originally an agricultural festival celebrating the vintage harvest, but in the course of time it came also to celebrate the constant renewal of the covenant between God and his people. This latter fact makes it natural to take up here the theme of Jesus as the one who fulfills the old covenant as the Jewish Messiah. So in this section the evangelist explores the messianic claims of Jesus and also makes extensive use of the literary device of dramatic dialogues between Jesus and his Jewish opponents about those claims.

Action
Jesus in the Temple at Booths, 7:14.

Dialogue
The claim of Jesus to be the Christ, 7:15–36. This is a series of three dramatic dialogues. The first (verses 15–24) concerns the authority of Jesus to heal on the Sabbath; the second (verses 25–31) deals with the claim of Jesus to be the Christ by the signs he has done; the third (verses 32–36) introduces the theme of the death of Jesus. This last will loom larger and larger from this point on in the gospel, until it dominates everything else as the theme of the farewell discourses.

Action
Jesus makes a personal claim to be the Living Water, 7:37–39. At the Feast of Booths, water was ceremoniously carried from the Pool of Siloam to the Temple as a reminder of the water miraculously supplied in the wilderness (Num 20:2–13) and as a symbol of the coming of the Messiah as the "water of life" (Isa 12:3). The evangelist has the opportunity to return to the theme of Jesus as the water of life, which he had first stated in the dialogue between Jesus and the woman of Samaria in chapter 4.

Dialogue
The Jews dispute among themselves concerning the claim of Jesus to be the Christ, 7:40–52. Unlike the previous dialogues, these do not feature Jesus at all but present the Jews in dispute among themselves concerning the validity of his claims.
[The adulteress story, 7:53–8:11, is not part of the original text of the gospel.]

Action
Jesus makes a personal claim to be the Light of the World, 8:12. A further feature of the symbolism of the Feast of Booths was the ceremonious lighting of lamps in the Temple court. The evangelist can return to the theme of Jesus as the Light of the World, a theme first stated in the prologue (1:4–5, 9).

Dialogue
The validity of Jesus' claims, 8:13–20. The Jews are presented as disputing with Jesus the validity of the claims he is making. This dialogue concludes on a further note of anticipation of the passion (verse 20).

Action
Jesus condemns the Jews, 8:21. The theme of the death of Jesus understood as his going where he cannot be followed (that is., back to the heavenly region from which he came) is developed at length in the farewell discourses (13:31–14:7). Here is its first statement in the context of a condemnation of the Jews, who cannot follow him. In the farewell discourses, the disciples are promised that they will be able to follow them.

Dialogue
Jesus and the Jews who do not believe in him, 8:22–30. Jesus is here presented as debating vigorously with, and condemning, the Jews who did not believe in him.

Action
Jesus and the Jews who did believe in him, 8:31–32. Jesus is now presented as making promises to the Jews who did believe in him.

Dialogue

Jesus and the natural claims of the Jews on God, 8:33–59. This dialogue begins with the Jews who did believe in Jesus and ends with those same Jews taking up stones to throw at him. Here the evangelist is wrestling with the problem of the Jewish rejection of Jesus. Jesus himself had some success in his mission to the Jewish people—he had attracted disciples—yet the Jews had finally engineered his crucifixion. Similarly, the Christians had some success in their mission to the Jews, especially among the Greek-speaking Jews of the Dispersion, yet the Jews at Yavneh had finally produced the benediction that drove the Christian Jews out of the Jewish community. The evangelist anguishes over this tragic pattern in the literary form of a dialogue between Jesus and his Jewish contemporaries.

Action

Jesus gives sight to a man born blind, 9:1–7. Continuing the theme of Jesus as the Light of the World, the evangelist now presents an account of Jesus giving light to a man born blind.

Dialogue

The fate of Jesus and his followers in the Jewish community, 9:8–41. What is at issue here in this series of dialogues is the fate of Jesus and his followers in the Jewish community.

The first dialogue is between the man and his neighbors (verses 8–12). It reflects the original impact of Jesus on his Jewish contemporaries and the questions to which it gave rise.

The second dialogue is between the man and the Pharisees (verses 13–17). Here the Pharisees represent not only the Jewish authorities who finally condemned Jesus, but also those Pharisees at Yavneh who produced the Prayer Against the Heretics (*Minîm*), making it uncomfortable for the Jews who had beliefs about Jesus of the Johannine type to remain in the synagogue. Perhaps the ban was implied.

The third dialogue is between the Jews and the man's parents (verses 18–23). It reflects the problems and divisions within the Jewish community produced by Christology. As we indicated above, verse 22 refers to the ban.

The fourth dialogue concerns the man himself and his fate at the hands of the Jewish authorities (verses 24–34). It reflects the fate of the Jewish convert to Christianity as the evangelist knows it; perhaps even the fate of the evangelist himself.

The fifth dialogue mirrors the further fate of the man who, now banned by the Jewish community, finds his new home in the community of those who come to faith in Jesus (verses 35–41). The members of this sectarian community in turn reject the community that had rejected them, as they reject the world. These dialogues reveal the actual situation of the evangelist and his readers, just as Mark 13 revealed the situation of the evangelist Mark and his readers.

Concluding Monologue

Jesus as the shepherd and the sheepgate, 10:1–18. The evangelist closes this section with a monologue and a dialogue on the messianic claims of Jesus and the response of the Jews. The monologue concerns Jesus as the shepherd and the sheepgate. The discourse is an involved allegory in which various images on the care of sheep appear in connection with Jesus. In verses 1–6 Jesus is the shepherd responsible for the sheep and to whom the sheep are responsive. In verses 7–10 he is the gate through which sheep enter and leave their fold. Verses 11–15 introduce the theme of Jesus as the good shepherd prepared to die for his sheep, and Jesus is contrasted in this respect with other shepherds. Finally, in verses 16–18 Jesus is the shepherd who lays down his life not only for his flock, the Jewish people, but also for the Gentiles.

Concluding Dialogue

The Jews disagree with the claims of Jesus, 10:19–21. The section concludes with a dialogue on the varied responses of the Jews to Jesus. This dialogue probably reflects the experience of the evangelist as he became a Christian in his own Jewish community.

Jesus and the Feast of Dedication, 10:22–39. The term "dedication" translates the Hebrew word *hanŭkkāh.* You will recall that the Feast of Dedication celebrates the rededication of the Temple in 164 B.C.E. after its desecration by Antiochus Epiphanes, who erected an altar to the Greek god Zeus in the Jerusalem Temple. This is the "desolating sacrilege" to which such frequent reference is made in Jewish and Christian apocalyptic (for example, Mark 13:14). Since the festival celebrated a major victory of the people of God against their enemies and was seen as a renewal of the covenant between God and his people, it becomes a suitable occasion for the evangelist to return to his theme of the messianic claims of Jesus.

Action

Jesus at the Feast of Dedication, 10:22–23.

Dialogue

The climactic claims of Jesus and the response of the Jews to them, 10:24–39. In this dialogue the evangelist presents Jesus as summarizing the claims he has already made for himself. He is the shepherd and the giver of life; he and the Father are one. At the same time a new note is introduced in accordance with the symbolism of the rededication of the Temple, which lies behind the Feast of Dedication: Jesus is the one consecrated by God and sent into the world (verse 36). Similarly, the negative response of the Jews is also summarized, and it is presented as reaching a climax. The Jews attempt to stone Jesus (verse 31) as they had before in 8:59; they also attempt to arrest him (verse 39) as they had before in 7:30, 32, 44; 8:20. Do these events represent fear of local persecutions in the Johannine community?

Transition: The End of the Public Ministry of Jesus, 10:40–42.

The thought of the evangelist is now turning more strongly to the Cross, and the last section of his Book of Signs deals with the meaning of the death of Jesus. So this transitional passage marks the end of the public ministry of Jesus; from this point forward we are concerned only with the death of Jesus and its meaning. However, the evangelist thinks in a spiral manner. We pointed out that the first part of the Book of Signs began and ended in Cana. Similarly, Jesus appeared on the scene for the first time in this gospel at the place where John was baptizing (1:29–34), and his public ministry must end at that same place, as it does in these transitional verses.

Jesus Moves Toward the Hour of His Glorification, 11:1–12:50

This is the last section of the Book of Signs. Jesus is still presented as working and teaching in public, but in the mind of the evangelist the public ministry is over, and now everything is dominated by the Cross. In this section, therefore, the evangelist begins the meditation on the death of Jesus and its meaning.

Action

The raising of Lazarus, 11:1–44. For the reader who comes to the Gospel of John after a reading of the synoptic gospels this is a most startling narrative. Not only is it a major miracle of Jesus about which the canonical synoptic gospels appear to know nothing—the Secret Gospel of Mark is related—but also it is presented as the actual occasion for the crucifixion (verses 45–53). Moreover, the Martha and Mary of this story appear also in the Gospel of Luke (Luke 10:38–42), where, however, there is absolutely no mention of Lazarus. The historical problems in connection with the story are all but insurmountable, and the best that scholars can do is suggest that the evangelist John is meditating upon an element of early Christian tradition otherwise lost to us. At this level the story comes alive as a dramatic presentation of Jesus as the resurrection and the life to those who believe in him. Note Martha's full confession of faith, probably representing true Johannine believers.

Reaction

The Jewish authorities condemn Jesus to death, 11:45–53. The normal pattern of the Johannine literary construction is shattered by the nearness of the Cross. So here we have the reaction of the Jewish authorities to the raising of Lazarus rather than the dialogue and monologue that would normally follow the action.

Transition: Will Jesus come to Jerusalem for the Passover? 11:54–57. The evangelist dramatically heightens the tension of his narrative in this transitional section.

Action

The anointing at Bethany, 12:1–8. This scene relates both to Mark 14:3–9, the anointing at Bethany, and to Luke 7:36–38, an anointing of Jesus in Galilee (see above). In the Gospel of John, as in Mark, the anointing anticipates the burial of Jesus. Jesus defends Mary's actions.

Transition: The tension in Jerusalem heightens, 12:9–11.

Action

Jesus enters Jerusalem in triumph, 12:12–19. This parallels the synoptic gospel accounts of the same incident (Mark 11:1–10; Matt 21:1–9; Luke 19:28–38). In John, however, the incident is interpreted as an anticipation of the glorification of Jesus (verse 16).

Action

The Greeks come to Jesus, 12:20–22. The evangelist has been concerned thus far in his narrative with Jesus and the Jews, which no doubt reflects his personal position as a member of a Jewish community who became a Christian. However, now he turns to Jesus and the Greeks in an incident referring to his being a Christian in a Greek city and preaching the gospel to Greeks.

Dialogue

The meaning of the Cross, 12:23–36. The evangelist now returns to his favorite literary device and explores the meaning of the Cross in dialogue between Jesus and the voice from heaven and between Jesus and the crowd.

The ending of the Book of Signs, 12:37–50. The evangelist brings his Book of Signs to an end with a summary of the meaning of the signs of Jesus, meditating on their meeting with the reactions of both nonbelief and belief.

Farewell Discourses and Prayer for the Church, 13:1–17:26

In this third major section of the gospel the evangelist explores the meaning of Christ for the believer and the church in a series of discourses and a prayer by Jesus as the Last Supper. They probably originated as a series of meditations at the celebration of the Christian Eucharist.

Opening Dramatic Scene

The Last Supper, 13:1–30. This is the Johannine version of the Last Supper between Jesus and his disciples, narratives of which we also find in 1 Corinthinans 11:23–26; Mark 14:17–25; Matthew 26:20–29 and Luke 22:14–38. Unlike those, John does not mention the eucharistic words, or words of interpretation spoken by Jesus over the bread or the wine, and he has an incident of foot washing the other narratives do not. We have no idea why the Eucharistic words are missing. Earlier we suggested that the evangelist has no concern for the sacraments and puts his emphasis elsewhere, and the omission of the Eucharistic words may be part of this general trend. On the other hand, these words were especially sacred to Christians in other circles. Did the evangelist regard this aspect of the narrative as too sacred to be written down?
The matter of the washing of the feet lends itself more readily to an explanation. The evangelist casts his thought in the imagery of incident and dramatic dialogue. He dramatizes the sacrifice of Jesus and its significance by means of an acted parable of humility and service. The humility of the action is the more striking in light of the evangelist's concentration on the passion of Jesus as his glorification. This section contains the first reference to the disciple whom Jesus loved who "was reclining next to him" (13:23, 25).

Christ's departure and return, 13:31–14:31. In this dialogue between Jesus and his disciples, the evangelist explores the glory of the relationship between the believer and the glorified Christ. 14:31, "Rise, let us be on our way," is one of the more obvious aporias noted above.

Monologue

Christ and the believer, 15:1–16:15. The evangelist now turns to the pattern of the Christian believer's life in the world. The believer abides in Jesus (15:1–11); he enters into a relationship of love with the fellow believer (15:12–17); and he separates himself from the world (15:18–27). In this last connection we are introduced to a particular Johannine conception, the *paraklētos,* the Paraclete (15:26: RSV, "Counselor"; NEB and NRSV, "Advocate"; TEV, "Helper"). In John's thinking it represents the thought that the risen Lord is spiritually present to the believer as that believer wrestles with the problems of Christian existence in the world.

Dialogue

Jesus and his disciples, 16:16–33. Turning now from monologue to dialogue, the evangelist explores the relationship of the risen Lord with those who believe in him. As is uniformly the case in these discourses, the Lord who speaks is the Jesus who died and rose again from the dead, who came from the Father and returned to him, and whose spiritual presence can now be known by the believer in the world.

Monologue

Christ's prayer for his church, 17:1–26. This is the evangelist's climactic statement of the significance of Jesus for the believer. It falls naturally into three parts. In part one (verses 1–5), the prayer is concerned with Jesus himself, with his death as his glorification, and with his power to give eternal life to those who believe in him. In part two (verses 6–19), the thought turns to the believer who is still in the world. Jesus is now glorified, but the believer still has to live out his life in the world and to represent Christ in the world. Finally, part three (verses 20–26) considers the corporate body of believers, the church, and the prayer is that the church may know the indwelling love of God as it fulfills its mission in the world of leading that world to belief in God.

The Passion Narrative, 18:1–20:31

The fourth major section of the Gospel of John is the passion narrative. John covers the same ground as do the synoptic gospels, and we have noted the parallels between John and Mark, and a few between John and Luke. However, the narrative in John has its own particular emphases. First, it has a distinctively apologetic tendency. The Jews are presented as the only villains of the plot, while Pilate is portrayed as sympathetic to Jesus, and interested in his welfare. Second, the Jesus of the Johannine passion narrative is not merely a victim, but a sovereign figure, a superhuman Being who could at will cause the whole process to cease.

The betrayal in the garden, 18:1–11 (compare Mark 14:32–48). John omits any reference to the prayer of Jesus, but then he has just completed the great prayer for the church.

Jesus before the high priest and Peter's denial, 18:12–27 (compare Mark 14:53–72). The narrative has the same structure as Mark, even to the extent of intercalating the trial scene into the account of the denial by Peter (see above). However, compared with the Markan narrative there are some new elements. There is the informal appearance before Annas (18:12–14), which has the effect of bringing Jesus before two high priests: "then the high priest questioned Jesus..." (verse 19) and "Annas then sent him bound to Caiaphas the high priest" (verse 24). The historical fact was that Annas was deposed from the high priesthood by the Romans in 15 C.E., but he remained enormously influential, and it may well have been that the Jews continued to grant him the courtesy of the title, if only as a protest against the Roman power to appoint and depose the chief representative of the Jewish people before God. In itself then, there is nothing intrinsically improbable about the Johannine narrative of the two hearings, and it may be that John here does have access to a tradition about the appearance of Jesus before Jewish authorities that is otherwise lost to us. At the same time, however, it is obvi-

ous from the comment in verse 14 that John's interest is in the symbolic significance of the high priest as the chief representative of the people before God.
With dramatic irony he puts on the lips of Caiaphas the key to understanding
the meaning of the death of Jesus. Another new element in the Johannine narrative is the appearance of "another disciple" who was known to the high priest
and who brings Peter into the courtyard (verses 15–16). He appears again in
20:2–10, where Mary Magdalene runs to Peter "and the other disciple" to tell
them that Jesus' body is not in the tomb. In that context the "other disciple" is
identified as "the one whom Jesus loved" (20:2), and this brings us to other references to the Beloved Disciple, of which there are five in the gospel. In 13:23–26
the disciple whom Jesus loved is intimately close to Jesus at the Last Supper. In
19:25–27 Jesus from the Cross commits his mother to the care of Beloved Disciple. In 21:7 "that disciple whom Jesus loved" recognizes the resurrected Jesus, and
in 21:20–23 there is a dialogue between the risen Jesus and Peter about "the disciple whom Jesus loved, who had reclined next to Jesus at the supper." Finally,
in 21:24 this disciple is identified as the ultimate source for the tradition in the
Gospel of John: "This is the disciple who is testifying to these things, and who
has written them, and we know that his testimony is true." We have indicated
several views on the fascinating problem of his identity and importance for the
Johannine community above.

Jesus before Pilate, 18:28–19:16 (compare Mark 15:1–15). This narrative is particularly interesting for its presentation of Pilate as a sympathetic figure earnestly
interested in Jesus' welfare and of "the Jews" as the real villains of the plot. One
gets a very strong impression that the author is himself a Jew reacting bitterly to
the treatment of Jesus by his own people. The bitter note of rejection in John
19:15 is an echo of that in Matthew's gospel (Matt 27:25). There is no evidence
that John knows the Gospel of Matthew; it is rather the case that both John and
Matthew are reacting equally strongly to a situation in which they feel themselves,
as Jews, personally involved.

The crucifixion, 19:17–37 (compare Mark 15:22–41 and Luke 23:33–49). This
narrative is close to Mark's with the exception of the mention of "the disciple
whom he loved," who is entrusted with his mother, and the reference to the giving up of the spirit (verse 30), which is reminiscent of Luke 23:46.

The burial, 19:38–42 (compare Mark 15:42–47). All the gospels stress the role of
Joseph of Arimathea in the burial of Jesus (Mark 15:43; Matt 27:57; Luke 23:50),
but John is alone in introducing the figure of Nicodemus, whom he identifies as
the one who had come to Jesus by night (verse 39; compare 3:1–15; 7:50–52).

The discovery of the empty tomb, 20:1–10 (compare Mark 16:1–8). All the gospel
narratives diverge dramatically after the point at which Mark ends: the discovery
of the empty tomb and the astonishment of the women. In Matthew the women
run to tell the disciples and are met by the risen Jesus on the way (Matt 28:9–10);
then the risen Lord appears to the disciples in Galilee. In Luke the women tell of
their discovery of the empty tomb, but they are not believed until a series of resurrection appearances in and around Jerusalem convinces the disciples that "The
Lord has risen indeed" (Luke 24:34). In John's gospel Mary Magdalene tells Peter
and the "other disciple" of the empty tomb, and Jesus appears to her and to the
disciples both in Jerusalem (20:19–23, 26–29) and in Galilee (21:1–14).

The appearance to Mary Magdalene, 20:11–18. The Gospel of John puts a major emphasis on the spiritual presence of Jesus with the believer. Both in 6:62–63 and 16:7 the evangelist emphasizes the eventual return of Jesus to the heavenly realm from which he came and the consequent possibility of his spiritual presence with the believer. Now he returns to this note in the story of the appearance to Mary Magdalene as Jesus tells her that he is about to ascend to the Father. That will make possible his spiritual presence with the believer and the promise of that presence is the point of the next story.

The appearance to the disciples as a group, 20:19–23. The evangelist now dramatizes the possibility of the spiritual presence of Christ with the believer through this story of the risen Lord appearing to his disciples and breathing on them. Both in Hebrew and Greek the word for "spirit" is the same as the word for "breath."

The appearance to Thomas, 20:24–29. In this story the evangelist brings his gospel to a climax by dramatizing doubt so as to highlight the possibility of belief. By means of the story of Thomas' coming to faith the evangelist presents a paradigm of the possibility for everyone everywhere to reach the point of saying to the risen Jesus, "My Lord and my God" (20:28).

The purpose of the gospel, 20:30–31. The evangelist climaxes his work with a statement of its purpose: to bring the reader to belief in Jesus and to the life that belief makes possible.

Epilogue: The Appearance in Galilee, 21:1–23

Surely the evangelist intended his gospel to end at 20:31, and chapter 21 has been added as an epilogue by another writer. The language is not quite that of the evangelist; yet the epilogue certainly echocs his concerns. It emphasizes the role of Peter, it uses the imagery of shepherd and sheep, and it features the Beloved Disciple. In many respects it is like the prologue to the gospel (1:1–18), which also shares the concerns of the gospel and yet at the same time differs in language from the text of the gospel itself. R. E. Brown makes the interesting suggestion that both the prologue and the epilogue may have been added to the main text of the gospel by the same redactor.

The major purpose of the epilogue seems to be ecclesiastical. The author of this chapter is concerned with the continuing life and work of the church and appears to feel that from this viewpoint something needs to be added to the gospel narrative. In particular, four matters concern him. He knows a tradition of a resurrection appearance to the disciples in Galilee as they were fishing, and he preserves it as a supplement to the accounts of the appearances in Jerusalem (verses 1–8). Second, he is concerned with the Christian sacred meal, the Eucharist, and he presents an account of a meal between the risen Lord and his disciples (verses 9–14), which is evocative of the Eucharist (Jesus takes the bread and gives it to the disciples in a solemn manner, verse 13). The Eucharist celebrated in the church is interpreted as a solemn meal between the risen Lord and those who believe in him. Third, there is the restoration of Peter after his denial of Jesus (verse 15–19). The Gospel of Mark already hinted at the restoration of Peter and of a resurrection appearance to him: "But go, tell his disciples and Peter that he is going ahead of you to Galilee; there you will see him . . . ."

(Mark 16:7). The epilogue to the Gospel of John develops this theme further. Finally, the author of the epilogue identifies the "disciple whom Jesus loved" as the ultimate "author" of the gospel. We cannot be certain whether this disciple is a historical or an ideal figure.

THE FIRST LETTER OF JOHN

Much of what we wish to say about 1 John has already been said at various places in this chapter and now only needs to be brought together. While there are many similarities, for example, its spiral structure and its dualism, it is probably not from the same author as the main text of the gospel. We noted the poverty of the style of this letter compared to that of the gospel and the real differences in thought between them, for example, on eschatology and the sacraments. At the same time we have joined the majority of interpreters in holding that it was not impossible that the author of 1 John had redacted the main text of the gospel, especially in the case of chapter 21.

A few other points need to be noted. The author is not mentioned by name or title. The date of 1 John will not have been too many years after the gospel (about 100 C.E.?) the major reason being that the attention has shifted from external opponents ("the world"; "the Jews") to false teachers within the community. What do they teach? In a word, a Christology that denied that Jesus is the Christ, the Son of God (2:22–23), and especially that he came "in the flesh" (4:2–3). How might this false teaching have arisen?

The Christology of the Johannine writings stresses Jesus as the Son of God who came into the world to empower and glorify those who accept him. Nevertheless, the gospel and letters of John show a strong dualism, a strong sense of the contrast between above and below, light and dark, good and evil, the spirit and the flesh. Under these conditions it is natural that Christians particularly influenced by these writings and their authors should be susceptible to the view that the world and the flesh are essentially evil and that the heavenly redeemer can not truly have come in the flesh, but maintain his heavenly nature while only appearing to be in the flesh. This way of thinking is natural in the larger Hellenistic world, and when it is applied to Jesus it becomes the Christological heresy "docetism," that is, he only "seemed" to be human (Greek *dokeō:* "I seem"). It is especially characteristic of later Gnosticism. In any case, a schism over true and false Christology arises within the Johannine church. For the author of 1 John, the opponents' "docetic" Christology leads to disobeying the commandments, to hating one's brother, to lies and falsehood.

Formally, 1 John is not so much a letter as it is a theological treatise or sermon. It is written with obvious love and concern for the spiritual welfare of its recipients. Indeed, some have supposed that there is also a source behind 1 John, and have tried to reconstruct it. For our purpose, it will suffice to note that whereas the gospel is more akin to proclamation, 1 John exhibits a balance of proclamation and parenesis. It may be outlined as follows:

1:1–4 PROCLAMATION.
The eternal life has been made manifest through the Son.

1:5–2:17 PARENESIS.

Right behavior is walking according to the light and keeping the commandments. It depends on true knowledge of God and renunciation of the world.

2:18–27 PROCLAMATION.

True knowledge of God depends on recognizing that Jesus is the true and only Son of God. He rewards with eternal life those who abide in him now. The dissidents are those who deny Jesus in the flesh; they are deceivers (2:26).

2:28–3:24 PARENESIS.

Those who abide in him now and exhibit the love of one another that naturally flows from that relationship avoid sin and have no need to fear his parousia.

4:1–6 PROCLAMATION.

Jesus Christ actually came in the flesh as the Son of God; those who do not believe this belong to the world or to the spirit of the Antichrist.

4:7–5:5 PARENESIS.

To abide in God is to be "of God," and to be "of God" is to exhibit love in the world. "We love because he first loved us" (4:19).

5:6–12 PROCLAMATION.

Jesus Christ is the Son of God, and acceptance of him is the means to eternal life.

THE SECOND AND THIRD LETTERS OF JOHN

2 and 3 John are true letters written by a member of the Johannine school who calls himself the "presbyter" or "elder." This word came to designate an official in the church, for example, 1 Timothy 5:17 "Let the elders who rule well..." and probably the author is simply referring to himself by the title of his office in the church.

One interesting question is the kind of authority the author exercises over the churches to which he writes. It seems to have been moral or even spiritual rather than formal (compare 3 John 9–12). This fact, together with the very nature of the gospel and letters of John themselves, indicates that the writer's authority stems primarily from his function as a preacher prominent in the conduct of Christian worship. It is perhaps not too much to say that in the second and third letters of John we have a much-loved leader of Christian worship and celebrator of the Eucharist attempting to extend his influence into matters of doctrine and polity.

The second letter of John is notable for its reference to churches as "the elect lady" and the "elect sister" and to the members of the churches as "her children" (2 John 1, 13). This indicates that the Christian church is now a definite and separate entity in the Hellenistic world and that individual churches are coming to be recognized as integral units in that entity. We are now in the middle period of New Testament Christianity. The second letter of John continues the theme of loving one another and the argument against docetism (2 John 7–11).

The third letter of John is a letter from the presbyter to a certain Gaius commending him for his earlier hospitality, recommending that he receive Demetrius (who possibly brought the letter) in hospitality, implying that a certain Diotrephes has refused such hospitality for the presbyter's emissaries. Apparently Diotrephes has seen the presbyter as a threat to his local authority. For his part, the presbyter attempts to exert his moral or spiritual authority (3 John 13; compare 2 John 12). For the rest, the letter testifies that the Christian Churches are recognizing that they are separate entities in the world and, as such, have a definite responsibility for Christians who come to them from another place (3 John 5–8). This hospitality to other Christians was to become an important sociological factor in the development of the church.

FURTHER READING

In this chapter we are particularly indebted to Dodd's *Interpretation of the Fourth Gospel*, to Martyn's *History and Theology in the Fourth Gospel* and *The Gospel of John in Christian History*, to W. Meeks' "The Man from Heaven in Johannine Sectarianism," *Journal of Biblical Literature* 91 (1972), pp. 44–72, and to the studies of Barrett, Brown, Culpepper, Fortna, Kysar, Neyrey, Smith, and Rendsberger, and to the commentaries of Bultmann and Brown.

Important Theories, Sketches, and Recent Bibliography

D. A. Carson, "Recent Literature on the Fourth Gospel," *Themelios* 9 (1983), pp. 8–18.

R. Kysar, "The Fourth Gospel in Recent Research," *Aufstieg und Niedergang der römischen Welt* II.25.3 (1985), pp. 2389–2480.

——, "The Gospel of John in Current Research," *Religious Studies Review* 9/4 (1983), pp. 314–323.

S. S. Smalley, "Keeping Up with Recent Studies. XII. St John's Gospel," *Expository Times* 97 (1985–1986), pp. 102–108.

G. Van Belle. *Johannine Bibliography 1966–1985. A Cumulative and Classified Bibliography of Books and Periodical Literature on the Fourth Gospel.*

One-Volume Commentaries and Dictionary Articles

ABD: "Beloved Disciple" (B. Byrne); "Cana of Galilee" (J. F. Strange); "Footwashing" (H. Weiss); "John (Disciple)" (R. F. Collins); "John the Baptist" (P. W. Hollenbach); "John, Epistles of" (R. Kysar); "John, Gospel of" (R. Kysar); "Lamb" (J. R. Mills); "Lazarus" (R. F. Hock); "Logos" (T. H. Tobin); "Thomas" (R. F. Collins).

IDB: "John, Gospel of" (J. N. Sanders); "John, Letters of" (C. B. Caird); "John the Apostle" (F. V. Filson).

IDB Suppl.: "John, Gospel of" (D. M. Smith); "John, Letters of" (D. M. Smith).

NJBC: "The Gospel According to John" (P. Perkins); "The Johannine Epistles" (P. Perkins)

Historically Influential Studies

R. Brown, *The Gospel According to John.* 2 vols. (The Anchor Bible Commentary).

R. Bultmann, *The Gospel of John.* (Commentary).

A. Culpepper, *The Anatomy of the Fourth Gospel.*

C. H. Dodd, *Historical Tradition in the Fourth Gospel.*

R. Fortna, *The Gospel of Signs: A Reconstruction of the Narrative Source Underlying the Fourth Gospel.*

J. L. Martyn, *History and Theology in the Fourth Gospel.*

W. Meeks, "The Man from Heaven in Johannine Sectarianism," *Journal of Biblical Literature* 91 (1972), pp. 44–72.

Collected Essays:

J. Ashton, ed., *The Interpretation of John.*

C. K. Barrett, *Essays on John.*

D. M. Smith, *Johannine Christianity.*

Among the many articles on John and its context (apart from research reports and collected essays above), we may note:

S. Katz, "Issues in the Separation of Judaism and Christianity after 70 C.E.: A Reconsideration," *Journal of Biblical Literature* 103/1 (1984), pp. 43–76.

R. Kimelman, *"Birkat Ha-Minîm* ["Prayer Against the Heretics"] and the Lack of Evidence for an Anti-Christian Jewish Prayer in Late Antiquity," pp. 226–244, 391–403 in E. P. Sanders, ed., *Jewish and Christian Self-Definition, Vol. 2: Aspects of Judaism in the Greco-Roman Period.*

G. MacRae, "The Fourth Gospel and *Religionsgeschichte* ["History of Religions"]," *Catholic Biblical Quarterly* 32 (1970), pp. 13–24.

A. J. Malherbe, "Hospitality and Inhospitality in the Church," pp. 92–112 in Malherbe, *Social Aspects of Early Christianity,* 2d ed.

B. J. Malina, "The Received View and What It Cannot Do: III John and Hospitality," pp. 171–189 in John H. Elliott, ed., *Social Scientific Criticism of the New Testament and Its Social World.*

S. M. Schneiders, "Women in the Fourth Gospel and the Role of Women in the Contemporary Church, " *Biblical Theology Bulletin* 12 (1982), pp. 35–44.

D. M. Smith, "Judaism and the Gospel of John (plus 'Discussion')," pp. 76–99 in J. H. Charlesworth, *Jews and Christians.*

C. Talbert, "The Myth of a Descending-Ascending Redeemer in Mediterranean Antiquity," *New Testament Studies* 22 (1975/76), pp. 418–40.

Commentaries Apart from Brown and Bultmann:

C. K. Barrett, *The Gospel According to St. John.*
————, *The Johannine Epistles.* (Hermeneia).
R. E. Brown, *The Epistles of John.* (Anchor Bible 30).
F.F. Bruce, *The Epistles of John.*
R. T. Fortna, *The Fourth Gospel and Its Predecessor.*
E. Haenchen, *A Commentary on the Gospel of John 1–6.* Trans. R. W. Funk (Hermeneia Series).
E. Haenchen, *A Commentary on the Gospel of John 7–21.* Trans R. W. Funk (Hermeneia Series).
E. Hoskyns and N. Davey, *The Fourth Gospel.*
J. L. Houlden, *The Johannine Epistles.*
R. Kysar, *I, II, III John.* (Augsburg Commentary on the New Testament).
J. Lieu, *The Second and Third Epistles of John: History and Background.*
R. H. Lightfoot, *St. John's Gospel.*
R. Schnackenburg, *The Gospel According to St. John.* 2 vols.

Introductory Studies:

D. Harrington, *John's Thought and Theology. An Introduction.*
R. Kysar, *John the Maverick Gospel.*
G. MacRae, *Faith in the Word: The Fourth Gospel.*
J. Painter, *John: Witness and Theologian.*
P. Perkins, *The Gospel According to St. John.* (Commentary).
D. M. Smith, *John.* 2nd ed. (Proclamation Commentaries).

Background of John:

C. K. Barrett, *The Gospel of John and Judaism.*
J. H. Charlesworth, ed., *John and Qumran.*

Literary:

A. Culpepper, *The Anatomy of the Fourth Gospel.*
P. Duke, *Irony in the Fourth Gospel.*
R. Kysar, *John's Story of Jesus.*

G. O'Day, *Revelation in the Fourth Gospel.*

Social Historical and Sociological:

R. Brown, *The Community of the Beloved Disciple.*

O. Cullmann, *The Johannine Circle.*

R. A. Culpepper, *The Johannine School.*

W. Meeks, "The Man from Heaven in Johannine Sectarianism," *Journal of Biblical Literature* 91 (1972), pp. 44–72.

J. H. Neyrey, *An Ideology of Revolt.*

G. C. Nicholson, *Death as Departure: The Johannine Descent-Ascent Schema.*

D. Rendsberger, *Johannine Faith and Liberating Community.*

F. Segovia, *Love Relationship in the Johannine Tradition: Agapē/Agapan in I John and the Fourth Gospel.*

R. A. Whitacre, *Johannine Polemic: The Role of Tradition and Theology.*

D. Bruce Wohl, *Johannine Christianity in Conflict: Authority, Rank, and Succession in the First Farewell Discourse.*

Other:

P. Borgen, *Bread from Heaven.*

E. Käsemann, *The Testament of Jesus.*

B. Lindars, *Behind the Fourth Gospel.*

F. Manns, *John and Jamnia: How the Break Occurred Between Jews and Christians c. 80–100 A.D.*

J. L. Martyn, *The Gospel of John in Christian History.*

W. Meeks, *The Prophet-King.*

E. Pagels, *The Johannine Gospel in Gnostic Exegesis.*

D. M. Smith, *The Composition and Order of the Fourth Gospel.*

U. C. von Wahlde, *The Johannine Commandments. I John and the Struggle for the Johannine Tradition.*

G. A. Yee, *Jewish Feasts and the Gospel of John.*

This manuscript portrays Jesus as the lamb standing on Mt. Zion, surrounded by the 144,000 redeemed (holding lutes). See Revelation 14:1–5; 7:1–8.

CHAPTER 13

REVELATION

The book of Revelation, the only full-blown apocalypse in the New Testament, has received a great variety of interpretation down through the ages. Christians who have been relatively well integrated into the larger society have usually found its otherworldly Messiah and array of beasts, numbers, colors, and the like difficult to understand, even disturbing. In contrast, marginal and persecuted Christians have often identified with its message about salvation and encouragement for martyrs. Fundamentalist Christians have seen in it prophecies of modern events. Political and religious revolutionaries have drawn on its political, anti-establishment rhetoric. Literary figures and artists have found in its bizarre images a source of great inspiration. Some students during the turbulent 1960s have wondered whether its author came from some ancient drug culture. Other students have found its symbolism fascinating to probe. There are also a variety of scholarly interpretations, but it would be generally agreed that historical and literary approaches provide the best avenues to its interpretation.

Revelation is in two respects quite different from the apocalyptic texts of ancient Judaism: It is not pseudonymous, and it takes the overall form of an open letter to seven churches in Asia Minor. So striking are these unusual characteristics that one might even ask whether the book that gives its name to the type of literature known as an apocalypse (Greek *apocalypsis* = "revelation") is really an apocalypse! On the other hand, it can scarcely be doubted that the book of Revelation is full of apocalyptic eschatology and illustrates an apocalyptic movement that experiences a threat of persecution, whether real or imagined. If this book comes from the middle period of Christianity, as we shall suggest, it represents a new outbreak of apocalyptic fervor in a period when most Christians were beginning to come to terms with the world. As such, it is an outstanding example of the complex interaction of history, myth, proclamation, and parenesis.

CHURCH TRADITION ABOUT REVELATION

An early tradition about Revelation comes from a Church Father named Justin Martyr, about 155 C.E.

> And further, there was a certain man, even with us, whose name was *John, one of the Apostles of Christ,* who prophesied in a revelation which came to him that those who believed in our Christ will spend a thousand years in Jerusalem, and after that, the general and, in short, the eternal resurrection and judgment of all will come to pass at one and the same time.
>
> (Justin Martyr, *Dialogue with Trypho* 81.4)

The references to the thousand-year reign of Christ (the millennium) and the final resurrection and judgment are clearly from the book of Revelation (Rev 20), and the author is clearly identified as "John, one of the apostles of Christ," in other words, John son of Zebedee. About 185 C.E., Irenaeus claims that the son of Zebedee wrote both the gospel and Revelation (*Against Heresies* 3.1.1–3; 4.20.11), though we have seen that his information about John is very suspect (see Chapter Twelve). The traditional view that John son of Zebedee wrote the Apocalypse is also implied by its inclusion in the list of the Muratorian Fragment at Rome (about 200 C.E.) and the writings of Hippolytus of Rome (170–236 C.E.) and Tertullian in North Africa (155–220 C.E.).

In addition to the remark above, Irenaeus also claimed that John's revelation was "seen" at the end of Domitian's reign (81–96 C.E.; compare *Against Heresies* 5.30.3), having already claimed that he lived into the time of Trajan and died in Ephesus (*Against Heresies* 2.22.5). Most ancient Christian writers in the West followed this view. Thus, in the western churches, despite the objections of the Alogoi in Asia Minor and Gaius at Rome, John the son of Zebedee was gradually considered to have been the author of the Apocalypse, and to have written it in the latter part of Domitian's reign on the island of Patmos (see below). The fully developed tradition was stated by Jerome in the late fourth century:

> Therefore, in the fourteenth year [of his reign], when Domitian began the second persecution after Nero, when he [John] had been banished to the island of Patmos, he wrote the Apocalypse, which Justin Martyr and Irenaeus interpret[ed]. But when Domitian had been killed and his decree rescinded by the Senate because of excessive cruelty, he returned to Ephesus under Nerva [96–98 C.E.] and, continuing there even until [the time of] the Emperor Trajan [98–117 C.E.], he established and directed all the churches of Asia, and, weakened with age he died in the sixty-eighth [year] after the passion of the Lord. He was buried near the same city.
>
> (Jerome *Illustrious* Men 9)

In the East, Revelation was accepted into the canon by the Alexandrian scholar Clement (about 150–215 C.E.) and his successor Origen (185–253 C.E.). Origen, who was widely traveled, put it in his list of generally "uncontested" books; he himself accepted it as written by John, son of Zebedee. However, about 250 C.E. another scholar from the same school, Dionysius of Alexandria, analyzed the vocabulary and style of Revelation and concluded that it could not have been written by the author of the Gospel and 1 John (compare Eusebius, *Ecclesiastical History* 7.24–25). Thereafter, others in the East, including a number of prominent bishops, doubted the Johannine authorship of Revelation and excluded it. Though Athanasius' *Festal Letter* of 367 C.E. included it, doubts persisted in the East. Indeed, some Syriac churches did not include it until the sixth century and other Syriac churches have never accepted it. Though the Greek Orthodox churches of the East followed the trend in the West, they have generally ignored it.

GENERAL HISTORICAL CRITICISM OF REVELATION: AUTHOR, DATE, PLACE

Information about John, son of Zebedee, was presented in Chapter Twelve, and we shall not repeat it here. Rather, we shall look more closely at external and internal evidence with respect to Revelation.

You will recall from previous discussions of Jewish and Christian apocalyptic that apocalypses were usually pseudonymous. Apocalypticists normally wrote in the name of some famous person from the past—Abraham, Enoch, Daniel, Ezra —and a number of apocalypses attempted to show how the ancient worthy prophesied historical events down to and including the present and near future of the apocalypticist. All of this was to demonstrate that the external course of history is determined by God and that the ancient prophets were correct in their predictions about the rapidly approaching End in the seer's own day. In contrast, the author of Revelation does not claim to be some ancient worthy writing in the distant past, nor does he claim to have prophesied the events that are now occurring. Rather, he explicitly identifies himself as John (Rev 1:1, 4, 9; 22:8) and he claims to be a contemporary of the events about which he writes. For Revelation, authority does not come from a famous ancestor who is believed to have accurately predicted the present, but from Jesus Christ, whose martyrdom inaugurated the last days and provided the basis for understanding potential martyrdom in the present.

We pointed out in Chapters Four and Five that a distinguishing feature of earliest Christianity was the consciousness that prophecy had returned. John's work is dominated by apocalyptic thought; yet, he himself implies that he is a prophet: By writing that he was exiled "because of the word of God and the testimony of Jesus" (Rev 1:9) which is "the spirit of prophecy" (19:10); by stating that he was told to prophesy after eating what is certainly a prophetic scroll (Rev 10:11; compare Ezek 1–3; *Shepherd of Hermas* 1:3–4, here a heavenly book of prophecy); and by describing his work as "the words of prophecy" (Rev 1:3; 22:7, 10, 18; compare 22:19). His work also contains many traditional prophetic forms and acts, though they are often colored by apocalyptic judgment pronouncements (Rev 2–3); symbolic actions like eating the scroll (Rev 10:8–11); seven blessings (Rev 1:1; 14:3; 16:15; 19:9; 20:6; 22:7–14); words and promises of God (Rev 1:8; 16:5; 21:5–8); interpretations of visions by intermediaries or the prophet himself (Rev 1:20; 7:13–17; 13:18; 14:4–5; 17:7–18; 19:8b); and many others. He describes the ecstatic vision that qualifies him: "I was in the Spirit on the Lord's day..." (1:10). The vision itself is an interesting example of the kind of experience that classical

Hebrew prophets claimed as validating their message (for example Isa 6). We may think of John, then, as an apocalyptic prophet.

Was this apocalyptic prophet John, the son of Zebedee? The author of Revelation never identifies himself as such. Nor does he refer to himself as a disciple or an apostle. After Dionysius, ancient scholars of the East who had come to accept the son of Zebedee as the author of the gospel and letters did not think that he also wrote the Apocalypse. Modern scholars note that while the Gospel of John is the least apocalyptic of the gospels, Revelation is the most apocalyptic writing in the New Testament. It has some Johannine words, but they are not used in Johannine ways. It also has different words for the same thing. When all of the differences in vocabulary and style between Revelation and the other Johannine literature are put into this mix, modern scholars agree with Dionysius and those who followed him that the Johannine gospel and letters were not produced by the same person or persons who produced the Apocalypse. At best, he might have been an apocalypticist within the Johannine School, but even that solution does not seem very likely.

If the author or authors of Revelation and the author of the Johannine gospel and letters were not the same person, it is in theory still possible that John the son of Zebedee wrote Revelation because, in the modern view, John did not write the gospel and letters. However, this position also has difficulties. Some critics think that the Apocalypse was not an immediate transcription of visions just experienced, but falls within a *literary* apocalyptic tradition that builds on other apocalypses and uses oral and written sources. This does not necessarily deny the existence of a seer's recent vision in the process; it does, however, suggest that its composition was complex, not the sort of thing one would expect from a Galilean fisherman.

The **date** of Revelation, which is related to authorship, is a difficult problem. The earliest possible date was probably sometime after 70 C.E. While it is true that Revelation 11:1–13 implies that the Jerusalem Temple, destroyed in 70, is still standing, most scholars think that this passage contains pre-70 traditions that have not been updated; in other words, the passage does not represent the time of composition. More important, Revelation refers to Rome symbolically as "Babylon" (Rev 14:8; 16:19; 17:5; 18:2, 10, 21). You will recall from Jewish history that both Babylon and Rome destroyed Jerusalem and the Temple, the former in 587 B.C.E., the latter in 70 C.E. The connection between these two destructions was commonly made in Jewish apocalyptic texts of the post-70 period (IV Ezra; *Apoc Bar; Sib Or* 5), that is, Babylon symbolizes Rome. Thus, a date sometime after the second destruction in 70 C.E. is very likely.

The latest possible date is still more problematic. Irenaeus claimed that John "saw" his visions near the end of the reign of Domitian, who was assassinated in 96 C.E. Though this might imply that they were *written* later, it is not so stated. Irenaeus' dating raises a number of issues, most important of which is the question of the so-called Domitian "persecution."

Even the casual reader of Revelation cannot doubt that John of Patmos believes that the Christians face an imminent and terrible crisis. He speaks of a past persecution of Christians and he expects a persecution of Christians in western Asia Minor. The following are some of the key persecution passages in Revelation:

1:9   "I John, your brother, who share with you in Jesus *the persecution and the kingdom and the patient endurance,* was on the island called Patmos because of the word of God and the testimony of Jesus."

2:10   Jesus speaks through John to the city of Smyrna: "Do not fear what you are *about to suffer.* Beware, the devil is *about to throw some of you into prison,* so that you may be tested, and for ten days you will have *affliction.* Be faithful unto *death,* and I will give you the crown of life."

2:13   Jesus speaks through John to the city of Pergamum: "...you did not deny your faith in me even in the days of *Antipas my witness (= martyr),* my faithful one, *who was killed among you, where Satan lives.*"

3:10   Jesus speaks through John to the city of Philadelphia: "Because you have kept my word of patient endurance, I will keep you from the *hour of trial which is coming* on the whole world, to test the inhabitants of the earth."

6:9–11 "When he opened the fifth seal, I saw under the altar the souls of *those who had been slaughtered* for the word of God and for the testimony they had given; 10) they cried out with a loud voice, 'Sovereign Lord, holy and true, how long will it be before you *judge and avenge our blood* on the inhabitants of the earth?' 11) They were each given a white robe and told to rest a little longer, until the number would be complete both of their fellow servants and their brothers and sisters, *who were soon to be killed as they themselves had been.*"

16:6a "*For they shed the blood of saints and prophets...*"

17:6a "And I saw the woman was drunk with the *blood of the saints* and the *blood of the witnesses* to Jesus."

18:24 "And in you was found the *blood of prophets and of saints,* and of *all who have been slaughtered on earth.*"

What kind of persecution of Christians is envisaged here? Various passages in the New Testament point to both Jewish and Gentile mistreatment of Christians. Jewish communities tended to be tightly knit, with a certain authority over their own members. Paul says that "five times I have received from the Jews the forty lashes minus one" (2 Cor 11:24), which was a Jewish punishment, just as "three times I was beaten with rods" (2 Cor 11:25) was a Roman one. Similarly, Mark 13:9 anticipates Christians being "beaten in synagogues" and standing "before governors and kings because of me"; these, again, refer respectively to Jewish and to Roman persecution of Christians. We have also noted general oppression of Christians in Hebrews. All of these references leave the impression that maltreatment of Christians was sporadic and spontaneous.

References in Revelation, however, suggest fears of a Roman persecution of major proportions. By way of background, the Roman government was generally tolerant of local religions but at the same time eager to guarantee overall loyalty to the empire. A polytheistic society presented no real problems; local inhabitants were asked to acknowledge formally the gods of Rome and sacrifice to the Roman emperor, and having done so, they were free to continue their local religious beliefs and practices, if they chose. The Jews, however, were monotheists and could not acknowledge the gods of Rome. Yet, their special position was recognized by the Romans. Their religious scruples were duly noted by the Roman authorities and they were freed from the requirement. They had to pay their taxes, of course, and after 70 C.E., the traditional Temple tax was required to be paid to the temple of Jupiter Capitolinus in Rome as part of their punishment (the *fiscus iudaicus;* Josephus, *Jewish Wars* 7.6.6 para. 218; Suetonius, *The Twelve Caesars,* "Domitian," 12). As Christians became increasingly separate from Jews, and were therefore in the position of having to refuse to acknowledge the gods of Rome while lacking the protection of a recognized legal religion, they were liable to harassment at any time. A local Roman official could demand that they acknowledge the gods of Rome; they would have to either recant or refuse; if they refused, they would then be liable to banishment, torture, or even execution. This everpresent possibility hung over the early Christian churches wherever they severed their ties with Judaism.

Another related element that might have led to the persecution of Christians was the widespread tendency for the Roman emperor to be worshiped as a god (compare Chapter Three). This emperor cult took its inspiration from the East, where pharaohs and kings could be considered gods or sons of gods. During and after the conquests of Alexander, it spread to the West, where it was fostered, partly for political utility; but in some provincial settings, for example, Asia Minor, it was often taken quite seriously. Moreover, by Roman times, and despite resistance from the Roman Senate, a few Roman emperors demanded that they be worshipped as gods, though other emperors deplored the practice. Similarly, some local Roman authorities pressed for it but others did not. Again, the Jews were in a privileged position that most Christians increasingly could not share.

The first known persecution of Christians by Romans mentioned in Roman sources took place at Rome under the emperor Nero (54–68 C.E.). In listing Nero's many vile, scandalous, and depraved deeds, the ancient Roman historian Suetonius remarks, "Punishments were also inflicted on the Christians, a sect professing a new and mischievous religious belief…" (Suetonius *The Twelve Caesars,* "Nero" 16). The Roman historian, Tacitus, is more explicit. He tells about the terrible fire that destroyed a quarter of Rome in 64 C.E. and says that when the rumor persisted that Nero himself had ordered the fire started to make space for his building operations, he found a scapegoat among the Christians:

> But all human efforts, all the lavish gifts of the emperor, and the propitiations of the gods did not banish the sinister belief that the conflagration [fire] was the result of an order [by Nero]. Consequently, to get rid of the report, Nero fastened the guilt and inflicted the most exquisite tortures on a class hated for their abominations, called Christians by the populace…. Accordingly, an arrest was first made of all who pleaded guilty; then, upon their information, an immense multitude was convicted, not so much of the crime of firing the city, as of hatred against mankind. *Mockery of every sort was added to their deaths. Covered with the skins of beasts, they were torn by dogs and perished, or were nailed to crosses, or were doomed to the flames and burnt, to serve as a nightly illumination when daylight had expired.* Nero offered his gardens for the spectacle, and was exhibiting a

show in the circus, while he mingled with the people in the dress of a charioteer or stood aloft on a car. Hence, even for criminals who deserve extreme and exemplary punishment, there arose a feeling of compassion; for it was not, as it seemed, for the public good, but to glut one man's cruelty, that they were being destroyed.

(Tacitus, *Annals* 15.44)

According to Roman sources, the persecution at Rome in 64 C.E. was the first major persecution of Christians. We gain a very strong impression of the situation of some Christians in Asia Minor from the correspondence between Pliny, the governor of Bithynia in northern Asia Minor, and Trajan, the Roman emperor (98–117 C.E.). About 112 C.E. Pliny wrote to Trajan:

It is my rule, Sire, to refer to you in matters where I am uncertain. For who can better direct my hesitation or instruct my ignorance? I was never present at any trial of Christians; therefore I do not know what are the customary penalties or investigations, and what limits are observed. I have hesitated a great deal on the question whether there should be any distinction of ages; whether the weak should have the same treatment as the more robust; whether those who recant should be pardoned, or whether a man who has ever been a Christian should gain nothing by ceasing to be such; whether the name itself, even if innocent of crime, should be punished, or only the crimes attaching to that name.

Meanwhile, this is the course that I have adopted in the case of those brought before me as Christians. *I ask them if they are Christians. If they admit it I repeat the question a second and a third time, threatening capital punishment; if they persist I sentence them to death.* For I do not doubt that, whatever kind of crime it may be to which they have confessed, their pertinacity and inflexible obstinacy should certainly be punished. There were others who displayed a like madness and whom I reserved to be sent to Rome, since they were Roman citizens.

Thereupon the usual result followed, the very fact of my dealing with the question led to a wider spread of the charge, and a great variety of cases were brought before me. An anonymous pamphlet was issued, containing many names. *All who denied that they were or had been Christians I considered should be discharged, because they called upon the gods at my dictation and did reverence, with incense and wine, to your image which I had ordered to be brought forward for this purpose, together with the statues of the deities; and especially because they cursed Christ, a thing which, it is said, genuine Christians cannot be induced to do.* Others named by the informer first said that they were Christians and then denied it; declaring that they had been but were so no longer, some having recanted three years or more before and one or two as long ago as twenty years. They all worshiped your image and the statues of the gods and cursed Christ. But they declared that the sum of their guilt or error had amounted only to this, that on an appointed day they had been accustomed to meet before daybreak, and to recite a hymn antiphonally to Christ, as to a god, and to bind themselves by an oath not for the commission of any crime but to abstain from theft, robbery, adultery, and breach of faith, and not to deny a deposit when it was claimed. After the conclusion of this ceremony it was their custom to depart and meet again to take food; but it was ordinary and harmless food, and they had ceased this practice after my edict in which, in accordance with your orders, I had forbidden secret societies. I thought it the more necessary, therefore, to find out what truth there was in this by applying *torture to two maidservants, who were called deaconesses.* But I found nothing but a depraved and extravagant superstition, and I therefore postponed my examination and had recourse to you for consultation.

The matter seemed to me to justify my consulting you, especially on account of the number of those imperiled; for *many persons of all ages and classes and of both sexes are being put in peril by accusation,* and this will go on. The contagion of this superstition has spread not only in the cities, but in the villages and rural districts as well; yet it seems capable of being checked and set right. There is no shadow of doubt that the temples, which have been almost deserted, are beginning to be frequented once more, that the sacred rites which have been long neglected are being renewed, and that sacrificial victims are for sale everywhere, whereas, till recently a buyer was rarely to be found. From this it is easy to imagine what a host of men could be set right, were they given a chance of recantation.

Trajan responds:

You have taken the right line, my dear Pliny, in examining the cases of those denounced to you as Christians, for no hard and fast rule can be laid down, of universal application. They are not to be sought out; if they are informed against, and the charge is proved, they are to be punished, with this reservation, *that if anyone denies that he is a Christian, and actually proves it, that is by worshiping our gods,* he shall be pardoned as a result of his recantation, however suspect he may have been with respect to the past. Pamphlets published anonymously should carry no weight in any charge whatsoever. They constitute a very bad precedent, and are also out of keeping with this age.

(Bettenson, *Documents of the Christian Church,* p. 10)

The internal evidence of the book of Revelation suggests that its author believed that a persecution of Christians living in western Asia Minor was imminent, that the persecution would come from the Romans, and that it would be sparked by demand for emperor worship (13:4, 12–17; 16:2; 19:20), which Christians would have to refuse (14:9–12). Revelation 17:10 refers to a series of seven heads or kings, five of whom have fallen, *one "who is" (the sixth),* and a seventh who is to come. The sequence is usually thought to intimate a sequence of Roman emperors, with the writer implying that he lives during the reign of the sixth of these, the one "who is." Various attempts have been made to identify the sequence, and thus the sixth emperor, who would be reigning at the time of the composition of Revelation. If we begin with Julius Caesar, the sixth would be Nero. A few scholars have taken this option. In our discussion of symbolism below, we shall note that the number of the beast, 666, in Revelation 13:18 refers in Hebrew to the name Nero. New Testament Christians certainly lived with the memory of the sudden persecution of the Christians in Rome under the emperor Nero, at which time tradition has it that both Peter and Paul perished (for example, *1 Clement 5*). However, since this persecution was limited to Rome and the issue was not emperor worship, scholars generally agree that the number 666 refers not to Nero himself, but to a Nero *redivivus*, that is, a new Nero. This theory is based on the ancient belief that Nero would come back to life and invade the empire from the East, a theme also found in Revelation (compare Rev 13:3, 12, 14; 17:8, 11). Since Nero committed suicide in 68 C.E., we should look for a later emperor, which would also fit the post-70 date based on the Babylon/Rome correlation noted above.

If the six Roman emperors begin with Augustus and we omit the three short reigns from 68–70, the sixth would be Vespasian, the emperor from 70–79 C.E. However, Vespasian did not demand worship of himself as a god, and there is no knowledge of a persecution of Christians in Asia Minor during his reign. The conditions implied by the book as a whole simply do not fit.

A third suggestion would be that the first five emperors are those who were deified by the Roman Senate after their deaths (Julius Caesar, Augustus, Claudius, Vespasian, and Titus). The sixth, or one "who is," would be Domitian, who, however, did demand divine honors. An alternative possibility would be to start with the ruler who encouraged the emperor cult, Gaius Caligula (37–41 C.E.), in which case Domitian would again be the sixth. Was Domitian the Nero *redivivus?* Was Irenaeus correct in placing Revelation in the last years of Domitian's reign?

We have arrived at the crucial question: Did Domitian undertake a major persecution of Christians in Asia Minor as a matter of imperial policy, as Nero did at Rome in 64 C.E.? Christian tradition beginning with Melito, bishop of Sardis (one of the seven cities of Revelation), certainly held this view in the latter second century, and Eusebius mentions others who held it thereafter (Melito, *To Antoninus* in Eusebius *Ecclesiastical History* 4.26; compare 3.17–20, 39; 4.18; 5.8, 18; 6.25; 7.25). Jerome's statement quoted above under the traditional view is a good fourth-century summary of it. Furthermore, a number of second-century Roman writers were also very critical of Domitian's policies. The problem is that some modern historians of Rome think that the opinion about Domitian among Roman writers was biased and unfounded, that is, it represented post-Domitianic polemic by Senatorial forces opposed to him. For example, when Suetonius claimed among other things that Domitian demanded to be addressed as "our Lord and our God" (for example, Suetonius *The Twelve Caesars*, "Domitian," 13.1–2; compare Martial *Epigrams* 5.5,8; 7.2,5,34; 8.2,82; 9.28,66; 9.56,3), such words were used by persons who wished to flatter the emperor, not demands by the emperor himself. It is also well known that when the Christian Melito wrote his apology for Christianity to the Roman emperor Marcus Aurelius (*To Antonius*), he told the emperor what he wanted to hear, namely, that only those emperors whom the Romans also considered bad emperors had persecuted the Christians. The revisionist view of Domitian, when combined with the lack of hard evidence for imperial persecutions of Christians in this period and some positive evidence that Domitian was sensitive to the needs of provincials, leaves us historically with two options: either Revelation was written later, in the period of actual persecution represented by the Pliny and Trajan correspondence (about 112 C.E.), or the author of Revelation, perhaps concerned about local enthusiasm for the emperor cult in western Asia Minor, feared a persecution that was local or regional. The latter seems more probable. Pliny's letter to Trajan (quoted above) implies some previous persecution in Asia Minor—"I was never present at any trial of Christians; therefore I do not know what are the customary penalties or investigations, and what limits are observed"—and there are also a number of minor details in the work that can be interpreted to refer to the time of Domitian. For example, Revelation 6:6 possibly alludes to an edict by Domitian in 92 C.E.; both Domitian and Jesus are compared with the morning star (2:28); problems of poverty may have been intensified by a famine in Asia Minor in 93 C.E.; and tensions between Jews and Christians (2:9; 3:9) may have been intensified by the "Prayer Against the Heretics" about 80–90 C.E. (see Chapters Eleven and Twelve; compare Ignatius, *Philadelphians,* 8.2). Thus, while there is no absolute certainly, we prefer to stay with traditional viewpoint and continue to date the book of Revelation about 95–96 C.E. (see Yarbro Collins).

The **place** of composition would appear to be one of the lesser problems connected with Revelation. John states that his first vision took place on the island of Patmos (1:9), a small rocky island in the Aegean Sea about forty miles off the coast of Asia Minor, and thus not far from the seven churches to which he wrote in western Asia Minor (Rev 1–3). He states that he was "on the island called Patmos because of the word of God and the testimony of Jesus," suggesting that he might indeed have been exiled. In any case, the ancients drew that conclusion, and modern scholars call him simply John of Patmos, in part to distinguish him from the writers of the other Johannine literature (see map, p. 459).

SOCIAL-HISTORICAL CONTEXT OF REVELATION

Whether there was an actual "Domitian persecution" of Christians or not, it seems clear from our persecution passages above that John has been exiled (1:9), that he expects the persecution, imprisonment, and possible martyrdom of Christians at Smyrna (2:10), that Antipas has already been martyred at Pergamum, and that John is preoccupied with martyrdom in relation to the emperor cult that is known to have been thriving in the cities of western Asia Minor. In short, he perceives an impending political crisis in connection with the Gentiles in western Asia Minor.

Revelation also implies that there are conflicts with the Jews. The vision message to Smyrna refers to those who "say that they are Jews and are not, but are a synagogue of Satan. Do not fear what you are about to suffer..." and thereafter come statements about imprisonment and potential death (2:9–11). Similarly the vision message about Philadelphia refers to a "synagogue of Satan who say that they are Jews and are not, but are lying" (3:9). There are tensions between Jews and Christians who consider themselves the true Israel, and, as noted above, one may speculate whether this split was intensified by the "Prayer Against the Heretics" about 80–90 C.E. (see Chapters Ten, Eleven, and Twelve; compare Ignatius, *Philadelphians,* 8.2). Perhaps there was collaboration between Jews and Gentiles against the Christians.

Finally, non-Biblical sources indicate that there was sharp conflict between rich and poor in western Asia Minor. This conflict is also reflected in statements about wealth in Revelation. In the message to the church at Laodicea, the Laodiceans who say, "I am rich, I have prospered, and I need nothing" (3:17) are warned to repent. "Babylon," or Rome, is attacked for her lavish display of wealth and luxury, and her crass commercialism (17–18). Poverty is also related to famine and inflation (6:6).

Such political, social, and economic conflict led the Johannine author to advocate sectarian exclusivism and rejection of the ways of the world. His attack on the Nicolaitans (2:6, 15), Balaam (2:14), and Jezebel (2:20) is an attack on eating meat sacrificed to idols (2:14, 20) and the practice of fornication (2:14, 20–23), that is, acts often considered by Jews and Christians to be idolatrous Gentile practices to which lax Christians were accommodating themselves (compare 1 Cor 8, 10). Such marginality, sometimes accompanied by what moderns think to be bizarre behavior, is typical of groups that consider themselves to be oppressed. Such separatist movements with apocalyptic beliefs are often called by anthropologists "millenarian" movements, a term derived from the 1000-year reign of Christ and the martyrs in Revelation (Rev 20). We shall comment further on this phenomenon in our conclusion to this chapter.

LANGUAGE, STYLE, AND FORMAL FEATURES OF REVELATION

Revelation reads as if it is written by someone who is not a native speaker of Greek, that is, it has numerous grammatical errors that suggest its author spoke a Semitic language. It also contains a number of interesting literary features. There are not only apocalyptic and prophetic, but also liturgical, mythical, and parenetic materials and forms. There are antiphonal hymns (4:1–11; 5:9–12, etc.); the so-called *trishagion* ("Holy, Holy, Holy," 4:8c); doxologies (1:6; 4:9; 5:13b–14; 7:12); acclamations of worth (4:11; 5:9b–10, 12); a thanksgiving formula (11:17–18); the *amen* and *hallelujah* responses (22:20; 19:1); a woe oracle (12:12b); the lament or dirge (18:1–24); the curse (22:18–20); and others. The language of myth is also common. The world is viewed as heaven above, earth in the middle, and hell below, and great portents occur in the heavens and the stars. It is inhabited by angels and demons and by animals that speak and act. There are also a number of traditional myths such as the birth and attempted destruction of the divine child (12:1–6); the sacred marriage (19:6–10 Christ, the Lamb and his bride); the combat myth with the victory of the good angel (Michael) and his followers over the primeval dragon and his angels and the divine warrior (portrayed throughout Revelation as a martyred Lamb who overcomes and rules the universe from his glorious throne; compare especially 12; 19:11–22:9); and the divine city (21:9–22:5). Parenetic materials are found not only in the prophetic commands, but virtue and vice lists (for example, 9:20–21; 13:4–8; 14:4–5). All of this points to the use of oral traditions and written sources, but its continuity of language, style, and imagery also suggests a unified composition.

Symbolism

We have seen again and again that apocalyptic draws heavily on the symbolic language of earlier literature, especially prophetic books of the Old Testament, primarily Ezekiel, and apocalyptic literature, notably Daniel. This is part of its quest for an all-encompassing vision of reality. Several kinds of symbols in Revelation are worth mentioning. Sacred numbers such as four (various parts or divisions of the created order), seven (completeness, totality, fullness), and twelve (Israel) abound. The numbers four and twelve are illustrated by Revelation 7:1–8, where the seer has a vision of the four angels standing at the four corners of the earth holding back the four winds (which cause plagues, compare Dan 7:2–3). A fifth angel ascends from the rising of the sun with God's seal and orders the four others to hold back the four winds until the servants(–martyrs, compare 6:11) should be sealed as a form of supernatural protection (compare Isa 44:5; Ezek 9:1–8). The number of the sealed is 12,000 from each of the twelve tribes of Israel, or 144,000, which refers to the Christian martyrs from all nations (5:9; 7:9), presumably the true Israel. The number seven usually stands for perfection. There are seven stars (1:13), seven letters to seven churches (2–3), seven seals (6:1–1, 8:1), seven trumpets (8:7–9:21, 11:15–19), seven bowls of wrath (16:1–12, 17–21), and seven heads, which are seven kings (17:9–15). It is so significant (occurring fifty-four times) that we shall outline the book by groups of seven (see below).

A final example of numbers symbolism is the famous number of the beast who symbolizes the Roman empire and its imperial line, as well as the Antichrist. He forced all the people to place a number on their right hands or foreheads, a number standing for the emperor-beast's name (Rev 13:18). In most texts, the number is 666; in one fifth-century manuscript, the number is 616, which was also known by Irenaeus in the late second century. Who is the mysterious emperor-beast 666 (616)? Many theories have been suggested, but most agree that it symbolizes the name Nero. The letters of the Hebrew alphabet are also its numbers (for example, A = 1, B = 2, and so on) and "Neron Caesar" spelled in Hebrew as *N-RōN C-S-R* (Hebrew uses only consonants, some of which are occasionally used as vowels) adds up to 666, while Nero Caesar (without the final "n") spells 616.

N =	50		N =	50
R =	200		R =	200
ō =	6		ō =	6
N =	50			
C =	100		C =	100
S =	60		S =	60
R =	200		R =	200
	666			616

In many respects, the visions of Revelation are psychedelic. An excellent example is the "four horsemen of the Apocalypse" (later used to describe a famous Notre Dame backfield!), each of whom rides a horse of a different color (6:1–8). Thus, white = victory (not purity; contrast 19:8); red = violence and war; black = famine and suffering; and pale green = decomposition and death. As is typical in apocalyptic, white also symbolizes the brilliance of the divine glory (6:11; 7:9, 13–14; 22:14).

There are many animals and beasts in Revelation. The lamb and the lion represent the sacrificial martyrdom and royal kingship of Jesus respectively. Beasts are Satanic figures, for example, the Roman emperor 666. Horns represent power (6:6; 12:3), and wings mobility (4:8; 12:14).

The seven cities of the Roman Province of Asia mentioned in Revelation 2–3. To the church in each city, a certain John writing from the island of Patmos addressed a letter.

There are many other symbols, for example, a woman = a people or a city (12:1–6; 17); eyes = knowledge (for example, 1:14; 2:18); the sharp sword = judging and punishing word of God (for example, 1:16; 2:12, 16); crowns = rule and kingship (for example, 2:10; 3:11); and the sea = chaos and evil (13:1; 21:1).

The Son of Man symbolism from Daniel 7:13 also occurs in Revelation 1:7, 12–16, as it does in other New Testament apocalyptic writings. We have already noted that the Q community turned to Daniel 7:13, that prophets in that community produced Son of Man sayings to put on the lips of Jesus, and that the apocalyptic discourses also turned to that passage and its central symbol. When one gets to a certain level of experience or expectation, the normal structure of language is simply shattered, and what is experienced or expected can be described only in symbols, often in archetypal symbols that have deep roots in the human consciousness. So it is with the consciousness of evil, sin, and guilt and with the expectation of a cataclysmic, eschatological act whereby evil, sin, and guilt will be no more. The Jewish myth explains the existence of sin as the result of the rebellion of primordial man, Adam, and its natural consequence is the expectation that the act of another representative man would redeem that sin. When Paul says, "as one man's trespass led to condemnation for all, so one man's act of righteousness leads to justification and life for all" (Rom 5:18), he is reflecting the natural consequence of accepting the myth that sin resulted from the rebellious act of the primordial man, Adam. In the language of apocalyptic symbolism, the same natural consequence is the idea of the coming of a redeemer figure "like a son of man," a figure human yet more than human, and it is undoubtedly this fundamental propensity of the human mind to think in such terms that accounts for the prominence of Son of Man symbolism in early Christian apocalyptic.

STRUCTURE AND OUTLINE OF REVELATION

We have seen that Revelation contains a great deal of apocalyptic eschatology and can be seen as a representative of apocalyptic literature, to which it gives its name, "apocalypse," or "revelation." Yet, it is written by one who, in contrast to Jewish apocalyptic, does not assume the role of an ancient worthy in order to predict events moving toward their climatic end, but who identifies himself by name as John of Patmos, thinks of himself as a prophet, and as analysis shows, incorporates many prophetic forms. Furthermore, he is familiar with and uses liturgical materials and forms as well as mythical themes. There is also a whole set of compositional techniques in the work such as the distribution of symbols and images over the whole work, announcements that are developed later, cross references, contrasts, numerical structures, interludes of material, insertions (intercalations) and various combinations of these techniques. Finally, we have seen that he incorporates letters and that the structure of his writing as a whole takes the form of a letter.

Perhaps the most unusual aspect of the book of Revelation is its seven letters to the seven churches in Asia Minor: Ephesus, Smyrna, Pergamum, Thyatira, Sardis, Philadelphia, and Laodicea (Rev 2–3). This feature is unparalleled in apocalyptic writing and may be a result of the effect of Paul's letter writing on the early church. We may also note that the seven letters have a common pattern of five parts: address and command to write; a prophetic messenger introduced with the formula, "Then says...," (sometimes translated with "These are the words of..." [NRSV]); a section about the individual church that begins "I know..." containing praises and/or warnings, and concluding with an exhortation; a formula call to hear the message ("Let anyone who has an ear listen to what the Spirit is saying to the churches"); and a prophetic promise to the martyr as one "who overcomes" or "conquers."

The influence of the letter form is even greater than the letters to the seven churches, for the book of Revelation as a whole has the external form of a letter. It begins with an opening salutation (1:4–6) and closes with a benediction (22:21). The contrast in literary form between the direct address of the letters and the symbolic drama of the remainder of the book is startling, but no more so than the fact that an apocalyptic writer identifies himself as a prophet and calls his work a prophecy.

The fact that we have here the outward form of a letter (see Chapter Six) helps us to grasp the essential thrust of the work. It begins with a salutation in the Pauline style: "To him who loves us and freed us from our sins by his blood and made us a kingdom, priests to his God and Father, to him be glory and dominion forever and ever. Amen" (Rev 1:5b–6; compare Gal 1:3–5). But then it continues: "Look! He is coming with the clouds; every eye will see him, even those who pierced him; and on his account all the tribes of the earth will wail. So it is to be. Amen" (1:7). This is a classic statement of the early Christian hope for the return of Jesus as apocalyptic judge and redeemer. Similarly, the closing benediction, "The grace of the Lord Jesus be with all the saints. Amen" (22:21), is in the Pauline style, but it is preceded by a prayer for the coming of the Lord, "Come, Lord Jesus" (22:20). However, this is the early Palestinian Christian Eucharistic prayer *Maranatha,* which Paul himself used at the end of a letter: "*Our Lord, come!* The grace of the Lord Jesus be with you. My love be with all of you in Christ Jesus. Amen" (1 Cor 16:22–24). It is a reminder that for all its surface strangeness, the book of Revelation is not to be separated from the rest of the New Testament. The hope it represents is a fundamental feature of a major part of the New Testament.

The natural question that arises from these considerations is this: Can one really develop an exact analysis and a precise outline of a work as complex as this, a work that includes in its purpose the attempt to stun its readers by the power of its visions so that the readers lose their fear of the present and are caught up in the hope for the future it presents? It may be that a structural analysis is somewhat arbitrary and in a sense a denial of its very quality as literary text. Nonetheless, frequent attempts have been made, many of them revolving around the book's clear references to the symbolic number seven. A simplified outlined based on two cycles of visions with three series of seven in each cycle would look like this (compare Yarbro Collins 1984; 1990):

I. Prologue	1:1–8	
Preface		1:1–3
Letter framework		1:4–8
II. First Cycle of Visions	1:9–11:19	
Seven messages to seven churches		1:9–3:22
Seven seals		4:1–8:5
Seven trumpets		8:2–11:19
III. Second Cycle of Visions	12:1–22:5	
Seven unnumbered visions		12:1–15:4
Seven bowls		15:1–16:21
Babylonian appendix		17:1–19:10
Seven unnumbered visions		19:11–21:8
Jerusalem appendix		21:9–22:5
IV. Epilogue	22:6–21	
Sayings; letter authentication		22:6–20
Letter Benediction		22:21

EXEGETICAL SURVEY OF REVELATION

Prologue, 1:1–8

1:1–3 PREFACE: DESCRIPTIVE INTRODUCTION AND BEATITUDE.

Christ reveals God's word to his "servant" John through the mediation of an angel. The reader and hearers (probably in a house-church) are blessed (compare beatitudes also in 14:13; 16:15; 19:9; 20:6; 22:7, 14).

1:4–8 LETTER FRAMEWORK.

John greets the seven churches in western Asia Minor. The greeting, to a redeemed priesthood, is from God, the seven spirits, and the resurrected King of kings who is pictured in the imagery of the coming Son of Man (Dan 7:14; Zech 12:10). Verse six contains a doxology.

First Cycle of Visions, 1:9–11:19

1:9–3:22 SEVEN LETTERS TO SEVEN CHURCHES.

After an inaugural vision come the seven prophetic messages of Christ as seven letters to seven churches. They follow a common form pattern or the form noted above. Since the seven cities were on a major highway, perhaps Revelation was meant to be a circular document read in each city.

> **1:9–20 Inaugural vision.** John, "your brother," exiled on Patmos, shares the "persecution" and receives the prophetic spirit "on the Lord's day" (Sunday?). He is commanded to write on a scroll to the seven churches, symbolized by seven lampstands. He has a vision of the heavenly Son of Man (compare especially Dan 7:9–14). The seven stars, which are seven angels of the churches, may be multidimensional symbols, perhaps suggesting a constellation and universal rule, as they do in the Persian mystery religion Mithraism (see Chapter Three).

> **2:1–7 The message/letter to Ephesus.** Ephesus was the prosperous capital of the Roman province of Asia (compare Acts 2:9; 18, 19; 1 Cor 16:8; Eph; Chapter Eight). The famous temple of the goddess Artemis was there (Acts 19:23–40), and so was a temple to Domitian, suggesting a revival of the emperor cult. The Ephesians are praised for their works. They have tested and exposed wandering missionaries (compare Q; *Didachē* 11–13; 2 Cor 10–13; Chapter Five) and have endured suffering. They are blamed for allowing their love to grow cold. They must repent or lose their standing. On the Nicolaitans, see verses 14–15. Revelation 2:7 contains the first reference to the Christian who, like the martyr Christ, is "everyone who conquers" (2:7, 11, 26–28; 3:5, 12, 21; 5:5; 21:7; compare 1:7–8; 12:10–11; 12:10–11; 13:7; 15:2; 17:14).

> **2:8–11 The message/letter to Smyrna.** Smyrna was a beautiful commercial city about thirty miles north of Ephesus. It was also a center of the imperial cult. The church there suffers, apparently persecuted by the large Jewish community (2:9; compare 3:9), and is materially poor, though praised for being spiritually rich.

> **2:12–17 The message/letter to Pergamum.** Pergamum, forty–five miles north of Smyrna and ten miles from the Aegean coast, was a major Hellenistic and Roman granite citadel-hill city and the original capital of Asia. It remained politically influential and had a famous library. It was also known for its many religions. The "Satan's throne" (2:13) may refer to such religions, and especially to the emperor cult, since Pergamum had temples to both Rome and Augustus. The Christians of Pergamum are praised for remaining loyal, even when Antipas was martyred, but are blamed for following Balaam (Num 25:1–3; compare 2 Pet 2:15; Jude 11)

and the Nicolaitans, that is, accommodating themselves to their environment. They are exhorted to repent.

2:18–29 The message/letter to Thyatira. Thyatira was a small town forty miles southeast of Pergamum. The church is praised for its love, faith, and works, but is blamed for tolerating the mysterious prophetess Jezebel (1 Kings 19:1–2; 21:1–14; 2 Kings 9:22, 30–34), who also leads the Christians to accommodation, perhaps in connection with the cult meals of Thyatira's well-known trade guilds.

3:1–6 The message/letter to Sardis. Sardis was about thirty miles southeast of Thyatira, was once the capital of Lydia, and had a Jewish community. A few Christians are praised and it is said that they will have their names inscribed in the "book of life" (3:5), perhaps recalling citizen-registers of antiquity. Had they had their names removed from the synagogue register?

3:7–13 The message/letter to Philadelphia. The church at Philadelphia, about thirty miles southeast of Sardis, is modestly praised for its endurance under persecution from the Jewish community (3:9–10). The "key of David" (3:7) from Isaiah 22:22 suggests Christ's power to include or excommunicate (compare Matt 16:17–19; 18:18). For the "new Jerusalem," see Revelation 21:10–22:5.

3:14–22 The message/letter to Laodicea. Laodicea, the last city in the circuit, was about forty miles southeast of Philadelphia and due east of the first city, Ephesus. It was a very wealthy commercial city, its citizens having had the funds to rebuild the city after an earthquake in about 60/61 C.E. Its Christians are blamed for being "lukewarm" (3:16) and complacently wealthy (3:17), but they are spiritually poor.

4:1–8:5 SEVEN SEALS.

The vision in chapter 4 portrays the heavenly worship of God sitting on his throne (4:10) and that in chapter 5 notes that in his right hand is a scroll sealed with seven seals (5:1). These two visions introduce the visions of the seven seals in chapter 6 and two supplementary visions in chapter 7.

4:1–11 The heavenly worship of God. The image of God on his heavenly throne is derived in part from Ezekiel 1 and 10 and Isaiah 6. The twenty-four elders seated on twenty-four thrones, who with the four living creatures also worship God, may have been suggested by the imperial cult, as well as the twelve tribes and twelve apostles (compare Matt 19:28). The four living creatures are described in Ezekiel 1:5–21; in Ezekiel 10:20–22, 14–15, they are cherubim; for their six wings, see Isaiah 6:2.

5:1–14 The scroll and the lamb. The scroll in God's right hand has seven seals; no one can open it (inaugurate the events of the End) but "the Lion of the tribe of Judah, the Root of David," that is, the Davidic Messiah (Isa 11:1, 10; compare Rev 22:16), who "has conquered" (see note on 2:1–7). The sacrificial lamb with seven horns (power) and seven eyes (knowledge) is Christ, who is also worshipped.

6:1 The opening of the seals by the Lamb. This symbolizes what must happen before the End. When the first four seals are broken, the four horsemen are revealed.

6:2 The first seal. A white horse symbolizes victory. The Parthian armies are probably implied by the rider with a bow (compare Rev 17).

6:3–4 The second seal. A red horse symbolizes violence and war.

6:5–6 The third seal. A black horse symbolizes famine and suffering.

6:7–8 The fourth seal. A pale green horse symbolizes plague (decomposition, death).

6:9–11 The fifth seal. This seal reveals the faithful martyrs.

6:12–17 The sixth seal. This seal reveals the apocalyptic cataclysm (compare Mark 13:5–37 = Matt 24:4–36 = Luke 21:8–36).

7:1–17 Two supplementary visions. In the first vision (7:1–8), the 144,000 elect (12 tribes × 12,000 from each tribe; see above) are sealed on their foreheads (compare Ezek 9; 14:1–5). In the second (7:9–17) a great multitude of the elect are unnumbered and from "every nation, from all tribes and peoples and languages" (7:9; compare 10:11; 13:7; 14:6; 17:15). These elect will survive the final tribulation.

8:1–5 The seventh seal. The seventh seal is a transition to the seven trumpets.

8:6–11:19 SEVEN TRUMPETS.

Each trumpet blast announces a cosmic catastrophe (Exod 19:16, 19; Matt 24:31; 1 Thess 4:16; compare Rev 1:10). In general the catastrophes are based on the plagues of Egypt (Exod 7–10).

8:7 The first trumpet. Hail and fire are mixed with blood (Exod 9:22–26).

8:8–9 The second trumpet. One-third of the sea becomes blood (Exod 7:14–25).

8:10–11 The third trumpet. One-third of the fresh waters becomes bitter wormwood (compare Jer 9:15–16).

8:12 The fourth trumpet. One-third of the sun, moon, and stars are darkened (compare Exod 10:21–23).

8:13 The three woes. Each woe represents one of the last three trumpets or catastrophes (Rev 9:12; 11:14).

9:1–12 The fifth trumpet (first woe). A star (demon) falls to earth. He opens up the abyss (Rev 20:1–3, 7–10) and lets loose a plague of locusts (Exod 10) with scorpionlike stingers, led by Abaddon (Aramaic: "destruction") or Apollyon (Greek: "Destroyer").

9:13–21 The sixth trumpet (second woe). This trumpet heralds an invasion from the East (verse 14, the Euphrates River). Probably the invaders are the Parthians who rivaled the Romans (compare the sixth bowl, 16:12–16).

10:1–11:14 Two supplementary visions. These two visions point ahead to the second cycle of visions (12:1–22:5). In the first supplementary vision (Rev 10) "another mighty angel" (compare 5:2) descends with a little open scroll (compare 5:1) and announces that when the seventh trumpet is blown, there will be no more delay; the plan of God will be revealed (10:7). John is commanded to eat the scroll (Ezek 2:8–3:3), which is sour (suffering) and yet sweet as honey (salvation of the elect), and then to prophesy about many peoples, nations, tongues, and kings (10:11; compare 7:9; 13:7; 14:6; 17:15). In the second vision (Rev 11:1–14), two mysterious witnesses prophesy that the time of woes will be limited to three and one half years (11:2–3; compare Dan 7:25; 12:7; Rev 12:6, 14; 13:5). The beast from the abyss (compare 9:1–12) may be the Roman emperor or Antichrist (compare 13:1–10; 17:8).

11:15–18 The seventh trumpet (third woe). This trumpet marks the final woes, resurrection of the dead for judgment, and salvation of the elect who are ruled over by the Lord and his Anointed.

Second Cycle of Visions, 12:1–22:5

12:1–15:4 SEVEN UNNUMBERED VISIONS.
The visions are usually marked by the formula "And I saw" (13:1, 11; 14:1, 6, 14; 15:1, 2). The main theme in this series is persecution.

12:1–18 First vision. The cosmic clothing of the woman (12:1–6) is characteristic of goddesses in antiquity, and so is the myth of a goddess who is pregnant with a savior and pursued by the many-headed monster of the abyss, or Leviathan (compare Babylonian and Canaanite myth; the birth of Apollo; Ps 74:12–14). Here the woman is also the heavenly Israel, which is the heavenly church; the archangel Michael defeats the serpent, the monster who is the Devil, and the serpent is expelled from heaven (12:9); and the woman is aided in her escape by the great eagle (12:14).

13:1–10 Second vision. The beast from the evil sea has ten horns (power) and seven heads (compare Dan 7:2–28), which symbolizes the Roman Empire, and it has power over all (compare 7:9; 10:11; 14:6; 17:15). On the seven heads/seven kings, see 17:10–14 and the discussion above. The head that is mortally wounded and then healed (13:3) may symbolize the Nero *redivivus* in the following vision.

13:11–18 Third vision. The second beast is from the earth; elsewhere it is identified with false prophets and false Messiahs (for example, 16:13; 19:20; compare Mark 13:22). Its authority (13:12) may refer to imperial cult functionaries. Its miracle working is reminiscent of the lawless one (2 Thess 2:9). The number 666 (13:18) refers to a Nero *redivivus* (see above).

14:1–5 Fourth vision. The vision of the Lamb and his followers contrasts with that of the beast. For the 144,000 (14:1), see 7:1–8; they are the first fruits of the resurrection of the dead, presumably the martyrs of the first resurrection (20:4–6).

14:6–13 Fifth vision. Of the three angels, the first announces good news to all (compare 7:9; 10:11; 13:7), the second announces the fall of Babylon or Rome (see above), and the third divine judgment on all.

14:14–20 Sixth vision. In Joel 4:13 and Isaiah 63:3, the harvest and vintage images symbolize victory of the divine warrior and angry judgment on the nations; a similar use is found here, the harvest representing the salvation of the elect (compare Matt 13:24–30), the vintage representing the judgment of wicked. compare Rev 19:13, 15.

15:2–4 Seventh vision. The victors sing the song of Moses, recalling the victorious hymn of Moses and the escaping Israelites in Exodus 15.

15:1–16:21 SEVEN BOWLS.
The main theme in this series is judgment, and the opponents of God are more specific.

15:1; 15:5–16:1 Seven angels; the last seven plagues = seven bowls. Revelation 15:1 introduces 15:5–19:10.

16:2 The first bowl. Sores appear on those who have the mark of the beast (compare Exod 9:8–12)

16:3 The second bowl. The sea becomes blood (compare Exod 7:14–24).

16:4–7 The third bowl. The rivers and springs also turn to blood.

16:8–9 The fourth bowl. The sun burns people.

16:10–11 The fifth bowl. The kingdom of the throne of the beast turns into darkness (compare Exod 10:21–23).

16:12–16 The sixth bowl. This bowl is linked to the sixth trumpet (9:13–21) by the Euphrates. The heavenly battle has its earthly counterpart, and again the kings of the East point to the Parthians. For the frogs, see Exodus 7:25–8:15; for the thief, see Matthew 24:43–44; Luke 12:39–40; 1 Thessalonians 5:2, 4; 2 Peter 3:10. Hebrew Armageddon means "Mountain of Megiddo." The plain before the ancient Israelite city of Megiddo was the site of many ancient battles.

16:17–21 The seventh bowl. God judges "Babylon" (Rome) and rains hailstones on it (Exod 9:23–24). See the following Babylonian appendix.

17:1–19:10 BABYLONIAN APPENDIX.

The punishment of "Babylon" = Rome is now detailed. She is the great harlot who has intercourse with the kings of the earth. She sits on a beast with ten horns and seven heads (see 13:1–10). In 17:12–16 the ten horns, or ten kings from the East, will leave the beast desolate but will be defeated by the Lamb. Revelation 18:1–19:4 is a dirge about the fall of Babylon. It is followed in 19:5–10 by a victory song celebrating the marriage of the Lamb to the elect.

19:11–21:8 SEVEN UNNUMBERED VISIONS.

These visions reveal the destruction of Satan's evil age, the millennium, God's eternal age, and the divine city. They recall the ancient combat myth (see Rev 12).

19:11–16 The first vision. The seer has a vision of heaven open and the heavenly Christ, called the Word of God and wearing a robe dipped in blood, astride a white horse. Following him are the heavenly armies clad in white linen, also astride white horses. All this is reminiscent of the holy war (2 Macc 10:29–31). He is "King of kings and Lord of lords" (19:16).

19:17–18 The second vision. God's banquet anticipates the following battle. Both visions recall Ezekiel 39:4, 17–20.

19:19–21 The third vision. Opposing this army are the Antichrist (the beast 666, Rev 13:1–10, 18) and the kings of the earth with their armies, along with the false prophet (the second beast, Rev 13:11–17), that is, a miracle-working helper, a pseudo-Christ. The Antichrist and the false prophet are caught and thrown into the lake of fire, a place of eternal damnation and punishment, and the rest are slain with a two-edged sword issuing from the mouth of the heavenly Christ. So ends the reign of idolatrous Rome and the Antichrist!

20:1–3 The fourth vision. Then an angel descends from heaven, binds Satan, who is the mythical dragon, and locks him in the bottomless pit.

20:4–10 The fifth vision. The martyrs for Christ are now raised (the first resurrection) and reign with Christ for 1000 years (the millennium) as priestly judges. However, all is not ended. After the millennium Satan is released to deceive the nations, called Gog and Magog (Ezek 38–39), and they surround the martyrs and Christ in Jerusalem; but fire comes down from heaven and destroys them, once and for all. Now the devil is thrown into the lake of fire with the Antichrist and the false prophet, and there they are tormented forever.

20:11–15 The sixth vision. John perceives God on his great white throne, and from God's presence heaven and earth disappear. The dead (except the martyrs) are raised for judgment (the second resurrection), and Death and Hades, along with those evil ones whose names are not written in the book of life, are also cast into the lake of fire.

21:1–8 The seventh vision. Next, the seer has a vision of a new creation, a new heaven and new earth (compare Isa 65:17;2; Baruch 32:6; 48:50; 51:3; 1 Enoch 45:4–5), and a new Jerusalem descends to earth, prepared as a bride adorned for her husband. The new age has begun! God and Christ now join the saints in the new Jerusalem in eternal joy and bliss.

21:9–22:5 JERUSALEM APPENDIX.

Finally the seer is transported by one of the seven angels to a high mountain, where he is shown the divine city, the bride of the lamb, in all of its magnificent glory.

Epilogue, 22:6–21

22:6–20 SAYINGS; EPISTOLARY AUTHENTICATION.

22:21 EPISTOLARY BENEDICTION.

THE ENDURING INFLUENCE OF EARLY CHRISTIAN APOCALYPTIC

The most obvious influence of early Christian apocalyptic is the continuing existence of apocalyptic sects and movements, or millenarian movements. Throughout Christian history, groups of believers have fed their hopes on New Testament apocalyptic literature and calculated the date of the coming of Jesus as Son of Man, as many still do. Similarly, the beast whose number is 666 (Rev 13:18) has been identified with every tyrant in western history, including Hitler and Stalin.

The apocalypse has also influenced worldwide millenarian movements that have come in contact with Christianity. A vivid example is the native American movement related to the great vision of Black Elk, a holy man of the Oglala Sioux, as reported by him to John G. Neihardt. Here is a scene taken random from that vision:

And as I looked and wept, I saw that there stood on the north side of the starving camp a sacred man who was painted red all over his body, and he held a spear as he walked into the center of the people, and there he lay down and rolled. And when he got up, it was a fat bison standing there, and where the tree had been in the center of the nation's hoop. The herb grew and bore four blossoms on a single stem while I was looking—a blue,

a white, a scarlet, and a yellow—and the bright rays of these flashed to the heavens. I know now what this meant, that the bison were the gift of a good spirit and were our strength, but we should lose them, and from the same good spirit we must find another strength.
(J. Niehardt, *Black Elk Speaks,* p. 32)

Like John of Patmos, Black Elk speaks for his oppressed people and, recalling the past, hopes for a future day when the white man will be gone and the bison will return.

In modern times historical scholars have had problems with the book of Revelation, but as we noted at the outset, poets and artists have found it an unending source of inspiration precisely because it uses images of immense evocative power. The human mind's fundamental propensity to embrace myth or symbol when attempting to approach the ultimates of human experience or expectation is found in Amos Wilder's poetic expression of his experience in the First World War.

There we marched out on haunted battle-ground,
There smelled the strife of gods, were brushed against
By higher beings, and were wrapped around
With passions not of earth, all dimly sensed.

There saw we demons fighting in the sky
And battles in aerial mirage,
The feverish very lights proclaimed them by,
Their tramplings woke our panting, fierce barrage.

Their tide of battle, hither, thither, driven
Filled earth and sky with cataclysmic throes,
Our strife was but the mimicry of heaven's
And we the shadows of celestial foes.

In thinking of apocalyptic we have to think of the human mind at a level of ultimacy and at that level turning naturally to the use of myth and symbol. In the case of the ancient Jewish and early Christian apocalyptic the ultimacy came from a total despair of the oppressive course of human history and an absolute trust in the final purposes of God.

FURTHER READING

ABD: "Babylon in the New Testament" (D. E. Watson); "Christianity in Asia Minor" (R. E. Oster, Jr.); "Lamb" (J. R. Miles); "Millennium" (W. H. Mare); "New Earth, New Heaven" (D. F. Watson); "Nicolaitans" (D. F. Watson); "Pliny the Younger" (B. W. Jones); "Revelation, Book of" (A. Yarbro Collins); "Seven Churches" (D. F. Watson).

IDB: "Revelation" (J. W. Bowman).

IDB Suppl.: "Revelation" (E. Schüssler Fiorenza).

NJBC, pp. 996–1016 (A. Yarbro Collins).

Introductory

J. Pilch, *What Are They Saying About the Book of Revelation?*

E. Schüssler Fiorenza, *The Apocalypse.*

Important Articles

D. E. Aune, "The Social Matrix of the Apocalypse of John," *Biblical Research* 26 (1981), pp. 16–32.

F. G. Downing, "Pliny's Prosecutions of Christians: Revelation and 1 Peter," *Journal for the Study of the New Testament* 34 (1988), pp. 105–123.

D. L. Jones, "Christianity and the Roman Imperial Cult." *Aufstieg und Niedergang der römischen Welt.* II.23.2, pp. 1023–1054.

E. Schüssler Fiorenza, "Composition and Structure of the Book of Revelation," *Catholic Biblical Quarterly* 39 (1977), pp. 344–366.

L. Thompson. "A Sociological Analysis of Tribulation in the Apocalypse of John." Pp. 147–174 in Yarbro Collins, ed., *Early Christian Apocalypticism.*

Commentaries

M. E. Boring, *Revelation.* (Interpretation).

G. B. Caird, *A Commentary of the Revelation of St. John the Divine.*

J. M. Ford, *Revelation.* (The Anchor Bible Commentary).

G. A. Krodel, *Revelation.* (Augsburg).

E. Schüssler Fiorenza, "The Apocalypse," pp. 99–120 of R. H. Fuller, et al., *Hebrews, James, 1 and 2 Peter, Jude, Revelation.* (Proclamation Commentaries.)

————, *Invitation to the Book of Revelation.*

A. Yarbro Collins, *The Apocalypse.* (New Testament Message).

Literary

D. L. Barr, "The Apocalypse as a Symbolic Transformation of the World," *Interpretation* 38 (1984), pp. 39–50.

A. Yarbro Collins, ed., *Early Christian Apocalypticism: Genre and Social Setting.*

Social History

A. Yarbro Collins, *Crisis & Catharsis. The Power of the Apocalypse.*

A. Yarbro Collins, ed., *Early Christian Apocalypticism: Genre and Social Setting.*

J. G. Gager, *Kingdom and Community: The Social World of Early Christianity.*

C. J. Hemer, *The Letters to the Seven Churches of Asia in their Local Setting.*

Other

J. J. Collins, *The Apocalyptic Imagination.*

E. Schüssler Fiorenza, *The Book of Revelation: Justice and Judgment.*

The above discussion of Revelation is heavily indebted to the writings of A. Yarbro Collins (from whom the outline is derived) and E. Schüssler Fiorenza.

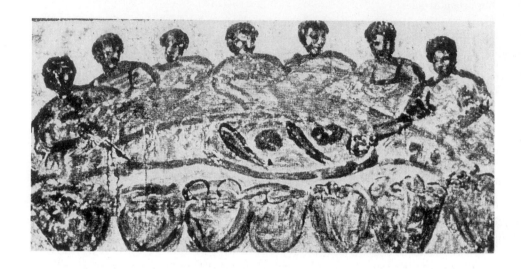

The Eucharistic Meal mural in the catacombs of Callistus in Rome, second century C.E. The reclining position at meals was usual. By the time the Christian literature in Chapter Fourteen was written, Jesus' last meal (1 Cor 11:11–23–24; Mark 14:22–25; Matt 26:26–29; Luke 22:15–20; John 13; 6:11) was becoming a sacred rite separate from a meal (1 Cor 11:27–34; *Didachē* 9, 10; Ignatius *Letter to the Smyrneans* 6; Justin Martyr *Apology* 1.65–67). The fish became a "condensed symbol" for Christianity itself ("fish" = Greek *ICHTHYS*, an acrostic: *I* = *Iēsous* [Jesus]; *CH* = *CHristos* ["Christ"]; *TH* = *THeou* ["God's"]; *YS* = *YioS* ["Son"], or "Jesus Christ God's Son"). Compare the Meal of the Loaves and Fishes and its caption at the beginning of Chapter Five.

CHAPTER FOURTEEN

THE CHURCH ON THE WAY TO BECOMING AN INSTITUTION

1 Peter; James; 1, 2, Timothy; Titus; Jude; 2 Peter

Traditionally, the letters in the New Testament are divided into two groups: "the Pauline epistles" (including 2 Thessalonians; Colossians; Ephesians; 1, 2 Timothy and Titus; and Hebrews) and "the Catholic epistles" (James; 1, 2 Peter; Jude; and 1, 2, 3 John). The latter group is called "Catholic" because the letters are addressed to the church in general rather than to a particular congregation or individual. In contrast to this traditional division, we have preferred, where possible, to group the letters according to literary and historical considerations. In Chapter Seven we discussed the letters that scholars agree were actually written by Paul. In Chapter Eight we took those written in Paul's name by his early pupils and followers, that is, the Pauline School, and tacked on Hebrews, which, while it was probably from the same general period as the early deutero-Paulines, was probably attributed to Paul only later in Christian tradition. In Chapter Twelve, we grouped 1, 2, and 3 John with the Gospel of John because the four texts have literary and theological connections as products of the Johannine School. We now consider 1 Peter, James, the so-called Pastorals (1 Timothy, 2 Timothy, Titus), Jude, and 2 Peter, because for the most part they are the common products of the final period of New Testament history, the early second century. The possible exception to this generalization is 1 Peter, which recent scholarship tends to push back into the late first century. Despite our willingness to accept this option below, in which case it might have been placed chronologically in an earlier chapter, we have elected to put it here in line with the first and second editions of this textbook, but to consider it first. We also need to note that we put Jude before 2 Peter, that is, between 1 Peter and 2 Peter, because 2 Peter reproduces Jude almost in its entirety. The Pastorals and 2 Peter also come last, and stand together as the most complete representatives of the emerging institutional church.

In the period roughly 90–125 C.E. new difficulties and needs are developing for some of the Christian movements. While Revelation attests to the revitalization of apocalyptic in a situation of perceived persecution, many, perhaps most, Christians believe that the parousia is no longer immediately expected and must learn to adjust to the destruction of Jerusalem and the Temple, and relations with non-Christian Jews, Greeks, Romans, and others in more "acceptable" ways. Religious movements that survive usually have to settle down to the process determining their relationship to the rest of society. They usually develop more formalized sets of beliefs to determine who "we" are, as contrasted with who "they" are. Thus, the varieties of Christian movements stemming ultimately from Judaism, with their consciousness of revelations enshrined in written texts, need their own authoritative texts. For example, by this time some of Paul's letters, as well as three attributed to him, have been formed into a collection. Gospels are beginning to become authoritative, as well. Moreover, to survive and function in society, the churches will normally begin to develop their own institutions, their own corporate and organizational structures, their decision-making apparatus, and a definition of the functions of those who wield power, especially at the local level, their officers and servants. In other words, to meet these needs the Christian churches at the end of the New Testament period are beginning to establish a more formalized creed, a canon, a liturgy, and an organized ordained ministry. Thus, the major characteristic of this final period of New Testament history is a beginning of institutionalization that will ultimately reach some degree of basic self-identity in the fourth century.

In this chapter we shall discuss primarily the literature in the Christian canon. However, it should not be forgotten that we are dealing with a *choice* of books that were only *eventually* accepted by the *majority* of the churches. We have seen, for example, that some forms of Christian literature survived only by being incorporated into the literature that did survive, for example, Q, the anecdotes, and the miracle stories. Other written documents were used by churches that did not unite with the growing majority, for example, the *Gospel of Thomas* and many other apocryphal documents. Still others hovered on the edge of being accepted into the emerging canon, for example, a letter written by Clement, bishop of Rome, to the church at Corinth (*1 Clement*); letters written by Ignatius, bishop of Antioch, to various churches as he was on his way to martyrdom in Rome; and a church order called the *Didache* ("Teaching [of the Lord to the Gentiles by the Twelve Apostles]"). In addition, some Christians of this period were being influenced by a growing Gnostic movement still in contact with Judaism, and it produced much literature. In this period of Christian history many oral traditions and books in use by many different churches were ultimately rejected by the majority; moreover, as we noted in Chapter Thirteen, no unanimity was ever reached by all Christian churches on the book of Revelation, and a study of manuscripts from the third century will show some books ultimately rejected by the majority were still being used and that some ultimately accepted were missing. From a strictly historical point of view, then, all books in use in the early second century should be considered along side the canonical books. To conserve space and stick with the New Testament itself, we shall simply refer to the "Apostolic Fathers" and other literature in passing, as necessity demands, and we shall note Gnosticism and the opposition to growing Gnostic forms of Christianity (especially 2 Peter and 1 Timothy) in the literature that was finally accepted as normative.

In short, our procedure in this chapter will be to discuss the New Testament texts in this order: 1 Peter, James, the Pastorals, Jude, and 2 Peter. Then we shall offer a summary of the characteristics of emerging institutional Christianity and remarks on its literature, and an Excursis on pseudonymity.

THE FIRST LETTER OF PETER AND THE PETRINE SCHOOL

1 Peter purports to be a letter written by Peter and his companions in Babylon "...to the exiles ['resident aliens'] of the Dispersion in Pontus, Galatia, Cappadocia, Asia, and Bithynia..." (1:1; 5:12–13; compare James 1:1). We shall now look more closely at these references and note the problems and some solutions related to them.

Peter, Babylon, and the Dispersion in Asia Minor

Peter is one of four names given to the same person, the three others being Symeon (Acts 15:14; 2 Pet 1:1); Simon, the Greek equivalent of Symeon (many times, especially in the gospels and Acts); and Cephas, the Aramaic word for "rock" (John [once], 1 Cor [four times], Gal [four times]). Peter comes from the Greek *Petros,* which translates the Aramaic Cephas; it occurs by far the most frequently, largely in the gospels and Acts. According to the gospel stories, the name *Petros* was the name given to him by Jesus: "Blessed are you, Simon son of Jonah.... You are Peter *(Petros)* and on this rock *(petra)* I will build my church" (Matt 16:17).

We cannot go into great detail about a figure as central to the New Testament as Peter. He was the son of Jonah (*bar-Jonah*), married (Mark 1:30 = Matt 8:14 = Luke 4:38; 1 Cor 9:5), and had a brother Andrew who also became Jesus' disciple (Mark 1:16–20 = Matt 4:18–22). They and another set of brothers, James and John, the sons of Zebedee, were fishermen who worked with Zebedee on the northwest corner of the Sea of Galilee near Capernaum, where Peter lived. Some archeologists think they have identified Peter's house there. The synoptic gospels portray Peter as the leading disciple and usually their spokesman. In John he is rivaled by the Beloved Disciple (John 20). Despite his denial of Jesus, Peter is said by Paul to have been the first to see the resurrected Jesus (1 Cor 15:3; compare Luke 24:34) and in Acts, he is the first major leader of the Jerusalem church (Acts 1–5). Paul says he was a pillar at Jerusalem and an apostle to the Jews (Gal 2:9). Tradition places his death in Rome under Nero (*1 Clement* 5).

Babylon, claimed to be the location of the writing of 1 Peter, was the capital of ancient Babylonia (modern Iraq). In Jewish and Christian apocalyptic, however, it had become symbolic for Rome because both Babylon and Rome had destroyed Jerusalem (see Chapter Thirteen). The regions to which 1 Peter are written are five Roman provinces in central and northern Asia Minor. The exiles are said to be facing various kinds of trials and sufferings (1:6; 2:12, 19–20; 3:14–16; 4:1, 4, 12–16, 19; 5:9).

Church Tradition about 1 Peter

1 Peter was clearly accepted as the composition of Jesus' disciple Peter by the late second century C.E. (Irenaeus, *Against Heresies* 4.9.2). It is likely that this

belief was current earlier. A Church Father, Polycarp, was later remembered as quoting from "the former epistle of Peter" (fourth-century Eusebius, *Ecclesiastical History 4.14.9*). Polycarp lived and flourished in the early second century (about 70–156 C.E.). This tradition about Polycarp appears to be confirmed since Polycarp's letter to the Philippians, written before 140 C.E., has survived, and he often refers to 1 Peter (Polycarp *To the Philippians* 1:3 [1 Pet 1:8]; 2:1 [1 Pet 1:15, 21]; 6:3 [1 Pet 3:13]; and so forth). Also, 1 Peter mentions "my son Mark" (5:13) whom Papias in about 135–40 C.E. thought was the "interpreter of Peter" (Eusebius, *Ecclesiastical History,* 3.39.15). Mark was being associated with Peter at this time, and there is an implied reference about this association in 1 Peter. Thus, Peter's name was associated with the document by the second quarter of the second century, which would also be the latest point 1 Peter could have been written.

Historical Criticism

Did Jesus' disciple Peter, who was martyred about 64 C.E., write 1 Peter? It is unlikely. Petrine authorship is related to a variety of disputed issues: the literary style, form, traditions, date and place of origin, and recipients of 1 Peter. Like James, the literary style of 1 Peter is characterized by Hellenistic Greek rhetorical devices: the play on words, for example, "perishable/imperishable" *(phthartēs/aphthartou)* (1:23); parallel clauses, for example, "whoever . . . ; whoever . . ." (4:11); the series of similar compound words, for example, "imperishable, undefiled and unfading" (all words constructed in Greek in the same way) (1:4); and others. 1 Peter is written in excellent Greek, and all quotations from and allusions to the Jewish Scriptures come from the Greek translation of those Scriptures, the Septuagint. Would such language have been typical of a Galilean fisherman whose native tongue was Aramaic? Probably not. Modern scholars who have defended Petrine authorship have usually suggested that its style came from Peter's secretary Sylvanus (5:12). Most, however, do not accept this view because of an accumulation of other problems.

One major problem is that like James, 1 Peter knows Jesus traditions (1:13 [Luke 12:35]; 2:12c [Matt 5:16]; 3:9 [Matt 5:44]; 3:14 [Matt 5:10]; 4:14 [Luke 6:22]). Yet, the author does not attribute them to Jesus. Would the leading disciple of Jesus have failed to attribute Jesus traditions to Jesus?

Another issue is that 1 Peter incorporates a variety of traditional materials, especially Christological hymns. Though precise reconstructions are probably not possible, we recall one possibility in 1 Peter 3:18–19, 22:

> Having been put to death in the flesh,
> Having been made alive in the spirit,
> Having gone to the spirits in prison,
>   He preached.
> Who is at the right hand of God,
> Having gone into heaven,
> Angels and authorities and powers having been
>   made subject to him.

If this hymn were prefaced with 1 Peter 1:20,

He was foreknown before the foundation of the world,
He was made manifest at the end of the times,

the preexistence, earthly existence, and postearthly existence pattern of the
Christ myth would be evident. A Christological hymn with this pattern is known
and cited by Paul (Phil 2:5–11) and other early Christians. The question is: Would
an immediate disciple of Jesus who was a Galilean fisherman have thought about
Jesus this way?

The form of 1 Peter also presents us with some problems. 1 Peter purports to
be a letter; yet, there are no direct personal relations developed between author
and recipients. Also, some have argued that the document has two distinct sections, with a break coming between 4:11 and 4:12. Certainly, there is a shift in
tone at 4:12. The references to suffering and persecution in 1:6, 3:14, and 4:1, as
well as "trials," suffering "for righteousness' sake," and "abuse" are general. In
4:12, however, the readers are said to endure some "fiery ordeal," and in 5:8
they are warned that "like a roaring lion, your adversary the devil prowls around,
looking for someone to devour." Do these latter references imply an actual persecution? One theory is that up until 4:11 we are dealing with the general possibility of suffering, but that after 4:11 we are in a concrete situation of actual
persecution. However, if the references are to an oppressed minority, they do not
need to refer to actual political persecution.

A related problem is the *baptismal theme.* 1 Peter 1:3 speaks of "new birth into
a living hope." 1 Peter 1:23 says, "You have been born anew, not of perishable but
of imperishable seed, through the living and enduring word of God." 1 Peter 2:2
states, "Like newborn infants, long for the pure, spiritual milk, so that by it you may
grow into salvation...." 1 Peter 3:21 reads, "And baptism, which this [the eight persons who in the days of Noah were saved from the flood waters] prefigured, now
saves you—not as a removal of dirt from the body, but as an appeal to God for a
good conscience, through the resurrection of Jesus Christ..." These phrases about
water, rebirth, and infancy are the language of early Christian baptism, that is, of
entering the state of childlike innocence and growing in the faith of the new
community (compare also 2:9–10, 24b–25; 4:1). Some scholars have suggested that
1 Peter is a reworked baptismal homily, or sermonette, that the author was in the
habit of using, and that at a time of oppression or persecution served as a
reminder to his readers of the spirit in which they first became Christians. If so, the
author added 4:12–5:11 as a reflection on the current situation of the recipients in
Asia Minor and circulated the whole to comfort his readers.

Social-Historical Context

Related to all these issues is the problem of the recipients and their social context.
Again, 1 Peter is addressed to "exiles [resident aliens] of the Dispersion in Pontus,
Galatia, Cappadocia, Asia, and Bithynia...." (1:1; compare 5:12–13) in Asia Minor.
You will recall that the term "Dispersion" refers to the Jewish Diaspora; thus, these
Christians are being compared to Jews who no longer live in their homeland. They
are later said to have an "exile," that is, "alien residence" (1:17) or to be "aliens
and exiles [visiting strangers]" "among the Gentiles" (2:11). "Resident alien" is a
single word in Greek, *paroikos,* and it had a technical meaning (J. Elliott). It

referred to a registered, displaced person living abroad, a "foreigner" with certain political, economic, legal, and social restrictions. *Paroikos* was used in the Septuagint and other Greek literature of Jewish origin to refer to displaced Jewish persons of the Diaspora. Such persons were beneath the status of full citizens, on the one hand, but above the status of mere "transients" *(xenoi,* "strangers"), freedmen, and slaves, on the other. Longer residence at one location could naturally change one's status from "transient" to "resident alien," and in exceptional cases, freedmen and slaves were also granted the "resident alien" status. Yet, *paroikos* could have symbolic significance for someone who was not "at home" in the environment. While it had such overtones in 1 Peter, it was nevertheless not simply symbolic and spiritual. Rather, "resident aliens" in 1 Peter refers in the first place to members of a sectarian Christian group, an oppressed minority that was being exhorted to maintain its purity in a non-Christian, sometimes hostile, environment. Some were of Jewish background, but most were Gentile Christians. Perhaps the group included newly relocated rural villagers. In any case, as Christians the members of the group were not "at home" in non-Christian social environment of these provinces of Asia Minor. Whatever symbolic overtones are associated with the term are grounded in social reality.

A key term related to *paroikos* by etymology and social context is *oikos,* or "house." *Oikos* is used as a metaphor in 1 Peter. The term describes its recipients: They are a "spiritual house(hold)" (2:5) and the "household of God" (4:17). Yet, the term is also grounded in social reality. We have previously noted that Pauline Christians usually met in houses belonging to the wealthier members of the local congregation (Chapter Six). When the head of the household converted and was baptized, so usually were the members of that household. In such houses the *paterfamilias* had absolute authority over his wife, children, and servants. Well-ordered household management *(oikonomia)* was thought to be the foundation of the well-ordered and stable society. All of this was expressed in the "household code." 1 Peter contains one of the New Testament household codes (2:13–3:9); moreover, the "house" or "household" is a way of referring to the Christian community itself. Thus, one might say that the *oikos,* or household of God, was composed of actual *paroikoi,* or "resident aliens," who experienced *paroikia,* or "homelessness." The "household" thus symbolized the community. A byproduct of this sort of social analysis is that the possibility of an actual *political* persecution is less certain.

Also related to these issues is the problem of dating 1 Peter, and again there is no scholarly consensus. If one accepts the theory that the last section of 1 Peter (4:12–5:11) reflects an actual, concrete, political persecution, there are three known possibilities: the persecution at Rome under Nero about 64 C.E., accepted as the occasion for Peter's martyrdom; some local persecutions under Domitian in the 90s, the time usually suggested for the local persecutions related to the book of Revelation; and the early second century under the emperor Trajan (98–117 C.E.; see Chapter Thirteen, the Pliny-Trajan correspondence). Those who have defended actual Petrine authorship have attempted to account for the Greek style with a secretary hypothesis and have defended the earliest date. Because of the difficulties noted above, however, most critical scholars have favored the latest date. It receives support because the Trajan persecution was the first large scale persecution of Christians. Moreover, Bithynia in northern Asia Minor is one known location of that persecution, and Bithynia is mentioned in 1 Peter 1:1. Thus, a pseudonymous author would have composed 1 Peter in the second century.

The position adopted here is the second position, from the latter period of the first century, that is, the middle period of Christianity. This date does not require an actual Roman political persecution under Domitian (81–96 C.E.). Rather, it is built on the oppression of Christian minorities in non-Christian environments. If Babylon (1:1) symbolized Rome, as it did in apocalyptic literature in general (for example, *2 Baruch* 11:1; 67:7; *Sibylline Oracles* 5:143, 159), including Revelation (14:8; 16:19; 17:5; 18:2, 10, 21), the work could have come from Petrine circles, or a Petrine School, at Rome. Peter had been influential there and had been martyred there. The work stresses persons known from Paul's contacts with the Romans, that is, Sylvanus (1 Pet 5:12 [Acts 15:22, 27 (= Silas)]), John Mark (1 Pet 5:13 [Phlm 23; Col 4:10], and certain ideas related to Paul's letter to the Romans, for example, the saving significance of Jesus' resurrection to God's right hand (1 Pet 1:21; 2:24; 3:21–22 [Rom 4:24; 8:34; 6:11], and so on). In short, 1 Peter is best understood as a pseudonymous letterlike work written about 80–90 C.E. at Rome by some person from a Petrine School who used the pseudonym of the apostle to address oppressed Christian groups in central and northern Asia Minor. Perhaps the communities addressed had been missionized by followers of Peter (compare Galatians; Acts 2:9). In any case, the purpose of 1 Peter was to express concern for, solidarity with, and encouragement of, the Christians in Asia Minor at a time when the Roman church was growing in importance (compare *1 Clement;* Ignatius, *Romans*).

Structure

It is difficult to recognize a structure in 1 Peter because so much of it is parenesis. Even where there is proclamation celebrating what God has done through Jesus, there is parenesis interwoven with it. We can recognize the opening greeting (1:1–2), the section related to a possible baptismal homily (1:3–4:11), the exhortation to stand fast in the face of oppression (4:12–5:11), and the closing greetings (5:12–14). Beyond that the most we can do is try to follow the writer's train of thought.

Exegetical Survey

1:1–2 OPENING GREETINGS.

1:3–4:11 THE FIRST SECTION, PERHAPS BASED ON A BAPTISMAL HOMILY.

1:3–9 An opening blessing. It was (and is) customary in Jewish worship to bless God for saving humanity. Here we may have a Christian development of that liturgical practice. The language of "rebirth" occurs in 1:3. Note how the author moves from "him" to "us" to "you" as his thought moves from God to Christians in general and then to the group he is addressing.

1:10–12 Christian salvation as the fulfillment of prophecy.

1:13–2:10 An exhortation to be God's holy people. Parenesis based upon key Biblical passages for holiness, "[You shall] be holy, for I am holy" (Lev

11:44–45) and related to rebirth (2:2, 22–23). Interwoven with the parenesis is reflection upon the significance of Christ: He is preexistent; he is the
lamb of God; he is the precious stone. The first theme may come from a
Christological hymn. The latter two are metaphors developed from Old
Testament passages much used in the New Testament, the lamb from Isaiah 53 and the stone from Psalm 118:22, which has led to other scriptural
passages mentioning stones. The community is also a "spiritual house"
(2:5) and a "holy priesthood" (see Hebrews, Chapter Eight).

2:11–3:12 An exhortation on the obligation of Christians. A long parenetical
section dealing with the relation of Christians as strangers and resident
aliens to the outside Gentile world. It begins with an emphasis on maintaining good conduct among the outsiders (2:11–12) and moves to the
necessity for accepting the authority of earthly rulers (2:13–17). In this latter passage we see the practical necessity for Christians to adjust to the real-
ities of life in the world. As the author of Luke-Acts addresses the subject
of the Christian's relationship to the Empire, so the author of 1 Peter finds
it necessary to speak to the Christian's relationship to institutions of
authority. Next the writer turns to a household code, a summary of duties
and responsibilities (2:13–3:7). Here the code itself becomes the basis for
homiletical development.

A feature of this development is the use of Isaiah 53. Let us compare
1 Peter 2:21–25 with Isaiah 53.

1 Peter 2:21–25	Isaiah 53
21) ... (Christ) ...also suffered for you, leaving you an example, so that that you should follow his steps.	4) ...he has borne our infirmities....
22) Who did no sin neither was guile found in his mouth.	9) ...he had done no violence, and there was no deceit in his mouth.
23) When he was abused, he did not return abuse; when he suffered, he did not threaten; but he entrusted himself to the one that judges justly;	7) He was oppressed, and he was afflicted, yet he did not open his mouth; like a sheep that before its shearers is silent..., so he did not open his mouth.
24) He himself bore our sins in his body upon the cross, so that, free from sins, we might live for righteousness; by his wound you have been healed.	11) he shall bear their iniquities (compare 4-6) 5) by his bruise we were healed
25) For you were going astray like sheep...	6) all we like sheep have gone astray

The parallels are too close to be accidental. 1 Peter 2:21–25 is a meditation upon Isaiah 53 as fulfilled in the crucifixion of Jesus.

3:13–4:6 Further exhortation. This passage deals in general with Christians
preparing to suffer for their faith, and in their prospective suffering to
follow the example of Christ. The passion of Jesus as an example for individual Christians to follow in their suffering is a major theme of the liter-

ature of the early church concerning martyrdom, and it is prominent in this passage. We have noted the strong possibility that there are Christological hymns and confessions in this section.

4:7–11 The End is at hand. The section climaxes on the note of anticipation of the parousia, but even this is interwoven with parenesis.

4:12–5:11 THE SUFFERING PARENESIS.

The suffering that was thought of as prospective in the first section has now become sharper. The writer exhorts his readers to stand fast and reiterates many themes.

5:12–14 CLOSING GREETINGS.

Mark, Sylvanus, and Babylon are mentioned.

THE LETTER OF JAMES

Church Tradition about James

In this "letter" James is said to be "a servant of God and of the Lord Jesus Christ" writing "to the twelve tribes in the Dispersion" (1:1). Who is this James? The son of Zebedee, the disciple of Jesus (Mark 1:19)? The son of Alphaeus, another disciple of Jesus (Mark 3:18)? James, the son of Mary (Mark 15:40)? The father of Judas (Luke 6:16; Acts 1:13)? Some unknown James? Later church tradition (Eusebius *Ecclesiastical History* 2.23.4) identified him with James, the brother of Jesus (Mark 6:3) who became the conservative leader at Jerusalem (Gal 1:19; 2:9, 12; 1 Cor 15:7; Acts 12:17; 15:13). No doubt this person is meant. Is it accurate?

Historical Criticism

The book of James begins with greetings (1:1) and contains direct address (1:2–5, 16, 19; 2:1, 5, and so on), but it is formally not a letter. Rather, it is a collection of moral maxims that focus on ethical exhortation or encouragement. In its 108 verses are 54 verbs that command in the imperative! Thus, James is parenesis.

Parenesis, or moral exhortation, is a common feature of the literature of the ancient world—Hellenistic, Jewish, and Christian. "Household codes" existed in Hellenistic moral philosophy and were borrowed by Christians. Proverbs and practical wisdom were borrowed from the Jews. There were also in the New Testament collections of ethical teachings ascribed to Jesus in the gospels (especially Matthew's Sermon on the Mount) and the parenetical sections of the Pauline and deutero-Pauline letters. Thus, there was a strong tradition of moral exhortation in the Christian environment and within the Christian movement that often borrowed from it, though Christianity also developed its own.

The existence of a vigorous Christian parenetical tradition is important for understanding James. One consequence is that verbal similarities between James and other New Testament texts do not mean that James necessarily knows those texts; they may have depended on a common oral tradition.

The book of James contains sayings that are ascribed to Jesus in the gospels, especially in the Matthean Sermon on the Mount. In James, however, they are not ascribed to Jesus. Compare the following:

James	Gospels
James 1:5, 17: If any of you is lacking in wisdom, ask God, who gives to all generously and ungrudgingly, and it will be given you. . . . Every generous act of giving, with every perfect gift, is from above, coming down from the Father of lights, with whom there is no variation or shadow due to change.	**Matt 7:7–12:** "Ask, and it will be given you; search, and you will find; knock, and the door will be opened for you. For everyone who asks receives, and everyone who searches finds, and for everyone who knocks, the door will be opened. Is there anyone among you who, . . . "
James 1:6: But ask in faith, never doubting, for the one who doubts is like a wave of the sea, driven and tossed by the wind. . . .	**Mark 11:23–24:** "Truly I tell you, if you say to this mountain, 'Be taken up and thrown into the sea,' and if you do not doubt in your heart, but believe that what you say will come to pass, it will be done for you. So I tell you, whatever you ask for in prayer, believe that you have received it, and it will be yours."
James 1:22: But be doers of the word, and not merely hearers who deceive themselves.	**Matt 7:24–27:** "Everyone then who hears these words of mine and acts on them will be like a wise man who built his house on rock. The rain fell, the floods came, and the winds blew and beat on that house, but it did not fall, because it had been founded on rock. And everyone who hears these words of mine and does not act on them will be like a foolish man who built his house on sand. The rain fell, and the floods came, and the winds blew and beat against that house, and it fell—and great was its fall!"

James 4:12: There is one lawgiver and judge who is able to save and to destroy. So who, then, are you to judge your neighbor?

Matt 7:1 "Do not judge, so that you may not be judged."

James 5:12: Above all, my beloved, do not swear, either by heaven or by earth or by any other oath,

Matt 5:33–37 "Again, you have heard that it was said to those of ancient times, 'You shall not swear falsely, but carry out the vows you have made to the Lord.' But I say to you, Do not swear at all, either by heaven, for it is the throne of God, or by the earth, for it is his footstool, or by Jerusalem, for it is the city of the Great King. And do not swear by your head, for you cannot make one hair white or black. Let your word by 'Yes, Yes' or 'No, No'; anything more than this comes from the evil one.

but let your "Yes" be yes and your "No" be no, so that you may not fall under condemnation.

There is also parenetical material similar to that in 1 Peter:

James

1 Peter

James 1:2–3: My brothers and sisters, whenever you face *trials of any kind,* consider it nothing but joy, because you know that *the testing of your faith produces endurance;* . . .

1 Peter 1:6–7: In this you rejoice, even if now for a little while you have had to suffer *various trials,* so that *the genuineness of your faith—* being more precious than gold that, though perishable, is tested by fire—may be found to result in praise and glory and honor when Jesus Christ is revealed.

James 4:1–2: Those conflicts and disputes among you, where do they come from? Do they not come from your *cravings that are at war within you?* You want something and do not have it; so you commit murder. And you covet something and cannot obtain it; so you engage in disputes and conflicts. You do not have, because you do not ask.

1 Peter 2:11: Beloved, I urge you as aliens and exiles to abstain from the *desires of the flesh that wage war against the soul.*

Again, it is not that James necessarily knows the gospels or 1 Peter, but rather that there is a Christian parenetical tradition into which sayings ascribed to Jesus in the gospels have been taken up, although not in the form of sayings of Jesus.

A further feature of James, as incidentally also of 1 Peter, is that the author uses Hellenistic Greek literary rhetorical devices. There are plays on words: 4:14, "That appears for a little time and then vanishes" (Greek: *phainomenē/aphanizomenē*); 1:1–2, "greeting/joy" *(chairein/charan);* 2:4, "made distinctions/become judges" *(diekrithēte/kritai);* and others. There is alliteration: 1:2, "you meet various trials" *(peirasmois/peripesēte/poikilois);* 3:5, "little member/great things" *(mikron/melos/megala).* James also uses the Hellenistic literary device of the diatribe, which is characteristic of parenetic literature. This device presents an argument in the form of a dialogue between the writer and an imaginary interlocutor (2:18–26; 5:13–15). It also has a number of aphorisms, a form also characteristic of Jesus' teaching.

Yet, James has almost nothing distinctively Christian about it. Jesus Christ is mentioned only twice (1:1; 2:1), and both verses could be omitted without any harm to the flow of thought in the text. When the "coming of the Lord" is mentioned (5:7) there is nothing to denote the specifically Christian hope of the parousia. It could equally be a reference to the coming of the Lord God. "Faith" in this text is not specifically Christian faith but rather the acceptance of monotheism (2:19). These facts have led some scholars to suggest that the text is a Jewish homily lightly Christianized. Yet, some features seem to favor Christian origin, especially the evidence of contacts with Christian parenetical tradition already noted and the discussion of the Pauline "faith" and "works" in 2:14–26, which seems to presuppose Galatians 3 and Romans 4. The discussion of faith and works in James 2:14–26 caused Martin Luther to contrast James unfavorably with the main texts in the New Testament as "a right strawy epistle in comparison with them, for it has no gospel character to it" (Introduction to his German New Testament, 1522).

The author's use of Hellenistic Greek rhetorical devices, his lack of specific references to Jesus, and his tendency not to exhibit the conservatism about the Jewish Law we know to have been characteristic of Jesus' brother pose problems for the identification of the author as James. Moreover, if the issue of faith versus works (2:14–26) echoes Paul, which is very likely, a date at least a generation after Paul suggests itself, and this does not easily comport with various traditions claiming that James was martyred in the 60s (Josephus *Antiquities* 20.9 197–203; Eusebius *Ecclesiastical History* 2.23–4–18).

A final problem is that the book was not widely known until it was popularized by the Church Father Origen in the third century C.E. By that time other pseudonymous books circulated under the name James, some of which can be found in the New Testament Apocrypha, for example, the Protoevangelium of James and the Acts of James. It is not impossible that the author of James developed some traditions that came from James, Jesus' brother, or that he thought that his traditions came from James, but that does not add conviction that James actually wrote the work. Thus, most scholars are convinced that it is pseudonymous.

Structure

James defies the categories of our approach to the New Testament in more ways than one. Not only is it purely parenetical; it also has no obvious structure. It moves from theme to theme, making connections by the association of ideas or catchwords. The insights we used in our structural analysis of other texts in the New Testament simply do not apply to the homily of James.

Exegetical Survey

1:1 ADDRESS.
James, God's servant, addresses the twelve tribes (true Israel) in the Diaspora, that is, all Christians.

1:2–18 INITIAL EXHORTATIONS.
James calls on the reader to remain joyful and steadfast under persecution, which leads to perfection (1:2–4), to pray with wisdom and faith (1:5–7), and to boast of poverty, not riches. The stress on poverty may have spiritual overtones, but is fundamentally economic. James stresses the downfall of the rich, thus reversing worldly human values (see 2:1–12, 4:13–16, 5:1–6). "Faith" means stability without doubt; passion leads to sin and death.

1:19–27 BOTH HEAR AND DO THE WORD OF GOD AND BRIDLE ONE'S TONGUE.
True religion is caring for orphans and widows, and maintaining purity from worldly defilement.

2:1–12 SHOW NO PARTIALITY, BUT FULFILL THE ROYAL LAW OF LOVE.
The literal poor are spiritually rich. Honor the poor, not the rich. The royal law: "You shall love your neighbor as yourself" (2:8 [Lev 19:18]; compare Mark 12:31; Gal 5:14). For Paul's view of the impossibility of keeping the whole law, see Galatians 5:3.

2:13 THE NECESSITY OF MERCY.
This verse is attached by a catchword to the preceding (Prov 14;21; Tob 4:10).

2:14–26 FAITH WITHOUT WORKS IS DEAD.
This passage presents the central theme on which the exhortations are based. It is concerned either to contest the Pauline doctrine of "justification by faith" or, more probably, to argue against an extreme interpretation of that view, one that denied the necessity for "works" at all. To be sure, Paul and James see "faith" in very different terms. For Paul faith is a dynamic relationship to the risen Lord allowing human beings to appropriate that which God has wrought through Jesus. For James faith is subscription to a sound monotheism. The two views could scarcely be further apart within the same tradition. Paul himself would never have denied the importance of works, as his parenetic sections show, especially when freedom led to moral excesses; faith had to have consequences. Yet, in his struggles with the Judaizers, Paul declared that works of the law were insufficient for salvation and thus the emphasis on them, symbolized by circumcision, misplaced. In James, however, the tables are turned. Here the author argues against the libertarians of his own day. Thus, the book of James exposes the early stages of institutional Christianity. There can be no direct comparison between James

and Paul because they come from different periods in New Testament history and correspondingly different social contexts.

3:1–12 WATCH YOUR TONGUE.
After a statement about the honorable role of teacher, the section exhorts: guard your tongue, the potential damage of which is disproportionate to its size (compare 1:19).

3:13–18 EARTHLY AND HEAVENLY WISDOM.
Abandon earthly wisdom and seek heavenly wisdom (compare 1:5; 1 Cor 1–4).

4:1–10 FRIENDSHIP WITH GOD VERSUS FRIENDSHIP WITH THE WORLD.
Avoid the conflicts brought on by the passion within and seek the peace that comes only from God.

4:11–12 AGAINST JUDGING YOUR NEIGHBOR.
Do not speak evil against, or judge, one another.

4:13–16 AGAINST ARROGANT PLANNING.
The business plans of rich, arrogant merchants who place commercial life first will be subject to God.

4:17 DOING RIGHT.
Appended by catchword: the failure to do right is a sin.

5:1–6 WARNINGS TO THE RICH.
Woes upon the rich who defraud and oppress their laborers.

5:7–11 PATIENT SUFFERING.
Be patient until the coming of the lord (the delay of the parousia theme). The judgment of God is imminent.

5:12 AGAINST SWEARING OATHS
(compare Matt 5:33–37).

5:13–18 THE HEALING POWER OF PRAYER.

5:19–20 BE CONCERNED FOR THE ERRING BROTHER
James has no formal conclusion.

THE PASTORAL LETTERS: 1 TIMOTHY, 2 TIMOTHY, TITUS

These three letters are known as the Pastoral Letters because, like a shepherd who cares for his sheep, they exhibit a serious, but sometimes affectionate, concern for churches, their leaders, and their ministry. They are purportedly written by Paul to individuals known from the Pauline letters, Timothy and Titus.

Timothy and Titus

Timothy is mentioned as coauthor and close companion with Paul in the greetings of both Pauline and deutero-Pauline letters (1 Thess 1:1; 2 Cor 1:1 ["our brother"]; Phil 1:1 ["slaves of Christ"]; Phlm 1 ["our brother"]; compare 2 Thess 1:1; Col 1:1 ["our brother"]). Paul sent his "brother" Timothy to Thessalonica from Athens, and he had reported back, probably to Corinth (1 Thess 3:1–5; see Chapters Six, Seven). He was also sent from Ephesus to Corinth to remind the Corinthians of Paul's "ways" (1 Cor 4:17; 16:10–11). It is implied that Timothy had preached to the Corinthians (2 Cor 1:19). Paul also said that he would send Timothy to Philippi and in passing told of his trust and very deep respect for Timothy (Phil 2:19–24). Since Philippians is a "prison letter," this remark implied that Timothy was with Paul in prison, perhaps in Ephesus (compare Phil 1:1). Acts fills in some details: Timothy met up with Paul in his hometown Lystra in southern Galatia and had a Greek father and a Jewish mother (compare 2 Tim 1:5: his mother is named Eunice, his grandmother Lois). According to Acts, Paul had him circumcised because of Jews in the area of Lystra and Derbe (Acts 16:1–3), and he then traveled with Paul (Acts 17:14–15; 18:5; 19:22; 20:4). Hebrews 13:23 also says "our brother Timothy has been set free."

Titus was also a trusted companion and emissary of Paul's. He was a Gentile convert whom Paul used as an example of one not compelled to be circumcised by the pillars at the Jerusalem Conference (Gal 2:1, 3). Titus was sent to Corinth to help inaugurate the collection for the poor among the saints at Jerusalem (2 Cor 8:5–6, 16–24; 12:18; compare 9:2). After Paul's "painful visit" to the Corinthians, he was sent to Corinth with a letter, probably the "tearful letter" (2 Cor 2:3–4; 7:6–8), and on this occasion he reported back to the anxious Paul in Macedonia that tensions between Paul and the Corinthians had eased (3:13; 7:6–16, esp. 7:6, 13–14). Nothing about Titus is reported in the book of Acts.

Church Traditions about the Pastorals

The first reference to the composition of the Pastorals is not until the Muratorian Canon, probably about 200 C.E. from Rome. It says that Paul wrote ".... one [letter] to Titus, but two to Timothy for the sake of affection and love." Apart from this reference, it is necessary to ask whether the Pastorals were quoted earlier in the century. There is a bit of parallel language between the Pastorals and Polycarp, who wrote before he was martyred about 155/156 C.E. (compare *Martyrdom of Polycarp*). However, it is also possible that they simply shared oral or written traditions. Otherwise, we do not find certain quotations from the Pastorals before Irenaeus' *Against Heresies* about 185 C.E. Other Church Fathers accept them in the early third century and eventually they were included in the all-important *Festal Letter* of Athanasius in 367 C.E. They are also found in the important Codex Sinaiticus from the fourth century.

That the Pastorals do not seem to be mentioned or quoted in the early second century becomes all the more interesting when it is remembered that Marcion's "canon" of Paul's letters about 150 C.E. does not seem to have included them. It is very unlikely that he simply rejected them, as Tertullian says (Tertullian, *Marcion*

5.21), if he knew them. Also, the important papyrus of the Pauline collection, P[46], perhaps as early as 200 C.E., does not have the Pastorals, though it is not impossible that the manuscript was damaged, since it breaks off at 1 Thessalonians 5:5. Finally, when the Muratorian Canon does include them, it places them at the end of the Pauline letters as a sort of appendix.

In short, certain evidence for the Pastorals dates from the late second century C.E. (Irenaeus), just about a generation before the time when they are included in the Muratorian Canon. Even then they are not yet firmly accepted everywhere.

Historical and Literary Criticism of the Pastorals

There are a few interpreters who argue that Paul could have written these letters to Timothy and Titus late in his life when the church was changing, and a few try to solve some of the language and stylistic problems by hypothesizing that he dictated them to a secretary. However, no secretary is mentioned in the Pastorals and, more importantly, where Paul uses a secretary elsewhere (1 Cor 16:21; Gal 6:11–18; Rom 16:22), we do not encounter the problems noted below. Thus, the large majority of critical interpreters think that Pauline authorship is impossible on the following grounds:

1. Vocabulary.
While statistics are not always as meaningful as they may seem, of 848 words (excluding proper names) found in the Pastorals, 306 are not in the remainder of the Pauline corpus, even including the deutero-Pauline 2 Thessalonians, Colossians, and Ephesians. Of these 306 words, 175 do not occur elsewhere in the New Testament, while 211 are part of the general vocabulary of Christian writers of the second century. Indeed, the vocabulary of the Pastorals is closer to that of popular Hellenistic philosophy than it is to the vocabulary of Paul or the deutero-Pauline letters. Furthermore, the Pastorals have a special set of theological terms that are not Pauline for example, "piety"; "sound teaching"; "a good conscience"); key Pauline terms are missing ("cross"; "covenant"; "freedom"); and Pauline words are found in a non-Pauline sense (*dikaios* in Paul means "righteous" and here means "upright"; *pistis,* "faith," has become "the body of Christian faith"; and so on).

2. Literary style.
Paul writes a characteristically dynamic Greek, with dramatic arguments, emotional outbursts, and the introduction of real or imaginary opponents and partners in dialogue. In contrast, the Pastorals are written in a quiet meditative style, far more characteristic of Hebrews or 1 Peter, or even of literary Hellenistic Greek in general, than of the Corinthian correspondence or of Romans, to say nothing of Galatians.

3. The situation of the apostle implied in the letters.
According to Titus, Paul has left Titus, behind on the island of Crete to organize the churches (1:5). He would at some time have gone to Ephesus (Titus 1:1; 3:12; compare Acts 20:4; Col 4:7; 2 Tim 4:12). In 1 Timothy, Paul is depicted as hav-

ing written from Macedonia to the younger Timothy (4:11), whom he has left behind in Ephesus to correctly instruct and exhort the people who have taken up false doctrines (1:3), probably Gnostic (6:20–21; compare 1:4). In 2 Timothy Paul is portrayed as imprisoned at Rome (1:8, 16–17; 2:9; compare 1:15–18; 3:10–17; 4:9–18), near death (4:6–8, 18), and he has had a preliminary hearing and most of his friends (except Luke) have abandoned him (4:16–17). He requests that Timothy, who is perhaps in Ephesus (2:17), should come and bring Mark (4:11, 13).

However one construes the sequence of these situations, they can in no way be fitted into any reconstruction of Paul's life and work as we know it from Paul's undisputed letters or the Acts of the Apostles. They can have happened only after his Roman imprisonment (Acts 28), in which case he might have carried out his intentions to go to Spain (Rom 15:24, 28; compare *1 Clement* 5:7; Muratorian Canon; Eusebius *Ecclesiastical History* 2.22.2), and somehow have made it to Crete, Ephesus, Macedonia, and Rome for a second imprisonment (2 Tim). However, the Pastorals mention no "first" imprisonment, and such meager tradition as we have seems to be more a deduction of what must have happened from Paul's plans as detailed in Romans than a reflection of known historical reality.

4. The letters as reflecting the characteristics of emerging institutional Christianity.

The arguments presented above are forceful, but a last consideration is overwhelming, namely, that together with 2 Peter, the Pastorals are the most distinctive representatives of the emphases of emerging institutional Christianity in the New Testament. Thus, we see concerns about doctrine, officers, behavior, church decorum, and the like. We agree with the large majority of scholars: It is highly unlikely that the apostle Paul could have written the Pastorals. They are, therefore, pseudonymous.

Yet, vocabulary, style, viewpoint, and concerns in the three letters are homogeneous enough to make it almost certain that they were written by the same person. The question is why the author chose to write in the name of the apostle Paul. The answer probably is that the author, a third-generation member of the Pauline School, believed himself to have been in the tradition of Paul. Also, the false teachers about whom he warned may have been using Pauline material in their teaching, and he wished to present a true understanding of Paul.

No place for the Pastorals can be documented, though they seem to be related to the Aegean region, that is, the island of Crete (Titus 1:5) and Ephesus (1 Tim 1:3). The affinity of perspective between the Pastorals and 2 Peter, and of language between the Pastorals and second-century Christian literature in general, indicates a probable **date** for these letters somewhere in the first half of the second century, more likely in the first quarter, 100–125 C.E.

"Opponents"

The author warns about those who are interested in "Jewish myths," "commandments" (Titus 1:14), and "quarrels about the law" (Titus 3:9), and in 1 Timothy they desire to be "teachers of the Law" (1:7). All of this sounds Jewish, or at least Jewish Christian: ". . . there are also many rebellious people, idle talkers and deceivers, especially those of the circumcision" (Titus 1:10). However, opponents also "forbid marriage and demand abstinence from foods" (1 Tim 4:3), claim that the resurrection has already taken place (2 Tim 2:18), and presumably are concerned about genealogies (Titus 3:9). This sounds somewhat more like Gnosticism, and there is also the comment, "Avoid the profane chatter and contradictions of what is falsely called knowledge" (*gnōsis;* 1 Tim 6:20). Clearly there are tensions and they may have been intensified by widows who chose celibacy as a means to freedom, especially when some of the Gnostic groups perpetuated this lifestyle. Thus, either we have indications of a kind of Jewish Christian Gnosticism, or there are several irreconcilable views that pious Christians should avoid.

Social-Historical Context of the Pastorals

The Pastorals reveal several interrelated concerns. The various recommendations show that the author wants to put on a good face for the rest of society: the bishop, for example, must "be well thought of by outsiders" (1 Tim 3:7). The church is also threatened internally, as the section on opponents has just indicated. All of this leads to a focus on order, to which we now turn.

In Chapter Eight we said that the large Greco-Roman family household with its "household code" was a pattern of social organization behind the deutero-Pauline literature and 1 Peter. You will recall that traditional male-dominated, authoritarian family structures were thought to be necessary to preserve a stable social and political order. The head of the family or head of the household (*paterfamilias*) ruled, and order was achieved primarily from three principles:

> wives subject to husbands,
> children subject to parents,
> slaves subject to masters.

We also noted that conformity to this code, in contrast with certain innovations of the Baptist and Jesus movements, and to a certain extent the apostle Paul, was typical of the church's growing adaptation to cultural norms, values, and practices, or "enculturation," in the late first and early second centuries (compare Col 3:18–4:1; Eph 5:22–6:9; 1 Pet 2:13–3:7; compare *1 Clement* 21:6–9; *Polycarp To the Philippians* 4:1–6:3; Ignatius *To Polycarp* 4:1–6:1; *Didachē* 4:9–11; *Barnabas* 19:5–7). Finally, we have also discussed in this connection the theme of household hospitality, or gracious reception of visitors, in 3 John (Chapter Twelve).

The family household and its organization is also the most important theme for understanding the social situation of the church in the Pastorals: "...I am writing these instructions to you so that,...you may know how one ought to behave in the household of God, which is the church of the living God...." (1 Tim 3:14–15; compare 2 Tim 2:20). "Do not speak harshly to an older man, but speak to him as to a father, to younger men as brothers, to older women as mothers, to younger women as sisters—with absolute purity" (1 Tim 5:1–2). The codes about household relationships are also clear in the Pastorals: Women should learn in silence in complete submission, and never teach or have authority over men (1 Tim 2:11–15); older women should train younger women to love their husbands and children and to be good homemakers under control of their husbands (Titus 2:4–5); church leaders should manage their households well and keep their children under control (1 Tim 3:4, 12); slaves should be under the control of their masters, not talk back (Titus 2:9–10), and regard their masters with honor, especially not taking advantage of Christian masters who are "brothers" (1 Tim 6:1–2). This implies on the one hand that some Christian slaves in the group had non-Christian masters, and on the other that master-patrons deserve benefits from their slave-clients. As in 1 Peter, no recommendation is given to masters, perhaps suggesting a worsening position of slaves in the social setting of some of the churches.

The household model of organization in the Pastorals seems to reflect households of rather large size, influence, and wealth (2 Tim 2:20). Yet, they have social diversity, and thus mirror a cross-section of social strata found in any Hellenistic city. The house must be large enough and the householder well-off enough to have slaves and take care of widows (1 Tim 5:3–8). The wealthy are exhorted not to be haughty or put their trust in riches (6:17–19) and women are warned not to adorn themselves in worship with braided hairstyles, gold ornaments, pearls, and expensive clothes, implying that they were wealthy enough to do so (1 Tim 2:9). There is also evidence that some officers of the church were paid (1 Tim 5:17–18).

The author of the Pastorals emphasizes that the church must be decent and well ordered. In 1 Timothy he describes offices with qualifications: bishop or overseer (*episcopos;* 1 Tim 3:1–7; Titus 1:7–9), deacon (*diakonos;* 1 Tim 3:8–13), elder or presbyter (*presbyteros;* 1 Tim 5:17–25), and apparently also a special group of widows (*chēra;* 1 Tim 5:9–11). A most important question historically is the relationship of the bishop/overseer to the elder/presbyter. By way of background, elders were local leaders in ancient Israel (Josh 24:31; Judg 2:7) and Judaism (the Mishnah; Jerusalem synagogue inscriptions). In the Christianity represented by Acts they, along with the apostles, had decision-making roles at the Apostolic Assembly in Jerusalem (Acts 15:2, 4, 6, 22–23; 16:4). The elder who claims to have written 2 and 3 John also assumed authority. In the Pastorals, there is a council of elders who "lay on the hands," that is, have the power to transfer authority, and it should not be done casually (for example, Num 27:18–23; Deut 34:9; compare Acts 6:6; Acts 13:3; 1 Tim 4:14; 5:22; 2 Tim 1:6). Indeed, "elders who rule," especially "those who labor in preaching and teaching," deserve to be paid (1 Tim 5:17–22). The problem is that their relationship to the bishop/overseer (*episcopos*) is murky. The letter to Titus seems to equate them (Titus 1:5–9), as does 1 Peter 5:1. Yet, 1 Timothy discusses them separately and "bishop" is in the singular (1 Tim 3:2; compare Titus 1:7), suggesting to some interpreters that they have a certain preeminence. Was the bishop/overseer virtually the same as the presbyter/elder? If so, the Pastorals might represent a community in which such offices were in transition and not yet clearly defined (compare *1 Clement*). Another possibility is that there is a modest development from Titus, where they are not distinguished, to 1 Timothy, where they are distinguished, thus suggesting that the bishop was in the process of gaining some preeminence (contrast Phil 1:1; compare Acts 20:28). If so, perhaps he was the the head of the council of elders. In this case, we would see a further development of the bishop's role in *Didachē* 13 and especially in the single "episcopate" of the writings of the Church Father Ignatius of Antioch from about the same time (the monepiscopate). Yet, in the Pastorals there is not yet any hint of an ordained succession of the bishops/presbyters (apostolic succession; compare *1 Clement* 44).

Structure of the Pastorals

The form of the Pastorals as letters must have been a stratagem by the author. They were directed to the church or to churches in a particular area, and the address to individuals known to be companions of Paul is a literary device to lend plausibility. Despite their literary form, like 2 Peter, they are essentially manifestos, written partly in response to the threat of a spreading Gnosticism within the church, partly as an answer to the growing need for organizational structure in the church. Additionally, 2 Timothy approximates a "testament," that is, the last words of an eminent figure, often a father to his son, or a central person to his coworker, in ancitipation of his impending death.

The structure of the Pastorals is simple. The author argues against the false teachers and urges organizational structure on the church. He exhorts "Timothy" or "Titus" to correct behavior and practice as ordained ministers of the church. He characteristically holds up the false teachers as bad examples to avoid and the apostle Paul (according to his literary device, himself) as a good one to follow.

The present order of the Pastorals in the New Testament is probably based on the number of lines in them, that is, from the longest to the shortest. Thus, the longest received the name 1 Timothy. There have been a variety of scholarly attempts to rearrange this order based on considerations of content and chronology. Some have suggested the sequence Titus, 1 Timothy, 2 Timothy, because bishops/elders are not separated in Titus and they are separated in 1 Timothy, and because "Paul" expects his impending death in 2 Timothy. Others place 2 Timothy first because it is more personal and mentions no specific offices, thus giving the following order: no specific offices mentioned (2 Timothy)—> bishops/elders not separated (Titus)—> separation of bishops and elders (1 Timothy). The most important point in this rearrangement is the shift from Titus (no separation of offices) to 1 Timothy (separated offices). There can be no absolute certainty in this matter, especially if we are in a transitional stage with all three letters, but we shall follow the second suggestion and take them up in the order 2 Timothy, Titus, and 1 Timothy. The basic reasons are that 2 Timothy may have been developed first on the basis of either a Pauline fragment about Paul's personal relations with Timothy or the attempt to create this impression, as Luke does in Acts 20. In this chronological sequence, the letters are increasingly less personal and increasingly more concerned with separated offices.

Exegetical Survey of 2 Timothy

1:1–2 ADDRESS AND GREETING.

1:3–5 THANKSGIVING.

1:6–2:13 EXHORTATION TO WITNESS ON THE BASIS OF THE EXAMPLE OF PAUL.
In 1:6, the laying on of hands is a "gift." 1:8 states that Paul is prisoner. Verses 13 and 14 of chapter 1 exhibit the view of Christian faith characteristic of the emerging institutional church. In essence it is the "standard of sound teaching" (1:13),

which was heard from the apostles, and which is to be guarded and followed. Note also 2:2, which stresses preservation of the truth in later generations. 2 Timothy 2:8 alludes to the Christological confession Romans 1:3; the author knows a collection of the Pauline letters.

2:14–4:8 EXHORTATION TO GOOD BEHAVIOR IN ALL RESPECTS.
The author now turns to the behavior expected of the true minister of God. Characteristically, the false teachers are examples to avoid and the apostle Paul an example to follow. In this section we learn more about the false teaching: It is "profane chatter" (2:16); it holds that "the resurrection has already taken place" (2:18); it features "myths" (4:4). We also learn more about the characteristics of the emerging institutional church: It regards its time as the last time, separate from the time of the apostles (3:1; compare Jude 18; 2 Pet 3:3); it is coming to regard Scripture in a very formal way as "inspired by God" and "useful" (3:16).

4:9–18 PAUL'S PERSONAL SITUATION.
This has been constructed to add verisimilitude to the pseudonymity.

4:19–22 CLOSING GREETINGS.

Exegetical Survey of Titus

1:1–4 SALUTATION.

1:5–9 THE ORDAINED MINISTRY.
Titus has been left in Crete to organize the church, and the function of the letter is a guide. This section is not a church order such as we find in 1 Timothy but rather some directions with regard to bishops and elders. As noted above, Titus seems to equate the two offices, whereas 1 Timothy seems to separate them. Yet, there is some commonality with the section on bishops in 1 Timothy 3:1–7. If there is a development in the letters, at the writing of Titus the situation with regard to the relationship between the two offices was still fluid, and separation of the two was only beginning to take place at the time of the writing of 1 Timothy.

1:10–16 AN ATTACK ON THE FALSE TEACHING.
The false teaching apparently had some connection with Crete (1:12) and certainly with Judaism (1:14; compare 1:10). See the section on the opponents above.

2:1–3:7 EXHORTATION TO A PROPER CHRISTIAN BEHAVIOR.
Here are the moral norms of the household and its organization found in emerging institutional Christianity (compare 1 Pet 2:11–3:7). Note also the renewed parousia hope and the description of Jesus as "our great God and Savior" (2:13; compare 2 Pet 1:1).

3:8–11 RENEWED ATTACK ON THE FALSE TEACHING.
The author appears to know Ephesians 2:3–12.

3:12–14 PERSONAL NOTES.

3:15 CLOSING GREETINGS.

Exegetical Survey of 1 Timothy

1:1–2 SALUTATION.

1:3–20 ATTACK ON THE DOCTRINE OF THE FALSE TEACHERS.
The false teaching seems to be a form of early Gnosticism with a strong Jewish element (compare 6:20). The reference to "myths and endless genealogies" (verse 4) would fit the Gnostic tendency to speculate about the hierarchy of heavenly beings, and the reference to the Law in verses 8–9 indicates the Jewish element. Faith in this passage has become a synonym for the Christian religion. In verse 5, "sincere faith" can be read as "sincere profession of the Christian religion" (see also 5:8; 6:10, 21). Moreover, that faith has become a matter of accepting doctrinal propositions (verse 15). All of this is quite different from Paul's view of faith.

2:1–3:16 A CHURCH ORDER: PART ONE.
Reflecting institutional Christianity's concern with the organizational structure of the church, 1 Timothy includes what is to all intents and purposes a church order, divided into two parts, 2:1–3:16 and 4:11–6:19. The first part covers worship in the church (2:1–15) and the ordained ministry (3:1–16).

    2:1–15 Worship in the church. The regulation to pray "for kings and all who are in high positions" and the grounds given for it (2:1–2) reflect the concern of emerging institutional Christianity for accommodation to the larger society outside the church and for the good reputation of Christians in that society. The ideal of good citizenship reflects Hellenistic philosophical values. The section on the subordination of women, that is, charging that they dress modestly in worship, forbidding them to teach, and emphasizing their roles as wives and mothers, is an accommodation to patriarchal values and the household code, although it is also a way of combatting ascetic opponents (compare 1 Tim 4:3–5). Compare 1 Corinthians 14:33b–36, which may have been added to 1 Corinthians on the basis of 1 Timothy 2:11–14.

    3:1–7 The ordained ministry: bishops. The church is the "household of God" and must be orderly. The qualifications for "bishop" are described separately from the qualifications for "elder" (5:17–25). In Titus the two are not clearly distinguished (Titus 1:5–9). Thus, we may be only at the beginning of their separation since in the Church Father Ignatius the bishop has emerged as the chief officer of the local church, especially in charge of worship. The bishop's functions are not absolutely clear in this passage, though he in some way takes care of the household of God (3:5). In Titus the bishop = elder is something like a pastor or minister. Both bishops and deacons are appointed in *Didachē* 15:1 where their ministry is identical with prophets and teachers, while preaching and teaching is connected with elders in 1 Timothy 5:17–23.

3:8–13 The ordained ministry: deacons. The term "deacon" is found in Philippians 1:1 and in Romans 16:1 where a woman Phoebe is called a deacon. It is unclear whether 1 Timothy 3:11 implies women deacons or the wives of deacons. As with the bishop, the qualifications are given, but the precise function of the deacon is not clear; in Acts 6 the deacons appear to be those in charge of the distribution of food for widows, but later in Acts they also preach (Acts 7; 8:4–8, 26–40).

3:14–16 Ethics and Christology. This section climaxes in one of the great New Testament Christological hymns (3:16), no doubt taken by the author from the liturgy of his church. (See Chapter Five.)

4:1–10 AN ATTACK ON THE ETHICS OF THE FALSE TEACHERS.

The writer contrasts the ethics of the false teachers with the behavior expected of the true teacher.

4:11–6:19 A CHURCH ORDER: PART TWO.

4:11–5:2 In the form of instructions to "Timothy" the author develops the **ideal of a Christian minister.** Note that in 4:14 "the laying on of hands by the council of elders" (compare 5:22; 2 Tim 1:6) should not be neglected by "Timothy."

5:3–16 Widows. The author details regulations concerning all widows (5:3–16; compare Polycarp *To the Philippians* 4). The specific qualifications for widow in 5:9–10 in comparison with those of bishop in 1 Timothy (3:2–7, 8–12) suggest that there was an office of "widow" (compare "enrolled" or "put on the list"), as in the letters of Ignatius. If this inner group chose celibacy as a means to freedom (already in 1 Cor 7:8–9, 25–38?), there was tension between their office and the other widows who were charged to conform to patriarchal models.

5:17–25 Elders. In Acts and probably in Titus the "elder" appears to be the same as the "bishop" (Acts 20:17, 28; Titus 1:5–9; *1 Clement* 44, too?), but now qualifications for elders are discussed separately (5:17–22; compare 3:1–7). They rule and are especially responsible for preaching and teaching (5:17); they are worthy of pay (possibly implied by "double honor" and certainly implied by the Scriptural reference; compare 1 Cor 9:9; Luke 10:7 [Deut 25:4]). In 4:14 a council of elders has the power to lay on hands; here, elders should not lay on the hands hastily (compare 2 Tim 1:6).

6:1–2 Slaves. Slaves are warned to honor their masters, and not to take advantage of masters who are also Christian brothers. Compare Titus 2:9–10.

6:3–16 Further instructions to the ideal minister. Avoid false teachers and act in a pious way.

6:17–19 Exhortations to the rich.

6:20–21 CONCLUSION.

Even in his concluding greeting the author continues his polemic against the false teachers. The reference to "what is falsely called knowledge (Greek: *gnōsis*)" strengthens the case that the false teaching was a form of Gnosticism.

THE LETTER OF JUDE

The author calls himself Jude, the "brother of James" (1:1). Unless "brother of James" was added, for which there is no textual evidence, this ascription would make him also the brother of Jesus, or Judas (Mark 6:3 = Matt 13:55: compare 1 Cor 9:5), not the apostle Jude, son of James (Luke 6:16; Acts 1:13; compare John 14:22: "Judas, not the Iscariot").

Church Tradition and Historical Criticism of Jude

Clement and Origen, both of Alexandria, followed later by Eusebius, listed Jude among the "disputed books" (Clement in Eusebius *Ecclesiastical History* 6.14.1; 6.13.6; 3.25). Gradually, however, church tradition accepted it and it appears in the Muratorian canon of about 200 C.E. and Athanasius' *Festal Letter* of 367 C.E.

There are problems with this ascription of authorship. The letter looks back on the time of the apostles as in the past (verses 17–18), and this, together with features of fine Greek, citation of several apocryphal sources, and especially emerging institutional Christianity make authorship by Jude impossible. The letter is pseudonymous, as is all the literature of the emergent institutional church in the New Testament. While the identity of opponents suggests Asia Minor, the place of composition cannot be known with any certainty. The outer limit for Jude's date is indicated by its incorporation into 2 Peter (see below). Its thought represents institutional Christianity. Thus, it was probably written sometime between 100 and 125 C.E.

"Opponents"

The letter of Jude is mainly a polemic against a group of opponents who seem to have been at one time outsiders (verse 4), but are now insiders creating dissidence within the church (verses 4, 12, 18, 23). They are accused of all manner of vices (flattery, gluttony, greediness, godlessness, licentiousness, ignorance, sexual deviance, grumbling, and so on); as such, they fulfill prophecies about ungodliness before the End (verses 14–15). Yet, they claim to be Christians and participate in the cultic meals of the community (verse 12). Who are they?

Identification of these opponents is very difficult, especially because the vices listed are general and very typical of such ethical lists in antiquity, and they are not explained further. Moreover, the writer does not rationally argue against them, which might clarify them, but simply denounces them, calls them names, and threatens them with dire examples of punishment from the Scriptures. They were certainly libertarians; despising the world of the flesh, they saw no fault in abandoning themselves to fleshly practices (verses 7–8). Perhaps they were early Gnostics because they considered themselves to be superior to the angelic powers (vs. 8: "the glorious ones"); this would be consistent with the word used of them in verse 19, *psychikoi,* a technical term used by Gnostics (compare 1 Cor 2:14).

The most interesting features of this letter are the characteristics of emerging institutional Christianity it exhibits. The letter speaks of "the faith that was once for all entrusted to the saints" (1:3); faith is the acceptance of authoritative tradition, and the writer denounces the heretics and admonishes the faithful on the authority of that tradition. There is also evidence of a developing Christian liturgy. In verses 20–21, "...pray in the Holy Spirit; keep yourselves in the love of God; look forward to the mercy of our Lord Jesus Christ" testifies to the liturgical development of a trinitarian formula. The closing doxology (verses 24–25) is a magnificent piece of liturgical language, so different in style and tone from the remainder of the letter that the writer has probably taken it from the liturgy of his church.

Structure

This polemical letter is an invective piece that defies structural analysis beyond the obvious fact that it opens with a greeting and closes with a doxology. The writer simply denounces the heretics and warns his readers against them.

Exegetical Survey of Jude

1–2 ADDRESS AND SALUTATION.

3–4 THE EMERGENCE OF FALSE TEACHERS.
It becomes an urgent necessity to contend for the faith that was once and for all delivered to the saints.

5–7 SCRIPTURAL INSTANCES OF SIN AND PUNISHMENT.
The writer warns his readers that God punishes sin, using as examples the traditions of God punishing the unfaithful Israelites in the wilderness (compare 1 Cor 10:1–11; Heb 3:7–4:11), the fate of the rebellious angels (Gen 6), and of Sodom and Gomorrah (Gen 19). The reference to the fallen angels seems to exhibit an awareness of how this myth was developed in the apocalyptic works *Enoch, Jubilees,* and *2 Baruch.*

8–16 DENUNCIATION OF THE FALSE TEACHERS.
The reference to the archangel Michael in verse 9 is a reference to a legend in an apocalyptic work, the *Assumption of Moses,* where Michael digs a grave to bury Moses, and Satan appears and unsuccessfully claims the body. Cain (Gen 4) and Balaam (Num 22–24) figure prominently in both Jewish and Christian tradition. Korah led a rebellion against Moses (Num 16:1–11). "Love feasts" are a form of the Christian sacred meal in which the cultic aspect was blended into a regular communal meal. In Corinth, and no doubt elsewhere, this blending led to excesses and loss of the cultic aspect (compare 1 Cor 11:20–22), and the communal meals were eventually separated from the cultic Eucharist. The reference to the wandering stars is from the apocalyptic book of *Enoch.* The quote in verses 14–15 is from Enoch 1:9.

17–23 EVILS OF HERETICS CONTRASTED WITH ATTITUDES REQUIRED OF THE FAITHFUL.
If verse 19 is a quotation, we do not know its source. It may represent the author's understanding of apostolic teaching and is notably apocalyptic in tone.

24–25 CLOSING DOXOLOGY.

Jude's Use of Apocalyptic Texts

A remarkable aspect of Jude is its use of apocalyptic texts. You will recall that apocalyptic flourished in both Judaism and Christianity throughout the New Testament period, and its Jewish and Christian forms were closely related. Jude is eloquent testimony to this relation because its author is aware of the myth of the fallen angels in Jewish apocalyptic in general, and he knows the myth of the burial of Moses from a Jewish-Christian apocalypse, the *Assumption of Moses*. He also alludes to a major apocalyptic work, the book of *Enoch,* in the matter of the wandering stars, and he explicitly quotes *Enoch* 1:9. His own understanding of apostolic faith is notably apocalyptic. The letter shows that apocalyptic, revitalized in the late first century (Revelation), is still a living force in the period of emerging institutionalism. Nevertheless, when Jude is reused in 2 Peter 2, the author of 2 Peter removes all references and allusions to apocalyptic works that were excluded from the Jewish canon of Scripture.

THE SECOND LETTER OF PETER

Peter, Church Tradition, and Historical Criticism of 2 Peter

We have given information about Peter, the first letter attributed to him, 1 Peter, and the Petrine School above. There is no church tradition about 2 Peter in the second century; indeed, the first to mention 2 Peter explicitly is Origen (217–51 C.E.) who places it among the "disputed books" (*Commentary on John* 5:3 in Eusebius, *Ecclesiastical History* 6.25), and the early Fourth Century Eusebius also has this judgment (*Ecclesiastical History* 3.25.3). Also, in the fourth century Jerome notes the doubts of many but accepts it. It is included in Athanasius' *Festal Letter* of 367 C.E. Yet, some churches still rejected it in the fifth century.

Modern scholars doubt that Peter wrote 2 Peter, despite its emphatic claims to the contrary (1:1, 18; 3:15). There are a number of reasons. 2 Peter explicitly mentions 1 Peter (2 Pet 3:1) and Jude 4–16 is incorporated into 2 Peter 2 (see Chapter Four and below). The writer knows the synoptic gospel account of the transfiguration (1:17–18) and the letters of Paul as a collection and as Scripture (3:15–16). The first generation of Christians has died (2:2). All of this points to a date in the early second century, many years after Peter's martyrdom. Moreover, 2 Peter, together with the Pastorals, is the most thoroughgoing representation in the New Testament of the views of emerging institutional Christianity in the early second century. This evidence makes it impossible for the apostle Peter to have written it, and it is universally recognized among critical scholars as pseudonymous. Its author is probably the latest of all the New Testament writers, and a date about 125 C.E. (some place it as late as 140 C.E.) would be appropriate.

Social Context of 2 Peter

The church to which this "letter" is written is pluralistic, that is, it contains Christians of both Jewish and Greek background. It has a number of references to ideas in the Bible that are paralleled in Greco-Roman literature, and several Greek concepts. Such features of the work suggest a Hellenistic, erudite urban setting, which corresponds to its stress on institutional features.

Literary Character, Contents, and Structure of 2 Peter

This "letter" has a double purpose: to reiterate the hope for the parousia against a growing skepticism (3:4) and to combat false teachers in the church. The two have a single root in that the false teachers were probably Christian Gnostics who emphasized knowledge of salvation now and eventual translation to the heavenly sphere, despised the world and the body, and therefore had no concern for a future parousia. The sheer passage of time and the continuing delay of the parousia had undoubtedly sharpened their polemic against the traditional Christian hope.

2 Peter is written in very good Greek, but in a style quite different from 1 Peter. Although it has an opening greeting, it has no further literary characteristics of a letter. Its main text is a manifesto, a strong statement of what the author regards as correct and authoritative teaching against false and disruptive teaching in the church. It opens with a greeting we would find in a Christian letter, but the greeting, like the pseudonymity, is characteristic of emerging institutional Christianity itself.

The structure of 2 Peter is simple.
Address and Salutation, 1:1–2
Exhortation to holiness, 1:3–21
    1:3–11 Exhortation.
    1:12–18 The certainty of the promise is grounded in the
       revelation the apostle encountered.
    1:19–21 An appeal to scriptural prophecy.
Attack upon the false teachers, 2:1–22
True teaching concerning the day of the Lord, 3:1–10
Parenesis and concluding doxology, 3:11–18

Exegetical Survey of 2 Peter

1:1–2 SALUTATION.
The salutation is important for an understanding of the author's viewpoint and the emerging institutional Christianity he represents. It sees faith as something originally obtained by the apostles and now available to those who stand in succession to them.

1:3–21 EXHORTATION TO HOLINESS.
    1:3–11 Exhortation. Note the characteristic Hellenistic emphasis on the corruption of the world and on escaping it to partake of the divine nature (verse

4). It is only a short step from this to the Gnosticism of the false teachers. The list of virtues in verses 5, 6, and 7 is a Christianization of the kind of virtue lists popular in the Hellenistic world. Verse 11 represents a Hellenizing of much earlier Christian language about "entering the Kingdom of God."

1:12–18 The certainty of the promise. The certainty of the promise is grounded in the revelation encountered by the apostles. This is a difficult passage, but its general meaning seems clear. The apostles were eyewitnesses to the transfiguration of Jesus and so eyewitnesses of his majesty—that is, they saw him partake of the divine nature on one occasion in anticipation of the moment after his resurrection when he would partake of it fully. Having been granted this vision, the apostles can testify to the reality of the promise that Christians also will one day partake of that divine nature.

1:19–21 An appeal to scriptural prophecy. The promise is also guaranteed by the Scriptures. All Scripture, not only particular books or passages, is understood as prophecy and a very high, albeit somewhat mechanical, view of the inspiration of Scripture is presented. In such a view the question of canonicity is crucial, and we shall see that 2 Peter is in fact our earliest witness to the development of a definite, distinct, and limited view of the canon of Christian Scripture.

2:1–22 ATTACK ON THE FALSE TEACHERS.

This section is based on Jude 4–16 (see Chapter Four). It portrays the false teachers in Jude's language and uses many of his examples. It is interesting that 2 Peter purges Jude of all references to works outside the canonical Scriptures, as the Jewish canon was by this time coming to be defined. Jude has a reference to the myth of the burial of Moses from the *Assumption of Moses,* an allusion to the book of *Enoch* in the reference to the wandering stars, and a quotation from Enoch 1:9. The myth of the burial of Moses, the wandering stars, and the quotation are all missing in 2 Peter. It is not that the author of 2 Peter has an objection to apocalyptic; far from it. His objection is apparently to the use of books now regarded as suspect insofar as a canon was developing among the Jews and as it should be accepted by Christians.

3:1–10 TRUE TEACHING CONCERNING THE DAY OF THE LORD.

This section begins with a renewal of the pseudonymous claim to Petrine authorship, which is at the same time a recognition that, for the writer, 1 Peter was already achieving the status of Scripture (verse 1). It continues with a clear recognition of the sacredness of the apostolic age, which is now past (verse 2). The present of the writer is separated from that age as "the last days" (verse 3; compare Jude 17–18, where we have exactly the same distinction between the apostolic age and "the last time"). The scoffing of the false teachers is met by claiming that God's time is different from human time and that the parousia is imminent in God's time and certain in human time. It is an ingenious argument, but it loses the dynamic of the imminence of the parousia in Mark or of the attempt to make theological sense of the delay of the parousia in Matthew or Luke. Verse 10 represents a theme known to us from the synoptic gospels (Matt 24:43 = Luke 12:39) and from 1 Thessalonians 5:2, except that it is considerably embellished.

3:11–18 PARENESIS AND CONCLUDING DOXOLOGY.

The most interesting element in this concluding passage is the reference to Paul's letters. In verses 15–17 they are clearly known as a collection and regarded as "Scripture." We are approaching a Christian canon that excludes Jewish apocalyptic works that the Jews themselves were excluding from their canon and that includes Christian writings. The Christian writings embrace at least the synoptic gospels (see 2 Pet 1:17 and its reference to the transfiguration—this is scriptural because 2 Peter does not use nonscriptural material in this way), 1 Peter (see 2 Pet 3:1), and a collection of the letters of Paul. Another important aspect of these references is the characterization of the letters of Paul as "hard to understand, which the ignorant and unstable twist to their own destruction..." (verse 16). This seems to imply that the false teachers the author is directing his polemic against are using the letters of Paul, or some aspects of them, as a basis for their position. The remainder of this passage is parenesis based on reiterating the expectation of the "day of the Lord" in 3:1–10.

THE CHARACTERISTICS OF THE EMERGING INSTITUTIONAL CHURCH

Self-Definition

There is a great deal of labeling, or name-calling, in the literature of the growing institutional church. Opponents in the Pastorals are accused of being greedy, deceptive, quibblers, sayers but not doers, full of vices, and appealing to women. In Jude we find libertarian heretics with traditional vices denounced, condemned for despising the world of the flesh, and reviled for considering themselves to be superior to the angelic powers. In 2 Peter the opponents are said to emphasize knowledge of salvation now and eventual translation to the heavenly sphere, and to despise the world and the body. Much of this sort of labeling is known from contemporary denunciations of "sophists" by other philosophers. This makes it difficult to establish concrete groups. Yet, we have indicated above that we may be encountering early stages of what became in the second century the Gnostic heresy. What is clear is that the institutional churches are in the process of self-definition over against those they believe to be heretics. This move toward orthodoxy, of course, eventually affected the choice of books in the New Testament canon itself.

The Apostolic Tradition

Another obvious characteristic of the emerging institutional church is its concern for the apostolic age and its reliance on the idea of apostolic tradition as a way of combatting its opponents. The church is now separated from the age of the apostles by a considerable period, and the tendency is to look back on that time as one of perfection, as the golden age of the church, as the time of revelation by God through Jesus to the church in the persons of the apostles. This process begins in the legends of the early church in the Acts of the Apostles, but the author of Luke-Acts himself stresses the parallels between that heroic age and that of his readers, thus blurring the distance in time between them. The writers in this period, however, characteristically see themselves and their readers as separated from the age of the apostles. That time was the time of revelation and perfection; theirs is the time of apostasy, of falling away. These are the "last days," and they are days of trial and corruption (Jude 17–18; 2 Pet 3:3; 2 Tim 3:1–5).

In many respects this understanding is strikingly parallel to the apocalyptic writers' understanding their days as the last days of a history hastening to its close. The representatives of the emerging institutional church share the Christian apocalyptic hope of the parousia. Yet, there is an important difference. The apocalyptic writers look to the future *and live out of that future;* the representatives of the emerging institutional church look to the future *but live out of the past,* the past of the apostolic age. An apocalyptic writer's expectation of the future dominates everything; a representative of emerging institutional Christianity, such as the author of 2 Peter, has an expectation of the future but is dominated by the past of the apostolic age, and the tradition that is believed to come out of that past.

The concept of an apostolic tradition is, therefore, essential to emerging institutional Christianity and this tradition must be guaranteed both in its origin and transmission. If it is to carry the authority of the apostles, then the apostles must themselves be the guarantors of the origin of the tradition. But if it is to carry the authority of the apostles into the "last days," there must be a separate agent guaranteeing its purity in transmission. That agent is the Holy Spirit; as the apostles are guarantors of the origin of the tradition, so the Spirit is the guarantor of its transmission (Jude 3; 2 Pet 1:12–18; 2 Tim 1:14).

In such circumstances these writers have a particular way of meeting the false teaching. They do not argue the issues or debate with the false teachers. Instead they confront the teaching and the teachers and, standing squarely on the authority of the apostolic tradition, denounce both as not being in accord with the apostolic truth.

The Concept of Faith

Emerging institutional Christianity conceives of revelation as given in the past, in the apostolic age, and handed on in the church as an object, sacred to be sure, but nonetheless an object. It follows from this that its concept of faith is very different from that of earlier periods of the church's history. It is no longer a belief in the imminent coming of Jesus as Son of Man, nor is it a similarly relationship to the risen Lord; it has become the acceptance of a revealed truth that can be expressed in propositional sentences, that is, creedal statements. It is even a synonym for the Christian religion. The Gospel of Matthew prepares for this with its concept of obedience to a verbal revelation authoritatively interpreted; and Hebrews, where faith is "the assurance of things hoped for, the conviction of things not seen" (Heb 11:1), represents a transitional stage. But in the literature of emerging institutional Christianity, faith becomes the acceptance of authoritative tradition (Jude 20), something originally obtained by the apostles and available to those who stand in true succession to them (2 Pet 1:1–2), and a synonym for the Christian religion (1 Tim 1:5). The key passages are 2 Timothy 1:13–14 with its "standard of sound teaching" to be guarded and passed on; 2 Timothy 2:2 with a similar emphasis; and the propositional statements scattered through the Pastorals that are "sure"—that is, part of the structure of faith, the adjective coming from the same root as the noun "faith" (1 Tim 1:15; 3:1; 4:9; 2 Tim 2:11; Titus 3:8).

The View of "Scripture"

The emphasis on authoritative apostolic tradition and on the Spirit as its guardian leads naturally to a high view of the written deposit of that tradition and of its Jewish counterpart, Scripture. 2 Peter 1:20–21 says that Scripture does not come "by human will, but men and women moved by the Holy Spirit," and 2 Timothy 3:16 says, "All scripture is inspired by God..." This view of Spirit-inspired texts naturally brings with it a concern for defining what constitutes a sacred book and what does not. The concern for a canon is intensified by the beginnings of the Jewish definition of Scriptures in this period (about 90 C.E., at Yavneh) and also by the fact that the Gnostic false teachers depend on their own sacred books, which are often thought to be secret. Motivated by their own high view of Scripture, challenged by the successful Jewish promulgation of a canon and confronted by the necessity for authoritative writings with which to confront the Gnostic false teachers and their secret books, the representatives of the emerging institutional church take the first step toward defining their own Christian canon of Scripture.

The most dramatic example is the contrast between Jude and 2 Peter 2. Jude makes indiscriminate use of the texts the Jews were accepting into their canon— what Christians were to call the Old Testament—and the texts the Jews were rejecting, in this instance apocalyptic texts. Jude is typical of earlier phases of the Christian movement. But when Jude is used as the basis for 2 Peter 2, all reference to anything outside the Jewish canon of Scripture is removed. The author of 2 Peter is paying eloquent testimony to the force of the Jewish example taking significant steps toward a Christian equivalent. This author's treatment of Jude reveals the first Christian writer to accept the Jewish canon of the Old Testament. Similarly, 2 Peter refers to Paul's letters—*precisely* which letters we do not know — as "Scripture" (2 Pet 3:15–16), and in treating the transfiguration of Jesus (2 Pet 1:16–19) and refering to "the second letter I am writing to you" (2 Pet 3:1), the author is also prepared to accept the gospels and 1 Peter as "Scripture."

Enculturation

The church settling down to the task of witnessing in the society around it must necessarily deal with its relations with that society, as the author of Luke-Acts deals with the Roman Empire and its authorities. In the literature of the emerging institutional church, there is a parallel concern for authorities—governors, kings, and the like—and also for the good reputation of Christians and the church among "those outside" (1 Pet 2:11–17; Titus 2:7–8; 3:1–2).

The concern for those outside the church and church order have as their counterpart a focus on accommodation to the established social order and its cultural beliefs, norms, and behavior. The strong stress on the orderly pattern of the household and the ethics of the household codes in the Pastorals provide clear examples of this enculturation. Especially obvious is the adaptation to patriarchal society, that is, the way in which the roles of women, children, and slaves are perceived in relation to men, parents, and masters.

An Ordained Ministry

A natural outgrowth of the emerging institutional church's concern for its organizational structure is its emphasis on a regular ordained ministry. There is in the Pastorals lack of clarity about church offices, especially in Titus, but also the beginning of the separation of offices of bishop and elder in 1 Timothy 3:1–7. Thus, there are explicit qualifications for the offices of bishop, elder, and deacon (1 Tim 3:8–13), and perhaps an office of widow (1 Tim 5:9–10). There is also reference to the actual act of ordination to the ministry of the church by the laying on of hands (2 Tim 1:6).

The Epistolary Form

Outstanding in the literature of the emerging institutional church is the deliberate use of the form of the letter. Only one of the texts is actually a letter (1 Peter), and the bulk of that is a baptismal homily. Of the others, Jude, 2 Peter, and the Pastorals are manifestos. Why, then, are they all given, artificially, the form of letters? The answer is probably twofold. In the first place, at this time the letters of Paul are known and are being circulated as Scripture. To imitate the literary form is to present the churches with something familiar and hence more likely to be accepted. In the second place, and actually much more important, imitating the form of a letter provides an opportunity for pseudonymity—an opportunity to write in the name of someone from the apostolic age—and pseudonymity is crucial to this literature.

Pseudonymity

We have already discussed pseudonymity in the New Testament at several points, but since pseudonymity is a major characteristic of the literature of the emerging institutional church, we must now give the subject closer attention.

EXCURSIS: PSEUDONYMITY IN THE LITERATURE OF THE EMERGING INSTITUTIONAL CHURCH

The synoptic gospels and the Acts of the Apostles are not pseudonymous; they are anonymous. They were originally circulated without any author's name, and the names they now bear were ascribed to them in the early church. Similarly, the literature of the Johannine School first circulated anonymously, except that the writer of the second and third letters identifies himself as "the elder," and the author of the appendix to the gospel, chapter 21, identifies the evangelist as "the disciple whom Jesus loved." The apocalyptic author of the book of Revelation identifies himself as "John" with no further qualification, and we have no reason to doubt that a John "of Patmos" was in fact the author of the book, though we have every reason to doubt that we may identify him with any other "John" known to us from the early days of the church.

Outside the literature of the emerging institutional church, pseudonymity confronts us in the New Testament only in the case of the deutero-Pauline letters: 2 Thessalonians, Colossians, and Ephesians. These are in a sense a special case, for they are an instance of pupils deliberately writing in the name of the master. This was a wholly acceptable practice in the ancient world—Plato wrote in the name of Socrates—and need occasion no further comment. Analogous to the pseudonymity of the deutero-Pauline letters is the quite remarkable gospel practice of putting everything in the form of sayings of Jesus and stories about him, even when the contents come from the church.

It is in the literature of the emerging institutional church that pseudonymity becomes a major factor in the New Testament. Every single text in this literature is pseudonymous. Neither Jude, the brother of Jesus, nor Peter nor Paul are the authors of the texts claiming their names in this literature. There is no single text in this literature that bears the name of its author; all without exception are written in the name of a figure from the apostolic age.

In claiming authorship, the other Christian literature of this period is also interesting. Clement of Rome does not write to the church at Corinth in his own name, but in the name of the church at Rome. The letter begins, "The church of God which sojourns in Rome to the church of God which sojourns in Corinth," and the actual author is nowhere mentioned in the letter. Ignatius of Antioch writes in his own name, but he is writing personal letters to churches and to an individual (Polycarp). The *Didachē* is technically "The Teaching of the Lord to the Gentiles by the Twelve Apostles." In other words, in this period there is a reluctance to write in one's own name; the important thing is not oneself, but the church one represents, or still more, the apostolic tradition in which one stands. Ignatius is the exception, but then his letters are distinctly personal letters; they are not parenesis, manifestos, or incipient church orders.

We say "Ignatius is the exception," but what we should perhaps say is that Paul, Ignatius, and John of Patmos are all the exceptions. Of all the literature we are discussing—the New Testament literature plus *1 Clement,* the letters of Ignatius, and the *Didachē*—only these few intensely personal texts are written in the names of their authors. Paul writes personal letters to churches he has founded, to an individual he knows, and to a church from which he hopes to get support. John of Patmos writes an account of a personal revelation granted to him. Ignatius writes personal letters to churches and to an individual, Polycarp, known to him. The gospels and Acts are anonymous, as are 1 John, Hebrews, and the *Didachē*. The second and third letters of John are written by someone who identifies himself with his office in the church, and 1 Clement is written in the name of the church in Rome. The deutero-Pauline letters are written in the name of Paul, and the literature of the emerging institutional church is written in the names of persons from the apostolic age, including Paul.

We can see that the pseudonymity of the literature of the emerging institutional church is not something exceptional; rather, it is part of a pattern. What we need to do is distinguish the highly personal from the remainder. Paul and Ignatius are writing personal letters, and John of Patmos is giving an account of a personal revelation granted to him. But the others do not think of their work in this way. They are writing by the authority of the risen Lord, or of the church, or of an office within the church, or of their teacher, or of the apostolic age. So anonymity or pseudonymity is the rule; it is personal authorship that is the exception.

Once we recognize this, the pseudonymity of the literature of the emerging institutional church becomes readily understandable. The writers view themselves as defenders of a faith once and for all delivered to the apostles and transmitted in the church by means of an apostolic tradition. So they write in the name of apostles and even go to considerable lengths to establish "authenticity," as when the author carefully constructs situations in the life of Paul out of which to write. The apostolic age and the apostolic tradition are the source of their inspiration and their authority. To write in the name of someone from the apostolic age is for them the next step.

THE INTERPRETATION OF THE LITERATURE OF THE EMERGING INSTITUTIONAL CHURCH

The interpretation of this literature depends very much on the personal standpoint of the interpreter (as does the interpretation of any literature). One who shares the concern of the writers for the apostolic age and tradition will find that these texts speak directly to him or her, as will one who shares the concern of the authors for proper order and sound doctrine. Others will perhaps see these texts as representing the church hammering out a new vision of its faith and purpose in drastically changing historical circumstances, which is what in fact they do represent, and they will find that these texts speak to similar situations of drastically changing historical circumstances.

FURTHER READING

This chapter is especially indebted to G. Krodel, ed., *Ephesians, Colossians, 2 Thessalonians, The Pastoral Epistles* for the Pastorals (R. Fuller) and G. Krodel, ed., *Hebrews, James, 1 and 2 Peter, Jude, Revelation* for 2 Peter (F. W. Danker) and Jude (G. Krodel); to J. Beker's contributions in the *IDB;* to R. A. Wild on the Pastorals; to J. Elliott's approach to 1 Peter; and J. H. Neyrey on Jude and 2 Peter in the *NJBC.*

1 Peter

ADB: "Peter, First Epistle of" (J. H. Elliott).

IDB: "Peter, First Letter of" (J. C. van Unnik).

IDB Suppl.: "Peter" (R. E. Brown).

NJBC, pp. 903–908 (W.J. Dalton).

> D. L. Balch, *Let Wives Be Submissive: The Domestic Code in 1 Peter.*
> E. Best, *1 Peter.* (New Century Bible).
> R. Brown and J. P. Meier, *Antioch and Rome.*
> J. H. Elliott, *A Home for the Homeless. A Sociological Exegesis of 1 Peter, Its Situation, and Strategy.*
> J. N. D. Kelly, *A Commentary on the Epistles of Peter and Jude.*
> G. Krodel, "The First Letter of Peter," in G. Krodel, ed., *Hebrews, James, 1 and 2 Peter, Jude, Revelation* (Proclamation Commentaries), pp. 50–80.
> C. H. Talbert, ed., *Perspectives on First Peter.* NABPR Special Studies Series 9.

James

ABD: "James, Epistle of" (S. Laws).

IDB: "James, Letter of"(A. E. Barnett).

IDB Suppl.: "James, Letter of" (R. B. Ward).

NJBC, pp. 909–916 (T. W. Leahy).

C. E. B. Cranfield, "The Message of James," S*cottish Journal of Theology* 18 (1965), pp. 182–193.

M. Dibelius and H. Greeven, *James.* (Hermeneia).

P. U. Maynard-Reid, *Poverty and Wealth in James.*

S. Laws, A *Commentary on the Epistle of James.* (Harpers).

G. S. Sloyan, "The Letter of James," in G. Krodel, ed., *Hebrews, James, 1 and 2 Peter, Jude, Revelation* (Proclamation Commentaries), pp. 28–49.

The Pastoral Letters:

ABD: "Timothy and Titus, Epistles to" (J.D. Quinn).

IDB: "Timothy, First and Second Letters to" (J.C. Baker); "Titus, Letter to" (J.C. Beker).

NJBC, pp. 891–902 (R. A. Wild).

J. Bassler, "A Widows' Tale: A Fresh Look at 1 Tim 5:3–16," *Journal of Biblical Literature* 103 (1984) pp. 23–41.

M. Dibelius and H. Conzelmann, *The Pastoral Epistles.* (Hermeneia).

B. Fiore, *Pastoral Example in the Socratic and Pastoral Epistles.*

J. L. Houlden, *The Pastoral Epistles.* (Pelican New Testament Commentaries).

A. J. Hultgren, I–II Timothy, Titus in A. J. Hultgren and R. Aus, *I–II Timothy, Titus; II Thessalonians.* (Augsburg Commentary on the New Testament).

R. J. Karris, *The Pastoral Epistles.* (New Testament Message 17).

D. C. Verner, *The Household of God. The Social World of the Pastoral Epistles.*

————, "The Background and Significance of the Polemic of the Pastoral Epistles," *Journal of Biblical Literature* 92 (1973), pp. 549–564.

Jude

ABD: "Jude, Epistle of" (R. Bauckham).

IDB: Jude, "Letter of" (J. C. Beker).

NJBC, pp. 917–919 (J. H. Neyrey).

J.N.D. Kelley, *A Commentary on the Epistles of Peter and Jude.*

G. Krodel, pp. 91–98 in Krodel, ed., *Hebrews, James, 1 and 2 Peter, Jude, Revelation.*

D. E. Rowston, "The Most Neglected Book in the New Testament," *New Testament Studies* 21 (1974–1975), pp. 554–63.

2 Peter

ABD: "Peter, Second Epistle of" (John H. Elliott).

IDB: "Peter, Second Letter of" (J. C. Beker).

NJBC, pp. 1017–1022 (J. H. Neyrey).

T. Fornberg, *An Early Church in a Pluralistic Society.*

E. Käsemann, "An Apologia for Primitive Christian Eschatology," pp. 169–95 in Käsemann, *Essays on New Testament Themes.*

J. N. D. Kelley, *A Commentary on the Epistles of Peter and Jude.*

J. H. Neyrey, "The Form and Background of the Polemic in 2 Peter," *Journal of Biblical Literature* 99 (1980), pp. 407–31.

The Good Shepherd mosaic from the Basilica in Aquileia, Italy, ca. 320 C.E. Psalm 23 begins, "The Lord [=God] is my shepherd...." Greco-Roman "pagan" art portrays the good shepherd with the sheep on his shoulders. For Jesus' parable of the shepherd who searches for the one lost sheep, see Luke 15:4–7, Matthew 18:12–13. The Gospel of Mark says that Jesus had compassion on the crowds because they were "like sheep without a shepherd" (Mark 6:34) and in the Gospel of Matthew Jesus refers to the crowds as "lost sheep of the house of Israel" (Matt 10:6; 15:24; compare Matt 25:31—46). Hebrews 13:20 refers to "our Lord Jesus, the great shepherd of the sheep." Finally, in the Gospel of John Jesus himself claims, "I am the good shepherd. The good shepherd lays down his life for the sheep" (John 10:11).

CHAPTER 15

THE PRESUPPOSITION OF THE NEW TESTAMENT

Jesus

Jesus of Nazareth is the presupposition for everything else in the New Testament. Had the carpenter not left his village and wandered about Galilee preaching, teaching, and healing, and eating with all sorts of people, had the Romans not executed him as a politically dangerous revolutionary prophet, and had some of those devotees who heard him and followed him not come to believe that God had vindicated him by raising him from the dead, there would have been no Christian movements, no Christian writings, and thus no New Testament. Yet, the books of the New Testament were produced by Christians who were for the most part more interested in the living Lord they believed to be still present among them. Since most modern people have many historical questions about Jesus, we must say something further about this difference.

"JESUS IMAGES" IN THE NEW TESTAMENT

As our surveys of early Christian oral traditions, sources, and writings have shown, early Christianity was characterized by a rich variety of individuals, groups, beliefs, and practices. It is thus not so surprising that there was a great diversity of tradition and opinion about who Jesus was, and what he said and did. For example, Paul was interested almost exclusively in the crucifixion and resurrection of Jesus; he recorded almost nothing about Jesus' life and teachings. In contrast, other Christians, some of whom Paul opposed, stressed Jesus as a charismatic miracle-working hero, and it was just this sort of Jesus who was perpetuated in miracle collections that survived only by being absorbed into gospels. Similarly, Paul was very cautious about early Christian "wisdom," but Jesus as a sage who spoke wise sayings came to be a very important part of Q and the *Gospel of Thomas*. Paul also had many difficulties with the Jewish Law, but the evangelist Matthew saw Jesus as the true interpreter of the Law and Jesus' story its very fulfillment. The words of early Christian prophets who spoke in Jesus name soon became Jesus' words.

Some believed that the Jesus about whom they spoke and wrote was also the one whom they expected suddenly to appear "on the clouds of heaven" to redeem them and judge their enemies. They created a whole tradition portraying him in his earthly ministry as exercising the authority that would be his when he would return as Son of Man. Of all the writers of the New Testament, only the author of Luke-Acts came close to a modern historical interest when he depicted Jesus as the model of Christian piety. Yet, even he was reinterpreting traditional materials and composing in characteristically ancient historiographical fashion; his gospel remained far from being a life of Jesus in any modern sense.

That earliest Christianity created a number of "Jesus images" makes the task of portraying the Jesus who actually lived very difficult. Yet, many scholars think that some progress, however limited, is possible. We will now say something about how that progress has been made.

THE QUEST OF THE HISTORICAL JESUS

The modern "Quest of the Historical Jesus" had its birth in the late eighteenth century, usually called the period of the Enlightenment. In this period European and American intellectuals, including such notables as John Locke, Jean-Jacques Rousseau, Thomas Paine, Benjamin Franklin, and Thomas Jefferson began to use reason as the norm for deciding all sorts of questions, regardless of what those who appealed to traditional "revelation" or church authority said. A common question for understanding the Christian religion was this: If we set aside the later creeds and confessions of the churches, what really happened in the first century? Attempts to answer this question have led to over two hundred years of study of the life and teachings of Jesus. Indeed, the study of the study of Jesus has become something of a scholarly discipline in its own right! Here we shall give only the contours of this modern quest in order to indicate why certain key questions have surfaced.

You will recall from Chapter Four that about 185 C.E. Irenaeus of Lyons wrote a treatise, *Against Heresies*. In it he offered his "reason" for accepting four gospels, namely, the number four is the mythic foundation of the world (*Against Heresies* 3.11.8; on the mythic four, compare Rev 7:1–8 and Chapter Thirteen). Actually, there are more plausible reasons for explaining why second-century Christians settled on four gospels. They can be summed up with the word **"apostolicity"**: These four gospels were believed to have been written by four apostles; they were used in large and powerful "apostolic" churches, that is, churches that claimed to have been founded by apostles; and they were used to support "apostolic," that is, emerging orthodox, doctrine.

However, there was a problem sometimes pointed out by non-Christian opponents: The four gospels do not agree with one another. Usually this problem was solved by either favoring one gospel over another—the churches generally favored Matthew for their liturgies and John for their creeds— or "harmonizing" the four into one, as Christian pageants still do when they put together Matthew's story of the wise men with Luke's story of the shepherds. Indeed, as you remember, about 170 C.E. Tatian actually produced such a harmony by weaving all four gospels together into one, the *Diatessaron* ("Through the Four"). When Augustine wrote

On the Harmony of the Evangelists in the fourth century, he defended the gospels against opponents who claimed that gospel differences meant that they were untrustworthy. Augustine claimed that they were written in the order in which they are now found in the canon: Matthew, Mark, Luke, and John. Meanwhile, the church of the fourth and fifth centuries was forming creeds by interpreting especially the New Testament hymns and the Gospel of John with the aid of Greek philosophy. Such official creeds were forged in heat of theological battle, and indeed virtually every statement was framed to counter some opposing position. These creeds tended to place emphasis on the nature of Jesus as the supernatural Christ, or as having the "same substance" as God the Father. While the classic formula of Chalcedon in 451 C.E. said that Jesus Christ was "truly God, truly man," "truly God" grew to dominate most Christian faith and practice, and it was this orientation that increasingly governed the minds of most pious Christians when they read the New Testament stories. Such an orientation was not totally inconsistent with the lack of interest in the Jesus of history on the part of most New Testament writers, but it was not quite the orientation of New Testament writers, either.

One problem was that the New Testament, despite its apparent lack of empirical historical interest, was taken as historical among believing Christians. In the period of the eighteenth-century European/American Enlightenment, both the traditional harmonizing of the four gospels and the creedal view of Christ as a divine figure in history received serious challenge. A number of famous thinkers, upset by the terrible wars of religion in Europe, sought intellectual freedom through human reason alone ("Rationalists"). Having by this time learned more about nonliterate and preliterate myth-making peoples around the world (the "age of exploration"), they came to think, somewhat like Freud a century later, that religion was either the product of the childlike phase of human evolution or the result of deceptive control of more educated religious authorities over childlike masses—or both. Their goal was to uncover the truth behind the "superstition." At the very least, they thought, something significant had transpired between the historical events and the record of those events. They were most bothered by the miracle stories. They claimed that since for enlightened, scientific-minded people miracles no longer happen, Jesus' miracles could not have happened, at least in the manner in which they are recorded in the New Testament. *Something else* must have actually happened. While their attempt at rational explanations seems quaint today, their desire to know "what actually happened" contained an important insight: Texts held to be inspired by God were also human documents written by human beings from a different time and place and with a different view of reality, and to interpret them one must understand more about this human, historical, contextual question.

While the rationalistic Enlightenment could be found in many places, especially in Europe and the Americas, the leading developments of "the quest of the historical Jesus" took place in Germany. In the late 1700s and early 1800s many "rationalistic" scholars attempted to explain the miracles, especially the nature and feeding miracles, by some "more believable" event. Then, in 1835 two important German publications pointed the way to the future: David Friedrich Strauss wrote a *Life of Jesus* in which he argued that the gospels contained mostly "myth," not history, and Karl Lachmann argued that the best solution for the Synoptic Problem was the **Two-Source Theory.** The former view implied that the Gospel of John, the most "mythical" of the four, was, despite its beautiful spiritual qualities, least valuable for the historical reconstruction of the life Jesus. The latter view led to **"the priority of Mark,"** that is, the Gospel of Mark, not the Gospel of Matthew, was earliest of the three synoptics. These theories gave birth to what was eventually called "Q." Both were very important for further study of the gospels, as we have seen, and especially for the life and teaching of Jesus. For a number of decades, the general outline of Mark was defended as being fundamentally historical (partly in opposition to Strauss' mythical theory) and thought to trace accurately Jesus' own idea of his spiritual messiahship (Jesus' "messianic consciousness"). This theory about Mark was called **"the Markan hypothesis."**

By the late nineteenth century, thousands of historical lives of Jesus were being written on the basis of the Markan hypothesis. During the same period, however, there emerged the German **"History of Religions School,"** which studied further the Hellenistic environment of the whole New Testament, especially the apostle Paul, and the Jewish environment of Jesus. Most important for understanding the teaching of Jesus was the rediscovery of Jewish apocalyptic literature, made famous by Johannes Weiss' study of the Kingdom of God (1892) and Albert Schweitzer's famous *The Quest of the Historical Jesus* (1906). At the same time, the ghost of Strauss was still alive, for in 1901 the German William Wrede published *The Messianic Secret,* which convinced most scholars (in Germany, at least) that a driving theme for the course of Jesus' life in the Gospel of Mark, the secret of his suffering messiahship, was not Jesus' secret; rather, it was created by the evangelist. This blow to the Markan hypothesis was followed in 1919 by K. L. Schmidt's *The Framework of the Story of Jesus ,* which showed that the writer of Mark himself had created the outline for Jesus' life, into which he had inserted the many Jesus episodes from oral tradition. In 1921, Rudolf Bultmann's classical work *The History of the Synoptic Tradition,* which made major advances in the exploration of the history of the individual oral traditions in the Christian communities before the gospels, was written. In the same period pioneering work on the social context of early Christianity was also being done in the United States ("the Chicago School"), and much Jesus research was also carried on by other European scholars, especially in England, France, and Scandanavia. The work of the two pioneering form critics, Schmidt and Bultmann, was continued and especially developed in the study of the parables. Then, in the 1950s scholars in Germany returned to Wrede's task: They carried out redaction critical studies of the "theologies" of the Evangelists, which has since become a more international enterprise. All of this study tended to deemphasize the historical-empirical nature of the gospels. Yet, recently, scholars have returned to investigating the social history and social contexts of the early Christian groups, thus combining literary, social-historical, and social-anthropological study of the gospel sources, and in the past decade there has been a decided renewal of interest in Jesus from these perspectives.

In short, the modern "quest of the historical Jesus" has traversed about two and a quarter centuries. In that quest, scholars have learned to treat the gospels as "faith stories" that reflect the historical and social contexts of the transmitters of the Jesus tradition and the authors of the gospels, not just the historical record about the life and teaching of Jesus. The implication is that digging through the layers of tradition and interpretation to find the historical Jesus is a difficult task; indeed, a variety of perspectives on his life and teaching have arisen depending on particular methods and emphases of the interpreter. What follows is not the only approach to the Jesus of history, but it is the one that has resulted from the main contours of this sketch.

CULTURAL AND SOCIAL-HISTORICAL CONTEXT

One legacy of the German History of Religions School, form criticism, and the American Chicago School is the understanding of the cultural and social historical context of Jesus, especially the social strata of the Palestine in which Jesus lived and taught, sketched in Chapters Two to Four. You will recall that Mediterranean society in antiquity was an advanced agrarian society. The Roman Empire regulated the land and its agricultural produce, and this regulation provided the basis for political and economic power. As with other agrarian societies, there was increasing plague and famine; there were also miserable sanitary conditions in the cities, and thus high infant mortality rates. Regional economic specialization emerged (grains, figs, olive oil, ores). The economy was controlled by the politically powerful, especially the emperor and his family, senators and their families, and regional native kings and their families, permitted to rule if they collected the taxes and kept the peace. Such client kings were given the honor of being called "friend" and "ally" of Caesar. They were in turn supported by local aristocracies. These powerful people probably made up only about 1–2 percent of the total population. The system was undergirded by the military. In all respects it was a male-dominated world (see Chapter Two, social stratification).

A small percent of the population, perhaps about 5 percent, were "retainers." These were mainly scribes who could write—most people could not—and who became administrative and financial bureaucrats, as well as tax collectors, household stewards, judges, professional soldiers, and educators. These groups mostly served the ruling elites and shared in their economic surplus. They were primarily urban and, as those who benefitted by the system, were moderate, conventional, pious, and relatively well-off. The growth of commerce also led to the emergence of traders and merchants, only a few of whom gained much status.

There was no large "middle class" as we understand it. The great majority of people, perhaps about 90 percent, were near the bottom of the social ladder. Most them, perhaps 75 percent of the total, were peasants, the poverty-stricken urban poor, and tenant farmers. Another 5 percent or so were artisans, those who worked with their hands—considered by the elite to be distasteful—to produce everyday goods. In many cases they were even below the peasants because they had been displaced from their ancestral lands. At the very bottom of the social ladder were the expendables—beggars, prostitutes, and the destitute—and the "unclean," perhaps another 10 percent, mostly all living at a bare subsistence level.

Palestine was part of this ancient Mediterranean and Roman colonial context. In Palestine there was no longer a native, independent, Jewish king. The region had fallen under political and economic control of a "superpower," the Romans, whom pious and pure Jews regarded as godless and unclean Gentiles. The client kings of the Romans, the Herodians, were considered by many Jews to be only half-Jews because they came from Idumea. Yet, they were supported by the Jewish priestly ruling classes and their retainers. Thus, Palestine was a Roman client kingdom, or when Roman governors controlled Samaria and Judea directly, a mixed client kingdom and mini-imperial province. Greco-Roman towns were scattered here and there, Roman soldiers were everywhere present, and the burden of Jewish taxation was doubled by Roman taxation. Most people were peasants or urban poor and lived at a subsistence level. The whole system went against the native Jewish ideal that the "land of Israel" was a promised ancestral land, sacred to them as the chosen people of God. Its center was Jerusalem with its Holy Temple and Holy of Holies, the special place of God's presence. Most Jews thought that Roman control of their Holy Land, Holy City, and Holy Temple was an abomination in the sight of God. Many believed that God himself was about to remedy the matter. The only questions were how soon God would act and in what ways.

In the midst of this political and economic oppression there emerged various geographical, ethnic, and religious factions and larger, more permanent groups, which often centered on issues of Torah purity. Most established politically and economically were the compliant and cooperative Sadducees, who were among the aristocratic elites, but there were also other groups such as the Pharisees and Essenes who offered alternatives to belief and lifestyle. For some Jews, the very presence of the godless Gentiles in the Holy City, for example, had to be the result of the sins of the people of God; therefore, they had to cleanse themselves in God's eyes so that God might find them more worthy. It is also possible to track an intensification of colonial oppression and an increase of social, economic, and political conflicts and crises in Palestine. The apocalyptic hope was widespread, and those Jews who held it believed that God would irrupt into history to deliver the chosen people. Probably many Jews among the masses were inspired by this hope, and a number of resistance, reform, and terrorists groups emerged. The result was the growth of various prophetic, popular-messianic, and revolutionary movements. Some were eager to start a war against Rome that they believed God would terminate in their favor. Still others were interested in social reform. Whatever form the movements took, there was mounting pressure from the urban poor and peasant masses against the rich and powerful, which included the Jewish leaders. Sporadic violent activity eventually led to the outbreak of war against Rome in 66 C.E., and tragically it included within it a civil war among the Jews themselves. During that time Jew murdered Jew in the name of God and Torah, and there was a vicious internecine strife in Jerusalem itself that aided the Romans in their siege of the city.

Jesus of Nazareth, a wandering artisan who carried out his activity primarily among the lower strata of Palestine, lived in the early decades of this period. We need to fill in some of the particulars, but first we note some references to Jesus outside the New Testament and develop some problems of method.

JESUS IN ANCIENT SOURCES OTHER THAN THE NEW TESTAMENT

The major references to Jesus outside the New Testament are of three types: Roman, Jewish, and Christian. There are also a few scattered Christian and non-Christian sayings ("Agrapha").

Roman Sources

The first of the Roman sources is a work of the historian Tacitus written about 112–113 C.E. You will remember from our discussion of Revelation that Tacitus described a great fire in Rome in the summer of 64 C.E. while Nero was emperor. Tacitus said that the emperor made the Christians scapegoats to account for the fire. He then gave a brief account of the "sect" (see Chapter Thirteen). As part of that description, he says,

> The founder of this sect, Christus, was given the death penalty in the reign of Tiberius [14–37 C.E.] by the procurator Pontius Pilate [ruled 26–36 C.E.]; suppressed for the moment, the detestable superstition broke out again, not only in Judea where the evil originated, but also in the city [of Rome] to which everything horrible and shameful flows and where it grows.
> (Tacitus, *Annals* 15.44.)

This represents the information available to the Roman historian at the beginning of the second century. If it is based on the police interrogation of Christians, it is not actually independent of the New Testament or Christian tradition; if it is not, it represents the most valuable piece of Roman evidence about Jesus.

The second reference is also from a Roman historian, Suetonius (75–160 C.E.), who published his *Lives of the Twelve Caesars* around 121 C.E. He says that Claudius, who was emperor 41–54 C.E., "expelled from Rome the Jews who were constantly rioting at the instigation of a certain Chrestus" (Suetonius, *Life of Claudius* 25.4). This is the expulsion referred to in Acts 18:2, and the reference is to disturbances in the Jewish community at Rome resulting from the preaching of Christian missionaries. Suetonius understood Chrestus to be the individual responsible for the riots. If the expulsion was in 49 C.E., which is held by a majority of scholars, it was long after the death of Jesus. Thus, either "Chrestus" was another person, or, what is more likely, Suetonius was misinformed or confused about Jewish-Christian conflicts at Rome.

These are the most important Roman sources. They do not offer us any information beyond that which could be deduced from the New Testament itself. They do confirm that Christian missionaries reached Rome quite early, which is evident from Paul's letter to the Romans. Only Tacitus says anything explicit about Jesus, and his information may have come indirectly from Christians. He tells us that Roman historians accepted as factual the Christian tradition that the founder of the Christian movement had been crucified by Pontius Pilate. We can probably conclude that while these writers know of Jesus and early Christian movements, Christians were not yet deeply affecting Roman society.

Jewish Sources

There are several possible references to Jesus in the Jewish sources, of which there are two kinds: the historian Josephus and the Babylonian Talmud. In reporting the execution of James, Josephus (37–100? C.E.) refers to him as "the brother of Jesus, who was called Christ" (*Antiquities of the Jews* 20.9.1 paragraph 200). Most scholars have seen this offhand reference as actually having come from Josephus, not a Christian copyist. Josephus' second passage, however, has some problems. It says:

About this time there lived Jesus, a wise man, *if indeed one ought to call him a man.* For he was one who wrought surprising feats and was a teacher of such people as accept the truth gladly. He won over many Jews and many of the Greeks. *He was the Messiah.* When Pilate, upon hearing him accused by men of the highest standing among us, had condemned him to be crucified, those who had in the first place come to love him did not give up their affection for him. *On the third day he appeared to them restored to life, for the prophets of God had prophesied these and countless other marvelous things about him.* And the time of the Christians, so called after him, has still to this day not disappeared.

(Antiquities of the Jews 18.3.3–4, para. 63–64)

The italicized phrases can hardly have been written by a Jewish author. Since Josephus' works were copied by Christians through the centuries, either the Christian copyists created the whole passage or added these phrases. If the latter, which appears to be the majority scholarly opinion today, Josephus did indeed have a note about Jesus as a wise man who gathered followers, taught, worked miracles, and was crucified under Pontius Pilate.

In the Talmud, the second Jewish source, we find, first, a *Baraitha* (a tradition ascribed to the first or second centuries C.E.) that reads as follows:

On the eve of Passover they hanged Yeshu [of Nazareth] and the herald went before him forty days saying, "[Yeshu of Nazareth] is going forth to be stoned in that he has practiced sorcery and beguiled and led astray Israel. Let everyone knowing anything in his defense come and plead for him." But they found nothing in his defense and hanged him on the eve of Passover.

(Babylonian Talmud, Tractate *Sanhedrin* 43a)

This is a reference of quite extraordinary interest. Independent of any Christian sources, it offers us three items of information. It tells us that the Jews remembered Jesus as having practiced "sorcery," which here means magic, and gained a following; it links the death of Jesus with Passover, as do the Christian gospels; and it has a reference to some sort of pleading in his defense, probably implying a formal trial before authorities, and implies that Jesus was "hanged" (presumably crucified, compare Gal 3:13).

The second reference to Jesus in the ancient Jewish literature directly follows the first in the Babylonian Talmud. "Jesus had five disciples, Mattai, Maqai, Metser, Buni and Todah" (b. *Sanhedrin* 43a). The names given here are different from any we find in the New Testament, although Mattai could be a corruption of Matthew and Todah a corruption of Thaddeus. However, the important point is not the names but the testimony to the fact that Jesus had disciples.

There are several other references to Jesus in ancient Jewish literature but they are either indirect or cryptic or both, they are polemical, and they do not add much to what we have already learned.

In summary, the Jewish sources tell us six things about Jesus. First, Jesus was a wise man. Second, he practiced magic and gained a following. This must mean that Jesus had a reputation as a miracle worker, perhaps particularly as a successful exorcist, and that he made a strong impression. This latter point is reinforced by the third thing, namely, that Jesus made disciples, indicating that his activity among the people had some success. Fourth, there is the implication that Jesus was formally tried by the Jewish authorities. Fifth, he was hanged (crucified) on the evening before a Passover. Finally, the execution took place when Pontius Pilate was governor. Again, these references offer no new information about Jesus, but they are important because they generally confirm what we learn from the gospels, though we shall question the formal trial. An important byproduct is that the ancients never doubted that Jesus actually existed, as a few modern interpreters have claimed.

Christian Apocryphal Gospels

You will remember from Chapter Four that there are a number of gospels that did not achieve recognition in the final formation of the canon of the New Testament. They are known as "apocryphal" ("secret" or "hidden"), originally because they were considered sacred, but eventually for the opposite reason, that is, they were to be kept from the orthodox faithful. There are several types of apocryphal gospels; one common classification is: 1) New Testament type, especially Jewish-Christian, gospels; 2) Gnostic gospels; and 3) gospels that are legendary supplements to New Testament stories, for example, Jesus as the miracle-working child, or Mary as a virgin child-bride of old Joseph. Most of these gospels offer nothing that can help the historian's quest for the historical Jesus, though they are fascinating and offer information about various Christian ideas and groups in the early centuries of Christianity.

However, there are exceptions to this generalization. We have studied the *Gospel of Thomas* as an important "sayings gospel." It is particularly important in the historical Jesus discussion because it has versions of sayings and parables of Jesus that appear to be literarily independent of the versions we find in the New Testament, and which therefore offer us an additional source to use in our attempt to reconstruct the original form of these sayings or parables. Further, it offers us new sayings and parables, a few of which might have been spoken by Jesus. A particularly instructive example of this latter type is the parable of the Assassin.

> Jesus said: "The kingdom of the Father is like a man who wishes to kill a powerful man. He drew the sword in his house, he stuck it into the wall, in order to know whether his hand would carry it through; then he slew the powerful [man]."
>
> *(Gospel of Thomas 98)*

This passage is similar to the Tower Builder and the King Going to War in Luke 14:28–32, and therefore could have been spoken by Jesus. A growing number of interpreters think that the *Gospel of Thomas* offers us some new material to use in our attempt to reconstruct the teaching of Jesus (see Chapters Four, Five).

The *Gospel of Thomas* has received by far the most positive evaluation as a noncanonical historical source for Jesus' sayings. Some scholars attempt to reevaluate a few other noncanonical gospel fragments and argue that they are also on a par with the canonical gospels. These include, first, the Egerton Gospel (Egerton

Papyrus 2), which contains four episodes from Jesus' life that overlap mainly with the Gospel of John and, second, the so-called *Gospel of Peter,* the surviving parts of which contain a few scenes about Jesus' passion and resurrection. In this connection, we should also mention, third, the Secret Gospel of Mark, which some scholars have accepted as originally a longer, but earlier, version of canonical Mark, two passages of which are purported to have been discovered in 1957. Positive judgments on these apocryphal gospel fragments, even if they gain wide currency, do not automatically or necessarily mean that the sayings or episodes they record are historical; they must be evaluated critically just as are the canonical gospel sayings.

Isolated Sayings Attributed to Jesus (Agrapha)

There are several agrapha, or isolated sayings, attributed to Jesus in sources inside and outside the New Testament. The most interesting saying completely outside Christian literature is the following.

> Jesus, on whom be peace, has said: The world is a bridge, go over it, but do not install yourselves on it.

This saying is found inscribed on the south portal of a mosque in India and is also attested elsewhere in Islamic literature. It is a very beautiful saying, but it does not have the same claim to authenticity (see later in this chapter) as the following one:

> When on the same day he saw a man doing work on the Sabbath, he said to him: Man, if you know what you are doing then you are blessed. But if you do not know what you are doing then you are cursed and a transgressor of the law.

This saying is found in only one manuscript of the New Testament (Codex D) after Luke 6:4. Otherwise unattested, it is nonetheless very much like a saying in the canonical tradition: the challenge of Jesus to make one's own decisions (see below, the Criterion of Coherence). Another possibility is this same manuscript's saying in Acts 20:35: "To give is more blessed than to receive." A third example that ranks very highly is a little papyrus fragment from the fourth or fifth century that comes from Oxyrhynchus, Egypt:

> Woe unto you blind that see not! Thou hast bathed thyself in water that is poured out, in which dogs and swine lie at night and day, and thou hast washed thyself and hast chafed thine outer skin, which prostitutes also and flutegirls anoint, bathe, chafe, and rouge, in order to arouse desire in men, but within they are full of scorpions and of [bad]ness [of every kind]. But I and [my disciples], of whom thou sayest that we have not im[mersed] ourselves, [have been im]mersed in the liv[ing . . .] water which comes down from [. . . B]ut woe unto them that. . . .
> (Oxyrhynchus Papyrus 840)

You will recall that oral tradition continued at least down to the time of the Church Father Justin Martyr in the middle of the second century C.E. Therefore, in some cases it is very valuable to compare gospel sayings with variant forms of the same sayings preserved in the early Church Fathers.

IMPORTANT CRITICAL PROBLEMS ABOUT THE LIFE AND TEACHING OF JESUS

The canonical gospels give us some narrative outlines of a short period of the adult life of Jesus, and two of them, Matthew and Luke, also have birth narratives. However, we have learned that for the most part, these outlines are part of the gospel writers' "Jesus images." While it is true that some details in John's gospel —for example, that Jesus made more than one visit to Jerusalem, or that his final meal was not a Passover meal—have historical merit, most modern critics have followed Strauss in concluding that the "spiritual" Johannine story is largely the faith creation of its author. The outline of Mark fared better during the nineteenth century but, since Wrede, it, too, has been judged by most to be the creation of its author, and it is the basis for the gospels of Matthew and Luke. In short, we cannot use gospel outlines to sketch a biography of Jesus.

If we disregard the outlines of the narrative gospels and ask about the smaller units within those gospels, we recall that this material was transmitted orally in forms that functioned in the life and work of the Christian churches. In the complex history of oral transmission in the tradition of the churches, some of it was altered in form before it reached written form, and some of it was created anew by anonymous prophets and scribes in the various communities. From time to time the Christian communities made collections of various types of materials, for example, miracle stories, sayings (compare Q, *Gospel of Thomas*), parables (compare Mark 4), anecdotes, and words embedded in the passion story. Finally, some material was altered or created by the writers, or evangelists.

You will recall that the form critics divided the smaller units of material into *narratives about* Jesus and *sayings of* Jesus and have attempted to trace the course of their development in early Christianity through the communities that preserved them. Miracle stories, for example, were narratives so retold that they often sound very much like other miracle stories known from Greco-Roman and Jewish antiquity. Though the specifics of Jesus' healing activity have become clouded by such traditional retelling, scholars generally agree that Jesus was an exorcist and healer—some would say a magician, as statements in the Talmud claim. Moreover, there are other aspects of Jesus life that are "inherently probable." The narrative of Jesus' crucifixion, for example, was, if not an embarrassment, at least not always easy to explain to potential converts. Yet, it is central to early Christian confessions, dominates Paul's thought, and offers the central drama at the conclusion of the gospel stories. Some historians conclude that it is therefore the most certain event of Jesus' life. There are other historical and cultural probabilities about narratives: Mary and Joseph as the parents of Jesus; Jesus' peasant/artisan origins; his baptism by the apocalyptic prophet John the Baptist; Galilee as the location of his activity; the calling of disciples; and meals with disciples, peasants, unclean, and expendables.

Other narratives are less certain. One kind of short narrative form that has to do with Jesus' life is the "biographical" anecdote, a story from the life of a wise man that culminates in a witty, figurative, or argumentative saying, or sayings, or in a brief dialogue. These biographical anecdotes occur in several versions; usually the biographical setting varies but the saying or dialogue remains constant. What this means for the historical study of the life of Jesus is that one usually finds more historical value in the saying, or dialogue, not the biographical setting, though some settings are necessary for understanding the saying or dialogue and other settings (for example, controversies with opponents) may have been quite typical.

Another complicating factor with the narratives is that so many of the events portrayed in the gospels are told as the fulfillment of Jewish Scriptural texts, and their details are often hidden allusions to, or seen as specific fulfillments of, those texts. This is especially the case in the "formula quotations" in the Gospel of Matthew, but it is a phenomenon in all the gospels, as we saw especially with respect to the use of psalms in the passion story (Chapter Five). This phenomenon inevitably raises the question as to whether the details of the events, or even the events themselves, have been built up out of Scripture and whether, therefore, they "actually happened." To add details from Scripture to interpret an event, or even to create an event from a Scriptural text, would be quite in keeping with ancient Jewish practice, and certainly Christians did both of these things. For example, we can see Matthew adding the details of the second animal from Zechariah 9:9 to his account of the triumphal entry (Matt 21:7; compare his source, Mark 11:7), and it would be generally agreed that most material of the birth and infancy stories in Matthew's gospel was created from the Old Testament texts it is held to fulfill. Thus, each event or narrative detail in which there is a quotation from or an allusion to Scripture—very many indeed—has to be investigated on its own merit.

Many scholars think that more can be said about the second major type of material, the "discourse" material, that is, Jesus' *sayings* or *message,* than about the precise events of his life. The teaching material attributed to Jesus also went through a long process of transformation before it reached the stage of gospel composition, and this process continued as the gospels were written. The clearest example is that Jesus' discourses in the Gospel of John are so "Johannine," and for the most part so different from what we find in the other canonical gospels, that, as important as they are for understanding the Fourth Gospel, they cannot be judged characteristic of Jesus' own teaching. In the synoptic gospels, the difficulties are similar, but somewhat more promising. We remember, for example, that Mark, Matthew, and Luke incorporate previously written documents, sources, and traditions and place them at various locations in their writings, thus giving them different settings and correspondingly different interpretations. This phenomenon is easiest to show with Matthew and Luke. For example, Matthew assembles various Mark, Q, and Special M teachings together, thus creating the five great discourses (Chapter Ten). Similarly, Luke relocates Mark's story of Jesus' teaching in the synagogue at Nazareth (Mark 6) to the beginning of Jesus' public ministry, expands it with teaching about the Messiah (Isa 61:1–2), and uses it as basic theme for his gospel (Luke 4:16–30; Chapter Eleven). In short, the placement and consequent interpretation of materials by the evangelists may sometimes give a few general clues, but we can never assume that they represent Jesus' own views; rather, we must look at the teachings themselves.

When we look at the isolated teachings, we must examine their forms and their histories. We listed forms of oral tradition in Chapter Four and discussed some of these in Chapter Five. With respect to teaching, these are aphorisms, parables, allegories, and anecdotes. The most stable parts of the anecdotes, as we stated earlier, are the sayings; they, along with parables and isolated aphorisms, will be important to examine for the teachings of Jesus.

In Chapter One, we analyzed in some detail Jesus' teaching about the Lord's Prayer. In that context, the major point was to illustrate the problems and the methods that have been used to solve these problems. We shall say a bit more about the Lord's Prayer in this chapter. For the moment, let us consider another kind of example to reinforce the way we attempt to arrive at the earliest stages of the many sayings traditions. It is the "sign of Jonah" saying. As with the Lord's Prayer, the material is found in Q (Matt 12:38–42 = Luke 11:16, 29–32). In this case, however, there is also a parallel of sorts in Mark 8:11–13 (compare also Matt 16:4). We begin with Mark. The Markan version says that the Pharisees sought to test Jesus by seeking a (cosmic, apocalyptic) sign from heaven to prove his powers. Jesus responds: "...*no sign* will be given to this generation" (Mark 8:12). The Q version (Matt 12:38–42 = Luke 11.29–32) stresses, first, that "this generation" is "evil," but now an exception to the refusal to give a sign is mentioned: "no sign ... *except the sign of Jonah*." It interprets the sign as Jonah's preaching to the Ninevites who repented (Jonah 3), implying that the only sign will be Jesus' preaching and those who respond with repentance. The passage continues with the comment that "something greater than Jonah is here" (Matt 12:39, 41 = Luke 11:30, 32; compare Matt 16:1, 2, 4). In Matthew alone, "adulterous" is added to "this generation," and the implication is that it is led by "scribes and Pharisees." Matthew further interprets the sign of Jonah exception as *three days and three nights in the belly of the whale,* that is, the resurrection of the Son of Man, which for Matthew means Jesus (see Matt 8:20), perhaps reflecting the Jewish tradition that Jonah was the widow's son resuscitated by Elijah (compare 1 Kings 17:17–24).

We have presented this tradition in the order that most critics would claim represents its history. The logic is that exceptions about Jesus' teaching and life were added to the absolute refusal to give a sign. Thus:

1. No sign will be given.
2. No sign will be given *except* the sign of Jonah: Jesus' preaching and those who repent forming the new community opposed to "this generation."
3. No sign will be given *except* the sign of Jonah: Jesus' preaching/the believers' repentance, and *especially* Jesus resurrection (see Matt 17.9).

If this analysis is correct, only version No. 1 would become a candidate to be considered as part of the teaching of Jesus.

We have attempted to illustrate something about form and function in the various communities of early Christianity, and noted the possibility of tracing the history of certain forms in early Christianity and of recovering presynoptic versions. We shall offer a further example below in connection with the parables. Now comes the crucial question: When we work back through the material to the earliest possible form, how can we decide whether it actually came from Jesus? This requires criteria, a subject of some debate.

CRITERIA OF PROBABLE AUTHENTICITY

Despite the subjectivity involved, scholars have attempted to develop some satisfactory criteria for determining the probable authenticity of material attributed to Jesus. Some years ago, R. H. Fuller and N. Perrin, working independently of each other, arrived at virtually identical criteria (see bibliography). Fuller suggested four criteria, Perrin three. They may be tabulated as follows.

1. Fuller: Distinctiveness
   Perrin: Dissimilarity
2. Fuller: The cross-section method
   Perrin: Multiple attestation
3. Fuller: Consistency
   Perrin: Coherence
4. Fuller: Linguistic and environmental tests
   Perrin: Assumed this, but did not define

Some of these criteria have been highly debated and modified, in some cases rejected. Nonetheless, we think that some form of them still exists in most contemporary attempts to rediscover "the historical Jesus."

The Criterion of Distinctiveness

For Fuller and Perrin, dissimilarity (Perrin) or distinctiveness (Fuller) is the most important criterion. As originally formulated, it says that especially *sayings material* may be accepted as probably going back to Jesus if it can be shown to be distinctive in relation to characteristic and "acceptable" teachings in ancient Judaism and early Christianity, implying that such material was gradually assimilated or became acculturated to Jewish and Greco-Roman ideas in the course of its transmission. Such a criterion, of course, requires a basic knowledge of the cultural environment and social history of early Christianity as sketched earlier in this chapter. As we noted in Chapter Three, an example of this is the use of "Father" (Aramaic *'Abbā'*) in addressing God in the Lord's Prayer (Luke 11:2) and in Jesus' prayer in Gethsemane (Mark 14:36). While it could be used also by *adult* children, and therefore was not equivalent to the child's illiterative "Dada" in English, it seems to have been a mode of address in the family that the Jews at the time of Jesus seem not to have used in prayer, having preferred "Our Heavenly Father," or something similar. Matthew's version "Our Father in heaven" (6:9b) is much closer to the common Jewish mode of address, thus illustrating a Christian writer's assimilation to typical Jewish usage. This sort of modification is typical of the history of Christian oral tradition and reinterpretation and literary modification.

Recent discussions of this criterion have added other dimensions to distinctiveness, for example, distinctiveness in the *forms* of Jesus' sayings and Jesus' *lifestyle*. Sayings that are distinctive in both content *and* form are more easily remembered in oral tradition; thus, it is not surprising to find that this criterion tends to focus on sayings that are short, pungent, and radically challenge culturally accepted beliefs, values, and practices, for example, pithy wisdom sayings and aphorisms—"Blessed are you poor" (Luke 6:20) or "Let the dead to bury their own dead" (Q 9:60b). Parables that challenge, disturb, provoke, or simply tease thought or shock the imagination are especially important possibilities for going back to Jesus. Similarly, a life-style that deviates from the usually accepted norms about following in the footsteps of one's father, or about normative patterns of family, home, and village life, or associating with people whom most would think ritually unclean or socially expendable appear to be striking and distinctive. Finally, the tendency of the developing Christian tradition about Jesus was usually to formulate less radical versions of Jesus' sayings and behavior, illustrating an accommodation to more conventional and acceptable cultural beliefs, values, and practices, in other words, of toning them down, a process of "socialization" or "acculturation." We can see this tendency especially with the redaction of the evangelists.

Some scholars see problems with the criterion of distinctiveness, at least as it was originally formulated by the form critics. They make the valid point that its use can lead to the rejection of sayings and narratives that might accurately portray Jesus as *like* "Judaism" or that were accurately preserved in early Christianity. In other words, they charge, the criterion is circular: By concentrating on what is new, unusual, shocking, or radical, it discovers a Jesus who is new, unusual, shocking, or radical. This becomes an especially pungent critique when several points are remembered. First, "laws" of developing tradition have received scrutiny and are often wanting; such criticism requires great caution. Second, we simply do not possess everything that ancient Jewish and Christians teachers —or Jesus himself—said. Third, as we shall indicate with the criteria of linguistic and environmental tests below, Jesus could not have been so utterly distinctive that he failed to communicate to his peers. It is especially important in this regard to beware of a certain tendency among Christian anti-Jewish scholarship to caricature the Jews as "legalists" or "ritualists" and then to see Jesus as the spiritual purifier of the Jewish religion. We must never forget that Jesus was a Jew operating within the context of his ancestral religion. Yet, it is equally true to ask if Jesus had said *only* what others were saying, why did he make such an impact on his followers? Furthermore, there were other teachers in antiquity that did not accept commonly held beliefs, values, and behavior, for example, Jewish charismatic miracle workers or Cynic teachers.

The cautious and judicious use of this criterion has led to the most distinctive elements in reconstructing the teaching of Jesus: his proclamation of the kingdom, his special use of aphorisms and parables, and elements of the prayer he taught his disciples. It also points to his unusual life-style. Moreover, it is only a starting point; its use must always be supplemented by the use of other criteria.

The Criterion of Multiple Attestation

This criterion has usually (though not always) referred to material that is found in several *synoptic* sources—Mark, Q, Special M, and Special L—where it does not seem that these sources are dependent on each other. The theory is that the more widespread a tradition is— attested in several sources *independently*—the greater chance it has of going back to an earlier point of origin. It has been also extended to refer to multiple *forms* of the same or similar material. The criterion has usually been thought to be most successful in determining the probable authenticity of *themes* that occur frequently in the message of Jesus rather than of particular sayings. So, for example, Jesus' association with marginal people, often called "tax collectors and sinners," is most likely authentic because it occurs in all of the synoptic sources and it is attested in multiple forms (sayings, parables, and controversy anecdotes).

With the reevaluation by some scholars of the antiquity and independence of some sayings in the agrapha and apocryphal gospels, multiple attestation, an essentially quantitative approach, is being used to examine other versions of sayings material. Thus, for example, a saying found in multiple sources and in multiple forms, some of them outside the New Testament, leads to an attempt to critically reconstruct the original form as possibly going back to Jesus, especially if the extracanonical sources are judged to be from a very early period.

Again, a note of caution is in order with respect to this criterion. The quantity of sayings or forms does not *prove* that Jesus said them. As an analogy, you will recall that modern textual critics have determined that the quantity of manuscripts or readings does not prove a version of the text correct. The majority of manuscripts were produced later—*after* many changes had already "corrupted" them. In other words, in this case the majority does not rule. Age and quality must be assessed. Similarly, multiple attestation of Jesus' sayings alone will not be decisive. Judgment calls about quality (distinctiveness) and age must also be made.

The Criterion of Coherence

This criterion grew out of a desire to go beyond what can be established through distinctiveness and multiple attestation. Essentially it says that material that on other grounds is uncertain can probably be accepted as generally authentic if it is consistent with the core material established as probable by the other criteria. For example, arguments are sometimes made that sayings in the *Gospel of Thomas* not found elsewhere might go back to Jesus if they sound very much like what Jesus would have said, given the material already isolated in the canonical gospels by the other two criteria. An example given above was the parable of the Assassin in *Gospel of Thomas* 98.

The Criterion of Cultural Environment and Language

This criterion has tended to be negative rather than positive, and only supplementary. In other words, material is *rejected* if it is *totally* incompatible with the languages or immediate environment of the Jesus' Palestinian environment. For example, while Jesus' teaching on divorce in Mark 10 is distinctive, it is not likely that all of it goes back to Jesus *in its present form* because it concludes with ideas based on Roman and not Jewish divorce law, that is, that a woman can divorce her husband. To be sure, it is not impossible that Jesus knew Roman divorce law, since there were towns in Palestine dominated by Roman military personnel; the greater probability, however, is that the story was altered in a social environment more influenced by Roman law. As for language, the allegorical interpretation of the parable of the Sower in Mark 4:13–20 hardly goes back to Jesus, because it uses much language from the technical vocabulary of the early church. *This criterion does not work in the opposite direction.* Material cannot be accepted as authentic *only* because it reflects the linguistic or environmental circumstances of the Palestinian ministry of Jesus for the obvious reason that the earliest Palestinian followers of Jesus shared his language and culture.

Other Criteria

Other criteria have been proposed. One is the "criterion of embarrassment" or "criterion of contradiction." It is argued that in some cases, sayings or episodes may have been preserved in a somewhat conservative manner even though they created some embarrassment for the early Christians. For example, though the one baptizing is normally "superior" to the one being baptized, Christians told stories about the baptism of Jesus by John the Baptist, but then later had to explain the event because John was clearly believed to be a mere "forerunner," or Jesus' inferior (compare Matt 3:14–16). Another example is that Jesus is portrayed as clearly knowing the future at times, yet he does not seem to know the day or hour of the parousia (Mark 13:32). Again, the crucifixion for sedition would seem to be the most solid historical event we have, yet we can see early Christians struggling with it. The obvious problem with this criterion is that what would be embarrassing to an ancient Mediterranean person is a judgment call, and not all scholars agree. There are other attempts to break up the above criteria into more extensive lists (see Boring), but for purposes of simplicity, we shall remain with these.

Our discussion thus far has established that the Gospel of John is so much the end product of intensive meditation and reflection, and so absorbed with the interpretation of Christ as the descending-ascending redeemer, that no way has yet been found of deriving important historical information about Jesus from it beyond a few probabilities. The Acts of the Apostles offers us an isolated saying (20:35, "It is more blessed to give than to receive"). Though Paul knows something of Jesus' teachings (see Chapters Six, Seven), he reveals very little interest in anything about Jesus beyond his death and resurrection. We find occasional variants of a saying of Jesus, though not attributed to him, in the letter attributed to James (see Chapter Fourteen). The remainder of the New Testament by its very nature cannot be expected to reveal much about the historical Jesus. We are primarily limited, therefore, to the synoptic gospels, the *Gospel of Thomas*, some isolated sayings preserved in various places, with some small supplementary help from the Jewish and Roman sources. This material must be carefully evaluated, using criteria of probable authenticity, with special help from a general knowledge of the cultural environment and social historical context. It is on this basis that we proceed.

MAJOR FEATURES OF JESUS' LIFE

Early Years

Jesus was probably born sometime before the death of Herod the Great (4 B.C.E.). The reason for putting the birth of Jesus at least four years "before

Christ," which sounds like a contradiction, is that the calculation of Jesus' birth in the sixth century C.E. was inaccurate by at least by four years. There are passages that locate the birth in Bethlehem of Judea, but that tradition is not unanimous (compare John 7:40–42) and it may have been an inference from the conviction in some circles that he was the Davidic Messiah and must have been born in David's city (compare Mic 5:2; Rom 1:3–4; Acts 2:36). More likely, he was born in Nazareth of Galilee, his hometown (see below). Mark calls Jesus a "carpenter" (Mark 6:3), and Matthew makes the deduction that he was the "son of a carpenter" (Matt 13:55). If these phrases are not simply metaphors for "teacher," as is sometimes the case in Rabbinic literature (for example, *j. Kiddushin* 66a), he was an artisan, presumably a woodworker. This probably meant that Joseph, or Joseph's father, or some more distant ancestor, was a peasant who had been displaced from his ancestral plot of land. Joseph's wife was named Mary. In a context where his village and family members do not accept him, the texts say that Jesus had brothers, four of whom are named (Mark 6:1–6 = Matt 13:53–58), one of whom (James) eventually became prominent in the Jerusalem church (Acts 12:17; 15:13; 21:18; compare 1 Cor 15:7; Gal 2:9, 12). Sisters are also mentioned (Mark 6:3).

Though the actual place of Jesus' birth remains uncertain, he probably grew up in the village of his father and mother, Nazareth of Galilee, for he was known as "Jesus of Nazareth" or "a Nazarene" (compare Mark 1:24; 10:47; John 18:5; Matt 2:23). Nazareth was located about twenty miles inland from the Mediterranean Sea and fifteen miles west of the southern tip of the Sea of Galilee. It was situated in one of the most fertile sections of Galilee, and we may assume that agriculture was its major activity, an assumption reinforced by agricultural images in Jesus' teachings, especially the parables. Curiously, Nazareth is not mentioned in the Hebrew Scriptures or ancient writings contemporary with the New Testament, but there is archeological evidence that indicates the presence of Jewish burial sites. We may conclude that Nazareth was a relatively insignificant Jewish peasant farming village, and that Jesus' native tongue was the language usually spoken by rural Palestinian Jews, Aramaic, as some terms in the gospels also testify (for example, *'Abbā'*). Whether he knew Greek is uncertain, but it certainly would not have been unusual for peasants to be able to speak some Greek, even if they could not write it, if only for trading purposes.

Given the size and environment of Nazareth, pejorative comments in the Rabbinic literature about Galileans who do not strictly keep the Torah laws, offbeat Galilean "charismatic" miracle workers such as Hanina ben Dosa and Honi the Circle Drawer, and the agricultural imagery of Jesus' parables, many scholars in the past concluded that the region in which Jesus was reared was a cultural backwater, relatively free from Greco-Roman culture and Judean control, and that all Galileans were merely uneducated peasants. Also, recall that a certain "teacher" named Judas the Galilean opposed the enrollment for taxes newly instituted in Palestine in 6 C.E., when Jesus would have been about ten years old, and that there was thereafter general unrest throughout Palestine (for example, Josephus *Antiquities* 20.5.2 paragraph 100–102). Judas' sons, James and Simon, were crucified in 47 C.E. Another descendant, Menahem, became a "popular king" who captured Masada from the Romans. Finally, Menahem's nephew, Eleazar, was the leader of the Jewish resistance to Rome at the end of the wars.

These indicators have often led scholars to say, further, that Galileans were independent and prone to political revolution. In this connection there is a substantial body of critical literature about the extent to which Jesus might have been a revolutionary (or was sympathetic to the revolutionaries), and the effect of his Galilean homeland on his views.

Today, caution about these historical deductions is in order. Nazareth was situated in Lower Galilee, or southern Galilee (Josephus *Wars* 3.3.1 paragraph 35–39; the Mishnah), which archaeologists say was much influenced by Greco-Roman Hellenism, in contrast to Upper Galilee in the North, which indeed was more remote, less under Roman control, and a likely outpost for the revolutionaries. Moreover, Nazareth was only about three miles south of Sepphoris, a small Jewish city of probably about 30,000 that was situated on the major highways from the Mediterranean Sea to the Sea of Galilee and from the north to the south, to Jerusalem. Sepphoris contained many of the architectural edifices of a city influenced by Hellenism. Although it had been razed for its central role in the revolt of 4 B.C.E., by 66 C.E. it remained loyal to Rome. All of this suggests that while Jesus' origins in the lower artisan strata of a village might naturally have led him to certain revolutionary ideas, we can no longer rule out the possibility that he had also come into contact with a somewhat more cosmopolitan and urbane environment than has often been supposed. That does not necessarily mean that he accepted or rejected it, but some scholars are now willing to suggest that he was influenced by strains of Greek philosophy, especially the wandering Cynic sages (see below).

John the Baptist

The gospels portray John as an apocalyptic prophet of judgment who baptized in the Judean wilderness along the Jordan River (Mark 1:4 = Matt 3:4; Luke 3:3–4), a view reinforced by the writings of the ancient Jewish historian Josephus (*Antiquities of the Jews* 18.5.2 paragraph 116–19). The core of his apocalyptic message was the call to repent and be baptized in preparation for "one who is coming" (Mark 1:7; Matt 3:11; Luke 3:16; Luke 7:19 = Matt 11:3), about which we shall say more momentarily. John is also said to have dressed in camel's hair with a leather belt around his waist (Mark 1:6 = Matt 3:4) and to have eaten an unusual (though ritually pure!) diet of locusts and wild honey (Mark 1:6; compare Lev 11:22). Luke adds the tradition that John came from a family of priests (Luke 1:5), and was born shortly before Jesus (Luke 1:26, 36). John's diet and priestly connections were not elsewhere attested and are therefore uncertain, especially when it is seen that John's dress was an obvious attempt to identify him with the prophet Elijah, who was taken off in a whirlwind (2 Kgs 2) and expected to return at the End (compare 2 Kgs 1:8; Zech 13:4; Mal 3:1; 4:5). Yet, the Judean wilderness, and the priestly, baptizing, and apocalyptic associations are intriguing when it is recalled that the Essenes had a community in that same wilderness not far away and that they were a priestly sect that baptized and wrote much apocalyptic literature. There is no real proof that John had connections with the Essenes, but it is one of those hypotheses that makes a lot of sense. It is interesting that a baptizing, Gnostic-oriented sect that claims connections with John the Baptist, that is, the Mandaeans, still exists in Iran and Iraq today. We may also note that John was imprisoned and executed at the hand of the Galilean client king, Herod Antipas, the gospels say because he criticized Herod's marriage to his brother Philip's wife (Mark 6:17–29), Josephus says because Herod feared that John's popularity might lead to rebellion (*Antiquities of the Jews* 18.5.2 paragraph 118–119).

Besides baptism, certain aspects of the life-style of John's core followers—prayer, fasting, abstinence from strong drink, and strict morality—can also be inferred from the gospels (Mark 1:6; 2:18; Matt 11:16–18; Luke 11:1; 3:7–14). John's apocalyptic message about "one who is coming" noted above undoubtedly referred to the Lord *God* coming for final judgment (Matt 3:11–12 = Luke 3:16b–17; compare Luke 1:76; Mal 3:1, 4:5). Christians who believed in Jesus as Messiah, however, developed a tradition that John meant the Lord *Jesus* (Q: Matt 11.2–6 = Luke 7:18–19, 22–23; Matt 3:11–12 = Luke 3:16–17; Mark 1.7–8; compare John 1:26b–27, 29–31), and this is what they meant when they spoke from Scripture of John's preparing the way of "the Lord" (Isa 40:3; compare Mark 1.2–3). So John was explicitly portrayed as the returning prophet Elijah (for example, Matt 11:15); as such he is said to be "the beginning of the gospel" (Mark 1:1), and as distinctly subordinate to Jesus.

Yet, there is some hint that Jesus and perhaps some of his disciples had once been among the followers of John (Acts 1:22). This is consistent with the tradition from Q that Jesus praised John (Matt 11:18–19 = Luke 7:33–35). However, Jesus' message was less apocalyptic and there are remnants of the tradition that imply that Jesus' life-style was not as "ascetic" as John's:

> For John the Baptist has come eating no bread and drinking no wine, and you say, 'He has a demon' [a "witchcraft accusation"]; the Son of Man has come eating and drinking, and you say, 'Look, a glutton and a drunkard [the rebellious son accusation (Deut 21:20; Prov 23.21; 11QT 64)], a friend of tax collectors and sinners!'
>
> (Matt 11:18–19a = Luke 7:33–34).

Whether Jesus actually spoke of himself as the Son of Man (which makes sense only in Hebrew or Aramaic, not in Greek) is much debated; if he did, he did not refer to himself as either the apocalyptic "one like a human being" who would come on the clouds (see Chapter Three; below) or the suffering Son of Man, a creation of the Markan author (see Mark 8:31; 9:31; 10:33–34; Chapter Nine); rather, he would have used the Semitic idiom for "human being," including himself, as English speakers sometimes use "people say" and include themselves. By the time Q was written in Greek, however, the phrase had become a specific title, indeed, a messianic title for Jesus, in several senses. It was so used of Jesus in this saying. Thus, there was an implied contrast between John and Jesus, both of whom had the same opponents. The dominant Christian view that John was only the forerunner of the Son of Man = Messiah = Jesus probably developed along side the split between John's and Jesus' followers (compare Mark 2:18–20). Indeed, there are indications that competition developed between the two groups, and that some of John's followers shifted over to the Jesus movement (especially Matt 9:14; John 3:22–30; Acts 19.1–7).

We can conclude from all this that Jesus and probably some of his disciples had close connections with John the Baptist and his disciples, that they probably been in John's prophetic movement at one time, and that Jesus had been baptized by John (Mark 1:9–11 = Matt 3:13a, 16–17 = Luke 3:21–22). Further, Jesus maintained a high opinion of John though he did not fully share John's strong apocalyptic judgment emphasis and certainly not his "ascetic" lifestyle. We can also see the increasing tendency of Christian tradition to subordinate John as "merely" the forerunner of "the Lord" who was now the Messiah Jesus, and indeed, observe some competition between the surviving followers of John and the Jesus movement.

The Itinerant Holy Man

The gospel portraits of Jesus indicate that he did not follow in the footsteps of his artisan father at Nazareth, but moved to Capernaum on the Sea of Galilee, and from there wandered about from house to house, village to village, town to town, preaching, teaching, exorcising demons, healing the sick, and offering hope to the poor, the unclean, and the outcast. This image of Jesus was that of a Spirit-filled (some scholars say "charismatic") Jewish prophet, preacher, teacher, exorcist, and healer, a "holy man" who nonetheless appeared unconcerned about, or at least was willing to break with, the legal-ritual traditions of holiness that so concerned the strictly pious among his own people.

Jesus chose from among his followers a group of disciples who exhibited in his name something of his power and authority. Thus arose what has recently been called a "Jesus movement," a social-religious movement spearheaded by a band of itinerants who, in the pattern of Jesus, went to the houses, villages, and towns of Palestine, preaching and healing (see Theissen). Jesus' mission charge to the disciples in Q may have become something of a model mission handbook in Christianity after Jesus' death, but buried in it were certain patterned features of the activity of Jesus and his first followers:

> Carry no purse, no bag, no sandals; and greet no one on the road. Whatever house you enter, first say, "Peace be to this house!" And if anyone is there who shares in peace, your peace shall rest upon that person; but if not, it will return to you. Remain in the same house, eating and drinking what they provide, for the laborer deserves to be paid. Do not move about from house to house. Whenever you enter a town and its people welcome you, eat what is set before you; cure the sick who are there, and say to them, "The Kingdom of God has come near to you." But whenever you enter a town and they do not welcome you, go out into its streets and say, "Even the dust of your town that clings to our feet, we wipe off in protest against you. Yet know this: the Kingdom of God has come near.
> (Q: Luke 10:4–11, 16 = Matt 10:12–14, 40; compare
> GTh 14.2)

The ideal in this passage, and others like it (compare Mark 6.7–13; 9.36–37; Matt 18:2, 5; Luke 9:47–48a; *Didachē* 11:4–5; John 5:23b; 12:44–50; 13:20), is in many respects similar to (influenced by?) the wandering Cynic ideal (see Chapter Three). "The harvest," sometimes developed into an image of the End (for example, Mark 4:29; Matt 13:30, 39), here combined with "laborers," suggests the mission and its urgency (compare *GTh* 73). "No purse" implies an ideal of poverty, as well as solidarity with the poor peasantry, unclean, and expendables, who were forced into poverty (compare Luke 6:20: "Blessed are you poor..."). "No bag" symbolizes dependence on others, that is, not begging for food, but sharing meals together, in contrast to the Cynic notion of self-sufficiency and begging (symbolized by the bag). We shall need to say more about this feature (see Crossan). "No sandals," that is, barefoot, was a familiar symbol of poverty. One is not to greet people on the road, perhaps a sense of urgency, but greetings do occur upon entering a (Jewish) house— "*Shālōm* to this house!—and if anyone who shares in peace ("son of peace") is there, the greeting will be received and you will receive hospitality, including a meal. "What they provide" and "what they set before you" is acceptance of hospitality of the host of the house, perhaps regardless of strict kosher rules. "The laborer deserves his wages" was a Jesus saying often recalled in early mission Christianity (compare 1 Cor 9:14; compare 1 Tim 5:18; *Didache* 13:1–2). Two other very important elements in the charge are "heal the sick" and say, "The Kingdom of God has come near to you," which we need to consider in more detail. Jesus' charge continues: If there is no hospitality extended, one either wipes off (Luke 9:5) or shakes off (Matt 10:14) the dust from one's feet, the reverse of an act of hospitality, that is, washing the guest's feet by the host's slaves (compare John 13:1–20). Thus, Jesus and his earliest disciples engaged in a rural and village mission, eventually extended to the towns. Again, such a mission was in many respects a religious-social revolution directed toward people on the margins of a society oppressed by Roman colonialism, and to that extent it had political implications. By the time of Paul, the mission had been extended to major cities in the Roman Empire, and it is clear that in these later days, some women ("sister-wives") accompanied the men on the missions (1 Cor 9:5), which might have been already developed in Jesus' day (for example, Luke 8:1–3; see the sections on eating together and healing).

Three special characteristics of the above description need to be highlighted: eating together (symbolized also by not carrying a bag), healing, and proclaiming the Kingdom of God. Though they are linked, we shall discuss the latter in the following section on Jesus' message; here we concentrate on meal practices and healing as part of Jesus' activity.

Eating Together

Sociologists and anthropologists have often stressed that meal practices symbolize social relationships: meal times and places, hospitality, who is invited, invitation customs, permitted and unpermitted foods, methods of food preparation, order of menu, persons with whom one may or may not eat, use of eating implements, seating place at the "table," appropriate table talk—all are very important social indicators. Major examples of meal practices in Greco-Roman antiquity are banquets and symposia, and in Judaism the stress on kosher foods, the Passover ritual, and not eating with Gentiles. You will recall that in early Christianity major controversies about meal practices took place, for example, at Antioch, where there was Jewish Christian scorn about eating with Gentile Christians, leading Peter to separate himself (Gal 2:11–14), and at Corinth, where the questions were whether one should eat meat sacrificed to idols (1 Cor 8; 10:14–22) and whether the rich should "banquet" with the poor at the Lord's Supper (11:17–22). Thus, it is instructive to look at Jesus and his followers in relation to meal practices.

The practice of eating together was very important to the life of the early Jesus movement (noted in Chapter Four). As the above quotation from Q indicates, the wandering Jesus and his followers were often guests in the houses of those who received them with hospitality, and there were also meals in the open. Such shared common meals celebrated unity in the new relationship with God, a unity based response to Jesus' proclamation of the kingdom reinforced by his gift of healing.

The gospels, especially expanded by Luke, show Jesus banqueting with all sorts of people; meals were inclusive, not exclusive, in itself a distinctive practice. We may assume that Jesus and his close followers often ate in the houses of the poor peasants and villagers to whom they went. Another group especially despised in polite society was labeled "tax collectors and sinners." Tax collectors were notoriously hated by colonial subjects not only for economic reasons—they were extortioners—but also because political and religious reasons: They worked for the "godless" Roman occupying powers. "Sinners" are more difficult to delineate. Apparently they were people whose activities or occupations were, according to strict interpretations of the Torah, an offense to God. For example, the earliest forms of several stories suggest that in some cases women sinners were sometimes present at meals. Prostitutes would have been an obvious example, especially if their clientele included Roman soldiers; thus, Matthew interprets the expression as "tax collectors and harlots" (Matt 21:31, 32). Whether or not the woman who showed up while Jesus was banqueting at a Pharisee's house was "a woman of the city, who was a sinner," as Luke says (Luke 7:27), and thus presumably a prostitute, may be debated (Luke 7:36–50; compare Mark 14:3–9 = Matt 26:6–13). That she showed up at all is striking. In any case, within the spectrum of those whom religious authorities considered most holy in Judaism (priests, levites) to those who were virtually beyond the bounds of the holy (for example, eunuchs, those with deformed sexual features, hermaphrodites), it is likely that the "tax collectors and sinners" were considered near the latter end of the spectrum, among the unclean. Thus, the expression "tax collectors and sinners" was a stereotyped phrase for marginal, unclean people in Jewish society. To strict religious Jews, their activities or occupations were considered an offense to God.

The following anecdote illustrates Jesus' general practice; note that it is correlated with healing, our next topic, by way of a metaphor:

> And as he sat at dinner in Levi's house, many tax collectors and sinners were sitting with Jesus and his disciples—for there were many who followed him. When the scribes of the Pharisees saw that he was eating with sinners and tax collectors, they said to his disciples, "Why does he eat with tax collectors and sinners?" When Jesus heard this, he said to them, "Those who are well have no need of a physician, but those who are sick; I have come to call not the righteous, but sinners."
> (Mark 2:15–17)

It appears that Jesus attempted to bring together such marginal people into a unified group no matter what their previous background or history, and apparently even their sex. We may also suppose that Jesus frequently ate with ordinary peasants who could not always follow the strictest Torah observance, and perhaps even women, who normally ate separately, were included. From this perspective, it is not surprising that Jesus was accused by outsiders of being "a glutton and a drunkard, a friend of tax collectors and sinners" (Matt 11:19 = Luke 7:34).

Healing the Sick

A second major activity of Jesus, also commanded of his followers, may be considered under the general term "healing." All the specific elements in the miracle stores did not happen the way in which they are recorded in the gospels; rather, they have been developed and conformed to the typical miracle stories of antiquity. Nonetheless, contemporary reconstructions of the historical Jesus do not doubt that he was an exorcist and a healer, and with some careful definition, some would include magician.

You will recall that natural disasters and widespread poverty contributed to a high level of physical disease and mental illness in Greco-Roman antiquity. Colonialism contributed further to oppression—excess taxation, military occupation, confiscation of ancestral lands, and the like—and thus to the problems of health. As the Romans and their local aristocratic supporters were viewed by common people as an attack on traditional society, so demons were viewed as an attack on the body. In Chapter Three we noted a variety of healing options, for example, health spas, prophets, charismatics, heroes, heroines, and magicians. Jesus looks most like a Jewish "charismatic" healer, for example, Honi the Circle Drawer and Hanina ben Dosa (see Chapter Four). He exorcised demons and healed the sick and, as a result, his enemies did something analogous to "witch-craft accusations," that is, they accused him of being possessed by Beelzebul, the Prince of Demons, from whom his power to exorcise demons came (compare especially Mark 3:22; Matt 12:27 = Luke 8:19). Recall that the later Jewish literature remembered him as having practiced sorcery or witchcraft, as a magician who led the people astray. By this time "magician" had become a pejorative label for healers who were not part of one's own group ("we" heal; "they" practice magic). Yet, the recollection that he was a magician was probably not just an outsider's accusatory label; traces of what on the grounds of pure description can be termed "magical technique" have not been fully erased from the exorcism and healing stories, for example, Jesus' use of spit to cure the blind (Mark 8:22–26; John 9:1–7; omitted by Matthew and Luke!). Thus, in a world that believed in warring powers of good and evil on all levels, Jesus was able, in the name of God and his kingdom, to help those who believed themselves to be possessed by demons, and to cure the sick. What Jesus and the disciples received in hospitality they returned with their gifts of health and healing, accompanied by the offer of the kingdom and a new, inclusive group.

In this concern for the unity of the group that responded to the kingdom proclamation, Jesus opposed the tendency toward exclusivity based on holiness, a common emphasis among certain priestly and sectarian Jewish leaders of his day. Among the early miracle collections there were certain miracles that revolved around meals (Feeding of 5000: Mark 6:34–44, 53; Feeding of 4000: Mark 8:1–10; John 6:1–21); healing of women who were unclean, either by a flow of blood (Woman with a Hemorrhage: Mark 5:25–34) or by death (Jairus' Daughter: 5:21–23, 35–43) or by Gentile background (Syrophoenician Woman:

7:24b–30); and the healing of the blind (Mark 8:22–26; 10:46–52), deaf and dumb (7:32–37), and demoniacs (Geresene Demoniac: 5:1–20). Also included in the early miracle collections was the healing of those whose social and economic oppression symbolized opposition to evil powers, whoever or whatever they might be. As Jesus' following among the peasant people grew, he aroused deep-rooted opposition among the political and religious Temple establishment in Jerusalem, as well as those who demanded strict Torah observance. The religious and social radicalism of Jesus and his followers was not explicitly a "political program," but it nonetheless had real political implications, just as it had in the case of John the Baptist. Jesus' unusual activities contributed heavily to an opposition at the centers of power. This opposition climaxed during a Passover celebration in Jerusalem, and led to his arrest, condemnation by the Jewish authorities on a charge of blasphemy, and final execution by the Romans on a charge of sedition . Before turning to those last days, we must first take up the third major feature of the mission discourse above, Jesus' message, which was centered in the Kingdom of God.

THE MESSAGE OF JESUS

The Proclamation of the Kingdom of God

The third major element in the mission discourse to the disciples and was the proclamation of the Kingdom of God. There is no doubt that this proclamation was the central aspect of the message of Jesus. Never, however, did he clearly define what it meant. To clarify his meaning, it is necessary to remember that in ancient Israel, prior to the time of the Babylonian Exile, there had arisen a myth about God and his kingdom. This is not surprising since the political form of government in the ancient Near East was the male-ruled monarchy, and the Israelites had developed their own version of it. God was imagined as a great king (Matt 5:35) who was so powerful that he created the world, brought his enslaved people out of Egypt, guided them through the wilderness, defeated their enemies like a conquering warrior, and gave them the promised land. He was a universal king, judging the nations, and his reign was thought to encompass his whole creation. This universal reign could be called the "Kingdom of God" (*malkuth Yahweh*), though the expression itself is not often found in Scripture (1 Chron 28:5). The myth of the God who created the world and constantly acted to preserve, protect, and judge the people became the very foundation of the nation Israel, and the myth was told and indeed acted again and again.

When Israel was finally destroyed and taken into exile by Babylon, the myth that had expressed national solidarity began to be more of a hope than a reality. It became an "eschatological myth," a millennial myth to which people clung in times of oppression and persecution, whether real or imagined. When the myth was taken up by apocalyptic seers in the years before the birth of Jesus, the tendency was to think in terms of "this (evil) age" and "the (good) age to come," "this age" being marked by a succession of four evil kingdoms that God, in one great cataclysmic and cosmic event, would overthrow and judge, preparing the way for an everlasting and victorious paradisiacal kingdom like his kingdom of old. For the apocalypticist, the more difficult and tragic conditions in this world became, the closer was the end of time—and all of this was observable by signs, the political and cosmic "signs of the times." Many apocalypticists undoubtedly took signs quite literally. Examples of this kind of thinking were frequent in Jewish and early Christian apocalyptic writing, as we have seen. However, not all of Jewish thought stressed literal apocalyptic "signs to be observed" in connection with the coming of God's Kingdom (for example, the daily synagogue prayer called the Kaddish prayer: ". . . May he establish his kingdom in your lifetime and in your days and in the lifetime of all the house of Israel even speedily and at a near time.") But whether apocalyptic signs were stressed or not, it is clear that the use of the phrase "Kingdom of God" would have called up the totality of the experience of Israel, that is, it was a *symbolic phrase recalling the kingdom myth*, the myth in which God created the world and the people, protected and sustained all of the creation, judged and defeated enemies, even judged the people when they did not conform to the covenant. This language would also give an accent to the future: The hope in Jesus' time was for the reestablishment of God's Kingdom.

There are a number of important Kingdom sayings that pass the criteria of probable authenticity and that can be easily correlated with the activity of Jesus. Consider the following distinctive sayings in relation to itinerancy and homelessness:

> As they were going along the road, someone said to him, "I will follow you wherever you go." And Jesus said to him, "Foxes have holes, and birds of the air have nests; but the Son of Man has nowhere to lay his head."
>
> To another he said, "Follow me." But he said, "Lord, let me first go and bury my father." But Jesus said to him, "Let the (spiritually?) dead bury their own (physical) dead; but as for you, go and proclaim the Kingdom of God."
>
> (Luke 9:57–58 = Matt 8:19–20 [see *GTh* 86]; Luke 9:59–60 = Matt 8:21–22)

The first saying has already received some Christian interpretations. The variant in the *Gospel of Thomas* has nothing about the followers of Jesus and, as noted above, "Son of Man" in Jesus' saying probably originally referred to human beings in general, not to Jesus as Messiah; thus, while members of the animal kingdom have their "homes," humanity in general, which includes Jesus in particular, is "homeless" and, perhaps like Wisdom, rejected. It would appear that a saying in which Jesus referred to himself has been interpreted by a Son of Man confession and extended to include his itinerant followers. The second saying is extremely radical, indeed! In Jewish antiquity, the code of honor required burial of one's parents as an absolute necessity (for example, Tobit 4:3–4; 6:13–15; *Berakoth* 3:1); the saying therefore implies that following Jesus and proclaiming the Kingdom take precedence over such family obligations.

There are other "hard sayings" affirming that Jesus' believing followers, not his "biological" family, are his true family. Note in the following sayings the mention of meals, the Kingdom, and the opposition to Jesus' exorcisms.

> Then he went home; and the crowd came together again, so that they could not even eat. When his family heard it, they went out to restrain him, for people were saying, "He has gone out of his mind." And the scribes

who came down from Jerusalem said, "He has Beelzebul, and by the ruler of demons he casts out the demons...." [the "witchcraft accusation"].

Then his mother and his brothers came; and standing outside [the house], they sent to him and called him. A crowd was sitting around him; and they said to him, "Your mother and your brothers and sisters are outside, asking for you." And he replied, "Who are my mother and my brothers?" And looking around on those who sat about him, he said, "Here are my mother and my brothers! Whoever does the will of God is my brother, and sister, and mother. [*GTh:* It is they who enter the kingdom of my father."]

> (Mark 3:19b–22, 31–35 = Matt 12:46–50 = Luke 8:19–20; plus *GTh* 99)

Following Jesus "into the Kingdom" may require rejection of the customary values about home and family.

Contemporary scholars of Jesus' teaching generally agree that among the authentic kingdom sayings is the following:

> The Kingdom of God is not coming with things ("signs") that can be observed; nor will they say, "Look, here it is!" or "There it is!" For, in fact, the Kingdom of God is among you.
>
> (Luke 17:20b–21)

With this version we may compare one from the *Gospel of Thomas:*

> His disciples said to him, "When will the Kingdom come?" [Jesus said,] "It will not come by waiting for it. It will not be a matter of saying 'Here it is' or 'There it is.' Rather the kingdom of the father is spread out upon the earth, and people do not see it."
>
> (*Gospel of Thomas* 113)

Both versions use the symbol of the Kingdom, but both deny the common apocalyptic interpretation of the eschatological myth: the Kingdom is *not* coming "with (cosmic, apocalyptic) signs to be observed"; no one will be able to say "Look, here it is!" or "There it is!" In a number of passages Jesus refused to give a sign (Matt 12:39; 16:4; Luke 11:29–32). We noted above that the earliest form of the Sign of Jonah sayings was the refusal to give any cosmic sign whatsoever: "Truly I tell you, no sign shall be given to this generation" (compare Mark 8:11–12). The exceptions related to Jonah were added in connection with the story of Jonah later. Thus, it is likely that this earliest form went back to Jesus, and was related to his view of the Kingdom.

One implication of these sayings is that Jesus is not an apocalypticist: The Kingdom is not coming with "signs to be observed"; it is already mysteriously present "among you." The phrase "Kingdom of God" is symbolic; it will have called up the myth of God's Kingdom to Jesus' hearers. It is in the nature of such language that it cannot be limited to literal, descriptive statements. Symbolic language calls forth a whole set of interrelated ideas and emotions. In other words, the eschatological mythical reality symbolized by kingdom language is confronting the hearers of Jesus already in the present; one is not simply to expect it, but to respond to it now.

Another aspect of the Kingdom can be seen in the following saying,

> From the days of John the Baptist until now the kingdom of heaven has suffered violence, and the violent take it by force.
> (Matthew 11:12)

Part of the eschatological myth in Judaism involved a cosmic battle between God and Satan, between the forces of good and the forces of evil, in which God and the forces of good would ultimately triumph. In this light, the saying expresses the view that the death of John the Baptist and the prospective suffering of Jesus and his followers is part of the eschatological war. The future battle is already taking place.

Another important kingdom saying is the following:

> But if it is by the finger of God that I cast out demons, then the Kingdom of God has come to you.
> (Luke 11:20)

This saying refers to the activity of Jesus as itinerant exorcist in the battle against the demons. As such, Jesus acts in behalf of God, or manifests his power to defeat evil. Again, the Kingdom "has come" in this activity; it is a present reality, certainly for those who are exorcised, and more, for those who can accept the saying itself. One aspect of "kingdom reality" is exorcism, and exorcism challenges the hearers of Jesus' message to take the kingdom myth seriously as an aspect of their own present experience.

To summarize, then, "Kingdom of God" is a symbol that evokes the whole range of meanings associated with the myth of God's activity as king, of his visiting and redeeming his people, not in the sense that it is simply a future reality proved by the demonstration of literal signs, but as a present reality available already through the preaching and activity of Jesus. This Kingdom reality is the central theme of the message of Jesus. It will now be helpful to clarify it through a discussion of other aspects of his message.

The Parables

Intensive work on the material in the synoptic gospels shows that there are three other areas of Jesus' message where we can come especially close to the words of the historical Jesus. These are the parables, the aphorisms, and the Lord's Prayer.

Modern research on the parables of Jesus has established a number of points about them that may be stated in summary fashion. (*a*) As discussed in Chapter Five, it is usual to contrast parable and allegory. The parable, on the one hand, makes its point as a whole story, not in its parts. Moreover, this point can never be exhausted by any one understanding; the parable is, within certain cultural limits, open-ended, so that its meaning can be newly perceived in different situations. For that reason the parable, like a poem, cannot be translated into an exact meaning, or restated as a proposition or descriptive statement of fact; rather, it must be retold. The allegory, on the other hand, makes its point in the parts; each part bears a one-to-one relationship with what it represents. Once that secret relationship is discovered, the message of the allegory becomes clear, and the allegory itself can be abandoned, for its cryptic message can now be—and should be—expressed in noncryptic language. It is generally argued that Jesus taught in parables, but the early church understood them as allegories and in many cases revised them so that they became more allegorical.

(*b*) Adjacent allegorical interpretations, transformations of the parables into allegories, and the present contexts and applications of parables in the gospels are the work of early Christian communities and the evangelists. To interpret a parable as a parable of Jesus, therefore, one must first reconstruct the original nonallegorical form of the parable and then interpret it as a parable in the context of the message of Jesus without reference to its context or function in the gospel narratives.

(*c*) The fundamental element in a parable is metaphor. *A* is compared to *B*, so that meaning may be carried over from *B* to *A*. Normally, *A* is the lesser known and *B* the better known. For example, when the Kingdom of God is the lesser known, aspects of its meaning are illuminated by something better known or more readily envisaged: the story of a man finding a treasure in a field or of a merchant finding a pearl (Matt 13:44–46).

(*d*) There is, therefore, in the parable a literal point, the meaning of the story or image, and also a metaphorical point, the meaning, the story, or image as it is transferred to what it is intended to refer.

(*e*) The purpose of a parable is normally pedagogical; Jewish rabbis used it extensively to illuminate, illustrate, and instruct. In the case of Jesus, however, this normal use of the parable seems to have been subordinated to proclamation.

The best example of parable followed by its allegorical explanation in the New Testament is the Sower (Mark 4:3–8, 13–20), already analyzed in Chapters Four and Five. Having discussed the importance of meals for Jesus' activity earlier in this chapter, we shall first illustrate parable and allegory with the parable of the Great Supper, of which we have three versions: Matthew 22:1–10, Luke 14:16–24, and the *Gospel of Thomas* 64.

In the Matthean version, the story is about a king who gives a wedding feast for his son; he sends his servants to fetch those who have been invited, but they do not come; he sends other servants who explain all the preparations for the wedding feast. Now the invited guests make excuses and some abuse the servants and kill them (verse 6). The king is angry. He sends his troops to kill the murderers and burn their city (verse 7). Then he sends servants to the thoroughfares and they invite everyone they find, "both good and bad," and the wedding hall is filled. Prior to this parable is another parable, the parable of the wicked tenants who have killed the son of the owner of the vineyard (compare Isa 5:2), who responds by putting "those wretches to a miserable death" (21:41), after which comes a quotation from Scripture, "The very stone which the builders rejected has become the cornerstone..." (compare 21:42). Prior to that is still another parable about two sons, the one obedient, the other not, the point being that tax collectors and harlots will go into the Kingdom of God before the chief priests and the elders of the people (compare 21:23, 45). This whole section indicates that the Matthean author views the parable as an allegory about Israel and the church: When Israel does not respond to the wedding feast for God's son, and indeed, kills his servants (by persecution), God destroys them, burns their holy city, Jerusalem, and invites the outsiders, "both good and bad." The allegory implies that in the light of the destruction of Jerusalem by Rome in 70 C.E., the church has succeeded Israel as the people of God. These are minivariants of the Matthean "salvation history" encapsulated in parables.

The Lukan version of the parable is much simpler (Luke 14:16–24). There is no king, but a man; no wedding feast, but a great banquet; no son; and no destruction of the city. Hints of allegorization are present in the two sets of servants (14:21, 23), but there is nothing like the highly developed allegory in Matthew's story. Yet, the story contains a point typical of Luke: those who are subsequently invited are "the poor and maimed and blind and lame" (14:21), a point that he has just made in the previous section (14:13). Indeed, the gospel for the poor is a major theme throughout the Lukan writings (for example, Luke 1:18–19; 4:22; 7:22–23). What we observe here is that Luke, who has a highly developed salvation history in his writings as a whole, interprets the story, but without nearly as much salvation-history allegory. Again, the story is simpler, more to the point, with a general moral teaching. A natural conclusion would be that Luke's version of the story is earlier.

Is this the version that Jesus told? Was Luke's concern about the "poor, maimed, blind, and lame" also typical of Jesus? Before drawing any conclusion, we must note a third version of the story, that found in the *Gospel of Thomas* 64. In this version again there is no king, but a man; again, no wedding feast, but a dinner; again, no son; and again, no destruction of a city. There are no advance invitations to special groups, but only immediate invitaions to those whom the servant finds on the roads. There are four refusals instead of three, and three of the four are based on businessmen conducting their business. The conclusion of the Thomas version is "tradesmen and merchants [shall] not [enter] the places of my Father." In this version what is new, apart from the unusual fourfold refusal, is the suddenness of the invitation and the condemnation of the merchant classes.

In these versions, we can observe an original story in three interpretations: God's rejection of Israel and acceptance of the Christians (Matthew); the good news for the "poor, maimed, blind, and lame" (Luke); and the condemnation of merchant materialism (in other Thomas sayings materialism is a hindrance to achieving true *gnōsis,* or "knowledge"). These interpretations represent the interests of the writers, though concern for the poor was prior to Luke and even part of Jesus' teaching, as we have seen. However, in terms of *form,* the original parable of Jesus was probably a simple story that had none of these specialized applications. Jesus spoke simply of an anonymous, wealthy man of the elite classes who held a sudden dinner, and without the usual advance notice, invited guests (probably three sets, common in oral tradition) who could not come. So a servant was sent to invite anyone who could come. The story beckons the hearer into a world where the unusual, the dishonorable, occurs: The invited elite do not come, but the uninvited marginal people do. This reversal of the customary is like many of Jesus' parables, and the original version probably was something like it.

A second example is the famous parable of the Good Samaritan.

"A man was going down from Jerusalem to Jericho, and he fell into the hands of robbers, who stripped him, beat him, and went away, leaving him half dead. Now by chance a priest was going down that road; and when he saw him, he passed by on the other side. So likewise a Levite, when he came to the place and saw him, passed by on the other side. But a

Samaritan while traveling came near him; and when he saw him, he was moved with pity. He went to him and bandaged his wounds, having poured oil and wine on them. Then he put him on his own animal, brought him to an inn, and took care of him. The next day he took out two denarii, gave them to the innkeeper, and said, 'Take care of him; and when I come back, I will repay you whatever more you spend.' Which of these three, do you think, was a neighbor to the man who fell into the hands of the robbers?"

(Luke 10:30–36)

This form of the parable is close to what Jesus taught. However, the present context of the discussion with the lawyer (10:25–29, 37) has been supplied by Luke, mainly relocated from his Markan source (Mark 12:28–31). In its present context the parable is an example of how to live, illustrating the principle of good neighborliness to a man in need. This is absolutely in keeping with the use of parables by later Jewish rabbis. However, the Lukan context must be ignored in an attempt to understand the parable as a parable of *Jesus*. Then it is not an example. You will recall that the Jews of Jesus' day despised the Samaritans on ethnic and religious grounds (see Chapter Two), and relations between the two groups were such that no one could expect hospitality in a Samaritan village if he were on his way to Jerusalem (Luke 9:52–56). So when the parable confronts—indeed, shocks—the Jewish hearer of Jesus at the literal level with the combination *good* and *Samaritan,* and does not value the usual code of holiness emanating from the priestly hierarchy, it is asking the hearer, at least if he or she is pious, to rethink an accepted norm of behavior related to purity, to see the outsider as insider and the insider as outsider.

What happens when one is confronted by the demand to conceive the inconceivable, to say what cannot be said? Either the demand is rejected, or the person concerned begins to question all that he or she has taken for granted. It becomes necessary to reexamine the very grounds of one's being by a challenge at the deepest level of existential reality. The parable has become proclamation.

A third, almost exact, parallel is the parable of the "Unjust Steward," or Manager.

"There was a rich man who had a manager, and charges were brought to him that this man was squandering his property. So he summoned him and said to him, 'What is this that I hear about you? Give me an accounting of your management, because you cannot be my manager any longer.' Then the manager said to himself, 'What will I do, now that my master is taking the position away from me? I am not strong enough to dig, and I am ashamed to beg. I have decided what to do so that, when I am dismissed as manager, people may welcome me into their homes.' So, summoning his master's debtors one by one, he asked the first, 'How much do you owe my master?' He answered, 'A hundred jugs of olive oil.' And he said to him, 'Take your bill, sit down quickly, and make it fifty.' Then he asked another, 'And how much do you owe?' He replied, 'A hundred containers of wheat.' He said to him, 'Take your bill, and make it eighty.'"

(Luke 16:1–7)

Verse 8 says, "And his master commended the dishonest manager because he had acted shrewdly; for the children of this age are more shrewd in dealing with their own generation than are the children of light." Beginning with this verse there are a series of moral applications to the story. These were added later and must be ignored as attempts to understand how it is that Jesus told a story about a character who was dishonest and compounded his dishonesty in the solution to his problem.

Instead of asking how this character can be seen as admirable, as did the author of verse 8, we should rather recognize the dramatic affront to moral standards that the Unjust Manager represents. In the case of the Good Samaritan, one needs to be aware of the situation between Jews and Samaritans at the time of Jesus, but with the Unjust Manager, the character's decision and actions challenge the moral standards that make possible any business relationship, any delegation of financial responsibility. The story itself focuses attention on the manager's dialogue with himself and his decision, and it implies that he was successful in his endeavor to avoid the evil consequences of his first dishonesty by compounding it. In a sense, then, the interpretation that concentrates on his "shrewdness" or the element of decision is correct. This is the focal point of the story. However, we should not remain content with recognizing that the story teases the mind of the hearer into applauding an act of decision in critical circumstances. We must go on to understand that the content of that decision is an affront to the accepted canons of moral behavior that make possible an ongoing world of business relationships. As the Good Samaritan is a challenge to say what cannot be said, this story is an effective challenge to the hearer to do what cannot be done. The story confronts accepted norms of behavior in human relationships. The Unjust Manager is a more radical form of proclamation than is the Good Samaritan. It is very difficult to applaud a decision that involves such blatant dishonesty; yet, that is what Jesus challenges his hearers to do.

A major theme of the parables is "reversal." In Luke 16:19–31, the Rich Man and Lazarus, the rich man will be punished and the poor man rewarded. In the case of the Pharisee and the Publican (Luke 18:10–14), the supposed righteous man turns out to be self-righteous, and the sinner is the righteous man. For Jesus the parable becomes a form of the proclamation of the Kingdom. As the hearers are challenged to say what cannot be said, to applaud what should not be applauded, to recognize in the reversal of human judgments and human situations the sign of the breaking in of God's Kingdom, so the Kingdom "comes." The power of Jesus to transform the parable into a form of proclamation was at the same time a power to express the experience of the Kingdom as existential reality.

Yet, Jesus did not always use the parable form in this way. Many of his parables instruct or teach, that is, they function as *parenesis*. This must have been so, because the message of Jesus could never have been as effective as its historical consequences demonstrate had it not included instruction in the mode of response to the proclamation.

Those of Jesus' day who heard the Hidden Treasure and the Pearl (Matt 13:44–46) would certainly have understood that the Kingdom evokes a response of overwhelming joy. The Tower Builder and the King Going to War (Luke 14:28-32), along with the Assassin in the *Gospel of Thomas* 98, were three kinds of people preparing themselves for their responsibilities. The Importuned Friend (the

Friend at Midnight, Luke 11:5–8) and the Importuned Judge (the Unjust Judge, Luke 18:1–8) are rabbinical arguments "from the lesser to the greater." The metaphorical position in both is the same. The friend is no real friend at all— otherwise he would be out of bed immediately—and the judge is certainly no true judge; yet, both could be pressed into doing what they should. If they can be so pressed, how much more can we not trust God, who does not need to be pressed?

We lack the space here to discuss all the parables of Jesus, but we have said enough to make the point that some of the parables of Jesus functioned as proclamation and others as parenesis. Some mediated the experience of the Kingdom of God to those who heard them, while others instructed the hearer to respond to the proclamation in various ways. An aspect of the use of the parables by Jesus we have not discussed is that which apparently refers to the future; we return to this under the rubric "Jesus and the future" below.

The Aphorisms

Collections of proverbial wisdom sayings can be found in the Hebrew Scriptures, or the Wisdom of Solomon and the Wisdom of Jesus the Son of Sira in the Apocrypha. Consider the following proverb:

> For the Lord honored the father above the children, and he confirmed the right of the mother over her sons. Whoever honors his father atones for sins, and whoever glorifies his mother is like one who lays up treasure.
> (ben Sira 3:2–4)

Note that this proverb is an expression of conventional wisdom about everyday family relationships (its lesson about parental authority is taken for granted as true) and that it is seen to conform to God's just and orderly rule of the world (it is "the way things are"). With this we may contrast the following aphorism:

> Whoever comes to me and does not hate father and mother, wife and children, and brothers and sisters ... cannot be my disciple."
> (Luke 14:26 = Matt 10:37; see GTh 55:1–2a; 101)

While the word "hate" in this saying may be hyperbolic, the point generally agrees with the other sayings noted earlier in this chapter about Jesus' true family: They are those who do the will of God and follow Jesus. Jesus' wisdom is not conventional. Thus, an aphorism is like a proverb in form but normally unlike a proverb in *content,* that is, it does not conform to the collective social wisdom of the ages about everyday life being God's orderly plan for the universe. Rather, it is a more personal flash of insight. Another example has been used in connection with homelessness of Jesus as an itinerant: "Foxes have holes, and birds of the air have nests; but the Son of Man has nowhere to lay his head" (Luke 9:58).

It must be admitted that occasionally traditional proverbs can be used in a more aphoristic sense, for example, "A prophet is not without honor, except in his own country" (Mark 6:4a = Matt 13:57 = Luke 4:24; John 4:44; compare GTh 31). An aphorism can also become a command, "Do not throw your pearls before swine, or they will trample them underfoot and turn and maul you" (Matt 7:6b). Aphorisms in oral traditions can also be slightly varied, doubled, grouped with other aphorisms or parables, worked into a dialogue, and concluded with an anecdote.

This, then, is the general background against which we must set Jesus' use of the aphorism. There are some aphorisms among the sayings already discussed. The following are important ones that Bultmann held to be authentic on the basis of what later came to be called the criterion of distinctiveness/dissimilarity. They will be at least typical of Jesus' sayings. We examine these in groups according to our own analysis.

(a) The most radical sayings: Luke 9:60a; Matt 5:39b–41

Luke 9:60a	"Let the (spiritually?) dead bury their own (physically?) dead" (already discussed in connection with Jesus' activity).
Matt 5:39b–41	"If anyone strikes you on the right cheek, turn the other also; and if anyone wants to sue you and take your coat, give your cloak as well; and if anyone forces you to go one mile, go also the second mile."

These are the most radical of the aphoristic sayings of Jesus. Indeed, they overturn normal social behavior. To "let the dead bury their own dead" by any usual norm of family behavior is to act irresponsibly. Giving the "cloak as well" and going the "second mile" are commandments that are impossible to take literally as moral imperatives. Since the Palestinian peasant at the time of Jesus wore only those two garments, the result would have been indecent exposure! Moreover, it refers to the privilege of Roman soldiers to impress local citizens into service; the result of obeying it would be a lifetime of forced servitude.

As the message of Jesus these are part of the proclamation of the Kingdom of God. They challenge the hearer to radical questioning. They jolt the hearer out of normal ways of thinking and acting by creating a judgment against them. They exactly match the function of the parable as proclamation in the message of Jesus.

(b) The eschatological reversal sayings: Mark 8:35; 10:23b, 25; 10:31; Luke 14:11 and parallels.

Mark 8:35	"For those who want to save their life will lose it; and those who lose their life [for my sake, and for the sake of the gospel] will save it" (The original may have been something like "...for the sake of the kingdom of God") (= Matt 16:25 = Luke 9:24; Matt 10:39 = Luke 17:33 [Q]; John 12:25).
Mark 10:23b, 25	"How hard it will be for those who have wealth to enter the Kingdom of God!...It is easier for a camel to go through the eye of a needle than for someone who is rich to enter the kingdom of God" (= Matt 19:22b = Luke 18:25).
Mark 10:31	"But many who are first will be last, and the last will be first" (= Matt 19:30; Matt 20:16 = Luke 13:30 [Q]; *GTh* 4b).
Luke 14:11	"For all who exalt themselves will be humbled, and those who humble themselves will be exalted" (= Matt 23:12; 18:4; Luke 18:14; Mark 10:33–34 = Matt 20:26–27; compare Luke 22:26)

In these sayings the theme of eschatological reversal is one of the best-attested themes of the message of Jesus. It proclaims the Kingdom as eschatological reversal of the present and so invites, indeed demands, judgment on that present. Again, this use of the aphorism exactly parallels a use of the parable in the message of Jesus.

(c) The conflict sayings: Mark 3:27; 3:24–26

Mark 3:27	"No one can enter a strong man's house and plunder his property, unless he first binds the strong man; then indeed the house can be plundered" (= Matt 12:29 = Luke 8:21).
Mark 3:24–26	"If a kingdom is divided against itself, that kingdom cannot stand. And if a house is divided against itself, that house will not be able to stand. And if Satan has risen up against himself and is divided, he cannot stand, but his end has come" (= Matt 12:25–26 = Luke 11:17–18).

Here we have the same kind of thinking expressed in the sayings in Luke 11:20 and Matthew 11:12 (discussed earlier) where the Kingdom is proclaimed in terms of the present exorcisms of Jesus, the fate of the Baptist, and the potential fate of Jesus and his disciples. These sayings understand human existence as an arena of conflict in which the Kingdom of God becomes a matter of human experience.

(d) The parenetical sayings: Luke 9:62; Matt 7:13–14; Mark 7:15; 10:15; Matt 5:44–48.

Luke 9:62	"No one who puts a hand to the plough and looks back is fit for the kingdom of God."
Matt 7:13–14	"Enter through the narrow gate; for the gate is wide and the road is easy that leads to destruction, and there are many who take it. For the gate is narrow and the road is hard, that leads to life, and there are few who find it (= Luke 13:23–24).
Mark 7:15	"There is nothing outside a person that by going in can defile, but the things that come out are what defile" (= Matt 15:11).
Mark 10:15	"Whoever does not receive the kingdom of God as a little child will never enter it" (= Matt 18:3; Luke 18:17; see *GTh* 22a, 46b).
Matt 5:44–48	"Love your enemies and pray for those who persecute you, so that you may be children of your Father...; for he makes his sun rise on the evil and on the good, and sends rain on the righteous and on the unrighteous. For if you love those who love you, what reward have you? Do not even the tax collectors do the same? And if you greet only your brothers and sisters, what more are you doing than others? Do not even the Gentiles do the same? Be perfect, therefore, as your heavenly Father is perfect" (= Luke 6:27–36).

In these sayings the normal use of the proverbial saying as parenesis reasserts itself, and Jesus uses the form exactly as his contemporaries among the rabbis would have. There is, of course, one great difference: These sayings are set in the context of the proclamation of the Kingdom of God. Like all the pareneses of Jesus, they are concerned with response to the reality of the Kingdom. Thus, though Jesus does not have a system of ethics in the usual sense, there are some implications for ethical reflection: The radical questioning of one's easy acceptance of his or her state of existence, the reversal of conventional morality, the battle against the forces of evil, and the necessity of responding to the kingdom proclamation with spontaneous, radical, self-giving love.

The Lord's Prayer

We reconstructed Lord's Prayer in great detail in Chapter One as follows:

> Father,
> Hallowed be your name.
> Your kingdom come.
> Give us this day our daily bread.
> And forgive us our debts,
> As we also have forgiven our debtors.
> And do not lead us to the test.

Clearly Jesus was echoing his Jewish heritage. Yet, the simplicity and brevity of the prayer—some scholars have broken down the prayer into sentence fragments—express a formal and majestic, but intimate, understanding of the relationship between the petitioner and God.

Second, we note again that the three most distinctive elements in the prayer are: use of the familiar Aramaic term for "father" ('*Abbā*'); the petition that the Kingdom "come"; and the willingness of humans to forgive as a condition for God's forgiveness of them. Jesus would also have viewed God's name as holy, have petitioned God for "daily bread" or "bread for tomorrow" and have stressed God's forgiveness of actual "debts," which in Aramaic can metaphorically mean "sins" (see Chapter One). The setting of the prayer would probably have been Jesus' meals with his disciples and marginal people. In the villages of Galilee, the Lord's Prayer was revolutionary "wisdom" and "prophetic" teaching in these circles. Finally, we would add that for those who prayed the prayer, the kingdom had already come.

JESUS AND THE FUTURE

We come now to an extraordinarily difficult point in the message of Jesus, his expectation and teaching concerning the future. We are convinced that all sayings or teaching ascribed to Jesus in the gospels that give a definite form to an expectation—for example, a future coming of the Son of Man—fail the test of the criteria for authenticity. But to say this is not to resolve the problem, for the question is not whether Jesus expected a future coming of the Son of Man, but whether he looked toward the future for something different from what was already present in the experience of those confronted by the reality of his activity and his message.

To bring this question into focus we must call attention to one result of our discussion of the message of Jesus, namely, that Jesus claimed to mediate the reality of the Kingdom of God to his hearers in a distinctive way. His proclamation of the Kingdom of God necessarily claims to mediate a reality to those of his hearers who appropriately responded to his proclamation. He took the literary form of the parable and pushed it beyond its normal limits, so that it became a medium of proclamation, and the hearers found the kingdom breaking abruptly into their consciousness as they were forced to say what could not be said and to applaud what should not be applauded. Similarly, on the lips of Jesus the proverbial saying also became aphoristic, a medium of proclamation in its power to jolt the hearer out of the effort to make a continual whole of existence in the world and into a judgment about that existence. In this "jolting" the Kingdom is also "breaking in." Finally, the Lord's Prayer envisages and expresses a relationship with God different enough from that in the Jewish prayers that for many persons who can pray that prayer the Kingdom has, in a real sense, already "come."

Yet, there is another aspect, for within the Lord's Prayer itself we find the petition "Your Kingdom come." Since we have already recognized it to parallel the petitions of the Jewish prayers in sentiment and meaning, we are forced to recognize that this petition looks toward the future, as the petitions in the Jewish prayers certainly did. Furthermore, there is a group of parables, the Sower (Mark 4:3–9), the Mustard Seed (Mark 4:30–32), the Leaven (Matt 13:33), and the Seed Growing of Itself (Mark 4:26–29), all challenging the hearer to look toward the future. At the literal level they move from the present of the sowing, or of the leavening of the dough, to the future of the result of the sowing or the leavening. At the metaphorical level also, therefore, they challenge the hearer to move from his or her present to a future. Finally, the eschatological reversal sayings seem to have an accent on the future insofar as the present is unacceptable.

At this point it becomes important to remind ourselves of several things. First, it is not necessarily the case that a modern conception of time and history can be ascribed to Jesus, a person of the first century. This consideration is reinforced by recalling that at one time, when first-century Jewish apocalyptic came very close to a modern understanding of signs as expressing a one-to-one relationship to temporal, historical events and figures, Jesus dissociated himself from such thinking. We are therefore justified in claiming that Jesus looked toward a future, but not necessarily a future conceived in what we would recognize as literal apocalyptic or temporal and historical terms. His message promised his followers a future that would be a consummation of what they already knew when they responded to the challenge of his proclamation. In their turn, they came to interpret this message in terms of a temporal and historical event drawn from apocalyptic expectations, the coming of the Son of Man, whom they now identified with Jesus. They were not necessarily correct in so doing.

THE LAST DAYS OF JESUS

Jesus' final days in Jerusalem received, like other narrative materials, a great deal of interpretation in early Christianity. In Chapter Five, we suggested that the connected passion story is increasingly judged by redaction critics to be a creation of the evangelists and is filled with prophecies that might give rise to events to fulfill them. At the same time the suspicion persists that there is some historical core underneath the accounts. We noted, for example, that the crucifixion of Jesus by the Roman authorities is judged by some historians to be the most certain event of Jesus' life, even though its details often appear to be developed from reflections about the psalms of suffering in the Scriptures. We now make some judgments about the salient points of Jesus' final days in Jerusalem.

We note first a discrepancy. The Gospel of John does not agree with the synoptic gospels that Jesus made only one trip (as an adult) to Jerusalem; rather, he made several trips to attend several festivals, and thus the length of his public life was not one year, as the synoptics imply, but at least two to three years. While this is not impossible—indeed, some think it probable—we shall focus our attention on that most important, final visit.

As an oriental temple state, the seat of holiness in Judaism was the holy city Jerusalem, its holy Temple, and within it the Holy of Holies, all under the control of the priestly hierarchy. Recall that Jesus' Kingdom message and his meal practice opposed the tendency toward exclusivity based on holiness, all of which implied an anti-Temple stance; that Jesus' healings of sick bodies was opposition to oppressive evil powers, which in antiquity could imply the realms of the economic, political, and social; and that there was always a basic distrust on the part of official and established political and religious groups of those who were outside the mainstream. As Jesus' following among the peasants and outcasts grew, he aroused opposition among the political, economic, and religious elite, as well as their "retainers," some of whom were among the religious parties, such as the Pharisees. From this perspective, it is not so surprising, then, that Jesus' inclusive, unusual meal practices, his healings and contact with the sick and marginal, his Kingdom message—itself drawn from a metaphor with potential political interpretation—contributed to an opposition that culminated in his arrest in Jerusalem, his trial by the Jewish authorities on a charge of blasphemy, and his execution by the Romans on a charge of sedition against the state.

While the facts are difficult to recover, it is possible that Jesus rode into Jerusalem on a donkey, though the gospel portraits of his tremendous reception and acclamation as the King Messiah have undoubtedly been expanded by reflection on the prophecy of the procession and entry of the humble messianic king into the holy city from Zechariah 9:9, specifically added to the story in Matthew and John (Matt 21:5; compare John 12:15). The Hosannas from the well-known and well-used texts in Jewish festival liturgies were no doubt added and received messianic interpretation (Ps 118:25–26).

An important event in the synoptics is Jesus' violent act of "cleansing of the temple" (Mark 11:15–19; Matt 21:12–13; Luke 19:45–48). In its present form, Jesus enters the Temple, drives out the money-changers, and overturns their tables, as well as those of pigeon sellers; he then quotes Scripture: "My house shall be called a house of prayer for all the nations" (Isa 56:7c) and "You have made it a den of robbers" (Jer 7:11).

There are some problems with the story. The outer precincts of the Jerusalem Temple had become a place where sacrificial animals could be purchased and money exchanged in order that the Temple tax might be paid without coins on which there were forbidden images. This was accepted practice; indeed, it was necessary to preserve purity. We have also noted the tendency of the gospel writers to relate various traditions to Scriptural prophecies. What, then, lies behind Jesus' violent act? Scholars have sometimes tied the event to a key prophecy from the trial scene that the canonical gospel writers say was spoken by false witnesses: "I will destroy this temple [made with hands] and in three days I will build another[, not made with hands]" (*GTh* 71; Mark 14:58 = Matt 26:61; compare Mark 15:29–30 = Matt 27:40–41; compare John 2:19), which is echoed in Stephen's temple polemic (Acts 7:48: "The Most High does not dwell in houses made with human hands..." (Acts 7:48). The *Gospel of Thomas* has what appears to be another variant: "I shall [destroy this] house, and no one will be able to build it [...]." The Markan version's "in three days" is probably an interpretation after the fact based on early Christian belief in Jesus' resurrection, found also in John 2:21–22. The Thomas version has no rebuilding at all; either it is more original or it is an interpretation based on the destruction of the Temple in 70 C.E. While there is no absolute certainty, it may well be that Jesus symbolically enacted in deed what he prophesied, all of which would have been consistent with his inclusive views that went beyond the kind of purity norms associated with the Temple. Indeed, it may be asked whether Jesus opposed the Temple and its sacrificial system altogether; if so, the gospels have toned down his views considerably: The Temple is only "cleansed," the words about its destruction are said by false witnesses and interpreted by the resurrection, and his opposition in the Temple is from a variety of "religious" opponents (Mark 12). While the view that Jesus literally attacked the Temple cannot be supported, it seems likely that his act, and probably the Temple destruction saying, engendered further opposition by the Jerusalem priestly establishment supported by the client kings and the Roman governor.

The second major event of Jesus' Jerusalem period was his last meal with his disciples. The synoptic gospels' overall view portrays Jesus as eating a Passover meal with his disciples on the first evening of the Passover feast (Mark 14:22–25). Afterwards, he was arrested and condemned for blasphemy at a late night trial before the Sanhedrin (Mark 14:53–72) and then crucified the next afternoon, still the first day of Passover by Jewish reckoning of the day, from sunset to sunset (Nisan 15; Mark 15:22–41). Matthew and Luke follow this general Markan Passover emphasis.

Yet, it has often been suggested that the comment in Mark 14:2, which says that the chief priests wished to arrest Jesus *before* the Feast of Passover began, "lest there be a tumult among the people" (Mark 14:2), hides a strong historical probability: The final meal was not a Passover meal. This opinion is supported by a number of other facts. First, neither of the two eucharistic rituals in the *Didachē* (10, 9) link Jesus' final meal with the Passover, and neither does Paul (1 Cor 11:23–26); indeed, the Gospel of John explicitly contradicts the Passover view by placing Jesus' crucifixion on the Day of Preparation, when the Passover lambs were slain, *before* the Passover evening meal (13:1; 19:31). The objection that John's version has symbolic significance—Jesus is the slain Passover lamb—is not sufficient; the synoptic version also has symbolic significance (new Passover, new Israel) and is highly interpreted. Second, crucial features of the Passover meal, particularly the Passover lamb and the unleavened bread, are not mentioned in the synoptic account. Third, in Jewish law, at least in somewhat later sources, night trials and single sessions of the Sanhedrin were strictly prohibited for capital cases; indeed, the courtroom was locked at night, and capital cases required a second verdict on a second day. Fourth, according to the same law, Jesus said nothing at the "trial" that was blasphemous (he said nothing against the Divine Name); moreover, the traditional Jewish punishment for blasphemy was execution by dropping a large stone on the convicted person standing in a pit ("stoning"). This problem, to be sure, is complicated by the question whether the Jews could themselves carry out capital punishment in this period (compare John 18:31: It is not lawful).

Some scholars still defend the Passover meal of the synoptics, but to us the greater historical probability is that Jesus ate one of his customary meals, perhaps with only his disciples, some time before the Passover began (the previous evening, as the Gospel of John suggests?). This would explain the problem that the earlier *Didachē* version (*Didachē* 10) appears to be a common meal of food and drink and why neither version (*Didachē* 10, 9) refers to Jesus' body and blood, the symbol for his death. It would also explain the tradition in Paul that the cup was drunk "after supper" (1 Cor 11:25), that Paul decried the social distinctions at the meal, and that such fellowship meals mentioned elsewhere as having been practiced in the early church (for example, Acts 2:46). Paul exhorts the Corinthians that if people (the elite?) could not wait (for the poor?) and eat *together*, and if they get drunk, they should eat at home, a recommendation that contributed to the eventual separation of the ritual from the common meal (compare 11:17–22, 33–34). Meanwhile, the proximity of Jesus' death to the time of the Passover contributed to the development of a "Christian Passover," and thus the synoptic tradition.

The third major historical question is this: Who was directly responsible for the execution of Jesus? The tradition that one of Jesus' disciples betrayed him may be accurate, though we can only guess at the motive. It is also possible that he was arrested in the Garden of Gethsemane by Jewish authorities as a threat to the Temple establishment and then handed over to the Roman authorities as a potential political threat, like John the Baptist before him. While it is not unreasonable to think that the Jerusalem aristocratic elite who controlled the Temple were deeply involved, it must be emphasized that gospel attempts to exonerate the prefect Pontius Pilate—a distinctly pro-Roman, pro-Gentile position—do not comport with what we otherwise know of Pilate's nasty character. Josephus relates several dramatic episodes in which Pilate crushed Jewish and Samaritan demonstrations (see Chapter Two), and Philo says that Pilate was responsible for "... acts of corruption, insults, rape, outrages on the people, arrogance, repeated murders of innocent victims, and constant and most galling savagery" (*Legation to Gaius*). We may assume that after the Roman-Jewish wars of 66–70 C.E., the gospel writers took a distinctly pro-Roman stance, thus fixing the guilt for the death of Jesus much more directly on the Jewish participants. This was all colored by the Christian belief that Jesus was the Messiah.

What we cannot doubt is that Jesus was crucified by the Romans for sedition, apparently deserted by his followers. Probably a sign was carried about his neck, as was the custom, and affixed to the Cross. It read, "King of the Jews."

FROM JESUS TO THE NEW TESTAMENT

The Jesus we can reconstruct historically from the New Testament was the pro-claimer of the Kingdom of God. More than that, he is one who had the power to mediate to his hearers that which he proclaimed and how to respond to it. On this basis he taught those who responded to the proclamation to look to the future with confidence.

There are two things conspicuously absent from this picture compared to that given in the gospels. The first is a specific claim by Jesus himself to be the Messiah. It is a striking feature of modern historical research that there is general agree-ment that the Messianic claims *put on* the lips of the Jesus of the gospels are exactly that: claims put on the lips of the Jesus of the gospels. As far as we can tell, Jesus proclaimed the Kingdom of God, exorcised demons and healed the sick, gathered together and ate with disciples, outcasts, and peasants, but made no explicit claims for himself. Of course, the very fact that he proclaimed the Kingdom of God and challenged his hearers as he did no doubt *implied* claims about himself, but Jesus did not make such claims explicit. The explicit claims in the gospels reflect the piety and understanding of the early churches and the writers of the gospels, not certain historical data about Jesus of Nazareth.

The second element conspicuously absent from this picture is an interpreta-tion by Jesus of his own death. The fact is that we simply do not know what Jesus thought about his own death. In view of the fate of the Baptist and of the saying Matthew 11:12, it is inherently probable that Jesus did recognize the dangers to himself of his last visit to Jerusalem, but the sayings in the gospels and in 1 Corinthians 11 that reflect on his death are also products of the piety and under-standing of the early church about martyrdom, and they do not tell us anything about Jesus himself.

We do know, however, that within a short time after his death the followers of Jesus were claiming that God had raised him from the dead. Where he him-self had proclaimed the Kingdom of God, they were proclaiming not only that, but Jesus himself. The proclaimer became the proclaimed (Bultmann). We have traced the various forms of this proclamation throughout the New Testament; our concern now is simply to note that the one who proclaimed the Kingdom of God began himself to be proclaimed as (*a*) the one who was about to return on the clouds of heaven as Son of Man and agent of God's final judgment and redemption of the world (so apocalyptic Christianity); (*b*) as the one who "died for our sins and was raised for our justification" (so Paul); and (*c*) as "the lamb of God, who takes away the sin of the world" (so the Johannine School). The precise historical details of the movement from the Jesus who proclaimed the Kingdom of God to the New Testament and its various proclamations of Jesus as the Christ, the Son of God, are probably forever lost to us. What we have is the New Testament itself, its proclamation and its parenesis, its myth and its history.

FURTHER READING

The literature on Jesus is much too extensive to cite; what follows is a selective sampling. We have been especially influenced by the studies of M. Borg, G. Boring, J. D. Crossan, R. A. Horsley, B. Mack, D. Oakman, G. Vermes, B. B. Scott, G. Theissen, and the discussions of R. Funk's Jesus Seminar.

ABD: "Jesus Christ" (B. F. Meyer); "Jesus, Quest for the Historical Jesus" (N. T. Wright); "The Actual Words of Jesus" (J. Riches); "Jesus, Teaching of" (M. J. Borg); "Parable" (J. D. Crossan); "Trial of Jesus" (T. Prendergast).

IDB Suppl.: "Teaching of Jesus" (W. R. Farmer); "Form Criticism, NT" (C. E. Carlston); "Parable" (C. E. Carlston); "Trial of Jesus" (D. R. Catchpole).

A. Vögtle, "Jesus Christ," in *Sacramentum Verbi* (ed. J. B. Bauer), vol. 3, pp. 419–437.

Important Recent Books (See below, Kingdom of God and Parables)

J. D. Crossan, *The Historical Jesus. The Life of a Mediterranean Jewish Peasant.*

E. Schüssler Fiorenza, *In Memory of Her. A Feminist Theological Reconstruction of Christian Origins.*

A. E. Harvey, *Jesus and the Constraints of History.*

R. A. Horsley, *Jesus and the Spiral of Violence.*

B. Mack, *A Myth of Innocence.*

J. P. Meier, *A Marginal Jew. Rethinking the Historical Jesus.* Vol. 1.

D. Oakman, *Jesus and the Economic Questions of His Day.*

E. P. Sanders, *Jesus and Judaism.*

M. Smith, *Jesus the Magician.*

G. Vermes, *Jesus the Jew.*

John the Baptist

ABD: "John the Baptist" (P. W. Hollenbach).

Jewish Culture

See Chapter Three, "Further Reading": "History, Culture, and Religion of Judaism"; "Collections of Texts."

Kingdom of God

ABD: "Kingdom of God/Kingdom of Heaven. OT, Early Judaism, and Hellenistic Usage" (D. Duling); "Kingdom of God/Kingdom of Heaven. New Testament and Early Christian Literature" (D. Duling).

NJBC, pp. 1364-1369, "The Parables of Jesus" (J. Donahue); pp. 1316-1337 "Jesus" (J.Meier).

N. Perrin, *Jesus and the Language of the Kingdom.*

Criteria of Probable Authenticity

M. E. Boring, "Criteria of Authenticity. The Lucan Beatitudes as a Test Case," *Forum* 1/4 (1985), pp. 3–38.

D. Duling, "Binding and Loosing (Matt 16–19; 18:18; John 20:23)," *Forum* 3/4 (1987), pp. 3–31.

R. W. Funk, "Criteria for Determining the Authentic Sayings of Jesus," *The Fourth R* 3/6 (November, 1990), pp. 8–10.

The Quest of the Historical Jesus

D. Duling, *Jesus Christ Through History.*

A. Schweitzer, *The Quest of the Historical Jesus.*

Classic Books

G. Bornkamm, *Jesus of Nazareth.*

H. Braun, *Jesus of Nazareth.*

R. Bultmann, *Jesus and the Word.*

H. Conzelmann, *Jesus.*

N. Perrin, *Rediscovering the Teaching of Jesus.*

Introductory Books

M. Borg, J*esus. A New Vision.*

H. Kee, *Jesus in History.*

W. B. Tatum, *In Quest of Jesus.*

Agrapha

J. Jeremias, *Unknown Sayings of Jesus.* 2d Eng. ed.

W. D. Stoker, *Extracanonical Sayings of Jesus.*

Old Testament Pseudepigrapha; New Testament Apocrypha

J. H. Charlesworth, ed., *The Old Testament Pseudepigrapha.* 2 vols.

E. Hennecke and W. Schneemelcher, eds., *New Testament Apocrypha.* 2 vols.

Anecdotes and Miracle Stories

See Bibliography, Chapter Five.

NJBC, pp. 1369–1373 (D. Senior: "The Miracles of Jesus").

Aphorisms and Parables

NJBC, pp. 1364–1369 (J. Donahue: "The Parables of Jesus").

J. D. Crossan, *In Parables. The Challenge of the Historical Jesus.*

J. Donahue, *The Gospel in Parables.*

R. W. Funk, B. B. Scott, and J. R. Butts, *The Parables of Jesus.*

J. Jeremias, *The Parables of Jesus..*

J. W. Miller, *Step by Step Through the Parables.*

B. B. Scott, *Hear Then the Parable. A Commentary on the Parables of Jesus.*

Social Issues

R. Horsley, *Sociology and the Jesus Movement.*

B. Mack, *A Myth of Innocence. Mark and Christian Origins.*

D. Oakman, *Jesus and the Economic Questions of His Day.*

L. Schottroff and W. Stegemann, *Jesus and the Hope of the Poor.*

G. Theissen, *Sociology of Early Palestinian Christianity.*

Other

V. Harvey, *The Historian and the Believer.*

L. Keck, *A Future for the Historical Jesus.*

W. Marxsen, *The Lord's Supper as a Christological Problem.*

B. Meyer, *The Aims of Jesus.*

W. Thompson, *The Jesus Debate.*

EPILOGUE:
WAYS OF BEING RELIGIOUS
IN THE NEW TESTAMENT

It is not possible to read the New Testament without being impressed by its immense variety, and especially by the variety of ways of being religious it exhibits. Although the New Testament is a unity in that all of its books accept the centrality of Jesus Christ, nonetheless it is diverse in that both the understanding of Jesus and the understanding of what it means to accept him are almost infinitely varied. Ascetic and mystic, warrior priest and worker priest, apocalyptic visionary and social revolutionary, ecclesiastical dignitary and street-corner pamphleteer—all these and many more have taken their inspiration from the New Testament or from some part of it. We have constantly been calling attention to this variety within the New Testament; now in this epilogue we briefly summarize some of its major orientations.

Apocalyptic

Apocalyptic is a major element in the synoptic gospel source Q, in portions of Paul's letters, in the Gospel of Mark and, of course, in the book of Revelation, the only full-blown New Testament apocalypse. The apocalyptic visionary is one caught up in the drama of a history hurrying to its close, preparing for the imminent future in which all will be different. Christian apocalypticism developed the concept of Jesus as the Son of Man, the powerful redeemer who would descend to the earth on the clouds of heaven to judge and redeem, destroy and remake. Yet, it did more than that, because it claimed not only that Jesus was the Son of Man; it claimed that the Son of Man was Jesus. That claim meant that characteristics of the redeemer figure were always subject to the control of the lineaments of Jesus. Thus, for example, the evangelist Mark was able to blend together the elements of power and authority and the necessity of suffering. In many respects, Christian apocalyptic was indistinguishable from Jewish apocalyptic, and certainly Christian apocalyptic writers made extensive use of Jewish apocalyptic literature. The central feature of their visions, however, was always Jesus. Nonetheless, the movement was apocalyptic, with its sense of a world being caught up in the throes of catastrophic change and its belief in the imminence of the final intervention of God that would make all things new and different. Like all apocalyptic writers, the Christian apocalypticist was alienated from the dominant social and religious structures; so the apocalypticist despaired of the world and its history, but had faith in God, who was about to change it. As a Christian the apocalypticist believed that Jesus would be the means of that change, and thus made preparations for the imminent coming of Jesus as Son of Man by obeying the teaching that was given in the name of Jesus.

The Apostle Paul

> For I am not ashamed of the gospel: it is the power of God for salvation to everyone who has faith, to the Jew first and also to the Greek. For in it the righteousness of God is revealed through faith for faith, as it is written, "He who through faith is righteous shall live." (Rom 1:16–17)

> There is therefore now no condemnation for those who are in Christ Jesus. For the law of the Spirit of life in Christ Jesus has set me free from the law of sin and death. (Rom 8:1–2)

With such deeply rooted convictions Paul put forth his view of the good news about Christ and his Cross-resurrection. That which he could not do himself, that which he believed the Law could not help him to do, Christ has done for him. Paul can now stand in the presence of God, from which presence he would before have had to flee, for he now bears not his own righteousness but Christ's. He now lives in the world not the life of fear and condemnation but of freedom and power within the bounds of faith and love. This life is Christ's gift to him. Here we recognize a classical form of the Christian experience of religious reality. It is the conviction that one is justified in the sight of God, and the discovery that this can be received only as a gift. Central to this understanding is a concentration on the Cross of Christ, interpreting it as a means of reconciling human beings to God. This understanding of religion is loaded with the symbolism of evil and focuses attention on the means whereby that evil is overcome and a quality of life from it can be known.

The Evangelist Matthew

With the evangelist Matthew we reach another of the classical options of New Testament religion. Here the central point is the concept of a verbal revelation authoritatively interpreted. The essence of religion is obedience to the revealed truth, and such obedience is possible because the world and life are ordered by the God who has revealed this truth to humanity. There is order and stability to be experienced, there is the firm basis of a revealed truth on which to build; there are appointed means both to make possible the necessary understanding and also to help attain the necessary level of obedience. These means are present in the church, in the structure and organization of the community of which the individual is a member and in which the risen and glorified Christ is present. In this understanding of what it means to be religious in the world, the essential elements are those of revelation and of obedience to revelation, and the conviction that there is a correspondence between the revealed truth and the experienced reality of life in the world such that life in the world, can be successfully organized on the basis of obedience to the revelation, and only on that basis.

The Author of Luke-Acts

The author of Luke-Acts is also concerned with revelation but with revelation in the form of a sacred person and a sacred time, and with a structured means of relating to that time. That person is Jesus, and that time is the time between the descent of the Spirit upon him at his baptism and the return of the Spirit to God at the Cross. One relates to him and to his time by means of the Spirit, which returned to the church and the believer at the baptism of Pentecost. In his own life Jesus was a paradigm of the possibilities for human existence in the world and the model of what it means to be religious in the world. The presence of the spirit of Jesus in the world, linking the believer with the sacred life and sacred time of Jesus, empowers the believer to exhibit the same quality of life in the world that Jesus did. This is borne out by the heroes and heroines of the church whose lives paralleled Jesus' in many respects. To be religious in the world is to imitate Jesus, the one who offers salvation to all, men and women, Jew and Greek, rich and poor, slave and free. This imitation made possible by the presence and work of Jesus' spirit in the world. To imitate Jesus means to care for the outcast, to concern oneself for the neighbor, to live the life of love in the world and for the world.

The Evangelist John

In the case of the evangelist John we have a concentration on the Cross of Christ almost as strong as that in the case of the apostle Paul. In John, however, the context is not the symbolism of evil but rather the symbolism of glory. The Christ of John's gospel is the descending/ascending redeemer, and the Cross is the moment of his glorious return whence he came—having achieved that for which he was sent. While the Cross itself is the moment of supreme glorification, there is a series of earlier majestic "signs" by means of which the Christ also manifests his glory. Moreover, a series of solemn discourses explores the glory of this Christ by using primary symbols of life-giving power—water, light, bread—and by claiming explicitly that he gives life and "eternal life" to those who believe in him. Further, he does the Father's work; he is at one with God. Combined with this emphasis on glory and power and on the Christ's oneness with God is an emphasis on the concern of the Christ for the believer, for example, by the use of shepherd and sheep symbolism, and on the believer's oneness with him. This last point is the key to the Johannine understanding of what it means to be religious in the world. The believer contemplates the glorious majesty of the Christ and of the Christ's oneness with the Father, and then finds himself or herself at one with the Christ in a mystical union by means of which he or she experiences the life of love in the world and against the world. But the emphasis now is on the rapture of love as experienced with other believers through knowledge of Christ, whereas in Luke-Acts the emphasis is on the manifestation of love in human relationships. Of course, neither excludes the other (see 1 John 2:1-11), but the emphasis is different. The gospel and letters of John are the charter of Christian mysticism.

The Other Ways

There are other understandings of what it means to be religious in the world in the New Testament. There are parts of the Jesus tradition in the gospels that focus on "the social gospel," that is, political, social, and economic liberation for oppressed peoples. Most, however, are variations, sometimes very important variations, on the main themes just mentioned. So, for example, the Gospel of Mark reshapes the apocalyptic way of being religious in the world by systematizing the mysterious apocalyptic drama, by developing the theme of the Son of Man who "must" suffer, and by showing what these things mean to faith and discipleship. Similarly, the writers of the period of the emerging institutional church develop, systematize—and further institutionalize—the "way" of the Gospel of Matthew. It is therefore not so surprising that many kinds of Christianity have developed from the New Testament, each in its own way finding some basis in these marvelous texts.

APPENDIX:
MAJOR ARCHEOLOGICAL AND TEXTUAL
DISCOVERIES AND PUBLICATIONS

In Chapter One we noted that in the narrow sense archeology refers to the science of recovering and evaluating the material remains of everyday life from past civilizations, but that in the broader sense it includes manuscript discoveries. We have had occasion to mention a number of such discoveries throughout this textbook, for example, the inscription from Delphi, Greece, which is the most important evidence we have for helping to date the Pauline letters (Acts 18:12–18; see Chapters Four and Six).

Because archaeological and textual discoveries and publications relating to the period of the New Testament are much too numerous to describe in a short appendix, we shall highlight only some of the most important ones.

THE DEAD SEA SCROLLS AND KHIRBET QUMRAN

In the spring of 1947 two Arab shepherd boys of the Bedouin Ta'amireh tribe were grazing their flocks of sheep and goats at the foot of the cliffs about a mile west of the Dead Sea, the lowest point on the earth's surface. They were about twelve miles east of Jerusalem and adjacent to the ancient ruins of the Wadi Qumran (a wadi is a dry riverbed that fills up in the rainy season). According to the boys, one of the animals strayed; in their search for it, Muhammed ed-Dib threw a stone into one of the cave openings high up the face of the cliff. Instead of the thud of stone against stone, he heard a shattering sound and, perhaps because of fear of demons, he fled. Later, when his fear subsided, Muhammed and his companion, Ahmed Muhammed, returned to the cave, went exploring, and found elongated jars—one of them containing leather scrolls—partly buried in the cave floor. Muhammed ed-Dib had discovered the first of what became known as the Dead Sea Scrolls, a discovery the eminent American archeologist W. F. Albright called, in a letter to Dr. John Trevor of the American Schools of Oriental Research, "the greatest manuscript discovery of modern times."

The following period was characterized by clandestine and illegal excavations and by the intrigue of buying and selling the valuable manuscripts. Some of the scrolls were finally purchased in a Jerusalem antiquities shop by Prof. E. L. Sukenik for the Hebrew University in Jerusalem. Another lot was acquired from the Bethlehem shoemaker and middleman Kando by the Syrian Orthodox Metropolitan of Jerusalem. It was identified by scholars at the American School of Oriental Research, smuggled to the United States by the Metropolitan, and finally purchased for the Hebrew University at the highly inflated price of $250,000 in 1954. After the initial discovery, Arab-Israeli fighting frustrated attempts to find the site of the discovery and carry out scientific excavations until the spring of 1949. The fantastic episode seemed closed. However, further digging by the

Ta'amireh tribesmen in 1951 uncovered more scrolls in caves at nearby Wadi Murabba' at. These scrolls also ended up in the hands of antiquities dealers. More bargaining took place, and a series of scientific excavations of the caves was begun in the general area.

In 1951 the first digging at the nearby site known as Khirbet ("ruin" of) Qumran convinced most scholars that it was the ancient monastery of the Essenes, who were described by Josephus, Philo of Alexandria, and Pliny the Elder, descriptions conveniently collected and discussed in A. Dupont-Sommer, *The Essene Writings from Qumran*. Though under challenge in some quarters, this Essene theory still predominates among scholars. More discoveries by the Ta'amireh tribesmen and further scientific explorations in eleven caves by the Wadi Qumran, as well as at several nearby sites, unearthed the remains of about 800 books, mostly in small fragments but including about ten complete scrolls. This was a library of significant proportions. Most of the manuscripts were written on parchment (leather), though a few were on papyrus and two were on copper. The most valuable finds were discovered in Cave I (the first discovered), Cave IV, and Cave XI. After many years of delay, in part due to the material's fragmentary nature, all the texts are now being published (1993).

The usual theory about the archeological excavations of Khirbet Qumran is that, on top of an eighth-century-to-seventh-century B.C.E. fortress, the Essene community built a monastery that it occupied in two periods, the first from about 135 B.C.E. to 31 B.C.E., when it was destroyed by an earthquake, and the second from about 4 B.C.E. to 68 C.E., when it was destroyed by the Romans. The elaborate site contained a water supply system with an aqueduct, cisterns and baths, assembly and banquet halls, kitchen and pantry, laundry, scriptorium (a room for copying texts), pottery workshops, storerooms, stables, watchtower, and cemetery. Other excavations were undertaken two miles south at Khirbet Feskhah, where there was an agricultural complex; nine miles inland at Khirbet Mird, where there was a Hasmonean fortress; and twelve miles south at Wadi Murabba'at, where four caves contained Greek, Aramaic, and Hebrew materials related to the bar Cochba Revolt of the Jews in 132–35 C.E., including letters of the revolutionary Jewish leader Simon bar Kosibah (see Chapter Two). A few other valleys and caves to the south were explored.

About one-fourth of the Dead Sea Scrolls are books that were eventually included in the Hebrew Bible, all thirty-nine books being represented except the book of Esther. Other categories of literature in the scrolls are Apocrypha and Pseudepigrapha (see below); Biblical commentaries exemplifying the *pesher* method of interpretation; apocalyptic, sectarian writings such as the War of the Sons of Light Against the Sons of Darkness; and rules for the community (the Manual of Discipline). All three languages—Hebrew, Aramaic, and Greek—are found in the scrolls, Hebrew predominating. The presence of books from the Apocrypha and Pseudepigrapha is further testimony that before the scholars of Yavneh or Jamnia began to narrow down the number of sacred texts, there was current prior to 70 C.E. a much larger and more diversified body of literature in use, and that some of what became Biblical texts were current in different types (recensions).

The organization of the community was based on several texts, especially the Manual of Discipline. It included divisions into priests and laity; the domination of the priests, including a priest-president who presided at the sacred meal; an overseer who had power over admissions, instruction, and various practical matters; a guardian of all the "camps"; a Council of the Community; a future lay leader (perhaps a royal Messiah); a Court of Inquiry to try offenders; an annual assembly at the Feast of the Renewal of the Covenant; nightly study and prayer; and a two-year initiation for new members. Several important beliefs and practices were that the community is the elect, purified remnant of Israel that will be vindicated in the final days (apocalyptic eschatology); that the Jerusalem Temple and its priesthood are polluted and are replaced by the community and its worship life; close adherence to ritual laws and seasonal festivals according to a solar calendar; the maintenance of purity by ritual baths; a sacred meal in which bread and wine are served and that anticipates the messianic banquet; a dualistic eschatology that opposed light, good, and angelic powers against darkness, evil, and the demonic powers; the hope for a prophet, as well as a Messiah of Aaron (priestly) and a Messiah of Israel (royal); and the anticipation of a postmessianic age that includes a new Jerusalem.

The discovery of the Dead Sea Scrolls was an amazing event. Old Testament texts in Hebrew predated previously known texts by a thousand years; the history of the Old Testament textual traditions was illuminated; knowledge of a little-known Jewish sect was impressively revealed; the understanding of pre-70 C.E. Judaism was totally transformed; and a sectarian movement parallel to early Christianity was uncovered, one that continues to provide invaluable information for the environment of Christian origins.

MASADA

About thirty miles south of Khirbet Qumran along the Dead Sea is a magnificent mesa, the flat top of which covers about twenty acres, with steep rock cliffs rising about 600 feet on the west side and about 820 feet on the east. This natural fortress was accessible only by two paths, one of which was the treacherous "snake path," and the other of which narrowed at one point, making it easy to defend. On the top Herod the Great built a walled fortress that he named Masada ("mountain stronghold"). The Jewish writer Josephus has immortalized the location with his exciting, but tragic, tale of the last stand of the Jewish revolutionaries and their mass suicide in order not to be taken alive by the Romans (Josephus, *Wars* 7.8–9). The site is symbolic of Israeli patriotism to this day.

Initial surveys of the well-known site in 1953 and 1955–1956 led to a full-scale archeological expedition in 1963–1965 headed by the noted Israeli archeologist Yigael Yadin. The discoveries revealed three main periods of occupation: (1) Herodian (37–4 B.C.E.); (2) the period of the Jewish-Roman wars and their aftermath (66–73 C.E.); and (3) the Byzantine period (fifth-sixth centuries C.E.). Since there was no water supply, Herod built dams on two small wadis below, and in the rainy season the water flowed by channels to two huge reservoirs cut into the cliff on the northwest side; from there the water was carried by slaves to cisterns on the top; all together the cisterns held about 1,400,000 cubic feet of water. His casemate (double-walled) wall surrounding the top (except for the villa) had thirty towers and four gates. Also on the top Herod constructed a series of storerooms for provisions, an intimate and luxurious three-tiered palace-villa at the north end, a huge western palace for administration and ceremony, several small palaces for family members and high-ranking officials, a luxurious bath-house, and a swimming pool.

Prior to the beginning of the revolt in 66 C.E., a Roman garrison was bivouacked on Masada. At the outbreak of the war, the revolutionaries took it by trickery and adapted it for themselves and their families. They also constructed ritual baths, a synagogue, and what may be a religious study house. Excavators uncovered in the western palace many burnt arrows and coins and in the smaller palaces scrolls of the Scriptures, of the famous second-century B.C.E. sage, ben Sira, and of some Qumran literature, indicating that some point of contact existed between the Essenes and the Masada revolutionaries. About 700 ostraca (pieces of pottery often used for ballots) show not only Hebrew and Aramaic writing, but also Greek and Latin. There is still visible a gigantic dirt ramp, on which a huge battering ram was brought forward by the Romans in their siege of the fortress. A Roman garrison remained after the siege. Subsequently, Masada was deserted until some Christian monks settled there and built a church, as well as a few rooms and cells.

THE NAG HAMMADI TEXTS

The precise details leading up to the discovery at Nag Hammadi are not clear. Late in 1945, an Egyptian peasant boy, Abu al-Majd, discovered twelve papyrus codices plus part of a thirteenth (tucked into Codex VI) bound in portfolio-like leather covers and stored in a ceramic jar under an overhanging rock at the base of the Jabal el-Tarif, located near the Nile River towns of Chenoboskia, a monastic center, and Nag Hammadi, both in southern ("Upper") Egypt. The peasant boy was accompanied by six others, one of whom was his oldest brother, Muhammad 'Ali, who took charge. Muhammad broke open the jar and, upon finding the codices, decided to divide them up among the seven camel drivers present; when the fearful and unknowing drivers refused their shares, Muhammad put them in a pile, wrapped them in his white headdress, and slinging them over his shoulder, mounted his camel and headed for his home in Chenoboskia. The usual confusion and intrigue followed: the scrolls made their way to middlemen, then to antiquities dealers, and finally to the Coptic Museum in Old Cairo, Egypt. The Jung Codex was an exception; it went to the United States and then to Brussels, Belgium, where it was purchased for the C. G. Jung Institute in Zurich and presented to the eminent psychiatrist Jung as a birthday present; subsequently (after its publication) it was returned to Cairo.

The announcement of the discovery of the Nag Hammadi texts officially began in 1956. The texts consist of copies of Coptic translations of fifty-one Greek texts (Coptic is an Egyptian language written with mostly Greek letters). In their present form as copies, they date from about the middle of the fourth century C.E., but some of the original autographs are much older and the Greek still earlier. The collection represents many literary types (genres), some like those of the canonical New Testament. It contains gospels, apocalypses, acts, letters, dialogues, secret books, speculative treatises, wisdom literature, Biblical interpretations, revelation discourses, and prayers. The texts also represent various types of Gnosticism known from the early Church Fathers, as well as the Egyptian Hermetic literature and non-Gnostic writings, such as Plato's *Republic*. Moreover, the texts show strong influence of Jewish traditions and interpretations, for example, the Genesis myth of creation, the Wisdom myth, various techniques of scriptural interpretation, and the apocalyptic periodization of history.

The question of the origin of Gnosticism in general has been hotly debated, and these texts add to the debate. Some of the texts seem to be non-Christian, but this does not answer the question whether they are pre-Christian. Nonetheless, it has been demonstrated that a non-Christian text in the collection (Eugostos the Blessed) has been reworked and made into a Christian version (the Sophia of Jesus Christ), that is, a Gnostic Christian has made use of a non-Christian text. This is all the more interesting when it is observed the Nag Hammadi text called The Apocalypse of Adam appears to be non-Christian, maybe dating as early as the second century C.E., yet it contains the full-blown Gnostic redeemer myth. Such an instance would seem to support the *possibility* that early Christianity could have been influenced by such a myth in its interpretation of Jesus.

One of the most important texts for the interpretation of Christian literature is the Coptic *Gospel of Thomas* from Nag Hammadi. It contains a collection of Jesus' sayings, including some thirteen parables that are variants of synoptic gospel parables. The genre of a "sayings-collection" is important for the Q hypothesis; moreover, a comparison of the forms of the Thomas parables with those of the synoptic tradition shows that the *Gospel of Thomas* has reserved simpler, probably earlier, forms of some of Jesus' parables. Its value for the Jesus tradition can therefore not be overestimated (see Chapters Five, Fifteen).

Until the discovery of the Nag Hammadi texts, what was known about Gnosticism came primarily indirectly, that is, through the critical attacks of early, anti-Gnostic Christian writers. Now there is available a group of texts that show what some Gnostics themselves believed. These texts are extremely valuable for the light they shed not only on the Gnostic movement but also on the history of Judaism and early Christianity, which interacted and had to come to terms with it.

THE OLD TESTAMENT PSEUDEPIGRAPHA

The term "Pseudepigrapha" means literally "false superscriptions," or false writings, not because they are not true, that is, spurious, but because they are noncanonical writings that for the most part are inspired by, in honor of, and attributed to Old Testament heroes who did not write them; that is, they are pseudonymous (see Glossary). The term is not totally satisfactory because Old Testament writings, like those in the New Testament, are also pseudonymous, and not every book in the collection called Pseudepigrapha is pseudonymous. Yet, no better term has been found for these books. Briefly, they are books that are either partially or totally Jewish or Jewish-Christian, from the approximate period 250 B.C.E. to 250 C.E.; they are normally considered to be inspired by or related to the Jewish Scriptures (Old Testament); and they are usually attributed to some Old Testament figure. Usually excluded are most (but not all) of the books from the same period called the Apocrypha (though most of the Apocrypha is found at various places in the Old Testament canon for Roman Catholics; the Protestant churches returned to the Hebrew Bible); also excluded are the Dead Sea Scrolls as a special discovery, and the Coptic Gnostic Nag Hammadi Texts as another special discovery, though some would like to include the (apparently non-Christian) Apocalypse of Adam, and certainly *by definition* many of the Dead Sea Scrolls could be included. The rabbinic literature (especially the Mishnah and the Talmuds) that has been preserved among Jewish scholars for centuries since its earliest sections were codified about 200 C.E. is excluded as well; this body of literature has traditions that go back to the period covered by the Pseudepigrapha, though most of it is later.

The Pseudepigrapha or parts thereof can be found in a number of modern editions. The classic is volume 2 of the two-volume collection by R. H. Charles called *Apocrypha and Pseudepigrapha of the Old Testament.* The Pseudepigrapha volume contains seventeen writings, introduced and extensively annotated. More recent and comprehensive is the two-volume edition edited by J. H. Charlesworth, *The Old Testament Pseudepigrapha.* Because of new discoveries, publications of little-known manuscripts, further evaluation of previously known documents, and the inclusion of a few documents that might, strictly speaking, fall outside the dating boundaries, this edition contains sixty-three documents with introductions and annotations, clearly a significant increase in the amount of material available to the Biblical student for historical and literary study. There is a wide variety of forms and genres, including apocalypses, testaments, prayers, psalms, hymns, odes, oracles, and legends. The material contains not only apocalyptic eschatology, but also much information about some of the more esoteric aspects of Judaism and Jewish Christianity, for example, astrology and magic. In short, though the Pseudepigrapha is not a completely new discovery in the sense of the Dead Sea Scrolls or the Nag Hammadi texts, much of it is either new or scarcely known and it is an important addition to the noncanonical materials of the period.

SINAITICIUS FROM THE MONASTERY OF ST. CATHERINE'S AT MOUNT SINAI

An especially interesting example of a "rediscovery" of a manuscript is Codex ("Book") Sinaiticus, a fourth-century manuscript that originally contained the whole Bible in Greek translation, plus two noncanonical works, the *Epistle of Barnabas* and the *Shepherd of Hermas.* Codex Sinaiticus is considered to contain one of the two most important more or less complete manuscripts of the New Testament. In 1844 a German textual critic, Constantin von Tischendorf, went to the Sinai Peninsula east of the Red Sea looking for manuscripts. If the story can be trusted, he saw in the Monastery of St. Catherine's at the foot of Jebel Musa ("Mount of Moses"), the traditional site of Mount Sinai, a basket of manuscripts that had been used by the monks to start fires. Allowed to examine them, von Tischendorf discovered that they included the Greek version, or Septuagint, of four books of the Old Testament, as well as Tobit and 2 Esdras, a total of forty-three pages, the monk having claimed that some baskets had already perished! Von Tischendorf was granted permission to take these forty-three leaves to the University of Leipzig, where they were presented to his patron, the king of Saxony, and where they remain in the university library. Keeping silent about their place of origin, he returned in 1853, but was unsuccessful in his effort to see the rest of the codex. However, on the last day of his third visit in 1859, von Tischendorf showed the steward of the monastery his own 1846 printed edition of the other pages, whereupon the steward showed him a great portion of the rest of the codex, 347 leaves, wrapped in a red cloth. When the secretly excited von Tischendorf stayed up all night looking at its contents, he discovered that it also contained the New Testament. Refused permission to buy it, he went to Cairo, prevailed upon the abbot to have it sent there, and then copied it, eight pages at a time. Eventually, for certain monetary gifts and ecclesiastical favors to the Greek Orthodox monks by the czar of Russia, von Tischendorf's current patron, the codex was presented to the czar and a facsimile edition published at Leipzig. Finally, after the Russian Revolution, the Russian government, in need of cash, sold it to the British Museum, whence it was delivered in 1933 and where it is prominently displayed today. Curiously, a dozen more leaves of the codex turned up in 1975 in the wake of a fire at the monastery and are in the process of being published.

MISCELLANEOUS PALESTINIAN ARCHEOLOGY

Herod the Great's Building Projects

The Jerusalem Temple. The rebuilding of the magnificent Jerusalem Temple began about 20 B.C.E. and, while the basic construction was completed about eighteen months, work probably was still being done until it was destroyed in 70 C.E. by the Romans. Because of destruction, much of the imaginative reconstruction must be done with the aid of 1 Kings and Josephus' works as literary sources. The bottom sections of the Western Wall, or Wailing Wall, are Herodian, and on it can be seen Robinson's Arch and Wilson's Arch (see photo, Chapter 9. There is also an excavation from Roman times on the North Wall at the Damascus Gate.

The Herodian palace area, city buildings, streets.

Masada. Herod's most famous palace-fortress complex (See above).

Herodium. Another of Herod's opulent palace-fortresses built atop a high hill not far from Bethlehem.

Jericho. Herod's luxurious winter palace in the warm Jordan valley.

Caesarea Maritima. A human-made seaport-city on the Mediterranean Sea, the "Roman capital of Judea".

Other Discoveries In and Near Jerusalem

Theodotus Inscription. One important find is the Theodotus Inscription (pre-70 C.E. date now debated). It is a dedicatory inscription that shows that a

Greek-speaking synagogue had existed in Jerusalem.

The crucifixion of Jehohanan. A small slab containing a spike and heel bones discovered in tombs northeast of Jerusalem represents the only surviving archeological remains of the crucifixion of a first-century Jew.

The pool of Bethesda (John 5:2).

The tomb of Caiaphas.

The "Burnt House," destroyed by the Romans in 70 C.E.

Jewish Synagogues

Archeological evidence that *Palestinian* synagogue *buildings* existed before 70 C.E. is sparse. (There is, however, first-century evidence for synagogues *outside* Palestine.) Palestinian evidence is limited to a few rooms (Masada, Herodium, Magdala, Gamala), possibly a first-century structure underneath a fourth/fifth-century synagogue at Capernaum, and possibly a Greek-speaking synagogue in Jerusalem (note the uncertain date of the Theodotus Inscription). Since this small amount of evidence conflicts with Josephus' writings and the New Testament, the problem may be one of definition: There may have existed rooms in houses used as synagogues ("house-synagogues" similar to Christian "house-churches").

Galilean Towns/Cities

Excavations in Lower (southern) Galilee and along the Sea of Galilee show that much of Galilee was not a "cultural backwater" as used to be thought. Discoveries at **Sepphoris,** an administrative capital along a major trade route, reveal a Greco-Roman cultural and religious presence only four miles from the village of Nazareth, Jesus' hometown. Such excavations play a role in the discussions about possible Greco-Roman (Hellenistic) influences on Jesus and earliest Christianity. One example is the use of Greek as well as Hebrew and Aramaic. Another is unconventional "wisdom" in Q as the literary context of the Lord's Prayer. **Capernaum**, a center of Jesus' activity, preserves the remains of a house under which may be more remains of a house belonging to Jesus' disciple Peter. It also has the ruins of a synagogue (see above).

Other Greco-Roman Cities and Religious Sites

Forums, main streets, town squares, market places, theaters, baths, stadiums, hippodromes, aqueducts, coliseums, houses, banquet rooms, and the like give glimpses of "urban" social life throughout the Roman Empire. Temples, groves, caves, theaters, hippodromes, mosaics, vase and wall paintings, and the like reveal the awe and mystery of Greco-Roman religious life.

FURTHER READING

The literature in this area is vast; the following represents a minimal selection and focuses primarily on Palestinian archeology.

General

C. Evans, *Noncanonical Writings and New Testament Interpretation.*

The Dead Sea Scrolls and the Khirbet Qumran Area

ABD: "Community, Rule of the (1QS)" (J. Murphy-O'Connor); "Damascus Rule (CD)" (P. R. Davies); "Dead Sea Scrolls" (J. J. Collins); "Pesharim, Qumran" (D. Dimant); "Qumran, Khirbet" (J. Murphy-O'Connor); "Zadokite Fragments (Damascus Document)" (L. H. Schiffman).

NJBC, pp. 1055–1077, "Dead Sea Scrolls" (R. Brown).

IDB: "Dead Sea Scrolls" (O. Betz).

IDB Suppl.: "Dead Sea Scrolls" (G. Vermes).

T. Beall, *Josephus' Description of the Essenes Illustrated by the Dead Sea Scrolls.*
F. M. Cross, *The Ancient Library of Qumran and Modern Biblical Studies.*
A. Dupont-Sommer. *The Essene Writings From Qumran.* Trans. by G. Vermes.
J. A. Fitzmyer, *The Dead Sea Scrolls. Major Publications and Tools for Study.*
J. T. Milik, *Discoveries in the Judean Desert* (standard edition, several volumes).
H. Ringgren, *The Faith of Qumran.*
H. Shanks, et al. *The Dead Sea Scrolls After Forty Years.*
K. Stendahl, *The Scrolls and the New Testament.*
G. Vermes, *The Dead Sea Scrolls in English.*
———, *The Dead Sea Scrolls. Qumran in Perspective.*
L. H. Schiffman, *Archeology and History in the Dead Sea Scrolls.*

Masada

ABD: "Masada" (E. Netzer).

IDB: "Masada" (R. Funk).

IDB Suppl.: "Masada" (Y. Yadin).

S. Cohen. "Masada: Literary Tradition, Archeological Remains, and the Credibility of Josephus," *Journal of Jewish Studies 33* (1982), pp. 385-405.
Y. Yadin, *Masada.*
———, "The Excavation of Masada, 1963-1964," *Israel Exploration Journal* 15 (1965), pp. 1-120.

Nag Hammadi Texts

ABD: "Nag Hammadi" (B. A. Pearson).

IDB Suppl.: "Nag Hammadi" (G. MacRae).

J. Doresse, *The Secret Books of the Egyptian Gnostics.*
J. M. Robinson, ed., *The Nag Hammadi Library.* 3d ed.
K. Rudolph, *Gnosis: The Nature and History of Gnosticism.*
Biblical Archeologist 42/4 (Fall 1979).

Pseudepigrapha

ABD: "Pseudepigrapha, OT" (J. H. Charlesworth).

IDB Suppl.: "Pseudepigrapha" (M. E. Stone).

R. H. Charles, *Apocrypha and Pseudepigrapha of the Old Testament,* vol. 2.

J. H. Charlesworth, *The Old Testament Pseudepigrapha.* 2 vols.

————, *The Pseudepigrapha and Modern Research.* 2d ed.

Codex Sinaiticus

ABD: "Codex Sinaiticus" (J. H. Charlesworth).

J. H. Charlesworth, *The New Discoveries in St. Catherine's Monastery: A Preliminary Report on the Manuscripts.*

B. M. Metzger, *The Text of the New Testament.* 3d ed.

Miscellaneous

ABD: "Archeology, Syro-Palestinian and Biblical" (W. G. Dever); "Caesarea" (R. H. Hohlfelder); "Capernaum" (V. G. Corbo); "Temple, Jerusalem" (C. Meyers); "Theodotus" (S. T. Carroll); "Coinage" (J. W. Betlyon); "Palestine Funerary Inscriptions" (E. Puech, trans. S. Rosoff); "Papyri, Early Christian" (S. R. Pickering); "Palestine, Archaeology of (NT)" (J. F. Strange); "Sepphoris" (J. F. Strange).

IDB: "Archeology" (G. W. Van Beek).

IDB Suppl.: "Archeology" (W. G. Dever); "Caesarea" (R. J. Bull); "Capernaum" (J. F. Strange); "Crucifixion" (O. Wintermute); "Jericho" (G. M. Landes); "Manuscripts from the Judean Desert" (G. Vermes); pp. 992–993 (map of archeological sites). Numerous other archeological studies in the *IDB Suppl.* are listed by location.

NJBC, pp. 1196–1218, "Biblical Archeology" (R. North; P. King).

W. F. Albright and W. G. Dever, *The Archeology of Palestine.*

M. Avi-Yonah, *Oriental Art in Roman Palestine.*

I. Browning, *Petra.*

R. J. Bull and D. L. Holland, eds., *The Joint Expedition to Caesarea Maritima.*

S. J. D. Cohen, "The Temple and the Synagogue," pp. 151–174 in T. G. Madsen, *The Temple in Antiquity.*

D. R. Edwards, "First Century Urban/Rural Relations in Lower Galilee: Exploring the Archaeological and Literary Evidence," pp. 169–182 in *Seminar Papers Society of Biblical Literature Annual Meeting 1988.*

J. Finnegan, *The Archeology of the New Testament.*

E. R. Goodenough, *Jewish Symbols in the Greco-Roman Period.*

J. Finnegan, *The Archeology of the New Testament.*

K. G. Holum, et al. *King Herod's Dream: Caesarea on the Sea.*

L. J. Hoppe, *What Are They Saying About Biblical Archeology?*

Jerusalem City Museum. *Finds from the Archaeological Excavations Near the Temple Mount.*

L. Kelso, et al. *Excavations at New Testament Jericho and Khirbet En-Nitla.*

K. M. Kenyon, *Digging Up Jericho.*

————, *Excavations at Jericho.*

————, *Jerusalem. Excavating 3,000 Years of History.*

L. I. Levine, *Roman Caesarea: An Archaeological-topographical Study.*

————, *Caesarea Under Roman Rule.*

E. M. Meyers and J. F. Strange, *Archaeology, the Rabbis, and Early Christianity. The Social and Historical Setting of Palestinian Judaism and Christianity.*

S. S. Miller, *Studies in the History and Traditions of Sepphoris.*

A. Negev, *Archeological Encyclopedia of the Holy Land.*

E. Netzer, *Greater Herodium.*

D. W. O'Connor, *Peter in Rome. The Literary, Liturgical and Archeological Evidence* (compare G. F. Snyder, "Survey and 'New' Thesis on the Bones of Peter," *Biblical Archeologist* [1969], pp. 2–24).

K. and L. Ritmeyer, "Reconstructing Herod's Temple Mount in Jerusalem," *Biblical Archeology Review* 15/6 (1989), pp. 23–42.

J. Zias, and E. Sekeles. "The Crucified Man from Giv'at ha Mivtar—A Reappraisal," *Biblical Archeologist* 48 1985), pp. 190–191.

V. Tzaferis. *Excavations at Capernaum.*

Videos

Masada: A Story of Heroism.

Mona Lisa of the Galilee (Sepphoris). Raanana: Biblical Productions, 1988.

The Temple at Jerusalem. Tel-Aviv: Doko Video, 1989.

Rebuilding Caesarea. Steven Spielberg Jewish Film Archive.
Jerusalem: Hebrew University, 1990.

Search for Herod's Harbor. Solving a 200-Year-Old Mystery. New York: Drew/Fairchild, 1989.

BIBLIOGRAPHY

This bibliography contains references to the books and articles at the end of each chapter; it does not contain the articles in the dictionaries and encyclopedias. Articles by an author are listed alphabetically before books.

Achtemeier, P. J. "The Origin and Function of the Pre-Marcan Miracle Catenae." *Journal of Biblical Literature* 91 (1972) 198–221.

————. "Toward the Isolation of Pre-Markan Miracle Catenae." *Journal of Biblical Literature* 89 (1970) 265–91.

————. *Mark.* Proclamation Commentaries. Philadelphia: Fortress Press,1975.

————. *Romans.* Interpretation. Louisville, KY: John Knox Press, 1985.

Adams, H. *The Interests of Criticism: An Introduction to Literary Theory.* New York: Harcourt Brace Jovanovich, 1969.

Agourides, S., and Charlesworth, J. H. "A New Discovery of Old Manuscripts on Mt. Sinai: A Preliminary Report." *Biblical Archeologist* 41 (1978) 29–31.

Aharoni, Y. *The Land of the Bible. A Historical Geography.* Philadelphia: Westminster Press, 1980.

Aland, K. "The Problem of Anonymity and Pseudonymity in Christian Literature of the First Two Centuries." *Journal of Theological Studies* 12 (1961) 39–49.

Aland, K. and B. *The Text of the New Testament.* Trans. E. F. Rhodes. Grand Rapids: Eerdmans, 1987.

Albright, W. F. *The Archeology of Palestine.* Baltimore: Penguin Books, 1960.

Althaus, P. *The So-Called Kerygma and the Historical Jesus.* Edinburgh: Oliver and Boyd, 1959.

Amiot, F. *The Key Concepts of St. Paul.* Trans. J. Dingle. New York: Herder and Herder, 1962.

Archeological Discoveries in the Holy Land. Compiled by the Archeological Institute of America. New York: Bonanza Books, 1967.

Arnold, C. E. *Ephesians: Power and Magic.* SNTSMS 63. Cambridge: University Press, 1989.

Ashton, John, ed. *The Interpretation of John.* Issues in Religion and Theology 9. Philadelphia: Fortress Press, 1986.

Attridge, H. *Hebrews.* Hermeneia. Philadelphia: Fortress Press, 1989.

Auerbach, E. *Mimesis.* Garden City, NY: Doubleday, Anchor Books, 1957.

Aune, D. E. "The Social Matrix of the Apocalypse of John." *Biblical Research* 26 (1981) 16–32.

————. *Prophecy in Early Christianity and the Ancient Mediterranean World.* Grand Rapids: Eerdmans, 1983.

————. *The New Testament in Its Literary Environment.* Philadelphia: Westminster Press, 1987.

Aus, R. *II Thessalonians.* Part II of A. J. Hultgren and R. Aus, *I–II Timothy, Titus; II Thessalonians.* Augsburg Commentary on the New Testament. Minneapolis: Augsburg, 1984.

Avi-Yonah, M. *Oriental Art in Roman Palestine.* Rome: Centro di studi semitici, Instituto di studi del Vicino Oriente, Universita, 1961.

Avi-Yonah, M., ed. *The World History of the Jewish People—The Herodian Period.* New Brunswick: Rutgers University Press, 1975.

Avigad, N. *Discovering Jerusalem.* Nashville: Abingdon, 1983.

Bacon, B. W. *Studies in Matthew.* New York: Holt, Rinehart & Winston, 1930.

Bailey, K. E. *Luke Through Peasant Eyes: More Lucan Parables, Their Culture and Style.* Grand Rapids: Eerdmans, 1980.

————. *Poet and Peasant: A Literary-Cultural Approach to the Parables in Luke.* Grand Rapids: Eerdmans, 1976.

Balch, D. L. *Let Wives Be Submissive: The Domestic Code in 1 Peter.* SBLMS 26. Chico, CA: Scholars Press, 1981.

Balch, D. L. ed. *Social History of the Matthean Community.* (Contributions by A. F. Segal, A. J. Saldarini, R. H. Gundry, D. L. Balch, A. C. Wire, P. Perkins, W. R. Schoedel, J. P. Meier, R. Stark, L. M. White, F. Norris, J. D. Kingsbury). Minneapolis: Fortress Press, 1991.

Banks, R. *Paul's Idea of Community: The Early House Churches and Their Historical Setting.* Exeter: Paternoster Press, 1980.

Baron, S., and Blau, S., eds. *Judaism, Postbiblical and Talmudic Period.* New York: Liberal Arts Press, 1954.

Barr, D.L. *New Testament Story. An Introduction.* Belmont, CA: Wadsworth, 1987.

———. "The Apocalypse as a Symbolic Transformation of the World." *Interpretation* 38 (1984) 39–50.

———. "'Abbá' Isn't 'Daddy.'" *Journal of Theological Studies* 39 (1988) 28–47.

Barrett, C. K. "Paul's Opponents in II Corinthians." *New Testament Studies* 17 (1970–1971) 233–254.

———. *A Commentary on the Epistle to the Romans.* Harper's. New York: Harper & Row, 1957.

———. *Essays on John.* Philadelphia: Westminster Press, 1982.

———. *Essays on Paul.* Philadelphia: Fortress Press, 1982.

———. *Freedom and Obligation: A Study of the Epistle to the Galatians.* Philadelphia: Westminster Press, 1985.

———. *From First Adam to Last: A Study in Pauline Theology.* New York: Scribners, 1962.

———. *Luke the Historian in Recent Study.* London: Epworth Press, 1961.

———. *The First Epistle to the Corinthians.* HNTC. New York: Harper & Row, 1973.

———. *The Gospel According to St. John.* London: SPCK, 1955.

———. *The Gospel of John and Judaism.* Philadelphia: Fortress Press, 1975.

———. *The New Testament Background: Selected Documents.* Rev. ed. Harper Torchbook No. 86. New York: Harper & Row, 1989.

———. *The Second Epistle to the Corinthians.* HNTC. New York: Harper & Row, 1973.

Bartchy, S. Scott. *First Century Slavery and 1 Corinthians 7:21.* SBL Dissertation Series 11. Missoula, MT: The Society of Biblical Literature, 1973.

Barth, M. *Justification. Pauline Texts Interpreted in the Light of the Old and New Testaments.* Trans. A. M. Woodruff III. Grand Rapids: Eerdmans, 1971.

Bartsch, H. W., ed. *Kerygma and Myth.* Harper Torchbook No. 80. New York: Harper & Row, 1961.

Bassler, J. "A Widows' Tale: A Fresh Look at 1 Tim 5:3–16." *Journal of Biblical Literature* 103 (1984) 23–41.

Bauer, D. R. "The Interpretation of Matthew's Gospel in the Twentieth Century." *Proceedings of the American Theological Library Association* 42 (1988) 119–45.

Beall, T. *Josephus' Description of the Essenes Illustrated by the Dead Sea Scrolls.* Cambridge: University Press, 1988.

Beardslee, W. A.. "The Uses of the Proverb in the Synoptic Tradition." *Interpretation* 24 (1970) 61–76.

———. *Literary Criticism of the New Testament.* Guides to Biblical Scholarship, New Testament Series. Ed. Dan O. Via, Jr. Philadelphia: Fortress Press, 1970.

Beare, F. W. *A Commentary on the Epistle to the Philippians.* HNTC. New York: Harper & Row, 1959.

Beker, J. *Paul the Apostle: The Triumph of God in Life and Thought.* Philadelphia: Fortress Press, 1980.

Bellinzoni, A. J., with J. B. Tyson and W. O. Walter, eds. *The Two-Source Hypothesis. A Critical Appraisal.* Macon, GA: Mercer University Press, 1985.

Belo, F. *A Materialist Reading of the Gospel of Mark.* Trans. M. J. O'Connell. Maryknoll, NY: Orbis Books, 1981.

Best, E. *1 Peter.* New Century Bible. Grand Rapids: Eerdmans, 1971.

———. *1 Peter.* New Century Bible. London, Oliphants, 1971.

———. *Disciples and Discipleship: Studies in the Gospel According to Mark.* Edinburgh: T. & T. Clark, 1986.

Best, E. F. *A Commentary on the First and Second Epistles to the Thessalonians.* HNTC. New York: Harper & Row, 1975.

Bettenson, H. *Documents of the Christian Church.* New York: Oxford University Press, 1942.

Betz, H. D. "2 Cor. 6:14–7:1: An Anti-Pauline Fragment?" *Journal of Biblical Literature* 92 (1973) 88–108.

———. *Essays on the Sermon on the Mount.* Trans. L. L. Welborn. Philadelphia: Fortress Press, 1984.

———. *Galatians.* Hermeneia Series. Philadelphia: Fortress Press, 1979.

Betz, H. D., ed. *The Greek Magical Papyri in Translation.* Chicago: University of Chicago Press, 1986.

Bianchi, U. *The Greek Mysteries.* Leiden: E. J. Brill, 1976.

Bickerman, E. *From Ezra to the Last of the Maccabees.* Foundations of Postbiblical Judaism. New York: Schocken Books, 1947.

Bilde, P. *Josephus Between Jerusalem and Rome: His Life, His Works, and Their Importance.* Sheffield: JSOT, 1988.

Bilezikian, G. G. *The Liberated Gospel: A Comparison of the Gospel of Mark and Greek Tragedy.* Grand Rapids: Baker Book House, 1977.

Boobyer, G. H. "Galilee and Galileans in St. Mark's Gospel." *Bulletin of the John Rylands Library* 35 (1952–53) 334–348.

Borg, M. *Jesus. A New Vision. Spirit, Culture, and The Life of the Discipleship.* San Francisco: Harper & Row, 1987.

Borgen, P. *Bread From Heaven*. Leiden: E. J. Brill, 1965.

Boring, M. E. "Criteria of Authenticity. The Lucan Beatitudes as a Test Case." *Forum* 1/4 (1985) 3–38.

———. *Revelation*. Interpretation. Louisville, KY: John Knox Press, 1989.

———. *Sayings of the Risen Jesus. Christian Prophecy in the Synoptic Tradition*. New York: Cambridge University Press, 1982.

Bornkamm, G. "On Understanding the Christ-Hymn, Phil 2:6–11." *Early Christian Experience* (New York: Harper & Row) 112–122.

———. "The Risen Lord and the Earthly Jesus: Mt. 28:16–20." In *The Future of Our Religious Past*. J. M. Robinson, ed. New York: Harper & Row, 1971, 203–209.

———. *Early Christian Experience*. Trans. P. L. Hammer. New York: Harper & Row, 1969.

———. *Jesus of Nazareth*. New York: Harper & Row, 1960.

———. *Paul*. New York: Harper & Row, 1971.

Bornkamm, G., G. Barth, and H.J. Held. *Tradition and Interpretation in Matthew*. Philadelphia: Westminster Press, 1963.

Bousset, W. *Kyrios Christos*. Nashville and New York: Abingdon Press, 1970. German original 1913.

Bovon, F. *Luke the Theologian: Thirty-three years of Research (1950–1983)*. Trans. K. McKinney. PTM 12. Allison Park, PA: Pickwick Publications, 1987.

Bowman, J. W. "The Revelation to John. Its Dramatic Structure and Message." *Interpretation* 9 (1955) 436–453.

Brandon, S. G. F. *The Fall of Jerusalem and the Christian Church*. London: SPCK, 1951.

Braun, H. *Jesus of Nazareth*. Trans. E. R. Kalin. Philadelphia: Fortress Press, 1979.

Bright, J. *A History of Israel*. Philadelphia: Westminster Press, 1976.

Brinsmead, B. H. *Galatians—Dialogical Response to Opponents*. SBLDS 65. Chico, CA: Scholars Press, 1982.

Brown, R. E. *New Testament Essays*. Milwaukee: Bruce Publishing, 1965.

———. *The Birth of the Messiah*. Garden City, NY: Doubleday, 1977.

———. *The Community of the Beloved Disciple*. New York: Paulist Press, 1979.

———. *The Epistles of John*. Anchor Bible 30. Garden City, NY: Doubleday, 1982.

———. *The Gospel According to John*. 2 vols. Garden City, NY: Doubleday, 1966 (I–XII), 1970 (XIII–XXI).

Brown, R.E., K. P. Donfried, and J. Reumann. *Peter in the New Testament*. Minneapolis: Augs-

burg Publishing House, 1973.

Brown, R.E., and J. P. Meier. *Antioch and Rome*. New York: Paulist Press, 1983.

Browning, I. *Petra*. Park Ridge, NJ: Noyes Press, 1973.

Bruce, F. F. *1 & 2 Thessalonians*. Word Biblical Commentaries 45. Waco, TX: Word, 1982.

———. *Jesus and Christian Origins Outside the New Testament*. Grand Rapids: Eerdmans, 1974.

———. *New Testament History*. Garden City, NY: Doubleday, Anchor Books, 1972.

———. *The English Bible. A History of Translations*. Rev. ed. New York: Oxford University Press, 1978.

———. *The Epistle to the Hebrews*. Grand Rapids: Eerdmans, 1990.

———. *The Epistles of John*. Grand Rapids: Eerdmans, 1970.

Buchanon, G. W. *To the Hebrews*. Anchor Bible 36. Garden City, NY: Doubleday, 1972.

Bull, R. J., and D. L. Holland, eds. *The Joint Expedidition to Caesarea Maritima*. Missoula, MT: Scholars Press, 1975–.

Bultmann, R. "The Primitive Christian Kerygma and the Historical Jesus." In *The Historical Jesus and the Kerygmatic Christ*. Carl A. Braaten and Roy A. Harrisville, eds. New York and Nashville: Abingdon Press, 1964.

———. "The Study of the Synoptic Gospels." In R. Bultmann and K. Kundsin, *Form Criticism: Two Essays on New Testament Research*. New York: Harper & Row, 1962.

———. *Jesus and the Word*. New York: Scribners, 1934, 1958. German original 1926.

———. *Jesus Christ and Mythology*. New York: Scribners, 1958, and London: SCM Press, 1960.

———. *Primitive Christianity in Its Contemporary Setting*. New York: Meridian, 1956.

———. *The Gospel of John: A Commentary*. Oxford: B. Blackwell, 1971.

———. *The History of the Synoptic Tradition*. New York: Harper & Row, 1968.

———. *The Johannine Epistles*. Semeia. Trans. R. P. O'Hara et al. Philadelphia: Fortress Press, 1973.

———. *Theology of the New Testament*. 2 vols. New York: Scribners, 1951 and 1955.

Byrne, B. *Paul and the Christian Woman*. Collegeville, MN: 1988.

Cadbury, H. *The Making of Luke-Acts*. 2d ed. London: SPCK, 1968.

Caird, G. B. *A Commentary of the Revelation of St. John the Divine*. Harper New Testament Commentaries. New York: Harper & Row, 1966.

———. *The Gospel of St. Luke*. Pelican Gospel Commentaries. Baltimore: Penguin Books, 1963.

Cambridge History of the Bible II. The West from the Reformation to the Present Day. New York: Cambridge University Press, 1963.

Cameron, R. "The Gospel of Thomas: A *Forschungsberich*t [Research Report] and Analysis." *Augstieg und Niedergang der Römischen Welt* II 25.6. New York: De Gruyter, 1988. Pp. 4213–4224.

Campbell, Joseph. *Myths to Live By.* New York: Viking Press, 1972.

Campbell, T. H. "Paul's Missionary Journeys as Reflected in His Letters." *Journal of Biblical Literature* 74 (1955) 80–87.

Carson, D. A. "Recent Literature on the Fourth Gospel." *Themelios* 9 (1983) 8–18.

Cartlidge, D. R., and D. L. Dungan. *Documents for the Study of the Gospels.* Cleveland: Collins, 1980.

Cassidy, R. *Jesus, Politics, and Society: A Study of Luke's Gospel.* Maryknoll, NY: Orbis, 1978.

Cassidy, R., and P. J. Scharper, eds., *Political Issues in Luke-Acts.* Maryknoll, NY: Orbis, 1983.

Cerfaux, L. *Christ in the Theology of St. Paul.* Trans. G. Webb and A. Walker. New York: Herder and Herder, 1959.

———. *The Church in the Theology of St. Paul.* Trans. G. Webb and A. Walker. New York: Herder and Herder, 1959.

Charles, R. H. *The Apocrypha and Pseudepigrapha of the Old Testament in English.* 2 vols. Oxford: Clarendon Press, 1913.

Charlesworth, J. H. "St. Catherine's Monastery: Myths and Mysteries." *Biblical Archeologist* 42 (1979) 174–179.

———. "The Manuscripts of St. Catherine's Monastery." *Biblical Archeologist* 43 (1980) 26–34.

———. *The New Discoveries in St. Catherine's Monastery: A Preliminary Report on the Manuscripts,* with G. T. Zervos. Forward, D. N. Freedman. ASORMS 3. Winona Lane, IN: Eisenbrauns, 1981.

———. *The Pseudepigrapha & Modern Research* (with Supplement). Missoula, MT: Scholars Press, 1981.

Charlesworth, J. H., ed. *John and Qumran.* London: Geoffrey Chapman, 1972.

———. *The Old Testament Pseudepigrapha.* 2 vols. Garden City, NY: Doubleday, 1983, 1985.

Church, F. F. "Rhetorical Structure and Design in Paul's Letter to Philemon." *Harvard Theological Review* 71 (1978) 17–33.

Cohen, S. J. D. "Masada: Literary Tradition, Archeological Remains, and the Credibility of Josephus." *Journal of Jewish Studies* 33 (1982) 385–405.

———. "The Significance of Yavneh: Pharisees, Rabbis and the End of Jewish Sectarianism." *Hebrew Union College Annual* 55 (1984) 27–53.

———. "The Temple and the Synagogue." Pp. 151–174 in T. G. Madsen, ed. *The Temple in Antiquity: Ancient Records and Modern Perspectives.* Religious Studies Monograph 9. Provo, UT: Religious Studies Center, Brigham Young University, 1984.

———. *From the Maccabees to the Mishna.* Philadelphia: Westminster Press, 1987.

Collins, A. Yarbro. "The Political Perspective of the Revelation to John." *Journal of Biblical Literature* 96 (1977) 241–256.

———. *Crisis & Catharsis. The Power of the Apocalypse.* Philadelphia: Westminster Press, 1984.

———. *The Apocalypse.* New Testament Messages. Wilmingdon, DL: Michael Glazier, 1979.

———. *The Combat Myth in the Book of Revelation.* Missoula, MT: Scholars Press, 1976.

Collins, A. Yarbro, ed. *Early Christian Apocalypticism: Genre and Social Setting.* Decatur, GA: Society of Biblical Literature, 1986.

Collins, J. J. "Pseudonymity, Historical Reviews and the Grace of the Revelation of John." *Catholic Biblical Quarterly* 39 (1977) 329–343.

———. *Between Athens and Jerusalem: Jewish Identity in the Hellenistic Diaspora.* New York: Crossroad, 1986.

Collins, J. J. , ed. *Apocalypse: The Morphology of a Genre.* Semeia 14. The Society of Biblical Literature, 1979.

Collins, J. N. "Georgi's 'Envoys' in 2 Cor 11:23." *Journal of biblical Literature* 93 (1974) 88–96.

Collins, R. F. *Letters That Paul Did Not Write: The Epistle to the Hebrews and the Pauline Pseudepigrapha.* Wilmington, DE: Michael Glazier, 1988.

Conzelmann, H. *1 Corinthians.* Hermeneia. Philadelphia: Fortress Press, 1975.

———. *An Outline of the Theology of the New Testament.* New York: Harper & Row, 1969.

———. *History of Primitive Christianity.* New York: Abingdon Press, 1973.

———. *Jesus.* Philadelphia: Fortress Press, 1973.

———. *The Theology of St. Luke.* New York: Harper & Row, 1960.

Cope, L. *Matthew, A Scribe Trained for the Kingdom of Heaven.* CBQ Monograph 5. Washington, DC: The Catholic Biblical Association of America, 1976.

Countryman, L. W. *Dirt, Greed, and Sex. Sexual Ethics in the New Testament and Their Implications for Today.* Philadelphia: Fortress Press, 1988.

Cousar, C. B. *Galatians.* Interpretation. Atlanta: John Knox Press, 1982.

Cowan, D. *Bridge Between the Testaments.* 3d rev. ed. Allison Park, PA: Pickwick Publications, 1986.

Crane, R. S. *The Languages of Criticism and the Structure of Poetry.* Toronto: University of Toronto Press, 1953.

Crane, R. S., ed. *Critics and Criticism, Essays in Method.* Abridged ed. Chicago: University of Chicago Press, 1957.

Cranfield, C. E. B. "The Message of James." *Scottish Journal of Theology* 18 (1965) 182–193.

———. *A Critical and Exegetical Commentary on the Epistle to the Romans.* International Critical Commentary. Edinburgh: T. & T. Clark, 1975, 1979.

Cross, F. M. *The Ancient Library of Qumran and Modern Biblical Studies.* Rev. ed. Grand Rapids: Eerdmans, 1980.

Crossan, J. D. "Parable and Example in the Teaching of Jesus." *New Testament Studies* 18 (1971–72) 285–307.

———. *Four Other Gospels. Shadows on the Contours of Canon.* Minneapolis: Winston Press, 1985.

———. *In Fragments. The Aphorisms of Jesus.* San Francisco: Harper & Row, 1983.

———. *In Parables. The Challenge of the Historical Jesus.* New York: Harper & Row, 1973.

———. *The Cross That Spoke. The Origins of the Passion Narrative.* San Francisco: Harper & Row, 1988.

———. *The Historical Jesus. The Life of a Mediterranean Jewish Peasant.* San Francisco: Harper, 1991.

Cullmann, O. *The Johannine Circle.* Trans. J. Bowden. Philadelphia: Westminster Press, 1976.

Culpepper, R. A. *1 John. 2 John. 3 John.* Knox Preaching Guides. John H. Hayes, ed. Atlanta: John Knox Press, 1985.

———. *The Anatomy of the Fourth Gospel. A Study in Literary Design.* Philadelphia: Fortress Press, 1983.

———. *The Johannine School.* SBL Dissertation Series. Missoula, MT: Scholars Press, 1975.

Cumont, F. *Oriental Religions in Roman Paganism.* New York: Dover Publications, 1956 [1911].

Dahl, N. A. *Jesus in the Memory of the Early Church: Essays.* Minneapolis: Augsburg Publishing House, 1976.

———. *Luke.* Proclamation Commentaries. Philadelphia: Fortress Press, 1976.

———. *Studies in Paul.* Minneapolis: Augsburg, 1977.

Danker, F. W. *Jesus and the New Age, According to St. Luke.* 2d. ed. St. Louis: Clayton Publishing House, 1988.

Daube, D. *The New Testament and Rabbinic Judaism.* New York: Arno, 1973.

Davies, W. D. *Paul and Rabbinic Judaism.* Harper Torchbook. New York: Harper & Row, 1967.

———. *The Sermon on the Mount.* Cambridge: Cambridge University Press, 1966.

———. *The Setting of the Sermon on the Mount.* Cambridge: Cambridge University Press, 1964.

Davies, W. D., and D.C. Allison *The Gospel According to Matthew.* 3 vols. International Critical Commentary. Edinburgh: T. & T. Clark, 1988.

Dawsey, J. M. *The Lukan Voice. Confusion and Irony in the Gospel of Luke.* Macon, GA: Mercer University Press, 1988.

Deissmann, A. *Paul: A Study in Social and Religious History,* 2d ed. New York: Harper & Row, 1927.

DeJonge, M. *Outside the Old Testament.* New York: Cambridge University Press, 1985.

DeJonge, M., and A. S. van der Woude, "11Q Melchizedek and the New Testament." *New Testament Studies* 12 (1966) 301–326.

Delcor, M. "Melchizedek from Genesis to the Qumran Texts and the Epistle to the Hebrews." *Journal for the Study of Judaism* 2 (1971) 115–135.

Dewey, J. "Mark as Interwoven Tapestry: Forecasts and Echoes for a Listening Audience." *Catholic Biblical Quarterly* 53/2 (1991) 221–236.

———. "Recent Studies on Mark." *Religious Studies Review* 17/1 (1991) 12–16.

———. "The Literary Structure of the Controversy Stories in Mark 2:1–3:6." *Journal of Biblical Literature* 92 (1973) 394–401.

———, *Markan Public Debate: Literary Technique, Concentric Structure and Theology in Mark 2.* Chico, CA: Scholars Press, 1980.

Dibelius, M. *From Tradition to Gospel.* New York: Scribners, 1935.

———. *Studies in the Acts of the Apostles.* New York: Scribners, 1956.

Dibelius, M., and H. Conzelmann *The Pastoral Epistles.* Hermeneia Series. Philadelphia: Fortress Press, 1972.

Dibelius, M., and H. Greeven. *James.* Hermeneia Series. Philadelphia: Fortress Press, 1976.

Dibelius, M., and W. G. Kümmel. *Paul.* Trans. F. Clarke. Philadelphia: Westminster Press, 1953.

Dodd, C. H. *Historical Tradition in the Fourth Gospel.* Cambridge: Cambridge University Press, 1963.

———. *The Interpretation of the Fourth Gospel.* Cambridge: Cambridge University Press, 1953.

———. *The Johannine Epistles.* Moffatt New Testament Commentary. London: Hodder and Stoughton, 1946.

———. *The Meaning of Paul for Today.* New York: Meridian Books, 1957.

Dodds, E. R. *The Greeks and the Irrational.* New

York: W. W. Norton, 1966.

Donahue, J. R. "Jesus as the Parable of God in the Gospel of Mark." *Interpretation* 32/4 (1978) 369–386; reprinted in J. L. Mays, ed., *Interpreting the Gospels*.

———. "Tax Collectors and Sinners." *Catholic Biblical Quarterly* 33 (1971) 39–61.

———. *The Gospel in Parable. Metaphor, Narrative, and Theology in the Synoptic Gospels*. Philadelphia: Fortress Press, 1988.

———. "The Changing Shape of New Testament Theology." *Theological Studies* 50 (1989) 314–335.

———. *Are You the Christ? The Trial Narrative in the Gospel of Mark*. SBL Dissertation Series 10. Missoula, MT: Scholars Press, 1973.

Donfried, K. P. "A Short Note on Romans 16" in Donfried, ed., *The Romans Debate*, pp. 50–60.

———. "False Presuppositions in the Study of Romans." *Catholic Biblical Quarterly* 36 (1974) 332–355.

———. *The Romans Debate*. 2d ed. Minneapolis: Augsburg, 1991.

Doresse, J. *The Secret Books of the Egyptian Gnostics*. New York: Viking Press, 1960.

Doty, W. G. *Letters in Primitive Christianity*. Guides to Biblical Scholarship. Philadelphia: Fortress Press, 1973.

Downing, F. G. "Pliny's Prosecutions of Christians: Revelation and 1 Peter." *Journal for the Study of the New Testament* 34 (1988) 105–123.

Dugmore, C. W. *The Influence of the Synagogue upon the Divine Office*. Oxford: Oxford University Press, 1944.

Duke, P. *Irony in the Fourth Gospel*. Atlanta: John Knox Press, 1985.

Duling, D. "Binding and Loosing: Matthew 16:19; Matthew 18:18; John 20:23." *Forum* 3/4 (1987) 3–31.

———. "[Do not swear . . .] by Jerusalem because it is the City of the Great King (Matthew 5:35)." *Journal of Biblical Literature* 110/2 (1991) 291–309.

———. "Interpreting the Markan Hodology [Thinking about 'the Way']." *Nexus* 17 (1974) 2–11.

———. "Matthew's Plurisignificant 'Son of David' in Social Scientific Perspective: Kinship, Kingship, Magic, and Miracle," *Biblical Theology Bulletin* 22 (1992), 99–116.

———. "Norman Perrin and the Kingdom of God: Review and Response." *Journal of Religion* 64 (1984) 468–483.

———. "The Eleazar Miracle and Solomon's Magical Wisdom in Flavius Josephus' *Antiquitates Judaicae* 8 42–49." *Harvard Theological Review* 78 (1985) 1–25.

———. "The Promises to David and Their Entrance into Christianity—Nailing Down a Likely Hypothesis." *New Testament Studies* 20 (1973–74) 55–77.

———. "The Therapeutic Son of David: An Element in Matthew's Christological Apologetic." *New Testament Studies* 24 (1978) 392–410.

———. *Jesus Christ Through History*. New York: Harcourt Brace Jovanovich, 1979.

Dungan, D., and David R.Cartlidge, *Documents for the Study of the Gospels*. Cleveland: Collins, 1980.

Dunn, J. D. G. "The Incident at Antioch (Gal 2:11–18)." *Journal for the Study of the New Testament* 18 (1983) 3–57.

———. "The Relationship Between Paul and Jerusalem According to Galatians 1 and 2." *New Testament Studies* 28 (1982) 461–478.

Dupont-Sommer, A. *The Essene Writings from Qumran*. Trans. G. Vermes. Cleveland: World, 1961.

Edwards, D. R. "First Century Urban/Rural Relations in Lower Galilee: Exploring the Archaeological and Literary Evidence." Pp. 169–182 in *Seminar Papers Society of Biblical Literature Annual Meeting 1988*. Atlanta: Scholars Press, 1988.

Edwards, O. C. *Luke's Story of Jesus*. Philadelphia: Fortress Press, 1981.

Edwards, R. A. "An Approach to the Theology of Q." *Journal of Religion*, 51 (1971) 247–269.

———. "Uncertain Faith: Matthew's Portrait of the Disciples." Pp. 47–61 in F. F. Segovia, ed., *Discipleship in the New Testament*. Philadelphia: Fortress, 1985.

———. *A Theology of Q*. Philadelphia: Fortress Press, 1976.

———. *Matthew's Story of Jesus*. Philadelphia: Fortress Press, 1985.

———. *The Sign of Jonah in the Theology of the Evangelists and Q*. Studies in Biblical Theology. London: SCM Press, and Naperville, Ill.: Allenson, 1971.

Eliade, M. "Myth." *Encyclopaedia Britannica* 15 (1968) 1132–1142.

———. *Cosmos and History: The Myth of the Eternal Return*. Harper Torchbook No. 2050. New York: Harper & Row, 1959.

———. *Myth and Reality*. Harper Torchbook No. 1369. New York: Harper & Row, 1963.

———. *The Quest: History and Meaning in Religion*. Chicago: University of Chicago Press, 1969.

Elliott, J. H. "Patronage and Clientism in Early Christian Society." Polbridge Press Bookshelf, *Forum* 3/4 (1988) 39–48.

———. *A Home for the Homeless. A Sociological Exe-*

gesis of 1 Peter, Its Situation, and Strategy. Philadelphia: Fortress Press, 1981, 1991 ("Introduction").

Elliott, J. H., ed. *Social-Scientific Criticism of the New Testament and Its Social World. Semeia 35.* Decatur, GA: Scholars Press, 1986.

Epp, E. J., and G. W. MacRae, eds., *The New Testament and Its Modern Interpreters.* Atlanta: Scholars Press, 1989.

Esler, P. F. *Community and Gospel in Luke-Acts.* Society for New Testament Studies Monograph Series 57. Cambridge: Cambridge University Press, 1987.

Evans, C. A. *Noncanonical Writings and New Testament Interpretation.* Peabody, MA: Hendrickson, 1992.

Evans, C. F. "I Will Go Before You into Galilee." *Journal of Theological Studies* n.s. 5 (1954) 3–18.

Fallon, F. T. *2 Corinthians.* New Testament Message. Wilmington, DE: Michael Glazier, 1980.

Farmer, W. R. "The Post-Sectarian Character of Matthew and Its Post-War Setting in Antioch of Syria." *Perspectives in Religious Studies* 3 (1976) 235–247.

Farmer, W. R. *The Synoptic Problem. A Critical Analysis.* New York: Macmillan, 1964.

Feeley-Harnik, G. *The Lord's Table: Eucharist and Passover in Early Christianity.* Philadelphia: University of Pennsylvania Press, 1981.

Feine, P., J. Behm and W.G. Kümmel. *Introduction to the New Testament.* New York and Nashville: Abingdon Press, 1966.

Feldman, L. *Josephus and Modern Scholarship (1937-1980).* New York: Walter de Gruyter, 1984.

Fenton, J. C. *The Gospel of St. Matthew.* Pelican Gospel Commentaries. Baltimore: Penguin Books, 1963.

Festugiére, A. J. *Personal Religion Among the Greeks.* Berkeley: University of California Press, 1960.

Fiensy, D. A. *The Social History of Palestine in the Herodian Period. The Land Is Mine.* SBEC 20. Lewiston: Edwin Mellen Press, 1991.

Filoramo, G. *A History of Gnosticism.* Trans. Anthony Alcock. London: B. Blackwell, 1990.

Filson, F. V. *A New Testament History.* Philadelphia: Westminster Press, 1964.

Finkelstein, L. *The Pharisees; The Sociological Background of Their Faith.* Philadelphia: Jewish Publication Society of America, 1958.

Finley, M. I. *The Ancient Economy.* Berkeley: University of California Press, 1973.

Finley, M. I., ed. *The Portable Greek Historians: The Essence of Herodotus, Thucydides, Xenophon, Polybius.* New York: The Viking Press, 1959.

Finnegan, J. *The Archeology of the New Testament.* Princeton: University Press, 1969.

Fiore, B. *Pastoral Example in the Socratic and Pastoral Epistles.* Rome: Biblical Institute Press, 1986.

Fiorenza, E. Schüssler. "Composition and Structure of the Book of Revelation." *Catholic Biblical Quarterly* 39 (1977) 344–366.

———. "The Apocalypse." Pp. 99–120 of R. H. Fuller, et al., *Hebrews, James, 1 and 2 Peter, Jude, Revelation.* Proclamation Commentaries. Philadelphia: Fortress Press, 1977.

———. *Bread Not Stone: The Challenge of Feminist Biblical Interpretation.* Boston: Beacon Press, 1984.

———. *In Memory of Her: A Feminist Theological Reconstruction of Christian Origins.* New York: Crossroad, 1983.

———. *Invitation to the Book of Revelation.* Garden City, NY: Doubleday, 1981.

———. *The Apocalypse.* Herald Biblical Booklets. Chicago, IL: Franciscan Herald Press, 1976.

———. *The Book of Revelation: Justice and Judgment.* Philadelphia: Fortress Press, 1985.

Fitzmyer, J. A. "Now This Melchizedek (Hebr 7:1)." *Catholic Biblical Quarterly* 25 (1963) 305–321. Reprinted in *Essays on the Semitic Background of the New Testament* (London: Chapman, 1971) 221–244.

——— "Qumran and the Interpolated Paragraph in 2 Cor. 6:14–7:1." *Catholic Biblical Quarterly* 23 (1961) 271–380.

———. "The Languages of Palestine in the First Century." *Catholic Biblical Quarterly* 32 (1970) 501–531.

———. "The Qumran Scrolls and the New Testament After Forty Years." *Revue de Qumran* 13 (1988) 609–620.

———. A *Pauline Theology: A Brief Sketch,* 2d ed. Englewood Cliffs, NJ: Prentice Hall, 1989 (=*NJBC,* pp. 1382–1416).

———. *The Dead Sea Scrolls. Major Publications and Tools for Study.* Rev. ed. Decatur, GA: Scholars Press, 1990.

———. *The Gospel According to Luke I–IX* and *The Gospel According to Luke X–XXIV.* (Anchor Bible). Garden City, NY: Doubleday, 1981, 1985.

Foerster, W. *From the Exile to Christ.* Philadelphia: Fortress Press, 1964.

———. *Gnosis. A Selection of Gnostic Texts.* 2 vols. Trans. R. McL. Wilson. Oxford: Clarendon Press, 1972.

Forbes, C. "Comparison, Self-Praise, and Irony: Paul's Boasting and the Conventions of Hellenistic Rhetoric." *New Testament Studies* 32 (1986) 1–30.

———. "Early Christian Inspired Speech and Hellenistic Popular Religion." *Novum Testamentum* 28 (1986) 257–270.

Ford, J. M. *My Enemy is My Guest: Jesus and Violence in Luke-Acts.* Maryknoll NY: Orbis, 1984.

———. *Revelation.* Anchor Bible. Garden City, NY: Doubleday, 1975.

Fornberg, T. *An Early Church in a Pluralistic Society: A Study of 2 Peter.* Lund: Liber-Laromedel/Gleerup, 1977.

Fortna, R. T. *The Gospel of Signs: A Reconstruction of the Narrative Source Underlying the Fourth Gospel.* London: Cambridge University Press, 1970.

———. "Christology in the Fourth Gospel: Redaction-Critical Perspectives." *New Testament Studies* 21 (1975–76) 489–504.

———. *The Fourth Gospel and Its Predecessor. From Narrative Source to Present Gospel.* Philadelphia: Fortress Press, 1988.

Fortna, R. T., and B. Gaventa, eds. *The Conversation Continues: Studies in Paul & John.* Studies in Honor of J. Louis Martyn. Nashville: Abingdon Press, 1990.

Fowler, R. *Let the Reader Understand: Reader-Response Criticism and the Gospel of Mark.* Minneapolis: Fortress Press, 1991.

———. *Loaves and Fishes. The Function of the Feeding Stories in the Gospel of Mark.* SBLDS 54. Chico, CA: Scholars Press, 1981.

France, D. "Matthew's Gospel in Recent Study." *Journal of Theological Studies* 14 (1989) 41–46.

Francis, F. O. "Humility and Angelic Worship in Col 2:18." *Studia Theologica* 16 (1962) 109–134.

Francis, F. O., and W. Meeks. *Conflicts at Colossae.* Missoula: University of Montana, 1973.

Freyne, S. *Galilee from Alexander the Great to Hadrian: 323 B.C.E. to 135 C.E. A Study of Second Temple Judaism.* Wilmington, DE: Michael Glazier, 1980.

———. *Galilee, Jesus, and the Gospels: Literary Approaches and Historical Investigations.* Philadelphia: Fortress Press, 1988.

———. *The World of the New Testament.* Wilmington, DE: Michael Glazier, 1982.

Fujita, N. S. *A Crack in the Jar: What Ancient Jewish Documents Tell Us About the New Testament.* New York: Paulist Press, 1986.

Fuller, R. H. "Hebrews." Pp. 1–27 in R. H. Fuller, et al., *Hebrews, James, 1 and 2 Peter, Jude, Revelation.* Proclamation Commentaries. Philadelphia: Fortress Press, 1977.

———. "The 'Thou Art Peter' Pericope and the Easter Appearances." *McCormick Quarterly* 20 (1966–67) 309–315.

———. "The Letter to the Hebrews." Pp. 1–27 R. H. Fuller, et al., *Hebrews, James, 1 and 2 Peter, Jude, Revelation.* Proclamation Commentaries. Philadelphia: Fortress Press, 1977.

———. *A Critical Introduction to the New Testament.* London: Duckworth, 1966.

———. *The Foundations of New Testament Christology.* New York: Scribners, 1965

Funk, R. W. "Criteria for Determining the Authentic Sayings of Jesus." *The Fourth R* 3/6 (November 1990) 8–10.

———. *Language, Hermeneutic and Word of God.* New York: Harper & Row, 1966.

Funk, R. W., B. B. Scott, and J. R. Butts, *The Parables of Jesus.* Sonoma, CA: Polebridge Press, 1988.

Funk, R. W., ed. *Journal for Theology and the Church.* VI: Apocalypticism. New York: Herder and Herder, 1969.

Furnish, V. P. *II Corinthians.* Anchor Bible. Garden City, NY: Doubleday, 1984.

———. *The Moral Teaching of Paul.* 2d ed. Nashville: Abingdon, 1985.

———. *Theology and Ethics in Paul.* 2d ed. Nashville: Abingdon, 1985. Gager, J. "The Gospels and Jesus: Some Doubts About Method." *Journal of Religion* 54 (1974) 244–272.

Gager, J. G. "Some Notes on Paul's Conversion." *New Testament Studies* 27 (1981) 697–704.

———. *Kingdom and Community: The Social World of Early Christianity.* Englewood Cliffs, NJ: Prentice-Hall, 1975.

Gamble, H. Y. *The New Testament Canon: Its Making and Meaning.* Philadelphia: Fortress Press, 1985.

———. *The Textual History of the Letter to the Romans.* Grand Rapids: Eerdmans, 1977.

Garland, D. E. "The Composition and Unity of Philippians." *Novum Testamentum* 27 (1985) 141–173.

———. *The Intention of Matthew 23.* Novum Testamentum Supplement 52. Leiden: E. J. Brill, 1979.

Garrett, S. R. *The Demise of the Devil. Magic and the Demonic in Luke's Writings.* Minneapolis: Fortress Press, 1989.

Gasque, W. W. *A History of the Criticism of the Acts of the Apostles.* Tübigen: Mohr, 1975.

Gaston, L. "Paul and Jerusalem." Pp. 61–72 in Peter Richardson and John Hurd, eds., *From Paul to Jesus.* Waterloo, Ont.: Wilfrid Laurier University Press, 1984.

———. *No Stone on Another. Studies in the Significance of the Fall of Jerusalem in the Synoptic*

Gospels. Leiden: E. J. Brill, 1970.

Georgi, D. "Forms of Religious Propaganda." In *Jesus in His Time.* H. J. Schultz, ed. Philadelphia: Fortress Press, 1971.

———. *The Opponents of Paul in Second Corinthians: A Study of Religious Propaganda in Late Antiquity.* Philadelphia: Fortress Press, 1986.

Getty, M. E. *Philippians and Philemon.* New Testament Message. Wilmington, DE: Michael Glazier, 1959.

Gillman, J. *Possessions and the Life of Faith. A Reading of Luke-Acts.* Zacchaeus Studies. Collegeville, MN: Michael Glazier, 1991.

Gnilka, J. "2 Cor. 6:14–7:1 in the Light of the Qumran Texts and the Testaments of the Twelve Patriarchs." Pp. 46–68 in J. Murphy-O'Connor, ed., *Paul and Qumran.* London: Geoffrey Chapman, 1968.

Godwin, J. *The Mystery Religions in the Ancient World.* San Francisco: Harper & Row, 1981.

Goguel, M. *Jesus and the Origins of Christianity.* Harper Torchbooks. 2 vols. New York: Harper & Row, 1960.

Goodenough, E. R. *An Introduction to Philo Judaeus.* Oxford: Basil Blackwell, 1962.

———. *Jewish Symbols in the Greco-Roman Period.* 13 vols. Bollingen Series 37. New York: Pantheon Books, 1953–1968.

Goodspeed, E. J. *A History of Early Christian Literature.* Rev. and enlarged by R. M. Grant. Chicago: University of Chicago Press, 1966.

Goulder, M. *Midrash and Lection in Matthew.* London: SPCK, 1974.

Gowan, D. E. *Bridge Between the Testaments.* Pittsburgh Theological Monograph Series. Pittsburgh: Pickwick Press, 1980.

Grant, F. C. *Hellenistic Religions.* New York: Liberal Arts Press, 1953.

Grant, M. *The World of Rome.* Cleveland: World, 1960.

Grant, R. M. "The Origin of the Fourth Gospel." *Journal of Biblical Literature* 69 (1950) 305–322.

———. *A Historical Introduction to the New Testament.* London: Collins, 1963.

———. *The Bible in the Church: A Short History of Interpretation.* New York: Macmillan, 1948.

Grant, R. M., ed. *Gnosticism: An Anthology.* London: Collins, 1961.

Green, H. *The Gospel According to Matthew.* London: Oxford University Press, 1975.

Guelich, R. *The Sermon on the Mount.* Dallas: Word, 1982.

Gundry, R. *Matthew: A Commentary on His Literary and Theological Art.* Grand Rapids: Eerdmans, 1982.

———. *The Use of the Old Testament in St.*

Matthew's Gospel. Leiden: E. J. Brill, 1967.

Hadas, M. *Hellenistic Culture.* New York: W. W. Norton, 1959.

———. *Imperial Rome.* New York: Time, 1965.

Hadas, M., and M. Smith, *Heroes and Gods. Spiritual Biographies in Antiquity.* New York: Harper & Row, 1965.

Haenchen, E. "History and Interpretation in the Johannine Passion Narrative." *Interpretation* 24 (1970) 198–219.

———. "The Book of Acts as Source Material for the History of Early Christianity." Pp. 279–389 in L. Keck and J. L. Martyn, *Studies in Luke-Acts.*

———. *A Commentary on the Gospel of John 1–6* and *A Commentary on the Gospel of John 7–21.* Hermeneia. Trans. R. W. Funk. Philadelphia: Fortress Press, 1984.

———. *The Acts of the Apostles.* Philadelphia: Westminster Press, 1971.

Hagner, D. A. *Hebrews.* Good News Commentaries. San Francisco: Harper & Row, 1983.

Hammond, G. *The Making of the English Bible.* Manchester: University Press, 1982.

Hanson, P. D. *The Dawn of Apocalyptic.* Philadelphia: Fortress Press, 1975.

Hanson, P. D., ed., *Visionaries and Their Apocalypses.* Philadelphia: Fortress Press, 1983.

Hare, D. *The Theme of Jewish Persecution of Christians in the Gospel According to St. Matthew.* Cambridge: Cambridge University Press, 1967.

Harnack, Adolf. *What Is Christianity?* New York: Harper & Row, 1957.

Harrington, D. "Matthean Studies Since Joachim Rhode." *Heythrop Journal* 16/14 (1975) 375–388.

Harrington, D. J. *Interpreting the New Testament. A Practical Guide.* Wilmington, DE: Michael Glazier, 1983.

———. *John's Thought and Theology. An Introduction.* Good News Studies 33. Wilmington, DL: Michael Glazier, 1990.

Harris, R., and Mingana, A. *The Odes and Psalms of Solomon. II. The Translation.* New York: Longmans, Green, 1916–20.

Harrison, R. K., ed. *Major Cities of the Biblical World.* Nashville: Thomas Nelson, 1985.

Hartman, L. *Prophecy Interpreted.* Coniectanea Biblica New Testament Series No. 1. Lund, Sweden: G. W. K. Gleerup, 1966.

Harvey, A. E. *Jesus and the Constraints of History.* London: Duckworth, 1982.

Harvey, V. A. *The Historian and the Believer.* New York: Macmillan, 1966.

Hayes, J. H., and C. R. Holladay, *Biblical Exegesis. A Beginner's Handbook.* Atlanta: John Knox, 1982.

Heitmüller, W. "Hellenistic Christianity Before Paul." Pp. 308–319 in W. Meeks, *The Writings of St. Paul.* New York: W. W. Norton, 1972.

Hellholm, D., ed. *Apocalypticism in the Mediterranean World and the Near East: Proceedings of the International Colloquium on Apocalypticism, Uppsala, August 12–17, 1979.* Tübingen: Mohr-Siebeck, 1982.

Hemer, C. J. *The Letters to the Seven Churches of Asia in their Local Setting. JSNT* Supplement 11. Sheffield: JSOT Press, 1986.

Henderson, I. *Myth in the New Testament.* Chicago: H. Regner, 1952.

Hengel, M. *Acts and the History of Earliest Christianity.* Trans. J. Bowden. Philadelphia: Fortress Press, 1980.

———. *Acts and the History of Earliest Christianity.* Trans. J. Bowden. Philadelphia: Fortress Press, 1980.

———. *Judaism and Hellenism.* 2 vols. Philadelphia: Fortress Press, 1974.

Hennecke, E., and Schneemelcher, W. *New Testament Apocrypha.* 2 vols. Philadelphia: Fortress Press, 1965.

Hill, D. *New Testament Prophecy.* Atlanta: John Knox Press, 1979.

Hills, J. "Tradition, Redaction, and Intertextuality: Miracle Lists in Apocryphal Acts." *Seminar Papers 29, SBL* (1990): 375–390.

Hock, R. F. "Paul's Tentmaking and the Problem of His Social Class." *Journal of Biblical Literature* 97 (1978) 555–564.

———. "The Workship as a Social Setting for Paul's Missionary Preaching." *Catholic Biblical Quarterly* 41 (1979) 438–450.

———. *The Social Context of Paul's Ministry. Tentmaking and Apostleship.* Philadelphia: Fortress Press, 1980.

Holladay, C. H. *Theios Anēr (Divine Man) in Hellenistic Judaism: A Critique of This Category in New Testament Christology.* SBL Dissertation Series 40. Missoula, MT: Scholars Press, 1977.

Holmberg, B. *Paul and Power. The Structure of Authority in the Primitive Church as Reflected in the Pauline Epistles.* Philadelphia: Fortress Press, 1980.

———. *Sociology and the New Testament. An Appraisal.* Philadelphia: Fortress Press, 1990.

Holum, K. G., R.L. Hohlfelder, R. J. Bull, A. Raban. *King Herod's Dream. Caesarea on the Sea.* New York: Norton, 1988.

Hooker, M. D., and S. G. Wilson, eds. *Paul and Paulinism. Essays in Honor of C. K. Barrett.* London: SPCK, 1982.

Hoppe, L. J. *What Are They Saying About Biblical Archeology?* New York: Paulist, 1984.

Horsley, R. A. "'How Can Some of You Say That There Is No Resurrection of the Dead?' Spiritual Elitism in Corinth." *Novum Testamentum* 20 (1978) 203–231.

———. "Questions About Redactional Strata and the Social Relations Reflected in Q." *Seminar Papers, SBL* (1989): 186–203.

———. "Wisdom of Word and Words of Wisdom in Corinth." *Catholic Biblical Quarterly* 39 (1977) 224–239.

———. *Jesus and the Spiral of Violence.* San Francisco: Harper & Row, 1987.

———. *The Liberation of Christmas. The Infancy Narratives in Social Context.* New York: Crossroad, 1989.

———. *Sociology and the Jesus Movement.* Crossroad: New York, 1989.

Horsley, R. A., and J. S. Hanson, *Bandits, Prophets, and Messiahs. Popular Movements at the Time of Jesus.* Minneapolis: Winston Press, 1985.

Hoskyns, E. *The Fourth Gospel.* F. N. Davey, ed. London: Faber and Faber, 1940.

Hoskyns, E., and N. Davey. *The Riddle of the New Testament.* London: Faber and Faber, 1948.

Houlden, J. L. *Ethics in the New Testament.* New York: Oxford University Press, 1977.

———. *The Johannine Epistles.* New York: Harper & Row, 1973.

———. *The Pastoral Epistles.* Pelican New Testament Commentary. New York: Penguin Books, 1976.

Howard, G. *Paul: Crisis in Galatia.* SNTSMS 35. Cambridge: University Press, 1979.

Howard, W. F. *The Fourth Gospel in Recent Criticism and Interpretation.* K. Barrett, ed. London: Epworth Press, 1955.

Hull, J. M. *Hellenistic Magic and the Synoptic Tradition.* SPT Second Series 28. Naperville, IL: SCM Press, 1974.

Hultgren, A. J., and R. Aus. *I–II Timothy, Titus; II Thessalonians.* Augsburg Commentary on the New Testament. Minneapolis: Augsburg Publishing House, 1984.

Hunter, A. M. *Paul and His Predecessors.* Philadelphia: Westminster Press, 1961.

Hurtado, L. *One God, One Lord. Early Christian Devotion and Ancient Jewish Monotheism.* Philadelphia: Fortress Press, 1988.

Jacobson, A. *The First Gospel. An Introduction to Q.* Sonoma, CA: Polebridge Press, 1992.

Jeremias, J. *Jerusalem and the Time of Jesus.* Philadelphia: Fortress Press, 1969 (German 1967).

———. *Jesus' Promise to the Nations.* Naperville, IL: Allenson, 1958.

———. *New Testament Theology.* New York: Scribners, 1971.

———. *Rediscovering the Parables.* London: SCM Press, 1966.

———. *The Eucharistic Words of Jesus.* Trans. A. Ehrhardt. Oxford: Blackwell, 1955.

———. *The Lord's Prayer.* Trans. J. Reuman. Phildelphia: Fortress Press, 1964.

———. *The Parables of Jesus.* Rev. ed. New York: Scribners, 1963.

———. *The Prayers of Jesus.* Naperville, IL: SCM Press, 1967.

———. *The Problem of the Historical Jesus.* Philadelphia: Fortress Press, 1964.

———. *Unknown Sayings of Jesus.* 2d Eng. ed. London: SPCK, 1964.

Jerusalem City Museum. *Finds from the Archaeological Excavations Near the Temple Mount.* Jerusalem: Israel Exploration Society, 1975.

Jervell, J. *Luke and the People of God.* Minneapolis: Augsburg, 1972.

Jewett, R. "Conflicting Movements in the Early Church as Reflected in Philippians." *Novum Testamentum* 12 (1970) 361–390.

———. "The Agitators and the Galatian Congregation." *New Testament Studies* 17 (1971) 198–212.

———. "The Epistolary Thanksgiving and the Integrity of Philippians." *Novum Testamentum* 12 (1970) 40–53.

———. *Letter to Pilgrims: A Commentary on the Epistle to the Hebrews.* New York: Pilgrim Press, 1981.

———. *The Thessalonian Correspondence: Pauline Rhetoric and Millenarian Piety.* Philadelphia: Fortress Press, 1986.

Johnson, L. T. *The Literary Function of Possessions in Luke-Acts.* Missoula, MT: Scholars Press, 1977.

———. *The Writings of the New Testament. An Interpretation.* Philadelphia: Fortress Press, 1986.

Johnson, M. D. *The Purpose of the Biblical Genealogies with Special Reference to the Setting of the Genealogies of Jesus.* Cambridge: University Press, 1969.

Johnson, S. E. *Paul the Apostle and His Cities.* Good News Studies 21. Wilmington, DE: Michael Glazier 1987.

Johnson, W. G. "The Pilgrimage Motif in the Book of Hebrews." *Journal of Biblical Literature* 97 (1978) 239–251.

Jonas, H. *The Gnostic Religion.* Boston: Beacon Paperback, 1963.

Jones, A. H. M. *The Cities of the Eastern Roman Provinces.* 2d ed., revised by M. Avi-Yonah et al. Oxford: Clarendon Press, 1971.

Jones, D. L. "Christianity and the Roman Imperial Cult." Pp. 1023–1054 in *Aufstieg und Niedergang der römischen Welt.* II.23.2.

Jones, G. V. *Christology and Myth in the New Testament.* London: Allen and Unwin, 1956.

Jonge, M. de, and A. S. van der Woude, "11Q Melchizedek and the New Testament." *New Testament Studies* 12 (1966) 301–326.

Judge, E. A. "St. Paul and Classical Society." *Jahrbuch für Antike und Christentum* 15 (1972) 28–32.

———. *The Social Pattern of Christian Groups in the First Century.* London: Tyndale, 1960.

Kähler, Martin. *The So-Called Historical Jesus and the Historic Biblical Christ.* Philadelphia: Fortress Press, 1964.

Kaiser, O., and W. G. Kümmel, *Exegetical Method: A Student's Handbook.* New rev. ed. Trans. E. V. N. Goetchius and M. J. O'Connell. New York: Seabury Press, 1981.

Karris, R. J. "Poor and Rich: The Lukan *Sitz im Leben.*" Pp. 112–125 in C. Talbert, ed., *Perspectives on Luke-Acts.* Danville, Va.: Association of Baptist Professors of Religion, 1978.

———. *Luke: Artist and Theologian. Luke's Passion Account as Literature.* New York: Paulist Press, 1985.

———. "The Background and Significance of the Polemic of the Pastoral Epistles." *Journal of Biblical Literature* 92 (1973) 549–564.

———. *The Pastoral Epistles.* New Testament Messages 17. Wilmington, DE: Michael Glazier, 1979.

———. *What Are They Saying About Luke and Acts?* New York: Paulist Press, 1979.

Käsemann, E. *Commentary on Romans.* Trans. G. W. Bromily. Grand Rapids, MI: Eerdmans, 1980.

———. *Essays on New Testament Themes.* Studies in Biblical Theology 41. London: SCM Press, 1964.

———. *New Testament Questions of Today.* Philadelphia: Fortress Press, 1969.

———. *Perspectives on Paul.* Trans. M. Kohl. Philadelphia: Fortress Press, 1971.

———. *The Testament of Jesus: A Study of the Gospel of John in the Light of Chapter 17.* London: SCM Press, 1968.

———. *The Wandering People of God. An Investigation of the Letter to the Hebrews.* Trans. R. A. Harrisville and I. L. Sandberg. Minneapolis: Augsburg Publishing House, 1984.

Katz, S. "Issues in the Separation of Judaism and Christianity after 70 C.E.: A Reconsideration." *Journal of Biblical Literature* 103/1 (1984) 43–76.

Keck, L. E. *A Future for the Historical Jesus.* New York and Nashville: Abingdon Press, 1971.

———. *Paul and His Letters.* Proclamation Commentaries. Philadelphia: Fortress Press, 1979.

Keck, L. E., and J. L. Martyn, eds. *Studies in Luke-Acts.* Nashville: Abingdon Press, 1966.

Keck, L. E., and V. P. Furnish. *The Pauline Letters.* Nashville: Abingdon Press, 1984.

Kee, D. "Who Were the 'Super-Apostles' of 2 Corinthians?" *Restoration Quarterly* 23 (1980) 65–76.

Kee, H. C. *Christian Origins in Sociological Perspective.* Philadelphia: Westminster Press, 1980.

———. *Community of the New Age. Studies in Mark's Gospel.* Philadelphia: The Westminster Press, 1977.

———. *Jesus in History.* New York: Harcourt Brace Jovanovich, 1970.

———. *Knowing the Truth: A Sociological Approach to New Testament Interpretation.* Atlanta: John Knox Press, 1989.

———. *Medicine, Miracle, and Magic in the New Testament.* New York: Cambridge University Press, 1986.

———. *The Origins of Christianity. Sources and Documents.* Englewood Cliffs, NJ: Prentice-Hall, 1973.

Kelber, W. *Mark's Story of Jesus.* Philadelphia: Fortress Press, 1979.

———. *The Kingdom in Mark.* Philadelphia: Fortress Press, 1974.

———. *The Oral and Written Gospel.* Philadelphia: Fortress Press, 1983.

Kelber, W., ed. *The Passion in Mark.* Philadelphia: Fortress Press, 1976.

Kelber, W., A. Kalenkow, and R. Scroggs. "Reflections of the Question: Was There a Pre-Markan Passion Narrative?" In *The Society of Biblical Literature One Hundred Seventh Annual Meeting Seminar Papers* (1971) 503–585.

Kelly, J. N. D. *A Commentary on the Epistles of Peter and Jude.* New York: Harper & Row, 1969.

Kelso, L., et al. *Excavations at New Testament Jericho and Khirbet En-Nitla.* New Haven: American Schools of Oriental Research, 1955.

Kenyon, K. *Jerusalem. Excavating 3,000 Years of History.* New York: McGraw-Hill, 1967.

Kenyon, K. M. *Digging Up Jericho; the Results of the Jericho Excavations.* New York: Praeger, 1957.

———. *Excavations at Jericho.* London: British School of Archaeology, 1960–1963.

Kermode, F. *The Genesis of Secrecy. On the Interpretation of Narrative.* Cambridge: Harvard University Press, 1979.

Kilpatrick, G. D. *The Origins of the Gospel According to St. Matthew.* Oxford: Clarendon Press, 1966.

Kim, C. H. *Form and Structure of the Familiar Greek Letter of Recommendation.* SBLDS 4. Missoula, MT: Scholars Press, 1972.

Kimelman, R. "*Birkat Ha-Minîm* ["Prayer Against the Heretics"] and the Lack of Evidence for an Anti-Christian Jewish Prayer in Late Antiquity." Pp. 226–244, 391–403 in E. P. Sanders, ed., *Jewish and Christian Self-Definition: Vol. 2: Aspects of Judaism in the Greco-Roman Period.* Phildelphia: Fortress Press, 1981.

Kingsbury, J. D. "Reflections on 'The Reader' of Matthew's Gospel." *New Testament Studies* 34 (1988) 442–460.

———. "The Jesus of History and Christ of Faith in Relation to Matthew's View of Time: Reactions to a New Approach." *Concordia Theological Monthly* 37 (1966) 500–510.

———. *Matthew.* Proclamation Commentaries. Philadelphia: Fortress Press, 1977.

———. *Matthew as Story.* 2d ed. Philadelphia: Fortress Press, 1988.

———. *Matthew: Structure, Christology, Kingdom.* Minneapolis: Fortress Press, 1975.

———. *The Parables of Jesus in Matthew 13.* London: S.P.C.K., 1969.

Klausner, J. *Jesus of Nazareth.* New York: Macmillan, 1925, and Boston: Beacon Press, 1964.

Klijn, A. F. J. "Paul's Opponents in Phil 3." *Novum Testamentum* 7 (1964–1965) 278–284.

Kloppenborg, J. "*The Formation of Q* Revisited: A Response to Richard Horsley." *Seminar Papers, SBL* (1989) 204–215.

———. "Tradition and Redaction in the Synoptic Sayings Source." *Catholic Biblical Quarterly* 46 (1984) 34–162.

Kloppenborg, J. S. "Bibliography on Q." *Society of Biblical Literature of Biblical Literature Abstracts and Seminar Papers* 24 (1985) 103–126.

———. *The Formation of Q: Trajectories in Ancient Wisdom Collections.* Studies in Antiquity and Christianity. Philadelphia: Fortress Press, 1987.

———. *Q Parallels. Synopsis, Critical Notes, and Concordance.* Sonoma, CA: Polebridge Press, 1988.

Kloppenborg, J. S., M. W. Meyer, S. J. Patterson, and M. C. Steinhauser. *Q Thomas Reader.* Sonoma, CA: Polebridge Press, 1990.

Knigge, H. D. "The Meaning of Mark." *Interpretation* 22 (1968) 53–76.

Knox, J. "Acts and the Pauline Letter Corpus." Pp. 258–278 in Keck and Martyn, *Studies.*

———. *Chapters in a Life of Paul.* New York: Abingdon-Cokesbury, 1950.

Koch, K. *The Rediscovery of Apocalyptic.* SBT Second Series 22. London: SCM Press, 1972.

Koester, C. "A Qumran Bibliography: 1974–1984." *Biblical Theological Bulletin* 15 (1985) 110–120.

Koester, H. "The Gospel of Thomas (II,2)." Pp. 124–138 in J. M. Robinson, *The Nag Hammadi Library*, 3d ed. English translation and introduction.

———. "The Purpose of the Polemic of a Pauline Fragment (Phil III)." *New Testament Studies* 8 (1961–1962) 317–332.

———. *Ancient Christian Gospels. Their History and Development.* Philadelphia: Trinity Press International, 1990.

———. *Introduction to the New Testament.* 2 vols. New York: Walter de Gruyter, 1982.

Kraft, R. A., and G. W. E. Nickelsburg, eds., *Early Judaism and Its Modern Interpreters.* Atlanta: Scholars Press, 1986.

Krentz, E. *The Historical Critical Method.* Philadelphia: Fortress Press, 1975.

Krodel, G. "The First Letter of Peter." Pp. 50–80 in G. Krodel, ed., *Hebrews, James, 1 and 2 Peter, Jude, Revelation.*

Krodel, G. *Ephesians, Colossians, 2 Thessalonians, the Pastoral Epistles.* Proclamation Commentaries. Philadelphia: Fortress Press, 1978.

Krodel, G., ed. *Hebrews-James-1 and 2 Peter-Jude-Revelation.* Proclamation Commentaries. Philadelphia: Fortress Press, 1977.

Krodel, G. A. *Revelation.* Augsburg Commentary on the New Testament. Minneapolis: Augsburg Publishing House, 1989.

Kümmel, W. G. "Current Theological Accusations Against Luke." *Andover Newton Quarterly* 16 (1975) 131–145.

———. *The New Testament: The History of the Investigation of Its Problems.* New York and Nashville: Abingdon Press, 1972.

———. *The Theology of the New Testament.* New York: Abingdon Press, 1973.

Kysar, R. "Community and Gospel: Vectors in Fourth Gospel Criticism." In J. L. Mays, ed., *Interpreting the Gospels.* Philadelphia: Fortress Press, 1981 265–277.

———. "The Fourth Gospel in Recent Research." *Aufstieg und Niedergang der römischen Welt* II.25.3 (1985) 2389–2480.

———. "The Gospel of John in Current Research." *Religious Studies Review* 9/4 (1983) 314–323.

———. *I, II, III John.* Augsburg Commentary on the New Testament. Minneapolis: 1986.

———. *John the Maverick Gospel.* Atlanta: John Knox Press, 1976.

———. *John.* Augsburg Commentary on the New Testament. Minneapolis: 1986.

———. *John's Story of Jesus.* Philadelphia: Fortress Press, 1984.

———. *The Fourth Evangelist and His Gospel. An Examination of Contemporary Scholarship.*

Atlanta: John Knox Press, 1976.

Ladoucer, D. J. "Masada: A Consideration of the Literary Evidence." *Greek, Roman, and Byzantine Studies* 21 (1980) 245–260.

Laws, S. *A Commentary on the Epistle of James.* Harper's. San Francisco: Harper & Row, 1980.

Layton, B. *The Gnostic Scriptures. A New Translation with Annotations and Introductions.* Garden City, NY: Doubleday, 1987.

Lenski, Gerhard and Jean. *Human Societies. An Introduction to Macrosociology.* 5th edition. New York: McGraw-Hill, 1987.

Levine, L. I. *Caesarea Under Roman Rule.* Leiden: E. J. Brill, 1975.

———. *Roman Caesarea: An Archaeological-topographical Study.* Jerusalem: Institute of Archaeology, Hebrew University of Jerusalem, 1975.

Lewis, N., and M. Reinhold. *Roman Civilization: Sourcebook II, The Empire.* 3d ed. New York: Columbia University Press, 1990.

Liebermann, S. *Hellenism in Jewish Palestine.* New York: The Jewish Theological Seminary of America, 1950.

Lietzmann, H. *A History of the Early Church.* 4 vols. Trans. B. L. Woolf. Cleveland: World, 1961.

Lieu, J. *The Second and Third Epistles of John: History and Background.* Edinburgh: T. & T. Clark, 1986.

Lightfoot, R. H. *History and Interpretation in the Gospels.* The Bampton Lectures. New York: Harper & Row, 1934.

———. *Locality and Doctrine in the Gospels.* New York: Harper & Row, 1936.

———. *St. John's Gospel.* Oxford: Clarendon Press, 1956.

———. *The Gospel Message of St. Mark.* Oxford Paperbacks 41. New York: Oxford University Press, 1962.

Lindars, B. *Behind the Fourth Gospel.* Studies in Creative Criticism 3. London: SPCK, 1971.

———. *New Testament Apologetic.* London: SCM Press, 1961.

Listening. Journal of Religion and Culture 24/3 (Fall 1989) (Articles by M. McVann, F. H. Gorman, F. J. Matera, R. A. Edwards, J. J. Pilch, G. R. O'Day, P. Perkins).

Lohse, E. *Colossians and Philemon.* Hermeneia Series. Philadelphia: Fortress Press, 1971.

———. *History of the Suffering and Death of Jesus Christ.* Trans. M. O. Dietrich. Philadelphia: Fortress Press, 1967.

———. *The New Testament Environment.* Trans. J. E. Steely. Nashville: Abingdon, 1976.

Lüdemann, G. *Early Christianity According to the Traditions in Acts.* Trans. J. Bowden. Minneapolis: Fortress Press, 1989.

——. *Opposition to Paul in Jewish Christianity.* Trans. M. Eugene Boring. Minneapolis: Fortress Press, 1989.

——. *Paul, Apostle to the Gentiles: Studies in Chronology.* Philadelphia: Fortress Press, 1984.

Luz, U. *Matthew 1–7.* Trans. W. C. Linss. Minneapolis: Augsburg, 1989 (German 1985).

MacDonald, D. R. *The Legend and the Apostle. The Battle for Paul in Story and Canon.* Philadelphia: Westminster Press, 1983.

MacDonald, M. Y. *The Pauline Churches. A Socio-Historical Study of Institutionalization in the Pauline and Deutero-Pauline Writings.* SNTSMS 60. Cambridge: University Press, 1988.

Mack, B. M. "The Kingdom That Didn't Come: A Social History of the Q Tradents." *Seminar Papers, SBL* (1988) 608–635.

——. *A Myth of Innocence. Mark and Christian Origins.* Philadelphia: Fortress Press, 1988.

Mack, B. M., and V. K. Robbins. *Patterns of Persuasion in the Gospels.* Sonoma, CA: Polebridge Press, 1989.

MacMullen, R. *Roman Social Relations. 50 B.C. to 284 C.E.* New Haven: Yale University Press, 1974.

Macquarrie, J. *The Scope of Demythologizing; Bultmann and His Critics.* London: SCM Press, 1960.

MacRae, G. "The Ego-Proclamation in Gnostic Sources." Pp. 122–134 in E. Bammel, ed. *The Trial of Jesus.* London: SCM Press, 1970.

——. "The Fourth Gospel and *Religionsgeschichte.*" *Catholic Biblical Quarterly* 32 (1970) 13–24.

——. *Faith in the Word: The Fourth Gospel.* Chicago: Franciscan Herald Press, 1973.

Malbon, E. S. "Fallible Followers: Women and Men in the Gospel of Mark," *Semeia* 28 (1983) 29–48.

——. *Narrative Space and Mythic Meaning in Mark.* San Francisco: Harper & Row, 1986.

Malherbe, A. J. "Hospitality and Inhospitality in the Church." Pp. 92–112 in Malherbe, *Social Aspects of Early Christianity,* 2d ed.

——. *Paul and the Thessalonians.* Philadelphia: Fortress Press, 1987.

——. *Moral Exhortation: A Greco-Roman Sourcebook.* Philadelphia: Westminster Press, 1986.

——. *Social Aspects of Early Christianity.* 2d ed. Philadelphia: Fortress Press, 1983.

——. *The Cynic Epistles: A Study Edition.* Missoula, MT: Scholars Press, 1977.

Malina, B. J. "The Received View and What It Cannot Do: III John and Hospitality." Pp. 171–189 in J. H. Elliott, ed., *Social Scientific Criticism of the New Testament and Its Social World.*

——. *Christian Origins and Cultural Anthropology. Practical Models for Biblical Interpretation.* Atlanta: John Knox Press, 1986.

——. *The New Testament World. Insights from Cultural Anthropology.* Atlanta: John Knox Press, 1981.

Malina, B. J., and J. H. Neyrey. *Calling Jesus Names. The Social Value of Labels in Matthew.* Sonoma, CA: Polebridge Press, 1988.

Manns, F. *John and Jamnia: How the Break Occurred Between Jews and Christians c. 80–100 A.D.* Jerusalem: Franciscan Printing Press, 1988.

Manson, T. W. *The Sayings of Jesus.* London: SCM Press, 1949.

——. *The Teaching of Jesus.* Cambridge: Cambridge University Press, 1931.

Marrow, S. B. *Paul: His Letters and His Theology.* New York: Paulist Press, 1986.

Marshall, I. H. "The Present State of Lucan Studies." *Themelios* 14 (1989) 52–56.

Martin, L. H. *Hellenistic Religions. An Introduction.* New York: Oxford University Press, 1987.

Martin, R. P. *Carmen Christi: Philippians ii 5–11 in Recent Interpretation and in the Setting of Early Christian Worship.* Cambridge: University Press, 1967.

Martyn, J. L. *History and Theology in the Fourth Gospel.* New York: Harper & Row, 1968.

——. *The Gospel of John in Christian History.* New York: Paulist Press, 1979.

Marxsen, W. *Introduction to the New Testament.* Trans. G. Buswell. Philadelphia: Fortress Press, 1968.

——. *Mark the Evangelist.* Trans. R. Harrisville. New York and Nashville: Abingdon Press, 1969.

——. *The Lord's Supper as a Christological Problem.* Trans. L. Nieting. Philadelphia: Fortress Press, 1970.

Mason, S. *Josephus and the New Testament.* Peabody, MA: Hendrickson, 1992.

Mattill, A. J. "The Value of Acts as a Source for the Study of Paul." Pp. 76–98 in C. Talbert, ed., *Perspectives on Luke-Acts.*

Maynard-Reid, P. U. *Poverty and Wealth in James.* New York: Maryknoll, 1987.

Mays, J. L., ed. *Interpreting the Gospels.* Philadelphia: Fortress Press, 1981.

McClelland, S. E. "Super-Apostles, Servants of Christ, Servants of Satan: A Response." *Journal for the Study of the New Testament* 14 (1982) 82–87.

McDonald, J. I. H. "Was Romans XVI a Separate Letter?" *New Testament Studies* (1970) 369–372.

McKnight, E. V. *What Is Form Criticism?* Guides to Biblical Scholarship, New Testament Series. Dan O. Via, Jr., ed. Philadelphia: Fortress Press, 1969.

McNamara, M. *Targum and Testament.* Grand Rapids: Eerdmans, 1972.

Meeks, W. A. "The Man from Heaven in Johannine Sectarianism." *Journal of Biblical Literature* 91 (1972), pp. 44–72.

———. "Since Then You Would Need to Go Out of the World; Group Boundaries in Pauline Christianity." Pp. 4-29 in T. J. Ryan, ed. *Critical History and Biblical Faith. New Testament Perspectives.* Villanova, PA: Villanova University, 1979.

———. "The Man from Heaven in Johannine Sectarianism." *Journal of Biblical Literature* 91 (1972) 44–72.

———. *The First Urban Christians. The Social World of the Apostle Paul.* New Haven: Yale University Press, 1983.

———. *The Writings of St. Paul.* Norton Critical Editions. New York: Norton, 1972.

Meier, J. P. "Symmetry and Theology in the Old Testament Citations of Heb 1,5–14." *Biblica* 66 (1985) 504–533.

———. *A Marginal Jew. Rethinking the Historical Jesus.* Vol. 1. New York: Doubleday, 1991.

———. *Law and History in Matthew's Gospel.* Analecta Biblica 71. Rome: Biblical Institute Press, 1976.

———. *The Vision of Matthew.* New York: Paulist Press, 1979.

Metzger, B. M. *The Canon of the New Testament.* New York: Oxford University Press, 1987.

———. *The Text of the New Testament.* 3rd ed. New York: Oxford University Press, 1992.

Meyer, B. *The Aims of Jesus.* London: SCM Press, 1979.

Meyer, M. W. *The Ancient Mysteries. A Sourcebook.* San Francisco: Harper & Row, 1987.

Meyers, E. M. "Early Judaism and Christianity in the Light of Archeology." *Biblical Archeologist* 51/52 (1988) 69–79.

Myers, E. M., and James F. Strange. *Archaeology, the Rabbis, and Early Christianity. The Social and Historical Setting of Palestinian Judaism and Christianity.* Nashville: Abingdon, 1981.

Milgrom, J. "The Temple Scroll." *The Biblical Archeologist* 41 (1978) 105–120.

Milik, J. T. *Ten Years of Discovery in the Judean Desert.* SBT 26. Naperville, IL: Allenson, 1959.

Miller, D. G., and Y. Hadidian. *Jesus and Man's Hope.* 2 vols. Pittsburgh: Pittsburgh Theological Seminary, 1970.

Miller, J. W. *Step By Step Through the Parables.* New York: Paulist Press, 1981.

Miller, S. S. *Studies in the History and Traditions of Sepphoris.* Leiden: E. J. Brill, 1984.

Minear, P. "Luke's Use of the Birth Stories." Pp. 111–130 in L. Keck and J. L. Martyn, eds. *Studies in Luke-Acts.* New York: Abingdon, 1966.

Mitton, C. L. *Ephesians.* Grand Rapids: Eerdmans, 1976.

Montefiore, H. *A Commentary on the Epistle to the Hebrews.* Harpers. New York: Harper & Row, 1964.

Moore, G. F. *Judaism in the First Centuries of the Christian Era.* 2 vols. New York: Schocken Books, 1958.

Moule, C. F. D. *The Birth of the New Testament.* London: A. & C. Black, 1962.

Moxnes, H. *The Economy of the Kingdom. Social Conflict and Economic Relations in Luke's Gospel.* Philadelphia: Fortress Press, 1988.

Munck, J. *Paul and the Salvation of Mankind.* Trans. F. Clarke. Richmond: John Knox Press, 1959.

Murphy-O'Connor, J. "Pauline Missions Before the Jerusalem Conference." *Revue Biblique* 89 (1982) 71–91.

———. "Relating 2 Cor 6:14–7:1 to Its Context." *New Testament Studies* 33 (1987) 272–275.

———. "The Judean Desert." Pp. 119–156 of R. A. Kraft and G. W. E. Nickelsburg, eds., *Early Judaism and Its Modern Interpreters.*

———. "Tradition and Redaction in 1 Cor 15:3–7." *Catholic Biblical Quarterly* 43 (1981) 582–589.

———. *St. Paul's Corinth: Texts and Archeology.* GNS 6. Wilmington, DE: Michael Glazier, 1983.

Myers, C. *Binding the Strong Man: A Political Reading of Mark's Story of Jesus.* Maryknoll, NY: Orbis Books, 1988.

Negev, A. *Archeological Encyclopedia of the Holy Land.* New York: Putnam 1972.

Neihardt, G. *Black Elk Speaks.* Lincoln: University of Nebraska, 1960.

Neill, S. *The Interpretation of the New Testament, 1861–1961.* London: Oxford University Press, 1964.

Netzer, E. *Greater Herodium.* Jerusalem: Institute of Archaeology, Hebrew University of Jerusalem, 1981.

Neusner, J. "The Formation of Rabbinic Judaism: Yavneh from A.D. 70–100." *Aufstieg und Niedergang der römischen Welt* (n.d.) II.19.2, 2–42.

———. *Development of a Legend: Studies in the Traditions Concerning Yohanan ben Zakkai.* Leiden: E. J. Brill, 1970.

————. *Invitation to the Talmud.* Rev. ed. New York: Harper & Row, 1984.

————. *The Rabbinic Traditions About the Pharisees Before 70.* 3 vols. Leiden: E. J. Brill, 1971.

Neusner, J., W. S. Green, and E. Frerichs. *Judaisms and Their Messiahs at the Turn of the Christian Era.* Cambridge: University Press, 1987.

Neyrey, J. H. "The Form and Background of the Polemic in 2 Peter." *Journal of Biblical Literature* 99 (1980) 407–431.

————. "Unclean, Common, Polluted and Taboo." *Forum* 4/4 (1988) 72–82.

————. "Witchcraft Accusations in 2 Corinthians 10–13: Paul in Social Science Perspective." *Listening. Journal of Religion and Culture* 21 (1986) 160–170.

————. *An Ideology of Revolt. John's Christology in Social-Science Perspective.* Philadelphia: Fortress Press, 1988.

————. *Christ Is Community. The Christologies of the New Testament.* Good News Studies 13. Wilmington, DE: Michael Glazier, 1985.

————. *Paul, in Other Words. A Cultural Reading of his Letters.* Louisville, KY: Westminster/John Knox Press, 1990.

————. *The Passion According to Luke. A Redaction Study of Luke's Soteriology.* New York: Paulist Press, 1985.

Neyrey, J. H., ed. *The Social World of Luke-Acts. Models for Interpretation.* Peabody, MA: Hendrickson, 1991.

Nicholson, G. C. *Death as Departure: The Johannine Descent-Ascent Schema.* Chico, CA: Scholars Press, 1983.

Nickelsburg, G. W. E. "Genre and Function of the Markan Passion Narrative." *Harvard Theological Review* 73 (1980) 153–184.

————. "Social Aspects of Palestinian Jewish Apocalypticism." Pp. 641–654 in D. Hellholm, ed., *Apocalypticism in the Mediterranean World and the Near East.*

————. *Jewish Literature Between the Bible and the Mishnah.* Phildelphia: Fortress Press, 1981.

Nickle, K. *The Collection. A Study in Paul's Strategy.* SBT 48. Naperville, IL: Allenson, 1966.

Nineham, D. E. *The Gospel of St. Mark.* Middlesex: Penguin Books, 1963.

Nock, A. D. *Early Gentile Christianity and Its Gentile Background.* Harper Torchbook No. 111. New York: Harper & Row, 1964.

————. *St. Paul.* New York: Harper & Row, 1938.

Noth, M. *The History of Israel.* Rev. ed. New York: Harper & Row, 1960.

O'Brian, P. T. *Colossians, Philemon.* Word 44. Waco, TX: Word, 1982.

O'Connor, D. W. *Peter in Rome. The Literary, Liturgical and Archeological Evidence.* New York: Columbia University Press, 1968.

O'Day, G. *Revelation in the Fourth Gospel. Narrative Mode and Theological Claim.* Philadelphia: Fortress Press, 1986.

O'Neill, J. C. *The Puzzle of 1 John 2–7.* London: SPCK, 1966.

Oakman, D. *Jesus and the Economic Questions of His Day.* SBEC 8. Lewiston/Queenston: Edwin Mellen Press, 1986.

Oates, W. J. *The Stoic and Epicurean Philosophers.* New York: Random House, 1940.

Ogg, G. *The Chronology of the Life of Paul.* London: Epworth, 1968.

Orton, D. E. *The Understanding Scribe. Matthew and the Apocalyptic Ideal.* JSNT Sup. 25. Sheffield: JSOT Press, 1989.

Osiek, C. "The New Handmaid: The Bible and Social Sciences." *Theological Studies* 50 (1989) 260–278.

————. *What Are They Saying About the Social Setting of the New Testament?* 2d ed. New York/Ramsay, NJ: Paulist Press, 1992.

Overman, A. *Matthew's Gospel and Formative Judaism. The Social World of the Matthean Community.* Minneapolis: Fortress Press, 1990.

Pagels, E. *The Gnostic Paul: Gnostic Exegesis of the Pauline Letters.* Philadelphia: Fortress Press, 1975.

————. *The Johannine Gospel in Gnostic Exegesis: Heracleon's Commentary on John.* Nashville: Abingdon Press, 1973.

Painter, J. *John: Witness and Theologian.* London: SPCK, 1976.

Patte, D. *The Gospel According to Matthew: A Structural Commentary on Matthew's Faith.* Philadelphia: Fortress Press, 1987.

Patte, D. and A. *Structural Exegesis: From Theory to Practice.* Philadelphia: Fortress Press, 1978.

Patterson, S. J., and M. W. Meyer, "The Gospel of Thomas." Pp. 75–159 in J. S. Kloppenborg, M. W. Meyer, S. J. Patterson, and M. G. Steinhouse, *Q Thomas Reader* (introduction, text, translation, notes).

Pearson, B. A. "1 Thessalonians 2:13-16: A Deutero-Pauline Interpolation." *Harvard Theological Review* 64 (1971) 79–94.

————. *The Pneumatikos-Psychikos Terminology in 1 Corinthians: A Study in the Theology of the Corinthians Opponents of Paul in Relation to Gnosticism.* Cambridge: Cambridge University Press, 1973.

Perkins, P. "Crisis in Jerusalem? Narrative Criticism in New Testament Studies." *Theological Studies* 50 (1989) 296–313.

————. *Hearing the Parables of Jesus.* New York: Paulist Press, 1981.

———. *The Gospel According to St. John. A Theological Commentary.* Chicago: Franciscan Herald Press, 1978.

Perrin, N. "The Christology of Mark: A Study in Methodology." *Journal of Religion* 51 (1971) 173–187.

———. "The Composition of Mark IX.1." *Novum Testamentum* 11 (1969) 67–70.

———. "The Literary Gattung 'Gospel': Some Observations." *Expository Times* 82 (1970) 4–7.

———. "The Modern Interpretation of the Parables of Jesus and the Problem of Hermeneutics." *Interpretation* 25 (1971) 131–148.

———. "The Parables of Jesus as Parables, as Metaphors and as Aesthetic Objects." *Journal of Religion* 50 (1970) 340–346.

———. "The Son of Man in the Synoptic Tradition." *Biblical Research* 13 (1968) 1–23.

———. "The Use of (*para*) *didonai* in Connection with the Passion of Jesus in the New Testament." In *Der Ruf Jesu und die Antwort Der Gemeinde: Festschrift für Joachim Jeremias*. E. Lohse, ed. Göttingen: Vandenhoeck & Ruprecht, 1970.

———. "Towards the Interpretation of the Gospel of Mark." Pp. 1-78 in H. D. Betz, ed., *Christology and a Modern Pilgrimage: A Discussion with Norman Perrin*. Claremont, CA: New Testament Colloquium, 1971.

———. "Wisdom and Apocalyptic in the Message of Jesus." *Society of Biblical Literature One Hundred Eighth Annual Meeting (1972) Proceedings* 2, 543–570.

———. *Jesus and the Language of the Kingdom.* Philadelphia: Fortress Press, 1976.

———. *Rediscovering the Teaching of Jesus.* London: SCM Press, and New York: Harper & Row, 1967.

———. *The Kingdom of God in the Teaching of Jesus.* London: SCM Press, and Philadelphia: Westminster Press, 1963.

———. *The Promise of Bultmann.* The Promise of Theology. M. Marty, ed. Philadelphia and New York: J. B. Lippincott, 1969.

———. *What Is Redaction Criticism?* Rev. ed. Guides to Biblical Scholarship. New Testament Series. Philadelphia: Fortress Press, 1971.

Peters, F. E. *The Harvest of Hellenism.* New York: Simon and Schuster, 1970.

Petersen, N. R. *Literary Criticism for New Testament Critics.* Guides to Biblical Scholarship. Dan O. Via, Jr., ed. Philadelphia: Fortress Press, 1978.

———. *Rediscovering Paul: Philemon and the Sociology of Paul's Narrative World.* Philadelphia:

Fortress Press, 1985.

Pfeiffer, R. H. *History of New Testament Times with an Introduction to the Apocrypha.* New York: Harper & Row, 1949.

Pilch, J. *What Are They Saying About the Book of Revelation?* New York: Paulist Press, 1978.

Pilgrim, W. E. *Good News to the Poor. Wealth and Poverty in Luke-Acts.* Minneapolis: Augsburg Press, 1981.

Piper, R. A. *Wisdom in the Q-tradition. The Aphoristic Teaching of Jesus.* New York: Cambridge University Press, 1989.

Pollard, T. E. "The Integrity of Philippians." *New Testament Studies* 13 (1966–1967) 57–66.

Pollard, T. W. *Johannine Christology and the Early Church.* Cambridge: Cambridge University Press, 1970.

Pomeroy, S. *Goddesses, Whores, Wives, and Slaves: Women in Classical Antiquity.* New York: Schocken Press, 1975.

Powell, M. A. "Are the Sands Still Shifting? An Update on Lukan Scholarship." *Trinity Lutheran Seminary* 11 (1989) 15–22.

———. *What Are They Saying About Luke and Acts?* New York: Paulist Press, 1989.

Pritchard, J. B. *The Excavation at Herodian Jericho, 1951.* New Haven: American Schools of Oriental Research, 1958.

Rahtjen, B. D. "The Three Letters of Paul to the Philippians." *New Testament Studies* 6 (1959–1960) 167–173.

Räisänen, H. "Paul's Conversion and the Development of His View of the Law." *New Testament Studies* 33 (1987) 404–419.

Rajak, T. *Josephus. The Historian and His Society.* Philadelphia: Fortress Press, 1983.

Reddish, M. G., ed. *Apocalyptic Literature. A Reader.* Nashville: Abingdon Press, 1990.

Reicke, B. *The New Testament Era.* London: Adam and Charles Black, 1968.

Rendsberger, D. "2 Corinthians 6:14–7:1: A Fresh Examination." *Studia Biblica et Theologica* 8 (1978) 25–49.

———. *Johannine Faith and Liberating Community.* Philadelphia: Westminster Press, 1988.

Reumann, J. "Philippians 3:20–21—A Hymnic Fragment?" *New Testament Studies* 30 (1984) 593–609.

———. *Jesus in the Church's Gospels.* Philadelphia: Fortress Press, 1968.

Rhoads, D. *Israel in Revolution 6-74 C.E.: A Political History Based on Josephus.* Philadelphia: Fortress Press, 1976.

Rhoads, D., and D. Michie. *Mark as Story. An Introduction to the Narrative of a Gospel.* Philadelphia: Fortress Press, 1982.

Rice, D. G., and J. Stambaugh. *Sources for the Study*

of Greek Religion. Missoula, MT: Scholars Press, 1979.

Richard, E. "Luke—Writer, Theologian, Historian: Research and Orientation of the 70's." *Biblical Theology Bulletin* 13 (1983) 1-13.

Richard, E., ed. *New Views on Luke and Acts.* Collegeville, MN: Liturgical Press, 1990.

Richardson, P. *Paul's Ethic of Freedom.* Philadelphia: Westminster Press, 1979.

Ricoeur, P. *Freud and Philosophy: An Essay in Interpretation.* New Haven: Yale University Press, 1970.

———. *The Symbolism of Evil.* Boston: Beacon Press, 1969.

Ridderbos, H. *Paul.* Grand Rapids, MI: Eerdmans: 1975.

Ringgren, H. *The Faith of Qumran.* Philadelphia: Fortress Press, 1963.

Ritmeyer, K. and L. "Reconstructing Herod's Temple Mount in Jerusalem." *Biblical Archeology Review* 15/6 (1989) 23–42.

Robbins, V. K. "By Land and By Sea: The We-Passages and Ancient Sea Voyages." Pp. 215-45 in C. H. Talbert, ed., *Perspectives on Luke-Acts.*

———. "Text and Context in Recent Studies of the Gospel of Mark." *Religious Studies Review* 17/1 (1991) 16–23.

———. "The Chreia." Pp. 1–23 in D. E. Aune, ed., *Greco-Roman Literature and the New Testament: Selected Forms and Genres.* Sources for Biblical Study 21. Atlanta: Scholars Press, 1988.

———. *Jesus the Teacher. A Socio-Rhetorical Interpretation of Mark.* Philadelphia: Fortress Press, 1978.

Robinson, J. M. "On Bridging the Gulf from Q to the Gospel of Thomas (or Vice Versa)." Pp. 127–175 in C. W. Hedrick and R. Hodgson, Jr., *Nag Hammadi, Gnosticism, and Early Christianity.*

———. "The Discovery of the Nag Hammadi Codices." *Biblical Archeologist* 42 (1979) 206–224.

———. "The Johannine Trajectory." In J. M. Robinson and H. Koester, *Trajectories Through Early Christianity.* Philadelphia: Fortress Press, 1971.

———. *The Nag Hammadi Library in English.* 3d ed. San Francisco: Harper & Row, 1988.

Robinson, J. M., and J. B. Cobb, eds. *The New Hermeneutic.* New York: Harper & Row, 1964.

Robinson, J. M., and H. Koester. *Trajectories Through Early Christianity.* Philadelphia: Fortress Press, 1971.

Roetzel, C. *The Letters of Paul. Conversations in Context.* 3d ed. Atlanta: John Knox Press, 1991.

———. *The World That Shaped the New Testament.* Atlanta: John Knox Press, 1985.

Rohde, J. *Rediscovering the Teaching of the Evangelists.* Philadelphia: Westminster Press, 1968.

Rose, H. J. *A Handbook of Greek Literature: From Homer to the Age of Lucian.* New York: E. P. Dutton, 1960.

———. *Religion in Greece and Rome.* New York: Harper & Row, 1959.

Rowland, C. *Christian Origins: An Account of the Setting and Character of the Most Important Messianic Sect of Judaism.* London: SPCK, 1985.

Rowley, H. H. *The Relevance of Apocalyptic.* Rev. ed. New York: Association Press, 1964.

Rowston, D. E. "The Most Neglected Book in the New Testament." *New Testament Studies* 21 (1974–1975) 554–563.

Rubenstein, R. *My Brother Paul.* New York: Harper & Row, 1972.

Rudolph, K. *Gnosis: The Nature and History of Gnosticism.* Trans. R. McL. Wilson. San Francisco: Harper & Row, 1987 (German 1980).

Russell, D. S. *Between the Testaments.* Philadelphia: Fortress Press, 1965.

Safrai, S., and M. Stern, eds. *The Jewish People in the First Century.* 2 vols. Philadelphia: Fortress Press, 1974.

Saldarini, T. *Pharisees, Scribes, and Sadducees. A Sociological Approach.* Wilmington, DE: Michael Glazier, 1988.

Samply, J. P. "The Letter to the Ephesians." Pp. 9–39 in G. Krodel, ed., *Ephesians, Colossians, 2 Thessalonians, The Pastoral Epistles.*

Sanders, E. P. *Jesus and Judaism.* Philadelphia: Fortress Press, 1985.

———. *Paul and Palestinian Judaism. A Comparison of Patterns of Religion.* Philadelphia: Fortress Press, 1977.

———. *Paul, the Law, and the Jewish People.* Philadelphia: Fortress Press, 1983.

Sanders, E. P, and Margaret Davies. and Margaret Davies, *Studying the Synoptic Gospels.* Philadelphia: Trinity Press International, 1989.

Sanders, J. T. *Ethics in the New Testament.* Philadelphia: Fortress Press, 1975.

———. *The Jews in Luke-Acts.* Philadelphia: Fortress Press, 1987.

———. *The New Testament Christological Hymns: Their Historical Religious Background.* SNTS Monograph Series. New York: Cambridge University Press, 1971.

Sandmel, S. *The Genius of Paul.* Philadelphia: Fortress Press, 1979.

Schaberg, J. *The Illegitimacy of Jesus. A Feminist Theological Interpretation of the Infancy Narratives.* San Francisco: Harper & Row, 1987.

Schalit, A., ed. *The World History of the Jewish Peo-*

ple, vol. 6: *The Hellenistic Age; Political History of Jewish Palestine from 332 B.C.E. to 67 B.C.E.* New Brunswick, NJ: Rutgers University Press, 1972.

Schauss, H. *The Jewish Festivals, History and Observances.* New York: Schocken Books, 1974.

Schelke, K. H. "The Letters of Paul." In K. Rahner, ed. *Sacramentum Mundi.* 6 vols. New York: Herder and Herder, 1968–70. Vol. 4, pp. 198–203.

Schiffman, L. H. *Archeology and History in the Dead Sea Scrolls.* Sheffield: JSOT, 1990.

Schmidt, D. "I Thess 2:13–16: Linguistic Evidence for an Interpolation." *Journal of Biblical Literature* 102 (1983) 269–279.

Schmidt, K. L. *Die Rahmen der Geschichte Jesu.* Berlin: Trowitzsch & Sohn, 1919.

Schmithals, W. *Gnostics in Corinth.* Trans. John E. Steely. Nashville: Abingdon Press, 1971.

———. *Paul and the Gnostics.* Trans. J. E. Steely. Nashville: Abingdon Press, 1972.

———. *The Apocalyptic Movement: Introduction and Interpretation.* Nashville: Abingdon Press, 1975.

Schnackenburg, R. *The Gospel According to St. John.* 2 vols. vol. 1, trans. K. Smyth. New York: Herder and Herder, 1968; vol. 2, trans. C. Hastings et al. New York: Seabury Press, 1980. Now published by Crossroad.

———. *The Moral Teaching of the New Testament.* Trans. J. Holland-Smith and W. J. O'Hara from the 2d German ed. Freiburg: Herder, 1965.

Schneiders, S. M. "Women in the Fourth Gospel and the Role of Women in the Contemporary Church." *Biblical Theology Bulletin* 12 (1982) 35–44.

Schoeps, H. J. *Paul: The Theology of the Apostle in the Light of Jewish Religious History.* Trans. H. Knight. Philadelphia: Westminster Press, 1961.

Scholes, R., and R. Kellogg. *The Nature of Narrative.* New York: Oxford University Press, 1966.

Schottroff, L., and W. Stegemann. *Jesus and the Hope of the Poor.* Trans. M. J. O'Connell. Maryknoll, NY: Orbis Books, 1986.

Schürer, E., G. Vermes, and F. Miller. *The History of the Jewish People in the Age of Jesus Christ.* Vol. 1. Edinburgh: T. & T. Clark, 1973.

Schütz, J. H. *Paul and the Anatomy of Apostolic Authority.* New York: Cambridge University Press, 1975.

Schweitzer, A. *The Quest of the Historical Jesus.* New York: Macmillan, 1964.

Schweizer, E. *The Good News According to Luke.* Trans. David E. Green. Atlanta: John Knox Press, 1984.

———. *The Good News According to Matthew.* Trans. D. E. Green. Atlanta: John Knox Press, 1975.

———. *The Letter to the Colossians.* Minneapolis: Augsburg, 1982.

Scott, B. B. *Hear Then the Parable. A Commentary on the Parables of Jesus.* Minneapolis: Fortress Press, 1989.

Scroggs, R. "The Sociological Interpretation of the New Testament: The Present State of Research." *New Testament Studies* 26 (1980), 164–179.

———. "Paul and the Eschatological Woman." *Journal of the American Academy of Religion* 40 (1972) 283–303.

———. "The Earliest Christian Communities as Sectarian Movement." Pp. 1–23 in J. Neusner, ed. *Christianity, Judaism and Other Greco-Roman Cults. Studies for Morton Smith at Sixty.* Part II. Leiden: E. J. Brill, 1975.

———. "The Sociological Interpretation of the New Testament: The Present State of Research." *New Testament Studies* 26 (1980), 164–179.

———. *Paul for a New Day.* Philadelphia: Fortress Press, 1977.

———. *The New Testament and Homosexuality.* Philadelphia: Fortress Press, 1983.

Seccombe, D. *Possessions and the Poor in Luke-Acts.* Trans. M. J. O'Connell. Linz: Studien zum Neuen Testament und seiner Umwelt, 1982.

Segovia, F. *Love Relationship in the Johannine Tradition: Agapē/Agapan in I John and the Fourth Gospel.* Society of Biblical Literature Dissertation Series 58. Chico, CA: Scholars Press, 1982.

Senior, D. *The Passion Narrative According to Matthew.* Louvain: Leuven University Press, 1975.

———. *What Are They Saying About Matthew?* New York: Paulist Press, 1983.

Shanks, H. et al. *The Dead Sea Scrolls After Forty Years.* Washington: Biblical Archeology Society, 1991.

Shuler, P. I. *A Genre for the Gospels: The Biographical Character of Matthew.* Philadelphia: Fortress Press, 1982.

Simon, M. *Jewish Sects at the Time of Jesus.* Philadelphia: Fortress Press, 1967.

Slingerland, D. "The Transjordanian Origin of St. Matthew's Gospel." *Journal for the Study of the New Testament* 3 (1979) 18–28.

Sloyan, G. S. "The Letter of James." Pp. 28–49 in G. Krodel, ed., *Hebrews, James, 1 and 2 Peter, Jude, Revelation.*

———. *John.* Interpretation. Atlanta: John Knox

Press, 1988.

Smalley, S. S. "Keeping Up with Recent Studies. XII. St John's Gospel." *Expository Times* 97 (1985-1986) 102–108.

Smallwood, E. M. *The Jews Under Roman Rule: A Study in Political Relations.* Leiden: E. J. Brill, 1981.

Smith, D. "The Historical Jesus at Table." Pp. 466–486 in D. J. Lull, ed., *Seminar Papers Society of Biblical Literature.* Atlanta: Scholars Press, 1989.

Smith, D. M. "Johannine Christianity: Some Reflections on Its Character and Delineation." *New Testament Studies* 21 (1974–75) 222–248.

———. "John and the Synoptics: Some Dimensions of the Problem." *New Testament Studies* 26 (1979–80) 425–444.

———. "Judaism and the Gospel of John (plus 'Discussion')." Pp. 76–99 in James H. Charlesworth, *Jews and Christians.* New York: Crossroad, 1990.

———. "The Setting and Shape of a Johannine Narrative Source." *Journal of Biblical Literature* 95 (1976) 231–241.

———. *Johannine Christianity.* Columbia: University of South Carolina Press, 1984.

———. *John.* 2d ed. Proclamation Commentaries. Philadelphia: Fortress Press, 1986.

———. *The Composition and Order of the Fourth Gospel, Bultmann's Literary Theory.* New Haven: Yale University Press, 1965.

Smith, J. Z. "Social Description of Early Christianity." *Religious Studies Review* 1 (1975) 19–25.

———. *Drugery Divine. On the Comparison of Early Christianitities and the Religions of Late Antiquity.* Chicago: University of Chicago Press, 1990.

Smith, M. *Jesus the Magician.* New York: Harper & Row, 1978.

———. *Tannaitic Parallels to the Gospels.* Philadelphia: Society of Biblical Literature, 1951.

Smith, R. H. *Hebrews.* Augsburg Commentary on the New Testament. Minneapolis: Augsburg, 1984.

Snyder, G. F. "Survey and 'New' Thesis on the Bones of Peter." *Biblical Archeologist* 32 (1969) 2–24).

Soards, M. L. *The Passion According to Luke. The Special Material of Luke 22.* JSNTSuppl. 14. Sheffield: University Press, 1987.

Stambaugh, J. E., and D. L. Balch. *The New Testament in Its Social Environment.* Philadelphia: Westminster Press, 1986.

Stanton, G. "Matthew." Pp. 205–219 in D. A. Carson and H. G. M. Williamson, eds., *It Is Writ-*

ten: Scripture Citing Scripture: Essays in Honor of Barnabas Lindars. New York: Cambridge University Press, 1988.

———. "The Origin and Purpose of Matthew's Gospel: Matthean Scholarship from 1945–1980." *Aufstieg und Niedergang der römischen Welt* II.25.3 (1985). Pp. 1890–1951.

Stanton, G., ed. *The Interpretation of Matthew.* Philadelphia: Fortress Press, 1983.

Stein, R. H. "What is *Redaktionsgeschichte?*" *Journal of Biblical Literature* 88 (1969) 45–56.

———. *The Synoptic Problem. An Introduction.* Grand Rapids: Baker Book House, 1987.

Stendahl, K. "The Apostle Paul and the Introspective Conscience of the West." reprinted in W. Meeks, *The Writings of St. Paul,* pp. 422–423, and in Stendahl, *Paul Among Jews and Gentiles,* pp. 78–96.

———. *Paul Among Jews and Gentiles.* Philadelphia: Fortress Press, 1976.

———. *The School of St. Matthew.* Philadelphia: Fortress Press, 1968.

Stern, M. *Greek and Latin Authors on Jews and Judaism.* 3 vols. Jerusalem: The Israel Academy of Sciences and Humanities, 1976–1984.

Stirnewalt, M. L. "The Form and Function of the Greek Letter-Essay." Pp. 175–206 in C. P. Donfried, *The Romans Debate.*

Stoker, W. D. *Extracanonical Sayings of Jesus.* SBLSBS 18. Atlanta: Scholars Press, 1989.

Stone, M. *Scriptures, Sects, and Visions. A Profile of Judaism from Ezra to the Jewish Revolts.* Philadelphia: Fortress Press, 1980.

Stowers, S. K. *Letter Writing in Greco-Roman Antiquity.* Philadelphia: Fortress Press, 1986.

Strauss, D. F. *The Life of Jesus Critically Examined.* Philadelphia: Fortress Press, 1972 (original German 1835).

Strecker, G. "The Concept of History in Matthew." *Journal of the American Academy of Religion* 35 (1967) 219–230.

———. *The Sermon on the Mount. An Exegetical Commentary.* Trans. O. C. Dean. Nashville: Abingdon, 1988 (German 1985).

Streeter, B. J. *The Four Gospels.* London: Macmillan, 1924.

Suggs, M. Jack. *Wisdom, Christology and Law in Matthew's Gospel.* Cambridge: Harvard University Press, 1970.

Talbert, C. H. "Shifting Sands: The Recent Study of the Gospel of Luke." Pp. 197–213 in L. Keck and J. L. Martin, eds., *Studies in Luke-Acts.*

———. "The Concept of Immortals in Mediterranean Antiquity." *Journal of Biblical Literature* 94 (1975) 410–436.

———. "The Myth of a Descending-Ascending Redeemer in Mediterranean Antiquity." *New Testament Studies* 22 (1975/76) 418–440.

Talbert, C. H. *Literary Patterns, Theological Themes, and the Genre of Luke-Acts.* Society of Biblical Literature Monograph Series 20. Missoula, MT: Scholars Press, 1974.

———. *Reading Luke. A Literary and Theological Commentary on the Third Gospel.* New York: Crossroad, 1988.

———. *What Is a Gospel?* Philadelphia: Fortress Press, 1977.

Talbert, C. H., ed. *Luke-Acts. New Perspectives from the Society of Biblical Literature.* New York: Crossroad, 1984.

———. *Perspectives on First Peter.* NABPR Special Studies Series 9. Macon, GA: Mercer University Press, 1986.

———. *Perspectives on Luke-Acts.* Danville, Va.: Association of Baptist Professors of Religion, 1978.

Tannehill, R. C. "Introduction: The Pronouncement Story and Its Types." *Semeia* 21 (1981) 1–13.

———. "The 'Focal Instance' as a Form of New Testament Speech: A Study of Matthew 5:39b–42." *Journal of Religion* 50 (1970) 372–385.

———. "The Mission of Jesus According to Luke IV 16–30." Pp. 51–75, in E. Grässer, A. Strobel, R. Tannehill, and W. Eltester, *Jesus in Nazareth.* New York: de Gruyter, 1972.

———. *The Narrative Unity of Luke-Acts.* 2 vols. Philadelphia: Fortress Press, 1986.

Tannehill, R. C., ed. *Semeia 20. Pronouncement Stories.* Chico, CA: Scholars Press, 1981.

Tarn, W., and Griffith, C. T. *Hellenistic Civilization.* 3d ed. London: Arnold, 1952.

Tate, W. R. *Biblical Interpretation. An Integrated Approach.* Peabody, MA: Hendrickson, 1991.

Tatum, W. B. *In Quest of Jesus.* Atlanta: John Knox Press, 1982.

Taussig, H. "The Lord's Prayer." *Forum* 4/4 (1988) 25–41.

Taylor, V. *The Gospel According to St. Mark.* London: Macmillan, 1952.

———. *The Passion Narrative of St. Luke.* Cambridge: Cambridge University Press, 1972.

Tcherikover, V. A. *Hellenistic Civilization and the Jews.* New York: Atheneum, 1970.

Teeple, H. *The Literary Origin of the Gospel of John.* Evanston, IL: Religion and Ethics Institute, 1974.

Theissen, G. *Sociology of Early Palestinian Christianity.* Trans. J. Bowden. Philadelphia: Fortress Press, 1978.

———. *The Miracle Stories of the Early Christian Tra-dition.* Trans. F. McDonagh. Philadelphia: Fortress Press, 1983.

———. *The Social Setting of Pauline Christianity. Essays on Corinth.* Trans. J. H. Schütz. Philadelphia: Fortress Press, 1982.

Theological Studies 50 (1989) (Historical Criticism: J. A. Fitzmyer; Social Criticism: C. Osiek; Feminist Hermeneutics: Phyllis Trible; Literary Criticism: P. Perkins; New Testament Theology: J. R. Donahue; Contemporary English Translations: J. P. M. Walsh).

Thompson, L. "A Sociological Analysis of Tribulation in the Apocalypse of John." Pp. 147–174 in A. Yarbro Collins, ed., *Early Christian Apocalypticism.*

Thompson, W. G. *Matthew's Advice to a Divided Community.* Analecta Biblica 44. Rome: Pontifical Biblical Institute, 1970.

Thompson, W. M. *The Jesus Debate.* New York: Paulist Press, 1985.

Thrall, M. E. "Super-Apostles, Servants of Christ, and Servants of Satan." *Journal for the Study of the New Testament* 6 (1980) 42–57.

———. "The Problem of II Cor VI.14–VII.1 in Some Recent Discussion." *New Testament Studies* 24 (1977) 132–148.

Thurston, H. *Familiar Prayers. Their Origin and History.* London: Burns Oates, 1953.

Tiede, D. L. *Prophecy and History in Luke-Acts.* Philadelphia: Fortress Press, 1980.

———. *The Charismatic Figure as Miracle Worker.* Missoula, MT: Society of Biblical Literature, 1972.

Tödt, H. E. *The Son of Man in the Synoptic Tradition.* Philadelphia: Westminster Press, 1965.

Tolbert, M. A. *Sowing the Gospel: Mark's World in Literary-Historical Perspective.* Minneapolis: Fortress Press, 1989.

Toynbee, A., ed. *The Crucible of Christianity.* New York: World, 1969.

Tuckett, C., ed. *The Messianic Secret.* Philadelphia: Fortress Press, 1983.

Tyson, J. B. "Paul's Opponents in Galatia." *Novum Testamentum* 10 (1968) 241–264.

Tyson, J. B., ed. *Luke-Acts and the Jewish People. Eight Critical Perspectives.* Minneapolis: Augsburg, 1988.

Van Belle, G. *Johannine Bibliography 1966-1985. A Cumulative and Classified Bibliography of Books and Periodical Literature on the Fourth Gospel.* Leuven: Leuven University Press—Peeters, 1988.

Van Tilborg, S. *The Jewish Leaders in Matthew.* Leiden: E. J. Brill, 1972.

Vanderlip, D. G. *Christianity According to John.* Philadelphia: Westminster Press, 1975.

Vermes, G. *Jesus the Jew.* New York: Macmillan, 1973.

————. *The Dead Sea Scrolls in English.* 2d ed. Baltimore: Penguin Books, 1987.

Verner, D. C. *The Household of God. The Social World of the Pastoral Epistles.* Society of Biblical Literature Dissertation Series 71. Chico, CA: Scholars Press, 1983.

Via, D. O. "The Prodigal Son: A Jungian Reading." *Society of Biblical Literature 1975 Seminar Papers.* Missoula, MT: Scholars Press, pp. 219–232.

————. *Kerygma and Comedy in the New Testament: A Structuralist Approach to Hermeneutic.* Philadelphia: Fortress Press, 1975.

————. *The Ethics of Mark's Gospel: In the Middle of Time.* Philadelphia: Fortress Press, 1985.

————. *The Parables: Their Literary and Existential Dimension.* Philadelphia: Fortress Press, 1967.

Vielhauer, P. "Jewish Christian Gospels." In E. Hennecke and W. Schneemelcher, *New Testament Apocrypha,* vol. 1. Philadelphia: Westminster Press, 1963.

————. "On the 'Paulinism' of Acts." Pp. 35–50 in L. E. Keck and J. L. Martyn, *Studies in Luke-Acts.*

Viviano, B. V. "Social World and Community Leadership: The Case of Matthew 23:1–12, 34." *Journal for the Study of the New Testament* 39 (1990) 3–21.

Vögtle, A. "Jesus Christ." Pp. 419–437 in *Sacramentum Verbi* II. J. B. Bauer, ed. New York: Herder and Herder, 1970.

Von Wahlde, U. C. *The Johannine Commandments. I John and the Struggle for the Johannine Tradition.* New York: Paulist Press, 1990.

Waetjen, H. C. *A Reordering of Power. A Socio-Political Reading of Mark's Gospel.* Minneapolis: Fortress Press, 1989.

Walaskay, P. *"And So We Came to Rome." The Political Perspective of St. Luke.* Society for New Testament Studies Monograph Series 49. Cambridge: Cambridge University Press, 1983.

Walsh, J. P. M. "Contemporary English Translations of Scripture." *Journal of Theological Studies* 50 (1989) 336–358.

Watson, F. *Paul, Judaism and the Gentiles. A Sociological Approach.* SNTSMS 56. Cambridge: University Press, 1986.

Weeden, T. J. *Mark: Traditions in Conflict.* Philadelphia: Fortress Press, 1971.

Weiss, J. *The Preaching of Jesus Concerning the Kingdom of God.* Philadelphia: Fortress Press, 1971.

Wheelwright, P. *Metaphor and Reality.* Bloomington: Indiana University Press, 1962. Paperback 1968.

Wheelwright, P. *The Burning Fountain.* Rev. ed. Bloomington: Indiana University Press, 1968.

Whitacre, R. A. *Johannine Polemic: The Role of Tradition and Theology.* SBLDS 67. Chico, CA: Scholars Press, 1982.

White, J. L. *Light from Ancient Letters.* Philadelphia: Fortress Press, 1986.

White, J. L., ed. *Studies in Ancient Letter Writing. Semeia 22.* Chico, CA: Scholars Press, 1982.

Whiteley, D. H. *The Theology of St. Paul.* Philadelphia: Fortress Press, 1964.

Wilder, A. N. "Eschatological Imagery and Earthly Circumstance." *New Testament Studies* 5 (1958–59) 229–245.

————. "The Rhetoric of Ancient and Modern Apocalyptic." *Interpretation* 25 (1971) 436–453.

————. *Early Christian Rhetoric: The Language of the Gospel.* New York: Harper & Row, 1964. Rev. ed., Cambridge: Harvard University Press, 1971.

————. *The Language of the Gospel. Early Christian Rhetoric.* New York: Harper & Row, 1964.

Williamson, R. *Philo and the Epistle to the Hebrews.* Leiden: E. J. Brill, 1970.

Wills, L. M. "The Depiction of the Jews in Acts." *Journal of Biblical Literature* 110/4 (1991) 631–654.

Wilson, B. R. *Magic and the Millennium. A Sociological Study of Religious Movements of Protest among Tribal and Third-World Peoples.* London: Heinemann, 1973.

————. *Religion in Sociological Perspective.* Oxford: Oxford University Press, 1982.

————. *Sects and Society.* Berkeley: University of California Press, 1961.

Wilson, S. G. *Luke and the Law.* SNTSMS 50. Cambridge: Cambridge University Press, 1973.

Wimbush, V. *Paul: The Worldly Ascetic.* Macon, GA: Mercer University Press, 1987.

Wohl, D. B. *Johannine Christianity in Conflict: Authority, Rank, and Succession in the First Farewell Discourse.* Society of Biblical Literature Dissertation Series 60. Chico, CA: Scholars Press, 1981.

Wood, J. D. *The Interpretation of the Bible.* Studies in Theology. London: Duckworth, 1958.

Yadin, Y. "The Dead Sea Scrolls and the Epistle to the Hebrews." *Scripta Hierosolymitana* 4 (1958) 36–55.

————. "The Excavation of Masada, 1963–1964." *Israel Exploration Journal* 15 (1965) 1–120.

————. *Masada.* New York: Random House, 1966.

Yamauchi, E. *Harper's World of the New Testament.* San Francisco: Harper & Row, 1981.

Yarden, L. *The Spoils of Jerusalem on the Arch of*

Titus: A Reinvestigation. Stockholm: Svenska Institutete i Rom, 1991.

Yee, G. A. *Jewish Feasts and the Gospel of John.* Zacchaeus Studies. Wilmington, DE: Michael Glazier, 1989.

Zias, J., and E. Sekeles. "The Crucified Man from Giv'at ha Mivtar—A Reappraisal," *Biblical Archeologist* 48 1985) 190–191.

BIBLIOGRAPHY FOR RESEARCH PAPERS

A good research paper should have the best, most recent bibliography available. Currently there is an explosion in bibliographical resources, which is part of the information explosion. For the printed material that follows we are indebted to Fr. Bonaventure Hayes, librarian at Christ the King Seminary, East Aurora, New York. For the electronic material, I am indebted to Professor Robert Kraft of the University of Pennsylvania, to Ed Kroll and Michael Strangelove (see below), and to the Systems Librarian at Canisius College, Karen Perone.

I. Dictionaries and Encyclopedias

Dictionaries and encyclopedia articles are often the best introduction to a new subject of research, and many contain excellent bibliographies up to the time of their publication. The student should consult dictionaries and encyclopedias, especially *The Anchor Bible Dictionary* and the *Interpreter's Dictionary of the Bible*, as a first step for orientation to a new topic of research. NOTE: Research papers should cite *the authors* of the dictionary or encyclopedia *articles* first.

The Anchor Bible Dictionary. Ed.-in-chief, D. N. Freedman. New York: Doubleday, 1992. This relatively new, six-volume dictionary is virtually an encyclopedia and contains *the best source for bibliography on particular entries up to about 1988.* It is cited frequently in the "Further Reading" sections at the ends of the chapters.

Baker Encyclopedia of the Bible. 2 vols. Ed. W. A. Elwell. Grand Rapids, MI: Baker Book House, 1988. Conservative.

A Dictionary of Biblical Interpretation. Ed. R. J. Coggins and J. L. Houlden. Philadelphia: Trinity Press International, 1990. Includes critical methods and some scholars' biographies.

Dictionary of Jesus and the Gospels. Ed. J. B. Green, S. McKnight, and I. H. Marshall. Downers Grove, IL: InterVarsity Press, 1992. Excellent conservative scholarship.

Dictionary of New Testament Theology. 3 vols. Ed. Colin Brown. Grand Rapids: Zondervan, 1975–1978. Conservative.

Encyclopaedia Britannica. Excellent scholarly work on some selected topics. Bibliographies.

Encyclopedia Judaica. Ed. C. Roth. Jerusalem: Keter Press, 1972. 16 vols. plus supplements. The best recent encyclopedia in English on topics pertaining to Judaism.

Exegetical Dictionary of the New Testament, Vol. 1. Ed. H. Balz and G. Schneider. Grand Rapids: Eerdmans, 1990–. First of three volumes translated from German; a standard, useful work, with brief bibliographies.

Harper's Bible Dictionary. Ed. P. J. Achtemeier. New York: Harper, 1985. Many illustrations and maps.

Harper's Encyclopedia of Bible Life. Ed. M. S. and M. L. Miller. Rev. ed. B. M. Bennett and D. H. Scott. New York: Harper, 1978. Illustrations, maps, and concluding bibliography.

International Standard Bible Encyclopedia. Ed. G. W. Bromiley. Grand Rapids: Eerdmans, 1979–. Conservative; four volumes.

Interpreter's Dictionary of the Bible (IDB). Ed. G. A. Buttrick et al. 4 vols. New York: Abingdon, 1962. Supplementary volume five (1975). Brief to medium length, excellent articles. Along with the *Anchor Bible Dictionary* a good place to begin research. Bibliographies. The supplementary volume should always be checked for other scholarship and bibliographies.

Jewish Encyclopedia. Ed. I. Singer (1901–1906). Reprinted 1966. 12 vols. New York: KTAV, 1901-1906. Dated, but still excellent on many subjects.

Léon-Dufour, X. *Dictionary of Biblical Theology.* Rev. ed. New York: Seabury Press, 1980. Brief articles with references to Biblical passages.

———. *Dictionary of the New Testament.* New York: Harper & Row, 1980. Brief, cross-referenced word studies. Introductory survey article on the New Testament world. Helpful is a sixty-page survey on the New Testament world.

Mercer Dictionary of the Bible. Ed. W. E. Mills. Macon, GA: Mercer University Press, 1990.

New Catholic Encyclopedia. New York: McGraw-Hill, 1967–79. 15 vols. plus 2 supplementary vols. Generally high quality, but somewhat dated. Short bibliographies.

Sacramentum Verbi: An Encyclopedia of Biblical Theology. Ed. J. B. Bauer. 3 vols. New York: Herder and Herder, 1970. Excellent Catholic European scholarship, though somewhat dated.

Theological Dictionary of the New Testament. Ed. G. Kittel and G. Friedrich. 10 vols. Grand Rapids: Eerdmans, 1964–1976. Very scholarly word-study reference tool listed alphabetically by Greek words, but it can be helpful to non-Greek-reading students who can use the Greek alphabet. Extensive references to non-Biblical sources. Articles dated.

Turner, N. *Christian Words.* Edinburgh: T. & T. Clark, 1980. Arranged alphabetically by English translation of Greek words.

The Oxford Classical Dictionary. Ed. N. G. L. Hammond and H. H. Scullard. Oxford: University Press, 1970. Bibliographies.

II. Computer-Generated (Electronic) Bibliographical Aids

The electronic revolution is here, the electronic library is on its way, and electronic bibliographical resources are already increasing so rapidly that by the time this book is available, what is listed here will be dated. There are obviously many questions of ethics involved, for example, plagiarism and copyright. *The student is advised to check with his or her professors. reference librarians, and/or computer center to see what resources are available and how they should be used.* Presently the following items will be helpful:

INTERNET: INTERNET is a worldwide network of computer networks, the U.S. part being supported at the moment by federal government funding (National Science Foundation [NSFNet], and eventually by the National Research and Education Network [NREN]). It is a way of retrieving information electronically. It is rapidly becoming an important resource for scholars and students.

Introductory Books about INTERNET:

Kehoe, B. P. *Zen and the Art of the Internet. A Beginner's Guide.* 2d ed. Series in Innovation Technology. New York: Prentice-Hall, 1993.

Krol, Ed. *The Whole Internet. User's Guide & Catalog.* Sebastopol, CA: O'Reilly & Associates,

1993. The standard guide.

LaQuey, Tracy L., with Jeanne C. Ryer. *The Internet Companion: A Beginner's Guide to Global Networking.* Reading, MA: Addison-Wesley, 1992.

Polly, J. A. "Surfing the Internet: An Introduction." *Wilson Library Bulletin* 66 (1992), pp. 38–42. The second edition is available electronically via FTP (see below).

Tennant, R., J. Ober, and A. G. Lipow. *Crossing the Internet Threshold: An Instructional Handbook.* Berkeley, CA: Library Solutions Press, 1992.

Religion Via INTERNET.

Kraft, Robert A. "Offline," *Council for the Scientific Study of Religion Bulletin.* Sponsored by the Computer Assisted Research Group (CARG) of the Society of Biblical Literature, coordinated by Professor Robert Kraft of the University of Pennsylvania, Kraft's column "Offline" has published advances in computer-assisted research for Biblical studies since 1984. In "Offline 40: Computer Assisted Research for Biblical Studies," *CSSR Bulletin* 22/1 (February 1993) Dan Lester, Michael Strangelove, James J. O'Donnell, Robert Weiss, and Matt Patrick Graham evaluate some key items. In spite of its name, members of certain groups can obtain it electronically, "online." The best guide for information about religion via INTERNET is:

Strangelove, Michael. *The Electric Mystic's Guide to the Internet: A Directory of Electronic Documents, Online Conferences, Serials, Software, and Archives Relevant to Religious Studies.* This standard guide is freely available by computer network (FTP [PANDA1.UOTTAWA.CA in the directory/pub/religion/]; Listserv [LISTSERV@UOTTAWA or LISTSERV@ACADVM1.UOTTAWA.CA]; Gopher server; see below). It is published by Scholars Press (1993) in a three-ring binder, making it possible to periodically update.

Here are some possibilities for bibliographical research on INTERNET:

E-Mail: Scholars and students can gain much information by consulting other scholars and students. E-mail, for "electronic mail," is a communications system in which letters are sent and received by computer. Such information can be obtained quickly, without the expense of a personal telephone call. Several resources are available for research in religion. IOUDAIOS, AIBI-L, and RELIGION are electronic discussion groups that also offer various data bases. Students should consult librarians and computer centers to communicate by E-mail.

E-Journals: "E-journals" are also emerging, and there are some in Biblical studies. These journals sometimes provide access to articles immediately, without any lag in publication time, though they may not always have the peer review of hardcopy articles. An example is the CONTENTS Project from Michael Strangelove at the University of Ottawa. It makes available bibliographies, articles, and related material. REVIEW-L is a supplemental list that provides reviews. It also publishes the *Electric Mystics Guide* of Michael Strangelove (see above). Like print journals, they may require a subscription fee, but most are free.

Remote Login, or TELNET. Many libraries have public access catalogs (PACS) of their library holdings, or databases. Most of these can be accessed through TELNET over the INTER-NET. Check with your library to see if it has a list of such addresses and if it has developed a means of student access. Easy access to these catalogs can be through free software such as Hytelnet, LIBS, or Gopher. At your library, or from your room through an institutional mainframe, or from your modem at home, perhaps you can gain access to catalog holdings in such universities as Oxford, England, or Harvard and generate a bibliography. Another possibility would be to access local libraries other than your own and get material by courier in a day or two, or by interlibrary loan, which should take two to four weeks. An especially interesting example is the Colorado Alliance of Research Libraries (CARL), which lists millions of articles from more than 12,000 journals going back to 1989, currently updating at the rate of 3500 articles daily. You can scan the tables of contents of these journals. Moreover, the library is able to order an article and fax it with 24 hours for a small fee (you can charge it to MasterCard or Visa),which in emergencies is much better than the two to four weeks of interlibrary loan.

File Transfer Protocol (FTP). Similar to TEL-NET there exists the possibility of locating and transferring whole files of information from one computer to another. There are many public archives (more than 900 FTP sites are available) from which data can be accessed. The archive service allows you to locate retrieval information for these files.

Other: Gopher, Wide Area Information Servers (WAIS), and World Wide Web (WWW) are other networks making information more accessible. Through Gopher it is possible to access an FTP site that contains many Biblical reference tools. If you search for a term in WAIS, it will offer you a "weighted relevance index," that is, how many times the term occurs in the context of the citation.

CD-ROM and Diskette Data Bases: Disks with stored data will be increasingly helpful for New Testament research. Scholars, for example, use collections of texts in Hebrew, Greek, and other languages for their research. The *Thesaurus Linguae Graecae* (2d ed.; New York: Oxford University Press, 1986), for example, contains most of the Greek texts from antiquity, including the Bible, and can be searched for words and word chains. The American Bible Society's *Scholarly Scripture Resources* markets a CD-ROM containing ancient languages (including the *Thesaurus*), various modern translations, and other scholarly aids. Many products on the market contain standard translations of the Bible and other texts from antiquity, and these can also be searched for words, word patterns, and the like. Check to see if your library has any of these reference tools. The *Hermeneutika* catalog (P.O. Box 98653, Seattle, WA 98198) offers a list of many computer disks for sale; it can serve as a bibliography.

III. Periodical Indices

Just as there is a *Reader's Guide to Periodical Literature* in general, so various fields of study have more specific guides to journals and magazines. The following are especially important for Biblical study. NOTE: Some of the works in the Introductory Bibliography Tools section above are also useful for periodicals.

Anderson, N. E. *Tools for Bibliographical and Backgrounds Research on the New Testament* (TBBRNT2). 2d ed. South Hamilton, MA: Gordon-Conwell Theological Seminary, 1987. Useful for political, social, literary, and religious background of the New Testament.

Biblical Theology Bulletin (1971–). A journal that periodically contains summary articles and bibliographical essays.

Elenchus Bibliographicus Biblicus. Rome: Biblical Institute Press, 1920–. An excellent, thorough index arranged by topics numbered for cross-reference. Published as part of the journal *Biblica* until 1967. In 1985 it became *Elenchus of Biblica*, published in 1988 as Vol.

1. Annual.

Elenchus of Biblica. See *Elenchus Bibliographicus Biblicus.*

Index on Articles on Jewish Studies. Jerusalem: Magnes Press, 1969.

Index to Religious Periodical Literature (see *Religion Index One*)

Religion Index One (formerly *Index to Religious Periodical Literature,* 1949–1978). Available in most college and university libraries, it is *probably the most useful* because it indexes the best journals in the field. Check "Bible, New Testament," and its subdivisions by New Testament book. Includes author index. Indexes book reviews down to 1985; these are now indexed separately as *Index to Book Reviews in Religion* (see below).

Religion Index Two: Multi-Author Works (1976–). Supplements *Religion Index One* with volumes of collected essays. There are also two supplemental volumes back to 1960.

Religion Index Two: Festschriften ("Memorial Volumes" dedicated to scholars), 1970–1975. 2 volumes.

IV. Abstracts

New Testament Abstracts. Cambridge, Mass.: Weston College School of Theology, 1956–. The most useful English language abstracts of articles, numbered for cross-reference; appears three times a year.

Internationale Zeitschriftenschau für Bibelwissenschaft und Grenzgebiete (1951). Multilingual, topical, cross-referenced, including abstracts. Though more difficult to use, it will supplement *New Testament Abstracts.*

Religious and Theological Abstracts. Vol. 1–, 1958–. One of the five subjects abstracted is Biblical studies.

V. Reviews

Catholic Periodical and Literature Index. See "Book Reviews" section.

Critical Review of Books in Religion, Vol. 1–. Atlanta, GA: Scholars Press, 1988–. A collection of reviews, not an index.

Index to Book Reviews in Religion. Originally part of *Religion Index One,* it began to appear separately in 1986. The first four volumes have been reissued in expanded form.

Mills, Watson E. *An Index of Reviews of New Testament Books Between 1900–1950.* Perspectives in Religious Studies, Special Studies Series, 2. Danville, VA: Association of Baptist Professors of Religion, 1977.

VI. Introductory Bibliographical Tools

Danker, F. W. *Multipurpose Tools for Bible Study.* 3d ed. St. Louis: Concordia Publishing House, 1970. Narrative description of standard tools for Biblical research.

Fitzmyer, Joseph A., S. J. *An Introductory Bibliography for the Study of Scripture.* Rev. ed. Rome: Biblical Institute Press, 1981.

France, R. T., ed. *A Bibliographical Guide to New Testament Research.* Sheffield, England: JSOT Press, 1979. Excellent pamphlet describing 29 areas of New Testament study with standard works annotated.

Gorman, G. E., and Lynn Gorman. *Theological and Religious Reference Materials: General Resources and Biblical Studies.* Westport, CT: Greenwood Press, 1984. An annotated bibliography with 1164 entries.

Harrington, Daniel J., S.J. *The New Testament: A Bibliography.* Wilmington, DE: Michael Glazier, 1985.

Hort, Erasmus. *The Bible Book: Resources for Reading the New Testament.* New York, NY: Crossroad Publishing Company, 1983.

Kepple, R. J. *Reference Works for Theological Research.* Washington, D.C.: University Press of America, 1981. Recent, comprehensive, annotated. Chapters 19–25 list materials for Biblical studies.

Marrow, S. B. *Basic Tools of Biblical Exegesis: A Student's Manual.* Subsidia Biblica 2. Rome: Biblical Institute Press, 1976. Annotated bibliography on tools for Biblical interpretation. Also covers materials outside the Bible.

Scholer, D. M. *A Basic Bibliographic Guide for New Testament Exegesis.* 2d ed. Grand Rapids: Eerdmans, 1973. Little or no annotation, lists standard tools in areas of New Testament research.

VII. Specialized Bibliographical Tools for the Bible

Aune, D. E. *Jesus and the Synoptic Gospels: A Bibliographic Study Guide.* Madison: Theological Students Fellowship, 1980. Selective, partially annotated.

Belle, G. van. *Johannine Bibliography 1966–1986: A Cumulative Bibliography on the Fourth Gospel.* BETL, LXXXII. Leuven: Leuven University Press, 1988.

Berlin, C. *Index to Festschriften (Memorial Volumes) in Jewish Studies.* New York: KTAV, 1971.

The Bible: Texts and Translations of the Bible and the

Apocrypha and Their Books from the National Union Catalog, Pre-1956 Imprints. 5 vols. London: Mansell, 1980. The first four volumes list more than 63,000 books; the last indexes the first four.

Borchert, Gerald L. *Paul and His Interpreters: An Annotated Bibliography.* Madison: Theological Students' Fellowship, 1985. Topically arranged.

Bovon, François. *Luke the Theologian: Thirty-Three Years of Research (1950–1983).* Allison Park, PA: Pickwick Publications, 1987. Seven topical chapters.

Brock, S. P., C. T. Fritsch, and S. Jellicoe. *A Classified Bibliography of the Septuagint.* Leiden: E. J. Brill, 1973.

Catholic Periodical and Literature Index. Indexes 140 Catholic periodicals. Not the best place to begin, but excellent on official church statements about the Bible.

Evans, Craig A. *Life of Jesus Research: An Annotated Bibliography.* Leiden: E. J. Brill, 1989. More than 1300 items.

Garland, D. E. *One Hundred Years of Study on the Passion Narratives.* NABPR Bibliographic Series, 3. Macon, GA: Mercer University Press, 1989.

Gottcent, J. H. *The Bible as Literature: A Selective Bibliography.* Boston: G. K. Hall & Co., 1979. Annotated resources on various literary approaches, broadly understood, to the Bible.

Hultgren, Arland J. *New Testament Christology: A Critical Assessment and Annotated Bibliography.* New York: Greenwood Press, 1988. Almost 2000 items, annotated. Excellent.

Humphrey, Hugh M. *A Bibliography for the Gospel of Mark 1954–1980.* Lewiston, NY: Edwin Mellen Press, 1981.

Guide to Social Science and Religion in Periodical Literature. Flint, MI: National Periodical Library, 1965–. Formerly *Guide to Religious and Semi-Religious Periodicals*, it indexes about 100 journals.

Johnson, Luke T. *The Writings of the New Testament. An Interpretation.* Philadelphia: Fortress Press, 1986. Contains useful bibliographies at the end of each chapter.

Kissinger, W. S. *The Lives of Jesus: A History and Bibliography.* New York: Garland, 1985.

———. *The Parables of Jesus: A History of Interpretation and Bibliography.* ATLA Bibliography Series, No. 4. Metuchen, NJ: Scarecrow Press, 1979. A history of parable interpretation and a bibliography.

———. *The Sermon on the Mount: A History of Interpretation and Bibliography.* ATLA Biblical

Series, No. 3. Metuchen, NJ: Scarecrow Press, 1975. History and bibliography.

Longstaff, T. R. W., and A. T. Page. *The Synoptic Problem: A Bibliography, 1716–1988.* Macon, GA: Mercer University Press, 1988.

Malatesta, E. *St John's Gospel, 1920–1965: A Cumulative and Classified Bibliography of Books and Periodical Literature on the Fourth Gospel.* Rome: Pontifical Biblical Institute, 1967. Derived from *Elenchus Bibliographicus* and its supplement, *Verbum Domini.*

Mattill, A. J., and M. B. Mattill. *A Classified Bibliography of Literature on the Acts of the Apostles.* Leiden: E. J. Brill, 1966.

Metzger, B. M. *Index to Periodical Literature on Christ and the Gospels.* Leiden: E. J. Brill, 1965. Topical arrangement plus author index.

———. *Index to Periodical Literature on the Apostle Paul.* Rev. ed. Leiden: E. J. Brill, 1970.

———. *Index of Articles on the New Testament and the Early Church Published in Festschriften (Memorial Volumes).* SBL Monograph No. 5. Philadelphia: Society of Biblical Literature, 1951: supplement 1955. Dated.

Mills, W. E. *A Bibliography of the Periodical Literature on the Acts of the Apostles, 1962–1984.* Supplements to *Novum Testamentum* 58. Leiden: E. J. Brill, 1986.

Petersen, Paul D. *Paul the Apostle and the Pauline Literature: A Bibliography Selected from the ATLA Religion Database.* 4th rev. ed. Chicago: American Theological Library Association, 1984.

Segbroeck, F. van. *The Gospel of Luke: A Cumulative Bibliography 1973–1988.* BETL, LXXXVIII. Leuven: Leuven University Press, 1989.

St. John's University Library Index to Biblical Journals. Collegeville, MN: St. John's University Press, 1971.

Wagner, G. *An Exegetical Bibliography of the New Testament: John and 1, 2, 3 John.* Macon, GA: Mercer University Press, 1987.

———. *An Exegetical Bibliography of the New Testament: Matthew and Mark.* Macon, GA: Mercer University Press, 1983.

White, L. J. *Jesus the Christ: A Bibliography.* Wilmington, DE: Michael Glazier, 1988. First two-thirds is Biblical.

VIII. Specialized Bibliographical Tools for Ancient Literature Related to the New Testament

Charlesworth, J. H. *The Pseudepigrapha and Modern Research with Supplement.* Missoula, MT: Scholars Press, 1981. Descriptions of documents plus bibliographies.

Fitzmyer, J. A. *The Dead Sea Scrolls: Major Publica-*

tions and Tools for Study. SBLRBS 20; rev. ed. Atlanta: Scholars Press, 1990. Texts, studies, authors, Biblical passages.

Grossfeld, B. *A Bibliography of Targum Literature.* Cincinnati: Hebrew Union College Press, 1972. Describes literature from 1500s to 1971.

———. *A Bibliography of Targum Literature II.* Cincinnati: Hebrew Union College Press, 1977. Supplements vol. I.

Hilgert, E. *A Bibliography of Philo Studies 1963–1970* and *Abstracts of Selected Articles on Philo 1966–1970* in *Studia Philonica* 1 (1972) 57–91.

Neusner, J., ed. *The Study of Judaism: Bibliographical Essays.* New York: KTAV, 1972.

Nickels, P. *Targum and New Testament: A Bibliography, Together with a New Testament Index.* Rome: Pontifical Biblical Institute, 1967. Part I by author, Part II by New Testament passage.

———. *Targum and New Testament: A Bibliography, Together with a New Testament Index.* Rome: Pontifical Biblical Institute, 1967. Part I by author, Part II by New Testament passage.

Revue de Qumran. A periodical that contains bibliographical sections in the first three issues of each volume.

Rounds, D. *Articles on Antiquity in Festschriften (Memorial Volumes): the Ancient East, the Old Testament, Greece, Rome, Roman Law, Byzantium. An Index.*

Scholer, D. M. *Nag Hammadi Bibliography 1948–1969.* Leiden: E. J. Brill, 1971. Supplemented annually in the periodical *Novum Testamentum.*

Schreckenburg, H. *Bibliographie zu Flavius Josephus.* Leiden: E. J. Brill, 1968.

———. *Bibliographie zu Flavius Josephus: Supplementband mit Gesamtregister.* Leiden: E. J. Brill, 1979.

Vermes, G. *The Dead Sea Scrolls: Qumran in Perspective.* London: Collins, 1977. Select bibliographies.

Vogel, E. K. *Bibliography of Holy Land Sites: Compiled in Dr. Nelson Glueck.* Cincinnati: Hebrew Union College/Jewish Institute of Religion, 1974. Reprint of Hebrew Union College Annual, vol. 42. Arranged alphabetically by place. More than 200 sites.

IX. Concordances

There are many concordances (alphabetized word lists with their contextual references by chapter and verse) to the original languages and the various translations. It is most important that you have a concordance to the translation you use. The most important are:

An Analytical Concordance to the Revised Standard Version of the New Testament. Ed. C. Morrison. Philadelphia: Westminster Press, 1979. It contains the English terms, Greek original with a transliteration, book, chapter, verse, and usually a phrase in which the term occurs.

The Eerdmans Analytical Concordance to the Revised Standard Version of the Bible. Compiled by R. E. Whitaker et al. Grand Rapids: Eerdmans, 1988.

Nelson's Complete Concordance of the New American Bible. Ed. S. J. Hartdegen, OFM. Collegeville, MN: Liturgical Press, 1977.

Nelson's Complete Concordance of the Revised Standard Version Bible. Ed. J. W. Ellison. New York: Thomas Nelson & Sons, 1957.

Young, Robert. *Analytical Concordance to the Bible.* Ed. W. B. Stevenson. New York: Funk & Wagnalls, n.d. Based on the King James Version, it gives Hebrew and Greek roots, which can be consulted for frequency of occurrence.

New Revised Standard Version (NRSV) Exhaustive Concordance: Includes the Apocryphal and Deutero-Canonical Books. Ed. B. M. Metzger. New York: Thomas Nelson & Sons, 1991.

NOTE: many translations are now on computer disc or can be accessed by INTERNET. They can also be searched. See II. Computer-Generated (Electronic) Bibliographical Aids.

X. Commentaries

There are one-volume commentaries on the whole Bible, for example, the *New Jerome Biblical Commentary* (NRSV). Commentary series project commentaries on all the books of the New Testament or Bible, though new ones are often in process. Each volume contains one or more books depending on length. Likewise, one scholar will often do only one volume in the series. Important series include:

The Anchor Bible, 1964. Scholarly, mostly excellent. (Doubleday)

Barclay, W. *The Daily Study Bible Series.* 17 vols. Rev. ed. Philadelphia: Westminster Press, 1975. Simple and helpful British conservative scholarship.

Harper's New Testament Commentaries. 1960 (Harper & Row).

Hermeneia. A Critical and Historical Commentary on the Bible. 1971 (Fortress Press). Mostly translated from German. Excellent.

International Critical Commentary. (T. & T. Clark). Original series 1930–1960. Scholarly. A revised edition in is process.

Interpreter's Bible. 12 vols. 1952–1957 (Abingdon). Clear and still useful.

New Century Bible. 1967 (Nelson).

New Testament Message: A Biblical-Theological Commentary. 22 vols. 1979–1981 (M. Glazier). Varies in quality, but generally good.

Word Biblical Commentary. 1982– (Word Books).

XI. Biblical Atlases

Aharoni, Y., and M. Avi-Yonah. *The Macmillan Bible Atlas.* 2d ed. New York: Macmillan, 1993. Main events of the Bible are stressed by maps.

Beitzel, B. J. *The Moody Atlas of Bible Lands.* Chicago, IL: Moody Press, 1985.

The Harper Atlas of the Bible. Ed. J. B. Pritchard. New York: Harper & Row, 1987. Perhaps the best available atlas in English.

May, H. G., et al. *Oxford Bible Atlas.* 3d ed., rev. J. Day. London: Oxford University Press, 1984. Topographical maps, archeology, narrative, occasional photographs, and plan of Jerusalem.

Negenman, J. H. *New Atlas of the Bible.* Ed. H. H. Rowley et al. Trans. H. Hoskins and R. Beck-ley. Garden City, NY: Doubleday, 1969. Photographs, narrative, occasional maps, and helpful charts.

Rogerson, J. *Atlas of the Bible.* New York: Facts on File Publications, 1986.

Wright, G. E., and F. Filson. *The Westminster Historical Atlas to the Bible.* Philadelphia: Westminster Press, 1956. Narrative, photographs, and excellent maps stressing geography.

XII. Biblical Geography and Archaeology

The Archaeological Encyclopedia of the Holy Land. Rev. ed. A. Negev. Nashville: Thomas Nelson, 1986.

Encyclopedia of Archaeological Excavations in the Holy Land. 4 vols. Ed. M. Avi-Yonah and E. Stern. Englewood Cliffs, NJ: Prentice-Hall, 1975–1978. 4 vols.

The New International Dictionary of Biblical Archaeology. Ed. E. M. Blaiklock and R. K. Harrison. Grand Rapids: Zondervan, 1983.

Vogel, E. K. *Bibliography of Holy Land Sites. (Part I).* 3d printing. Cincinnati: Hebrew Union College, 1982.

Vogel, E. K., and H. Brooks. *Bibliography of Holy Land Sites. Part II (1970–1981).* Cincinnati: Hebrew Union College, 1982.

GLOSSARY

Apocalypse From the Greek *apokalypsis,* "an uncovering" or "revelation" (compare Rev 1:1), a book or part of a book that records visual and auditory revelations about the future and/or the heavenly world, believed to come from an otherworldly medium such as God or an angel, sometimes in the form of dreams about the heavenly world, to a human "seer" who "sees" in an ecstatic state ("in the Spirit"). Apocalypses contain many esoteric symbols and are typified by pseudonymity. See Chapter Three.

Apocalyptic An adjective derived from "apocalypse," but also used as an umbrella noun to encompass three overlapping phenomena: (1) apocalypses; (2) apocalyptic eschatology; and (3) apocalypticism. It is especially typical of Jewish and Hellenistic religions from about 250 B.C.E.–250 C.E. See Chapter Three.

Apocalypticism Describes a social movement, especially in Judaism and Christianity, that is typified by apocalyptic thought. See Chapter Three.

Apocalyptic Eschatology A particular kind of thought or teaching in the form of revelations about the end of the world. See **Apocalyptic** and **Eschatology**.

Apocrypha From the Greek *apocryphos,* "hidden," books that were not accepted into the final canon of Jewish or Christian Scripture. In the church such books were to be "hidden" from the faithful. When used alone, Apocrypha normally refers to the Old Testament Apocrypha, that is, to books rejected from the final Jewish canon of Scripture but transmitted by Christians as part of the Old Testament. After the Protestant Reformation, the Protestant churches accepted the Jewish canon of Scripture as defining the Old Testament. The Roman Catholic church continued to accept most of the books in the broader canon of the ancient church. When used of the New Testament, the expression is New Testament Apocrypha. See **Canon** and **Pseudepigrapha**.

Apostle From the Greek *apostolos,* "envoy," "messenger," or in the religious sense, "missionary." Though the term is sometimes used of Jesus' immediate disciples (especially in Luke-Acts, see for example, Luke 6:13; Acts 1:23–26), thus giving rise to the expression "the Twelve Apostles," usually in the New Testament it refers to a larger circle of early Christian missionaries. Paul, who had apparently never met Jesus, consistently designated himself "apostle (to the Gentiles)."

Apostolic Fathers See **Church Fathers**.

Aramaic Descended from ancient Hebrew, this dialect became the international language of the East in the pre-Hellenistic period, and was still the vernacular of most eastern Jews, including Jesus and the first Christians in the first century C.E. See **Targums** and Chapter Two.

Astrology From the Greek *astēr,* "star," the study of heavenly bodies, which are also deities, to ascertain the future.

Azazel In our period, a demonic being; traditionally associated with the Day of Atonement ritual.

Beatitude A literary form that begins with the word "blessed," praises a person, and promises a corresponding divine reward. See Matt 5:3–12.

Canon From the Greek *kanōn,* "reed," which could be used to measure like a yardstick, a list of books to be read by a group of religious persons to "measure" belief and practice; hence "Buddhist canon," "Hebrew canon" or "Old Testament canon," "New Testament canon." See **Apocrypha** and **Pseudepigrapha**.

Catholic From the Latin *catholicus,* "universal" or "general." It is used in connection with the later letters in the New Testament, the "Catholic Epistles," because they are addressed to the church at large rather than to individuals or separate churches. It is then used of the church as a whole as distinct from one particular part of the church, for example, the "catholic church" as distinct from the "Syrian church." In discussing the period after the Reformation it distinguishes the Roman Catholic church from the Protestant churches. In that last context it is always capitalized, "Catholic."

Christology From the Greek *Christos* (= Messiah, from Hebrew *m^{e}shiach,* "anointed") and *logos,* "word" or "teaching"; hence, teaching concerning the person of Christ.

Christological titles Titles of great honor taken over from the cultural environment and used by early Christians to describe Jesus, for example, Christ (Hebrew Messiah), Lord, Son of God, Son of Man, Son of David. See **Christology**.

Church From the Greek word *kyriakon,* "that which belongs to the Lord," the English term "church" translates a number of New Testament words, but especially Greek *ekklēsia,* a community summoned for a particular purpose. Early Christians did not meet in church buildings, but in houses, hence the modern term "house-church." See **Synagogue.**

Church Fathers (see **Apostolic Fathers**). Very important Christian writers in the early centuries of Christianity, a few of whose works almost became part of the New Testament. See Chapters One and Four.

Church order A text setting out the polity and discipline of a church with regard to its officers and members.

Codex Papyrus or leather (vellum) pages sewed together to make a book. The codex form made its appearance in the second century C.E. and gradually supplanted the scroll as the form on which New Testament books were written. See **Papyrus.**

Corpus The Latin word for "body." It is used of a complete or comprehensive body of writings. The "Pauline corpus" is the body of writings attributed to the apostle Paul.

Cynics Wandering street preachers who tried to convert people from normative human values such as the quest for fame, fortune, and pleasure to a life of austere virtue as the path to true freedom and happiness. See Chapter Four.

Dead Sea Scrolls A major discovery of Jewish manuscripts found near the Dead Sea in the caves above Khirbet Qumran, 1947–1956. See **Khirbet Qumran,** Chapters One and Three, and the Appendix, "Major Archeological and Textual Discoveries and Publications."

Diaspora (or **Dispersion**) From the Greek *diaspora,* "a dispersion," the community of Jews living outside their ancestral homeland, Palestine ("Land of Israel").

Divination A communication with supernatural powers by using natural things (stars, the liver, and so forth) or human-made objects (arrows, lots, and so forth) in order to learn answers to questions or the future.

Doxology From the Greek *doxologia,* "a praising," the act of praising God. In New Testament studies specifically used in connection with formal praises of God to be found in prayers, letters, and the liturgy of the church.

Dualism A type of thinking that views reality as a conflict of opposites, for example, good and evil, light and darkness, life and death. There are sometimes supernatural forces behind the opposites, for example, angels and demons. The major philosophical alternative to dualism is "monism," that is, all reality is one.

Eschatology From the Greek *eschatos*, "furthest," and *logos*, "word" or "teaching," teaching concerning the last things, the end of the world or the end of history.

Essenes A priestly sect from about 150 B.C.E. to 68 C.E., described by **Josephus** as one of the four "philosophies" of Palestinian Judaism, also described by **Philo of Alexandria** and Pliny the Elder. The Dead Sea Scrolls are usually thought to have been the library of Essenes living at Qumran, though this conclusion has been challenged. See **Khirbet Qumran**, **Dead Sea Scrolls**, and Chapters One and Three.

Evangelist From the Greek *euangelion*, "good news," "gospel," a preacher of the gospel, or, customarily in New Testament studies, the author of one of the four canonical gospels. See **Gospel**.

Exegesis From the Greek *ex*, "out of," and *hēgeomai*, "I lead," that is, to "lead out," or "bring out" the original, intended, meaning of the author of a text. It is sometimes contrasted with "eisegesis," to ("wrongly") "read into" the text one's own private meaning. The adjective is exegetical.

Form Criticism A translation of the German *Formgeschichte*, literally "form history," referring to the analysis of smaller forms, their function in various religiosocial contexts, and their historical development in oral tradition. See Chapter One.

Gallio Inscription Discovered at Delphi, Greece, beginning in 1905, this inscription helps to fix the date when L. Iunius Gallio Annaeanus was proconsular governor of Achaia, or southern Greece, about 51 C.E. Since Paul appeared before Gallio (Acts 18:12–17), having arrived at Corinth eighteen months earlier (Acts 18:11), or about 49 C.E., it gives the archeological basis for modern reconstructions of the chronology of Paul's life. See Chapter Six.

Glossolalia From the Greek *glossa*, "tongue," and *laleō*, "I speak," literally "speaking in tongues," that is, noncommunicative, pulsating noises that issue from the mouth of persons in what psy-chologists call "dissociative states" or "altered states of consciousness." For believers, the person is thought to have the special spiritual gift of receiving messages from God through the Holy Spirit, but they require interpretation. See 1 Cor 12–14.

Gnosticism From the Greek word *gnōsis*, "knowledge," a dualistic religious movement (see **Dualism**) that often cuts across and combines many streams of thought from Judaism, Christianity, and Hellenism (see **Syncretism**) and stresses special mythical *knowledge* about the origins, situation, and destination of the universe and humanity, especially salvation from this evil world and body. See especially Chapter Three.

Gospel From the Middle English *godspell*, "good spell," that is, "good news." It translated Greek *euangelion*, "good news." Originally, it referred to the good news of what God had done in Christ, then to the literary form created to narrate and proclaim the event.

Hellenism (adjective: **Hellenistic**) From the Greek *Hellenismos*, "imitation of the Greeks." The culture that developed in the world conquered by Alexander the Great as that world adopted the Greek language and imitated Greek ways.

Heresy, Heretic From the Greek *hairesis*, "sect," "party," "school," which has over time been contrasted with normative beliefs, values, and practices, or "orthodoxy" (Greek: "thinking straight").

Hermeneutics From the Greek *hermēneutēs*, "an interpreter." The science of interpretation, especially the interpretation of written texts. It is usual to use *hermeneutic* for a particular method of interpretation and *hermeneutics* for the science as a whole. See Chapter One.

Hero, Heroine Figures to whom are attributed superhuman powers, especially miracle working. See Chapter Three.

History of religions While the expression can mean the field of comparative religions with an emphasis on history, in New Testament study it translates the German *Religionsgeschichte* and has had a more particular meaning: the study and analysis of the history of early Christianity in comparison with the religions and philosophies of the ancient Mediterranean context in which it emerged. See **Social History.**

House-church See **Church.**

Josephus A Jewish historian (ca. 37–100 C.E.) whose works, preserved by Christians, trace the history of the Jews in the Biblical period and provide the best information for reconstructing the history of Palestinian Judaism in the first century C.E. He was also a politician and military commander in Galilee during the wars with Rome, 66–70 C.E.

Kerygma The Greek word for proclamation. It is used to denote the preaching, proclamation, or central message of the New Testament as a whole or of any part of it, and similarly of the church as a whole or of any part of it.

Khirbet Qumran Often spelled phonetically *Khirbet Qumrân*, Arabic for "ruin of *Qumrân*," named for the nearby *Wâdī Qumrân*, a *Wâdī* being a dry riverbed that fills up in the rainy season. The ruin was extensively excavated and partially reconstructed after the discovery of the Dead Sea Scrolls in the adjacent cliff caves in 1947. The prevailing view has been that the site represents the remains of community life of the "monastic" group within the Essene sect. See **Dead Sea Scrolls; Essenes;** Chapters One and Three, and the Appendix, "Major Archeological, Textual Discoveries and Translations."

Koinē The Greek word for "common," it describes the commonly spoken form of Greek that became the lingua franca of the Hellenistic world.

Levite Originally a person from one of the twelve tribes of Israel, the tribe of Levi, the hereditary tribe of the priests; in our period, they have become a group with subordinate status, that is, temple functionaries and musicians. See **Priest.**

Life of Jesus research A comprehensive term designating every possible kind of historical research in connection with the life and teaching of Jesus.

Magic An attempt by religious specialists to control the mysterious powers that determine one's fate, or to provide protection against demonic powers, or to occasionally cause evil, all by ritual recitation of the correct formula.

Mimesis (adjective: **Mimetic**) The Greek word for "imitation." It is used as a technical term for literature that is deliberately realistic, that is, imitative of life.

Minuscules Handwritten manuscripts with cursive script, dominating from the tenth to the sixteenth centuries. See **Uncials** and Chapter One.

Mishna(h) A compilation of Jewish legal material interpreting Biblical law, put into writing about 200 C.E. It emanates mainly from Pharisaic oral interpretation of the Torah and became the center of Rabbinic Judaism. See **Torah, Pharisees, Rabbi,** and Chapter Three.

Muratorian Canon (Muratorian Fragment) Discovered by Lodovico Antonio Muratori (1672–1750), an early list of New Testament books that excludes Hebrews, James, 1 and 2 Peter, 3 John, but includes the Wisdom of Solomon, the *Apocalypse of John,* and the *Apocalypse of Peter.* Its early date, ca. 200 C.E., and place, Rome, have been recently challenged by A. C. Sundberg, Jr., and others who suggest fourth-century Syria or Palestine.

Old Testament Apocrypha See **Apocrypha.**

Old Testament Pseudepigrapha From the Greek *pseud-,* "false," and *epigraphos,* "superscription," Jewish and Jewish-Christian works usually influenced by the Old Testament, written from about 250 B.C.E. to 250 C.E., often characterized by pseudonymity, and then considered by the church to be books with "false titles." See **Apocrypha** and **Pseudonymity.**

Orthodoxy See **Heresy.**

Oracle A revelatory statement of a priest, medium, or wise person; the person himself or herself.

Papyrus A 12-15-foot-high, wrist-thick plant that grows in marshy regions, especially in the Nile River valley. Its bark can be stripped, dried, layered, glued, and smoothed to make paperlike sheets on which writing can be preserved. Pieces glued side by side and then rolled make a papyrus scroll, usually not longer than 35 feet. The earliest manuscripts of the New Testament are written on papyrus sheets, or papyri (pl.). See **Codex.**

Parable C. H. Dodd defines a parable as "a metaphor or simile drawn from nature or common life, arresting the hearer by its vividness or strangeness, and leaving the mind in sufficient doubt about its precise application to tease it into active thought." See Chapter Five.

Parenesis From the Greek *parainesis,* "exhortation," "advice," a technical term used to denote exhortation, advice, instruction, or encouragement.

Parousia A Greek word for "presence," in Hellenistic Greek it became a technical term for the visit of a high official, especially a king or emperor, to a province or place. In the New Testament it came to be used of the expected coming of Christ in glory to judge the world and redeem his people, and in this sense it has become a technical term of theological and Biblical scholarship.

Passion When used alone ("Passion" or "the passion") this term always refers to the suffering and death of Jesus. The "passion narrative" is the narrative account of that suffering and death.

Pastorals (Pastoral Epistles or Letters) The letters written in the name of Paul and addressed to Timothy or Titus. They give advice to a "pastor" of a church with regard to his responsibilities to his "flock," hence their designation. See Chapter Fourteen.

Pentateuch The first five books of Hebrew Scriptures or Old Testament; it is traditionally called the Torah. See **Torah.**

Pericope From the Greek *peri,* "about," and *koptein,* "to cut": an extract from a larger work; a unit of narrative or discourse; thus, a shorter unit of material, or passage.

Pesher A Hebrew word meaning "interpretation," a form of it occurs at the beginning of a special kind of interpretation of Biblical texts in the Dead Sea Scrolls. See **Dead Sea Scrolls** and Chapter Three.

Pharisees Probably from the Hebrew *perūshîm* or the Aramaic *perishaya* ("the separated [ones]"), a mostly lay sect from about 150 B.C.E., described by **Josephus** as one of the four "philosophies" of Palestinian Judaism. Originally a politically oriented reforming faction, they became especially known for oral interpretations of the Torah and the acceptance of newer beliefs (angels, demons, resurrection of the dead) in contrast to their rivals, the Sadducees. They survived the Jewish Wars of 66–70 C.E., and their traditions form the heart of the Rabbinic literature. See **Rabbi, Mishnah, Talmud**, and Chapter Three.

Philo of Alexandria A Hellenistic Jewish philosopher (ca. 20–15 B.C.E. to 47 C.E.) known for interpreting the Jewish Scriptures by means of allegory.

Portent An omen predicting the future.

Priest A holy man who sacrificed at the Jerusalem Temple, and was descended from the tribe of Levi, but from the powerful family of Zadok, a priest at the time of David and Solomon. See **Sadducee.**

Proselyte A convert from another religion.

Pseudepigrapha See **Old Testament Pseudepigrapha**.

Pseudonymity From the Greek *pseudos,* "false," and *onyma,* "name," thus attributed authorship [literally, "false name"]). See **Apocrypha, Old Testament Pseudepigrapha**, and Chapters Three, Eight, and Fourteen.

Ptolemies From the Greek *ptolemaios,* "warlike," they were a dynasty in Egypt and along the North African coast, along with some islands in the Mediterranean, established by Ptolemy I of Egypt (ruled 305–282 B.C.E.), of Macedonian descent, lasting until 31 B.C.E. They dominated the Jews during the third century B.C.E. Their main rivals were the Seleucids. See **Seleucids** and Chapter Two.

Q Probably derived from German *Quelle,* "Source" (not the only explanation), this letter symbolizes the same or similar material shared by Matthew and

Luke, but mainly absent from Mark, and thus considered by those who hold the Two-Source Theory to have been a written source in Greek used by the authors of Matthew and Luke. It is largely sayings of Jesus, and has found a formal analogy in the *Gospel of Thomas*. See **Two-Source Theory; Thomas, Gospel of;** and Chapter One.

Qumran See **Khirbet Qumran.**

Rabbi, (adjective: **rabbinic**) From Hebrew *rabbî,* "my great one," "my master," a way of addressing an honorable teacher of Torah; it later became an official title for teachers in the Mishna; also literature that emanates from such teachers, such as the Mishna and the Talmud, is called "rabbinic" literature. See **Mishna, Talmud,** and **Targums**.

Redaction criticism The usual translation of the German *Redaktionsgeschichte* (literally "redaction history"), the study of the redaction or editing of traditional material as it is transmitted or used. See Chapter One.

Priest A holy man who offers sacrifices at the Jerusalem Temple and maintains purity according to the laws of Leviticus.

Sabbath Perhaps from Hebrew *shabbāt,* "to stop," "to cease," or perhaps from an Akkadian word for "seventh," it refers to the seventh day of the seven-day week on which, according to the Biblical creation story, God ceased from his work of creation (Gen 2:1–3). It thus became the holy day of rest from work in the Jewish weekly calendar.

Sanhedrin The Jewish High Court in Jerusalem, dominated by the Sadducee party. See **Sadducees.**

Scribe One of a small group of people in antiquity who wrote, who copied manuscripts, who thus became educated bureaucratic officials, and in religious circles, who became learned sages who copied sacred texts.

Seleucids A dynasty in Syria established by Seleucus I (ruled 305–282 B.E.C.), of Macedonian descent. They dominated the Jews during the early second century B.C.E. after defeating their main

rivals, the Ptolemies. See **Ptolemies** and Chapter Two.

Septuagint From the Latin *septuaginta* ("seventy"), the Greek translation of the Jewish Scriptures, transmitted to the Old Testament by Christians. It received its name from the legend that it was translated in seventy days by seventy-two translators, six from each of the twelve Jewish tribes. See Chapter Three.

Sitz im Leben A German term meaning "setting in life." It is used in form criticism as a technical term for the socioreligious context in which a given oral or literary form functions (for example, sermon, or ethical instruction) and for the purposes for which it was developed. See Chapter One.

Social History The study of historical documents from the perspective of social context, attempting thereby to understand what such documents (usually unintentionally) reveal about the "social world" of early Christian communities. It is concerned with such issues as the distribution of power, social organization, status, rural and urban environments, relation to the "world," and the like; it attempts to understand individuals and communities with sociological theory, but its emphasis is distinctly historical. See **Sociological Criticism** and Chapter One.

Sociological Criticism The study of the New Testament communities, their contexts, and their way of thinking with models from, or derived from, anthropology, sociology, economics, and the like. It is in some ways similar to social history, but has more theoretical interests. See **Social History** and Chapter One.

Soteriology From the Greek *sōtēr,* "savior," and *logos,* "word" or "teaching." Teaching about the death of Jesus as the means of man's salvation.

Stoicism From the Greek *hē poikilē stoa,* or "the Painted Porch," an open-air colonnade in the market place of Athens, where a Phoenician philosopher, Zeno from Citium in Cyprus (ca. 332–262), originally taught. The dominant philosophical school of the Hellenistic Age, it influenced some of Paul's ideas and ways of argument.

Synagogue From Greek *syn*, "together," and *agō*, "I lead," "I bring," that is, a place to bring people together for prayer and worship. Though synagogue buildings existed in the Diaspora (see **Diaspora**), evidence from such buildings in Palestine prior to 70 C.E. is sparse, if indeed it exists at all. Perhaps rooms in houses were set aside for such gatherings, that is, house-synagogues. See **Church.**

Syncretism A term in the formal study of religion used to describe the identification of gods, goddesses, myths, ideas, and so forth from one religion with another, usually "diffused" by contact throughout a larger cultural arena, for example, the regions surrounding the Mediterranean Sea.

Synoptic Gospels From the Greek *synoptikos*, "seeing the whole together." The Gospels of Matthew, Mark, and Luke are called the "synoptic gospels" because they tell the same general story in the same kind of way. A contrast to the Gospel of John is intended.

Synoptic Problem The problem of the direct and/or indirect literary connections between the first three gospels, Matthew, Mark, and Luke. See **Two-Source Theory** and **Q.**

Synoptic tradition The traditional material that has been used by the authors of the synoptic gospels.

Targums Paraphrasing translations of Hebrew sacred texts into Aramaic for use in Jewish worship when Aramaic had (mostly?) replaced Hebrew as the vernacular for common folk. See **Aramaic.**

Talmud From the Hebrew for "study" or "learning," the centuries-long, many-

layered commentary on the Mishnah by learned rabbis. See **Mishna(h)** and **Rabbi.**

Textual Criticism The evaluation of manuscript copies containing mistakes and intentional changes—no originals ("autographs") survive—in order to reconstruct what the author most likely wrote. See Chapter One.

Thomas, Gospel of Discovered in 1945 in Egypt as one of the Nag Hammadi texts, it consists of 114 sayings attributed to Jesus and is very valuable for comparison with the New Testament sayings. See Appendix.

Torah From Hebrew *tōrāh*, "instruction," "guidance," "the way," the term was gradually narrowed to refer to the Pentateuch as one of three traditional Jewish divisions of the Scriptures. See **Pentateuch.**

Two-Source Theory The dominant "solution" to the Synoptic Problem, it claims that the authors of Matthew and Luke used two written sources, the Gospel of Mark and Q. See **Synoptic Problem, Q,** and Chapter One.

Uncials Handwritten manuscripts in capital-letter block script, flourishing from the third to the tenth centuries. See **Minuscules** and Chapter One.

Witness One who bears testimony to his or her faith, or the act of bearing testimony. The Greek word is *martyrion;* later it came to be used specifically of those who "witnessed" to their faith to the point of dying for it.

Zealots From the Greek *zealos*, "zeal," the term refers to revolutionaries who emerged during the wars between Rome and the Jews, 66–70 C.E. In some modern study, the movement is thought to have antecedents in other politically revolutionary movements in first-century Palestine. See Chapter Two.

CREDITS AND
ACKNOWLEDGMENTS

We wish to thank the following for the photographs included in this edition:

Chapter 1:   Courtesy of the Masters and Fellows of Trinity College, Cambridge.
Chapter 2:   Harcourt Brace photograph
Chapter 3:   Harcourt Brace photograph
Chapter 4:   Photo by Elliot Faye from *In the Footsteps of Saint Paul* by Wolfgang E. Pax. Copyright © 1977 by Nateev, Printing and Publishing Enterprises Ltd., Israel, p.111.
Chapter 5:   Alinari/Art Resource, NY.
Chapter 6:   Alinari/Art Resource, NY.
Chapter 7:   Scala/Art Resource, NY.
Chapter 8:   Institute for Antiquity and Christianity, Claremont, California. Photo by Jean Doresse.
Chapter 9:   Harcourt Brace photograph
Chapter 10:   Archie Leiberman
Chapter 11:   Alinari/Art Resource, NY.
Chapter 12:   The John Rylands University Library of Manchester
Chapter 13:   M.644, f.174v. The Pierpont Morgan Library
Chapter 14:   The Bettmann Archive
Chapter 15:   Scala/Art Resource, NY.

INDEX